ECLIPSE

Books by Mark Perry

FOUR STARS

ECLIPSE

ECLIPSE

The Last Days of the CIA

Mark Perry

WILLIAM MORROW AND COMPANY, INC.

NEW YORK

It is the policy of William Morrow and Company, Inc., and its imprints and affiliates, recognizing the importance of preserving what has been written, to print the books we publish on acid-free paper, and we exert our best efforts to that end.

Library of Congress Cataloging-in-Publication Data

Perry, Mark, 1950–
    Eclipse : the last days of the CIA / Mark Perry.
      p. cm.
    ISBN 0-688-09386-8
    1. United States. Central Intelligence Agency. 2. Intelligence
service—United States. I. Title.
JK468.I6P454 1992
327.1′273—dc20   92-1288
                                            CIP

Printed in the United States of America

First Edition

1 2 3 4 5 6 7 8 9 10

BOOK DESIGN BY LISA STOKES

For Nina

———— ★★★ ————
Acknowledgments

This book could not have been completed without the assistance of a number of my colleagues and friends here in Washington.

Most important among them is independent reporter and television producer Jeff Goldberg, who spent weeks commenting on and critiquing this book. His work on the manuscript, his familiarity with the intelligence community, his advice on how this story could best be told, and his selfless devotion of time were an indispensable guide for me over the last three years. Jeff and I also worked with British reporter Tom Mangold, an immensely talented student of this subject, on a number of stories for the BBC newsmagazine *Panorama*. Several of those stories are further developed in this book. I owe Tom my deep appreciation, and Jeff a great debt of gratitude. He is an extremely talented, loyal, good, and honest friend.

Journalist Anthony Kimery provided me with the first in hundreds of pages of material that gave invaluable insights into the workings of the intelligence community. His talent at developing sources is truly amazing—and much appreciated. I also owe thanks to Washington reporter William Scott Malone, who worked with me on a number of other stories which also have found their way into this work. His continuing skepticism, outspoken opinions, and unique viewpoints were always valued by me.

Several other journalists contributed to this work. *Newsday* reporter Knut Royce and I worked for two years investigating the Pan Am 103 bombing. Knut willingly shared his findings with me as a way of shedding light on that terrible incident. Billie Vincent, Walter Korsgaard, and Vincent Cannistraro also provided an extraordinary amount of guidance to me on the conduct of the investigation and the effects of the tragedy on the intelligence community.

My gratitude also goes to Steve Kurkjian of *The Boston Globe,* David Ignatius of *The Washington Post,* Mark Feldstein and Mary Whittington of Cable News Network, Nayan Chanda (a reporter for the *Far Eastern Economic Review* when this book was being written), Bob Vasilak of *Regardies* magazine, and Victor Navasky and David Corn of *The Nation* for providing their advice and support. I owe thanks to Saul Friedman of *Newsday* for his invaluable comments on the CIA's role in the Washington bureaucracy.

Jack Blum, Jonathan Winer, Richard McCall, Deborah DeMoss, Jesse Helms, John Kerry, José Blandón, Bosco Vallarino, Augusto Villalaz, and many others provided special insights on Manuel Noriega's Panama.

CIA and other government officials, a number of them now retired, were kind enough to share their perspectives on the agency's inner workings. I wish to thank David Whipple, James Greenleaf, Graham Fuller, Thomas Polgar, Edward Proctor, Angus Thuermer, Peter Ernest, Bobby Ray Inman, Ray Cline, Joseph De Trani, Richard Allen, Mark Mansfield, and many, many others for their help. In addition, former Director of Central Intelligence William H. Webster was kind enough to provide me with an interview at the height of one of the agency's most public, and controversial, moments.

I wish to thank Michael Oksenberg, Al Wilhelm, and Robert Ross, who provided their own singular perspectives on China during the Tienanmen crisis. But I most especially want to thank Ambassador James Lilley, who willingly recounted his lifetime of experiences and his often painful memories of an emotional and sad time as American ambassador to China.

A book on the CIA simply cannot be written without the cooperation of those who have served in the agency. Most of those who helped cannot be cited here by name. I owe, in particular, thanks to three agency sources who provided me with anecdotal material about the inner workings of the CIA over the last three years. One in particular placed his reputation and his career on the line to help me write this book. His conversations with me over the last two years made this work possible. I hope that I can, in some small way, repay him in the future. Until that time comes, I can only reassure him that his confidence and trust are being repaid. He should know that there are some of us, out here, who wish him well.

My gratitude must also be expressed to Scott Armstrong, Chip Beck, Ken Berez, Richard Billings, Bill Cowan, Ken Cummins, Tom Cardamone, Jeff Danziger, Alexa Davis, John Dinges, Gayle Garmise, Bonnie

Goldstein, Jim Hougan, Frederick Kempe, Lori Kenepp, Marc Leepson, Ed Miles, Dan Moldea, Bobby Muller, Tom O'Neill, Joe Pichirallo, Michael Pilgrim, Margaret Porter, John Prados, Peter Ross Range, Robert Sorley, John Terzano, William C. Triplett, Bill Thomas, Julie Trotter, Tom Von Stein, Danny Wechsler, and Tim Wells for their support. My gratitude also goes to Washington Independent Writers and the National Security Archives for their cooperation and loyal friendship.

An important part of this work rests on a series of interviews I conducted in the Middle East over a period of two years. I wish to thank Thomas Martin for his friendship in helping me do that work. I also wish to thank David Aasen, whose knowledge of the Middle East and comments on important parts of this manuscript proved to be indispensable. My appreciation also goes to Robert Sensi, a good friend and listener, for making available his innumerable contacts in the region.

Most of all, however, I wish to thank those who were kind enough to take time to speak with me under sometimes difficult circumstances in Tunis and Jerusalem: Bassam Abu Sharif, Khalid al-Hassan, Yassir Abedrabbo, and Radwan Abu Ayyash, as well as dozens of others.

Finally, I hope that this book honors the memory of Abu Iyad, whose murder occurred just weeks after I interviewed him. If there is a tragedy in these pages, it is that Abu Iyad did not live to see the day when he could return to the home that he had so desperately sought.

As always, I owe a great debt to my agent and friend Gail Ross, whose confidence is apparently without limits, and to my editor at William Morrow, Lisa Drew, whose support, patience, good grace, and insightful comments were a constant source of inspiration.

Finally, I would like to thank my wife, Nina, my son, Cal, and my daughter, Madeleine, for seeing me through this difficult project. They cannot possibly ever realize just how much I owe them. They gave unfailingly of their time so that this book could be completed.

—MARK PERRY
Arlington, Virginia

Contents

$\star\star\star$

Glossary of Intelligence Acronyms and Titles

ADDO: The assistant deputy director for operations, responsible for the CIA's day-to-day conduct of foreign espionage and covert activities. The ADDO is a career operations officer.

Base: A small group of CIA operations officers who report to a station in a foreign country. The CIA's station in India is in New Delhi. The CIA *base* in Calcutta reports to the New Delhi station.

BKA: The Bundeskriminalamt, the German federal police.

BfV: The Bundesamt für Verfassungsschutz, the German interior intelligence agency.

BND: The Bundesnachrichtendienst, the German agency responsible for gathering foreign intelligence.

Bona fides: An agent's background. Checking out a foreign national or potential agent's bona fides means finding out whether he or she is who he or she *says* they are or, more generally, can be trusted.

CIA: The Central Intelligence Agency, whose headquarters is in Langley, Virginia, just across the river from the White House in Washington, D.C. There are approximately thirteen thousand employees working for CIA.

CIA agent: A foreign citizen who supplies a CIA officer with sensitive information on the policies or programs of a foreign nation. A CIA agent is not a CIA employee.

CIA officer: The name given a CIA employee working in the Directorate for Operations. A CIA officer working in a foreign station is responsible for contacting, developing, and working with foreign citizens who will act as agents, obtaining information for the CIA.

Clandestine service: The preferred name given by CIA employees to the Directorate for Operations. Sometimes referred to as the "black side of the house."

Compartmented: The term used for information that is restricted to a limited number of CIA officers or government officials through the use of code words. The CIA has its own code words, identifying documents as having originated with that agency. There are also government-wide identifiers; UMBRA and GAMMA are two such important compartments. There are others: NO-FORN (information not to be disseminated to foreign intelligence sources) or NOCONTRACT (information not to be disseminated to intelligence officials working under contract).

Com-symps: The name given by agency activists in the Directorate for Operations and the Directorate of Intelligence for operations officers and analysts who believed that the Soviet Union was undergoing radical changes and was not interested in extending its influence, especially in the third world. In the late 1970s and the early and mid-1980s the com-symps were heavily criticized for their views. Short for Communist sympathizer.

Consumers: Officials in the executive branch or, though less often, in the legislative branch of the U.S. government for whom intelligence reports are written.

COS: Chief of station; the head of an overseas post.

Counterintelligence: An intelligence activity designed to thwart foreign intelligence efforts to penetrate the CIA through the use of agents (or "moles"). In addition, an intelligence activity designed to penetrate a foreign intelligence service through the clandestine placement of a mole. In order to coordinate counterintelligence activities among varying U.S. intelligence bureaucracies, the CIA has established a counterintelligence center, or **CIC.**

Counternarcotics: An intelligence activity designed to thwart drug traffickers and drug trafficking networks, to identify and eliminate the threat of narcotics growth overseas and their import into the United States. In order to coordinate counternarcotics activities among varying intelligence bureaucracies, the CIA has established a counternarcotics center, or **CNC.** The CNC is still considered an analytic, or nonoperational, intelligence center.

Counterterrorism: An intelligence activity designed to thwart terrorist activities that will harm Western interests or U.S. citizens. In order to coordinate counterterrorism activities among varying U.S. intelligence bureaucracies, the CIA has established a counterterrorism center, or **CTC.** The CTC is headed by a counterterrorism official from the FBI who coordinates the CTC's activities with an official of the CIA. Unlike the CNC, the CTC is an operational arm of the intelligence community.

Covert action: A clandestine foreign intelligence activity designed to influence events in a foreign nation. A covert activity can involve CIA officers, military officers, or foreign nationals and must be approved by the President of the United States with a finding.

Cowboys: The agency nickname for activists inside the Directorate for Operations. For those who agree with such activism the nickname is used with pride; for those who do not it is a term of derision.

DA: The Directorate for Administration is responsible for administering and managing the CIA. A **DDA,** a deputy director for administration, heads the DA.

DCI: The director of central intelligence, the President and National Security Council's chief intelligence adviser. The DCI is the chief officer of the CIA and also heads the intelligence community. The DCI is responsible for overseeing, monitoring, and coordinating intelligence activities carried on by the military and a variety of independent intelligence bureaucracies.

DDCI: The deputy director of central intelligence, the DCI's deputy and the second-in-command of the CIA.

DI: The Directorate of Intelligence is responsible for gathering and analyzing intelligence, which is gleaned from a variety of overseas sources. A **DDI,** the deputy director of intelligence, heads the DI.

DO: The Directorate for Operations at the CIA is responsible for planning and carrying out covert destabilization campaigns, dissemination of propaganda, paramilitary operations, and other espionage activities. The DO is sometimes referred to by its shorthand title, the clandestine service. The DO is divided into six divisions: Soviet Bloc, Europe, Western Hemisphere, East Asia, Near East, and Africa. Each division is further subdivided into offices, branches, or task forces. For instance, the NE (Near East) Division contains an Office of Arab Affairs, an Iran branch, and an Iraq Task Force. The division is headed by a **DDO,** a deputy director for operations, who coordinates covert activities and oversees the day-to-day work of the DO.

DP: The Directorate of Plans at the CIA, responsible for coordinating and planning future intelligence needs of the CIA. It is the youngest CIA directorate and is headed by a **DDP,** a deputy director for plans.

DS&T: The Directorate of Science and Technology at the CIA, responsible for conducting the agency's scientific research, especially the development of new and improved intelligence collection systems. The directorate is headed by a **DDS&T,** a deputy director of science and technology.

Denied area: A hostile foreign environment, where the CIA operates under the constant threat of surveillance or arrest. During the cold war the Soviet Union was a denied area.

Deuxième Bureau: A reference to the French intelligence service of the 1950s, now superseded by the SDECE. Some Middle East intelligence bureaus, formerly under French control, still refer to their intelligence agencies as the Deuxième Bureau.

DIA: The Defense Intelligence Agency. The coordinating intelligence agency for the Department of Defense and U.S. military. The DIA's activities are, nevertheless, subject to the authority of the director of central intelligence.

ELINT: Electronic intelligence, usually intercepts of conversations of foreign leaders or military commanders.

Espionage: Any gathering of information from foreign nations or officials through surreptitious means, conducted by the Directorate for Operations. This activity is not to be confused with covert action. Conducting espionage is the everyday work of CIA officers posted overseas.

EXDIS: Special dispatch; a cable slug that indicates that information in the intelligence report is highly compartmented and intended for a very small and select group of policy makers—usually just the highest-level members of the National Security Council.

Finding: A presidential authorization for covert action, given in writing, in which the President states, in very general terms, the reasons for initiating the covert action and its intended goal.

Fluttering: Taking or administering a polygraph examination. If you have taken a polygraph examination, you have been "fluttered."

The Four Princes: The name given by agency employees to the heads of the CIA's four major directorates—Administration, Intelligence, Operations, and Science and Technology. The Four Princes are reputed to have enormous power inside the agency's bureaucracy.

HPSCI: The House Permanent Select Committee on Intelligence.

HUMINT: Human Intelligence. Intelligence gained from the firsthand knowledge of a human source operating in a foreign country.

Identifiers: On classified documents, identifiers are code words or symbols that identify who has sent the document and its compartment.

INR: Bureau of Intelligence and Research, the State Department's intelligence office.

Keyhole: An intelligence compartment for those with access to satellite information gathered by the KH-11, or Keyhole, reconnaissance satellite.

KG-84-HJ: The U.S. government's most sophisticated international communications encryption computer. Messages from the KG-84-HJ are sent and received in code, then deciphered and assessed, and eventually edited for use by U.S. government officials as part of daily intelligence briefings.

Knuckledraggers: A term of derision used by CIA employees to describe the military officers assigned to the agency.

KY–7: The CIA's standard encryption communicator.

Lacrosse: A high-image, digital reconnaissance satellite, the most sophisticated currently deployed by the NSA.

MI5, MI6: The British intelligence services.

Mossad: ha-Mossad le-Modiin ule-Tafkidim Meyuhadim, the institute for intelligence and special tasks, or Mossad, the Israeli intelligence service.

Mukhabarat: Arabic for "intelligence"; with some exceptions, the name of any intelligence agency in an Arab country.

NESA: The Office of Near East and South Asia Analysis, in the Directorate of Intelligence.

NIC: The National Intelligence Council (or "nic"), composed of sixteen national intelligence officers, responsible for producing national intelligence estimates. The NIC is also responsible for providing intelligence goals to DO divisions and special task forces. It operates under, and reports to, the DCI.

NID: National Intelligence Daily, a daily newsletter that summarizes the important intelligence events of the previous twenty-four hours. Access is highly restricted, to under 150 government officials.

NSC: The National Security Council, the highest policy-making body of the U.S. government, composed of the President, Vice President, secretaries of state and defense, and the national security adviser. The DCI serves in an advisory role.

NIE: A National Intelligence Estimate. A written assessment of probable future events in a foreign nation or on an intelligence topic. An NIE will lay out policy options based on intelligence gathered by the DO. An NIE brings together the views of experts on a region or country inside the CIA.

NIO: National intelligence officer. The sixteen NIOs are members of the National Intelligence Council. An NIO is responsible for a region or special topics area. An NIO reports directly to the chairman of the National Intelligence Council.

NRO: The National Reconnaissance Office. The jointly run CIA-Air Force office that manages the U.S. satellite reconnaissance program.

NSA: The National Security Agency, which is responsible for intercepting signals intelligence and breaking foreign intelligence codes. The NSA is also in charge of securing U.S. communication and cryptographic equipment and codes.

PDB: President's Daily Brief. The most highly restricted daily intelligence summary in the U.S. government, meant for the President and the administration's most senior officials.

Product: What agency employees call intelligence reports, analyses, or assessments. Intelligence product is given to intelligence consumers.

Proprietary: A cover operation or business used by the CIA or any other intelligence agency.

Roger channel: The State Department's secret international covert operations cable channel, which carries the most sensitive information on American overseas clandestine activities.

SDECE: Service of External Documentation and Counterespionage, the French foreign intelligence service.

SI: Special intelligence. Information gathered from interception of signals communications by the National Security Agency. SI contains information that is the most guarded in the U.S. intelligence community. Access to this material is very restricted and closely guarded.

SIGINT: Intelligence information derived from the interception of a foreign country's signals communications.

SITKG: Special Intelligence, Talent, Keyhole, Gamma. One of the highest intelligence compartments in the U.S. government. Officials with this designation have access to material gathered through signals interception (called SI, or special intelligence), Talent-Keyhole (access to intelligence gathered from technical systems, "overhead," satellite systems, but *not* to the systems themselves), and Gamma intelligence, which is restricted to collection from Soviet intelligence systems, either signals or overhead. Intelligence officers are sometimes known to designate their importance by referring, with each other, to their compartments classification, as in "I'm SITKG." A high-level intelligence compartment. Most high-ranking State Department and CIA officers are given access, through this compartment, to a broad range of human and technical intelligence reports.

SIRO: The State Department's cable designation for information to be given to the CIA, or information contained in a State Department cable that has been given it by CIA officers or agents. The CIA has an office at the State Department which is the CIA's liaison office. The acronym stands for Special Intelligence Reporting Office—or SIRO.

SNIE: A Special National Intelligence Estimate. A shorter assessment than an NIE of foreign policy and intelligence options during a time of crisis or opportunity.

SOVA: The Office of Soviet Analysis, which is inside the Directorate of Intelligence.

SSCI: The Senate Select Committee on Intelligence. In this book I refer to this committee in a shorthand version as the Senate Intelligence Committee. The Senate Intelligence Committee has primary oversight responsibility of the CIA in Congress.

Task force: A special intelligence group of the CIA, convened during a period of international crisis, that brings together intelligence analysts, operations officers, economic specialists, psychologists, technical experts, and regional experts to gather and assess intelligence data, and to plan and carry out covert operations.

TEFRAN: Teheran/Frankfurt, the CIA's Teheran station in exile, located in Frankfurt, Germany.

Tradecraft: The operations skills of CIA officers, including methods of surveillance, propaganda, espionage, weapons training, recruiting agents, and escape. Most tradecraft is taught at the CIA's training center at Camp Peary in Virginia.

201 File: An officer's personnel file, begun when he is training as a CIA officer and kept throughout his career. Every evaluation is placed in a 201, every result of a polygraph exam and every investigation conducted by the CIA's Office of Security.

Sources:

Burton, Bob. *Top Secret: A Clandestine Operator's Glossary of Terms.* Boulder, Colo: Paladin Press, 1986.
Richelson, Jeffrey T. *The U.S. Intelligence Community.* Cambridge, Mass.: Ballinger, 1989.

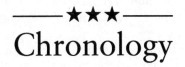

Chronology

1986

December 15: William Casey falls ill at CIA headquarters and is rushed to Georgetown University Hospital.

1987

May 6: William Casey dies at his home on Long Island.

May 26: William H. Webster is sworn in as the fourteenth director of central intelligence.

December 8: Richard Stolz is named new deputy director for operations.

December 17: Webster announces that he is disciplining seven agency employees for their role in the Iran-contra affair.

December 31: Clair George retires as deputy director for operations.

1988

January 9: Panamanian demonstrations call for the replacement of Manuel Noriega.

February 4: Noriega is indicted by a Miami grand jury on thirteen counts of drug trafficking and racketeering.

March 16: An opposition coup attempt in Panama fails; Colonel Moisés Giroldi is credited by Noriega with saving his regime.

Late March: Eduardo Herrera Hassan visits the United States at the invitation of the State Department.

Mid-April: A campaign of harassment against American citizens in Panama is launched by Noriega.

Mid-May: The CIA proposes the seizure of Noriega and his return to the United States for trial.

July: Three and a half million dollars in covert funding for the non-Communist resistance in Cambodia is found missing by CIA officers.

September: A CIA-State Department planning group continues efforts to launch a covert operation against Noriega. The group's efforts are paralyzed by bickering.

November 4: George Bush is elected President of the United States.

December 6: William Webster is renamed to head the CIA.

December 21: Pan Am 103 explodes over Lockerbie, Scotland; 270 die in the terrorist attack.

1989

January: National Security Directive 26 is adopted by the Bush administration. The paper calls for closer ties to Iraq.

January: CIA officer Charles Allen appeals his reprimand for his lack of cooperation with an agency investigation of the Iran-contra affair.

Early February: CIA experts and three other officials, including Ambassador James Lilley, brief Bush on the political situation in China and South Korea.

February 26: Colonel Gerald E. Clark, an American intelligence officer, dies in a car accident in Panama.

February 28: Deputy Director Richard Kerr tells the Senate Intelligence Committee that Gorbachev's reforms in the Soviet Union could be long-lasting.

March: The CIA and Pentagon publicly disagree over the scope of Gorbachev's reforms.

April 5: Kurt Frederick Muse, who runs a clandestine radio operation, is arrested in Panama.

April 15: Hu Yaobang dies in China. Pro-democracy demonstrations marking his death begin.

April 27: Pro-democracy demonstrators occupy Tiananmen Square.

May 7: Elections in Panama result in a humiliating defeat for Manuel Noriega, who then steals the election.

June 4: Chinese troops massacre students in Beijing.

October: The Pentagon finalizes plans for Operation Just Cause, the invasion of Panama.

October 3: Colonel Moisés Giroldi's coup against Noriega fails.

December 20: Operation Just Cause is launched against Panama. Kurt

Muse is rescued from his prison cell and returned to the
United States.
December 21: Romanian troops fire on demonstrators in Bucharest.
December 25: Romanian dictator Nicolae Ceausescu and his wife are
executed by a firing squad, ending a year of revolution
in Eastern Europe.

1990

March 7: The Bush administration accuses Libya of manufacturing
chemical weapons at its plant at Rabta.
March 15: The government of Yitzhak Shamir loses a vote of confidence
in the Knesset.
March 15: British journalist Farzad Bazoft is executed in Iraq.
March 15: The Rabta chemical plant in Libya is destroyed by fire.
April 1: Saddam Hussein threatens Israel with destruction.
Mid-April: A key clue in the bombing of Pan Am 103, a tiny piece of
a computer chip, is found in the fields near Lockerbie.
Early May: The CIA issues its first warning that Iraq may be moving
toward war in the Persian Gulf.
July 17: U.S. reconnaisance satellites report troops movements in south-
ern Iraq.
July 28: CIA officials tell President Bush that Iraq will invade Kuwait.
August 1: William Webster tells President Bush that Iraq will invade
Kuwait within twenty-four hours.
August 2: Iraq invades Kuwait.
Late August: CTC investigators tentatively conclude that Libya bombed
Pan Am 103.
December: William Webster tells Congress that economic sanctions
could eventually force an Iraqi withdrawal from Kuwait.
December 23: James Lilley visits President Bush at the White House.
December 31: Richard Stolz retires as deputy director for operations.

1991

January 16: The United States and its coalition allies launch Operation
Desert Storm.
February 22: CIA Director Webster is attacked as "weak and pathetic"
in a news article quoting administration sources.
February 23: U.S. and allied troops invade Iraq and Kuwait.
March 28: Saddam Hussein begins a counteroffensive to crush rebel-
lions in southern Iraq.
April: The CIA dispatches an eleven-man team to report on the Kurdish
rebellion.

May 8: William Webster announces that he will retire as director of central intelligence.

May 14: Robert Gates is nominated to head the CIA.

July 9: Former CIA officer Alan Fiers pleads guilty to two misdemeanor charges for his role in the Iran-contra affair.

July 12: The Senate Intelligence Committee postpones hearings on the Gates nomination.

September 16: Hearings open on the Gates nomination.

November 12: Robert Gates is sworn in as the fifteenth director of central intelligence.

December 14: Two Libyans are indicted for the bombing of Pan Am 103.

"Pay no attention to that man behind the curtain."

—From *The Wizard of Oz*

— ★★★ —
Prologue

As is the case with every government bureaucracy, the Central Intelligence Agency has a private, inner past that reflects conflicts rarely seen by the American people. But unlike those of any other federal agency, careers in the CIA can be made, or broken, on issues of life and death. A lifetime of work can be sidetracked or ended forever by a single unpredicted incident or an embarrassing flash of coincidence. Working for the CIA is an immensely demanding task and a high-pressure job.

For these reasons, internal CIA debates are intensely argued and its battles are vigorously fought. For each event of its public history over the last forty years, the agency has been divided by a series of unknown conflicts that have had a significant effect on the way our government collects and uses intelligence. Because the stakes involved in doing this job are so high, the CIA has always maintained that it produces information untainted by fear or favor and unslanted by outside political views. The American people have remained just as confident that the agency produces objective facts gleaned from trustworthy sources that are then used to mold U.S. foreign policy. They rest easy with the assurances that facts are never bent to serve political ends and that the CIA is an independent intelligence agency.

As history shows, that just isn't true.

In the 1950s, the agency's most experienced espionage officers succeeded in establishing far-flung networks of agents inside the Soviet empire. It was an enormously costly operation. By mid-decade, most of these networks were betrayed. Many of the CIA's top agents were executed or turned against the United States. The information they later provided was soon found to be sown with deception.

Because of the frightful toll these failed operations took on the agency at the height of the cold war, an influential group of CIA analysts argued that risky espionage operations were counterproductive. Their dissent over the scope of the CIA's overseas activities sparked an agency-wide review of such programs in Eastern Europe and the Soviet Union. But U.S. government officials decided the CIA should continue its wide-scale espionage programs because the Communist threat to the nation was too serious to ignore.

The Arbenz coup in Guatemala in 1954 and the Mossadegh coup in Iran in that same year reignited the internal debate over what role the CIA should play in trying to influence world events. A small number of agency analysts argued that covert interventions actually harmed U.S. interests because they were undemocratic. But because the Guatemala and Iran coups were so successful, this dissent was largely ignored.

In mid-decade, senior CIA officers in West Germany constructed a long tunnel that stretched from the American zone into East Berlin. The tunnel's end was directly under Soviet military headquarters. Agency technicians then tapped into the USSR's primary communications channels using sophisticated listening devices. The information retrieved from the tunnel was sent to the Berlin station and then back to Washington.

Unfortunately, the existence of the tunnel was betrayed to the Soviets almost immediately after it began. When this failure became known the agency was forced to discard many of the secrets it had deciphered because they were useless. This stark intelligence defeat rekindled concerns among the growing number of CIA dissidents, who now argued that the agency was exaggerating the Soviet threat and its own prowess. Their voices of concern, however, were drowned out by the nation's obsession with a drumbeat of nightmarish tales about how the U.S. government had been betrayed by the forces of evil and their "fellow travelers."

The millions of dollars spent deciphering the piles of useless paper from the tunnel may well mark a low point for the CIA during the 1950s. The tunnel operation, however, is still trumpeted by agency veterans as a stellar triumph.

The internal debate over the scope of agency activities reached a new crescendo in 1961, when CIA-supported Cuban exiles were decisively defeated at the Bay of Pigs in Cuba. The operation was poorly planned and executed. The CIA was internationally condemned for its activities. The agency's small group of dissidents—who looked on the CIA solely as an intelligence-gathering office—were now joined by a distinct group of operations officers who had disagreed with the covert Cuban invasion. Calls for internal reform were heard from all segments of the intelligence community. Instead, the CIA was given a new director.

The escalation of covert operations during the Vietnam War inflamed this growing internal conflict. Hoping to dampen the increasingly bitter debate, DCI John McCone worked diligently to separate those who thought the Vietnam War could not be won from those who didn't. McCone worked to make certain the CIA's intelligence product remained unblemished by those who wanted the agency to become more deeply involved in Vietnam.

The differences were apparent even inside McCone's personal staff, where a group of officers surreptitiously tried to circumvent his directives on agency involvement in Southeast Asia. In 1963, for instance, McCone let it be known that he opposed plans to replace Ngo Dinh Diem, South Vietnam's unpopular premier. Diem was overthrown anyway. CIA officers helped plan the coup.

McCone's position on Vietnam undermined his authority as the director of central intelligence. Agency activists let it be known that if he was replaced, the CIA would take a more helpful role in winning the war. It was even later suggested by a number of CIA officers that these activists had a hand in McCone's ouster. In mid-1966, he was replaced by Richard Helms.

The disagreements that divided the CIA were deepened by the agency's involvement in Vietnam. Those who had consistently argued that the agency should be an activist institution that promoted covert operations won a temporary victory for their position in mid-1967. In that year the agency expanded its training of South Vietnam Special Forces units. The small squads were given an extraordinarily important mission: to root out the Vietcong "infrastructure"—the political arm of the insurgency in South Vietnam. By the end of 1968, the CIA station in Saigon employed nearly one thousand agency officers. The CIA's influence was felt in every province, village, and hamlet.

The decision to enlarge the CIA's role in Southeast Asia caused an explosive debate at Langley. A growing chorus of critics argued that the agency had betrayed its mission and undermined its claim to objectivity. For years, these dissenters stressed, CIA analysts had been saying that the United States could not and would not win the war in Indochina. Now, with the start of what later was known as the Phoenix Program, the agency was participating in this inevitable defeat.

Richard Helms attempted to strike a delicate balance between these two contending views. He argued that so long as the CIA's tradition of separating espionage and paramilitary operations from intelligence analysis—in other words, those who supported the war from those who opposed it—the agency could maintain its position as a credible and valued part of the American government.

Eventually, however, Helms's strategy of isolating the policies followed by the Saigon station from the views of their Langley opponents came into conflict with Lyndon Johnson's commitment to the war. By 1969, the dissent over the war inside the CIA was slowly silenced, but at great cost. The first in a massive series of resignations took place at the CIA in the final years of the decade.

Despite this success, the agency's most outspoken activists never regained the ascendance they enjoyed during the salad years in Vietnam. By 1975, the CIA was under enormous congressional and public pressure to bare its dirtiest secrets. Congressional hearings on these transgressions were conducted in the wake of the worst political scandal in American history. They reflected the conflict that had raged inside the CIA for more than two decades.

The reforms put in place after the scandalous revelations of the mid-1970s were intended to transform the CIA by making it accountable to Congress. The agency underwent a period of soul-searching. But the debates that marked its first twenty-five years were not dampened. Starting in 1976, new pressures were brought to bear on the CIA by conservatives who believed its primary mission was being sacrificed by DCI Stansfield Turner. He was criticized for sacrificing the agency's traditional activism to the new technology provided by sophisticated reconnaissance satellites.

The CIA's internal debate was also becoming a topic of public controversy. For the first time in its history, a director of central intelligence actually sided with the agency's most outspoken reformers. A number of senior operations officers were forcibly retired during Turner's term, while others were given less controversial assignments. The dismissals were interpreted by many as a direct attack on the tradition of the Directorate of Operations (DO), which conducts agency espionage and covert activities.

Turner's tilt away from human espionage programs had a demoralizing effect at Langley, where even the agency's most outspoken critics of intelligence activism were disturbed by his emphasis on technical information-gathering systems. The result of this widespread skepticism was that the views of the agency's most highly regarded espionage activists were never totally discredited, even by their traditional opponents.

When William Casey took over as DCI after the election of Ronald Reagan, he reversed this trend and vowed that he would rebuild the DO. Almost immediately, however, his attempts to infuse the CIA with a new sense of activism met with opposition. To some senior DO officers, and to many in the directorate of intelligence (DI), some of Casey's ideas seemed dangerous. A small cadre of operations officers and analysts, many of whom would have welcomed a dose of risk-taking during Turner's term, now recoiled from such bald proposals during Casey's.

These officers did not mistrust Casey; they simply believed that if he wanted the CIA to enlarge its operations overseas, then President Reagan and his DCI could change the laws to make that possible. Their fears dated from an earlier time, when public disclosures of CIA activism shattered the careers and lives of a generation of agency employees who had too willingly carried out the orders of the White House. They did not want that to happen a second time.

Casey's persistence, however, was met with broad support among a large number of clandestine service officers. The CIA expanded its overseas operations. For a period of almost exactly six years, the agency was occupied by a series of crises that rivaled any in its history. In 1983, agency-trained guerrillas mined Nicaragua's harbor. In 1984, William Buckley, the CIA chief of station in Beirut, Lebanon, was kidnapped and tortured. In late 1985, the CIA helped the Reagan White House ship arms to Iranian moderates. Finally, in 1986, the most serious scandal since the Nixon presidency was sparked by revelations that profits from those sales were diverted to the contras. At the end of 1986 William Casey fell ill.

The public controversy about the CIA's role in the Iran-contra affair and William Casey's death are often cited as the end of an era at the CIA. That is hardly the case. For forty-five years, the CIA has maintained its position as the premier foreign-intelligence-gathering arm of the American government. That did not change with Casey's death.

The bitterly contested internal conflict over the agency's role in American foreign policy intensified following Casey's burial in May 1987. The war for the soul of the CIA was to be waged for another four years. That period was marked by the appointment of William Webster as DCI, the election of George Bush as President, and the elevation of former Deputy DCI Robert Gates to a position of immense power inside the White House and eventually inside the CIA.

Over the next years—from Casey's funeral to Gates's ascendence—these officials and a handful of agency officers at CIA headquarters in Langley, Virginia, presided over the most revolutionary transformation of American intelligence in the nation's history.

Part I
★ ★ ★
The Wizard

1

★★★

Rashid's Revenge

*I*t was not the way they expected him to die. While William Casey gave every appearance of infirmity through all six of his years as head of the CIA, few of his colleagues ever believed that his essential vitality would be sapped by anything so human as cancer. There was no warning. In fact, Casey came into his office at the CIA on that bright winter morning in December 1986 looking better than he had in several weeks, perhaps a little tired, his colleagues now say, but no more so than usual. A few minutes later, in the middle of an examination by Dr. Arvel Tharp, the CIA physician, there was a slight tremor in his right arm, then in his left leg. Casey peered at the doctor, then blinked in confusion. "What's happening to me?" he asked. Within minutes his aides had rushed him to an ambulance for the ten-minute ride to Georgetown University Hospital.

The first medical report said Casey would recover; the second, following surgery to remove a tumor from his brain, predicted that he would be incapacitated for a short time. Then the reports stopped, and it became clear to everyone that Casey was terminally ill. He died on May 6, 1987.

For his closest colleagues at the agency, William Casey was the golden knight, the perfect master spy, and the symbol of a proud calling. There were times when the CIA's senior officers disagreed with his views, argued vehemently with his most outrageous proposals, and feared his volcanic outbursts and his disturbing tendency to give voice to larger and then still larger claims. But they admired the way he took on his role. They knew that the thinly smiling aging warrior who walked with a stoop (he looked like a retired investment banker discomfited by an ill-fitting pin-striped suit) was a man whose very presence commanded respect. Those who knew him least said he was complex, but those who worked with him every day were attracted by his disarming simplicity. There was nearly unanimous agreement that the agency had not had someone like him as its head since Allen Dulles was DCI, back in the 1950s. When people saw William Casey, they saw the power of the CIA.

At the same time there was something vulnerable about Casey, as if he sensed that if he let down his guard, he would slip back to the neighborhood in Queens where he was reared. It was for this reason, perhaps, that he was always on the move, shambling down one of the CIA's back stairways to the sixth floor's East Asia Division, then to the fifth floor, where he talked with great animation to officers of the Technical Services branch, then further into the depths of the agency to the offices of the Cable Secretariat, and finally into his limousine to investigate the workings of agency scientists with their new satellite gadgets at a nearby technical laboratory. He listened intently during briefings, with his head cocked to one side and his mouth slightly askew, and everywhere he went he exuded confidence. He talked quickly, laughed oddly, and when he left, no one was quite sure what it was that he had said, but they liked him anyway and were complimented by his confidence and constant attention.

When President Reagan appointed him to head the CIA, Casey was independently wealthy. He was a respected lawyer and managed a stock portfolio that was the envy of many. The stock market was his obsession; when he stalked into his spacious office on the seventh floor at Langley each morning, trailing lean, dark-eyed bodyguards, he carried a copy of *The Wall Street Journal* tucked under his arm. It was an important moment of the day, coming just after the daily intelligence briefing, when his wide eyes scanned the Dow Jones quotes. Only after completing this vital reading would Casey heave himself from his office sofa to begin the day's work. Like an aging cathedral, he seemed beyond time, even though his eyes were sunken, his face mottled by age, and his gait an unnatural shuffle. His secretaries were in a continual lather over his pronouncements, all the more so because they could hardly understand him; his sentences were sometimes so badly skewed he dripped saliva. But Casey's wheezing declarations and bowed profile were a charade. Underneath it all he was solid and imposing, as if marked by heroic acts in ancient wars.

So it was with a distinct sense of disbelief that Casey's family, friends, and colleagues filed into St. Mary's Catholic Church in Roslyn Harbor, Long Island, on a bright May morning in 1987. Casey's frightening brain seizure in his seventh-floor office the previous December 15 had come as a shock. It would have surprised many in the church to know that at the time of his collapse he was undergoing treatment for prostate cancer, a fact he kept from everyone except his most trusted friends (he told President Reagan). If anything, this knowledge that his life was certainly ending spurred his efforts, so that when his seizure hit, he was carrying an enormous load.

Preparations for Casey's burial started early in the morning. The local police arrived first and came in force. They erected barricades across the streets leading to the church and diligently checked security badges to keep away the merely curious. Bryant Avenue, the long, tree-lined street that led to the front of St. Mary's, was blocked off in order to make room for the approximately three hundred dignitaries expected to attend. A detachment of Secret Service agents came next, walking through the wealthy neighborhood, then unobtrusively making their way through the center of the church and into the balcony. Finally the first mourners began to arrive.

President Reagan was ushered in, but said nothing. Former President Richard Nixon arrived next, quickly flashing his characteristic self-conscious and uncomfortable smile, and then deciding that he shouldn't be smiling at all. He ducked into the church without saying a word and sat near the Reagans. Defense Secretary Caspar Weinberger and Secretary of State George Shultz, both of whom had bitterly disagreed with Casey on a number of issues, appeared grim-faced before taking their places in a pew behind the Reagans. The acting DCI at the time, Robert Gates, whose close relationship with Casey caused him to lose his first chance to head the CIA, sat nearby. Finally, FBI Director William Webster, who soon became Casey's successor, silently took his place with other officials near the front of the church.

The seating of official Washington followed standard etiquette. Public officials were seated in pews that ran along the left side of the church; the President and his wife sat in the front pew, members of the Cabinet in the next, followed by members of Congress. Casey's CIA friends and colleagues filled the pews near the middle and back, their suit coats forming a solid sea of black. The pews on the right side of the church were reserved for family members and friends. Casey's widow, daughter, and son-in-law were seated in the front pew with family friends, including many of Casey's closest associates from his days as an investment and tax lawyer in New York City. Reporters crowded into the church balcony, where they strained to identify the great and near great in the congregation. There were crowds outside, held back behind the police barricades, and a large group of Casey's friends in the church basement, listening to the service on a loudspeaker system.

Casey's funeral was appropriately solemn, though unmarked by the presence of deep tragedy that often accompanies such ceremonies. The only controversy of the day came when Roman Catholic Bishop John McGann told the mourners that he regretted the "violence" of the war in Central America and then lightly chastised his lifelong friend for his continuing support of the contras. "Bill must have thought us blind to the potential of a Communist threat in this hemisphere as we opposed and continue to oppose the violence wrought in Central America by support of the contras," the bishop noted in his eulogy. "These are not light matters on which to disagree. They are matters of life and death. And I cannot conceal or disguise my fundamental disagreement on these matters with a man I knew and respected." McGann's words sparked an uncomfortable rustle in the balcony, where a row of reporters reached into their coat pockets for their notebooks and pens. On national newscasts that night and in front-page summaries of the funeral service the following morning, the bishop's words received a prominent place as the most remembered event of a day intended as a commemoration of Casey's life.

McGann's words were in stark contrast with those of U.S. Ambassador to the United Nations Jeane Kirkpatrick, a strong conservative, whose "rip-roaring" eulogy was a paean to Casey's dedication to destroying communism. Her speech was a perfect symbol of Casey's own unrepentant and unapologetic Catholic anticommunism. Her remarks contained a stinging repudiation of Casey's most recent critics. "These men and their comments would not overly disturb our friend," Kirkpatrick said with disdain. "Supporting Nicaragua's freedom fighters had a special priority for him—no question about it. But that had no more priority than law." She paused for effect, looking down at the congregation, and then quoted Casey, who defended his views by claiming he had a special place in heaven. "He lived his life to the hilt," she said, "and left it in the spirit of a man who was [as he said] 'ready—and not afraid of the devil.'"

The funeral service was marred by the McGann-Kirkpatrick disagreement; it was as if those in attendance had come to pay homage to two men, not one. In the months that followed, when all the early praise for Casey subsided, people began a more objective assessment of his career. Only then, after Casey's own role in the Iran-contra affair was diminished by his unexpected death, did Jeane Kirkpatrick's words of praise for him and her plea that he should be remembered as a man with respect for the law seem an inappropriate coda to his life. While the eulogy was intended as Casey's great defense, it contained the very reason why his judgment on intelligence matters was so often questioned—even by his closest colleagues. For although they didn't say so at the time, Casey's top CIA assistants later admitted that they were often puzzled by his relentless obsession with communism and his voracious appetite for conflict. There was something oddly discomforting in Casey's pronouncements, they said. On more than one occasion, they recalled, high-ranking agency officials exchanged concealed glances of disbelief over many of his proposals.

In a number of key instances during Casey's six-year tenure at Langley, the CIA's clandestine operations officers openly warned him about this lack of caution and, when that didn't work, circumvented his orders. At first Casey was puzzled by his staff's unwillingness to act on some of his schemes, but he passed this off as the result of what he viewed as the demoralizing years the agency spent under his predecessor. After a time, however, Casey's frustrations deepened, and the resulting tensions estranged him from his own most experienced colleagues. For this reason the discomfort caused by Casey's death was especially keen among CIA officials who attended his memorial service; they served and defended him through six controversial years, but at important points they undermined his dictates. There was irony in the fact that fate had timed his death to coincide with his impending public testimony on the Iran-contra scandal, but it was even more ironic that his Iran-contra program had less to do with one of his grand plans than with his frustrations over the DO's unwillingness to act on his beliefs. After several years of facing what he believed was purposeful obstruction on the part of several important clandestine service officers, Casey went ahead on his own.

Feeling betrayed and deceived, nearly disbelieving that the agency he envisioned would not heel to his every whim, Casey reached out to a fearless military officer with a can-do mentality. But the incident that finally convinced Casey that Oliver North was the activist patriot he was looking for had little to do with either Iran or the contras. Thinking back on it long after Casey's burial, a number of key officers of the CIA's clandestine service became convinced that the Iran-contra affair had really started when William Casey became obsessed by the actions of a young Arab by the name of Mohammed Hussein Rashid.

The CIA's terrorism experts knew all about Rashid. They even had photographs of him tucked away in the clandestine service's cache of top secret files. The agency spent three years gathering intelligence about Rashid, then sent its findings to its stations in Europe and the Near East. It made copies for the State Department, which passed the information on to U.S. embassies around the world. CIA officers kidded about it among themselves. When they'd finished with Rashid, they laughed, they knew as much about him as he knew about himself. "Born in Jordan on April 24, 1949," his file says. "He is between 5 feet eight inches and 5 feet ten inches; of slender build. He has slightly wavy black hair with a receding hairline and brown eyes." In the early 1970s Rashid was convicted of drug trafficking; he was a careless liar, was given to petty crime, and preyed on the innocent by using his uncommon good looks to pro-

Eclipse

mote himself and his cause. Rashid was an intelligent, self-assured world
traveler who was comfortable in both European and Middle Eastern
societies. By the early 1980s he had learned how to build bombs so well
that by the beginning of the next decade he was deemed "a menace to
international civil aviation."

The CIA had earlier decided to keep an eye on Rashid after it
spotted him learning his trade as an apprentice bomb maker for the
Baader-Meinhof gang in West Germany. A surveillance team was dispatched to West Germany to track the young Palestinian in the late 1970s,
while another group of officers busily documented his connections to
radical Palestinians in the Middle East. Although the agency managed
to successfully track Rashid's movements, it consistently failed to predict
his targets or interdict his bombs. He was especially dangerous because
he was not only extremely committed to his cause but also technically
brilliant. With the help of the Palestinian bomb maker Abu Ibrahim,
Rashid brought the fine art of aircraft explosions to new and graver
levels of sophistication. During the early 1980s he and Ibrahim pioneered a particularly well-disguised type of suitcase bomb that turned
out to be much more dangerous than its primitive predecessors; the
batteries of the explosive device were concealed in the false bottom of
a suitcase and contained a barometric trigger, a lethal combination that
made his bombs impossible to detect. (Aviation security officials were
consistently foiled by Rashid's simple but brilliant innovations; when
bomb-sniffing dogs were trained to uncover the chemical traces of the
explosives he used, he wrapped them in epoxy.) Rashid's talents, the
CIA discovered, were being used by the radical Baghdad-based 15 May
Group.

Rashid announced his arrival as an international terrorist on August
11, 1982, when a bomb he built detonated aboard Pan Am Flight 830
en route from Tokyo to Honolulu. The bomb killed a sixteen-year-old
Japanese citizen, Toru Ozawa, and injured fifteen others. According to
a file on the incident, the bomb had been placed under Ozawa's seat by
"individuals traveling as a Moroccan family using the name 'Harouk'
who had occupied seats in the same row as Ozawa's seat during the
earlier Hong Kong to Tokyo portion of the Pan American flight." The
Harouk family, the file went on to say, was actually Rashid, his wife, and
their young son.

Casey was enraged by the Pan Am episode and demanded that the
clandestine service take steps to destroy the 15 May Group, a task made
all the more important because this bombing was one of the first acts of
anti-American terrorism during his tenure as DCI. Casey treated the
Rashid incident as a personal affront, as if the bomb had been planted
solely to embarrass him. But Casey was confident of the clandestine
service's ability to bring Rashid to justice: He was a known international

traveler, had contacts throughout the Middle East and North Africa, and used a predictable method of operation.

The fact that Rashid often traveled with his Austrian-born wife and young son, however, made him difficult to capture because airport security officials weren't likely to question or detain an attractive, apparently middle-class family. While the CIA tried to track down Rashid and sent notices about his activities to stations in the Middle East and Europe, the young Palestinian continued to elude them.

The next clue came two weeks after the Pan Am explosion, when airline attendants in Rio de Janeiro discovered an unexploded bomb attached to the bottom of a seat on a jetliner that had just completed a flight from Miami. Within hours, CIA explosives experts had linked the bomb to Rashid. Over the next year the agency doubled its efforts to find him, while the DO's Near East field officers planned and mounted an operation to dismantle the 15 May Group. By late 1982 the agency's operation provided significant results. It identified the organization's key leaders and recruited one of its European bomb couriers, a Palestinian businessman known to the agency as "MJ Holiday." This businessman-courier, in turn, identified two of the 15 May Group's high-level operatives, code-named MJ Ticker 1 and MJ Ticker 2. After Tunisian security officers discovered a bomb concealed in the suitcase of a Palestinian at Tunis's International Airport, MJ Tickers 1 and 2 unknowingly led the CIA to a cache of Rashid-built suitcase bombs in the North African city.

The discovery stunned the CIA's Directorate for Operations. Rashid had not only stockpiled a large number of suitcase bombs but made them virtually impossible to detect. All the bombs the CIA discovered either were wired on the inside of Japanese-manufactured radio-cassette players (with their barometric devices and detonators elegantly screened by the radio's speakers) or were molded into the lining of suitcases. Rashid's progress in constructing and concealing bombs constituted what CIA officers viewed as a technological revolution among terrorists; they knew that eventually Rashid and Ibrahim could build a bomb that would be undetectable, that even the most sensitive airport X-ray machines could not keep up with their innovations. The agency confiscated Rashid's Tunis bombs but failed to intercept other, less sophisticated types that were hidden in Europe.

"Holiday" provided the agency with some of the most important information on terrorism it ever received. In particular he revealed that the 15 May Group had dispatched a courier (code-named MJ Ticker 3) to Geneva, Switzerland, for the purpose of planting a bomb in the Noga Hilton Hotel. He warned that it was probably too late to intercept this mission. Fortunately for the agency, however, MJ Ticker 3 got cold feet and blubbered a tearful confession to Swiss intelligence officials before he activated the bomb. The Swiss turned him over to the Americans. The CIA dispatched an interrogation team to Geneva, and he immediately confessed that he had been given the device by Abu Ibrahim himself. The explosive material for the bomb was molded into the suitcase's lining, a perfect fit with Rashid's own bomb signature. CIA officers speculated that the bomb's explosive power would have "decapitated" the hotel by destroying its top floors. The carnage might have caused hundreds of casualties.

Agency officials started to breathe more easily in the autumn of 1983, after learning that Portuguese officials had arrested Rashid for his involvement in the murder of Dr. Issam Sartawi, a Palestinian moderate who was gunned down in front of his hotel in the resort city of Albufeira. Rashid confessed that he was involved in Sartawi's murder but denied he was the gunman. The agency's celebration of Rashid's arrest was tempered by Sartawi's assassination, which was a blow to U.S. government efforts to promote him as a moderating influence on the Palestine Liberation Organization (PLO). Sartawi had not been a U.S. agent, as Rashid and his accomplices claimed, but he was respected by CIA officers who followed his career. ("He was a very courageous man," says one CIA veteran.)

Rashid was found guilty by a Portuguese court of participating in the plot to kill Sartawi and sentenced to three years in prison. But even though Rashid was out of circulation in a Portuguese jail, his suitcase bombs were still active. In December 1983 security agents at Istanbul airport intercepted a bomb similar to those pioneered by Rashid; the lethal device was set to detonate eight hours after the suitcase was to be transferred in London to a Pan Am flight bound for New York—at about the same time that the plane was on its final approach to JFK International Airport.

Just after the discovery of the Istanbul bomb, a CIA officer working undercover in the agency station in Athens traced explosives used by the 15 May Group to the apartment of a young Englishwoman. The officer broke in, photographed the suitcases, and presented the evidence to Greek authorities. He also found explosives hidden in the woman's flower pots. The woman turned out to be an unwitting accomplice in several other planned bombings; she was the girl friend of radical Palestinian Fuad Hussein Shara, a Rashid accomplice whose next target was to be Israel's El Al Airlines. Greek authorities averted further disaster by arresting Shara and holding him for questioning. The combination of Shara's arrest, Rashid's incarceration in Portugal, and the discovery of his bombs in Tunis took enormous pressure off the DO, which was the target of a number of Casey's sputtering lectures on the agency's inexplicable impotence.

Although Casey had approved the plan to penetrate and destroy the 15 May Group, he was skeptical of the program's eventual worth and pushed the clandestine service to take more radical steps to deal with terrorists. During one briefing Casey had vehemently argued that Rashid should be kidnapped, saying that the CIA couldn't trust European intelligence services to defend U.S. interests. The Swiss were a case in point, Casey noted, since they apparently believed that bombs were round and black with long fuses, "like the kind used by the coyote in *Roadrunner* cartoons."

Casey became increasingly enraged by his inability to persuade key clandestine service officers to take extreme steps to deal with the 15 May Group. By early 1984 he had convinced himself that his assistants were more concerned with saving their own careers than with defending the national security. The DO, however, was unimpressed by Casey's arguments. It counseled patience; it knew that breaking up a terrorist organization took time. In fact, its operation was working well; the agency had identified important 15 May Group operations in Europe and put pressure on a number of governments to expel the organization's agents. With both Rashid and Shara in jail, it looked as if the CIA had successfully shut down a major terrorist threat. Casey was silenced, at least temporarily.

That changed in mid-1984, when Greece freed Shara and expelled the CIA's deputy chief of station in Athens. The Greeks claimed that U.S. officials purposely violated Greek law by illegally searching the apartment of the accused terrorist's girl friend. Shara's release was followed within weeks by that of Rashid, who immediately left Portugal. A former CIA officer and veteran of nearly twenty years' service in the DO's Near East Division vividly recalls the scene at CIA headquarters in early August 1984 on the morning after Rashid's release. Casey bellowed his way onto the seventh floor, shouting at the top of his lungs. His face was beet red, and the veins on his neck stood out against his starched white collar. But Casey's frustration wasn't aimed so much at the Portuguese as at his own clandestine staff. The United States could not count on the Europeans, he stressed, and he angrily denounced Greece for "caving in" to a "bunch of murderers." Finally he mastered his anger and barked out a series of orders to his top aides. The DO— meaning the Near East Division specifically—was to come up with a plan to kidnap Rashid and bring him to the United States for trial. Casey said he wanted the final proposal on his desk within a week. The division, he said, should start working on this as soon as possible, that very morning.

Casey's rage sent aides scurrying. They knew that this time, at least, Casey's demand that the agency do *something* was more than just bluster; his talk of "snatching" Rashid had the force of a direct order. The DCI was fully capable of spreading fear in the agency, though not simply because of his power as one of the few men in the administration who had Ronald Reagan's trust. What really worried agency officers was that Casey could count on support from an emerging group of pro-Casey activists ("my shooters," he called them), who were only too happy to comply with his wishes.

It didn't take long for word of Casey's tantrum to make the agency rounds. The CIA's younger officers, in particular, were angered by his proposal; they believed he was asking them to break the law or, at the very least, to undertake an unsanctioned covert operation. They weren't willing to do it; nearly all of their generation of recruits (primarily those in their late thirties in the agency's mid-level positions) had joined the CIA at the end of the Vietnam era, when trust in American leadership was at its lowest ebb. They kept faith with the agency, but only because of firm reassurances from CIA executives that the excesses of the 1960s would not be repeated.

In fact, they had little to fear. Hunched over their desks in their sixth-floor cubicles, clandestine service moderates who opposed Casey's plans found a way of dealing with his latest kidnapping orders. They relied on a method that they'd perfected during his first years: Studies were completed, plans drawn up, and officers dispatched overseas, but in the end nothing was done. The clandestine service stood its ground— and for good reason. The DO's most experienced and highest-ranking officials knew that Casey's dangerous proposals could damage valuable intelligence programs in the Arab world, where the CIA had worked diligently to gain the confidence of a number of North African, Middle Eastern, and Asian intelligence agencies. While there was little doubt that Rashid was a mass murderer and would continue his bombings unless stopped, these officers were convinced that his abduction would do nothing more than escalate an already vicious terrorist war. And they knew that the operation fell into a large gray area of American law since the CIA and other government agencies did not yet have the requisite "long arm" statute they needed to conduct kidnappings overseas. Like many of Casey's other proposals, they believed, the Rashid kidnapping was dangerously counterproductive: It would focus congressional attention on the agency at a time when it didn't need it.

The DCI's most important intelligence advisers shook their heads whenever Casey dismissed their warnings about questionable intelligence operations; the Congress barred the agency from engaging in such activities, and they were determined to make sure they obliged. They weren't going to put the agency at risk. Nor was the DO going to be intimidated by Casey's argument that it lacked the courage necessary to deal with international terrorists. At best, Casey's memory was selective; he hadn't been at the CIA when James Schlesinger decided to clean it out, nor had he been present when William Colby aired the agency's dirtiest secrets—the assassinations, coups, and dirty tricks—that forever tarnished its reputation. The result was that the CIA was far less willing to take the kinds of risks it had during the Dulles or Helms years. This viewpoint prevailed through 1984 and into early 1985. So long as Rashid's whereabouts were unknown, Casey could do little to convince the Operations Directorate to act. But when Rashid showed up in the Sudan, the DCI again ordered his top officers to draft plans for his abduction. This time, to make *certain* his orders were followed, Casey announced that he had talked about the kidnapping with the head of the French overseas intelligence service.

The CIA's leading counterterrorism officers were horrified. Casey's orders tied the agency to a foreign intelligence service renowned for engaging in risky operations that were not only illegal but sometimes even murderous. They also resented Casey's decision because they were convinced that the French had made things difficult for the United States in the Middle East. The French had adroitly stood by in 1979, for instance, and allowed the Ayatollah Khomeini to leave Paris for Teheran. That Casey would now order the CIA's top clandestine officers to cooperate with the French on a "snatch" operation brought open mutters of complaint. "Friendly intelligence service, my ass," one case officer said bitterly. From Casey's point of view, however, the recruitment of the French as a friendly liaison in the Rashid case made perfect sense since France's intelligence chief, Pierre Lacoste, a former vice admiral in the French Navy, was an engaging personality with the same political opinions as the DCI.

In April 1985 CIA officers discovered the French weren't as interested in kidnapping Rashid as they were in killing him and his wife (the ultimate fate of Rashid's ten-year-old son was never mentioned). This was going to be a tough and dangerous operation, the French said; you never knew what would happen—Rashid might even be accidentally shot. The trigger-happy French appeared unconcerned by the trouble this might cause for the CIA, whose nightmare was that unnecessary gunplay could result in the death of innocent Sudanese citizens. (An even worse fear for the CIA was that such a "wet" operation would result in a congressional investigation.) Casey's top aides also knew the Sudanese government would take a dim view of a CIA abduction on its soil. These senior operations officers decided that Rashid just wasn't worth it.

Meanwhile, the group of CIA counterterrorism officers working with the French decided to inform agency lawyers that they were planning an abduction. While the lawyers studied the operation, Casey proceeded to short-circuit the mounting opposition by moving up the "go" date of the kidnapping. At the last minute, however, a full-scale internal skirmish over the program was averted when the French inexplicably withdrew their support. Later an interagency operation (involving FBI,

FAA, NSC, and CIA officers) to nab Rashid also went awry. Finally, on May 30, 1988, after receiving a tip that he would make an appearance in Khartoum, in Sudan, CIA officers waiting for him there were informed that he had been arrested in Athens. They rushed to Greece to put pressure on the government to hold him indefinitely, pending his extradition to the United States to stand trial.

The handling of the Rashid case was symbolic of Casey's style, but it was just one of a number of problems DO officers faced during his six years in office. There were others, some of them so intractable that a number of senior officials in attendance at his funeral in May 1987 were relieved they didn't have to wrestle with them again. Among those who had come to pay their respects to Casey was David Whipple, who earlier had been given the thankless task of escorting the DCI during his visits to Capitol Hill. It had proved to be one of the most frustrating experiences of Whipple's long career. The tall, plainspoken veteran was involved in several dangerous overseas missions during his thirty years at the CIA, but nothing compared with the danger caused by Casey's exaggerated claims about national security issues that were presented to Congress. In effect, Casey stretched the truth beyond believable bounds during his appearances in order to dramatize his, and the CIA's, position on complex intelligence questions. Whenever Casey finished his testimony and returned to the agency, it was always Whipple's job to repair the damage he'd done.

Another high-ranking career CIA officer had similar experiences with the Congress. By 1986, he says, Casey's inflammatory statements to the oversight committees forced him to adopt a strategy designed to derail the DCI's claims without raising questions about his competence. After Casey completed his testimony and departed, the aide normally stayed behind to provide more details on his major points. In fact, the aide's real strategy was to water down what Casey had said: The aide agreed with every point the DCI made but made sure that the committee understood the pressures that Casey was under. The CIA spokesman would indirectly apologize for Casey's testimony by suggesting that the pressures of his job sometimes caused him inadvertently to exaggerate some of his claims. Whenever the aide came under fire from skeptical committee members who were accustomed to this peculiar performance, he feigned anger and argued that the committee was putting too fine an edge on Casey's words. What Casey said was true "in principle," the aide protested, but as the committee well knew, certainty was a slippery thing. It was the committee's fault for demanding all the details, not Casey's.

"There was always this problem with Congress, and it just got worse and worse," David Whipple admits. "And we would go to him [Casey] and say: 'Listen, this time, when you go up there, just answer the question.' But it was absolutely useless. And don't get me wrong, Casey wasn't lying, not at all. He was just giving them William Casey's view of the world."

Reflecting on this delicate task in the aftermath of Casey's death, the CIA officer who often accompanied Casey to Congress admitted that his strategy of protecting Casey more often failed than succeeded. The most embarrassing failure came at the beginning of his tenure, when Casey told the Senate Select Committee on Intelligence that the CIA had obtained proof that the Soviet Union was financing and training international terrorists, an idea he'd adopted after reading journalist Claire Sterling's 1981 book *The Terror Network: The Secret War of International Terrorism*. Sterling claimed that all major international terrorist groups were controlled by the Soviet Union. (Then-Secretary of State Alexander Haig obtained a galley proof of the book and found it so compelling that he passed it on to Casey.) At Casey's insistence, top CIA terrorism analysts and Soviet experts dissected Sterling's argument and assigned a group to prepare a special national intelligence estimate, or SNIE, on the subject. Based on a collation of a mass of intelligence data and secret interviews with key sources from the third world, the finished SNIE gave only a backhanded endorsement to Sterling's claim: The assessment concluded only that there was some evidence that the Soviets provided support for revolutionary organizations in third world countries. But even that finding was a reach—and the authors specifically backed off from making claims that Moscow provided any direct support for terrorist organizations that threatened U.S. interests. The SNIE even presented evidence that the USSR attempted to dissuade certain Palestinian terrorist groups from taking violent actions against American targets. These official conclusions didn't bother Casey, however; he continued to support the claims in the Sterling book.

After Casey ended his congressional testimony and returned to Langley, his aide was left to answer detailed questions about the CIA's position on terrorism. The committee had clearly misunderstood the director, the aide lamely explained; there was no such thing as absolute proof. On the other hand, he added, Casey was actually right: After all, wasn't it true that the Soviets were allies of nations that harbored terrorists? The proof, the aide maintained, was right there for anyone to see. Leaning back in his chair, a pencil set to his pursed lips, Senator Barry Goldwater, the committee's co-chairman, shook his head in disgust. He didn't believe it, the rest of the committee didn't believe it, Casey's aide didn't believe it, and most important, the CIA didn't believe it. The committee session was adjourned.

Afterward Casey still remained deeply dissatisfied with the CIA's findings. During one subsequent review of the SNIE, he asked his staff: How could Claire Sterling find evidence of Soviet-backed terrorism and his own analysts find nothing? Look again, he insisted. But the CIA's top intelligence analysts still came up empty-handed. "It was just bullshit," recalls the top aide who accompanied Casey on Capitol Hill. "I had to tell the committee that, but without really saying it." Casey eventually dropped the matter, but only with great reluctance.

By 1984 Casey had become convinced the agency was crippled by a fear of failure and by years of ossified leadership; it had become a top-heavy bureaucracy, he thought, an incompetent force that was governed by an outdated code. Casey desperately wanted to reinvigorate the CIA, but four years into his tenure as its leader he still didn't know how. His disappointment focused itself on his key aides—the heads of the major directorates and especially the top division chiefs of the clandestine service. Despite their years of overseas espionage experience, to Casey these senior officers seemed incapable of following his simplest orders.

Although Casey came to the CIA with few illusions and was well aware that the previous fifteen years had gutted the clandestine service of its most talented officers, he was sorely disappointed by what he viewed as the DO's lack of creative thinking, a handicap caused by the clandestine service's fear of public scandal. By 1984 Casey was convinced that when it came to conducting operations that threatened the CIA's reputation in Washington, he would have to turn to someone outside the agency for help.

While CIA officers who became entangled in the Iran-contra scandal disagree about many of its details, they are convinced that Casey used Oliver North in order to circumvent the agency's unwillingness to participate in high-risk activities. North became Casey's unofficial director for operations and the acknowledged inheritor of his activist dream; in Casey's eyes North was a hero. Despite Casey's growing friendship with the young lieutenant colonel, only a small group of agency officers knew that North was running a mini-CIA inside the White House until the summer of 1985, when they were first brought into Casey's scheme to provide logistical support for North's secret arms shipments to Iran. Casey gave his DO officers a direct order to help North and assured them that his operation had White House approval. This tight circle of officers had deep doubts about the wisdom of this plan, but they had their instructions; the CIA served the President and they served the CIA. It was also obvious to this select group, without being stated, that they shouldn't ask too many questions. Thomas Twetten, then the deputy chief of the CIA's NE Division, said as much in a deposition he gave after the scandal had been made public. "I will tell you that [it] is not my job to investigate Colonel North," he remarked bitterly, while making it sound as if he wished somebody had.

Clair George, then the agency's deputy director for operations and its master of clandestine planning, also viewed the North-Casey initiative suspiciously. George, who spent a lifetime working on overseas operations, had developed a basic mistrust of Casey's judgment. While George was required to follow the DCI's orders, he continually questioned them. George had come to this view through close personal contact with Casey. Earlier, in 1982, after more than two decades as a clandestine service officer, for example, George's own career was sidetracked when Casey named him head of congressional relations. The appointment was a disaster, as many predicted it would be, because George was never able to acclimate himself fully to the openness that the job demanded. Senate Intelligence Committee members suspected that his natural career-inculcated reticence to share information with anyone was his way of showing disrespect for democratic principles, but they were wrong. George was normally ebullient, positive, and hardworking, but Casey's views wore him down.

In July 1984 George was finally appointed deputy director for operations, the pinnacle of a successful career and a position that suited him much better. The following year, however, he was horrified to learn that he would be involved at Casey's urging with Manucher Ghorbanifar, a man who was viewed as "a cheat and a crook and totally dishonest."

Ghorbanifar was a rotund, mustached, fast-talking Iranian businessman who'd lived in exile in France since 1979. He'd had contact with the CIA before; DO officers described him as a "rumormonger" and "a talented fabricator." His agency file said that information provided by him "consistently lacked sourcing and detail notwithstanding his exclusive interest in acquiring money." Nevertheless, Casey decided in 1985 to take the most recent of Ghorbanifar's contacts with the CIA seriously because he claimed to have a special relationship with moderates inside the Iranian government. Casey wasn't the only one who considered Ghorbanifar a valuable intelligence asset; the Mossad (the Israeli intelligence service) also presented him as a source with credible information on moderate Iranian government factions that would welcome an opening to the United States. CIA operations experts, led by George, strongly disagreed with both Casey and the Israelis, and to buttress their view, CIA officers gave Ghorbanifar a polygraph examination in January 1986. The test showed that he lied on all but one question: He told the truth about his name. That didn't seem to bother Casey, who remained as committed to Ghorbanifar in 1985 as he was to Claire Sterling in 1981. When George told Casey that he found it distasteful to have to deal with Ghorbanifar, Casey said he didn't have to; he would assign someone else. Charles Allen, one of the agency's top counterterrorism experts and a graying Middle East analyst, was given the job.

Ghorbanifar wasn't the only problem that officers in the clandestine service had with the proposed opening to Iran that was being pursued by Casey and the White House. The other problem was Richard Secord, a retired, politically conservative Air Force general who admitted that one day he wanted to take George's job as chief of the CIA's clandestine service. That wish was pure fantasy: Secord had gotten mixed up in a scheme orchestrated by CIA renegade Ed Wilson to sell weapons illegally to Libya in the early 1980s. As a result, Secord was forced to retire. But he'd kept his hand in by parlaying his knowledge of Iran into a number of international business ventures. Secord's partner was an Iranian-American by the name of Albert Hakim, a small man with intense eyes and a flair for making money. The CIA's file on Hakim, kept in the military liaison branch, described him as "a businessman with broad international contacts," a phrase that CIA officers interpreted to mean that Hakim would help the United States, but only for a profit. Nobody in the agency's upper reaches was happy to work with either Secord or Hakim, but no one had a choice; both men were North's operations officers.

In November 1985 Casey assigned the agency's head of clandestine operations in Europe, Dewey Clarridge, to help North smooth the way for his illegal arms flights—in this case, a shipment of TOW missiles from Israel, via Lisbon, to Teheran. Clarridge and North were friends. They had been introduced several years earlier when Clarridge, then concentrating on Latin American projects, had relied on North to keep Nicaragua's contras supplied. In effect, North became Clarridge's point man at the White House, a jack-of-all-trades who enjoyed clandestine operations nearly as much as his CIA counterpart. Clarridge, a flamboyant white-haired case officer with twenty-five years of operations experience, was a unique and legendary figure inside the DO. Breezy, brilliant, glib to a fault, the energetic and chain-smoking Clarridge often dressed in black suits and pink ties with a garish swatch of handkerchief peeking from his pocket. He was a master of the outlandish who, at the same time, was committed to anonymity. His disguise was to draw attention to himself. Those who served under him explained it this way: No one would ever mistake a man who dressed like Clarridge for a CIA officer. His colleagues at the CIA also knew well Clarridge's real strength: He was an operations genius, one of the rare breed who took to clandestine activities as if born to them.

Casey trusted Clarridge; he liked the man as he liked few others among his division chiefs. Clarridge was chief of station in Rome when Casey discovered him in the early 1980s. Later, at Casey's instigation, Clarridge rose to become chief of the Latin America Division and then head of all agency espionage operations in Europe. Clarridge was one of the few CIA officers with whom Casey developed a warm personal relationship. Casey valued Clarridge's views on the CIA's future but especially his judgments about the terrorist threat in the Arab world. Clarridge was born and bred in the Near East Division. ("He was dyed-in-the-blue NE," a former case officer who served with him attests.) On the basis of his years of experience overseas, Clarridge remained a widely respected Arabist. So when Oliver North needed help with Iran, it was only natural that Casey would give the job to Clarridge. In November 1985 Clarridge began working with North on the Iran account.

Almost immediately thereafter, Clarridge made a rare mistake, one that turned out to be fatal for his career. In late November 1985 he gave Richard Secord the name of a CIA airline proprietary when the retired general had trouble finding an aircraft for his covert Tel Aviv to Lisbon to Iran airlift. This slipup sent Deputy DCI John McMahon into a fit of anger and despair. Using a CIA airline tied the agency to the National Security Council's operation, McMahon said, and made the CIA an integral part of North's initiative. As patiently as possible McMahon reminded Clarridge's boss, Edward Juchniewicz (the assistant deputy director for operations [ADDO]), that in order to conduct a covert activity, the CIA needed a finding—a written presidential seal of approval. Up to this point the CIA hadn't needed one because it really hadn't been involved in the program. Now not only did it have to make it its operation, but the finding would have to be backdated to cover Clarridge's bonehead move.

As punishment for his gaffe, Casey decided to reassign Clarridge to another of his pet projects: conducting a study of the ways the CIA could combat international terrorism. In the meantime, the planning for North's arms shipments was turned over to the NE Division, headed by Bert Dunn and his deputy, Thomas Twetten. Twetten decided to take the lead in the operation despite his obvious "consternation" at having to deal with the likes of Ghorbanifar, Secord, and Hakim (all of whom, as he said, had a "little odor"). Twetten, an unassuming thirty-year CIA veteran, had built his career from the bottom up, as a case officer and then the station chief in the Middle East. Much of his career was spent at Langley, however, because he eschewed foreign assignments (primarily, as CIA scuttlebutt would have it, because his wife wanted him close to home). For a variety of reasons, Twetten was not viewed as a man with special talents by his colleagues. "We figured he wouldn't even make it as a mid-level officer," said one. After he served a stint in Cairo and Amman, most of his colleagues viewed him as "just an average" case officer, clearly not in the same league as either Clarridge or Dunn.

Twetten would prove his detractors to be wrong. Despite predictions that he would never make it into the agency hierarchy, his solid, if unexciting, tradecraft had paid off in 1970 in Cairo, where Americans were looked on with suspicion. According to a story on Twetten's career that circulated inside Langley when he was ADDO, Twetten made impressive contacts in Egypt's government, and reported his successes back to Langley. His success was all the more impressive because Egyptian President Gamal Abdel Nasser had transformed the Mukhabarat el-Aam, the Egyptian intelligence service, into a wing of the KGB, which made it incredibly difficult for the CIA to conduct operations in Egypt. When Nasser died in September 1970, his successor, Anwar el-Sadat, took only a few, tentative steps to change the previous intelligence relationships. The "Soviet Republic of Egypt," as the KGB termed it, remained solidly in the USSR's orbit. When Twetten was assigned to Cairo, he found it almost impossible to get a foothold in the country; his every move was monitored, his most innocent contacts were questioned and sometimes even tortured. (The Mukhabarat was established by former Nazis stranded in Egypt after World War II, and its methods hadn't changed much over the previous twenty-five years.)

In 1971 the CIA's Cairo station was located in the American Interests section of the Spanish Embassy. As one of the station's newest officers, Twetten decided he would try his best to open the Egyptian government to CIA penetration. With this in mind, he befriended Ashraf Marwan, a high-level Egyptian official who sat next to Sadat during Cabinet meetings and served as his closest adviser. Marwan seemed to be a possible recruitment target because he had deep doubts about Egypt's increasing dependence on Soviet largess. He was also an admirer of the United States, and he mistrusted the head of Egypt's intelligence service, Sami Sharaf, a portly, block-faced man who enjoyed watching the tortures he ordered. Sharaf was the KGB's top agent in Cairo and became its most outspoken defender in Sadat's inner circle. Twetten's eventual conversion of Ashraf Marwan was considered a nearly miraculous accomplishment; by early May 1971 high-ranking CIA officials at Langley were so impressed by Marwan's anti-Soviet stance that they began to believe he might be the key to taking Egypt out of the Soviet orbit. They were right.

On a hot morning in mid-May 1971, Twetten received a "flash" cable from Langley that warned of a KGB plan to overthrow Sadat. Precise evidence about the coup was difficult to obtain, especially since the Mukhabarat was under Sharaf's control. However, by putting together a complex series of intelligence reports from otherwise disparate sources, the CIA managed to learn that Sadat would be assassinated during a coup launched by a number of his top aides, who were in the pay of the KGB. One of these reports, which the agency viewed as authoritative, was provided by a career Soviet diplomat and KGB officer, Vladimir Nikolaevich Sakharov, who was then stationed in Kuwait and had previously served in Egypt. Sakharov—who had worked for the CIA throughout the 1960s—felt he had come under increasing suspicion by his KGB colleagues in Kuwait City. He reported his fears to his CIA handler, a career NE Division officer then serving as COS in Kuwait.

Sakharov's report about the coup plot in Cairo was coupled with intelligence gleaned from the agency's penetrations in Egypt—including transcripts of telephone conversations among the plotters. The overall picture indicated that the coup might succeed. The implications were stunning: Sadat's overthrow would lock Egypt in the Soviet camp, redeeming the billions of rubles the USSR had squandered on some of Nasser's grandiose projects.

It took Twetten three hours to shake the Mukhabaret tail that the KGB put on him during the early-morning hours of that bright May day in 1971, but when he finally met with his Egyptian contact, he had more than enough time to detail the outlines of the plot against Sadat. He explained to Marwan how Sadat's own intelligence service was suborned, how his military chiefs took favors from the KGB, and how Nasser's and now Sadat's top intelligence adviser was working for the Russians.

Within days of Twetten's meeting with his contact, Sadat broke the back of the coup and arrested the chief plotters. Twetten's primary evidence was taped telephone intercepts of conversations among the plotters, which Marwan laid on Sadat's desk on the morning of May 11. The tapes proved that intelligence chief Sami Sharaf and Sadat's vice-president, Ali Sabry, were both part of the secret plot. (Sabry had been designated by the KGB to take Sadat's place after he was murdered.)

Twetten became the unacknowledged hero of Egypt, a CIA officer whose diligent tradecraft paid off in an unexpected way. After the failed coup the United States worked at breakneck speed to make Egypt an American ally, including calling on Kamal Adham, then the chief of Saudi Arabian intelligence, to put increasing pressure on Marwan to convince Sadat to turn his country to the West. It was Twetten's crucial work, and a little luck, that made this effort possible, and in the postmortem he was credited with almost single-handedly taking the Sadat government out of the Soviet orbit. It was simply a major CIA victory that had been accomplished at a fraction of the cost of the billions of rubles that the Soviets had indulged on their future Soviet republic.

For the United States, the payoff was sweeter than anyone could have imagined; during the years following the arrests of Sharaf and Sabry, the Russians were kicked out of Egypt, their intelligence assets in the country were hunted, tried, and jailed, and their embassy in Cairo was isolated behind a high brick enclosure. Thanks to Sakharov's information, the CIA was able to identify every known Soviet intelligence asset in Egypt, in effect turning the former Soviet Egyptian republic into a KGB gulag. Another of the rewards of Egypt's transformation into an American ally was the establishment of the U.S. Army's desert "Red

Team," a fully armored battalion of Soviet tanks and troop carriers based in California that is still used by the American military to help train its soldiers in the tactics of the next war. It all was shipped to the United States from Egypt, as Sadat's way of showing gratitude.

Twetten's next major foreign assignment was not nearly as successful. In the late 1970s he became chief of station in Amman, Jordan, where he was given responsibility for working with King Hussein, then counted as one of America's most important allies in the Middle East. In Amman, Twetten inherited a divided and demoralized station rife with sexual intrigue. According to several CIA officers familiar with his Amman troubles, several months after becoming COS, Twetten discovered that one of the station's secretaries was having a romantic relationship with a Jordanian intelligence officer who was also a KGB source. The potential scandal might have ruined Twetten's career, but he acted as quickly as he had in Egypt: He fired the secretary, he made a full report to agency headquarters, and he cooperated with the security team dispatched from Langley to conduct a full station-wide investigation. The miniscandal was embarrassing but not fatal.

Twetten later had other troubles: King Hussein disliked him because, unlike his predecessor, he didn't ride and hunt, a talent that, in Hussein's opinion, was an absolute requirement for an American intelligence officer. Twetten went riding with the king once, and it didn't turn out well. Afterward Hussein badgered Langley to recall Twetten. While the DO's senior officers hesitated to do so, they finally agreed and brought him home to serve in the CIA's favorite dumping ground, the Office of Technical Services.

The next several years, until the mid-1980s, were Twetten's most productive years as a CIA officer. He became an expert on terrorist organizations and clawed his way to the top of the NE Division by proving his worth as a resident expert on the politics of the Middle East. By the time he was named deputy chief of the NE Division, he had a healthy respect for traditional tradecraft, the keep-it-simple-stupid philosophy that marks the agency's most successful operations. This was why Casey's support of the Oliver North initiative bothered Twetten. Something about the operation, to paraphrase Twetten's own description, just didn't smell right. Still, he had his orders, and the initiative had the support of the President; the best that he and others at the agency could do, Twetten believed, was to keep the CIA clear of the wreckage when the whole thing came crashing down, as it almost certainly would.

In February 1986 Twetten thought he had found a way to lessen the agency's vulnerability. Returning with North from a meeting in West Germany to iron out the details of future arms transfers, Twetten gingerly mentioned that Secord, Hakim, and Ghorbanifar were inappropriate intermediaries to be dealing with the CIA. He couched his criticism as a professional opinion, by suggesting that North needed a better translator than Ghorbanifar or Hakim ("I am not one who presses frontally very often," he later admitted). When North didn't respond, Twetten told him that it wasn't a good idea to have "these outsiders" involved in the operation, especially since the arms-for-hostages initiative was now official government policy. He added that he would be happy to provide North with a trusted officer who spoke fluent Farsi. What Twetten *didn't* tell North was that he feared the initiative to supply arms to Iran would cross paths with the administration support of the contras, as now seemed possible, since that part of the operation was being run by Secord. "... we never mix the mechanism for two separate operations if we can possibly get away from it," Twetten later explained.

It's clear from the evidence subsequently developed by congressional investigators that Twetten believed it was his job to keep the CIA as far away from North's Iran arms initiative as he possibly could, but without actually circumventing Casey's orders *or* the President's wishes. And while he kept insisting that it was an NSC operation (a plaintive plea at best, considering Dewey Clarridge's inadvertent mistake in November), Twetten knew that CIA officers would inevitably be implicated no matter how many protections he tried to install. When it all came out, Twetten knew, someone would have to be in place to draw the investigators' attention away from the CIA—someone who spoke Farsi, knew Iran, but wasn't currently tied in to the agency's inner circle.

Retired CIA veteran George Cave met all of Twetten's requirements: The graying, battle-hardened, and quick-tongued former chief of station in Teheran had a gift for languages, was familiar with the leading figures of the Iranian revolution, spoke excellent Farsi, and, like Twetten, knew a bad operation when he saw one. Like many other retired CIA officers of his generation, Cave was a born skeptic with a bad back, who was dedicated to spending his last years nurturing a family he'd ignored through all of his long career. Twetten's choice of Cave to head the North initiative was well suited for two other reasons: First, Cave was still an agency consultant, though not a full-time employee; second, Cave knew Ghorbanifar well; he'd terminated the CIA's relationship with the Iranian in the early 1980s and had designed the polygraph exam that Ghorbanifar had flunked two months before. Twetten and Clair George met with Cave at Langley on March 5.

Twetten knew that Cave would be surprised to learn the agency was involved with Ghorbanifar once again, so he tried to soften the blow. How would Cave like to meet Ali Akbar Hashemi Rafsanjani, the most powerful and important man in Iran aside from Khomeini himself? Cave waved off Twetten's opening question and asked him to come to the point. Unchastened, Twetten nodded curtly and plunged ahead, telling Cave that the agency was providing assistance to the NSC to ship arms to Iran. There were two goals, he said: first, to open Iran to the United States and, second, to gain the release of American hostages being held in Lebanon. The arms, Twetten added, were being shipped through Oliver North's intermediaries, who included Ghorbanifar.

Cave's response to this pitch was all that Twetten could have hoped: "After I heard about the initiative, I recommended to [Twetten] and I think also to Clair George, that the participation in the operation by serving officers should be as limited as possible in that it was quite apparent to me if this operation ever blew, you know, careers would be in jeopardy. And since I was an annuitant, it didn't matter."

Cave did his job well. He served as the agency's trusted intermediary on the North initiative and carefully kept his former employer clear of its seamier aspects. Put simply, the CIA's most senior operations officers—Twetten, George, and others—attempted to do to the Casey-North operation what others had done to Casey's Rashid operation: They tried to control it and hoped they could eventually kill it. While their effort ultimately failed, as they feared it would, they took steps to ensure that as few agency employees as possible were involved in the public scandal that resulted. When they failed in their effort to convince Casey that his scheme was based on a false premise (namely, that there actually *were* moderates in the Iranian government), their strategy was to minimize the scandal's impact on the CIA. In large measure, they succeeded—at least for a time.

The most important lesson learned by the CIA's senior operations officers was how to survive. Thomas Twetten survived Amman, George Cave survived the horrors of a revolution in progress in Teheran, Clair George survived the ugly underside of the cold war in Europe and Africa. And each of them survived six years of William Casey's leadership of the CIA. Those six years provide a commentary on how the agency views itself, as well as how its senior managers worked to protect it from attacks on its forty-plus-year tradition. The arms-for-hostages operation is a case in point.

The scandal bared the myth behind America's melodramatic, and sometimes even romantic, perception of the CIA as an uncontrollable behemoth, an all-powerful body of spies whose commitment to secrecy veils the seedy underside of its daily work. A more appropriate and more accurate metaphor is suggested instead by the scene in *The Wizard of Oz* when young Dorothy finally arrives at the Emerald City. Much to her disappointment, she finds that the Wizard (a stammering, sometimes confused, but kindhearted old man) is much less powerful than she had ever supposed. The true secret he possesses is that his power is based on an illusion; he can manipulate the levers that make him *look* powerful, but in the end he can do little else. His bag of tricks is empty; he's a charlatan. The Wizard's real message ("pay no attention to that man behind the curtain")—like Casey's—is that no one should look too closely at what he's doing.

Herein lies the basic paradox of William Casey's term as DCI. At the same time that the agency's most experienced clandestine service officers were celebrating his commitment to operational activism, they were acting to dampen the impact of his schemes. Where once they had pushed and prodded his predecessor, Stansfield Turner, they now held tightly to the reins. They praised him and defended him because he reminded them of what they once had been and, they hoped, could be once again.

Even Thomas Polgar, the outspoken former Saigon COS who was hired by the Senate to investigate the Iran-contra scandal, could not bring himself to denigrate Casey. "He did what he thought was right," Polgar says. "There were problems, sure, but he was respected over there."

Dr. Ray S. Cline, one of the deans of the CIA's retired set, puts it much the same way: "He had terrible administrative problems. I don't think that was his strong suit. But he understood the pride of the agency and the clandestine service's feeling of elitism." All this rationalization was by way of apology: If Casey made mistakes, his defenders maintained, it was only because he believed that the CIA could defeat America's enemies; the agency was the one part of the bureaucracy that could see things clearly. "He appreciated the agency's ability to get things done, even as he criticized it for not being creative enough," remarks one officer. "He was frustrated by its contradictions, pleased by its commitment. But in the end he knew it was just like any other part of the government, a bureaucracy."

Casey's tenure as director of central intelligence was fraught with danger, including the threat that the DCI himself could have brought down the agency. While there were great accomplishments during his six-year term (the agency fought and checkmated the Soviet advance in Afghanistan, broke up a major terrorist ring in Europe, and began rebuilding the human intelligence sources that provide a necessary foundation for all intelligence work), there were also critical setbacks: Casey quibbled with Congress over notification requirements on covert operations, was caught mining Nicaragua's harbors when he said he wouldn't, and was embarrassed by the publication of a counterinsurgency manual that winked at murder. He died just as the CIA was being scrutinized for its role in the Iran-contra affair. Despite these problems, the CIA emerged intact from the Casey years and ready to serve its new head, William Webster. Judge Webster's surprise appointment held out some hope, which even his most strident critics acknowledged, that he might actually accomplish for the CIA what Jeane Kirkpatrick claimed for

Casey: He would follow the law and in doing so return the CIA to a respected position at the head of the American intelligence community. The only question was whether an outsider like Webster, a man barely known inside the world of international intelligence, would fit into the Byzantine traditions at Langley.

At the end of the May 7 funeral service Casey's casket was carried by six pallbearers to a waiting hearse. The burial itself was private, at nearby Holy Rood Cemetery. Neither President Reagan nor any other dignitaries attended the ceremony at the grave site. They decided instead to return to Washington, where they faced a cascade of questions about the secret operation that Casey was thought to have commanded. Appropriately, the day ended on a confusing note—one that seemed to symbolize Casey's term as DCI—when Ronald Reagan misunderstood a reporter's question, yelled out over the sound of the presidential helicopter's revving engine. "Did you contribute to the Casey-contra fund?" the reporter asked. Reagan nodded yes. Later presidential spokesman Marlin Fitzwater cleared up the confusion, by explaining that the President thought he was responding affirmatively to the question, "Was it a nice service?"

2
★ ★ ★
Our Man in Teheran

*H*oward Baker was worried. Just seventy-two hours after becoming White House chief of staff, the former Tennessee senator and presidential candidate was in the midst of his first major crisis: The Reagan administration couldn't find anyone to replace Bill Casey as the nation's top spy. Long before Baker had arrived at the White House, the Senate had successfully derailed the nomination of President Reagan's first choice to become the new DCI, Robert Gates, who withdrew his name from consideration when questions were raised about his role in the Iran-contra scandal. With Gates out of the running Baker was now touting former Texas senator John Tower as the perfect nominee. When Baker mentioned the idea to Tower on Monday, March 2, 1987, just one day before the President intended to announce the selection, Tower seemed likely to accept. Although he hadn't yet said yes, he would absolutely take the job, as far as Baker was concerned, there was never any doubt that he would.

Even Gates, still the acting DCI, thought the Tower nomination would be welcomed at the agency. While it was true that Tower didn't have the required intelligence experience for the job, Gates knew that the CIA's top officers were desperate for the patina of respectability Tower's nomination would bring. Moreover, Gates knew that the agency didn't need an intelligence genius—someone like Allen Dulles, say—but a good administrator and a strong presence respected by Congress. Gates believed that his CIA colleagues would be satisfied with just about anyone, so long as the new DCI didn't use the Iran-contra scandal as an excuse to dismember the intelligence community.

As late as Monday afternoon, Tower's nomination seemed a certainty. He was to be ushered into the White House on Tuesday morning and introduced to the national press, after which he was expected to gain easy Senate confirmation. Tower was trusted on Capitol Hill, well known to the public, and, although a tough, conservative Republican, had recently added a reputation for objectivity when he was properly critical of Reagan during the Iran-contra scandal.

Tower's credibility came from his sometimes harsh censure of Reagan when he headed the three-man committee that assessed NSC procedures during the Iran-contra debacle. The final report that the Tower Commission issued (officially the "Report of the President's Special Review Board") concluded that Reagan never took responsibility for White House actions in the Iran-contra affair and allowed his staff to pursue a policy that contradicted his public statements. Tower's conclusions, while not shattering, showed his independence from the President, a quality that would help him during the confirmation process. Even so, if it seemed that the CIA job was a payoff for Tower's work as Ronald Reagan's chief damage control officer, as some suggested, Baker was willing to meet the charge head-on. The Senate, he believed, wouldn't dare deny Tower the job or question his ability to head the agency. He was one of their own.

Just as Baker was set to announce that Tower would be the new DCI, however, Tower called the White House to say that he wouldn't take the job after all. He was apologetic and fully aware of the embarrassment his apparent change of heart might cause Ronald Reagan's new chief of staff, but the decision was final. "I just can't do it," he told Baker. He'd always been interested in being defense secretary, not CIA director. Being head of the CIA was an honor, no doubt about it, he admitted, but it would take him out of the running for the Pentagon post forever. His heart was set on being secretary of defense, and he thought he still had a chance at that job in the future. Baker argued with Tower, but his words were perfunctory; he could tell the Texan had made up his mind.

Baker was exasperated. He knew that Tower's rejection could prove to be very embarrassing to Reagan, whose ability to lead was already the subject of widespread discussion. The chief of staff searched through his list of names. Gates was gone; Tower was waiting for a job that might never come. There was always Brent Scowcroft, of course, the former Air Force general who had served on the Tower Commission, but appointing Scowcroft now, so soon after the Texas senator had turned the job down, would make it look as if the President was searching around for someone to reward. That also meant that appointing former senator Edmund Muskie was also out of the question—since he had been the third Tower Commission member. Muskie was too much of a Democrat anyway, Baker decided, so he never seriously considered Muskie for the job, even though his name had appeared mysteriously in several newspaper accounts. With the press breathlessly waiting for an announcement ("They look like they're smirking," remarked one of Gates's friends to the acting DCI), Baker decided he needed to move quickly.

At this point Vice President George Bush entered the picture. During the previous weekend Bush had discussed with his staff the need to appoint a trusted government official to lead the CIA. Bush, himself a former DCI, believed he had a unique perspective to offer in selecting a new nominee. He and his staff came to the conclusion that the serving director of the Federal Bureau of Investigation, William Webster, was the best man for the job. Webster met the same criteria as Tower, Bush argued, because, like Tower, he was a lifelong, loyal Republican and was trusted by Reagan's top aides as well as by Bush himself. Bush considered Webster not only a friend but something of a kindred spirit. In light of his handling of the FBI over the previous nine years, Bush believed Webster almost certainly would win speedy confirmation from the Senate (particularly since he had done so before). Then, too, Webster had something Tower didn't: As head of the FBI he had gained nearly a decade of experience in working with the intelligence community and was familiar with the role of the CIA. Most important of all, Bush told his aides, he admired Webster's "steadiness" and "commitment." While Webster's appointment would leave the FBI job vacant, this was considered a minor problem, since his ten-year term was nearly over anyway. The White House believed it could take its time in appointing a successor. Baker readily agreed with Bush; he was surprised that he hadn't thought of Webster earlier. Getting Reagan's approval was a mere formality. On the afternoon of March 3 Baker phoned Webster to convey the offer.

Webster was intrigued with the idea of heading the CIA but wouldn't commit himself. Baker pushed him, saying that the President needed an answer within twenty-four hours. Webster told Baker that he would need only one night to make up his mind. Webster was flattered by Baker's call. He knew he would have to take the offer seriously despite the fact that he didn't want to stay in Washington. He had actually planned to leave the FBI in 1985 but had agreed to stay only at the urging of Attorney General Meese, who told him that leaving his post during the off-year election campaign was a bad idea. Webster made it clear to Meese that he was eager to return to St. Louis to practice law as soon as it was politically feasible to replace him. He had ended up staying nearly two more years. Now, with Baker's phone call, he was forced to make a decision he knew he couldn't make alone. Webster, a widower, telephoned his daughter Drusilla ("Dru," he calls her) with the news. She was silent at first and then clearly expressed her displeasure. "The FBI's one thing," she said. "But, Daddy, that other place is scary." He reassured her that he hadn't yet decided what to do but said he was inclined to take the job.

That night Webster made a second call, this time to Admiral Bobby Ray Inman, Casey's first deputy DCI, the former head of the National Security Agency, and one of the most respected intelligence officials in Washington. When Reagan was first elected President, Inman was at the top of everyone's list to be the new DCI. When Casey got the job, he swallowed his disappointment, agreed to be Casey's deputy, but left the agency after only sixteen months, when it became clear he had little real influence. Webster wanted to know whether Inman thought he should take the CIA job. Was it possible, he asked, for a CIA director to be a lawyer and still be an effective head of a spy agency? Wouldn't he be required to break the law? Inman reassured Webster that he could serve at the agency without compromising his principles. The CIA didn't break *U.S.* laws, Inman explained, though foreign laws were a different matter. Webster was reassured but wanted to know Inman's opinion of the agency's morale, especially after the Iran-contra scandal. Inman replied that morale had been damaged but could be quickly turned around if the CIA were given effective leadership. Finally, Webster asked, did Inman think that he'd be a good director of central intelligence? Inman sincerely answered that he thought that Webster would be a good DCI. The job, he said, was "a challenge."

Webster made his decision early the next afternoon, though a number of his FBI associates now recall that there was never really any doubt that he would accept Baker's offer. Webster, they say, was as convinced as Bush that he was a perfect choice for the position. Despite the inherent differences between the agency and the bureau, Webster was already familiar with some of what the CIA did; within one year of being named to the FBI, Webster had expanded the bureau's overseas intelligence operations as part of his program of cooperation with the CIA. Webster believed he could do for the CIA what he had done for the FBI. In his view, the two agencies weren't really that dissimilar in what they needed in terms of management styles. In fact, the CIA was in much the same position in 1987 as the FBI had been when Webster took it over nine years earlier. In 1978 the FBI was haunted by the ghost of J. Edgar Hoover, one of the most powerful and controversial figures in law enforcement history. Webster's predecessor, Clarence Kelley, provided new blood at the top of the FBI in the immediate wake of the Hoover years, but his time there had been too short to bring about permanent changes. Webster was left with that task. He had to revive a bureau that had been demoralized by interoffice gossip and political infighting, whose work was sloppy, and whose agents were viewed as gumshoe clock punchers. It took Webster three years to clean out the bureau's entrenched Hoover partisans and rebuild its sullied reputation on Capitol Hill.

Webster won plaudits for carrying out this job, but he was also not without his detractors. He was criticized heavily in 1981 for his handling of the confirmation investigation of Raymond Donovan, Reagan's nominee to head the Department of Labor. After Donovan was accused of accepting bribes, the Senate found that the FBI had withheld important information in preparing the background file on his nomination. The Senate then investigated the FBI's handling of the matter and issued a stinging criticism of Webster's leadership. The Senate found that the bureau's background material on Donovan was only a compilation of glowing endorsements from some of his closest friends; it was worse than useless. Donovan was indicted and tried and eventually acquitted. However, his courtroom drama probably never would have occurred if the bureau had acted more competently before his nomination was sent to the Senate. That was the best that could be said. On the other hand, Webster's critics claimed that the FBI's failure in the Donovan case showed that the bureau was as politicized as ever. Webster changed nothing.

Similar criticisms had emerged in the wake of the ABSCAM scandal, after the bureau's agents ran a "sting" operation that offered bribes to members of Congress in return for political favors. While Operation ABSCAM resulted in a number of indictments, the FBI's actions were the subject of an in-depth Senate probe that focused on whether Webster's men had unfairly selected, lured, and trapped their targets—most of whom were Democrats. The investigating committee found that the bureau kept sloppy records of tapes and telephone conversations and that communications between Webster and his agents were lacking. In other words, Webster suffered the same kinds of criticism during the ABSCAM investigation that plagued him during the Donovan probe. Though seven members of Congress were eventually convicted as a result of ABSCAM, the bureau's investigation was tarred by accusations that the FBI was being used as a political arm of the White House. Webster lashed out at his critics. "I'm proud of what we did," he said. "Our work stood up in court."

In Operation Corkscrew, in which the FBI's goal was to catch Cleveland judges taking bribes offered by a court bailiff, Webster's bureau expanded on its ABSCAM mistakes. FBI agents involved in this probe had failed to check the bailiff's criminal record, and it turned out that he was a convicted burglar. Nor did the FBI check to see whether the bribes he was offering were actually paid to judges; the bailiff in fact had pocketed the money and fingered judges he'd never approached. In the end the only party charged in the operation was the bailiff himself.

Questions of whether the FBI was used to serve political ends were again raised when it was learned that one of the bureau's most sensitive informants during the Webster years was Jackie Presser, the short, hugely overweight, and wheezing leader of the powerful International Brotherhood of Teamsters. Presser was serving as an FBI informant at the urging of Attorney General Edwin Meese, who said that Presser could be used to help clean up the then corrupt union (Presser had served on the 1980–81 Reagan transition team, after the Teamsters were one of the two national unions that supported Reagan for President). Presser fed the FBI a detailed account of the Teamsters' ties to organized crime, though he was suspected of playing both sides of the fence. Despite much internal debate about Presser's motives and trustworthiness, the bureau launched a three-year investigation that eventually removed many of the IBT's top leadership. The FBI takes pride in cleaning up the union. Senior FBI officials emphasize that the information given them by Presser was invaluable and that the use of the IBT president as an informer was essential to ending the union's corrupt practices. (Presser was eventually indicted for giving ghost jobs to relatives and organized crime figures, but he died of brain cancer before he could come to trial.)

Like Casey's years at the CIA, Webster's tenure at the FBI was also marked by a number of notable, well-publicized successes. The sting operation the FBI attempted in Cleveland, for instance, finally worked properly in Cook County, Illinois, where the bureau won indictments against scores of corrupt judges. But by far the greatest success was Webster's ability to reestablish the bureau's reputation as the nation's premier law enforcement agency in spite of its failures. This accomplishment, while tarnished in the end by revelations that the FBI had engaged in domestic spying operations against groups opposed to U.S. involvement in Central America, was no small feat. On the whole, Webster had successfully subdued the activists of the Hoover era and resuscitated the bureau's reputation as a home for hardened G-men.

On the afternoon of March 3, as Webster contemplated his future, he wasn't as concerned with his record as FBI director as he was with gaining Senate confirmation as the new head of the CIA. Motivated by an almost primordial belief in personal service, Webster was absolutely convinced he could do the job as DCI. Almost twenty-four hours after Howard Baker called him to offer him the new post, Webster picked up the phone to inform the White House of his decision. He was "complimented and honored," he said, that the President would think of him for the position as DCI. He would take the CIA job, he said, and pledge to do the best he could.

The official announcement of Webster's appointment came on March 5. Standing together in the press room at the White House, President Reagan described "Bill" Webster as "a man of honor and integrity" and cited his experience as a federal judge and as head of the FBI as solid qualifications for his nomination. But there was also a hint in Reagan's hesitant delivery that he did not understand why his original decisions to appoint Gates, and then Tower, were not honored. For one of the few times in his presidency Reagan looked like a grade B actor: He was unfamiliar with his material, and his remarks were poorly scripted. He smiled at all the wrong places and cast surreptitious glances at Webster, as if uncertain who he was. Webster, in turn, was gracious, self-effacing, and confident. He was ready for the Senate confirmation process, he said, but insisted on deferring all questions about his own views until he had time to get more familiar with his new job.

If Reagan was unsure of Webster, members of the Senate Select Committee on Intelligence had few doubts. For them, Reagan's appointment of Webster was a welcome relief from the months of deepening skepticism over the CIA's future. It was clear to the senators that Casey's team had damaged the agency's standing with the public and in Congress and just as clear that Robert Gates wasn't the right man to restore that lost reputation. When members of the committee heard that Reagan was considering naming John Tower to take charge at Langley, the skepticism deepened. It was not that Tower could not be confirmed (he could be, and might well have been); it was that the certainty of his confirmation just wasn't a good enough reason for proposing his candidacy. They believed the CIA needed someone instead with a reputation for rebuilding demoralized organizations. Webster, who had just that kind of track record, was well known and well liked on Capitol Hill. While he might have run into trouble during the Donovan and ABSCAM investigations, at least he believed in the concept and processes of oversight—which was more than anyone could ever say about Casey.

Senator David Boren, the articulate Oklahoma Democrat who chaired the Intelligence Committee, was adamant on just this point. If Reagan, battered by Iran-contra, wanted to save himself and his presidency, Boren told an aide, he could make a commitment to following the law and finding people who would cooperate with Congress.

Senator William Cohen from Maine, the committee's ranking Republican, felt the same way, though he couldn't say so openly due to party loyalty. Cohen believed that the committee had done its best to shut down Casey's private foreign policy operation. The only way to make certain it stayed that way, Cohen thought, was to appoint someone as DCI who was familiar with the law and was committed to obeying it. Publicly Cohen praised Reagan's appointment of Webster, but privately he suspected that the Iran-contra scandal went deeper than anyone knew. The White House and CIA could plead innocence or ignorance all they wanted to, Cohen confided to his staff aides, but he was not sure that the administration's private foreign policy operations had ended. What bothered him most was that there was absolutely no way to check. Cohen suppressed his discomfort and joined Boren in the chorus of Webster supporters.

It was the kiss of death: If David Boren thought William Webster would make a good CIA executive, it meant that the senator had received assurances that the FBI director was going to be an open, even pliant DCI—perhaps even Capitol Hill's snoop inside Langley. At least that was what many senior CIA officials thought on the day that Webster was named to head the agency. At Langley, Reagan's announcement was greeted with widespread skepticism and whispered doubts that Webster had the kind of background necessary to rebuild the agency's public image and internal morale.

Inside the clandestine service's offices on the sixth floor, the CIA's ranking operations officers talked in fitful clusters, concerned that Webster's nomination would only add to their problems. The deepest suspicions were harbored by the handful of officers who were involved in William Casey's scheme to trade arms for hostages. The chief of the CIA's Iran desk was especially concerned. "What do you think he'll do?" he asked a colleague. "What's he like?" The Near East Division's leading counterterrorism expert was also worried. "Just what does this guy know about intelligence?" he asked another officer.

Thomas Twetten, the recently named chief of the Near East Division, was more optimistic. He believed Webster would make a careful start at Langley, if for no other reason than to make sure he did not offend the people with whom he needed to work. Webster needed to get his feet wet, Twetten said. He'd met him, knew him, talked to him; he was "all right."

It was not really shocking that a large number of the CIA's senior clandestine officers were uncomfortable with Webster's appointment. The former Missouri judge was known inside the FBI for his occasional petty tirades, his impatience with bureaucratic infighting, and his willingness to punish subordinates who worked outside his own narrow definition of right and wrong. He was reputedly quick-tempered, demanding, and at times a martinet. Those at the CIA who worked as liaison officers with the FBI had noticed this behavior, and word got back to the agency that Webster was difficult to work for. On the other hand, Webster had gained the allegiance of a number of top FBI officials who were convinced that their boss was exactly the right person for the CIA job. Webster, they believed, would cleanse the agency of those even marginally involved in the Casey-North scandal. A handful of CIA officers who headed Casey's Iran operation, notably Clair George, Dewey Clarridge, Thomas Twetten, and their lieutenants, were the most vulnerable. Clarridge, especially, believed that Webster's appointment marked the end of his career. "I won't be staying here long now," he told an associate.

There were other worries. Some viewed Webster's nomination as politically motivated, a way of satisfying Congress's desire to punish the CIA for participating in North's operation. Now, they believed, congressional oversight of the agency, through Webster, would be even more intense than in the past. Still others said he didn't know as much about intelligence work as he claimed and had only passing knowledge of the Byzantine traditions of the intelligence community. Added to these doubts were the deep divisions among agency officers over Robert Gates's inability to get confirmed. Most of the CIA's senior leaders, especially those inside the clandestine service, disliked Gates but believed his inability to win Senate confirmation had eliminated other CIA professionals from consideration. His failure, despite his faults, was theirs, and it now looked as if it would be some time before any career intelligence officer could be named DCI. Gates's decision to remove his name from consideration was keenly felt by his closest colleagues inside the Directorate of Intelligence because he would have been the first DCI to have spent his years at the agency as an analyst. At the very least Gates was a known quantity; Webster wasn't.

The internal debate at Langley about Webster's knowledge of the inner workings of the intelligence community and his ability to handle the complexities at the agency was exacerbated by press reports of his positions on certain key issues. These news accounts gave ammunition to those who believed the Webster appointment would be bad for the agency; they cited three examples to buttress their position. First, in 1981, during the initial days of Casey's term as director, FBI Director Webster publicly opposed lifting restrictions on the agency's ability to gather foreign and domestic intelligence. Webster's surprising position on this issue looked like his way of thanking outgoing President Jimmy Carter (who put in place the restrictions) for giving him the job at the bureau.

Secondly, in 1984, Webster had tipped his hand against the CIA in a public statement that numerous CIA officials believed revealed his operational naïveté. He told the press that he opposed creation of military units to launch preemptive attacks against terrorist organizations. The United States should not do things, he said, that "in a later, more sober time, would appear reprehensible." To his most persistent critics, it sounded as if Webster were applying U.S. laws to foreign intelligence cases and saying the CIA should act against terrorists only after they struck, not before. His views were jeered by those inside the clandestine service.

Last, on a related topic, Webster had opposed a White House plan in 1986 that would have allowed the CIA to kidnap terrorists and bring them to trial in the United States. His views were ridiculed as naïve by the agency's paramilitary operatives, or "knuckledraggers," as they are disparagingly called inside the CIA. While it was true that senior agency officers had earlier fought Casey on just this point while he was trying to hunt down Mohammed Hussein Rashid, they did so for good reason. Then, in 1986, just when the agency was protecting itself by establishing a legal basis for such operations, Webster complained that the law was being stretched to the breaking point. CIA officers were aghast at his interpretation; they knew that followed to its logical extreme, Webster's position meant the end of the agency's foreign operations. There had to be some give somewhere. The CIA desperately needed a program to deal with terrorism. But every time it came up with one, Webster opposed it.

The single most important factor in raising agency doubts about Webster, however, was personal: He would be the first director to come to the CIA from the FBI and the first law enforcement officer to be given responsibility over agency operations. Moreover, everyone knew that the FBI and the CIA had a long history of disagreements that once led to an open breach between the two. At one point, on orders from J. Edgar Hoover, they stopped talking altogether. The most bitter break was in 1970, when separate CIA and FBI domestic spying operations ran afoul of each other. Hoover's subsequent vendetta against the agency was fueled by his mistrust of CIA domestic operations, as well as the CIA's reputation as a supersecret band of Ivy League–educated snobs. After the break the mere mention of the CIA drove Hoover to the edge of rage.

The break was eventually mended, but only after Hoover died. The congressional ban against CIA domestic operations also helped heal the breach, so that by 1975 the long and delicate process of reestablishing a climate of cooperation between the two organizations was well under way. Webster's predecessor at the FBI, Clarence Kelley, worked diligently to build a new relationship between the two organizations, but even in Webster's time there remained a certain stiff cordiality between the two organizations. The FBI is perceived at the agency as the older, but overrated service, filled with gray-suited flatfoots bent on busting illegal aliens and car thieves. The bureau thinks of the CIA as a cloak-and-dagger ivory tower, manned by pipe-smoking academics too busy theorizing to be effective. There is more than a little truth to the stereotypes. The CIA perceives itself as an intelligence elite, while the FBI regularly dismisses the agency's habit of putting simple problems in complex terms. These mutual hostilities had a powerful effect on the CIA's view of Reagan's choice to head the agency: Webster was considered an unknown outsider who would have to get on-the-job training. Most career agency officers were simply not prepared to give him anything approaching a warm welcome.

Nor did Webster seem particularly suited for the role of a classic CIA spymaster, a man in the mold of Allen Dulles, Richard Helms, or William Casey. He is an unassuming, five-foot-ten former Missouri judge who likes to read Hemingway, collects autographed books, plays tennis by the hour, and rides horses back on his farm in the Midwest. He has a fanatic's love of the law, and his incessant talk of the "rule of law" seems so quaint that even those closest to him sometimes think he is old-fashioned. He seemed unlike anything the CIA had ever seen: a tee-totaling, devout Christian Scientist, who didn't swear, who exercised daily, and who cited soppy aphorisms to make his point. "I never confuse movement with action," he once earnestly told an interviewer. His record as a government servant was nearly spotless; his personal life was above question. Nowhere in his background lurked the terrible unknown scandal, like a parking lot pickup, a sleazy payoff, or a hidden academic stain. The William Webster of 1987 actually looked a lot like Stansfield Turner had ten years earlier: religious, single-minded, and isolated—a comparison that was so immediately obvious that it brought groans to officers in the clandestine service.

Even the most dubious career CIA officers soon found Webster to be disarmingly friendly. He came out to Langley after he was nominated for a get-acquainted session, clasped hands with everyone, shook his head in amazement at all the right times, and listened intently to his first briefings as the DCI-designate. CIA officers who participated in these sessions found him a slower study than they had hoped; while he was apparently interested in the work of the agency, they discovered that his confidence in his own abilities sometimes blinded him to the enormous amount of knowledge he was required to digest. The impression he left was that he surpassed William Casey in administrative skills, but not in intelligence intuition; he still maintained that the agency's work overseas could be done in full accord with American laws, despite the fact that even attempting to recruit a foreign national was a dangerous task. For those agents recruited in "denied areas" (the Soviet Union, say, or Iran), it was an act of treason punishable by death. It was a significant blind spot. "Ever since I can remember," he told one audience, "I've wanted to be a lawyer."

Now William Webster was going to head the CIA.

* * *

Deciding that Webster should be the new DCI was one thing; getting him formally confirmed was another. While the official Washington establishment was certain there were no known embarrassing obstacles in the path of his confirmation, no one was willing to concede he was totally without blemish. The doubts had nothing to do with Webster's personal life (he was a hardworking, responsible, intelligent family man); rather, the most frightening prospect was that the Senate Intelligence Committee would discover that he had accidentally stumbled across evidence, as FBI director, of covert arms shipments to Iran or of Oliver North's diversion scheme and had failed to say anything about them. Put another way, no one wanted to find indications that Webster had knowingly participated in the cover-up of a crime.

What most disturbed the senior staffers in the CIA's Directorate for Operations and officials in the CIA's Office of Congressional Relations about Webster's chances was a little-known incident that began in mid-1985, when mid-level officers in the DO's Near East Division started sensing that something important was going on in Iran. "There were closed door meetings all the way through the end of the summer of '85," recalls a former intelligence officer. "It was Twetten, [Clair] George, [Iran branch chief Jack] Devine, just everyone imaginable—all the top NE officials—involved in these meetings. So some of us in the division went to Bert Dunn, the NE chief, and said: 'Look, if there's something we should know, you should tell us. We don't want to step on your operation.' We were told, 'There's nothing going on.' But we pressed him [Dunn] on it. 'Are we doing something ourselves? Are we putting arms in there?' But he waved us off. 'There's no way we would do that,' he told us."

The rumors persisted. According to this former officer, Bert Dunn—one of the agency's best overseas operators—and a group of his top assistants had been busily monitoring foreign arms shipments to Iran since the early 1980s in an effort to track Iranian military capabilities during its war with Iraq. In 1982 they heard unverified rumors of a covert shipment of sophisticated British tanks destined for Bandar Abbas, Iran's busy Persian Gulf port. If true, the report confirmed that America's closest ally was profiting from Khomeini's fanatical desire to depose Iraq's Saddam Hussein. The CIA also discovered that in 1983 the Iranians had opened a large office in London to purchase weapons from private international dealers. The discovery of this bustling Iranian arms bazaar run out of downtown London fueled rumors that the United States was also involved in arming Iran.

The rumors peaked in September 1985, when an NE Division officer received a call at Langley from a Washington, D.C., FBI agent on a secure CIA telephone. The FBI man revealed that the bureau had successfully recruited an Iranian student who was shortly to return to Teheran. Since he was headed overseas, the FBI thought that it might be a good idea for the CIA to get involved. The FBI officer added that the student was intelligent and articulate and could prove to be an invaluable source of information.

The CIA officer took the proposal to his supervisor. Over the next two weeks the NE Division's senior officers considered the offer. The decision on whether to recruit and train the Iranian student, recalls an officer involved in the incident, was passed "up the ladder, from the Iran desk officer to the branch chief, to the DC/NE [Twetten], to Dunn [the chief of the Near East Division], and then to George [the head of clandestine operations]." In the end the CIA decided to turn down the bureau's offer, even though the agency's Iranian networks were "decimated." The reason for the decision: It didn't seem likely that a mere student could provide any valuable information. The CIA gave the bureau permission to handle the case itself.

Just two weeks later, however, the agency's senior espionage officers quickly changed their minds when the FBI informed them that their new recruit had been able to land a well-placed job in Teheran. He had become personal assistant to one of Iran's highest officials, giving him access to some of that nation's most sensitive military and intelligence data. The FBI's information seemed too good to be true. If the CIA took full control, it would have a human intelligence source with unparalleled access to a veritable treasure trove of information from the inside of the Khomeini regime. The United States would have something it had not had in nearly ten years—an agent with access to the upper reaches of the Iranian government. The NE Division's most experienced officers moved quickly. At the beginning of October they set up a meeting in the conference room of the military liaison branch at Langley. In attendance were some of the highest-ranking foreign intelligence officers from the agency and the bureau. The FBI sent its chief and deputy chiefs for international terrorism to the meeting, as well as its agent's American handler. Agency officers in attendance included the deputy chief of the Iran branch and two experienced high-level case officers, including the CIA's liaison to the bureau, Larry Larkin (known as "Captain" Larry to the large Iranian exile community in America), perhaps the most knowledgeable Iran operations officer who ever served in the NE Division. In all, there were in the room nine high-level senior officials, each with more than two decades of experience in clandestine operations.

Larkin set the tone for the meeting by telling FBI officials that the Iranian student would be more valuable if he were handled exclusively by the CIA. Everyone in the room knew that by law the agency had first rights to foreign intelligence assets; as a practical matter, the CIA was far better prepared to handle the operation. It was a rude way to open a discussion, but it was the CIA's practiced manner of dealing with the bureau. The CIA's deputy Iran branch chief continued in a lower key: The agency was desperate for the asset, he admitted, since its human intelligence networks in Iran had never fully recovered from the Khomeini revolution.

One of the FBI's leading international terrorism experts reluctantly agreed with these observations but added that in exchange for its cooperation, the bureau wanted access to the agent's information as well as a full and detailed summary of the CIA's handling of him at every step. What this FBI spokesman said next, however, nearly horrified agency officials: The Iranian student, the FBI officer noted, was providing information to the bureau in direct voice-coded telephone contacts and through a series of letter drops inside Iran. The system seemed to be working well.

CIA officers were thunderstruck. They knew that no matter how careful the bureau was, Khomeini's intelligence service had probably intercepted the agent's overseas calls and it was likely he would be arrested at any minute. Not only did the Islamic republic conduct some of the most tenacious surveillance operations in southern Asia, but it had inherited the CIA's sophisticated and extremely expensive telephone wiretap technology that the agency had installed for the shah in the 1970s; the system had cost the CIA millions and was one of the greatest technical losses suffered by the U.S. intelligence community as a result of the 1979 Iranian Revolution. By using the system, Khomeini's intelligence service was able to monitor hundreds of telephones at a time. After a few moments of stunned silence an agency official let out a barely audible groan and suggested that the FBI end the phone calls immediately. The bureau was told to make one last contact with its Iranian agent in order to give him new instructions, while the CIA came up with a plan to reestablish contact with him.

Despite its problems with maintaining telephone ties to the Iranian student, the FBI's greatest vulnerability lay in its insistence on using letter drops, or dead drops, as an optional way to communicate with him. Dead drops were considered primitive and easily identified, and they were extremely difficult to monitor; it made for good spy fiction, but in an age of sophisticated reconnaissance satellites the technique was in disrepute. There was plenty of evidence that dead drops didn't work, as when a CIA officer retrieved a message from a highly placed agent in the Middle East and found a picture of the agent's mutilated body inside. Nor could anyone in the Soviet Division forget that one of the CIA's most valued Russian agents, a renowned woman scientist with access to sensitive information on the Soviet missile program, was arrested by the KGB on a Leningrad bridge while attempting to slip a small white envelope inside a hollow brick. While the agency hadn't given up the practice of using dead drops altogether, their experience with them had been so bad that the method acquired a damning slang: They were now widely referred to as "drop deads."

It was clear to the CIA that the bureau's recruit was an amateur playing at being a spy and was therefore unlikely to be schooled in the ways of sophisticated tradecraft. The probability was very high that he would be identified and executed, or else turned against the Americans ("doubled" is the term most often used). At least one of the CIA officers present during the bureau-agency meeting thought it likely the FBI had already botched the case. To run the operation properly, the student would have to be brought out of Iran; retrained; interviewed; polygraphed; provided with radio equipment and a set of identifiers and codes; and sent back into Iran—what the agency referred to as "establishing bona fides and setting up a commo system."

Following the meeting, the agency's NE Division and case officers in the Iran branch began to draw up a sophisticated plan to do just that. Within a few days they decided their new agent could be brought out of Iran for training and designated a CIA station in the Persian Gulf for the task. It was too risky to bring him all the way to Frankfurt, West Germany, they decided, though that would have been preferable. (The agency's Teheran station in exile is in Frankfurt and is known by the acronym TEFRAN, short for Teheran-Frankfurt, and is one of the largest of the CIA's overseas offices.)

The agency's final plan, agreed to within a week of the FBI-CIA meeting at Langley, called for bringing the agent out of Iran and training him for five days at a secret location. It was a crash program; the NE Division's clandestine officers knew they had to rush the training at the same time that they provided a credible cover story to make certain their operation wasn't discovered by Khomeini's intelligence service. The training was designed to eliminate the possibility of the agent's being compromised: He would receive sophisticated CIA communications equipment, as well as detailed instructions on when and how to transmit information to the United States. CIA officers were confident they could successfully protect their agent from discovery but they still understood that the operation would be extremely dangerous. As standard insurance, the CIA planned to designate a foreign official working in Teheran to monitor its new agent's work and devised an escape plan for him that it had used successfully in previous operations.

But just weeks before the agency planned to begin the training, in mid-October 1985, an officer in the NE Division received a troubling telephone call from the agent's FBI contact. The FBI man said he'd received a report from the Iranian student that could prove to be embarrassing to the United States. The Iranian student said he had been dispatched as an escort for his employer, the high-level Iranian government official, on a tour to inspect Iran's military installations. Their trip included a visit to a military base in Tabriz, near the Soviet border. While standing on the tarmac of the Tabriz Air Base, the FBI agent said, the Iranian student spotted what looked like an unmarked U.S. aircraft unloading sophisticated weapons. The FBI agent hesitated for a moment to gauge the CIA officer's reaction to this information and then inquired whether the DO had a secret arms supply program under way in Iran. The CIA officer's answer was curt: The agency had no knowledge of any U.S. arms shipments to Iran. He added that such shipments violated established American policy. Iran was branded a terrorist state, so the Iranian student *must* be mistaken. There was simply no other explanation.

While the agency officer's denial was categorical, the FBI report resurrected agency doubts about what might be happening behind closed doors in the DO's Near East Division. As word of the Tabriz sighting swept through the clandestine service, the officer who received the call reported the news to the NE Division's Deputy Chief Twetten. After bringing Twetten up-to-date on the operation with the Iranian student, the officer expressed his fear that another project being conducted at higher levels of the CIA might endanger the NE Division's own agent networks. Twetten acted quickly; he immediately ordered a complete review of the division's plan to train the FBI's Iranian agent. He also emphatically denied the existence of any other high-level covert operation to supply Iran with arms.

Twetten's review recast the CIA's relationship with its potentially vital Iranian human intelligence source. Within weeks of the report on the Tabriz incident, the agency decided to end its planned training of the Iranian student. The ostensible reason was that the information he provided was fabricated—immediately making him an unreliable source. A more likely reason, claims a clandestine service officer, is that the CIA's prospective agent had uncovered arms shipments meant to be secret.

No matter what the reason, just weeks after the CIA had agreed to take control of the FBI's man in Teheran, the agency scheduled a second meeting with its bureau counterparts. This time the head of the Iran branch began the meeting by informing the bureau that the CIA had changed its mind again: It was no longer interested in receiving reports from the Iranian student. While FBI officers present at the meeting were surprised by the sudden shift in the agency's position, they had little choice but to accept it, dismissing the CIA's decision as yet another instance of agency-bureau coolness.

The entire incident might well have been forgotten had it not been for Casey's death and Webster's confirmation hearings. Almost eighteen months after the CIA told the FBI that it was not interested in the Iranian student, agency officials assigned to marshal agency resources on Webster's behalf were worried that the incident could endanger his chances for confirmation. It was possible that the arms-for-hostages initiative had been reported back to Webster and that he had learned of the aircraft spotted by the FBI's man in Teheran. These fears were confirmed when the Senate Intelligence Committee, in a long pretestimony letter to Webster, questioned him on whether he had ever obtained "independent" knowledge of the arms-for-hostages operation "from FBI reports." The way the question was worded prompted CIA officers to conclude that the committee had somehow discovered the aborted FBI-CIA program. On a quiet morning in late April 1987 one of the CIA's legislative officers on Capitol Hill phoned Langley to confirm that details of its October plan to recruit the Iranian had indeed been leaked to committee members, apparently by someone at the FBI. The report, he said, included a summary of the agent's allegation that he saw a U.S.-manufactured aircraft on the ground in Tabriz in 1985—one month before the CIA admitted to cooperating with Oliver North's arms-for-hostages scheme.

The information was immediately forwarded to the new head of the Iran branch, Fred Lundahl, who then alerted Twetten, the new Near East Division chief. Twetten was stunned. In the midst of a process designed to show that William Webster had been a competent and honest FBI director (and so would presumably be just as competent and honest at the CIA), his own bureau came up with information that could be potentially fatal to his chances of becoming DCI. The report also endangered the agency's claim that it hadn't become involved in shipping U.S. arms to Iran until November 1985. It was the worst possible news. Given the shock of the Iran-contra revelations, Twetten knew that nobody would believe the CIA was not involved in masterminding the October shipment (if there was one), even if it was not true, as he insisted to his top aides it was not.

Twetten took what steps he could to deflect the threat by directing the officers involved in the agency-bureau meetings to write a summary of the proposed operation. In addition, the CIA privately reiterated to the Senate its own oft-repeated denials that it had conducted a covert arms resupply effort to Iran prior to November 1985 and added that even then, it was ordered to help facilitate landing rights for an aircraft in Portugal by the White House for an operation it thought had the approval of the President. Nor, it argued, was the CIA's role in the scandal germane to whether Webster had heard of any covert program; he was at the FBI at the time and had no knowledge of any American shipments to Iran. The CIA's answer on Webster's behalf left little doubt about the agency's own position: The report was mistaken, and that was why the CIA decided not to recruit the agent in the first place.

Within days the Senate Intelligence Committee had its own ready explanation; the evidence, it concluded, suggested that the aircraft spotted in Tabriz (if indeed, it added painfully, there actually was one) wasn't American, though no one could say for sure just what nation it was from. And the only thing that could prove conclusively that it *was* an American flight (that a resupply operation to Iran was planned and executed with the full knowledge of the CIA before it testified it was told to do so by the White House) was if the aircraft contained American markings. It didn't. In other words, evidence provided by the FBI was inconclusive; it proved nothing. "We can't say whether the story was true or not," an SSCI staff investigator explains. "It could well be that there was an American aircraft on the ground in Tabriz, that the CIA knew it and was running the secret supply operation—and had been—for quite some time. But we have no evidence of that, and we don't believe it."

The story remains tantalizing. No one has ever denied that there was some kind of plane unloading weapons on the ground in Tabriz that hot August day, only that there is any way to confirm the report. Nor has anyone denied that someone at the FBI leaked information that showed that the bureau recruited an Iranian student in 1985 to provide intelligence information on Iran to the United States, that he was trusted and had unparalleled access to Iranian military and political secrets. This information was clearly leaked to the Senate with the intention of de-railing Webster's confirmation and throwing into doubt his denial that he knew of the Iran-contra fiasco. Fortunately for Webster, however, the truth of the incident was as elusive then as it is now, and in the end, the Senate committee chose to be convinced by Webster's denials and those of the CIA.

The Tabriz report, and several others like it, continued to fuel nagging suspicions that William Webster knew more about the Iran-contra scandal than he admitted and sparked rumors in Congress that President Reagan had come to a belated realization that he had made a mistake in appointing Webster Casey's successor as DCI. In the wake of former Senator John Tower's refusal to consider the CIA job, the gossips claimed, Howard Baker and President Reagan rushed the Webster nom-ination because they assumed he could win easy confirmation—which was far more important to the White House than finding someone who could do the job at the CIA. The critics also maintained that Webster—as FBI director—knew quite a bit about the Iran-contra affair but had refused to follow up on his knowledge. There was a growing feeling that Webster had ignored evidence of CIA-sanctioned arms shipments to the Middle East at the same time that the FBI was providing infor-mation to the U.S. Customs Service on privateers engaged in similar arms transactions. Some members of Congress also believed that the FBI and Webster were fully aware of the contra diversion, though evidence documenting this wrongdoing had never been shown to Congress and the American public. Angered by these claims, Webster confided to several colleagues that he feared the Senate was going to use his nomination to further cripple Reagan's presidency. Webster categorically rejected all these accusations.

In response to written questions about the Iran arms deals put to him by the Senate Intelligence Committee, Webster replied: "The first knowledge I had of any possible activity by U.S. officials providing illegal or unauthorized assistance came to me during the press conference of the President and the Attorney General on November 25, 1986, and at the meeting in the Attorney General's office immediately following."

In a second questionnaire Webster was asked a more detailed question: Did he have knowledge of any arms shipments from the U.S. government to Iran from "other sources"? The question had the same impact on Webster that a prior question about knowledge of the operation had on the CIA: It seemed to imply that the committee knew that Webster hadn't told them the absolute truth. After a few days' hesitation Webster retracted his first answer and stated that he now remembered being told of "an ongoing strategic initiative authorized by the President toward an element of the Iranian Government" in August 1986. Webster said that when he heard about the program, he questioned Attorney General Meese and was told that the opening to Iran was "supported by a Presidential finding which he [Meese] had reviewed." Webster said he was satisfied with this explanation; since "the Attorney General had confirmed his awareness and approval of the initiative, there were no further actions indicated."

The answer was not what Chairman Boren or the rest of the Intelligence Committee expected; it looked as if Webster belatedly realized that Senate investigators had information about his August 1986 meeting with Meese and decided to test him to see if he would tell the truth. Not only that, committee aides pointed out, it looked as if Webster was skirting the issue. The point was not whether he was satisfied with Meese's response, or even whether the Iran initiative was supported by a presidential finding, but whether he had evidence of other government-supported initiatives—like the diversion of funds to the contras. Webster was head of the FBI and was supposed to enforce the law, not be satisfied with easy answers. The result was that when he finally appeared in person before the SSCI at the beginning of April 1987, he was more closely questioned than many in the CIA had predicted. The committee's questions revolved around Webster's discussions of arms sales with Meese. While these inquiries never degenerated into an adversarial cross-examination, they were pointed enough to raise hackles among Webster partisans. "They asked him the same question the same way dozens of times," one of his advisers remembers. "It was really very unnecessary."

This pro-Webster protest was actually no more than an oversensitive reaction to the Senate committee's desire to make it appear that Webster's nomination was not a certainty. Though Boren and his colleagues would have refused to confirm Webster if they discovered evidence of his partic- ipation in the Iran-contra scandal, it is now clear that anything short of that would have resulted in his confirmation. In the end the committee was more willing to believe Webster's explanation of his own role in the scandal than not. William Cohen, for instance, was certain that whatever knowledge Webster may have had about the Iran-contra affair "was purely tangential, at best," while Boren (who had already weighed in with praise for Webster on the day he was nominated) later told his colleagues in private that he saw "no reason why this man shouldn't be DCI."

For some of Webster's critics, however, the SSCI's final session left unanswered the question of what Webster knew about the White House's covert program to ship arms to Iran. These critics (from the CIA, FBI, and Senate) remain convinced that the FBI's man in Teheran may hold the key to unlocking the CIA's subterranean role in the NSC initiative; committee aides point out, for example, that the only thing that could have forced Webster to approach Meese in August 1986 was information that the FBI was gathering on the arms-for-hostages initiative from their student/agent working for a high-level Iranian official. Where else would Webster have even heard of such an operation? At the very least, the critics charge, Webster showed an incredible lack of curiosity about the White House program after he learned of it; at the most he perjured himself. Webster's defenders at the CIA, meanwhile, confine their re- sponse to these allegations to a simple statement about Webster's rep- utation for honesty. "The judge told the truth to the committee," they all say. "He wouldn't lie."

With Webster's explanation of his discussion on the Iran operation with Meese in hand, the committee turned its attention to Webster's own views of his job as CIA director. His responses to *those* concerns—whether he would insist on being a part of Reagan's Cabinet, for instance, or his views on congressional notification of CIA covert programs—were heart- ening. Webster told the committee that he would reverse Casey's practice of sitting in White House meetings as a Cabinet member and insisted that the DCI "should not be involved in policy discussions." Finally, under pressure, he agreed that he would keep the committee "fully informed" on covert activities. This is exactly what the members of the SSCI wanted to hear. On the last day of April they unanimously endorsed Reagan's choice as Casey's successor at the CIA. One month later, on May 20, the Senate followed their lead, and six days later William Web- ster was sworn in as director of central intelligence at CIA headquarters in Langley, Virginia. His daughter held the Bible for him as he took his oath. The next morning, flanked by a new security detail, Webster ar- rived at CIA headquarters to begin his first full day of work.

3

★★★

Just Off the Boat from the FBI

*D*irectors come and go, veteran officers retire (then sign on as consultants), aging researchers with encyclopedic memories of operations, biographies, and statistics are given their pensions, but the secret work of the agency continues uninterrupted through all the changes. On May 26, 1987, the day William Webster was sworn in as the nation's fourteenth director of central intelligence, the agency was involved in five major covert operations on two continents, was closely monitoring a burgeoning and embarrassing crisis in Panama, and was attempting to resolve a divisive internal dispute over a CIA defector. The five major CIA covert operations that Webster would now have to manage were secret in name only; each had been publicly revealed in print and scrutinized by the Senate Intelligence Committee. Details of the operations not only were generally known to the public and Congress but in a number of cases were the object of fierce administration arguments. In at least one case it even appeared that the agency's reputation and its practices might be seriously harmed.

In Southeast Asia the CIA was engaged in supplying aid to three non-Communist resistance groups fighting Cambodia's Vietnam-supported central government in Phnom Penh. In turn, the resistance was allied with the Khmer Rouge—perpetrators of some of the most heinous crimes in modern history—who received arms, munitions, and monetary support from China, America's most constant regional ally. Their Vietnamese adversaries depended on the Soviet Union for economic and military aid and, in return, provided a large naval base for

Soviet warships in the Far East. The CIA's Cambodia program was run by the DO's East Asia Division, which funneled thirty million dollars in aid each year through Singapore, Malaysia, and Thailand to Cambodian resistance fighters in eastern and northeastern Thailand.

The agency was also involved in an important military campaign in Afghanistan, supplying a loose coalition of battle-hardened Afghan tribal armies, the mujaheddin, with untold millions of dollars' worth of sophisticated weapons to fight well-armed Soviet troops who invaded the country in 1979. Funds for this program were disbursed through CIA proprietaries in Europe and southern Asia, and most of America's arms were shipped through Alexandria, Egypt. Some of the CIA's money was earmarked to pay for the cost of running the ground fighting in Afghanistan, which CIA officials monitored from nearby Pakistan, at the agency's base in Karachi and its well-staffed station in Islamabad. As in Cambodia, the agency's Afghan program was strengthened by the infusion of small arms shipped by China to the resistance fighters. A small CIA liaison office at Langley coordinated this entire massive logistical network and planned Afghani military attacks. This Afghan Task Force was housed on the agency's sixth floor, in the Near East Division, across the hall from the offices of the Iran branch.

In Angola, the agency gave fifteen million dollars each year to Jonas Savimbi's UNITA (National Union for the Independence of Angola), a resistance movement fighting the Soviet-allied government entrenched in Luanda. Savimbi's increasingly effective forces started receiving weapons from the United States in 1985, after a strict ten-year congressional ban on the agency's covert program to UNITA was lifted. The fifteen-million-dollar sum was paltry in comparison with the U.S. effort during the previous decade, which had earmarked nearly thirty million dollars a year in arms transfers to Savimbi's army. CIA officers were somewhat mollified, however, by the knowledge that the new Savimbi program was being enhanced by contributions from South Africa and China. Still, these combined efforts fell far short of the one billion dollars in Soviet aid being given to the Angolan government, whose power was further strengthened by the presence of thousands of troops from Cuba. Despite these handicaps, Savimbi's movement gained ground in 1986, when the Soviet-backed government in Luanda began tiring of the conflict. The CIA then stepped up its weapons shipments and enlarged its modestly staffed Angolan Task Force, whose most important agency field manager worked at the CIA station in Kinshasa, Zaire. From there the CIA coordinated secret air shipments of weapons through Lisbon into camouflaged airstrips in UNITA-controlled western Angola. It was a complex operation.

In Central America the CIA provided the anti-Sandinista contra forces with badly needed logistical equipment and medical supplies. While the contras succeeded in keeping political pressure on the regime in Managua they failed to win any major battles against the Sandinista army. The best that could be hoped for, especially after the details of the Iran diversion were publicly revealed in late 1986, was that the CIA's support would eventually force the Sandinistas to accept either open elections or the contra opposition in the government. The CIA's non-lethal aid program, which was covert in name only, was still controversial on Capitol Hill and a flash point for domestic discontent. In addition, the U.S. "freedom fighters," as Ronald Reagan called them, weren't popular either in Nicaragua or in Honduras, their host country. For these reasons, CIA officials did not hold out much hope for a successful resolution of the conflict or an early end to their aid program.

In Lebanon the CIA had installed a small and extremely vulnerable intelligence team to monitor the progress of the hostage situation. The team's task was to check the credibility of the many mysterious local people involved in providing information about the location of U.S. citizens held by pro-Iranian revolutionary groups. Invariably the information received by the CIA officers stationed in Beirut was useless or, if credible, unusable. The U.S. policy of refusing to provide money, weapons, or drugs—the three most valued commodities sought by hostage holders—was stringently maintained in the wake of the Iran-contra scandal. Nevertheless, the agency had successfully penetrated Lebanon's small intelligence service and was constructing a complex plan to rescue the hostages. The CIA also had opened a top secret communications channel to high-level officers in Syria's intelligence service to share hostage information. The only U.S. officials who knew of this channel were the CIA's top covert executors, the DCI, the President, Vice President, secretary of state, and NSC adviser. Not even the head of Syrian military intelligence was informed, because of his violently anti-American sentiments. The channel was opened in 1985; by early 1987 it was formalized in a series of meetings between Syrian intelligence officers and their CIA counterparts in Beirut.

Each of these five covert programs had come under fire since being established, usually as a result of congressional queries into their effectiveness or because of controversy generated by questions raised in the media. Ironically, the single most controversial of these CIA programs, that in Central America, was also its most stable. Even after a number of embarrassments (Casey's disastrous decision to mine Nicaragua's harbors and Oliver North's secret airlift of arms to the contras), the chances that the CIA's Central America program would succeed were improving. That surprising judgment was due to the fact that the Iran-contra scandal forced the agency to monitor more closely its Central America program or face further congressional censure. That kind of intense pressure clearly was not a factor in the CIA's other operations in Africa, Asia, or the Middle East.

On the day that William Webster was sworn in as DCI, the Directorate for Operations was investigating a number of miniscandals in its four other major covert projects. These messy situations showed just how vulnerable the agency was to its sometimes untrustworthy foreign clients. In Thailand, for example, the senior managers of the covert program were attempting to discover the whereabouts of millions of dollars destined for America's client armies fighting in Cambodia. CIA officers believed these U.S. funds had been stolen, but their findings were inconclusive because of the difficulty in tracing agency money through a three-tier organization comprised of U.S., Thai, and Cambodian officials, a handful of Thai and Singapore banks, and a welter of CIA- and Thai-hired independent contractors. The investigation was further complicated by the Byzantine character of Thai politics, in which military officers jockeyed for power with civilian officials to curry favor with the symbolically important Thai royal family.

In Afghanistan the CIA was having similar problems. Senior officers working in Langley's Afghan Task Force were especially concerned about complaints from client rebel groups that they had not been receiving the arms they were promised, although no one could find out just where they had gone. There were plenty of theories, one being that the arms were being sent into Iran, another that the CIA's weapons were showing up in the hands of the Baluchis, a rebellious and casually violent tribe on Iran's border, and still another, a very likely candidate, that a coterie of Pakistani military officers was siphoning CIA funds from the guerrillas as "the price of doing business in southern Asia." The program was also plagued by persistent reports from the task force in Pakistan that CIA weapons were resold to enrich Afghan tribal leaders. Another large percentage of the weapons sent to Afghanistan ended up on the black market in Peshawar or were sold to arms-hungry militias in exchange for drugs (which were then sold to provide "pocket money" for corrupt Pakistani military officers). The corruption generated by the agency program was clear to see for anyone with eyes: It was not unusual to be able to purchase a new Soviet-made Kalashnikov AK-47 rifle—brought in by the CIA—for as little as five hundred dollars in the street stalls of the cities of western Pakistan. One Pakistani official said his country had been transformed to a "Kalashnikov culture."

The problems with the CIA's program of resupplying the Angolan insurgency through bases in nearby Zaire were not nearly as significant. Still, the corruption that existed was becoming manifest, even in the sparsely populated plains and forests of West Africa. Just as U.S. funds threatened the stability of Pakistan, so the CIA's considerable presence in Zaire was fueling a massive black market in stolen U.S. goods. Much of America's aid to Zaire was finding its way into the pockets of the nation's richest and most powerful politicians, including its president. By 1987 Zairian President Mobutu Sese Seko, known in the early 1960s as Joseph Mobutu, was one of the richest men in the world although he led a nation that was one of the planet's most impoverished. The trade-off was all but a matter of public policy; the price of maintaining Savimbi's forces in Angola was paid in Kinshasa.

The lack of serious financial or corruption problems in the agency's program in Lebanon was more than outweighed by the fearsome vulnerability of working in an extremely dangerous "denied area." The agency had enemies everywhere in Lebanon in 1987: Among Maronite Christians who believed the United States was being chary in support of its natural allies, among the Druze militia, which resented America's 1983 intervention in its strongholds in the Chouf Mountains, and especially among Hezbollah militias holding U.S. hostages. The CIA attempted to break through the forces surrounding it in Beirut in early 1987 by successfully recruiting members of Nabih Berri's Amal militia, but Berri's forces were too scattered and mistrusted by Lebanon's other warring parties to yield substantial benefits. The CIA's senior covert officers were also hesitant to become too deeply involved in Lebanon because of the agency's tragic history in the region. In 1983 for instance, the CIA suffered the loss of two of its top officers—Robert Ames, the national intelligence officer for the Middle East, and Kenneth Haas, the CIA's deputy Beirut station chief—when a car bomb destroyed the U.S. Embassy. Ames's and Haas's deaths were followed by the kidnapping, torture, and death of William Buckley, the Beirut chief of station.

Unlike the CIA's covert operations in Cambodia, Afghanistan, Angola, and Nicaragua—all of which supported native insurgencies fighting Soviet-backed governments—the Lebanon program was less focused. Primarily the CIA was engaged in recruiting agents purely for information-gathering purposes (to locate American hostages and assess threats to U.S. interests). It also struggled to rebuild a multifactional Lebanese Army, but this was a task so daunting it seemed nearly impossible. In view of the nature of the objectives, it was difficult for senior DO officials to determine the success of the CIA's performance. The trade in hostage information, for instance, created a popular cottage industry that attracted dozens of Lebanese, Syrian, Iranian, and Druze profiteers who claimed to be cousins, brothers, fathers, sons, or friends of hostage holders. Their demands were always impossible to meet. In one instance a Lebanese employee of the U.S. government claimed that his cousin was holding an American and was prepared to give him his freedom in exchange for money. The CIA station in Beirut verified the claim by following the embassy's employee to a Beirut villa where the

American was being held. But the agency was barred from meeting the demand. Then, by the time a rescue operation could be planned, the hostage had been moved to an unknown location, and the CIA had to start all over again. The incident was emblematic of the frustrations of Beirut.

The job of assessing threats to American interests in Lebanon was comparatively simple since the United States had few interests to guard. The official White House position on Lebanon was droningly dull and starkly naïve: The United States sought an equitable end to the civil war and the establishment of a government to represent each of Lebanon's warring factions (that the factions were battling over just that point was, it seems, never considered).

In early 1987 it was clear that each of the CIA's five covert programs—which were either established or developed during Casey's tenure—needed to be refurbished or, in some cases, expanded. Everyone at the CIA involved in them, however, was waiting to see what changes the new DCI would make before that process could begin. One thing that seemed assured was that Webster would transform the CIA's internal covert review procedures, so that the most sensitive agency programs would be immune to the persistent corruptions that poisoned them. As significant as all these decisions were, when Webster took his oath as DCI these problems seemed minor in comparison with two controversies that were proving to be the CIA's most intransigent.

Panamanian dictator and CIA asset Manuel Noriega was the agency's most serious problem. The brutal military commander had created a scandal of such massive proportions that it threatened to spill over and expose the kind of corruption that infested each of its major secret operations. Noriega was not only a former CIA asset but a drug runner, gun trafficker, and money launderer whose broad international intelligence contacts and suspicious friendships threatened American interests. To make matters worse, inside the DO's Latin America (LA) Division there were two opposing factions having a heated argument about what to do with him. One of these factions, composed mostly of veteran LA Division anti-Communists, opposed U.S. intervention in Panama; the other group was just as firmly convinced that the United States had to help launch a coup to overthrow Noriega. This debate was unusually intense and surprisingly public, given the CIA's tradition of secrecy.

The real issue was whether the CIA should fund Panamanian opposition groups that were dedicated to Noriega's ouster or do nothing at all, in the hope that he would be deposed anyway by his fellow military officers. The debate was complicated by the fact that the two former heads of the Latin America Division—a volatile and aging activist named Nestor Sanchez and his successor, the flamboyant Dewey Clarridge—

were both virulent anti-Communists and Noriega supporters. As of 1987, Clarridge defended Noriega from his position as the CIA's leading guru on counterterrorism, while Sanchez then held a similarly powerful position at the Department of Defense. Together, Clarridge and Sanchez still had enough prestige that they effectively could untrack any plan to oust the Panamanian dictator. By the time that Webster became DCI, it was clear that the CIA would do little or nothing to remove him.

The Noriega controversy reversed the long-held positions of LA Division activists (the shoot-first crowd) and division minimalists (the reluctant interventionists). In an unusual flipflop, the minimalists—who should have traditionally favored doing nothing to destabilize the Panama regime—actually counted themselves as proponents of an activist Noriega policy, while those traditional activists—who normally argued vehemently for Noriega's ouster—now urged caution and a go-slow policy. Over the next two years these two factions inside the clandestine service became more and more strident, and their confrontation threatened to become public.

The controversy over Noriega was somewhat surprising because the LA Division has a long-standing reputation for being one of the most conservative parts of the agency, particularly since it had demonstrated a willingness to tolerate the antics of corrupt, pro-American dictators. This tradition was firmly grounded in failure; the division's support of Cuban strong man Fulgencio Batista in the 1950s and then the bumbling attempts to rid the Western Hemisphere of his Communist successor, Fidel Castro, was the most prominent example of these mistakes. The failed Cuban policy was followed by the agency's hamhanded plotting against Chile's Socialist president Salvador Allende (who was murdered by Chilean military officers during a CIA-supported coup); then by the CIA's impotence in convincing President Carter to continue support of Nicaraguan strong man Anastasio Somoza; and later by its inability to establish and gain support for any political group to oppose Somoza's Sandinista successors. Finally, under pressure to resolve its internal differences over Noriega, a truce was arranged that postponed the final showdown over Panama; in true bureaucratic fashion the CIA's leadership commissioned a secret study of the problem, which was due for release in December 1988. Until then things remained calm.

The same could not be said for the DO's Soviet and Eastern European (SE) Division, where officers were only beginning to recover from the defection of Edward Lee Howard, a former SE Division officer who had been trained to serve in Moscow. Howard betrayed a number of CIA agents and half a dozen sensitive intelligence-gathering programs when he hurriedly fled to the Soviet Union in 1985. Howard's access to the SE Division's case files also meant that he could identify all CIA officers who served in Moscow for the foreseeable future. No one knew for certain what Howard told the Soviets or what effect these secrets would have, but it was clear the SE Division would have to restructure its espionage operations, assess blame, and to determine how to keep the Howard incident from being repeated. Several internal studies were commissioned.

At the center of these controversial reviews was sixty-two-year-old Gardiner "Gus" Hathaway, the chief of the agency's counterintelligence (CI) staff, who was responsible for finding out what went wrong, why, and what it meant for the CIA. Despite Hathaway's well-earned reputation as a topnotch counterintelligence officer and a member of the CIA's senior inner circle, he was criticized for his handling of the Howard scandal—there was a widely held belief that he was tardy both in identifying the problem and in taking steps to repair it.

The criticism was unjust. The striking Virginia patrician with just a hint of an up-country, properly southern piedmont accent was not responsible either for assessing Howard's abilities or for making the final decision to post the young officer to the USSR in 1983. That job was left to officials in the DO's SE Division, who educated, trained, briefed, polygraphed, retrained, and repolygraphed Howard in preparation for his sensitive assignment. Even up to the time of his final polygraph exam, Howard appeared to be the perfect CIA officer. But in that exam he showed deception in answers to a series of routine questions about whether he had ever stolen classified documents from the CIA. He then finally admitted to what a senior SE officer charitably describes as "petty theft" and was dismissed from the service in June 1983. Howard's polygraph failure shook the agency after it became generally known within days of his firing. After Howard's dismissal Hathaway's CI staff was given responsibility for determining whether he posed an ongoing security risk. Initially Hathaway did not find any evidence to warrant the suspicion that Howard's theft included passing secrets to the Russians. But as time went on Hathaway and his top assistants slowly became convinced that Howard had indeed been a spy, or "mole," inside the CIA for at least a short time. But no further steps were taken against Howard, who had quietly returned to private life. This inaction was compounded by a decision made by Clair George, William Casey, and Hathaway himself that incriminating information about Howard should not be passed on to the FBI. This decision turned out to be one of the most controversial of Hathaway's thirty-year career.

The highly respected Hathaway had been promoted to head the CI staff after postings in Latin America and Europe, and after serving as the prestigious chief of station in Moscow and then deputy chief of the SE Division. His promotion to run the CIA's counterintelligence unit caught him and his colleagues by surprise because he was next in line to become head of all Soviet and Eastern European operations, a job that nearly everyone inside the SE Division covets. Nevertheless, Hathaway's appointment to head the counterintelligence staff was viewed throughout the agency as a brilliant personnel move because of his excellent reputation and extensive field experience. The judgment seemed confirmed when Vitaly Yurchenko defected to the United States in 1985. Yurchenko's sudden and stunning defection was an extraordinary stroke of good fortune for Hathaway and the CIA because he had served as deputy chief of the First Department of the KGB's First Chief Directorate. In essence, Yurchenko had been responsible for all Soviet civilian espionage activities in the United States and Canada.

Hathaway's triumph, however, was short-lived; the information provided by Yurchenko shattered the CIA. Soon after defecting, Yurchenko told Hathaway that the KGB was receiving vital information on CIA operations in the USSR from a U.S. citizen known by the code name of "Robert." His description of the KGB's American asset was detailed enough that the CI staff and SE Division quickly concluded that "Robert" was, in fact, Edward Lee Howard. In September 1985, two years after his dismissal, the agency finally told the FBI about Howard, and the bureau began trailing the former CIA officer. But Howard, alerted to their presence, used the same countersurveillance tactics he had been taught by the agency to evade the FBI watchers posted outside his home in New Mexico. Howard made his escape to Europe, traveling to Copenhagen, Helsinki, then to Frankfurt and Munich. According to his own account, he then spent time in Latin America and Canada "under an assumed name." He traveled to Vienna and eventually showed up at the Soviet Embassy in Budapest, Hungary.

The Howard disaster was soon followed by another crushing setback for Hathaway. After naming "Robert" as the KGB's mole, Yurchenko had second thoughts about his defection. In the weeks after he arrived in Washington, Yurchenko had been put in comfortable, well-guarded house, introduced to top agency officials (he attended an unusual dinner with William Casey), and even flown to Toronto, where the Canadian intelligence service helped locate his former mistress. But nothing the CIA did seemed to satisfy the former KGB chief, who was disturbed by the agency's selective leaks about his defection (which were undertaken, in part, to offset the bad press the agency was receiving for botching the Howard case) and its nonstop interrogations. On November 2, 1985, Yurchenko walked away from his CIA escort at a Georgetown restaurant and "redefected" to the Soviet Union.

The Howard defection and Yurchenko's sudden change of heart were two major blows to the CI staff and to Gus Hathaway's distinguished career. In May 1987 the two events still bubbled below the surface of the DO. Of the two scandals, however, the Howard defection had left the most serious lingering effects, since it cast a spotlight on the CIA's inability to recruit and retain talented and ambitious officers.

Edward Lee Howard was initially recruited by the CIA because he was a willing, intelligent, and highly motivated young man who appeared to show great potential and believed in the agency's mission. A previous stint in the Peace Corps had acclimated him to life in hostile foreign environments. He had a talent for languages and an innate grasp of foreign policy issues, was at ease at mastering the agency's training requirements, and had a remarkable capacity for working under pressure. Nevertheless, the agency should have been able to predict the problems that Howard would cause, for while the CIA routinely rejects applicants who have used drugs, it did not do so with Howard, who used marijuana, cocaine, and hashish during his time in the Peace Corps and then again as a young businessman working in Chicago. Nor did it question Howard about his badly strained marriage. These warning signs eventually combined to transform him from a potentially excellent case officer into a traitor working for the Soviet Union. The lasting tragedy of the Howard case, and the most serious crisis facing Gus Hathaway in 1987, was the organization's inability to police itself—to find out whether another Howard lurked inside the CIA.

Hathaway had reason to be concerned. The DO was rife with gossip about the changes that would be instituted after Webster's appointment, including reports that the CI staff would actually be restructured and transferred from Langley to form the core of a new intelligence group. The massive security checks of December 1986—after the Iran-contra scandal exploded—heightened these worries, and the clandestine service's work suffered as a result. Officials in the Office of Security were especially concerned that many of the agency's traditional security problems were more serious than they had understood. Again, the Howard case provided the best example. Many of the questions during Howard's polygraph exam centered on his drinking problem, which should have been a warning to the SE Division that he didn't belong in Moscow. The Office of Security concluded that barring other incentives to steal documents (there was no evidence that Howard had done so for money), Howard's alcohol problem had somehow turned him against the agency, which was a maddeningly simple explanation with frightening implications for the clandestine service.

A veteran agency officer claims that the CIA is "awash" in alcohol. Over the last years of Casey's tenure, four CIA officers were officially warned about drinking during working hours. The punishing routine of secret intelligence work contributes to the problem, but the CIA officer's predilection for alcohol lasts into retirement. Using old-fashioned agency terminology to describe the clandestine service as "the DDO," a retired officer laughingly describes his aging colleagues as "true DDOers: *d*runk, *d*ivorced, and *o*ver the hill." The CIA also has one of the highest divorce rates of any part of the American government, and there have been a few instances when the wife of a case officer has had to be medically evacuated from an overseas posting, an entire family put into counseling, or a case officer recalled for engaging in extramarital activities with the wives of foreign diplomats.

The problems of alcoholism and divorce are far more widespread than many CIA managers are willing to admit. The CIA's high-pressure environment contributes significantly to these problems. Another, far more important reason has to do with the agency itself. The CIA is the most insulated organization of the U.S. government. While agency employees assert that such isolation is necessary, they have paid a heavy price for it. CIA officers, especially those working in the clandestine service, form a tightly knit group. Entire families dedicate their lives to working at the CIA; sons (and daughters) follow fathers, and in some cases sons-in-law follow the careers established by their fathers-in-law.

No one contends that the CIA's clannishness has harmed U.S. intelligence activities, but there's little doubt that it has a negative impact on the agency's image in official Washington, where CIA employees are viewed as unapproachable. The Operations Directorate is the one part of the agency that has been most often described this way—as a bureaucracy within a bureaucracy dedicated to protecting its own members, where families work together, vacation together, party together, and grieve together. It's only natural that officers are suspicious of outsiders (employees of other agencies, the press, and the Congress, especially), who are not part of the clandestine service's world. While the agency's obsession with secrecy breeds this isolation, by May 1987 senior officials were beginning to worry that the CIA's seclusion was undermining its ability to fulfill its mandate.

Such isolation has an especially negative impact on the CIA's most senior executives, those career officers who report directly to a presidentially appointed director. After two decades or more of overseas assignments, the most successful career officers are required to serve a political appointee who often has little experience in dealing with foreign intelligence issues. It can often be an uncomfortable fit. Not unlike military officers who become increasingly jaded by having to mold their views to political exigencies, CIA officers have a visceral mistrust of politics and politicians. Even though the CIA is purposely structured to dampen the impact of politics on intelligence, in truth politics is as much a part of the inner workings of the CIA as a simple security check. The two—politics and intelligence—meet in the person of the DCI.

* * *

After Supreme Court Justice Lewis Powell, an "old and trusted friend," administered the oath, William Webster began his tenure as head of the CIA by reassuring careerists that he was someone they could trust. Looking out over the packed audience in the main lobby at the Langley, Virginia, headquarters the new director was well aware that some of his predecessors had never gained the trust of agency employees and their reputations had suffered as a result. So after paying the required obeisance to the three political figures most responsible for his appointment—Ronald Reagan, Edwin Meese, and, above all, George Bush—he turned his attention to those who had been at the agency for longer than he had been in Washington.

He began his remarks by mentioning William Casey's tenure at the agency: "I want very much to be worthy of Bill Casey, my good friend, and all of those who have led this great agency in the past. I come with profound respect for all that has been achieved and with a deep awareness of the enormous challenges that face the intelligence community in the years ahead."

This opening was a modest but necessary plea, as well as a signal that while Webster knew he was an outsider, he would take immediate steps to control the organization. It was the last such modest statement he would make that afternoon.

"There are some today who can hear my voice but who cannot share the sunlight of this occasion because our country needs their anonymity," he continued. "I simply want to salute these unseen soldiers of democracy and say that I am proud to join their team." This passage was something less than the required bended-knee attitude taken by past directors, but it was still effective and well-received. Webster's most important message in that passage was that he would be "joining their team"—whether they liked it or not.

For those members of the clandestine service who were present at the swearing in, Webster's final comment was less a formal bow to tradition than a clear indication of what he planned to do as DCI in the days ahead. And in light of the national attention then focused on the Iran-contra hearings, his words sparked a predictable apprehension. "We will diligently carry out our assignments around the world," he said, "however difficult, with fidelity to the Constitution and the laws of our beloved country."

Following the ceremony, a muted reception was held in the director's dining room (just off the DCI's suite of offices on the seventh floor). Immediately after that, Webster's new responsibilities were spelled out at his initial full briefing on agency operations. It was the first of many such briefings he received from CIA experts from all directorates during the next two years. While there were few operational decisions Webster was required to make at the outset, everyone realized that his reaction to this first briefing would, in large measure, set a tone and determine how well he could acclimate himself to established agency traditions and practices. Webster made his own views known at the start: Every major intelligence operation, especially those with the greatest risks, were to be passed through him, and all intelligence officers were to be informed that they were barred from any illegal activity. There were no gray areas, Webster stressed to the assembled chiefs of the CIA's principal directorates. There would be no room for interpretation. Turning to the deputy director for operations, Clair George, Webster added for emphasis that the agency was under increasing congressional scrutiny and that his first months as DCI would be closely monitored by the Senate Intelligence Committee.

The second test of Webster's leadership came three days later, on the morning of May 29, during a short speech he gave to officers of the agency's clandestine service. Webster faced the agency's rank-and-file clandestine officers in the CIA's "bubble," a secure auditorium reserved especially for such occasions. His tone had changed from the one that he had used two days before with their superiors; he was matter-of-fact and in no way cowed by those who faced him. He began by admitting he knew he was "an outsider" but then added that he was prepared for his new position. "I've worked with many of you," he said. "I know you. I trust you." But those in the DO who crowded the auditorium remained silent and applauded only when Webster was introduced, a chilling formality he didn't miss.

Webster explained in his remarks that he had a plan for the DO that he believed would disarm the CIA's congressional critics at the same time that it would ease from the service those most responsible for the Iran-contra disaster. "He was tough," one retired DO officer remembers, "but he let us down easy." While Webster said there would be a thorough investigation of the excesses of the Casey era, he distanced himself from the tradition of wholesale dismissals that had marked the previous fifteen years. "There will be no recriminations, no mass firings, no purges," he told his silent listeners, "but those who have violated our rules will be asked to account for their actions." He then bowed to the service's tradition of secrecy by pledging that he would continue to guard the CIA's most sensitive operations from the American press and public. But that pledge, he noted, did not extend to the "lawful" requirements of keeping Congress informed of agency activities. He concluded his remarks by reasserting the CIA's commitment to upholding the law, a view he repeatedly stressed in each of his briefings during his first week as DCI.

As the DO awaited word about who would lead the agency's internal investigation, Webster moved swiftly to rebuild the CIA's tarnished reputation. The next day, May 30, he appointed the FBI's public spokesman, William Baker, as chief of the agency's Public Affairs

Office. Baker, who had served loyally under Webster for three years at the FBI, came to the CIA with a reputation as one of the most open and effective press officers in recent bureau history. Yet his appointment sent a chill through the DO—it meant that the plea for openness that Webster had made the day before would be immediately put into place. The appointment marked a shift from Casey's preference of selecting career DO officers for the public affairs section because Casey believed they were the best judges of what should remain secret. Baker's predecessor, George Lauder, a twenty-year veteran of the clandestine service, was trusted inside the DO and widely viewed at the CIA as a perfect agency spokesman. To the press, however, Lauder was considered a public information officer in title only. "He was a tool of the DO," admits a former CIA officer. "His job was to keep the press out of the CIA's business." For this reason, Baker's appointment was widely resented in the DO—since they thought he did not understand the need for secrecy.

"We don't need this," the head of the DO's Iran branch told Webster the day after the Baker selection was announced. "We already have enough reporters around."

Webster disagreed. "Deniability can only go so far," he told his personal assistant in mid-June, after grumbling about the Baker appointment had reached a new pitch. "We can't deny there's a CIA." Baker came aboard at Webster's insistence, but the cascade of criticism continued in the clandestine service, where officers joked sarcastically that he would turn the CIA into one of the stops on a tour bus schedule. Baker was walking into an ambush. It was bad enough that he came from the FBI; it was much worse that Webster was asking him to take over public affairs from trusted agency activist and DO veteran Lauder, a tall, thin-smiling man who knew that his primary job was to deter media questioning and even, if the need arose, use the members of the press as sources for information that the agency itself might find interesting. At one point Lauder once even laughingly told a colleague that he used many of the same tactics with the press that he had used throughout his career to recruit foreign assets.

Webster's appointment of Baker revived a long-smoldering debate on how the CIA could best handle the press. For the most part, as former CIA counterterrorism expert David Whipple explains: "Most people are afraid that there will be a higher public profile for the agency, and they're totally opposed to that. The opposition isn't just in the DO; it's in every directorate and office, right down the line." For this reason the CIA's Public Affairs Office is viewed with almost universal suspicion inside the agency. Lauder knew this better than anyone. Soon after he became head of public affairs, he decided he would handle press questions the way they'd always been handled, by "keeping the lid on as tight as it can go."

Baker was different. Schooled by Webster in the art of opening doors to the press, Baker came to the agency after eighteen years in the FBI, where he had last served as the assistant director in the Office of Congressional and Public Affairs. He was proud that he had learned how to deal with the press by taking an FBI course on media relations, a fact that he nervously mentioned once too often as he toured the CIA's sixth floor during his second day on his new job. "They're [the press] going to eat you alive," a DO officer told him. "Don't volunteer anything, and you'll never be accused of lying." Another DO officer had offered similar advice: "Just get yourself a tape recorder, put 'no comment' on it, and go buy a sailboat." After Baker made the agency rounds, Webster scheduled a meeting for him in the bubble with top branch officers of the clandestine service to explain the kind of cooperation the new regime intended to forge with the press. "We didn't even give him polite applause when he was introduced," remembers one DO officer. "We just sat on our hands." Baker attempted to dampen the air of mistrust by saying he hoped he could do "half as good a job as George Lauder" (which would have suited the DO just fine) and added that the only way for the CIA to maintain the public's trust was to be open to media questions but without giving away its cherished "sources and methods."

Baker's reception was far worse than he had imagined it would be. "That day, I entered an auditorium full of intense and quiet people," he says. "Some were under administrative inquiry, all were concerned that secret intelligence operations were about to be examined by congressional committees, and all were *outraged* that media leaks on the Iran-contra case were endangering the lives of both CIA officers and CIA agents who were involved in covert operations." Like Webster, Baker was viewed as an outsider. "I was pretty sure," he later admitted, "they were less than enthusiastic about joining forces with an aggressive advocate of public affairs who had just gotten off the boat from the FBI."

William Webster's closest friends say he had a public relations plan for the CIA that went far beyond anything any previous director had attempted. He wanted to open up the agency and transform its image as a secret institution engaged in a dirty trade. He believed the only way to do so was to publicize its successes. Appointing William Baker head of public affairs was the first step in the process. Webster's proclamations to the CIA's congressional liaison staff against shading the truth were another part of this strategy. "Never lie," he told those aides, who were responsible for defending the agency on Capitol Hill. "Don't tell the Congress anything you shouldn't, but don't lie. If you have a problem answering a question, tell them to come see me."

Webster's views met with immediate opposition, primarily from the senior holdovers of the Casey regime, including Clair George, who was still serving as head of the Directorate for Operations, and Dewey Clarridge, who continued as a major figure (though defanged) inside the clandestine service. Both George and Clarridge were adamant opponents of an activist public affairs department. Clarridge was the more outspoken of the two, but both had reason to be steadfast, since they were vulnerable as key figures in the ongoing investigations of the Iran-contra affair. "This is a mistake, a big mistake," Clarridge warned. "We shouldn't be running a public relations campaign."

Webster countered these views by constantly reassuring the DO, through George, that he was as interested as they were in guarding the agency's most sensitive secrets. The new DCI insisted that the real threat to the CIA's integrity came from public mistrust; if the agency did not break the law, he maintained, then it would not matter how powerful, or obstructionist, the press became.

Gus Hathaway, the embattled head of counterintelligence, was considered the agency's elder statesman. So it was significant when he entered the debate a month after Webster took office. Hathaway had previously sided with George and Clarridge, taking a decidedly conservative stance toward the agency's handling of the press. But Webster's arguments began to sway him. During a senior staff meeting in Webster's office in June, Hathaway urged the other top CIA officials in attendance to give the Webster-Baker strategy a chance. "If this fails," he said "we go back to square one. We sure as hell can't do any worse."

After Hathaway spoke, Webster put a halt to the questioning of his new policy when he told George that Baker's instructions on how to handle the press would not be rescinded. When answering a reporter's questions, Baker had been told he could go beyond Lauder's frustrating "no comment" or flat denials. Whenever possible, Baker would also be empowered to take initiatives to short-circuit false stories or damaging revelations. This mandate had worked well for the FBI, Webster said, and it could work again. To buttress his point, Webster repeated a story often cited by Baker of how he had salvaged a bad situation for the FBI. This incident began when columnist Jack Anderson told the bureau that he was going to publish a story about how FBI employees had cheated on bureau examinations. After investigating the charges, Baker informed Anderson that the story was correct but added that the bureau was taking steps to remedy the problem. The story was printed, but it was not as damaging as it might have been.

Webster won this first internal debate that confronted him during his tenure as DCI by exerting his power as the new director. But this victory did not yet bring with it the trust of agency employees or the confidence of career officers serving with the clandestine service. Many agency veterans argue that this initial test of Webster's abilities should not be used to measure whether he succeeded during his first days on the job. These inside observers point out that a number of Webster's top staff assistants, but especially George and Clarridge, were hobbled by their participation in the Iran-contra scandal and, as a result, did not carry much weight with the new DCI. Nor was Webster's decision to expand the role of the Public Affairs Office a guarantee that the agency would be more open to public scrutiny than in the past. The success of Webster's policy would depend on his continuing ability to enforce compliance with his views; in order for Baker to be effective, the DO would have to trust in his ability to keep secrets. But only someone like Clair George, with his vast store of experience and his extensive network of friendships in the clandestine service, could ensure the kind of openness that Webster deemed essential. And George was under investigation.

In mid-June, at the height of the controversy over Baker's appointment, Webster came under increasing pressure to discipline Clarridge and, to a lesser extent, George for their roles in the Iran-contra scandal. But he was under the greatest pressure to dismiss CIA officer Joseph Fernandez, who, as the CIA's chief of station in Costa Rica, had helped plan and run contra resupply missions with Oliver North. Back in 1985–86 Fernandez had ignored the political fallout his contra support operation might cause the agency. At the same time that Thomas Twetten was attempting to distance the CIA from Iranian arms sales, Fernandez had pushed for increased aid to the contras and had approached private fund-raisers to keep the opposition forces alive. The Latin America Division conducted a separate investigation of Fernandez's handling of the Costa Rica station and determined that he had contravened agency regulations. In the words of one colleague, his actions were "way out of line." By mid-June Latin America Division officers were convinced Fernandez had to go.

In early July Webster met with LA Division officials to air these complaints and to assess blame for the scandal. The division's top officers were blunt. "Fire Fernandez," one urged. "Get rid of him." Webster decided to postpone any decision to dismiss the CIA officer. He said that it would be improper to do so without first allowing him a full hearing, but he repeated his promise to punish those who violated agency rules. Webster's decision to open a full internal investigation to determine who had violated agency regulations, however, took longer than expected. The delay occurred, in part, because the new DCI wanted to ensure that such an inquiry would be impartial and would be conducted by someone brought in from outside the CIA. Webster's sensitivity on this subject was heightened by a number of discussions he had with Deputy DCI Robert Gates, who cautioned him to move carefully in assessing blame for the scandal. The appearance of fairness, Gates argued, was as important as its reality; the final judgment had to be above question.

The delay was also caused by a more mundane reason: Webster was just too busy with other matters throughout his first months as DCI to turn his full attention to the problem. Webster's early schedule was taken up with intelligence briefings, introductory meetings with heads of other branches of the intelligence community, and preparations to visit CIA stations overseas. His senior advisers were particularly intent on making certain that he was given the opportunity to familiarize himself with foreign intelligence operations and to meet with those heads of state whose relationships with the CIA were essential to the success of a number of key foreign initiatives.

But Webster's own capabilities in absorbing new information hindered these ambitious plans. In mid-June, for instance, Webster underwent an intensive briefing for a proposed two-week trip to North Africa and the Middle East. As the team of CIA regional specialists began their talk, the new DCI interrupted to check his own notes. "Morocco," he said aloud to himself. "Let me see now." He then reached into his suitcoat to retrieve a pocket dictionary, which he thumbed through until he found an undersize map of the world. "That's in Africa, right?" he asked. The briefers exchanged startled glances. "That's right," one of them replied.

Reports that the DCI was a much slower study than many had hoped soon started to circulate in the offices of the clandestine service, where it was taken as a sign that whatever his plans were to upgrade the agency, he was going to need more time to acclimate himself to its programs. Webster also had difficulty accepting the idea that the CIA regularly violated foreign laws as part of its job. "We have to make ourselves welcome overseas," he said to one DO officer in mid-June, at the time of his briefings. The officer blinked, caught unawares, then smiled. "How do you think that we should do that, sir?" he asked.

In June 1987, Webster set off on his Middle East tour. He spent his first important days in Egypt getting briefed on the Afghan Task Force's complex Alexandria to Karachi resupply operation for the Afghan insurgency. Following his Cairo visit, Webster flew to Islamabad, Pakistan, where he met with President Muhammad Zia ul-Haq and was briefed by intelligence officers on the nearby war in Afghanistan. Two other major overseas trips followed during the next few months—to Europe and Central America—where the same ceremonial meetings and intelligence briefings took place. These tours were part of the well-crafted introduction that the CIA's top managers conceived and conducted for their new director.

By the end of August, however, rumors had started to circulate that Webster had not done as well on these trips as his top assistants had hoped. Senior officers in the clandestine service, in particular, were disturbed by what they perceived as Webster's inability to distinguish between separate operations. In one episode in Argentina, Webster confused a *liaison* operation (in which the CIA shares information with a foreign intelligence service) with a *unilateral* operation (in which the CIA conducts an intelligence operation in a foreign country without the host government's knowledge). In that instance Webster thanked the head of the Argentine foreign intelligence service for cooperating with the CIA, when no such congratulations were due (and thereby blowing the secrecy of the CIA's operation).

Perhaps the most comic, though far less dangerous, incident took place in Islamabad, when the new DCI introduced himself as "Judge Webster" to President Zia. The Pakistani leader eyed him for a moment before leaning across his desk. "Do you really mean to tell me that Mr. Reagan has appointed a *lawyer* to head the CIA?" he asked, clearly dumbfounded. Webster was unruffled. "That's right," he replied.

As word of Webster's Argentine gaffe quickly made the rounds of the DO, the officers at Langley chortled over this apparent confirmation of their belief that the former top FBI man was unfit to lead the CIA. Zia's comment, which was also widely repeated, reinforced the perception. Webster's supporters were embarrassed by his mistakes in Buenos Aires and angered by Zia's remark, but even they later admitted that the new DCI "had some catching up to do." Looking back, one Webster defender had a more ready excuse. "Sure, Webster made some mistakes early on," he said, "[but] that's because he brought over a new philosophy, a new openness, and he was absolutely dedicated to making that work." To the critics, such explanations were not very convincing, since Webster continued to confuse operations at a fearful rate. At one point he even reversed the names of two CIA branches during a White House briefing.

If the new DCI was embittered by grumbling that he wasn't up to the job, he didn't show it. He simply refused to respond to the criticisms. Instead, he embarked on a personal review of CIA complicity in the Iran-contra scandal. What he found convinced him that the innocent mistakes he'd made in his first weeks as DCI paled in comparison with those errors in judgment made at the height of the Iran-contra operation.

Webster was especially appalled by intelligence reports that were used to underpin the arms-for-hostages trade with Iran. He read through a number of these intelligence reports, but the May 1985 paper written by the CIA's top Middle East analyst, Graham Fuller, came in for special scrutiny. In this study Fuller suggested that the United States ease its worldwide arms embargo against Iran in order to contact "moderates" inside the Iranian government. He proposed that the Reagan administration sell arms to Iran and withdraw American warships from the Persian Gulf in order to gain Iranian trust. Webster learned that

Fuller's analysis contradicted a 1984 State Department study that concluded that the United States had few prospects for contacts inside Iran. A subsequent Special National Intelligence Estimate (SNIE) confirmed this latter view.

Persistent allegations that the CIA's intelligence product had been politicized during Casey's term surfaced throughout Webster's first months as DCI. The more he heard, the more he began to believe the stories and the more he suspected that the agency's senior managers, many of whom he had inherited, were responsible. Included at the top of that list was Robert Gates, who was acting director during Webster's confirmation process and now served as his deputy director. Gates's role as chairman of the National Intelligence Council was key, since he was responsible for approving all of the agency's national intelligence estimates. As disturbing as all this was, Webster wanted to give the allegations a fair hearing in order to satisfy his own curiosity and also to quiet the boiling discontent among the mid-level analysts in the DI over the past abuses that they perceived had been allowed to go unchecked.

To do this, Webster called in Mark Matthews, a trusted lawyer who had served with him at the FBI. Matthews's assignment was to interview major DI analysts about their complaints and report back to the DCI on his findings. It was a delicate task which had to be kept as cnfidential as possible. Matthews and an assistant appointed by Webster secretly interviewed agency analysts on the issue of politicization; many of them were twenty-year veterans whose rage over the Iran-contra scandal and the Fuller memo had brought them to the verge of resignation.

What Matthews heard apparently convinced him that the DI's product on Iran—especially its claim that there were moderates inside its government—was suspect. He concluded that the agency's intelligence product had been corrupted to serve political ends. While the precise details of the Matthews report remain classified and very controversial, pro-Webster officials adamantly insist that Webster brought Matthews to the CIA only for the express purpose of investigating the politicization of the DI. The Matthews inquiry was secret, they say, because it involved Robert Gates, Webster's chief deputy.

In the middle of this investigation, Deputy Director of Intelligence Richard Kerr passed Webster a memo about the problem that was written at the end of 1986 by Thomas Barksdale, one of the most senior and respected experts in the Office of Near East and South Asia Analysis. Barksdale's paper eloquently summed up the conclusions that Matthews and Webster were reaching. In it, Barksdale condemned the Iran initiative and detailed the perversion of the intelligence process that had made it possible. His words were also a plea for a restoration of the agency's good name. "I obviously have not conducted a poll of my colleagues," Barksdale wrote, "but I believe a sampling of opinion would reveal widespread malaise on the part of most employees connected with Iran, the hostages, and Iranian terrorism over the manner in which the issue of contacts with Iran have been handled by the Agency. Morale has been dealt a serious blow...."

The combination of the Matthews review of the Fuller SNIE, the pressures within the Latin America Division to do something about Fernandez, and the criticism over Webster's own gaffes on intelligence operations moved the DCI to an inevitable conclusion: The best way to deal with the remaining questions about the Iran-contra scandal was to appoint an outside counsel to conduct a complete investigation. Webster was also getting heavy pressure from the Senate Intelligence Committee to move quickly to assess blame for the agency's role in the debacle. In a telephone exchange at the beginning of August, Chairman Boren reminded Webster of his promise to discipline CIA employees who were involved in the scandal. But it wasn't until September 1987 that Webster named Russell Bruemmer to be special counsel to conduct the internal investigation. The appointment was greeted in the DO with even less acclaim than Baker's; Bruemmer was viewed as a strong Webster ally and another in the long line of those who were "just off the boat from the FBI." But no one underestimated Bruemmer's abilities or his commitment to search for the truth. The DO elite knew that he was to be given full access to any paper having to do with the CIA's role in the scandal and that he would report every detail to Webster, even if his investigation uncovered malfeasance among the CIA's top officers. He had until December to complete his work.

A well-known Washington lawyer, the studious-looking Bruemmer had made his reputation as a partner at the law firm of Wilmer, Cutler & Pickering, where he was known as a good administrator with an eye for detail, a ready smile, and a decided talent for putting people at ease. Bruemmer had two characteristics that Webster particularly valued: He was incapable of feeling uncomfortable around those he was investigating, and he was absolutely loyal to William Webster. At the FBI Webster hired Bruemmer from a field of candidates to serve as his special assistant, though bureau gossips claimed that Webster's choice was predetermined since Bruemmer had once served as his law clerk.

By late September, Bruemmer was an ever-present figure inside the agency and his memos asking for more files became a common sight in the CIA's sixth-floor offices. By November, as his investigation was nearing its end, he had briefed Webster nearly half a dozen times on his interim findings. While there were few surprises, it was clear there would have to be changes made at the top of the agency.

The highest-ranking CIA official to be felled by Bruemmer's investigation was the deputy director for operations, Clair George, whose tenure as head of the clandestine service had been marked by change and controversy. While Bruemmer did not single out George for an official reprimand, there was little doubt that his continued presence at the agency would cause displeasure on Capitol Hill. George was well liked and respected inside the Directorate for Operations, and he had succeeded in winning Webster's trust by defending the DCI at DO meetings. For these reasons, Webster was loath to act on Senator Boren's veiled warning that if the DCI didn't take action by year's end to discipline CIA employees involved in the scandal, the trust he had built with the SSCI would begin to disintegrate. Finally, on November 13, the day that joint Iran-contra committees in Congress published their findings of their investigation of the scandal, George took it upon himself to suggest to Webster that he thought it was time he retired. Webster didn't disagree.

The departure of Clair George ended the stellar career of one of the most respected officers in recent CIA history. His colleagues considered him one of the most "urbane," "gracious," "well-read," and "beloved" clandestine service officers who'd ever served as director for operations. In the years that followed 1987—even after George's reputation had been sullied by charges that he had known of the diversion of arms profits to the contras and had directed a chief subordinate to lie to Congress—his reputation as a brilliant espionage officer remained intact. Though many of the anecdotes characterizing his thirty years of service cannot be confirmed, one that *can* be verified best symbolizes what he meant to the CIA.

In late 1985 the agency's program to aid the Afghan rebels was stalled. The Soviets had responded to the increasing violence of the civil war by deploying thousands of men and arms to Afghanistan, including squads of Hind helicopters that were capable of wreaking havoc on guerrilla formations. Lobbying groups representing the guerrilla factions in Washington were terrified that the Soviets would overwhelm their poorly supplied forces. They were also enraged that CIA-purchased weapons were being siphoned off to the Pakistani intelligence service. Members of the House Permanent Select Committee on Intelligence were deeply affected by the emotional arguments presented by resistance supporters. Two groups, the Committee for a Free Afghanistan and the Federation of American Afghan Action, were instrumental in bringing pressure to bear on Congress to step up shipments of weapons to Afghanistan. The response inside the CIA, however, was cool—since few DO officers believed that the mujaheddin were capable of fighting a high-tech war against the USSR. The one exception was Clair George.

George recommended that the CIA dispatch U.S.-made Stinger antiaircraft missiles to the mujaheddin in response to the battlefield crisis.

He was strongly influenced by firsthand reports brought back by agency officers who had been sent to monitor the aid program on the ground in Afghanistan and by the arguments of Special Forces officers who testified before Congress. But George needed to convince Casey, whose view of the covert program was surprisingly low-key. Nearly everyone else in the U.S. administration who mattered also opposed the move, including the Joint Chiefs of Staff (who feared the missiles would fall into the hands of terrorists), the State Department (who doubted the missiles' versatility), and even officers of his own clandestine service. George prevailed anyway. He was eventually allowed to take his argument directly to Congress, where his eloquent plea that he was "absolutely convinced" the Stinger "could make the difference" swayed members of the Senate Intelligence Committee to take a chance on the risky program, which would tie the United States directly into the conflict. The operation was approved in February 1986.

Within two years George's controversial predictions about the effect of the missiles proved to be more accurate than even he could have hoped. During that period, as the long Soviet intervention in Afghanistan had turned the country into a bloody nightmare, nearly seven hundred Stingers were shipped to the rebels through Pakistan by CIA proprietaries. By 1989, Soviet military resources in the region had been virtually exhausted and the USSR's vaunted helicopter formations were being swept from the skies. A special U.S. Army report later confirmed that the deployment of the Stingers had "changed the nature of combat" in Afghanistan and become "the war's most decisive weapon." The toll exacted on the Soviet military by George's program was formidable: Mujaheddin guerrillas shot down 269 aircraft in 340 firings, better than any rate scored in tests of the ground-to-air missiles in the United States. Clair George's simple recommendation had won the Afghan War for the United States by forcing the withdrawal of Soviet troops. That outcome will remain the single most important CIA paramilitary victory in America's forty-year cold-war face-off with the Soviet Union.

The voluntary retirement of George served two main purposes for Webster: It not only rid the new DCI of a delicate problem (it was difficult enough to discipline a DO official, let alone the head of the clandestine service) it gave Webster a chance to name his own man to take his place. Soon after George decided to retire, Webster announced that his replacement would be agency veteran Richard Stolz, who, like Baker and Bruemmer before him, was a trusted personal friend of the DCI's (they had been classmates at Amherst College). But unlike Baker's and Bruemmer's, Stolz's appointment was welcomed. While he was one of Webster's closest friends, he had also served as an intelligence officer at the CIA for nearly three decades and was well known to officials of the clandestine

service. Webster announced the appointment on December 8, just one
week after he disciplined seven agency employees for their role in the
Iran-contra scandal.

Webster's selection of Richard Stolz to lead the agency's Directorate
for Operations was "probably the best decision he's ever made," remarks
a veteran officer. This officer acknowledges that one of Webster's reasons
for picking Stolz was embarrassment over the intelligence mistakes he
had made in his first few months on the job. "He [Stolz] was used to
guide Webster through the rough weather," he explains. But the Stolz
appointment was not universally hailed. Expressing the minority view,
one DO officer said at the time: "Stolz is too conservative. He won't take
any risks."

After the Casey years and the mounting criticism of the CIA in
Congress, that is exactly what Webster wanted. He told his top aides that
the agency needed a head of clandestine operations "who could weigh
the risks against the gains." Webster trusted Stolz's judgment so much
that he had privately relied on it since the time he had been appointed
as DCI. He also valued Stolz's personal characteristics. Stolz looked more
like a true spy than Clair George and was even ill-humored enough
to serve the classic stereotype of a spymaster. Stolz was just the kind
of man that Webster thought would bring a no-nonsense approach to
the DO.

For Stolz, being appointed director of the clandestine service must
have seemed like a just repayment for the previous slights that he had
suffered at the hands of Stansfield Turner and William Casey. Admiral
Turner had passed over Stolz for the job as head of the DO in 1977,
when he appointed John McMahon instead. While Turner later said that
he had flipped a coin to make the decision, the choice was a major
disappointment for Stolz. Nothing could compare, however, to the bitterness that Stolz felt three years later, when he was passed over a second
time. When Casey replaced Turner, he decided to appoint as operations
director his personal business friend Max Hugel, who had no CIA experience. Stolz retired from the agency in disgust, though he stayed in
close touch with his colleagues by signing on as a consultant to the
intelligence community. When the Casey regime collapsed seven long
years later, Stolz buried his bitterness and warned his former schoolmate
of potential troubles among DO officers.

Stolz had a clear knowledge of how the CIA works and how the
everyday controversies over intelligence policy can undermine even the
most respected director. He had served most of his career as a clandestine
service officer in the Soviet Union and Eastern Europe. He was ordered
to leave Moscow by the Soviet government in 1965 in retaliation for the

U.S. government's decision to expel a Soviet diplomat in Washington. After a short stint in Bulgaria he went on to become chief of the SE and European divisions, serving thirty-one years in all.

With Stolz in place, Webster was poised to make good on his promise to Boren to discipline CIA employees who had violated agency regulations during the arms-for-hostages operation. The task wasn't easy; while it was clear from the Bruemmer report that perhaps as many as twoscore DO officials had acted improperly during the last two years of Casey's reign, there was unimpeachable evidence against only seven of them. Webster resolved the ambiguities by disciplining only those whose guilt was unquestioned. On December 17 he fired two of the CIA officers and sanctioned five others through reprimands and demotions.

One surprising name on this latter list was Charles Allen, who had consistently warned his superiors against participating in the North operation. As the bearer of bad tidings during the last months of Casey's tenure as DCI, Allen was also widely mistrusted for telling NSC officials that Iranian middleman Manucher Ghorbanifar could not be believed. The only reason Allen was involved in the first place, as everyone knew, was that he had agreed to handle Ghorbanifar when Clair George refused. Allen's reprimand was puzzling.

Everyone else punished by Webster was known for his role in the scandal. Joseph Fernandez, the CIA station chief in Costa Rica, and Robert Atkins, the chief of the CIA's Honduras base, were fired. Four others, including Dewey Clarridge and Alan Fiers, chief of the Central America Task Force, were reprimanded, and in addition, Clarridge was demoted and dropped a pay grade. Both Fiers and Clarridge retired from the agency. Two other officers serving in the Latin America Division were reprimanded. The DO, which had been rife with rumors that Webster would cut a wide swath through their ranks, breathed a collective sigh of relief.

Nonetheless, in January 1988, as Webster completed his first seven months in office, he had yet to win the trust of the clandestine service. The widespread skepticism that greeted his appointment had not dissipated. While he had articulated his own vision for the agency, he had yet to survive an actual trial by fire, when his abilities and loyalty to the intelligence community could be clearly tested not only by those who had confirmed him on Capitol Hill, but by those powerful forces inside the agency whose view of the CIA had done the most to define its character. In the year ahead the CIA was to become deeply and bitterly divided by a debate on how best to handle one of its former agents. Webster's first test as DCI was to come at the hands of two enemies: an outspoken and widely feared U.S. senator and a discredited, and tyrannical, CIA asset.

4
★★★
Senator, Soldier,
Dictator... Spy

*T*he senator was North Carolina's Jesse Helms; the discredited CIA asset was Manuel Antonio Noriega, Panama's de facto dictator and head of the Panama Defense Forces (PDF). Helms and Noriega were as different as two men could be, but they had one thing in common: They both believed that the CIA was a powerless institution and they were dedicated to using their political muscle to prove it. The struggle between them had started back in 1977, when the conservative southern Republican accused Noriega, then Panama's second most powerful official, of being involved in international drug trafficking, money laundering, and passing U.S. intelligence secrets to foreign governments. The claims were dismissed as politically motivated by congressional Democrats, however, because Helms was waging a one-man battle to block President Carter's plan to grant sovereignty over the Panama Canal to the Panamanian government by the end of the century. Helms eventually lost the debate when the Senate voted to ratify Carter's proposal in April 1978. Politically bruised, Helms never forgot the indignities he suffered during the Panama Canal battle and he remained convinced that Manuel Noriega was dangerously corrupt.

Seven years later, in December 1985, Helms again urged the Senate to investigate Noriega's ties to drug trafficking. This time the senator's interest in Noriega was not motivated purely by politics, but was sparked by a visit from Winston Spadafora, the brother of Panamanian political activist Hugo Spadafora, whose decapitated and horribly mutilated corpse was discovered just north of Panama's border with Costa Rica. Spadafora told Helms that his brother was murdered by Noriega's henchmen because he had gathered incriminating evidence of the general's money-laundering schemes and growing drug empire. Sickened by the vivid photographs of Hugo Spadafora's bloodied corpse, Helms promised that he would bring the murderers to justice. In retrospect, Helms's promise marked a major turning point in U.S. relations with the Panamanian dictator; after his meeting with Spadafora, Helms announced that the Senate Foreign Relations Subcommittee on Western Hemisphere Affairs, which he chaired, would hold hearings on Noriega's ties to drug smugglers.

The hearings began four months later with the appearance of Elliott Abrams, the thin, chalk-faced assistant secretary of state, who was already notorious for his unbending defense of the Nicaraguan contras and his defiant criticism of congressional Democrats for their lukewarm support of President Reagan's Central America policies. Argumentative, ramrod-straight, and arrogant, Abrams defended Noriega as an American ally who opposed Soviet influence in the region. "The people of Panama do not want a foreign-dominated anti-democratic state, such as Nicaragua, fomenting armed conflict in the region," Abrams said. He pointed out that Noriega was an American ally, one of the few that the United States could count on to defend American policies in Central America.

Helms was unimpressed; he never took a second seat to anyone when it came to defending anti-Communists and was convinced that Noriega, whose anti-Communist credentials were highly suspect in any event, was not the same leader that Abrams was describing. "Jesse was just overcome by the Spadafora murder," Deborah DeMoss, Helms's primary investigator on the case, says. "It was the last straw."

Helms's hearings ended with a whimper several weeks later, when the subcommittee could not produce unimpeachable evidence of Noriega's crimes. Privately Helms was described as a poor loser by his Senate colleagues, who criticized his investigation and charged that he launched his attack on Noriega because of his failure to block the Canal treaty. Even in public his colleagues defended Noriega, saying that all the evidence Helms had collected was not convincing enough to paint the Panamanian leader with the broad brush of evil that Helms thought necessary. Finally, when Helms urged the full Senate Foreign Relations Committee to pass a resolution calling for economic sanctions against Panama, Senator Christopher Dodd (D-CT) diligently marshaled votes in Noriega's favor and questioned Helms's political motives on the Senate floor.

Despite these setbacks, the Helms hearings had raised enough questions about Noriega to catch the attention of acclaimed reporter-author

Seymour Hersh, whose own investigation of Noriega's drug ties resulted in a front-page story in *The New York Times* on June 12, 1986. Hersh's report, headlined PANAMA STRONGMAN SAID TO TRADE IN DRUGS, ARMS AND ILLICIT MONEY confirmed many of Helms's suspicions. It was followed the next day by a *Washington Post* report that cited a CIA study that showed Noriega was involved in a massive trade of illicit drugs and arms and had cooperated with the Cuban intelligence service.

The CIA study was prompted by agency fears that Noriega had purposely compromised U.S. intelligence sources working under cover in Central America. Vital secrets would have been lost to the Soviet Union, the CIA feared, because Noriega's closest confidants were co-operating with Cuban intelligence officials linked to the drug trade. Overall, the study reflected growing concern in the LA Division that Noriega was abusing his long-term relationship with the United States. The CIA study even suggested that Noriega might threaten to compromise agency sources and methods in an attempt at extortion against the Reagan administration.

While the CIA actually had begun investigating Noriega's criminal activities in the mid-1970s, its recent findings were the most disturbing yet uncovered. Its information was based largely on communications intercepts secretly gathered by the National Security Agency. This intelligence had led State Department officials to conclude that Noriega's intimidating tactics and political corruption had tipped the previous election in Panama in favor of Nicolás "Nicky" Ardito Barletta (a Noriega crony), when Arnulfo Arias actually won by about thirty thousand votes.

Despite the mounting evidence of Noriega's corruption, his ties to the Reagan administration were still solid in June 1986, when he began a whirlwind tour of Washington. (By design, Hersh's first piece on Noriega appeared in *The New York Times* on the day after he arrived in the United States.) Publicly, Noriega's visit was highlighted by a lecture on the Communist threat in Central America at a meeting of the Inter-American Defense Board at Fort McNair. Privately, the tour took on the trappings of a triumphal procession, including a pleasure cruise on the Potomac with White House officials (attended by the NSC aide Oliver North) and a visit to CIA headquarters for a meeting with William Casey (who was touting Noriega in public as an anti-Communist bulwark in Central America). This session was Noriega's third such face-to-face talk with the DCI. The first one was held in Panama in November 1983 (when Casey enlisted Noriega's help in the fight against the Sandinistas), and the second one occurred in November 1985 at the White House (when Casey scolded him for his "anti-democratic tendencies").

Their June 1986 meeting did not go nearly as well as the previous two. The discussion was much briefer than the others and devoid of any of the usual amenities. Casey mainly reiterated his view that Noriega's autocratic actions in Panama were making it difficult for the United States to continue supporting him despite his avowed hatred of communism. Their conversation ended after one hour. According to several of Casey's confidants, the DCI was finally starting to realize that the Noriega problem was much more complex than he had first thought. Even when he wanted to, Casey was finding it increasingly difficult to distance Langley from the Panamanian dictator. The snag was due, at least in part, to the Latin American Division's continued insistence that the CIA needed to use Panamanians to gather information on the Sandinistas in Nicaragua.

The CIA officer whom Casey relied on most for advice on this ticklish situation was Dewey Clarridge, then still head of the CIA's counterterrorism unit. Clarridge served as the catalyst to begin changing the agency's policy toward Noriega, despite activist arguments that Panama's strong man was a necessary evil and despite Clarridge's almost blind personal commitment to the contra cause. In a number of late-night talks with Casey, Clarridge broached the subject of Noriega, arguing that he was becoming the agency's primary public relations embarrassment. Clarridge pointed out that the internal debate over Noriega was undermining the commitment to activism that Casey had spent years building. Casey was forced to agree, but he still refused to cut all agency ties to the Panamanian dictator; the United States must be committed to fighting the Sandinistas first, Casey stressed, and only after their defeat would the CIA be free to deal with Noriega. Clarridge kept his private discussions with Casey secret from Noriega's most vocal critics inside the agency. In public the agency maintained the same attitude: Any questions about the CIA's dealings with Noriega were firmly brushed aside.

Unfortunately for the Reagan administration, calls for a full investigation of Noriega's alleged drug ties, money-laundering schemes, and intelligence betrayals were gaining momentum in Congress. In addition to the Helms inquiry, Massachusetts Democrat John Kerry had launched an investigation that touched on Noriega, although it focused primarily on allegations that the CIA-backed contras were involved in the drug trade. The FBI had begun following up similar charges in April 1986 that the CIA chief of station in Costa Rica was involved in illegally providing arms to the contras; in some cases, FBI investigators discovered, arms shipments to the contras were "married" to return flights of narcotics sent via the Bahamas to the United States. Under mounting public scrutiny the Reagan White House reluctantly conceded that some contra rebels may well have "engaged in" drug trafficking although, the administration quickly added, these drug runners were acting on their own. Once this admission was made, Kerry asked the Senate Foreign Relations Committee to open hearings on the matter.

Senator Kerry's initial attempts to prove contra involvement in smuggling drugs proved fruitless. At a meeting held in his office on May 6, 1986, FBI, Justice Department, State Department, Drug Enforcement Administration (DEA), and CIA representatives denied the drug allegations and also dismissed charges that NSC staffers were involved in a secret contra arms resupply operation. The CIA delegate was the most outspoken member of the administration group. According to a Senate aide who was present, the CIA officer adamantly and categorically denied that specific flights to and from Central America were used as a clandestine arms or drug network. He summarily dismissed such allegations as "ludicrous." From the strength of these denials, the evidence that Kerry was gathering produced little official or public impact; even as details of the NSC's private contra supply network were published, Kerry's allegations about contra drug running still failed to generate much interest.

It was an unlikely ally, Senator Helms, who gave Kerry's claims the impetus they needed to gain serious attention. Helms, whose Noriega hearings had ended by then, suggested to Kerry that they combine their efforts. Helms liked the arrangement because he thought Kerry, though normally a liberal adversary, was courageous for attending his subcommittee hearings on Noriega when all his other colleagues had shied away. For his part, Kerry refused to criticize Helms because he wanted to document the alleged connection between Noriega's drug activities and the contras. By combining the two investigations, both senators figured they would benefit from increased publicity. In May, Kerry and Helms publicly joined forces—with an agreement that Helms's allegations against Noriega would take prominence over Kerry's accusations against the contras.

Despite Senator Kerry's well-known liberalism and his reputation as a political neophyte, he was perhaps the best ally that Jesse Helms could find in his fight to unseat Manuel Noriega. Like the senior senator from North Carolina, the junior senator from Massachusetts was one of the CIA's most consistent critics and a passionate advocate for increased monitoring of agency operations. Both men mistrusted the CIA, albeit for different reasons: Kerry viewed the agency with suspicion because of its special status as a secret arm of the government; he thought that the CIA too often eluded congressional oversight requirements. Helms mistrusted the CIA because he believed its exemption from strict accountability made it flaccid and useless. It was strictly an alliance of political convenience. For Kerry, the CIA was too strong; for Helms, it was too weak.

The two men were different in almost every other sense. Kerry was tall with rugged features, a deep voice, and a smooth-as-silk delivery that was tailor-made for a career in politics. He had catapulted himself into the public arena through his opposition to the Vietnam War. Thereafter he was one of the leaders of Vietnam Veterans Against the War and frequently appeared as a witness on Capitol Hill. "He was running for the Senate even then," says a friend from those days. Helms, by contrast, was a typical southern pol: round, balding, open-faced, with a "hi, cousin" handclasp, a huge, straight-from-the-belly laugh, and a redneck tinge. His colleagues regularly underestimated his bulldog tenacity and uncompromising dedication to conservative principles.

The newly forged alliance between Helms and Kerry brought together what became one of the most highly respected investigative teams the Senate had seen since the days of Watergate—though it consisted of only four main people. Kerry assigned two of his prominent researchers to the task of chasing down leads and witnesses to Noriega's international drug ties: lawyer Jack Blum and staff aide Richard McCall. Blum had served as special counsel to Kerry's Subcommittee on Terrorism, Narcotics and International Communications—where the allegations against Noriega were first publicly aired. He was known as a tireless investigator, with a special talent for convincing unwilling, and often frightened, witnesses to testify under oath. McCall, a nuts-and-bolts investigator, was known for his almost encyclopedic knowledge of U.S. intelligence activities and his deceptively low-key approach. Also joining the team at Kerry's behest was Jonathan Winer, a lawyer of considerable skills, who was responsible for putting together the paper trail on Noriega's criminal acts. Senator Helms assigned his aide, Deborah DeMoss, to the effort so that she could lend her considerable expertise on Central America. DeMoss was a single-minded researcher with a knack for surviving dangerous situations on the ground in Central America.

After only one month of hurried preparation, the Helms-Kerry hearings began with the stage-setting appearance of two Bahamian drug runners. Then, on July 15, 1986, the subcommittee turned its attention to a more central question—Noriega's role in the international drug cartel. Kerry convened this second hearing and then quickly deferred to Helms, who questioned a convicted drug trafficker, Jorge Morales, about his knowledge of smuggling operations in Panama.

"I would like you to tell the committee as briefly as may be possible," Helms instructed Morales, "the extent of the money laundering in Panama and how did you go about it. And were any government officials involved in the money laundering in Panama?"

Morales responded: "I get the money in the briefcase, take a plane, a personal plane, a private plane and I fly to Panama—I would meet these guys who work for the [Panamanian] government, and they will take care of the situation with customs, and immigration people, the authorities, and the airport."

It was clear from the sensational testimony that Morales knew Noriega was involved in drug trafficking and money-laundering schemes, though he refused to identify Noriega by name. Still, this account was enough for Kerry and Helms. By September they had accumulated a library of information on the dictator that included a thick file of materials on his relationship with the CIA.

Manuel Antonio Noriega was recruited by the CIA's chief of station in Lima, Peru, in 1959, when he was asked to provide information on his fellow students at the Peruvian Military Academy. Noriega was paid a nominal sum for his services until 1962, when he returned to Panama. He was on the CIA's payroll with only minor interruptions almost continually thereafter until at least 1976. Noriega was a good investment. He became a powerful figure in Panama's military during the late 1960s, primarily by showing his loyalty to General Omar Torrijos, Panama's winsome military ruler whose 1969 coup was welcomed by his reform-minded countrymen. One of Noriega's jobs was to provide detailed reports to the CIA on Panamanian military and civilian officials who received training in Moscow, to furnish up-to-date news on Panama's political intrigues, and to identify fellow military officers who could be trusted as friendly to American interests. In 1969 Noriega was appointed as head of the PDF's military intelligence directorate after helping to foil an anti-Torrijos coup. By the early 1970s, the CIA had come to rely on him to such a degree that he was being paid more than one hundred thousand dollars each year.

Noriega first became a problem for the CIA in March 1976, when then-DCI George Bush learned that the U.S. Defense Intelligence Agency (DIA) had initiated an investigation of Noriega, code-named Operation Canton Song. The DIA produced evidence that Noriega had purchased sensitive intelligence from three U.S. Army noncoms in Panama—dubbed the "Singing Sergeants" by DIA officers—and turned the information over to Torrijos as a way of extorting concessions from the United States during negotiations over the status of the Canal. Similar classified information, including top secret U.S. documents on Cuba itself, the DIA feared, was being passed directly to Fidel Castro. The DIA's revelation, Bush realized, packed a wallop so explosive that it threatened to derail the Ford presidency, then under attack by former governor and Republican challenger Ronald Reagan, who was claiming that Ford was intent on giving away the Canal.

Bush decided that the CIA would take no action against the three Army sergeants because their indictment and subsequent trial could uncover secret agency actions in Panama, including efforts to recruit high-ranking Panamanian officials as U.S. agents. Bush also believed that a public trial would bare U.S. diplomatic strategy in the region at a fragile time in Panamanian-American relations. He concluded that it was up to the Army, and not the CIA, to punish the noncommissioned officers. Because of the DCI's power as head of the U.S. intelligence community, Bush's decision to ignore the scandal became government policy.

There were other important reasons why Bush refused to take action against the three sergeants. Bush fully understood that the DIA's findings meant they had uncovered a major intelligence leak involving a highly placed foreign official on the CIA payroll. If publicized, this revelation would cast the agency in the worst light, as either too incompetent or too naïve to conduct foreign espionage. Bush found himself in the middle of an intelligence operation that had a potentially enormous political impact; if Governor Reagan discovered that American soldiers were passing CIA secrets to Noriega, he could make good on his charges that President Ford's negotiations over the Canal were not in the U.S. interest. If Reagan further learned that Noriega was passing this same intelligence to Fidel Castro, the resulting public outcry could be used as a springboard to the presidency.

Also weighing on Bush was Noriega's considerable value as an intelligence asset; he was rated as one of the best agency sources of information in Central America. He was a credible anti-Communist and had proved it many times by providing useful political intelligence on the region to the CIA. Noriega was also an irreplaceable funnel for CIA funds to other intelligence agents in Panama, and he recruited Panamanian military officers to work for the Americans. To abruptly end Noriega's relationship with the CIA would mean the end of the U.S. relationship with virtually its entire network of Panamanian sources, which was something the CIA did not want to do. Moreover, Noriega was the second most powerful official in Panama and was next in line to succeed Torrijos as head of the PDF, thereby giving the CIA its highest-ranking intelligence asset in all of Central America. There was little argument with Bush's decision. While Noriega posed problems for the agency and was potentially a serious political embarrassment for the Ford administration, his long-term usefulness far outweighed what little damage CIA officers believed he had caused.

Seven months later Bush probably regretted his decision not to drop Noriega from the CIA pay list. In October 1976, the agency discovered that Noriega was responsible for three terrorist bombings in Panama designed to bring pressure on the Ford administration to hurry the Canal negotiations. No one was injured in the explosions, but the U.S. ambassador to Panama, William Jorden, confronted Torrijos with evidence linking them to Noriega. Jorden warned that the incidents could undo the progress made in the Canal talks.

A chagrined Torrijos sent Noriega to Washington to speak with Bush. The meeting was said to have been cordial and official, but little else; apparently both men decided to ignore the incident. This meant that until the end of Bush's tenure as DCI in early 1977 (two months into the Carter presidency), Manuel Noriega had remained one of Bush's most perplexing problems. Bush was tarred by Noriega and his frustration with the whole situation was nearly palpable. "He was always wondering," recalls one of Bush's CIA colleagues, "where Noriega's next boot would land."

Long after Bush left the CIA, his handling of the Noriega problem received both applause and heavy criticism. The most sympathetic readings came from his most strident supporters in Congress. They contended that Bush handled the Singing Sergeants scandal properly by protecting agency sources and methods. They argued that the Panama Canal negotiations and Ford's Republican party nomination victory could not be linked, since Ford's election chances were not affected by Bush's decision. These defenders further pointed out that the Senate Intelligence Committee gave Bush a clean bill for his decisions in the Singing Sergeants affair. CIA officers also defended Bush's actions. These officers argued that information provided by Noriega was consistently credible and that he provided an essential communications back channel to Cuba. This channel had proved valuable in several instances, most notably when Noriega secured the release of an American who launched a one-man seaborne raid (which appeared to be CIA-sanctioned) on a Cuban fishing village. Noriega continued to talk with Castro throughout the 1970s; he told the Americans as much about what was happening inside the Cuban government as he told Castro about what was going on in the United States. (Noriega later claimed that Bush used this same channel in 1983 to inform Castro of the American invasion of Grenada.) The officers felt the DCI was justly unwilling to spark a public scandal over a relatively minor incident and thereby sacrifice one of the nation's most important policy goals. Bush was well aware of the allegations of Noriega's wrongdoing, they say, and took proper steps to distance the agency from him.

Bush's critics are not nearly as sympathetic. They say Bush never considered ending the CIA's relationship with Noriega and never warned the Panamanian that the United States could not tolerate his theft of its national security secrets or his violent threats and direct attacks against its citizens. They also argue that Bush was more intent on continuing the CIA's relationship with Noriega than on protecting CIA secrets.

After Bush's departure from Langley, Stansfield Turner immediately severed all agency ties to Noriega, despite some internal protests over the decision. For instance, Nestor Sanchez, the head of the LA

Division, openly disagreed with Turner's decision. Sanchez was among those DO activists who felt a strong commitment to Noriega because he believed the directorate's human intelligence capabilities needed to be expanded.

Dewey Clarridge, however, refused to defend the Panamanian because Clarridge had been in charge of an internal CIA review of Noriega's role in the Singing Sergeants scandal. Although Clarridge was a relatively young officer in 1976, he had been marked as an up-and-comer and served as one of Bush's top intelligence advisers. According to several of Clarridge's colleagues from that period, he decided to maintain his silence over Turner's decision, though he believed Noriega could still be useful as a future CIA source in the region.

In 1981, within months after the Reagan/Bush team took office, William Casey approved the decision to put Noriega back on the CIA payroll, at a reported salary of $180,000 per year. If George Bush had doubts about Noriega's value in the mid-1970s, he failed to voice them. Nor was it surprising that the same CIA officials who were Noriega's defenders when Bush headed the agency remained his chief allies while Casey was DCI. First among these officers was Nestor Sanchez, who had retired from the CIA to become the assistant secretary of defense for Latin America in the International Security Affairs bureau at the Pentagon. Sanchez was described as "a kind of superspy for Latin America" by an ISA officer who served with him. Dewey Clarridge, Casey's most trusted operations officer, also believed that Noriega's powerful position in Panama could once again prove useful to the CIA. Clarridge came to this view after Casey made him the head of Latin American operations. But it turned out that Noriega's most important friend during the Reagan years was William Casey himself; Casey valued Noriega's blustering anticommunism ("Noriega could turn it on and off like a tap," says a former CIA officer), and his constant offers to help the United States fight Nicaragua.

Questions about Bush's relationship with Noriega were raised in public with increasing frequency during the second Reagan administration, reaching a fever pitch by late 1987. In early April 1988, when Senator Kerry opened a second set of hearings on narcotics trafficking, a number of reporters were dispatched to Panama in search of a tape allegedly made of a 1983 conversation between Bush and Noriega, during which money laundering was discussed. (The tape, if it ever existed, was never found.) Rumors of a so-called special relationship between Bush and Noriega reached their zenith just twenty-four hours prior to the April 1988 Super Tuesday presidential primary, when Bush faced off against Senator Robert Dole for the Republican nomination. Dole attempted to use Kerry's investigation as the basis for charges that Bush had condoned Noriega's illegal activities, both as DCI and as Vice President. "Don't sit on this evidence," Dole shouted at a congressional investigator during one telephone conversation. "I know you've got this stuff. Release it! Release it!" But Kerry never had any incriminating evidence, nor was he able to tie Bush directly to Noriega. Instead, Kerry's investigators concluded that Bush always maintained a formal, almost frigid attitude toward the Panamanian dictator, especially when Bush was DCI.

During a 1983 stopover in Panama, for example, Bush met with President Ricardo de la Espriella, Panama's titular leader, who was escorted to the meeting by Noriega. During their conversation Bush gave his whole attention to de la Espriella, while Noriega sat by in silence. The lack of evidence to prove embarrassing ties between Bush and Noriega did little to convince the Kerry-Helms's subcommittee in 1988 that Bush had not supported the Panamanian dictator and would not continue to defend him in administration circles. In April 1988 that same belief was also held privately by a group of DO officers who were strident Bush critics. As one of them put it: "You could draw a line from Bush to Noriega through the deputy director of the DO and the LA Division and right down to Nestor Sanchez. Hell, Sanchez was Noriega's case officer." Jack Blum, Kerry's talented investigator, heard these kinds of rumblings from intelligence sources in 1988, which convinced him the matter should not be dropped. "There were all these questions about the Vice President," Blum explains, "that he really had not answered. You have to wonder what he knew about Noriega and how much he did not want to become public."

Former DCI Turner was even more outspoken. "Bush is in the government during the Ford administration, and Noriega is on the payroll," Turner told an interviewer. "Bush is out of the government during the Carter years and Noriega is off the payroll. Bush comes back and so does Noriega. Those are the facts, and you have to figure it out for yourself."

The public scandal over Noriega's ties to international drug trafficking confirmed the harshest judgments about William Casey, who revived the agency's dormant relationship with Panama's strong man and even expanded it. By 1984, Casey's fourth year as DCI, Noriega was viewed as an indispensable part of America's anti-Nicaraguan Central American policy. But when support for the contras finally collapsed three years later, so, too, did the last vestiges of Noriega's backing inside the CIA. If the United States was going to scuttle the contras, what need was there to stay friendly with Panama's corrupt strong man? The drumbeat of continued congressional hearings also undermined the agency's willingness to promote Noriega as a valued intelligence asset. When Noriega was finally indicted in February 1988, that argument was abandoned. DDO Richard Stolz believed the CIA could not cooperate with prosecutors who brought the indictments. When they requested agency files on Noriega, they received only two thin folders of material of dubious value, one of which contained only newspaper clippings reviewing Noriega's drug ties. "The CIA's information was useless," says Richard Gregorie, then an assistant federal prosecutor in Miami. "It was almost as if they were sending a message: 'If you think you can do this [prosecute Noriega], go ahead. But we're not going to help.' "

The CIA's decision to stay at arm's length from the Kerry-Helms hearings and the prospective prosecution of Noriega in Florida was not taken lightly, or without dissent inside the agency. Richard Stolz, the new head of the clandestine service under Webster, was primarily responsible for molding this policy. During Stolz's first month on the job, he was approached by a small group of officers in the LA Division who were concerned that the CIA was not doing enough to distance itself from the Panamanian dictator. They argued that the agency should clearly condemn his ties to drug dealers. This small anti-Noriega faction was more than balanced, however, by a larger, and much more influential, group of officers who believed the CIA should remain silent about its relationship with Noriega.

In the final analysis, the argument that the CIA should purposely and publicly repudiate Noriega was not persuasive to either Stolz or Webster. They were convinced that the CIA had nothing to gain from publicizing evidence it gathered on Noriega's criminal activities. Stolz also argued that cooperation with congressional committees—other than doing what was mandated by law—would set a dangerous precedent. Once the CIA decided to cooperate, no matter how well-meaning the offer, it would inevitably lead to the uncovering of agency operations. "Sooner or later Kerry or Helms will ask us how we got our information," Stolz told a group of CIA officers. "And we just won't be able to tell them. So why open the subject?"

Stolz's decision had immediate ramifications. The first, and most important, was that the CIA's silence seemed to confirm public suspicions that the agency was either directly or indirectly involved in the narcotics trade. At the very least, it appeared that the CIA actively condoned drug trafficking in order to maintain its network of agents in Central and South America. Second, the CIA's policy meant that the agency could no longer be used as a force for change in Panama. Any attempt to destabilize Noriega's government or bring him to trial in the United States would have to be planned and executed without the CIA's help. Gregorie summarized the views of a growing number of officials in the U.S. government who believed the CIA could not be trusted to act against Noriega. "I will always have a hard time justifying what the CIA was doing about Noriega," he said. "They're basically cold warriors, and their policies fit into that world view. They say, 'Well, we know Noriega's a very bad guy, but he's our guy.' "

   The CIA's history of cooperation with Noriega poisoned the Washington establishment against any plan to have the agency do something about him. This reality was made plain in March 1988, when the State Department decided to launch its own covert program to establish a Panamanian opposition force that would eventually overthrow him. It was not unusual for the State Department to run such programs, but in this case there was a clear attempt to make certain the CIA knew as little as possible about the plan, and that *was* unusual. The State Department's plan even predated its diplomatic attempt to convince Noriega to retire. This reversal of traditional American policy procedures helped convince CIA officers that "those people across the river" (as they refer to their competitors at State) not only mistrusted the CIA but were acting more from desperation than from well-considered policies. At the center of the State Department's plan to build an opposition was Panama's ambassador to Israel, Colonel Eduardo Herrera Hassan, one of Noriega's most outspoken critics inside the PDF.
   In late March Herrera Hassan was spirited out of Israel and secretly flown under military escort to Washington for consultations. His visit, however, turned out to be an embarrassment. Midway through his tour Herrera Hassan sensed that U.S. government officials had changed their view of the operation's chance for success. The main signal was the chilly reception he received during a number of high-level meetings at the State Department. Angered and embittered by his welcome, Herrera Hassan counseled other Panamanian opposition figures living in exile in Washington to cooperate with the U.S. government only if they were certain they would not be betrayed. Then, without giving his U.S. hosts any explanation, and after spending only three days in Washington, Herrera Hassan returned to Israel completely disillusioned about the State Department's commitment to rid Panama of Noriega. (Herrera Hassan's anger was misplaced: The real opponents of the plan to use him as the leader of an opposition movement came from the Joint Chiefs of Staff. They viewed any covert destabilization plan as dangerous to U.S. military interests in Panama.)
   The CIA learned of the State Department plan purely by accident. A few days before his secret U.S. visit, Herrera Hassan routinely called the agency's chief of station in Tel Aviv in order to get details on his trip. The chief of station was caught flat-footed; he had no idea what Herrera Hassan was talking about. The incredulous Panamanian ended up giving the station chief the details of the State Department's clandestine program. The CIA officer was shocked to near silence by the

account. ("It was the first time he'd heard of such a thing," a colleague explains, "in all his twenty years.") The station chief finally repeated that he knew nothing about the scheme, then gave his own view: Any secret activity to unseat Noriega had to be well organized and have the full support of all segments of the American government. He added, needlessly, that he doubted this was the case since he would have been informed of such a plan if the CIA had been notified. After this discussion Herrera Hassan nearly called off his visit, but he decided at the last minute that any chance to get rid of Noriega far outweighed the risks involved.

Herrera Hassan's trip to the United States turned out to be poorly managed. The State Department even failed to take precautions to assure his security once he arrived, even though he made it clear several times that he would be killed if Noriega discovered he was in Washington. According to Senator Alfonse D'Amato, who had joined Senators Helms and Kerry as an outspoken critic of Noriega, the State Department's lack of concern with Herrera Hassan's security untracked U.S. plans to support a native opposition to Noriega and endangered the diplomat's life. To back up his contention, D'Amato cited an incident that took place on March 25, after opposition figures had concluded a meeting with Defense and CIA officers at the Pentagon. As military officers escorted their guests through the main Pentagon lobby, they were spotted by former CIA officer Nestor Sanchez. The chance hallway meeting was cordial; Sanchez was familiar with most of the Panamanians in the group and with their anti-Noriega views. "During a Saturday meeting at the Pentagon we ran into Nestor Sanchez in the Pentagon lobby," recalls one PDF participant. "The next day our names appeared in Noriega's newspaper [La Crítica]. There were six PDF officers there. Bob Pastorino, then with Panamanian Affairs at the Defense Department, was there. Ignatio Morales [a CIA officer], who had been in touch since we came over, was there. . . . Dr. [Anthony W.] Gray [deputy director, Inter-American Region of the DoD] was there. And Colonel John Cash of the DIA, who was later replaced by Colonel [James V.] Coniglio. The newspaper just named us as being at the meeting. It didn't describe the discussions."

Senator D'Amato remains convinced that Sanchez deliberately leaked the information and "compromised Herrera Hassan." He adds: "That son of a bitch [Sanchez] was behind it. And the CIA probably knew, too." Senator D'Amato questioned Sanchez about the incident in a fiery headline-making exchange during Senator Kerry's hearings on Noriega's narcotics ties several months after the incident. Sanchez admitted meeting the Panamanian officials that day in March, but denied under oath that he was the source of the leak. "I have no business relationship with him [Noriega]," Sanchez said. "I have not spoken to any member of his staff, his chief of staff, his secretary, or an interpreter. ... I was aware of the meeting because when they came out of that meeting I happened to be in the area."

"Yet you were aware of the meeting, though?" D'Amato asked, looking directly at Sanchez.

"They must have had a meeting," Sanchez replied, his voice rising. "I saw them coming out of the Deputy Assistant Secretary's office ... what are you trying to ask, Senator? Please be more specific. I don't like for you to leave the innuendo or intimate that Nestor Sanchez was the one who leaked this information to the Panamanian government. Is that what you are trying to say?" Sanchez's hand trembled as it lay on the witness table.

"Well, did you?" D'Amato asked.

"I did not," Sanchez answered.

"Did you tell anybody about the meeting?" D'Amato pressed.

"I did not know what was discussed in the meeting," Sanchez said, artfully dodging the question. "I knew that a meeting took place because they greeted me when they came out of the office...."

D'Amato interrupted. "Sure," he said, "so you knew there was a meeting. So, it is not an unrealistic question?"

The hatred between D'Amato and Sanchez was now palpable, the hearing room was snapping with emotion. Sanchez had had enough. "I had no way of knowing what took place in the meeting," he stated, "just because I saw them come out of the meeting, Senator. If you have that power, I do not."

D'Amato then dropped the subject, knowing that Sanchez had admitted far more than he should have, even if he had failed to answer the basic charge.

The attack on Sanchez was not only aimed at the Defense official but targeted at the CIA, which the senator publicly castigated as "a group of indolent fools." The agency's failure to respond to charges that it was protecting, and even abetting, the activities of an international criminal was almost too much for D'Amato to bear. As he told Kerry during the hearings: "The fact of the matter is, Mr. Chairman, as you and I know from sources—and I daresay the CIA will say 'we never make a comment one way or the other'—that Noriega, this thug and racketeer, has been on the payroll and in the employ of the CIA for many, many, many years and, I have been given to understand, up until rather recently. And I daresay the intelligence agencies of this country, by God, should be involved in this battle instead of working with the scum of the earth, which they have been doing."

There were CIA officers, especially in the DO's Latin American division, who heartily agreed with D'Amato (many others, of course, vowed to never forgive the New York senator). But for Richard Stolz and William Webster, D'Amato's comments meant nothing since they had already made the decision to steer the CIA clear of what they viewed as a purely political problem.

That decision left the State Department, DoD, and NSC in charge of planning and executing Noriega's removal, which was just fine with Assistant Secretary of State Abrams. With the contras now hobbled, Abrams designed a campaign that targeted the Panamanian leader—with the State Department playing the lead role. Abrams's program began when Ronald Reagan imposed economic sanctions on Panama; the second step was taken when Abrams dispatched the State Department's chief Panama expert, Michael Kozak, to Panama City to convince Noriega to retire. Abrams wanted to put extreme pressure on Noriega by making it clear that the option Kozak presented was the best offer Noriega would ever receive and far better than being brought to the United States to stand trial or squaring off against well-armed opposition forces led by his former colleagues.

In doing this, Abrams resuscitated the threat of the Herrera Hassan plan. Several weeks later, however, the State Department again failed to gain approval from high-ranking U.S. military officers to execute this plan. The Joint Chiefs of Staff stridently reiterated their opposition to any action in Panama that endangered their troops or dependents. JCS Chairman William Crowe was especially adamant. So long as U.S. military assets in the Panama Canal Zone were not being directly threatened by Noriega, he told members of the Senate Intelligence Committee, it was too dangerous to support a coup aimed at overthrowing him. By establishing an opposition group inside Panama, Crowe warned, the United States would endanger the Canal and create thousands of American hostages if the coup failed.

The CIA also weighed in on the side of the military. During a mid-April meeting at the White House, agency officials presented a detailed profile of Noriega, written by the CIA's Political Psychology Division, which characterized the Panamanian dictator as a wily opponent who would almost certainly find ways to survive the pressures of opposition groups. CIA officials stressed that the opposition figures had little credibility inside Panama. For instance, the exiled president, Eric Arturo Delvalle, was no more than an embarrassing spendthrift who was more interested in betting on horses at Hialeah than in establishing democracy in Central America.

At President Reagan's insistence, Abrams managed to overcome JCS and CIA doubters. He won a number of major concessions that assured the establishment of a titular opposition to Noriega, although it was to be underfunded and without the support of the most important parts of the U.S. bureaucracy. In April Reagan signed a presidential finding that directed the CIA to provide secret nonlethal assistance to anti-

Noriega forces inside Panama. This support included a radio transmitter and funding for a propaganda campaign to be run by opposition figures in the United States and the Canal Zone. The CIA chief of station in Panama City was put in charge of disbursing the aid and organizing a credible political alternative to Noriega. When these moves were coupled with the negotiating pressures that Abrams and Kozak were bringing to bear on Noriega, there was every confidence at the top of the Reagan administration that the Panama problem could be resolved without resorting to force.

After several months, however, it became clear that the program was having little success, in part because the CIA was negligently slow in keeping up its end of the bargain. Among other things, it mysteriously took the agency six weeks to find a suitable radio transmitter. (One former CIA officer derisively remarks: "I could have found one at Radio Shack.") Another problem was that the opposition to Noriega was more fragmented than U.S. officials had foreseen. Eric Arturo Delvalle was nearly useless in gaining the confidence of his colleagues in the exile community. It was also difficult to rally the democratic forces inside Panama because the people were beginning to complain that the economic sanctions ordered by Reagan were hurting them more than Noriega. More importantly, Michael Kozak's attempts to convince Noriega to resign had collapsed. Noriega just did not believe there was any reason for him to retire. He continued to believe he was immune to the pressure, in part because he thought he still had many allies inside the CIA willing to protect him.

The talks between the dictator and U.S. officials broke down in mid-May. Noriega refused to resign as head of the PDF in exchange for the dropping of federal drug charges against him. (Senator Robert Dole bitterly referred to this proposed deal as "a legal golden parachute.") It was clear by then that the only way to resolve the Noriega problem was through force. In June President Reagan's original nonlethal finding was expanded to include a paramilitary operation that was to be launched against Noriega from inside the Canal Zone. This new plan was dependent for its success on a soldier borrowed for that purpose from the Defense Intelligence Agency.

The soldier was Colonel Gerald E. Clark, a five-foot-nine-inch tough-talking veteran of Vietnam who was considered one of the most talented and capable Latin America experts in the U.S. military. In March, Clark had been given the task of making certain Herrera Hassan made his secret flight from Tel Aviv to Washington without being spotted by Noriega's friends in Israel. When the Herrera Hassan mission failed, Clark then began serving as an aide to Michael Kozak in the negotiations to persuade Noriega to leave office. When that initiative also failed, Clark was put in charge of running a covert operation to seize Noriega and bring him to the United States to stand trial. This highly sensitive plan was delicate, complex, and dangerous, all the more reason why Clark, a dedicated, well-trained, and fearless officer, was chosen to run it.

Clark was an anomaly, one of the few soldier-diplomats of the American Army, an experienced combat officer who was also inured to the unique dangers of intelligence operations. He had spent his twenty-year career as a military officer, but his work in intelligence circles, for the Defense Intelligence Agency, for the State Department, or on assignment to the CIA, constituted a lifelong mission.

Born in Puerto Rico in 1944, Clark was in the unique position to know Central America's culture and the region's deep mistrust of its powerful northern neighbor. After he served with distinction in Vietnam, his most important assignment occurred from 1981 to 1986, when he was U.S. defense attaché to the Honduran government. Honduras's most powerful military leaders, Clark soon discovered, feared that their nation's sovereignty was being undermined by the massive amount of American aid being given the Nicaraguan contras. The Honduran leaders also resented the arrogance of the contra leaders who established a nearly independent state in southern Honduras. Their dissatisfaction was only modestly ameliorated by a flood of U.S. aid; it was left to Clark to convince them that the money was more than just a bribe—a task that was somewhat complicated by the Honduran military's custom of protecting the lucrative Central American drug trade. Clark was particularly angered by the action of Honduras's chief of army intelligence, Colonel Leonides Torres Arias, who vehemently opposed the contra presence and protected Honduran drug lords from prosecution. No sooner had Clark set foot in Honduras than he was faced with the tricky question of how to convince the Honduran military to get rid of the corrupt colonel.

Relying on a combination of experience, savvy, and charm, Clark accomplished his assignment within weeks of his arrival in the Honduran capital, Tegucigalpa. Torres Arias was forced out of his position by pro-American Honduran officers whom Clark had befriended and was sent into exile as the military attaché to Chile. Clark soon learned, however, that Torres Arias's departure would not solve Honduras's drug problem. Soon after Torres Arias departed, he visited Bogotá, Colombia, where he befriended Jorge Ochoa, one of the leaders of the Medellín drug cartel. The Torres Arias incident was symbolic of the difficulty confronting the United States as it tried to break up the drug trade. Inevitably, just like nearly every other important American official in the region, Clark was forced to work with key officers in the region whose honesty was tainted by their drug ties. The policy was a prescription for disaster.

Clark was particularly unhappy that he was required to look the other way from Honduran officers he knew were corrupt. "Gerry told me they were keeping him under wraps," says a Clark colleague. "He wasn't being allowed to do what he wanted about corruption [in Honduras] because he thought the White House was afraid their contra program would be harmed."

Clark was especially incensed by the ease with which Honduran military corruption was brushed aside as the cost of doing business in Central America. His most outspoken criticism was reserved for Oliver North, the Reagan administration's most dedicated contra supporter. As Senator Helms's aide, Deborah DeMoss, puts it: "Ollie didn't like Gerry, and Gerry hated Ollie." For Clark, North's obsession with arming the contras was the chief obstacle in building an incorruptible Central American military leadership capable of providing a bulwark against the Sandinistas; there was little doubt that North would sacrifice Honduras to ensure the contras' survival. "Clark was the best intelligence officer the U.S. had in Central America," Panamanian opposition figure José Blandón says. "He was trusted by everyone. He never lied. And you knew that he wouldn't throw you away. I never really felt that about Ollie."

During his seven years as an unofficial ambassador to the Honduran military, Clark was able to dampen anti-U.S. feelings at the top of the Honduran government. He was also intent on cleaning up the corruption among those Honduran companies involved in supporting the contras and allegedly engaged in drug trafficking. One of the most notorious of these firms was SETCO, established in Tegucigalpa by international drug trafficker Juan Ramón Matta Ballesteros. In the mid-1980s SETCO was awarded a State Department contract to ship to the largest Honduras-based contra group. The deal included "at least a million rounds of ammunition, food, uniforms and other military supplies for the Contras."

Matta was strikingly handsome, obsessively concerned about physical conditioning, and inured to a life of wealth and crime. He grew up in poverty in a part of Honduras known as a training ground for the hemisphere's most notorious gangsters. He was arrested at an early age by U.S. Immigration and Naturalization Service agents and was sentenced to five years at a minimum security prison in Florida. But after serving three and one half years, he bribed his guards and fled to Mexico, where he became a powerful figure in a drug-smuggling ring with ties to Colombia's Medellín and Cali drug cartels. After he was implicated in the murder of DEA investigator Enrique Camarena Salazar in 1985, in Mexico, Matta fled to Cartagena, Colombia, where he met with leaders of the Cali and Medellín drug cartels, who wanted to use Honduras as the major transshipment point for drugs bound for the United States. When Matta was arrested yet again, in Colombia, his powerful drug allies successfully plotted his escape by offering prison officials $2 million to let him go. In 1987 he returned to Honduras as the head of a vast criminal empire that stretched from the jungles of Colombia and the barrios of Bogotá to the ghettos of Miami. By then, Gerry Clark had left Honduras and was serving in a new assignment at the DIA, planning to establish an opposition force in Panama. While Clark was shuttling between Washington and Tel Aviv (and with Michael Kozak between Washington and Panama City), Matta was enjoying his new life as one of Tegucigalpa's leading citizens. But Matta's stay in Tegucigalpa was cut short.

On the morning of April 5, 1988, six weeks after Clark returned to Washington, agents of the Customs Service, the U.S. Marshals Service, and the DEA watched intently as elements of the elite Cobra unit of the Honduran national police surrounded Matta's mansion in Tegucigalpa. The operation was primarily initiated because Clark had gained the permission of high-ranking Honduran military officers to move against the drug lord. Clark had also agreed to serve as the U.S. military's liaison officer to help the joint DEA-Justice Department team. Once Matta was seized the plan called for his surreptitious transfer to the United States. After flying first to the Dominican Republic, Matta would be put aboard an American aircraft for the short flight to Miami. As soon as the aircraft reached U.S. airspace, he would be placed under arrest and charged with drug trafficking, international flight, conspiracy, and murder.

At first nothing went according to plan. When the heavily armed group of Honduran commandos stormed Matta's home, they discovered only an empty shell—Matta was nowhere to be found. The recriminations immediately flew back and forth. DEA agents suggested that Matta had been tipped off by corrupt Honduran military officers opposed to his seizure, which sparked a shouting match between the Americans and Hondurans on the street in front of Matta's home. In the midst of this angry exchange, Matta himself appeared in the distance, after finishing his predawn jog through the streets of Tegucigalpa. Matta was seized and bundled aboard a Honduran aircraft bound for the United States via the Dominican Republic. When Matta's plane entered U.S. airspace, he was arrested.

DEA and U.S. Marshals officers were jubilant. They believed the seizure of Matta proved that the Reagan administration was serious about doing something to end the drug trade; they also thought it showed that American and foreign officials could cooperate in striking at the heart of the drug cartel's leadership. Perhaps as important, the DEA had planned and launched the operation without relying on help from the

CIA, which it deeply mistrusted. When reporters expressed skepticism that the operation could have gone forward without the consent of the CIA, Howard Safer, the U.S. Marshals Service's head of operations and mastermind of Matta's seizure, was scornful. "This [operation] was ours," he said. "We're the ones who pulled it off. They had nothing to do with it. Nothing."

This sharp criticism reflected the ongoing bitterness that existed between the DEA and Marshals Service on one side, and the CIA on the other. The resentment over the CIA's reputation as defender of Central American agents involved in drug trafficking had divided the American government. The Matta case, the CIA critics note, provided the best example of the agency's willingness to defend drug dealers so long as they remained strong anti-Communists. Members of Senator John Kerry's subcommittee staff point out that Matta's ownership of SETCO in the mid-1980s provides at least circumstantial proof that the CIA was willing to tolerate drug corruption if it meant aiding the chances of survival for the contras. They add that evidence of Matta's ties to Colonel Leonides Torres Arias, who in turn was friendly with Manuel Noriega, shows the agency had much to lose from Matta's arrest.

But the DEA's claim that the Matta operation went forward without the CIA's foreknowledge is not correct. While the DEA's target was not generally known inside the agency's LA Division, CIA officials did learn of the Matta plan two weeks before it was executed. The CIA's chief of base in Honduras warned Langley that high-level Honduran military officers were assisting the operation and that a feud had broken out inside the Honduran government over whether to let it go forward. Those officials in favor of Matta's seizure won this debate, but the losers insisted that the first leg of Matta's journey must not include the use of a Honduran aircraft. At least, then, they said, their government could claim that it had had nothing to do with a violation of its own laws, which barred forced extradition of Honduran citizens. The argument was re-solved when the Americans agreed that Matta would be transported to the Dominican Republic on an unmarked U.S. aircraft. The CIA's officer in Tegucigalpa reviewed the debate for his superiors in Washington and predicted that Matta's seizure would inflame anti-American passions. His prediction came to pass.

Two days after Matta's arrest anti-American riots broke out in Te-gucigalpa. On the night of April 7, 1988, a crowd of two thousand protesters tried to storm the U.S. Embassy and succeeded in setting its annex on fire. Six Hondurans were killed, including a fourteen-year-old girl who was burned to death. The United States protested to the Honduran government and claimed that urgent calls for assistance from the embassy to authorities had gone unanswered. It took two hours for the Honduran military to deploy police units to quell the riots.

Despite the bitterness between the DEA and CIA over the Matta caper, the anti-American crisis in Honduras passed, and in its wake the CIA assessed the possibility of using the seizure as a model for a similar operation against Manuel Noriega. High-level agency officers argued that Matta's arrest proved the United States could reap significant public benefits by showing a commitment to the war on drugs. At the end of April Richard Stolz won approval for an operation that looked remarkably like that which had snagged Matta: Panamanian opposition figures would seize Noriega, put him on a flight to the Dominican Republic, and then transfer him to another aircraft for the short trip to the United States. (There was also some consideration given to kidnapping him in the Dominican Republic, where he was occasionally seen visiting his daughter, who was married to a Dominican doctor.) It was the firm hope of Stolz and his advisers that Noriega's arrest, trial, and conviction would end the unseemly rumors of agency complicity in the international drug trade.

CIA planning for the Noriega operation went forward in mid-May 1988, after Stolz won approval for it from William Webster's new Covert Action Review Group (CARG), which had been set up to control the excesses that plagued the agency during the Iran-contra scandal. Webster was criticized by DO officers for establishing this high-level review group, which they perceived as "just another layer of bureaucracy." Webster responded by arguing that the covert action review process needed to be "strengthened" by being "institutionalized" among the agency's senior management. The group he established reviewed all prospective "findings" with an eye toward determining whether they met his new, tougher legal standards and whether they conformed to what Webster called "the traditions of the American government." Webster later said that he never opposed a finding that passed the CARG's review, but then he hesitated and quickly amended his comment. "Except," he added, "for one." The one exception was the Stolz proposal to snatch Manuel Noriega from Panama. "Webster was against this thing all the way," a CIA officer recalls. "He just thought it was ridiculous."

The CIA needed to gain Senate approval for the Noriega operation before it could go forward because funds for it had to be reallocated from other, already approved intelligence operations. According to a skeptical Senate Intelligence Committee staff aide, there was another reason why the CIA wanted to check fully with Congress before carrying out its operation. "The CIA wanted to show they were as interested in getting rid of Noriega as we were," this aide says, "but in reality I don't think they wanted to do anything. They came up here with a lethal option on Noriega knowing that the Pentagon would oppose it—like they had opposed everything having to do with Panama in the past. That way they could say: 'Well, we wanted to get rid of Noriega, but the military thought it was too dangerous.' "

One week before a scheduled Senate hearing on the CIA program, Secretary of State George Shultz wrote a memo about the plan to Deputy Secretary John Whitehead. "Your [Senator Daniel] Inouye testimony," Shultz began. "Just a reminder to mark-up your draft testimony for next Thursday [May 26]. We will try to get as much intelligence as we can on issues that might be raised in the questioning. What actually is raised, of course, will depend on who shows up and Inouye's horoscope for the day."

The State Department and CIA eventually decided to postpone their presentation until the Senate Committee had time to study the plan; that way, when the finding was actually presented, the committee would consider itself a partner in the enterprise. The CIA was not ready to go forward until July. State Department official Michael Armacost meanwhile cautioned Secretary Shultz to stay clear of the controversy that he expected the proposal would generate. "Dick Stolz, Rich Armitage [from the Defense Department] and I are scheduled to testify," Armacost wrote in a memo. "There is some feeling over in the White House that our chances of securing Congressional support for this—and their support is required, since monies must be reprogrammed—would be enhanced if you and Bill Webster handled the testimony. [General] Colin [Powell, then serving as the President's national security adviser] may even raise this with you at the Grove [an elite Washington watering hole]. They're undoubtedly correct in their assessment, but I would not urge you to take this on. You already have a tight schedule, and there are tricky questions that will require some preparation that is difficult to handle outside of Washington. I am prepared to do it. Rich, Dick and I are ready to give it our best shot."

Richard Stolz was pessimistic about the CIA's chances in Congress, since he had taken a straw poll of the Senate Intelligence Committee members long before Armacost wrote his memo for Shultz. Stolz had found that while Congress certainly wanted to do something about Noriega, it much preferred a "quick fix" to a controversial kidnapping that was only quasi legal. The committee was also concerned about the public reaction in Panama to such an operation, especially after Matta's seizure in Honduras had led to full-scale anti-American riots.

Michael Armacost was equally wary. As he confirmed to Shultz: "The initial reactions we have gotten back from the agency's consultations with the intelligence committees suggest that we face an uphill battle on this one."

Stolz and Armacost turned out to be correct. Following the CIA's July testimony, the Joint Chiefs of Staff once again told the Senate Intelligence Committee that such a plan was needlessly dangerous. "We have 15,000 Americans in the Canal Zone," warned JCS Chairman Crowe, "and every one of them is a potential hostage." The committee responded by temporarily postponing approval of the CIA program and asked Crowe for a study of how long it would take the military to complete removal of the Americans in Panama.

If it was the CIA's intent to uncover the military's intransigence on Noriega and thereby pin the blame on the Pentagon for not doing anything about him, then Crowe's answer to the Intelligence Committee's questions on removing military dependents was welcomed in Langley. At the beginning of August 1988 the JCS returned to the committee with a study that showed that a withdrawal of Americans from the Canal Zone could take months, perhaps even more than a year. "I'm surprised they didn't list the number of moving vans they needed," one of Senator Helm's investigators quipped in disgust. "All they could come up with was that they couldn't do this. They said a military option was out, and they did their damnedest to make sure the CIA's proposal didn't go anywhere."

By the end of August the committee had voted against approving the CIA's lethal finding, but directed Stolz to prepare an improved version of the agency's nonlethal program.

Yet even this proposal was eventually sidetracked. Privately, by then, President Reagan had assured Panama's president in exile, Eric Arturo Delvalle, that he had approved a finding that would bring about Noriega's removal from power. The truth was that the administration was actually unwilling, or unable, to resolve its problems in Panama. In September the chief of station in Panama City told his bosses at Langley that the deployment of a radio transmitter for opposition forces would endanger agency operations in Central America. As a result, the CIA scaled back its broadcast propaganda program. "This was a joke," explains a Panamanian opposition figure. "We got a small radio transmitter, but we could only get on the air for thirty minutes before Noriega would jam us. We were promised that the American military would help us, but they were planning another operation, so we got put on hold. We were told to get ready, then told to 'forget it.' We were very disappointed."

Investigators for Helms and Kerry were also disappointed. "The CIA and military were both involved in spiking the finding," says a subcommittee investigator. "Both groups thought getting rid of Noriega was too difficult and too risky." Jack Blum, Kerry's most outspoken expert on Noriega and international drug trafficking, agrees: "My first reaction [to hearing about the finding] was 'Boy, oh, boy, what craziness.' I think that it was the purpose of the administration to have the Congress turn it down. And that's not just paranoia."

After the Senate Intelligence Committee finally denied the revised Stolz proposal, the CIA, State Department, and Pentagon convened a special study group to assess U.S. options on Noriega for 1989. The Reagan administration wanted to find out whether economic sanctions were enough to force Noriega from power. If he resigned, U.S. policy makers also wanted to know what the chances were that a democratic government would take his place. The study was conducted by the GAMA corporation, a Washington, D.C.-based contractor that had worked for the CIA in the past. In essence, the GAMA Corporation's analysis would be a simulated replay of the debate over Noriega that had divided the agency during the five previous years. Participants in this simulation, which GAMA called "A Geopolitical Path Game," were drawn from both sides of the Noriega question. One of the prominent members of the GAMA study's Blue Team, which represented the U.S. government in the game, was Jerry Gruner, the real-life head of the LA Division at Langley. Gruner, who was called "Jay Grunin" in the GAMA report, was an outspoken Noriega opponent who had led the charge in support of a well-funded opposition program in Panama.

The Green Team, which represented America's friends in Central and South America, included an intelligence officer from the CIA's Directorate of Intelligence and officials from the Justice Department and Pentagon. The Red Team, representing Panama, was led by Colonel James Coniglio and included Major Mark Inniss (the DIA's Panama desk officer) and Nestor Sanchez (Noriega's chief defender in the U.S. government). According to several participants in the game, Sanchez's team "won"—the study concluded that Noriega could not be forced from power, and that even if he was, he would be succeeded by "another Colonel Noriega."

The study group also concluded that the "chances of Noriega leaving in 1989" if the United States continued its policies were "about 10 or 20 percent." If the United States toughened its policies in "the non-economic sphere," the likelihood increased to "20 to 40 percent." The group emphasized that U.S. military intervention, though unlikely, would have a serious domestic impact. The report noted: "If Noriega threatened U.S. security interests and a U.S. military operation ensued, there would likely be some dramatic television footage of fighting and the U.S. might lose more than ten soldiers, not least due to possible helicopter accidents."

The GAMA group's final summation was a prescription for doing nothing. "If Noriega did leave" the study concluded, "his successor would represent more of the same, not a significant shift toward a responsible, democratic government."

In other words, the GAMA study concluded that the devil the United States had created was probably better than a devil it did not know. Or as study participant Colonel Coniglio later remarked, "I was Noriega in the game, and I won every time."

5

★★★

354 Days

No one at the Central Intelligence Agency was surprised when Vice President George Bush defeated Massachusetts Governor Michael Dukakis in the 1988 election. The only surprise was that Bush's brief time as CIA director had played such a minor role in the contest. From the time Bush first won the Republican party nomination, the view was nearly universal inside the agency that he would be called to account, sooner or later, for his service as the nation's top spymaster.

That Bush avoided public condemnation for his suspected ties to Noriega came as a distinct surprise to his top political aides. They had felt certain that Dukakis would launch a major attack by claiming that the Vice President was fully aware of Noriega's drug ties, despite Bush's earlier claim to the contrary. In February 1988 Bush's chief GOP rival, Senator Robert Dole, had publicly demanded that Bush detail his knowledge of Noriega's drug ties and explain their past relationship through the CIA. Bush had artfully declined. "Part of what I don't do," he replied, "is go out and discuss [such matters] when I take an oath of office at CIA to protect sources and methods of intelligence." Bush's implied message was that he, and not Dole, was just the kind of person to keep an oath and that Dole should know better than to even ask.

The questioning about Noriega grew more intense in May 1988, when former national security aide Norman Bailey told *The Washington Post* that references to Noriega's drug ties were the subject of a number of national intelligence summaries circulated inside the White House from 1981 to 1983. Bailey suggested that Bush was almost certainly privy to these reports, called the National Intelligence Daily (NID). Bailey's revelation put a lie to Bush's claim that the first time he knew of Noriega's drug ties was when the dictator was indicted in February 1988.

Bush first denied the Bailey allegation through Donald Gregg, his top national security adviser. Gregg said that Bush, while serving as Vice President, never saw the references to Noriega in any NIDs. Gregg explained that Bush was cleared for a higher order of intelligence than the one given in the NID. ("He normally does not see the NID," Gregg noted.) Gregg added that it was therefore perfectly logical to assume that Bush had remained unaware of Noriega's drug ties.

Bush's own subsequent response to the press was more demonstrative. When asked whether he knew of Noriega's activities when he headed the CIA, Bush flashed with anger. "In terms of drugs, absolutely not," he said. "And nobody with any sense of decency in the political arena has alleged I have. And they had better not, because it's not true, And if they say it's true, let's see the evidence. . . . Let them be man enough to stand up to my face and tell me." He was even quicker to defend the administration's policy toward the Panamanian dictator. When Dukakis attacked Reagan, Bush counterattacked: "It is our administration that is trying to bring this man to justice, once we found out he had gone bad."

Officials inside the U.S. government who knew the real story were incredulous. To them it seemed nearly impossible that neither DCI Bush nor Vice President Bush had known of Noriega's drug ties. Norman Bailey was perhaps the most astonished observer. In March 1988 Bailey told a House panel that he had traced laundered money to the Panama Defense Forces to be used for gun and drug smuggling. The illegal activities had been going on since the mid-1970s. Bailey explained: "Available to me as an officer of the NSC, and available to any authorized official of the U.S. government is a plethora of human intelligence, electronic intercepts, and satellite and overflight photography that, taken together, constitute not just a smoking gun, but rather a 21-cannon barrage of evidence."

Bailey added: "The only possible reason or excuse for being ignorant of [Noriega's criminal activities] would be because the person involved did not want to know or find out, or willfully ignored the overwhelming evidence."

That is exactly what Bush claimed. In order for Bush not to have known of Noriega's drug ties and other illicit international operations, the President-elect would not only *not* have read the information contained in the NID but have had to be nearly comatose during the ten years that preceded Noriega's Florida indictment. The first authoritative public report about Panama's role in drug trafficking had appeared in *The Washington Post* in November 1977, when questions were raised about

Noriega's boss, Omar Torrijos. Noriega was designated to furnish the rebuttal—he responded that U.S. antinarcotics efforts in Panama were being used in an attempt to "discredit our government." A second *Post* report in February 1978 revealed that the Senate Intelligence Committee had made "explicit allegations" about Noriega and drug dealing. In 1985 *The New York Times* quoted a Panamanian government official as saying that Noriega was a "narcotics trafficker." In June 1986 the *Times* published Seymour Hersh's long investigative story on Noriega.

"It's hard to believe Bush didn't know what Noriega was doing," a Bush associate said long after the election, "or the kind of criminal activities Noriega was involved in. But I don't think there's any doubt that as Vice President, Bush wanted to get rid of Noriega just as much as anyone else." When Bush claimed the same thing, he was met with a chorus of doubters.

Among these skeptics was Senator Jesse Helms, who loudly criticized the Reagan administration's lukewarm policy toward Noriega in public throughout the summer preceding Bush's election. Helms also castigated Bush and his national security adviser Colin Powell, in private, for their "lack of backbone" in dealing with the Panamanian dictator. During a late-night telephone conversation in his Senate office, two months before Bush's election, Helms faced off against Powell and sharply criticized NSC planners for their "lack of creativity" on the Noriega situation. Powell repeated to Helms what he had said to a group of senators a few weeks earlier: that he, like JCS Chairman Crowe before him, could not approve any operation against Noriega "that would cause lives to be lost." When Helms received the report, he was incredulous. "Just what the hell do we have a military there [in Panama] for?" The conversation ended with Helms losing his temper. "You're not doing enough," he said, and slammed down the telephone.

The closer the election loomed, the shriller Bush's detractors on Capitol Hill became. They accused the Vice President of covering up his ties to Noriega for political ends and of issuing misleading public statements about whether he supported a program to remove the dictator from power.

On closer inspection, Bush appears to have been telling the truth about at least *one* point—he did not want anyone to claim that he was Noriega's patsy. As evidence of this, in September 1988, in the midst of CIA-State Department efforts to put in place a covert assistance program in Panama, Bush aide Sam Watson told the State Department's Panama Working Group that Bush had no desire to "avoid putting pressure on Noriega prior to the election." Watson explained that the Bush campaign actually wanted to sidestep another issue: "The kind of pressure they want to avoid is stories about bickering between the U.S. agencies. They do not mind in the least stories manifesting greater pressure on Noriega."

Not surprisingly Watson got his way on both counts, though not quite in the way that he might have imagined.

Six weeks before the national election the interagency Panama Working Group held a major meeting on the Noriega crisis that reflected widespread disagreement—"bickering," to use Watson's word—between the State Department and CIA. At issue was whether to supply a Panamanian opposition group headed by Bosco Vallarino with a high-powered radio transmitter. A classified memo of the meeting concluded:

> [The CIA] has not been back in contact with Bosco Vallarino's group at the Embassy on radio broadcasting, but will do so this week. [The CIA] now has the field report on the feasibility of broadcasting from mobile vans. Technically, this is highly feasible and would provide full coverage of Panama City with no risk that their location could be pinpointed. The transmitters could be on the air within three days of a decision to go forward. Nevertheless, both the COS and SOUTHCOM [the U.S. military's Southern Command] consider the risk unacceptable since Noriega will retaliate against U.S. assets if he believes that we have contributed to enhancing the effectiveness of opposition activities.

In other words, the State Department was faced with the same intransigence it had faced earlier in the year from the Pentagon, and to a lesser extent from the CIA.

In addition to Vallarino, the CIA had recruited a number of other Panamanians to serve as a titular opposition to Noriega inside Panama, including Chamber of Commerce president Aurelio "Yeyo" Barria and businessman Chinchoro Cárdenas. To this group was added the circle of disenchanted PDF officers around Eduardo Herrera Hassan, referred to at the agency as "the Herrera group." Unfortunately for the State Department, which put great stock in the abilities of the opposition figures, the CIA placed little trust in either Vallarino or Herrera Hassan. Vallarino was viewed as a lightweight whose naïve views would play into Noriega's hands, while Herrera Hassan was described by one CIA officer as "a common thug," who was "no better than Noriega himself."

Also numbered among the plotters was a group of former PDF officers who had been involved in coup planning in Panama since at least the mid-1980s. One of the leaders of this group was Panamanian Air Force Major Augusto Villalaz, who flew three separate secret shipments of weapons for Noriega from Cuba to Panama and was convinced he was storing them for what he called "an all-out battle against the United States." Villalaz had participated in a short-lived 1987 coup against Noriega that misfired after the battalion guarding the dictator refused to join the conspirators. This battalion was commanded by one of the PDF's most talented officers, Captain Moisés Giroldi. Showing almost chilling courage and fierce loyalty to Noriega, Giroldi turned the tables on Villalaz and his comrades by appealing to his soldiers to arrest the leaders of the coup. Noriega emerged from the crisis stronger than ever. He bragged to American journalists that the few shots fired during the attempted takeover were "kisses."

From then on Villalaz was a hunted man in Panama. He remained a loyal anti-Noriega oppositionist and was part of the Herrera Hassan mission to Washington in April 1988. But Villalaz eventually grew to mistrust U.S. intentions; he became embittered after the series of CIA and State Department plans to destabilize the Noriega regime had been thwarted by internal squabbling and by antagonism from U.S. military leaders in Washington and the Canal Zone. "The American government seemed to think that Noriega would go away if you just left him alone," he explains. Villalaz is especially critical of the September 1988 attempt to provide the Panama opposition with a full-scale anti-Noriega covert propaganda campaign. "The covert operation was a radio station," Villalaz recalls in disgust.

The disagreement between the CIA and the State Department over what actions should be taken to destabilize the Noriega government continued after the September Panama Working Group meeting. In the weeks leading up to the November election, the CIA station chief in Panama continued to express doubts about the State Department program. He told a group of CIA and State Department planners who were meeting secretly in Panama to assess the program's effectiveness, that he opposed support for Panamanian opposition figures because "they can't be trusted." The station chief's dispatches to Langley grew so pessimistic that he was ordered to end his negative reporting and show more cooperation with Herrera Hassan, Vallarino, Villalaz, and the other Panamanian opposition leaders.

The CIA was urging its station chief to put a better face on what was clearly a deteriorating situation in Panama. The CIA's warning was also Langley's way of showing a greater interest in destabilizing the Noriega regime. The CIA's operations directorate was telling its COS to "stop his whining" and begin cooperating with the State Department whether he liked its plan or not. The order was a fulfillment of Watson's fondest wish. By establishing a show of support for the Panamanian opposition, the CIA could at least never be criticized for doing nothing. At the same time, the agency would be meeting the wishes of the man who would almost certainly be the next President of the United States.

The CIA's new attitude also showed that it now agreed with the State Department's plan to help the Panamanian opposition. For those in the CIA who still found it distasteful to deal with the likes of Eduardo

Herrera Hassan or who believed it was naïve to suppose that someone like Vallarino could actually overthrow Noriega, there was always the calming knowledge that the next President would not tolerate such bureaucratic infighting. After all, he was one of theirs—the first President ever elected to have served as head of the CIA.

George Bush was nominated as the eleventh director of central intelligence by President Gerald Ford in November 1975 and was sworn in as head of the CIA the following January 30. Just ten days short of one full year later, Bush left the agency, thereby ensuring that he would forever be described as an "interim DCI."

Bush was a CIA director whose appointment was made by a President obsessed by the need to rebuild confidence in American institutions, to reestablish congressional trust in the agency, and to somehow invigorate his own diminishing chances for reelection. Bush, a former two-term Texas congressman, Republican national chairman, and U.S. ambassador to China, accepted his appointment without complaint and felt he did an exceptional job as DCI for the short time he served. But he also felt that his sacrifice went unnoticed and unappreciated by Ford and his fellow Republicans. When it came time for President Jimmy Carter to take office, many CIA officials thought Bush should be retained by the new Democratic administration. Bush himself had become quite taken with his job and took the highly unusual step of making this suggestion to Carter. Even though the request was gingerly ignored, Dewey Clarridge—then one of Bush's staff assistants—had agreed with the DCI's assessment that he should try to stay on. Clarridge told associates that Bush impressed him as "a quick study" and one of the few DCIs who "seemed to have a grasp of the job and its demands."

Clarridge's description was not shared by many other senior officers at the agency, then or after. When Bush was first named by Ford to head the CIA, he was viewed as an outsider who was using the agency for his own, narrow, partisan purposes. Bush had been born and reared in a straitlaced upper-crust New England family (his father, Prescott Bush, served as senator from Connecticut) and graduated a Skull and Bones man from Yale. He had no intelligence experience when Ford appointed him DCI and had spent nearly his entire adult life either pursuing money (as founder and owner of his own Texas petroleum company, Zapata Oil), or running for public office.

In both areas he had been modestly successful, though his sale of Zapata yielded far fewer riches than those of a number of his contemporaries. In politics, too, his reach had sometimes exceeded his grasp: While he won a House seat, he failed in his bid to reach the U.S. Senate. Later, in 1974, Bush was passed over as Vice President by Gerald Ford; at the last minute Ford named Nelson Rockefeller instead. After this disappointment Bush accepted Ford's offer to serve as the U.S. representative in Beijing. This assignment also turned out to be a frustrating experience; Secretary of State Henry Kissinger was firmly in control of China policy and allowed Ambassador Bush little leeway.

Bush continued to hope that he would eventually be considered for higher office. The best chance for that was coming in 1976, when President Ford would have another opportunity to name him Vice President. As the former Republican chairman, Bush believed he was a logical choice for the job, and a large number of Republicans, many of whom thought Ford should have selected Bush in 1974, agreed. But Ford decided instead to name Bush DCI and privately told him that the CIA needed his talents for the challenging job. It's much more probable that Ford simply wanted a free hand to name his own running mate. By naming Bush CIA director, Ford sparked a round of questioning on Capitol Hill, where the appointment was viewed as the President's way to give a Republican ally the experience necessary to seek national office. That was the last thing congressional Democrats wanted—they still feared that Ford wanted to make Bush his Vice President in 1976. So, during Bush's confirmation hearings, the Democrats elicited a promise that he would say "no to politics" while serving as DCI—and that he would not be a candidate on the Ford ticket in the next election.

It seemed at first that Bush wanted to be head of the CIA even less than Gerald Ford wanted him to be Vice President. Bush was acutely aware that being confirmed as DCI would ruin whatever near-term chance he had for higher office. He took the job at Langley mainly out of sense of party loyalty and because he had nowhere else to go. He was convinced that this assignment was just another in a string of jobs he was being shunted off to in his career. Yet his self-assured tenacity still persuaded him that his time in the limelight would surely come. Even so, Bush himself has indicated that he was embittered at being forced once again to undermine his own chance to one day inhabit the Oval Office. This attitude comes through most clearly in his autobiography, where he describes being named DCI with an uncharacteristic complaint: "Having lost out to Rockefeller as Ford's vice presidential choice in 1974, I might be considered by some as a leading contender for the number two spot in Kansas City [site of the 1976 Republican National Convention]—but not if I spent the next six months serving as point man for a controversial agency being investigated by two major congressional committees."

It was Bush's primary job to restore confidence in the agency and head off the potential resignations of CIA officers who were considering leaving their posts. Less important was the actual day-to-day task of running the agency, which, Bush soon realized, was best left to the intelligence professionals. The new DCI got a taste of just how difficult it would be to win the trust of his top officers during his first day on the job, when he showed up for the DCI's traditional "morning brief" to find his seventh-floor conference room full of men who were not only more experienced in intelligence matters than he was but were also, with few exceptions, older. On his immediate left at the large oval table sat Lieutenant General Vernon Walters, the deputy DCI and one of the deans of the U.S. military/intelligence community. Seven years Bush's senior, Walters was a block-faced, plainspoken Army officer whose towering demeanor was largely based on his thirty-five years of high-level military and diplomatic experience under five U.S. Presidents dating back to Eisenhower.

Arrayed to the left of Walters around the table were the heads of the CIA's most powerful principalities: John Blake, the experienced deputy director for administration; Carl Duckett, the deputy director for science and technology; Edward Proctor, the brainy deputy director for intelligence; and William Nelson, the new head of operations. These Four Princes and their chief deputies were joined by the head of the National Intelligence Council and Bush's primary staff assistant. Along the edges of the room (though not accorded a place at the table), was a group of aides, stenographers, and key officers from a number of other CIA departments.

Walters presided over this first official meeting of Bush's tenure, making certain that the newly arrived DCI led off the discussion by reviewing President Ford's mandate. "The CIA has been through some tough times," Bush said, "but the President resides absolute confidence in our abilities." He added that he was counting on their help to do well as the administration's new intelligence chief.

Everyone listening to Bush's pep talk knew why he was the new DCI: His appointment marked an end to the years of scandal that had plagued the agency and an end to the revelations that characterized the tenure of his immediate predecessor, William Colby. President Ford was taking steps to distance his administration from the "old" CIA in preparation for the 1976 election. He had chosen Bush as DCI to make certain the agency remained as unobtrusive as possible. As far as Ford was concerned, the less that he, Congress, and the voting public heard from the agency, the better. Bush understood this objective as well as anyone. Aside from the standard intelligence briefings that Ford received on a daily basis and the traditional congressional appearances, he made sure that he kept the agency well out of the public eye. During his year as DCI the agency disappeared from the front pages of the nation's newspapers. With Henry Kissinger firmly in control of the U.S. foreign policy establishment, the CIA had even less impact on the White House than it otherwise might have.

Within weeks of Bush's swearing in, morale at the agency noticeably improved, if for no other reason than its employees believed that they were finally out of the spotlight. It did not matter that Bush had no experience in the intelligence community, that he was a purely political appointment, or that he was typecast as an interim DCI; the agency desperately needed a return to anonymity. Bush could take some of the credit for that; he was a serious and hardworking director who regularly issued the kinds of reassurances meant to buoy the agency's self-confidence.

Bush's second day on the job set the tone for his entire term. After an early-morning meeting with President Ford at the White House, Bush again faced the agency's top officers in his seventh-floor conference room. This time the group seated before him was far more curious about what the President had said, and how Bush had responded, than they were about any other single topic. The new DCI did not disappoint them. "I met with the President this morning," he began, "and when he asked me how I liked my first day on the job, I told him that I was surrounded by the smartest people I'd ever met." That was a good start. Bush's remarks were well received, even if Walters and others knew deep down that the first thing Bush was convinced he *had* to do was win their trust.

Bush understood what President Ford wanted him to do and he did it well. When called by members of Congress to attend informal discussions, the new DCI took the unusual step of bringing along senior agency officers as briefers, something that had been done only rarely in the past. And when the Senate finally formed its intelligence oversight committee, established by the Hughes-Ryan Act of 1974, Bush made sure to refer questions he could not answer to his assistants. On more than one occasion, he even directed his aides to answer a question more clearly when they showed reticence. In every way Bush, the experienced politician, gave the appearance of being open and candid. Unlike many previous directors, former Congressman Bush seemed perfectly at ease on Capitol Hill. He understood full well that the rapport he established with the Congress would likely last well past his service as DCI. As a result, he always made sure that he never crossed the line or went too far. Bush continually reminded the Senate committee that its primary function, by law, was only to oversee the CIA budget through a complex audit process. Even though he and the CIA feared that congressional monitoring of CIA activities would be expanded, they knew that Congress had little real power, at least in this earliest era of oversight.

Bush's public performance as DCI reveals almost nothing about his effectiveness as a leader inside the secretive agency. It was one thing to satisfy Congress and give the appearance of openness and another entirely to gain the essential trust of the CIA's senior officers. Not surprisingly, those officers who believe Bush was an able and respected DCI are willing to say so publicly. Those who do not will not comment.

Veteran officer Angus Thuermer, who then headed the CIA's Public Affairs Office and attended many of the daily meetings, concurs. He says that Bush "quickly impressed all of us by his grasp of the issues." Thuermer remembers Bush as "one of the nicest guys you'd ever want to meet. There was never any doubt that he was a loyalist, that once he'd befriended you, he'd help you in any way he could. That kind of attitude is valued at the agency, and it certainly was then."

Bush's personal assistant, Dewey Clarridge, had a detailed and telling judgment of the oilman/politician-turned-intelligence-official. After one high-level Middle East briefing, Clarridge remarked to a subordinate that he was pleased to learn that Bush "knows the difference between a Sunni [Muslim] and a Shiite [Muslim]." This was the type of specific knowledge that impressed Clarridge and others in the clandestine service the most; they felt that Bush would wrap himself around a subject in a way that few previous DCIs had ever done.

Bush was a voracious reader and a hyperactive consumer of ideas. He often engaged in endless questioning of intelligence analysts on anything new or unique—especially if the subject involved the Muslim world. That interest should not have come as a surprise: Bush's Zapata Oil had won the contract in the mid-1960s to build Kuwait's first offshore oil rig, and Bush himself was at ease with Arab businessmen. "He understands that part of the world very well," one Bush friend notes simply.

Bush's interests as DCI were not confined to the Middle East. His staff assistants also discovered that he had a keen interest in the work of the agency's scientists and engineers, who were making extraordinary strides in developing what were to become the most technically sophisticated information-gathering systems in intelligence history. At the recommendation of his senior intelligence officers, Bush pushed for a substantial increase in the CIA's photoreconnaissance budget, with most of it earmarked for development of the KH-11 satellite. He strenuously argued that the agency needed an additional four hundred million dollars to develop an "all-weather" orbiter capable of producing digitized photographs despite clouds or darkness. Also included in Bush's requests was a top-secret signals project that called for the construction of four overseas ground stations to intercept foreign communications. Bush's interest in high-tech spying later paid huge dividends, agency officials say, and gave the United States a clear intelligence edge during a number of key international crises.

Bush's nine-month term as DCI was not without controversy, despite the almost universal judgment that he served well. Although career officers acknowledge that Bush had a positive effect on agency morale, they invariably mention what they call "Bush's betrayal" of the agency's reputation for producing independent intelligence assessments, especially the analyses of the Soviet nuclear threat. This criticism of Bush arose over what became known as the "Team B" episode, his attempt to deflect the growing controversy over the CIA's conservative estimate of Soviet intentions. (These estimates were based loosely on what CIA analysts called the "costing" of Soviet military expenditures.) When the CIA's 1975 Soviet estimate was completed during Colby's term, retired Admiral George W. Anderson, Jr., the head of the President's Foreign Intelligence Advisory Board, told the White House that the study underestimated Soviet capabilities. President Ford was fearful that a divisive public controversy would ensue. So Ford caved in to the partisan pressure and agreed that the CIA would no longer be the sole estimator on the Soviet threat. Instead, Ford appointed two teams to review the CIA's findings. Team A was headed by Howard Stoertz, the agency's national intelligence officer on the Soviet Union; Team B was headed by Richard Pipes, a conservative Harvard University Professor, Soviet specialist, and constant critic of CIA estimates.

Colby had provided the initial impetus for the two studies when he agreed that they were necessary. His decision was met with derision by the CIA's Directorate of Intelligence, whose national estimates on Soviet military capabilities were jealously guarded. These intelligence analysts were embittered by what they viewed as White House complicity in an attempt to politicize their intelligence product. Their complaint was not that Colby or Ford doubted what the CIA estimates said; it was that the DCI and President had succumbed to naked political demands.

When Bush became DCI, agency analysts hoped he would lobby to reverse Ford's decision or, at the very least, lessen the controversy's impact. The outcome would be a litmus test to see whether he stood up to political pressures. But within days of his swearing in, Bush made it plain that he would not intervene. He allowed the Team B study to go forward. "It wasn't my doing," Bush told an aide.

Word of Bush's decision led to a storm of protest inside the CIA, where both he and Colby were widely perceived as having bowed to conservative threats. President Ford's agreement with Bush's recommendation only served to reinforce this perception since Ford was seen as being desperate to increase his standing with Republican conservatives. (These right-wingers had been vocal in their criticism of the agency and believed it was a hotbed of Eastern establishment thinking.) Bush responded to the complaints by explaining that he only intended to provide another viewpoint on an important issue. He told his key aides that those analysts who wrote the CIA estimate had little to worry about. If they were right, he said, they had nothing to fear from an outside review.

Former DDI Ray Cline represents a large group of CIA veterans still embittered by the incident. "Why have outside experts?" he asks rhetorically. "The incident was a purposeful attempt to cast doubt on the agency's expertise. It was a bad decision." Cline reflects the widespread feeling among agency analysts that the Team B approach was being used to buttress the political standing of well-known conservatives. "It was a challenge to an institution," Cline says, "and it was clearly political, and it was anti-intellectual."

Bush did the best he could to mollify his critics inside the agency, but he never quite retrieved the great store of confidence and goodwill that he had spent months nurturing before being sworn in as DCI. He especially provoked grumbling after he made the unpopular announcement that he was replacing the retiring Lieutenant General Walters as deputy director by appointing E. Henry "Hank" Knoche, who was known more for his prowess on the tennis court than for his spy craft. Knoche has since become virtually lost to history as a result of the chilling impact his appointment had on senior CIA staff officers. He had never held any posts in the Directorate for Operations and was nearly unknown to the agency's scientists and analysts. His entire career had been spent in administrative positions, including a period back in the early 1960s as executive assistant to General Pat Carter, then the CIA's deputy director. While Knoche was a hardworking, personable fellow with a willingness to learn, his lack of experience in both the DO and as an analyst crippled his ability to be an effective deputy director. His stature was so weakened that much of what any other DCI might have delegated to his top assistant was never assigned to Knoche. Within a few short weeks of his appointment he was isolated from the CIA's decision-making process. Within four months after Bush's resignation, Knoche left the agency for good.

Knoche's appointment was perhaps the most revealing symbol of George Bush's tenure as DCI. While Bush was praised as an able administrator and astute politician, he was loyal to a fault. He had appointed Knoche more because of their personal friendship than because he was the best man for the job. Several of Bush's close associates admit that this misplaced loyalty was, and still is, Bush's most disturbing blind spot. Throughout his career George Bush has surrounded himself by a close corps of loyal advisers. He, in turn, remained loyal to them because they were his friends, not necessarily because they were willing, or able, to give him good advice. These friendships were more important to Bush than anything; he needed to insulate himself from outsiders and to enclose himself in a group of "good fellas." This habit gave his tenure at both the CIA and, later, the White House a collegial, clubbish feel.

The appointment of Knoche was not fatal to Bush's stature as DCI, but it definitely colored his relations with his other assistants and helped to erode his standing with the CIA's rank and file, where promotion by merit is an expected benefit of working for such a secret organization.

Bush's short time as DCI was marked by his impatience with the minutiae of intelligence. Even the most significant intelligence questions were left to his senior subordinates, while Bush focused on rebuilding the agency's reputation with Congress. In effect, the CIA was run by Bush's subordinates during his entire term at Langley, while he focused almost exclusively on political problems—such as the burgeoning Noriega scandal and the appointment of Team B to provide a competitive Soviet estimate.

If Bush had not eventually become President of the United States, his term as CIA director might well have been judged as one of the most forgettable in agency history. With the exception of three other low-impact DCIs (Sidney Souers, Hoyt Vandenberg, and James Schlesinger), Bush served less time as head of the agency than anyone in its four-decade existence. In the mid-1970s few praised him for his leadership or his innovative policies. The CIA under Bush was viewed as a moribund organization whose powers were harmed only slightly less by Bush's inability to give it a new vision than by William Colby's revelations of past sins. It was not only that the agency was recovering from the scandals of a prior era but that Bush himself had few ideas of where the CIA should go or where he should take it. Nor could he take credit for keeping the agency out of politics. The Team B incident showed otherwise.

It is important to strip away the myth of Bush's term as DCI so that his later relationship with the CIA during his presidency can be put in its proper perspective. While it is true that Bush has maintained close ties to agency officers through the rest of his political career, it is an exaggeration to say that he was as heavily influenced by his 354 days as CIA director as many claim. Bush did his best during his one year to resuscitate agency morale, but Langley's vaunted élan was not fully revived until five years later, during the early days of William Casey's term.

As far as CIA support for Bush's subsequent political ambitions, a small, tight-knit group of former CIA officers did indeed back Bush's run for the presidency in 1980 and again in 1988. From that group, Hank Knoche was the most prominent fixture during these two campaigns. But most agency officials who knew Bush best during his CIA tour either were still active (and therefore barred from political work) or decided to stay out of the political scene altogether. So for anyone to suggest that Bush was the "agency's choice" for President in either race or that the CIA as an institution somehow worked behind the scenes to ensure his election is laughable. Instead, Bush is remembered as a transitional DCI—a talented manager and politician who gained lasting friends at the CIA but whose term was fraught with as many failures as victories.

As one of Bush's CIA staff assistants soberly recalls, "Bush lurched from controversy to controversy during his term. It's important to remember that the real controversies of his time—the appointment of Team B, the decision not to prosecute the Singing Sergeants, and the naming of Hank Knoche as deputy director—were of his own making."

The first two of these three controversies were purely political, since both of them bore directly on President Ford's chances of winning another term. The third simply reflected Bush's penchant for confusing friendship with talent. None of these setbacks deterred Bush from his plans for higher office. Rather, his service as DCI was often cited by his friends as a primary reason why he should be elected President. Bush himself used the experience as one of his major selling points. Here was a man, it was said, who understood the value of intelligence. He played this theme again and again. In the summer of 1988 candidate Bush refused to divulge anything about his, or the CIA's, secret relationship with Manuel Noriega, citing his agency oath as the reason for his silence. He seemed to be saying that he was still one of them, that at heart he was not a politician at all but a former CIA officer who just happened to be running for President.

George Bush's landslide victory over Michael Dukakis coincided with the first CIA scandal in William Webster's term as DCI. While these revelations caused only a ripple in the national press and had a negligible effect on Bush's standing among the electorate, they raised the specter that the newly elected President's first job as commander in chief might be to initiate yet another housecleaning at Langley.

The tip of the scandal actually emerged during the first days of Bush's campaign in New Hampshire, when an internal CIA auditing team concluded that at least $3.5 million was missing, and presumably stolen, from the agency's covert fund used to support the non-Communist resistance in Cambodia. While modest in comparison with funding levels of other secret operations, the sum represented fully 25 percent of all monies earmarked for the use of the U.S.-sponsored rebels. At first the CIA officers who conducted this routine audit (which was a standard means of monitoring a program's effectiveness) could not determine where the funds had gone or who was involved in the massive diversion. After several weeks of investigation were completed, it became clear that a trio of Thai Army officers who helped the agency disburse the money were guilty of theft.

The incriminating evidence against these high-ranking Thai military officers was also a searing indictment of the small group of clandestine service officers who formed the core of the Cambodian Task Force. This special unit of paramilitary trainers and regional analysts was established to oversee the financial transfers and make certain the CIA's money was wisely spent. When the program began in 1982, experienced CIA operations experts from the East Asia Division recommended that the Thai military be made a part of the covert operation to ensure U.S. government deniability. They also argued that the United States needed Thai military cooperation to make the program work—since Thailand would be responsible for providing badly needed support for the non-Communist resistance (NCR). Analysts inside the task force—who were closest to the situation—strongly disagreed with this recommendation from their East Asia Division supervisors. They argued that most senior-ranking Thai military officials were corrupt and, in some cases, anti-American. These problems were particularly evident, they said, at the very top of the Thai military, where a group of officers led by the army commander, General Chavalit Yongchaiyudh, wielded enormous influence, though not always with the best interests of the United States in mind. Inevitably, senior division officers won the debate since, as they pointed out, it was not within normal CIA practices to conduct such a massive operation without the cooperation of the host government, no matter how corrupt the officials might be.

The United States eventually sent nearly $100 million of covert assistance to its Cambodian NCR allies between 1982 and 1988. During the same period nearly $35 million in overt aid voted by Congress also was sent to Cambodia through Thailand. At no time during those years was there even a hint of scandal associated with the operation, let alone the blatant theft that was uncovered in early 1988. When CIA auditors reported that more than $3.5 million in U.S. funds were unaccountably missing in Thailand, officers from the Cambodian Task Force were stunned. If the theft was made public, they knew it could spell the end to one of the most successful CIA programs of the Reagan era. They also feared that Congress, which rarely found reason to praise the agency for its handling of public funds, would lose confidence in the one program where strict accountability was particularly important. Senate Democrats had long been afraid that no matter how diligently the CIA monitored the program, some of the aid would end up in the hands of the genocidal Khmer Rouge.

With these concerns in mind, there was never any question of withholding the news of the theft from Richard Stolz or not providing him with a full copy of the audit report. The recriminations immediately revived the internal debate over the agency's Cambodia operation. The theft gave enormous leverage to those who had initially argued against the inclusion of top-ranking Thai military officers over those operations officers on the task force who had urged their participation. If anything, the analysts said, the theft of the money showed that the Cambodian program had outlived its usefulness. There was no chance, they thought, that a mere $12 million per year could ever hope to defeat either the Hun Sen government in Phnom Penh or the Khmer Rouge, both of which were infinitely better supplied.

Stolz short-circuited the argument. First, he briefed Webster on its ramifications. ("The judge was ashen," one of his assistants recalls.) Then Stolz dispatched a joint CIA-State Department audit team to Thailand to conduct a full investigation. They filed their report in late March, naming the three suspected high-ranking Thai military officers as the masterminds of the embezzlement scheme.

In April, Stolz told Senator David Boren, chairman of the Senate Intelligence Committee, about the theft and provided him with a report of the CIA-State Department audit. Boren immediately called a closed-door hearing to review the situation, which was later described by a committee staff aide as "one of the roughest sessions that Dick Stolz ever had." Despite all of the bad news about the theft, Stolz's strategy to be candid with the Senate worked. By involving important senators in the process of cleaning up the program, he won their support for its continuation. At Stolz's suggestion, the committee dispatched its own team of auditors to review the CIA-State Department investigation. This team spent nearly a month in Thailand before reporting back to the entire committee, on July 12, that their findings agreed with the agency's. For Webster, Stolz, and the Cambodia Task Force—who all attended this second meeting together—the committee's findings were a vindication of the program itself. Boren was especially impressed. He praised both Webster and Stolz for their "candor" and argued that the committee's audit proved that Webster's CIA could be trusted. Some of Boren's colleagues, however, weren't so sure.

Five Democrats on the fourteen-member committee argued vehemently that the entire Cambodia aid program should be scrapped. They were skeptical that an operation aimed at unseating a well-funded central government could ever succeed. They were exasperated by the agency's inability to police its own affairs. "Can you give us a good reason, in light of this audit, to suppose that the same thing won't happen again?" a senator asked Stolz. "Is there anything here that should give us that kind of confidence?"

By their count, this was the second time the CIA had bungled an important mission. The first time occurred when it became involved in something it should not have (the Iran-contra affair), the second time through its inability to run a program that it had actually established. Stolz insisted that U.S. credibility was at stake in Thailand and in other nations that supported the American program. In spite of the theft of CIA funds, he said, the program was still succeeding in keeping the

Cambodian resistance alive. Considering the growing strength of the Khmer Rouge guerrillas and the Soviet Union's continued support of the Hun Sen government, Stolz stressed, this covert operation was one of the few cards the United States still had to play in Southeast Asia. Support the program, he argued, or write off American influence in Indochina altogether.

Though these five Democratic critics carried considerable weight within the committee, Stolz eventually succeeded in driving a bargain that helped save the program. In exchange for keeping the covert operation alive, he promised that the CIA would be willing to give the committee greater oversight about future decisions. He even pledged to include a team of Senate investigators to help establish greater control over how American taxpayers' money was disbursed in Bangkok. This plan seemed to mollify several Democrats. It also satisfied the committee's vice-chairman, Senator William Cohen (R-ME), who argued that the accused Thai officers "should make restitution," as he said, no matter how high-ranking they were.

Stolz softly shook his head in disagreement. He patiently explained that the success of the program was as dependent on the cooperation of the Thai military as it was on the consent of the Senate committee. "They'll get the message," he told the senators.

By the end of the volatile session the Intelligence Committee members were convinced they should continue the program. In all, nearly eight million dollars was set aside for the CIA's Cambodia operation, most of it to be used in the purchase of uniforms, radios, and other "nonlethal" but military-related supplies.

And so it appeared in mid-July that the CIA had dodged another potentially embarrassing threat to its reputation; the Senate Intelligence Committee had endorsed one of the agency's most important covert programs and had even voted to continue funding its client, the non-Communist resistance groups, even if the amount was not as large as the Cambodia Task Force had hoped. It also appeared that the CIA had succeeded in keeping the scandal out of the public eye.

The apparent success was short-lived. In October, one week before the presidential election, the whole story was splattered across the pages of *The Washington Post,* which disclosed details of the theft in Thailand and how the Senate Intelligence Committee decided to cut funds from the program. The prominent *Post* report outraged Cambodia Task Force officers and sparked an intense government-wide hunt for the leaker.

The revelation also had a big impact in Thailand, where military officers tried to pass off the charges as an attempt by the Dukakis campaign to undermine Bush's candidacy. The Thai armed forces supreme commander, General Chavalit—one of the most powerful and intimidating officers in recent Thai military history—angrily denied that any of his officers were involved. The general used the front page of *The Bangkok Post* to carry his message, under a large banner headline that screamed: NAME NAMES OR GO TO HELL. Other senior Thai officers followed Chavalit's lead by dismissing the charges as "irresponsible." General Sunthorn Kongsompong, the armed forces chief of staff, told *The New York Times* that "corruption [in the program] is impossible." Within days of the initial report, a figure of *Washington Post* editor Ben Bradlee was burned in effigy in the center of Bangkok by an angry mob protesting the story.

Chavalit was not the only person deeply troubled by the *Post* story. When the revelation of the theft first appeared, candidate George Bush became concerned that questions would be raised about whether the CIA was on the path to reform that had been promised by DCI William Webster the year before. Considering Vice President Bush's key role in choosing Webster as Casey's successor, if Webster and the CIA looked bad, then Bush looked bad too. The fact that the Cambodian program was in jeopardy also raised doubts among Bush's top campaign officials about whether Webster should be retained as DCI after Bush's election. Bush was equally concerned that an important CIA program he had personally supported back in 1982 during its infancy could eventually be killed by the Senate's refusal to fund it. Bush viewed covert funding of Cambodia's non-Communists as a way to keep the United States involved in Asia, where its presence was severely curtailed by the defeat in Vietnam. He also knew that China approved of the U.S. program as a way of keeping pressure on Vietnam and counter Soviet influence in the region. Bush had been a key advocate for the CIA's Cambodian program in the White House. In 1982, he was one of William Casey's chief allies in convincing President Reagan of its worth. In many ways, when it came to this CIA program, Bush's personal reputation was as much at stake as his chances for election. If he became President, Bush knew, one of the first questions he would face would be whether he should appoint a new DCI.

James Greenleaf is a tall, slightly balding, and unassuming man with a knack for putting people at ease. He was the second CIA public affairs chief during William Webster's term as DCI (replacing William Baker, who returned to a higher post at the FBI). Greenleaf is an unabashed fan of George Bush. He enjoys speaking about the good relations between Bush and Webster and the remarkable similarities between the two men. "The President and the judge are close," Greenleaf observes. "They almost look like brothers. I can remember when the then Vice President invited us up to Kennebunkport when the judge was at the FBI. They would do things together. Tennis and all the other stuff. They knew each other well."

Greenleaf's description—"like brothers"—was a bit exaggerated, since Bush and Webster never developed the informality that is a hallmark of true friendship. Both before and after Bush was elected, the crucial role of being the President's closest buddy and most trusted adviser went to his longtime ally James Baker.

George Bush's fervent need to be well liked by a circle of close confidants is one of his most enduring and disturbing qualities. It sometimes borders on the quirky: When William Webster's wife died of cancer in 1984, Bush was almost overly solicitous, asking Webster again and again if there was anything he could do. Bush also had a bit of advice for the FBI director. "Just work, work, work," he said; "it's the best way to get over these things."

When Webster still appeared disconsolate, Bush offered his Kennebunkport home as an unofficial halfway house. "He basically turned over the keys to the house and insisted that Webster spend a week there," Greenleaf remembers. "And it was nothing but run, run, run all week long. It went from tennis to fishing to jogging back to tennis. By the end of each day Webster was exhausted, and it really brought him out of it. By the end of the week I think that Webster had gotten over his depression, and Bush told him, 'Go back and put this behind you. Keep working and you'll get over this.'" From that difficult time forward Webster was a Bush loyalist.

Webster was not the only recipient of Bush's friendship. When the first wife of Texas financier Robert Mosbacher died in the mid-1970s, Bush volunteered the same generous offer: a week of tennis, relaxation, and emotional recovery hosted by Bush himself. Earlier, when James Baker's first wife died, Bush had acted the same way. Mosbacher became a lifelong friend and commerce secretary during the Bush administration, while Baker was named secretary of state. Besides Webster, Mosbacher, and Baker, two other loyalists became key officials in his administration: John Sununu (who showed his support during the 1988 New Hampshire primaries, even when it appeared Bush would lose) and Robert Gates (who gracefully bowed out of contention as DCI after Bush recommended that Webster should be given the job). Each of these men owed Bush more than he owed them; and, in the four years ahead, each of them would go out of his way to repay the kindness.

Among this group, only Webster's fate in the new administration was in doubt in the days after Bush was elected. Many of the CIA's top officers felt certain that Webster would be replaced by Bush's old friend James Lilley, then serving as U.S. ambassador to South Korea. The tall, graying, and quick-tempered Lilley was a former highly regarded CIA operations officer who had topped off his long career by serving as the agency's national intelligence officer for China when Bush was DCI. Bush greatly respected Lilley for his expertise in intelligence matters.

Lilley had pursued the DCI's job with the diligence of a bulldog, though he had chosen a career track well outside the path usually taken by other ambitious CIA officers. Lilley was one of the CIA's top Asia experts, and they were not typically viewed as probable DCIs, at least certainly not in an era when outsiders—politicians (Bush), admirals (Turner), campaign managers (Casey), and judges (Webster)—most often succeeded to the intelligence community's top spot. Lilley's claim to being CIA director came as much from his association with Bush as from his experience as an intelligence officer; they became friends when Lilley was sent to China as the first CIA chief of station in Beijing, and he served there when Bush headed America's diplomatic mission. During the waning days of the 1988 campaign, Bush began considering Lilley's candidacy for DCI. Bush even mentioned the possibility of a Lilley appointment to his campaign manager, James Baker.

For several weeks after Bush's election, the names of other potential DCIs were circulated among the President-elect's closest advisers. Most prominently mentioned were: William Hyland, a former deputy director of the National Security Council and the editor of *Foreign Affairs;* Brent Scowcroft, who was eventually named as Bush's national security adviser; Colin Powell, who later was named chairman of the Joint Chiefs of Staff; and Frank Carlucci, President Reagan's secretary of defense. The President-elect, however, remained curiously silent on Webster's candidacy, though it was clear that the DCI wanted to continue on the job. Webster said as much to his three top assistants. He told Richard Stolz, Robert Gates, and DDI Richard Kerr on separate occasions during the days after the election that he would like to remain at the CIA. All of them replied that they supported his efforts to win reappointment. Stolz especially urged his former schoolmate to tell Bush personally that he wanted to keep the job.

Webster refused to provoke a confrontation. He confided to his colleagues that he wanted at least to "make the appearance" of not "openly pushing himself for the job." By maintaining a low profile, he felt he would make himself more valued by Bush.

Meanwhile, among Bush's advisers, especially James Baker, there was some confusion about whether Webster actually wanted to continue in the job. The effect of such doubts was that Webster's name was slowly losing its luster within Bush's inner circle. Even Webster told a top associate that he measured his chances for reappointment as "slim and none." He complained that he was "frustrated and depressed" and that his only contact with Bush since the election had been cursory at best. Webster had phoned to congratulate Bush soon after his landslide victory, but the conversation had skirted the issue of who would be the next DCI. Both Stolz and Kerr were disturbed by Webster's feelings of impotence. He had forlornly repeated to them at least half a dozen times in private conversations that he could return to his old law firm in St. Louis if he was not reappointed. Finally, in mid-November, Webster's inability to promote his own candidacy became so disturbing to Stolz that he addressed the subject head-on to Webster during one of their early-morning conferences.

Stolz told Webster that if he wanted to keep his job, he had to say so, because the President-elect obviously thought he was not interested. Stolz added that if Webster wanted to leave Langley, he should also make *that* preference clear since much of the agency was abuzz with unsettling rumors about who would take his place. Webster was visibly upset by Stolz's warnings. He admitted that he wanted to continue as CIA chief but did not know how to go about lobbying for the job. Such a campaign was, he said, "against every instinct I have."

Realizing that his old friend was not nearly the politician he'd supposed in spite of his adept handling of Congress, Stolz made several suggestions. The first thing Webster should do, he said, was make sure the President knew he wanted to continue on as DCI. Then Webster needed to stake out his own position as head of the nation's intelligence community; the one thing that Bush wanted from Webster was a reaffirmation that he would not attempt to be part of the White House foreign policy team. Finally, Webster should renew an invitation he had made to *Washington Post* publisher Katharine Graham to speak to a class of CIA recruits about the role of the press in the national security establishment.

That, Stolz said, would help get his name into the newspapers. Webster was still uncertain. He repeated that he did not want to lobby for the job. Stolz brightened. "Well then," he said, "at least *say* that."

Webster knew that Stolz was right. With his reappointment clearly in jeopardy, Webster needed to make a bid to retain his post. That effort, he agreed, included currying favor with the press. The next day Webster telephoned Mrs. Graham to revive the speaking invitation. She gladly accepted and appeared at CIA headquarters a few days later. She was warmly received, and her speech was a hit—especially with Webster.

Her remarks to the CIA's assembled recruits coincided almost exactly with his own opinions and reflected his inherent conservatism about matters of national security. "We live in a dirty and dangerous world," the *Post*'s publisher told the class. "There are some things the general public does not need to know and shouldn't. I believe democracy flourishes when the government can take legitimate steps to keep its secrets, and when the press can decide whether to print what it knows."

After Mrs. Graham left Langley, Webster hoped that he had gained a powerful ally in the Washington media establishment and looked forward to favorable coverage in the *Post*.

The Webster campaign shifted into high gear. During a morning briefing he announced to the agency's top officers that he had decided he wanted to remain as DCI because he believed it was important that the organization retain its reputation as an independent agency. To change directors before the inauguration of a new President, he said, would be to send "exactly the wrong kind of message to Congress and the American people. We don't want to politicize our work." He then instructed his public affairs director to promote these positions in his talks with the press. On November 16 a reporter was told that the reason Webster's name hadn't come up in discussions of who would head the agency was that Webster wasn't promoting his own candidacy. "[W]hat [Webster] wants is a smooth transition," the CIA spokesman said, "not politicizing the agency, but keeping it moving." A report of the conversation appeared in the *Post* on November 18. The *Post* story also included a litany of Webster's accomplishments as DCI.

The *Post* article could not have come at a better time for Webster. A number of retired agency officers who were close to Bush were pointedly criticizing Webster for having a lackadaisical attitude toward intelligence. They charged that Webster was neither the quick study everyone assumed nor the activist that many wanted. Despite his warm relations with Congress, they said, Webster was clearly a transitional figure, and Bush should appoint someone better known inside the CIA, "someone from the community." A number of Bush's top advisers agreed, including newly appointed chief of staff Sununu, who thought that Bush should appoint his own man to head the CIA. Bush was also getting pressure from a close group of foreign policy experts allied with Brent Scowcroft, who was under consideration as his national security adviser.

By the end of November, after weighing his options, Bush was leaning toward keeping Webster on as DCI. He was swayed in that direction primarily because his top adviser and the secretary of state-designate, James Baker, was convinced that it would be a mistake to replace a man whom Bush himself had helped get appointed. Bush also wanted to see just how effective Webster would be in managing the agency during an activist administration. Webster had not had much of a chance to run things during the Reagan presidency, Bush argued, and he should be given a chance to show whether he could do the job. Bush told his aides that he wanted to get off to a good start on key foreign policy issues during the first days of the administration and that it would take too long for a new director to be put in place, even if that person was someone as experienced as James Lilley. Baker strongly agreed. In the end Baker could take much of the credit for Webster's reappointment; the last thing the CIA needed now, he told Bush in one meeting, was another new start with another new director. The agency was in trouble and needed as much stability as it could get. On December 6 Bush made it official, naming Webster his administration's DCI.

Webster was obviously pleased by the decision. It meant that he would be presiding over perhaps the most important period in the agency's forty-year history. The Soviet target was fast dissolving, to be replaced by a whole menu of concerns. The agency could now take time to study the future, instead of lurching from crisis to crisis. Or at least that was the hope. But on December 21 the agency's normally quiet holiday season was shattered by the single most destructive terrorist event of modern times.

6
★ ★ ★

Out of a Clear Sky

On the night of December 21, 1988—before George Bush could even take office—the night air over the village of Lockerbie, Scotland, was shattered by a massive explosion. The tragedy that took place that dark winter night, which cost the lives of 270 innocent men, women, and children, was to inflame George Bush's presidency for the next three years.

How strange the incident must have seemed to the U.S. counter-terrorism center, and how ironic for the officers of the CIA's Near East Division—for the bloodiest terrorist incident in history had a chilling resemblance to an incident recounted at the beginning of one of the century's most controversial novels. The opening of Salman Rushdie's *The Satanic Verses* might well have served as the outline for the destruction of Pan Am Flight 103. The simple irony seemed to somehow prove that the world's most murderous gangsters were devotees of the grotesque, as well as politically astute. Their act of terror was a signal that the agency's long-running battle with a number of Middle East terrorist organizations that had begun more than a decade before was far from over.

Salman Rushdie gave the agency its first hint of the tragedy when no others were yet available: "Just before dawn one winter's morning, New Year's Day or thereabout, two real, full-grown, living men fell from a great height, twenty-nine thousand and two feet, towards the English Channel, without benefit of parachutes or wings, out of a clear sky."

Close enough: Pan Am 103, northwest bound to New York out of

London's Heathrow Airport in the early evening of December 21, 1988, reached a cruising altitude of 30,007 feet before a bomb hidden inside a passenger bag and placed in forward luggage container 14L blasted through the aircraft's fuselage, sprayed a chunk of the bolted exterior earthward, and immediately rendered the aircraft inoperable. During a subsequent investigation that thrived on details and involved hundreds of intelligence officers and law enforcement officials from dozens of nations, the hole the bomb caused was precisely measured at eighteen inches by twelve inches—not large by most standards, but big enough so that within a few short seconds after the detonation a structural wave buckled the jetliner and sheared off its front end, ripping the 747 into two distinct parts. Two seconds later a second wave moved through the fuselage, breaking the aircraft into five main pieces that plummeted gracelessly toward Lockerbie, where eleven unsuspecting people in the small Scottish town below would meet a horrible fate.

What fell from the sky, investigators now know, were thousands of pieces of metal, leather, carpet fragments, and flesh, the detritus of a massive calamity that left a huge, distinct cone of debris stretching for hundreds of miles to the northwest from Lockerbie to the North Sea. It took many months to locate even the barest fragments of the most important portions of the aircraft, though the crew cabin came down more or less intact. Up to two years later searchers were still combing the fields of Scotland for any clues to help solve the mystery of the flight's sudden demise.

So much was lost in the blast, including the cockpit voice record containing the crew's last words, that by the time the explosion had become apparent to the 747's captain, any expletive he might have uttered would have hung unheard in the air. When the jet's radio messages to ground trackers were reviewed hours later, all that could be discerned coming from the 747 before the abrupt, total silence was a short raspy sound ("like the ripping of a fine textile," explains one investigator). Although no one yet could exactly pinpoint the source, this brief sound was a disturbing clue, since other airline explosions had been preceded by exactly the same kind of noise. Perhaps the bombing of Pan Am 103 *did*, after all, have its inception in Salman Rushdie's polemic on Muhammad; it's as good an explanation as any other, and the parallels are chilling. "The aircraft cracked in half, a seed-pod giving up its spores, an egg yielding its mystery," Rushdie writes.

Not quite. In the hours, days, weeks, and months that followed, the terrorist bombing of Pan Am 103 remained one of the world's most baffling puzzles, an enigma so vast and complex that after a time it became difficult for even the most accomplished investigator to separate fact from fiction. Over the course of two years it seemed that as many theories on the aircraft's bombing were issued as there were pieces of the aircraft itself, which was painstakingly reconstructed in a large warehouse in southern Scotland. Even the most widely believed theories—that the bomb was put aboard by a drug-toting dupe on his way to Detroit, that a CIA officer on the aircraft had his bag switched for another in London, that an agency sting operation had somehow gone awry in Frankfurt—were thrown into disrepute. In the end the simplest, and also the least satisfying, explanation was accepted: The bombing of Pan Am 103 was a simple act of revenge.

Within hours of the Pan Am crash Director of Central Intelligence William Webster ordered the CIA's counterterrorism center (CTC) to begin an investigation of the bombing and identify the perpetrators. In many ways, Webster, Stolz, and their top assistants knew that the Pan Am 103 disaster would be a "showcase," as one report said, "for one of the CIA's promising recent innovations." It would serve as a way of showing that the CIA had entered the post-cold war world intact and was fully capable of cooperating with the FBI and other government agencies in solving an international crime. But if the bombing was the CTC's first public trial, it was also a test for DCI William Webster, Deputy Director for Operations Richard Stolz, and Thomas Twetten, the assistant deputy director for operations.

Webster was aware that any future judgment of his performance as DCI might well rest on whether the agency he headed could resolve the Pan Am mystery and help bring its perpetrators to justice. He was as outraged by the sudden, deadly attack on the aircraft as William Casey had been during a similar, but not nearly as catastrophic, incident six years earlier. For at least one CIA officer, the explosion that decimated Pan Am 103 looked suspiciously like an act that might be carried out by the Baghdad bomber, Mohammed Hussein Rashid.

The man in overall charge of the CIA's investigation was Fred Turco, a twenty-five-year agency veteran whose reputation as a steady, often insightful operations officer was confirmed by the fact that none other than Dewey Clarridge had recommended him as his successor to head the CTC. Turco had the clandestine service's confidence, though not simply because he was well known inside the DO; over his more than two decades of experience, he had befriended some of the CIA's most powerful officials, including Thomas Twetten, with whom he'd become fast friends. While Turco's background included tracking international terrorists, he was known more for his outspoken views on how to deal with them. He was, in Casey's term, a "shooter," one of a handful of CIA professionals who believed that the agency should wage a tit-for-tat war against terrorist organizations. But Turco's colleagues agree that he was no Clarridge; he was more adept at handling the bureaucracy and much less flamboyant. His one personal tic was his absolute commitment to secrecy and what one colleague described as "a predisposition to coldness."

William Webster liked Turco primarily because when he was head of the FBI, his own terrorism officers had given the CIA veteran high marks, describing him as one of the most cooperative agency officers they'd ever met. In addition, Turco had supported Casey's and Clarridge's proposal to set up the CTC primarily because of his frustration at having to coordinate operations with the State Department, Federal Aviation Administration, FBI, Secret Service, and Pentagon. When Casey and Clarridge decided that it would be a good idea to set up an interagency group to handle the deepening crisis over terrorism, Turco became one of its strongest supporters and Clarridge's designated heir. That Webster respected Turco's judgments was surprising to some senior agency officers, primarily because it was well known that the CIA veteran looked askance at Webster's appointment and believed he was too close to Congress to be effective.

Turco had access to the most extensive data base on terrorists in the world, a system known to the intelligence community as DESIST, which could identify locations of terrorists and cross-reference the information with their methods of operation. DESIST identified an organization's financing, its known members, their affiliations with other groups, whether any of them had ever provided information to any intelligence agency, and the specific terrorist acts in which they had taken part. "We could get information at fifteen different levels; it told us almost everything we wanted to know," a terrorism expert says. DESIST's sorting and organizing functions were unprecedented; even the name of its designer was one of the CIA's best-kept secrets. Within forty-eight hours of the bombing of Pan Am 103, the DESIST program had eliminated nearly 80 percent of the incident's original suspects.

But DESIST could not answer the CTC's most important questions: Who bombed the aircraft, and why? In the immediate aftermath of the disaster, and for more than two years later, no one really knew. Within twenty-four hours, CTC officers concluded that Pan Am 103 had been brought down by a terrorist bomb. This assessment was believed by almost everyone at the agency. The aircraft's sudden fall seemed to rule out a mechanical failure; everything about the flight was normal until its last seconds. So Turco did what any good senior manager would do during times of crisis: He set up a task force inside the CTC to focus attention on the crash and began working twelve- to fifteen-hour days, sifting through the piles of information provided to him by his top assistants. The Pan Am Task Force investigation was a massive undertaking; Turco called on the expertise of anyone at the CIA who had even passing knowledge of terrorist groups, including clandestine service officers, bomb experts, and Middle East political analysts. He also instructed communications officers at the National Security Agency (NSA) in Maryland to cull through thousands of communications intercepts looking for clues to who had bombed the aircraft.

For the first time in CIA history, Turco was also given full access to information from all other organizations that were part of the CTC; investigators from the FBI, Federal Aviation Administration, and Pentagon all reported to him on their own findings. The Pan Am Task Force, which was up and running within forty-eight hours of the crash, also began tracking airline routes, tracing passenger bags, and interviewing informants who might have any leads. Cables were immediately sent to the CIA's European and Middle East stations, seeking data from sources familiar with the activities of the two dozen terrorist groups that were the most likely suspects with both the expertise and motivation to destroy an intercontinental airliner. The CTC set up active liaison relationships with British and West German intelligence officers and maintained them throughout the investigation. All this preparation was accomplished in four days, so that by December 26 the CTC was ready to hear its first major report from the crash site. In Lockerbie, meanwhile, investigators had determined by then that Pan Am 103 was brought down by a bomb stored in one of its forward cargo holds. This conclusion was arrived at after an examination of several pieces of shredded metal found in the surrounding fields. No one was surprised by the finding.

The Pan Am puzzle was complicated by the many unknown possibilities of how the bomb got into the cargo hold. Anyone could have unwittingly brought the bomb on board the aircraft, or the device might have been slipped aboard by a "ramp rat,"—one of hundreds of baggage handlers who had access to Pan Am's gates at the London and Frankfurt airports. There were really two flights involved, since the Pan Am 103 flight had originated in Frankfurt, where it took on businessmen, students, and families (some of them from the Middle East) bound for London and New York. The Frankfurt passengers, in turn, had come from all parts of the globe, and any one of them might have unwittingly carried the bomb. Or the bag containing the bomb might have been secreted into the aircraft's cargo hold at London's Heathrow Airport, where some of the Frankfurt passengers disembarked while others replaced them. Connecting flights inbound to London from half a dozen other locations had fed passengers into the Heathrow terminal for the 747, known as "The Maid of the Seas." The final mix of passengers departing London came from a variety of starting points—from London and Frankfurt, as well as Beirut, Malta, Cyprus, Scandinavia, and Africa.

From the start of the investigation Turco relied on the expertise of several key officers who had actually rubbed shoulders with terrorists, the kind of rare experience that he knew might come in handy. One such expert was CIA veteran Vincent Cannistraro, a large, soft-talking man then in his mid-forties, who had a varied background with the CIA, including service as an operations officer with a reputation for getting to know everything he could about terrorists and terrorism. That was standard practice in the mid-1980s, when smart careerists who decided to stay with the CIA viewed counterterrorism work as chic and identified Dewey Clarridge as a patron of some influence.

Cannistraro spent most of his CIA career in a number of overseas assignments until late 1984, when he was named director of intelligence programs at the NSC. He had an office at the White House, where he befriended Oliver North. In February 1987 he became special assistant for intelligence at the Defense Department and was named head of operations and analysis at the counterterrorism center two months before the Pan Am disaster. Turco considered him one of his best analysts, but Cannistraro wasn't universally liked at the CTC, or in the CIA, because of his liberal views on the limited role the CIA should play in U.S. policy.

Cannistraro's relationship with senior CIA officers, especially Thomas Twetten, was also damaged by his decision to turn down an assignment that would have made him COS "in an important Middle Eastern country" in early 1987. "You just don't turn down those kinds of appointments," a CIA officer says of Cannistraro's decision, "if you want to keep going up the [career] ladder. The fact that he didn't take the job was a sign that he wasn't interested in staying with the agency." Instead Cannistraro asked Deputy DCI Robert Gates for permission to serve as special assistant for intelligence at the Department of Defense, a move he now admits "probably wasn't the best thing to do in terms of my career." Cannistraro's request for a transfer was frowned on by CIA officials; they took it as a sign that he felt more comfortable with military officers than with his colleagues. The Pentagon assignment lasted eighteen months, and it ended when Turco decided that he needed Cannistraro to head the CTC's intelligence unit.

The CTC's Pan Am probe also depended heavily on reports received from FAA explosives expert Walter Korsgaard, a self-effacing, thin-as-a-rail bomb sleuth who'd acquired a mythic reputation as a fearless operator. That was a huge compliment since members of the clandestine staff, in particular those who had signed on with Turco, never really wanted to believe anyone outside the agency was actually fearless. Korsgaard was the exception. Throughout his career Korsgaard followed the standard practice of typical government bureaucrats: He tried to keep his head down and stay out of trouble. The last thing in the world that he wanted to do was make a name for himself by being controversial.

Put simply, Korsgaard was the U.S. government's top antiterrorist bomb retriever. Some of his operations have become legendary.

In January 1984, for instance, Korsgaard was dispatched to Karachi, Pakistan, where he helped the French analyze a bomb that had blown a hole in a 747 jumbo jet bound for Dhahran, Saudi Arabia. "This was very unusual," a colleague says, "since the French never come calling. But Korsgaard's the best." After the preliminary investigation was completed, Korsgaard stopped off in Athens, Greece, to retrieve a bomb he was told would be waiting for him there. This was the Shara bomb, confiscated from the apartment of the Palestinian's girl friend. Korsgaard, whose memory is usually prodigious, says he just does not remember any details of that incident. "Oh, yes," he replies, when prompted. "I was in Athens all right, and I got a bomb, but I don't remember what bomb it was. Really, I don't." He smiles innocently. "There were so many bombs," he says. "You have to understand, I didn't care who made them; I only wanted to study them."

During another overseas trip Korsgaard was in the process of bringing home a bomb from Pakistan when he received instructions from Washington to stop off in Istanbul, on the off chance that he might be able to get his hands on a bomb that was confiscated by the Turkish intelligence service. That bomb had been put aboard an earlier Alitalia flight to Rome but had failed to explode. Korsgaard was in luck. As chance would have it, an old friend with whom he had served in a UN detachment during the Korean War was a career Turkish intelligence officer and had access to the Alitalia device. The two men first went out for a long drink at an Istanbul café and relived old times. Korsgaard almost forgot what he had come for until the Turkish officer reminded him. "Now then," he said, "what is it that you wanted?" Korsgaard smiled disarmingly. "A bomb," he replied. "I want you to let me look at a bomb." Korsgaard's Turkish friend allowed him to examine the bomb and make a diagram of it. But when the American asked if he could take it with him, the officer shook his finger at him. "Oh, no." He laughed. "I really don't think so."

Korsgaard packed up his diagram and his Pakistani bomb and tried to find a way home. It was not easy. "Walt had a hell of a time getting the Pakistan bomb out of there," a former colleague recalls. "We thought we would have to send a special FAA jet to get it—which was very expensive. But Korsgaard called at the last minute and said that he would hop a ride with a C-141 flight out of Istanbul that would come into Dover Air Force Base. So he went to the crew and told them who he was, and they said: 'Well, if *you're* going to ride with it, then I guess we can ride with it, too. You and your bomb are welcome to come along for the ride.' So we met him at Dover. He usually could get any kind of bomb from any government. Then the CIA and FBI would study and restudy it. How the bomb was made could tell you quite a bit."

On several other occasions Korsgaard solved his transportation problems in his own special way: He just didn't tell airline security officers that he was transporting a bomb aboard their plane. "He would just carry it on and bring it back," his former colleague explains. "He thought, 'Well, what the hell.' "

Just hours after the Pan Am disaster Korsgaard was hurriedly dispatched to Lockerbie. On the morning of the second day after the bombing Korsgaard was standing in a bog, talking with British investigators. "What are we looking for?" one of them asked him.

Korsgaard looked around for a moment, then spotted a stray piece of metal. He picked it up and bent it back and away from his body in a straight ninety-degree angle. "This is what we're looking for," he said, "but it has to be burned, like someone tried to solder it."

The next day a Scottish investigator came to Korsgaard's makeshift office at Lockerbie and dropped a metal strip on the desk. The piece was three feet long and only an inch wide. Korsgaard recognized it as a sliver from the 747's left-front metal frame. It was bent back just where he said it would be, and charred. The explosion had ripped the metal outward, and the heat of the blast almost snapped it off. It normally *would* have snapped, except that the frigid, thin air at thirty-three thousand feet froze the blasted metal piece into place at an odd outward angle. Korsgaard, nodded. "That's it," he said. "A bomb brought down this airplane."

Turco, Cannistraro, and Korsgaard all played important roles in solving the Pan Am riddle, though they were supported by a large number of other able officers. Most of the work compiling intelligence on suspected terrorist groups was handled by officers in the CTC. The fieldwork in Scotland was done by Korsgaard and a team of British forensics experts who painstakingly reconstructed the aircraft and slowly deciphered its secrets. Other inquiries were initiated by the global network of CIA officers in backwater stations throughout the Middle East and Asia. In Tunis the CIA dispatched one of its top officers to request cooperation from members of the Palestine Liberation Organization. (That meeting was held in the house of the PLO's intelligence chief, Abu Iyad.) As far away as Bangkok a CIA officer approached sources inside the Thai security service to determine if bomb threats they had received were somehow related to the events in Lockerbie.

From the start of the investigation high-ranking CIA officers believed that the solution to the Pan Am mystery would probably lie in a part of the world—the Middle East—where the agency was least capable of finding answers to some of its most intransigent questions. The CIA station for Iran, for example, was actually located in Frankfurt, Germany. This was a bit of a happy accident, considering the origin of the Pan Am 103 flight, but the station was really too far removed from Teheran to gather information that could tie the Islamic revolutionary government to the bombing. The CIA's human intelligence sources in Iran were useless, and its information-gathering capabilities on the political maneuverings inside the Iranian government were nonexistent. The same was true in Damascus, where the CIA had a titular presence. The agency's officers were under continual surveillance by Syrians dispatched expressly for that purpose by President Hafez al-Assad. In Jordan the agency was dependent for information on the local intelligence service, whose wide range of contacts in the Palestinian community ("no one is better on the Palestinians than the Jordanians," a CTC officer says) might have provided a treasure of information, but the CIA was barely on speaking terms with Jordanian intelligence officers.

Worse yet, the agency's top field officers in Lebanon, who might have been expected to provide the best information possible on links between the Pan Am bombing and terrorist groups located in Beirut and the Bekaa Valley, were no longer in the field. To the CIA, their absence was an added, crushing tragedy of Pan Am 103: that one of the CIA's foremost Arab experts and perhaps its most promising young Middle East officer, thirty-four-year-old Matthew Gannon, had died on the flight along with a young, unmarried Army major by the name of Charles McKee, who had been dispatched by the Pentagon to Lebanon to help rebuild that war-torn nation's military.

Gannon and McKee knew each other well. They had shared the same flight out of Beirut on the twenty-first bound for London via Nicosia, Cyprus. Later that day, as they awaited the flight to New York, they had shared a drink with two State Department security officers, Daniel O'Connor and Ronald Lariviere, in the Pan Am Clipper Club Lounge at Heathrow Airport. The four men were joined there by State Department diplomat Bernt Carlsson, who was returning from a successful negotiating mission to resolve the Namibia dispute. They all were in a festive, holiday mood. "They were happy to be going home," remarked a waitress at the lounge.

The deaths of Gannon and McKee only added to the complexities of the CTC's investigation, since it raised the obvious questions of whether the bombers had identified and targeted the two Americans, and whether their mission in Beirut had been compromised. The urgent need to resolve those questions gave an added intensity to the work of the CTC. "There was a tragic sense of loss because of Matt's death," explains Vince Cannistraro, "and we worked extraordinarily hard because of that. I think that's what we owed to ourselves, to the agency, and to all of those who were lost. This incident hit home like no other that I can remember. It definitely had an impact."

Gannon's loss marked more than just the death of a promising young CIA officer; it was a personal slap at the agency's ability to protect one of its own. While all those in the clandestine service knew that their lives were sometimes in danger, Gannon's death left a lasting impression far beyond the simple facts of the incident. He came from one of the agency's best-known families, his wife was a CIA officer, and his father-in-law, Thomas Twetten, was the assistant deputy director for operations.

Two days after the bombing, State Department spokeswoman Phyllis Oakley identified three "State Department employees" who were on Pan Am 103: Ronald A. Lariviere, "who had been assigned to Beirut as a security officer since June"; Daniel E. O'Connor, "who was assigned to Nicosia, Cyprus, as a security officer in April"; and "Matthew K. Gannon, of Orange, California, who was assigned to the State's Department's Middle East bureau and was returning home after serving in Beirut as a political officer."

Gannon was actually one of the graduates of the CIA's class of 1977, the second wave of Arabist recruits the agency spent so much time training. He was quickly identified by senior officials as one of the clandestine service's most well-liked and accomplished officers.

Prior to being sent to Beirut, Gannon served in posts in Jordan, Syria, and North Yemen. He also became a well-known figure among agency professionals in North Africa. Eventually his expertise brought him attention and respect at Langley, particularly because he routinely volunteered for overseas operations that were dangerous.

By 1985 Gannon had become a key officer in Langley's secret war against the Abu Nidal organization (ANO) in Europe. His exact role in this vital antiterrorist offensive was a closely held secret.

It was due to Gannon's unique experience that CIA officers speculated from the start that Pan Am 103 had been bombed because he was aboard and that the probable bombers were Abu Nidal agents based in Europe. That Gannon would be targeted stood to reason: He was widely known in Beirut as "an agency man" despite the CIA's best efforts to guard his identity. He was escorted in Beirut by a heavily armed agency security officer, presumably to deter kidnappers from abducting him (that was what had happened to William Buckley, only five years before), and was involved in tracking down U.S. hostages held in Lebanon. It was a pressure-cooker job that brought him in contact with intelligence officers from other countries stationed in the city.

Newspaper articles published in the days after the Pan Am bombing claimed that the CIA's Beirut chief of station was aboard the aircraft. These stories were incorrect. Gannon's job was much more important than that. Over a period of five years he had made more than half a dozen trips to Lebanon, most of them in search of information about the location of American hostages. At the same time he was involved in espionage operations as an officer of the counterterrorism center, where he helped identify terrorists and uncover their plans.

In the weeks that followed his death a number of CIA officers grumbled that Gannon need not have died on Pan Am 103 because the agency did not conscientiously preserve his identity as an American intelligence officer. The complaint was especially widespread among officers of the Near East Division, whose overseas missions were viewed as particularly harrowing. "Six temporary duty assignments in Lebanon over the course of half a decade is just too much," says a retired CIA official. "They shouldn't have sent Matt back in there, it was just too dangerous."

It was a complaint that Thomas Twetten, Fred Turco, and other CIA senior managers had heard before. When Beirut station chief William Buckley was abducted and tortured, his closest colleagues in the intelligence community had mounted a vigorous internal campaign to win his release. They were routinely frustrated, however, by the agency's seeming inability to conduct an effective search for his whereabouts. The problem was exacerbated by bureaucratic infighting over who was to be held responsible for Buckley's often swaggering, high-profile mission to Beirut, which had included the dangerous duty of cozying up to that city's militia captains. The blame *should* have been squarely placed on William Casey's shoulders, since he recruited Buckley for the Beirut job even though the former Army officer, paramilitary expert, and Vietnam veteran had had little experience in running a station. Instead, Twetten and Turco were blamed by a large number of Buckley's colleagues for their "cavalier attitude" toward his rescue and their inept handling of the internal fallout that occurred after his capture. There was even a hint that Buckley's death may have resulted, at least in part, from the wide circle of enemies he had made at the agency. "Buckley wasn't liked, he wasn't liked at all," observes a CIA contract employee.

A more damning explanation for the Buckley fiasco is issued by a former NSC employee who watched closely as the CIA struggled with the case. This observer contends that the CIA bureaucracy should be blamed for the deaths of both Buckley and Gannon. If the agency had more diligently recruited and trained officers for duty in the Middle East, he explains, then it would not have been stretched so thin in that part of the world and Gannon might not have been sent there so often. If the CIA fails to recruit a large number of talented officers, he says, it will also fail in its primary espionage missions and career employees will be put at risk. In the end, the CIA sent Gannon to Beirut because there just wasn't anyone else it could send.

The Gannon case differed from the Buckley tragedy in one important sense: CIA officers were firmly convinced that the agency would do everything it could to find Gannon's killers. The CIA might have been lax in going to Buckley's aid since he was a paramilitary officer, a knuckledragger, but Gannon was heir to the traditions of the clandestine service. By 1988 Gannon had already carved out a reputation inside the CIA as an affable and honest man. Few doubted that he would have been a very successful officer.

Despite the obvious differences in their ages and backgrounds, William Buckley and Matthew Gannon had several things in common. Their most important bond was that they both were victims of secret and extremely dangerous CIA operations that were never made public. Both were talented officers who were underestimated early in their careers, both were patriots who loved government service, both were slowly drawn into the political tendrils of the Middle East, and both died when unforseen circumstances intervened in their lives.

Buckley's legacy was based on the physical courage he demonstrated in Korea, Vietnam, and the long civil war in Lebanon. Gannon was more cerebral than Buckley. Gannon's reputation at Langley was based on a solid academic foundation (he graduated from the University of Southern California with a degree in international relations and Arabic). Both were marked men, the recognizable instruments of U.S. policy in a region whose people still remembered the humiliation of European occupation and where one leader, Muammar al-Qaddafi, was admired as the most implacable Arab enemy of the United States.

At the time of Gannon's death the CIA had been waging an undeclared, but ceaseless, war against Qaddafi for nearly fifteen years as part of an effort to rid North Africa of a leader whom Egypt's president, Hosni Mubarak, described as "an international terrorist." Through surrogates, secret agents, national proxies, armies developed from the crumbling remnants of Libyan opposition movements, and, in 1986, actual military intervention, the United States had been attempting to counter his influence since the late 1970s. These efforts were transformed into something far more serious during the Reagan years, however, when the CIA established a number of programs aimed at spurring the violent overthrow of his regime.

In the early 1980s the NE Division established links to the National Front for the Salvation of Libya in order to increase pressure on the North African leader among the Libyan exile community. The Near East Division strengthened the NFSL, headed by Libyan exile leader Aly

Abuzaakouk, and soon transformed it from a powerless and fearful group of exiles into a well-funded organization with international contacts among the most devoted opponents of Qaddafi's regime. In 1981 the CIA and Pentagon hatched an extraordinary plan, code-named Operation Early Call, to bait Qaddafi into attacking Sudan by faking a pro-Libyan takeover of the Sudanese government. The plan was uncovered by Qaddafi but caused minimal embarrassment for the United States.

In May 1984 the CIA supported a coup by Libyan military officers that was crushed bloodily. Qaddafi executed more than seventy-five of the plotters. By the end of 1984 the Reagan administration's top intelligence officers had become obsessed with the problem of getting rid of Qaddafi, and a senior intelligence group, headed by Libya Task Force chief Vince Cannistraro and NSC staff officer Donald Fortier, drew up a paper that proposed a two-part strategy to deal with him that included arming Libyan dissident groups in Egypt and Algeria. This plan was quickly followed, in July 1985, by publication of a paper written by Deputy Director of Intelligence Robert Gates, who suggested the United States support an Egyptian invasion of Libya that would "redraw the map of North Africa."

The Gates program, Operation Flower/Rose, gained the support of National Security Adviser John Poindexter but was short-circuited by Secretary of State Shultz, who looked on the suggestion with a mixture of horror and disdain. The man most responsible for actually killing the plan was President Mubarak, who was not convinced that the United States could keep the program a secret. His views were prescient; by the end of the year *The Washington Post* had published details of the plan after congressional leaders who opposed it wrote to President Reagan that they were going to shut it down. After Gates's idea for a military operation against Libya was rejected, American and French intelligence agencies continued to cooperate on another plan to destabilize Qaddafi's regime by diplomatically isolating him from his North African neighbors. This operation was far less extensive than the one proposed by Gates, but many officers at the CIA thought it had a good chance of success.

This latest CIA program intended to subvert the Libyan government by establishing a military threat in Chad, where pro-American President Hissen Habre had been engaged in a fierce border battle with Qaddafi since 1979. This fight had produced thousands of starving refugees in a nation already torn by famine. Despite a French-engineered truce between Habre and Qaddafi, Libyan troops continued to undermine Habre's government. The CIA's top adviser in Chad's capital of N'Djamena and the man serving as Habre's chief protector was the ever-present William Buckley. He put his military experience to good use training Habre's military advisers and an elite counterinsurgency force. By the mid-1980s, when Buckley was transferred out of the country,

Habre's military hold on Chad was formidable. The CIA believed it was permanent.

After a period of relative calm in U.S.-Libyan relations, however, Qaddafi inexplicably order his antiaircraft batteries in the Libyan port city of Sirte to fire on American aircraft patrolling the Gulf of Sidra. This March 1986 military action was an open provocation to test what he called his "line of death." Within hours U.S. aircraft carrier jets retaliated by knocking out Qaddafi's radar network and firing on Libyan patrol boats. After this unequal contest had ended, Qaddafi instructed his terrorist networks to attack American targets in Europe. On April 2 TWA Flight 840 was bombed as it made its descent into Athens, killing four passengers, all of them Americans. On April 5 a bomb was detonated at the La Belle discotheque in West Berlin, killing an American soldier.

The CIA determined that both the TWA and La Belle bombings were carried out by the 15 May Group at the direction of Qaddafi. The evidence linking the Libyan dictator and the 15 May Group to both bombings was overwhelming. On April 15 the United States struck back, sending a squadron of fighter bombers from England to Libya for a strike at Qaddafi's personal residence and the Jamahariyah Barracks. Some of the bombs missed their targets entirely and dropped in residential neighborhoods. Libya reported that thirty-seven people were killed; Qaddafi miraculously survived this veiled assassination attempt, though rumors spread that his fifteen-month-old adopted daughter had died in the attack.

The bombing of Tripoli marked the beginning of a pause in overt American efforts to overthrow the Libyan regime. But the anti-Qaddafi campaign was not shelved. Robert Gates, for example, was still intent on carrying out a program that would use American-supported Libyan exile groups to confront Qaddafi. A month before the bombing of Pan Am 103, the CIA received presidential authorization for the Gates program. The objective was to train an army of Libyan soldiers held prisoner by Chad, where President Habre was still enjoying American protection. This CIA program was by far the most intensive effort yet to spark an anti-Qaddafi coup.

The CIA's covert army was recruited from among the large group of Libyans who had been captured in border battles with Chad during four years of fighting in the early 1980s. These Libyan prisoners had refused to return to their homeland; instead, they had agreed to fight in the CIA-supported force in exchange for their freedom. This Libyan army in exile became the military arm of the U.S.-backed National Front for the Salvation of Libya, which sent opposition leaders to educate the soldiers on the evils perpetrated by their former commander. The program involved dozens of CIA paramilitary trainers, a score of Near East

Division case officers, and a logistics lifeline that ran from the Pentagon to a windswept camp on the outskirts of N'Djamena. Hundreds of Libyan soldiers enlisted in the CIA army.

The CIA program to defang Qaddafi was one of the most extensive in its history. Strangely, however, few operations officers involved in the effort believed that Qaddafi would respond to such overt threats against his rule by targeting Americans or a large U.S.-based airline. In 1988, therefore, the fact that the Libyan dictator had the means, motive, and opportunity to bring down an American 747 was dismissed. Most of the CTC's analysts believed that Qaddafi was too fearful of American retaliation to consider launching such an attack. The only exception was Vince Cannistraro, the former Libyan Task Force chief. Back in 1988 Cannistraro was so skeptical that the CIA's anti-Qaddafi program would work that he issued a warning against such flagrant use of American power, suggesting that the covert effort was reminiscent of the agency's attempt to assassinate Fidel Castro. Qaddafi, he was sure, would strike back. "Active American participation in anti-Qaddafi activity by the Libyan opposition," he warned in one classified study, "may result in the removal of the last restraints against Libyan-sponsored terrorism directed at American citizens and officials."

In December 1988 the restraints were loosed.

Gannon's death cast a pall over the agency. Thomas Twetten, now heir apparent to Richard Stolz, was shattered. "Matt's death took a lot out of him," a colleague says. The same was true for Gannon's wife, who was suddenly the sole parent of two small children. Tragically, CTC investigators concluded that Gannon should not have been aboard Pan Am 103 at all; at the last minute he changed his reservation from a later flight because he was eager to return home for the Christmas holidays. This fact did little to dampen speculation that he was the target of a terrorist bombing. CTC officials were particularly fearful that Gannon might have been identified by Beirut terrorists in the late spring of 1988, when he helped monitor a prospective hostage release that involved American Robert Polhill, who the CIA believed was being held separately from any other U.S. hostages in a suburb of Beirut. That information came by way of a U.S. Embassy guard related to one of Polhill's captors. The guard was also a former member of Imad Mughniyah's extremist Islamic Jihad. Mughniyah was intent on trading the hostages for the release of his brother-in-law, who was a member of the Daawa 17, a group of Shiite radicals who were jailed for six terrorist bombings in Kuwait in 1983.

Of all the intelligence received by the CIA and State Department about U.S. hostages up to that time, the information provided by the embassy guard about Polhill seemed among the most promising. According to the CIA's source, Polhill was being held in one of Beirut's southern suburbs, which was in imminent danger of being overrun by advancing Syrian military units. The hostage's chief guard was concerned that the Syrians might gain control of Polhill; therefore, he thought that it was best to strike a deal with the Americans as soon as possible. A secret cable from the American Embassy in Beirut to the State Department, dated May 17, 1988, reported that the U.S. source proposed a swap of Polhill for "$500,000–600,000." The offer was immediately vetoed by the State Department. The cable, sent through the department's secret Roger channel, had noted: "RSO [regional security officer] stated that the U.S. government would never agree to payment of ransom of any hostage but that if a rescue of hostage could be effected the U.S. government would be grateful." The cable also informed Washington that the RSO had sent a request to the hostage holders that a picture of Polhill with a current copy of a Beirut newspaper should be provided to show the organization's "bona fides." A copy of the cable was sent on to the CIA's counterterrorism center.

The proposed rescue of Polhill never took place. It is apparent from the details of the cables on the incident, however, that U.S. officials were satisfied that Polhill's captors were who they claimed to be and that Polhill was being held somewhere in the southern suburbs of Beirut. Gannon and other U.S. officers had attempted to ascertain the validity of the information on Polhill. In doing so, they were able eventually to identify the exact location where Polhill was being held. But as in all previous hostage cases, neither Gannon nor any of his colleagues recommended, or were given permission to launch, a rescue attempt. Such a mission, they decided, would place other hostage lives at great risk. In the end the Polhill incident was passed off as just another attempt to win "ransom" for hostage holders. As the American chargé in Lebanon concluded, "In my view, 'rescue money' equals 'ransom,' and half a million dollars is not 'operational expenses.' " In the wake of the Iran-contra scandal, the judgment seemed sound.

The death of Matthew Gannon in the bombing of Pan Am 103 did not end U.S. efforts to locate American hostages being held in Beirut. Nor did the loss of his colleague Major Charles McKee terminate the Defense Intelligence Agency's program in Lebanon, which was designed to help the battered central government reconstruct its divided army. Still, the loss of McKee was keenly felt since he was perhaps the most experienced military intelligence officer deployed by the DIA in the region. McKee, a six-foot-five, 270-pound bear of a man who was known to friends as Tiny, began his career as an intelligence officer with the 10th Special Forces Group in Munich, Germany, studied Arabic at the Defense Language School and served as a military attaché in Saudi Arabia. He was later assigned as a staff officer to the Army's Intelligence and Security Command, which, like the CIA, recruits foreign agents to gather intelligence. McKee's mission in Lebanon was secret. Army officials refuse to describe what he was doing in Lebanon, and in a telephone call from McKee to his mother just twenty-four hours before the bombing, the forty-year-old officer refused to divulge his whereabouts. "I said, 'Where are you?' " Mrs. McKee recalled to a journalist. "He sort of half laughed and said, 'Over here.' "

Army records from the months before McKee died indicate that McKee was involved in a dangerous mission in Lebanon. An Army report confirms that "Maj McKee continues to perform one of the most hazardous and demanding jobs in the United States Army" and adds that he was "deployed OCONUS [outside of the continental United States] on an extremely sensitive mission." According to another report, his job was "high threat" and "he survived [his assignment] through his exceptional knowledge...." From these and other clues, it stands to reason that McKee, with Gannon, was involved in a courageous search or rescue mission for U.S. hostages, as well as espionage activities targeting Lebanon-based terrorist groups.

After the Pan Am 103 bombing, rumors of Gannon and McKee's "real mission" in Beirut circulated in the press. (European news accounts focused primarily on their CIA ties. These stories were fed by reports that a suitcase full of cash belonging to them had been found in Lockerbie.) Nowhere was it accurately reported that Gannon spent a great deal of time in Beirut gathering intelligence on Abu Nidal cells operating in the city, or that he was recruiting agents for that purpose in southern Lebanon. Gannon's responsibilities were complex: He kept alive the CIA's presence in Lebanon (in part to make plain that the agency would not be cowed by the mounting violence); he maintained a network of agents to gather information on the U.S. hostages; and he gathered as much intelligence as possible to be used against Abu Nidal. Tiny McKee was an able deputy. McKee's assignment in Lebanon was also fraught with danger and intrigue.

Among the personal effects recovered from Lockerbie was a typed sheet of paper on which McKee listed the names of U.S. embassy officials. Next to these names appeared code names used to communicate with them. McKee was listed as "Capone" while other embassy officials were designated by the names of other gangsters or dictators, including: Dillinger, Bonnie and Clyde, Hitler, Stalin, and Pol Pot. (The slip of paper also cryptically referred to a prison, cemetery, and crematorium—none of which was ever explained.) While the paper did not mention Gannon or the CIA, rumors about McKee's actual employer began to circulate soon after the Lockerbie crash. The speculation was that the DIA officer was actually on loan to the CIA. Several months later, a colleague of McKee's in effect confirmed this rumor when he was quoted as saying that he was certain McKee "was either assigned to or worked for the CIA."

Like Gannon, McKee was eager to return home for the Christmas holidays. Like Gannon, he changed his flight plans so that he could arrive in New York a day earlier than originally scheduled. McKee's most recent tour in Lebanon had lasted only four weeks. A colleague remembers seeing him in a hallway at the State Department shortly after Thanksgiving. The major told him that he was returning to the Middle East, but he hoped it would not be for too long. "It's clear he wasn't looking forward to going back," the colleague recalls.

The return-trip booking to the United States for both Gannon and McKee was prepared by Beirut's Lutas travel agency, which was the subject of an immediate investigation by the CTC to determine whether anyone at the travel agency might have deliberately or inadvertently given information about the two to known terrorists. CTC investigators quickly concluded that it was not likely. On the flight from Nicosia, Cyprus, to London, the four Americans—Gannon, McKee, Lariviere, and O'Connor—sat near one another, then deplaned for the four-hour wait in the Pan Am Clipper Club lounge.

The next morning, on December 22, not yet a full day after the 747 fell out of the sky over Lockerbie, McKee's disfigured body was found on the ground near a small church in the village of Tundergarth.

There was good reason to believe that the bomb that brought down Pan Am 103 was tied in some way to Mohammed Hussein Rashid's terror network, though Rashid himself was then being held in an Athens jail. He had the experience, know-how, motivation, and nerve to carry off the attack. The bombing had all the markings of a sophisticated Rashid operation. Within eight weeks after the Pan Am investigation began, the CTC concluded that a volatile explosive secreted inside a suitcase was responsible for the blast that destroyed the 747. Later investigators were able to pinpoint the exact location of the explosion and detail how the bomb had gotten on the aircraft. They also determined that the device was contained inside a Toshiba Bombeat radio. But obviously the imprisoned Rashid could not have brought down Pan Am 103. Nor could the CTC tie the explosion in any way to Rashid's patron, Abu Ibrahim, who remained safely outside the reach of international law in Iraq. Even so, the Rashid-Ibrahim connection is where the CIA's initial Pan Am 103 inquiry had begun.

During the first seven days of the investigation CTC officials circulated a detailed organizational chart on Abu Ibrahim's complex, worldwide terrorist network. Rashid was listed just below Ibrahim on the chart. Below Rashid a welter of branches reached into shadowy front organizations and corporations in Syria, Libya, and Lebanon. Ibrahim's network in Libya appeared to provide the most fertile soil for further CTC snooping, since Qaddafi's foreign intelligence organization sometimes provided cover for Ibrahim's operations. Another disturbing problem was that apparently legitimate Libyan businessmen in Europe and North America had ties to the community of gunrunners and terrorists that Qaddafi employed in Geneva, Frankfurt, and Madrid and to the terrorist network that Ibrahim used in the Middle East. By early 1989 none of these intricate relationships between Ibrahim and Qaddafi had yielded any hard evidence bearing on the Pan Am probe. So the Ibrahim-Libyan connection was put aside in favor of other more promising leads that emerged in Europe.

When CTC investigators sifted through recent warnings of possible terrorist acts, they continually came across the name of one man, Ahmad Jabril, who was in nearly every major terrorist file kept by the U.S. government. Jabril headed a small, but dangerous, Palestinian splinter group, the Popular Front for the Liberation of Palestine—General Command (PFLP—GC), based in Damascus, Syria. The PFLP—GC was held responsible by American authorities for nearly a dozen violent acts of terrorism, including the 1969 hijacking of a TWA airliner en route to Tel Aviv from Athens. Like Rashid and Ibrahim, Jabril, a former military munitions specialist, loved to tinker with explosives and was known as an amateur inventor with a talent for coming up with new ways to commit acts of violence. Jabril had also recruited a skillful bomb maker named Marwan Kreeshat, whose favorite method of operation was to mold barometric-triggered explosives into transistor radios. "All you have to do to build such a bomb is buy an altimeter," former FAA security expert Billie Vincent says, "like the kind used by skiers. It's incredibly effective."

The most damning information on Jabril came from CIA officers monitoring the PFLP—GC's activities in Europe and the Middle East. For three months prior to the Pan Am attack, U.S., West German, French, and British intelligence officers knew that Jabril was planning a spectacular terrorist operation somewhere in Western Europe against an American target, but they didn't know when or where he would strike. Everyone was guessing. Five weeks before the attack, for instance, CTC officers filed a warning about a proposed Jabril-Abu Nidal operation in South America, where U.S. targets were thought to be particularly vulnerable. "As of mid-November 1988," the CIA report reads, "the Abu Nidal Organization (ANO) and the Popular Front for the Liberation of Palestine—General Command (PFLP—GC) were jointly planning an operation against a U.S. target in Latin America. (Headquarters comment: The ANO is a highly compartmented organization which generally does not become involved with other terrorist groups on an operational level. We have no additional information from other sources on a joint ANO/ PFLP—GC operation in Latin America)."

The CIA should have received its best information about a proposed PFLP—GC operation in Europe from West German authorities. But in this case, the German federal police, the BKA (Bundeskriminalamt), and the German foreign intelligence service, the BfV (Bundesamt für Verfassungsschutz), were uncooperative with their U.S. counterparts. They failed to freely share information due to competitive and nationalistic jealousy, ostensibly because it was a matter of professional pride to the Germans that they be given credit for being more vigilant against terrorists, who often targeted Israelis. So, on October 26, 1988, when German authorities broke up a PFLP—GC cell in a series of coordinated raids, code-named Operation Autumn Leaves, they acted without U.S. knowledge. The surprise German arrests netted sixteen PFLP—GC operatives; a search of the terrorists' apartments in Neuss, Frankfurt, Hamburg, Mannheim, and Berlin turned up batteries, fuses, a detonator, radio components, and a number of blank passports. It was not until several days later that German intelligence officers informed their U.S. counterparts that they had also uncovered what looked like a massive plot to bomb an airliner.

A top secret U.S. intelligence document written at the end of October dryly summarized the surprising outcome of Operation Autumn Leaves. After West German authorities arrested the PFLP—GC operatives, the report noted, they inexplicably released twelve of them, including Marwan Kreeshat, "for lack of evidence." This hasty move angered American intelligence officials. The secret report continued:

> Police raids on October 26 that netted over a dozen members of the PFLP—General Command were undertaken to prevent a possible attack on a Spanish airliner scheduled to fly to Israel on October 28, according to German intelligence. Other terrorist operations in the FRG [Federal Republic of Germany] and elsewhere may also have been in the works under the direction of one of the suspects—a PFLP—GC Central Committee member who traveled under a false name on a Syrian official passport and took orders from the group's headquarters in Damascus.

The U.S. report concluded with a political comment: "It remains likely that the PFLP—GC intended to embarrass moderate Palestinians on the eve of the PNC [Palestine National Congress]. The targeting of a Spanish airliner may be tied to Madrid's 1986 recognition of Israel."

German intelligence officers had also received information about the PFLP—GC's operations in Western Europe from Israel, which had been closely tracking the head of the organization's "western section," Hafez Machmed Kassem al-Dalkamouni. (He was the PFLP—GC "Central Committee member" mentioned in the U.S. intelligence report.) The devout Muslim Dalkamouni was a large, square-headed man with a distinctive full mustache and enigmatic smile. Several months before the Pan Am bombing, he was rumored to have completed a trip to Teheran, where he helped negotiate the payment of some ten million dollars to the PFLP—GC from Ayatollah Khomeini's government. The cash was a fee for carrying out a terrorist attack against the United States. U.S. intelligence officials believed that Iran wanted to bring down an American airliner in retaliation for the loss of Iran Airbus Flight 655, which was accidentally shot down in the Persian Gulf by the U.S. Navy destroyer *Vincennes* on July 3, 1988. While the American government apologized for the tragic mistake and agreed to pay reparations to the families of the victims, Iran publicly vowed to take revenge.

As the CIA officers investigating Lockerbie read through their thick file on Operation Autumn Leaves, they initially concluded that the PFLP—GC was the leading suspect in the bombing. The key evidence included in the material seized earlier by Germany's BKA was a radio-cassette player of the same general type that was later recovered from the Pan Am aircraft's remains. This specially designed bomb was described in vivid terms in a November 1988 FAA bulletin: "Preliminary analyses [have been completed] by West German authorities of improvised explosive devices [IED] found in various stages of preparation during the recent arrests of members of the PFLP—GC. [The Germans] discovered one IED consisting of a Toshiba BOMBEAT 453 radio containing approximately 300 grams of a plastic type explosive wrapped in a metallic coated 'Tobler' brand candy wrapper. The bomb contained an electrical detonator."

Finding a suspect who might have bombed Pan Am 103 was one thing; proving it quite another. Two months into the Lockerbie investigation, CTC officers were convinced that Jabril must have had something to do with the incident. They were angered, however, by the German decision to release his bomb maker, Marwan Kreeshat, who had been quietly deported back to Jordan. This led them to speculate that Germany and Jordan had struck a secret deal to bring about his release. Germany's freeing of Kreeshat was a terrible mistake because it immediately identified him to everyone as an informer and placed his life in jeopardy.

CTC officers also believed the Germans had bungled the case in other ways. They suspected that after the Kreeshat release, other PFLP—GC operatives carried out Jabril's plan in December.

The CTC had to follow up an almost endless series of leads it had developed on its own from information given by dozens of sources in Europe and the Middle East. For instance, CTC investigators discovered that one of the stewardesses slated to make the Pan Am flight had not been on board the aircraft because she had called in sick the day before. They learned that the young woman had an apartment in Moscow, which she shared with her Arab boyfriend, who happened to be a member of Jabril's organization. The information sent CTC officer hopes soaring. "This type of link is standard procedure for terrorist groups," explains a former CTC officer. "We've seen it dozens of times. We always watch stewardesses."

Three months after the Lockerbie bombing, high-level CIA officials asked their KGB counterparts to begin an unofficial investigation in Moscow of the stewardess and her boyfriend. They received an unequivocal answer just one week later: The KGB said it was convinced that neither the stewardess nor her boyfriend had anything to do with the attack. A CTC officer remembers that CIA officers, including Fred Turco, were incredulous that the Soviet investigation could be wrapped up in such a short time. "Turco basically asked, you know, 'How can you be sure?' But they were sure all right. One of the guys we talked with just shrugged his shoulders and said something like: 'Well, he [the PFLP—GC suspect] took a licking and kept on ticking.' Basically, they just kicked the shit out of him."

The CTC also had to pursue a number of unexplained threats that had been made against American airlines in Europe in the days and weeks before the Pan Am bombing. For instance, on December 5, in a message to the U.S. Embassy in Helsinki, an unidentified caller warned that European operatives of the Abu Nidal Organization would destroy a Pan Am aircraft on an international flight before the end of the year. The report puzzled the CTC. Although the ANO's reputation as a cold-blooded foe of the United States made it a likely suspect, the group's continuing internal strife, sparked by the CIA's most reliable Middle Eastern operatives, seemed to rule it out as a likely perpetrator. Nevertheless, the Helsinki report had to be taken seriously. An NSC intelligence officer, for example, remembers receiving details about the threat at the White House within a few hours after it was made. "We knew something was going on right away," he says. "We took it very seriously." CTC officials were dispatched to Helsinki but soon concluded that the threat was "phony."

Another lead that branched out from the PFLP—GC seemed even more promising. After the BKA arrested the sixteen PFLP—GC members (including Kreeshat) in West Germany in October, they discovered ties between that network and another Palestinian terrorist group based in Stockholm. Members of the Stockholm group had even visited PFLP—GC operatives in Germany prior to the Pan Am bombing. Swedish authorities arrested the suspects, who were also implicated in a series of bombings in Copenhagen, Denmark, in 1985 and 1986. Even more chilling, the suspects often traveled to Malta, where they purchased clothing at a Malta shop called Mary's House for resale among Palestinians living in Sweden.

Several months after the beginning of the Pan Am 103 investigation, British and American forensic experts told the CTC that the Toshiba cassette recorder that carried the bomb had been wrapped in clothing that came from that shop. At the time it looked like the biggest lead CTC investigators had, since it linked the Stockholm Palestinians directly to the bombing of the Pan Am aircraft. Coupled with the information developed by West German authorities and information on the kinds of bombs made by Kreeshat (now virtually imprisoned in a safe house in Amman, Jordan), CTC investigators were convinced they could make a "match," tying the fibers recovered from the aircraft's debris to the Stockholm group.

For a time it seemed as if the CTC had cracked the case. But just as the anticipation seemed to peak, the outer edges of the Stockholm investigation began to fray. The owner of Mary's House insisted that he could easily recognize the person who bought the articles of clothing that ended up on Pan Am 103. But when the shopkeeper was shown photographs of the Swedish suspects, he emphatically shook his head no. He told the team of U.S. and Scottish investigators that he was familiar with those Palestinians from Sweden, but they had not purchased the clothes found in the Pan Am wreckage. He was adamant. "If you show me the picture of the man who bought those clothes," he kept saying, "I will identify him." CTC investigators, however, were not able to produce such a photo. Many of them were beginning to believe that it might well be impossible.

Retired CTC official Cannistraro remembers the counterterrorism center's work on the Pan Am 103 bombing with pride. But he remains even more impressed by the painstaking work of the British forensics experts who were able to tie a few shreds of fiber found in the wreckage to the small shop in Malta that sold an unknown man a batch of clothing that was used to wrap the bomb that was hidden on board Pan Am 103. Cannistraro also vividly recalls the intense frustration from the Malta investigation and the long nights spent theorizing about the most puzzling question. If the Palestinians arrested in Stockholm did not buy the clothing in Malta, then who did?

Even more frustrating to Cannistraro and his colleagues was that all the facts the CTC took for granted as *facts* turned out to be false leads or incredible coincidences. "That the Stockholm suspects weren't suspects at all just stunned me," Cannistraro admits. "The evidence against them was just too much of a coincidence. We kept looking at it and looking at it, but we couldn't figure it out." These same doubts prey on former FAA security officer Vincent. "I still can't believe that those people [in Stockholm] didn't have anything to do with this," he says, in wonder.

The threads of the CTC's investigation that once seemed so certain—leading from Damascus to Frankfurt and Stockholm and then back to Damascus and perhaps even on to Teheran—were finally shattered by evidence that was both overwhelming and bizarre.

Before that could happen, the other significant leads had to be put to rest. Had Gannon been targeted? "It took us two months to eliminate that as a possibility," Cannistraro says. And what of reports that Khalid Jaafar, a student from Detroit, unwittingly carried the bomb aboard? "That took us a little longer to knock down," Cannistraro replies. "Nine months—something like that." And the Pan Am stewardess with the PFLP—GC boyfriend in Moscow? "We got that one resolved quickly," he says. That left only one other serious option: The bomb was made by Kreeshat and wrapped in clothing bought by some yet-to-be-identified Palestinian operatives in Malta. Now all the CTC had to do was prove it beyond the shadow of a doubt, so that it would stand up in court.

A smiling Cannistraro shakes his head in wonder as he tells the story of how the CTC finally came upon the single most important piece of evidence that changed the course of the Pan Am inquiry. "At one point in the investigation we thought we knew everything that we needed to know," he admits, "and then it was almost like we woke up one morning and we didn't know anything at all." That one morning occurred in Amman, Jordan, during the high heat of a desert summer. On that day in mid-1989, CIA officers were allowed for the first time to question Marwan Kreeshat, the PFLP—GC's master bomb maker. Kreeshat was still angry over the decision by the West German police to release him from jail (which proved to Ahmed Jabril that he was in the pay of a foreign intelligence service). Kreeshat looked at his CIA interrogators in disgust. "I did not make the bomb," he told them in ever-strident tones. They replied, just as certainly, that he must have. "I didn't make the bomb," he repeated, according to a CIA officer with knowledge of the interrogation. "You will see."

The bombing of Pan Am 103 and the death of Matt Gannon had echoed through the CIA like a thunderclap, bringing darkness to the holiday season and throwing the clandestine service into an unofficial state of mourning. There was nothing the CIA could do publicly to relieve the grief. There was little that the agency's leaders could even do privately to soften the blow. Although Gannon had died while returning from a classified mission in Lebanon, his death was not officially considered "in the line of duty". Because he was technically on Christmas vacation, there was some question about whether a star symbolizing his sacrifice could be added to the CIA's book of honor and replicated on

Langley's lobby wall. Even if such a star was dedicated to his memory, Gannon's often brilliant work in the Middle East could not be otherwise commemorated or even publicly acknowledged. As far as his CIA colleagues were concerned, Gannon would have to be buried in silence, but he had not died without reason. He was viewed as a martyr to the cause of the CIA's unrelenting war against terrorism. He was considered a hero, even if the details of his dangerous work would remain known only to the agency itself.

Gannon's death added to the sense of drift that permeated Langley during the eighteen months after Webster was appointed DCI. For senior officers in the clandestine service, it seemed as if agency morale had suffered an almost irreparable blow and sunk to a point lower than the one reached in the immediate wake of the Iran-contra revelations. The person most deeply affected was Gannon's father-in-law, Thomas Twetten.

Webster shielded Twetten from the ravages of Gannon's death by applying the same counsel that George Bush had used when Webster's wife died: He told Twetten to take some time off but to keep himself busy. When Twetten returned to his desk after a short leave, Webster flooded him with work. Webster thought this was a surefire way of guaranteeing Twetten's increasingly significant position as one of his most valued counselors. The strategy was only partly successful in keeping Twetten's mind away from the haunting images of Lockerbie. In his role as ADDO, Twetten was in constant touch with his old friend Fred Turco and had access to the CTC's weekly updates. He remained obsessed by the Pan Am investigation.

For Webster's other colleagues, the incredibly unjust terrorist attack on Pan Am 103 could not have come at a worse time. The DCI knew that the agency was still struggling to shake off the widespread demoralization caused by the Iran-contra morass. Webster himself continued to be victimized by this disheartening environment. Congress expected him to clean up the CIA at the end of the Reagan years. While he had done his best to limit the damage that his internal investigation had sparked, the fact was that reprimanding half a dozen agency employees deepened the sense of drift he was put in place to end. Nor had Webster yet succeeded in transforming the agency from an instrument of U.S. cold war policy to the kind of intelligence organization keyed to addressing America's international economic problems. The best that could be said for the CIA on the eve of George Bush's inauguration was that while it was still reeling from the revelations of Reagan's last days, things could only get better.

That was a faint promise. The challenges facing the agency at the beginning of 1989 must have seemed overwhelming. William Webster was still struggling to recast its mission, from hunting Soviet spies to tracking terrorists, from counting new Russian missiles to assessing the threat of emerging nuclear powers. Most important, Webster's CIA needed to familiarize itself with the agenda of a new President who had once been DCI but who paradoxically now saw a more diminished role for the agency than he had when he was its head in the mid-1970s. The agency's struggle to familiarize itself with Bush's new dispensation turned out to be the biggest challenge of all.

Part II
★ ★ ★
The Analyst

7

★ ★ ★

The Crisis of the CIA

*T*he CIA's most important battles are waged not on foreign soil but inside the long corridors and well-lit offices of the headquarters at Langley, Virginia. The men and women who fight these battles are unlike any of the spies Americans have met in fiction or on film. In fact, the most important spies of the CIA aren't really spies at all but analysts; schooled in the humanities, they are more obsessed with a region's customs, language, and political traditions than with the minutiae of agency tradecraft. Some of them are so highly regarded in their fields that they could be candidates for the most prestigious chairs of American academia. So while the American public and press are consumed by sensational accounts of buggings, break-ins, and black bag jobs, the CIA's most significant and unheralded task—of analyzing information and presenting intelligence assessments—goes virtually unnoticed.

Like so much else that has to do with the CIA, our perception of the agency has skewed the picture of what it actually does. On the left, the CIA is perceived as a kind of star chamber, a government within a government, whose sins are so manifest that to consider reforming its functions is viewed as tantamount to collusion with its policies. They believe that the agency needs to be dismantled. On the right, the CIA is viewed as a sword dulled by compromise with the forces of darkness, an instrument made cowardly by pretentious ivory tower eggheads incapable of mounting an effective defense of freedom. Their solution is the same: The CIA needs to be taken apart. Even sensible people whose opinions stand between these two extremes have a picture of the agency

that is based upon popular notions that have little to do with reality.
The picture of a man in a gray flannel suit—of a normal American who
leads a double life as an undercover spy—has been so deeply implanted
in our psyche that it has become a symbol for the agency itself. Americans
believe that the CIA is more capable now than at any time in the past
of running secret wars in far-off countries.

The truth is far more disturbing. The agency was actually a far less
competent arm of American foreign policy at the beginning of the Bush
years than the public could have believed and was less capable of conducting a successful covert operation than at any point in its forty-year
history. The truth is that the agency did not harbor a "secret team" that
was carrying out a foreign policy by other means; it did not harbor any
team at all. The problem was not with its courage but with its mission.
The man in the gray flannel suit had long ago passed from the scene;
he was replaced by those more concerned with pay grades and pensions.
The irony is that the CIA is not a unique government organization; it
has become the quintessential government bureaucracy.

In January 1989 America's perception of the CIA was largely dependent on its judgment of George Bush, the most public figure ever
to have been associated with the organization. Liberals thought that
Bush's election marked the institutionalization of American intelligence;
he was seen as a CIA advocate who would expand the dangerous programs initiated by William Casey. Conservatives, on the other hand,
feared that Bush's Ivy League background made him susceptible to the
views of the agency's naïve intelligence experts. But those without political axes to grind had the most interesting opinion of all: Bush's CIA
experience was good training for a President since it meant that he
understood the intelligence community's value as an essential American
institution.

Everyone was wrong. The next three years were to show that George
Bush was less influenced by what the CIA had to say than any President
in history. Bush showed time and again at crucial junctures that he placed
more faith in personal diplomacy than covert operations and that he
purposely liked to eschew the advice of agency experts.

In January 1989 Bush's forthcoming inauguration was viewed with
a mixture of pride and apprehension inside the CIA. To some people,
the new President was proudly looked upon as proof that a DCI could
ascend to the nation's highest office. Others felt far less confident that
Bush's presence in the Oval Office would trigger a golden age of intelligence. Many of Bush's former CIA colleagues believed that he was one
of the most complex individuals they had ever met. For them, Bush
defied definition, in large part because he assiduously refused to bare
even the most mundane facts about his past with his closest colleagues.
He was simply one of the most private people they had ever met. Despite

his apparent interest in the CIA, his associates suspected that he viewed his eleven months as DCI as little more than an interlude on his political journey to the top.

To assume that the election of Bush to the presidency marked the beginning of the agency's renaissance was considered laughable at Langley. He kept all but a handful of close friends from the agency at a distance. Aside from an unofficial clique of Bush boosters from among the retired agency officers and several intensely loyal former CIA officers who remained on his staff after he left Langley, Bush's ties to the CIA were neither deep nor significant.

A number of senior CIA officers believed that Bush's tenure as DCI in 1976 had accomplished little and had actually accelerated the decline of the agency's influence (particularly because of his stance on the Team A/Team B controversy). They also thought that Bush had failed to understand or master the agency's true character during his year there. To them, Bush had entered and left the CIA as nothing but an outsider. Yet they feared that he had come away convinced that his agency experience had actually made him an accomplished intelligence officer. As Bush moved into his new office in 1989, therefore, the danger for the professionals at Langley was not that he would use the agency to promote a risky foreign initiative or that he would transfer its functions to the White House, but that he would ignore it altogether—that his presidency would mark not the rise of the CIA but its fall.

The CIA that DCI George Bush inherited in 1976 was quite different from the one he was bequeathed as President in 1989. During the intervening thirteen years the CIA had been transformed from the nation's premier intelligence agency to just one of many in a long list of intelligence bureaucracies. In retrospect, it's clear that the revelations that occasioned Bush's nomination as DCI propelled the atomization of the CIA's responsibilities, at least so far as covert activities were concerned.

From at least 1975 forward the Pentagon assumed a greater role in overseeing paramilitary activities, and the military was given greater responsibility for providing expertise for some of the CIA's most important international programs. By the mid-1980s, for instance, specially trained teams under the direction of the U.S. Army were carrying out a number of highly secret foreign operations.

This shift, bitterly vilified as the "militarization of intelligence" by CIA veterans, had actually begun in the early 1960s, when the agency used military assets to launch the Bay of Pigs operation. The trend later became much more pronounced during the Vietnam era, when the armed services established special intelligence-gathering units whose competition with CIA officers was a constant source of friction in both

Indochina and Washington. The policy of using military units to carry out CIA operations, or allowing the various services to conduct their own covert operations, could not be reversed; many of the CIA's top officers were recruited from the fertile ground of regional military experts. By the time that Casey took office, the agency's civilian career employees complained that Langley was "filled with guys in uniform." Nor did it seem to matter that the agency was given the final right of approval for all military intelligence operations; the power of the nation's men and women in uniform was everywhere apparent.

In other important ways, the CIA's influence had actually shrunk since Bush was DCI. The advent of sophisticated intelligence-gathering satellites had provided the national security establishment with an unprecedented method for obtaining credible intelligence never before available. At first the CIA had a leading role in using this new technology. In 1973 the CIA had established the National Photo Interpretation Center (NPIC), which was run as a "service of common concern" for the entire intelligence community. An increasing number of offices in the CIA's Directorate of Science and Technology coordinated overhead reconnaissance information. By the mid-1970s this type of intelligence was becoming more and more valuable and was garnering a larger portion of the intelligence community's budget.

This trend toward overhead spying was given greater emphasis under each succeeding DCI, from William Colby to George Bush and then Stansfield Turner. William Casey continued the tradition during the 1980s, when the CIA oversaw the launch of a number of highly sensitive signals satellites, called "platforms." But in reality the CIA profited from these actions only indirectly: By then the National Security Agency (an arm of the Department of Defense) and the National Reconnaissance Office (run jointly by the Air Force and CIA) provided the largest portion of intelligence information to the government.

This technological revolution completely transformed the way that intelligence was gathered and interpreted. It also changed the status of the CIA. When Ronald Reagan was inaugurated, three major intelligence bureaucracies—the National Security Agency (NSA), the National Reconnaissance Office (NRO), and the Defense Intelligence Agency (DIA)—were vying with the CIA for attention, funding, influence, and status inside the national security establishment. This competition created a radical change in the CIA's position in Washington.

"It's impossible to play hunches," explains one agency veteran. "You're surrounded by evidence, evidence, evidence. And that's what the arguments are about, how to weigh what you actually see. The good old days of intelligence are long gone." Another, serving, thirty-year veteran complains that the real work of intelligence has been sacrificed: "It's nearly impossible to get anything done at the CIA. There's no time to think. You're surrounded by guys in uniform, scientists, interpreters, and analysts. The paperwork involved is astonishing. The work product of the clandestine service has suffered as a result. It's turned into one giant bureaucracy."

More precisely, the intelligence community actually is comprised of *many* bureaucracies.

The NSA is responsible for intercepting and analyzing foreign communications and running the U.S. cryptographic program. The publicity-shy agency inhabits a trio of huge modern green glass buildings at Fort Meade, Maryland. With a budget estimated at between ten and twelve billion dollars, the NSA employs well over fifty thousand people worldwide. Because of the sensitivity of its intelligence-gathering activities and the high quality of its intelligence product, the NSA has taken the CIA's place as the most exotic and valuable provider of foreign intelligence. In an age when the political intentions of foreign leaders, which are usually the province of CIA analysts, are difficult to assess and a nuclear war is potentially only minutes away, the NSA's reports have gained increasing attention in intelligence circles. Similarly, the National Reconnaissance Office, a sister intelligence bureaucracy whose workings are nearly as secret as the NSA's, spends between four and five billion dollars. The NRO employs more than a thousand analysts and scientists who manage the intelligence community's satellite program.

The separate intelligence branches of each U.S. military service account for over $850 million in total funding. The Army, Air Force, Navy, and Marines each have separate commands responsible for overseeing human intelligence, counterintelligence, signals intelligence, and communications security. Each service also has a variety of special intelligence functions: The Army operates a counterterrorism and threat analysis center, the Navy runs a maritime surveillance program, and the Air Force has a strategic studies division (whose target is the Soviet Air Force).

The total cost of all these military intelligence operations does not include expenditures for the Defense Intelligence Agency, which coordinates all armed service intelligence operations, runs a separate intelligence-gathering unit (along the same lines as the CIA's geographic divisions), and issues separate intelligence assessments on military topics. The DIA spends nearly $450 million per year and employs sixty-five hundred military and civilian personnel. In total, by the beginning of the Reagan years, the combined budgets of the military services outstripped the funding given to the CIA. At the same time, the DIA's own intelligence reports began to compete with the CIA's product among intelligence users.

During Casey's tenure as DCI it was increasingly evident that the agency was becoming a victim of its time; not only was it just beginning to rebuild the human intelligence networks that were dismantled during the previous decade, but it was struggling to reestablish its own credibility in the national intelligence establishment. It was a general misconception to attribute this progressive weakening of the CIA to Casey's shortsightedness or to the public furor over the agency's role in any number of previous scandals. Rather, its standing was being undermined by progress itself. In the skies the NSA and NRO were benefiting from the increasing importance of technically sophisticated intelligence-gathering mechanisms; on the ground and at sea the military's intelligence requirements far outpaced what Langley could provide.

By 1984, the midpoint of Casey's term, these changes had become institutionalized; enormous power had been ceded to technical intelligence experts and military officers who commanded the Pentagon's massive intelligence programs. While the DCI still directed the intelligence community and retained enormous influence on the conduct of intelligence policy, the CIA's rank and file were confined largely to the business of espionage and analysis. Their work was a critically important part of the U.S. intelligence capability, to be sure, but it was one far different in scope and power from that initially envisioned when the agency was officially created in 1947.

By 1988 the U.S. intelligence budget showed that the agency's power had been markedly constrained by boundaries established by the Pentagon and NSA. According to one authoritative estimate, only 10 percent of the total intelligence budget was earmarked for the CIA. Of that amount, fully 90 percent of the agency's total funding was allocated for administration, intelligence analysis, and the coordination of signals and satellite reconnaissance operations. These numbers showed that Casey had tried to slow the fifteen-year trend to increase U.S. technical intelligence-gathering capabilities, but even he could never quite stop the momentum.

By the time William Webster became DCI, the CIA faced a crisis unparalleled in its history: With a budget estimated at just over one billion dollars per year, the CIA spent just a hundred million dollars on espionage programs—money allocated for the training and deployment of agency officers, recruitment of foreign intelligence agents, maintenance of its overseas assets, and general upkeep for its worldwide network of bases and stations. While officers of the clandestine service—some three thousand in all—might still consider themselves the intelligence community's elite frontline spies, they were fast becoming the forgotten stepchildren of the intelligence bureaucracy.

To make matters worse Webster was faced with the rapid dissolution of the clandestine service, where nearly 20 percent of all operations officers resigned, retired, or were considering transfers to other posts within one year after he took over at the agency. The Far East and Near East divisions were particularly hard hit; only half a dozen officers who spoke Mandarin remained in the FE Division's mammoth China branch, while only a handful who spoke Arabic remained in the NE Division. The crisis was exacerbated by a number of key transfers, as people the CIA had spent years training decided to pursue careers in other parts of the government they believed wielded more influence.

Events in the agency's Near East Division were emblematic of the crisis. The CIA spent an enormous amount of money and energy recruiting Near East experts in the early 1970s; the agency sent at least six recruiting teams onto American college campuses looking for Arabists. It turned out that the NE Division's best recruiting ground came from the military, where a series of high-profile enlistments replenished the agency's training classrooms. The most important corps of these committed young Arabists graduated from the CIA's training program in two waves, in 1973 and 1977. These groups of new officers helped run a series of key agency campaigns in the Middle East during the late 1970s and early 1980s. They also conducted antiterrorist training programs for America's most important regional allies.

By January 1989, both classes were decimated: Most of the leading young Arabists either had been killed or had resigned to pursue other careers. One of the best young officers left to become an undersecretary of the air force. That was only one example. Other young NE officers left to take chairs at leading universities or hired themselves out as consultants to major international corporations. The NE Division has never really recovered.

The resignations, retirements, and transfers demonstrated a unique paradox that existed inside the agency. Career operations officers valued the increased stature and appreciation given to them by activist directors (like Casey). However, they were embarrassed when called upon to carry out activist programs of questionable merit that undermined the agency's public reputation. The history of the CIA shows that periods of agency activism have been punctuated by intervals of relative calm (directors who prize a dynamic operations policy inevitably have been followed by conservative administrators, like Webster). But then the periods of relative calm unavoidably yield to internal pressures for a return to more dynamic leadership. The agency survived these policy oscillations for forty years, but by the end of the 1980s they were beginning to take their toll.

Webster understood (as had Casey) that the CIA no longer enjoyed the widespread confidence of the nation's top policy makers. The harm done to the agency by scandal, sophisticated intelligence-gathering techniques, and the Pentagon's increasingly expert special operations teams seemed irreparable. In early 1989, with the approaching end of the cold

war and the breakup of the CIA's primary target, the final act in the
agency's four-decade drama was already scripted. At worst, the CIA
would be retired as the government's leading authority on threats to the
national security; at best, the agency would be treated as an ossified
remnant of an era since passed. A number of senior CIA officials foresaw
that this end was coming and had tried to take steps to postpone it. Even
William Casey, despite his almost genetic fear of world communism, had
realized that the CIA was entering a new era. It needed to review and
redirect its mission. Casey had believed that the place to start was in
Washington.

Webster and Casey were distinctly different DCIs. Webster was a
fitness fanatic who delegated authority. Casey was a more cerebral,
hands-on operator. Webster cautiously manipulated the levers of power;
Casey manhandled them. Webster was a poised and confident manager,
Casey a fiery crusader. Webster was perhaps the most public DCI in
history, while Casey cherished his privacy and reveled in the agency's
secrecy.

Casey confided his innermost thoughts to very few people. After he
spent long hours exercising his enormous clout as one of President
Reagan's closest advisers, Casey often drew the shades to his seventh-
floor office and poured himself a drink. Most times he invited several
of his close, high-ranking advisers to join him, including John McMahon,
Ed Juchniewicz, Robert Gates, or Dewey Clarridge, the one man he
trusted most in the CIA. Casey spent many of these evenings engaged
in long conversations with these men. It was during one of these typical
talks, on an autumn night in 1986, that Casey shared with them his vision
of the agency's future.

The agency was changing, Casey confided. There were many things
it did well and must continue to do—monitor the Soviet military threat,
conduct broad espionage programs, penetrate foreign intelligence operations, advise the President on American vulnerabilities. But the primary reason for its creation, and its very reason for being over four long
decades, was slowly passing into history. So, too, Casey explained, were
those officers who had spent their lives fighting communism. Although
the Soviet Union was still a major competitor, its empire would inevitably
disintegrate. The CIA, which probably contained more Soviet experts
than any other institution in the world, had to recognize that its primary
intelligence target was slowly disappearing.

Casey was not yet willing to declare a final victory. Soviet influence
in Central America proved the USSR was still capable of undermining
American interests when it chose to. There were, however, unmistakable
signs that the end of the cold war was near, which meant that the CIA
would have to reassess its mission. As this process evolved, there would

be attacks on the agency from outside. Long-standing enemies would find common cause in trying to destroy the institution. That was what the CIA had to prepare for.

Casey was right in more ways than he could ever have imagined. The world was being transformed, but so, too, was the American government. The CIA held less power inside the American government than ever before, but its failures were also more public; congressional oversight had taken its toll. The NSA and NRO, with their seemingly invincible new high-tech gadgets, were continuing to absorb more and more of the intelligence community's budget allocations. Casey could argue that the most important intelligence never came from satellites or decoded communications intercepts, but he knew that the logic of politics dictated that power flowed from money.

Casey commented at length during his private, after-hours discussions about how the CIA no longer retained its special privileged status. He noted that the arrogance and elitism that had motivated the CIA in its early years had largely dissipated in a skein of embarrassments that curtailed its power and thinned its ranks. Casey was unutterably opposed to the further erosion of the CIA's power. He wanted to reverse this trend, and he slowly began to put in place the changes he was convinced would carry the CIA into the next century. His first experiment in transforming the CIA from its role as a gatherer and disseminator of intelligence to its rightful place as a kind of in-house think tank for the entire intelligence community had involved Dewey Clarridge.

The blueprint for the future CIA that Casey diagrammed was modeled on Clarridge's earlier success in establishing the counterterrorism center—the CTC. Casey wanted to create a series of other, similar intergovernmental committees, comprised of experts and operations officers, to focus attention on critically important national security problems. If resources, information, and know-how were marshaled, Casey thought, a wide variety of perplexing problems could be resolved. (Casey was particularly intent on organizing intelligence groups that focused on the narcotics and security problems.)

The establishment of the counterterrorism center had marked the beginning of a revolution at the CIA. Never before had CIA officers been asked to cooperate openly with other government agencies in gathering and analyzing foreign intelligence information. Vince Cannistraro, a participant in this transformation, described it as nothing less than "one of the most controversial decisions that Casey ever made." Initially, Casey's decision was forcefully opposed by rank-and-file operations officers who feared that sharing secrets with other parts of the government would compromise agency sources and methods and would hasten the agency's decay. Clarridge forced the change on the CIA bureaucracy by invoking Casey's name and cajoling reticent officers and analysts. The rank and file in the DO, Clarridge threatened, could cooperate in the new enterprise or be left out of it altogether. Once the CTC was formed, he warned, it would be the sole arbiter of government policy on terrorism.

"The CTC was the model," Cannistraro explains. "Everything followed from that success. It was really the first time that we had opened up the CIA bureaucracy to the rest of the government in any substantive way."

Casey had two purposes in building on the success of the CTC: He wanted the CIA to gain access to new information and assets so it could better solve intelligence problems; he sought to increase the agency's profile inside the government, to make the CIA more of a "player." But Casey's broad program of restructuring the CIA to make it more competitive posed a threat to some of Langley's ingrained bureaucratic practices; his plans were viewed as a direct threat to the power of the Four Princes—those heads of the CIA's major directorates who had the most influence over the agency's policies and most important programs.

The CTC grew out of the crisis brought on by a series of unpredicted terrorist events in 1985, starting with the seventeen-day hijacking of TWA Flight 847, one of the most sobering illustrations of U.S. vulnerability to terrorism during that decade. "At the time of the TWA hijacking President Reagan was putting a lot of heat on Casey to do something about this problem," explains a former counterterrorism officer. "We just weren't able to conduct a foreign policy as long as we had to deal with terrorism on an everyday level."

In December of that same year, gunmen from the Abu Nidal organization murdered twenty-five people in separate incidents at the Rome and Vienna international airports. The pressure on Casey increased. Critics within the U.S. government charged that the CIA was either unable, or unwilling, to pool interagency resources to combat the terrorist threat. At that point, Casey called on Clarridge to begin the long process of restructuring the agency's approach to resolving national security problems. Casey thought that Clarridge was the one insider with enough stature to bend the parochial concerns of the CIA's disparate directorates and divisions to his will.

"We damn near had a civil war inside the clandestine service," one CIA officer admits. "It spilled blood all over the floor because it was one of the first times an office was organized outside directorate lines. Clarridge gathered people from each division in the clandestine service. He forced directorates to give up manpower. And fairly quickly we scored some very significant victories. When the agency pulled everything together, we found that we knew a hell of a lot more about terrorism than we had ever imagined. We were actually doing a very good job, but we just never knew it. We never shared information."

The establishment of the CTC also angered the Directorate of Intelligence, where the move was viewed as a strictly out-of-channels operation whose sole purpose was to bypass the unpopular or uncomfortable conclusions of the agency's ranking analysts. Some analysts contended that the CTC circumvented the experts, which undermined the CIA's claim of providing objective and unslanted intelligence reports. The role of the CTC, they believed, was nothing less than an in-house covert operation, an internal destabilization campaign launched by the clandestine service to slant the findings of the Directorate of Intelligence. "There's a very dangerous trend that Casey and Gates started in the CIA which was to create joint DO-DI centers," one senior analyst later argued. "One of their tasks was to prepare analysis on key subjects. The result of this was to create a DO slant on DI intelligence. This is surely the case of the counterterrorism center...."

By the time William Webster became DCI the counterterrorism center was the chief planning and operational focus for U.S. government antiterrorist policy. The center had also won Langley new friends inside other agencies, particularly after CIA officers made it clear that they were willing to relinquish control of the CTC to the FBI. This was done, in part, to highlight the FBI's role as a law enforcement agency. "We gave them the lead," Cannistraro says, "but we did it because really they should take the lead. It's a very fragile arrangement. We still don't talk sources and methods with them, but we give them what they need to function. I guess you could say we go in the back door and give them the keys to the front."

Webster inherited the CTC at the height of its power, when clandestine service officers were running one of the agency's most dangerous and secret operations. The program (run by the NE Division, using officers and resources from the CTC) began in mid-1988, after more than six months of planning. It involved officers serving in nearly a dozen countries. The CIA's target was the notorious Abu Nidal organization (ANO), which was responsible for more airline hijackings, bombings, and violent acts than any other terrorist group. In November 1985 the ANO hijacked an EgyptAir flight and executed five passengers, in December 1985 the ANO claimed responsibility for the slaughter of twenty-five people at the Rome and Vienna international airports, and in 1986 it bombed a synagogue in Istanbul, killing sixteen people. After ANO operatives murdered nine passengers aboard the Greek pleasure boat *City of Poros* in 1988, the CIA decided to take action.

The agency had been conducting an extensive and dangerous information-gathering operation on the ANO since 1981. The agency penetrated the organization by recruiting defectors and by establishing a number of front companies that did business with Abu Nidal agents in Europe and North Africa. The corporations the CIA established sold a variety of military-related equipment to the Palestinian fringe group—boots, hats, and knapsacks. Other CIA proprietaries sold the ANO electronic equipment.

Through the use of this campaign the CIA was also able to provide information to U.S. Customs Service officials on American corporations who were ANO contractors. A number of these companies, the CIA discovered, were front groups for the Mossad, the Israeli intelligence service, that were also attempting to penetrate the terrorist group using the same tactics as the CIA. Agency officers were gleeful about the treasure trove of information they were able to uncover about Mossad front companies operating in the United States and took particular pleasure in shutting them down. Several of these Israeli-backed companies were broken up, their executives put on trial, convicted, and jailed.

The CIA's penetration of the ANO was extensive. A handful of CIA proprietaries became exclusive suppliers for the terrorist group.

There were problems with this strategy from the very beginning. At what point did the CIA stop gathering information on the ANO and begin to destroy it? At what point did the CIA cross the line from being an intelligence agency to being an accomplice to ANO operations?

The *City of Poros* incident was the watershed event that convinced senior agency officers that they needed to put the information they had gained in the previous seven years to work. The *City of Poros* murders also had an enormous impact on the Palestine Liberation Organization (PLO), whose top officials met with CIA officers in North Africa in the autumn of 1988 to plead that the two groups work together to end Abu Nidal's terror campaign once and for all. The CIA agreed with the PLO's leaders.

Following the *City of Poros* incident, CIA officers began to work in cooperation with several European intelligence agencies to put into place a broad anti-ANO plan. Using moderate Palestinian and Jordanian operatives as penetration agents, CIA officers successfully recruited rank-and-file ANO informers, spread rumors and disinformation through the organization's widely dispersed cells, and sparked mass defections by setting up a false contest for power inside the ANO's leadership cadre. Within the first six months of the operation, nearly sixty high-ranking ANO members had defected to more moderate Palestinian organizations.

One of the best-kept secrets during this anti-ANO campaign was the agency's close cooperation with the Tunis-based PLO, which helped provide intelligence for dismembering Abu Nidal's European and North African terrorist networks. The CIA contacted PLO officials through intermediaries in Beirut, Morocco, and Tunis. Their most senior PLO contact was Salah Kahlaf, known as Abu Iyad, who served as Yasir Arafat's chief intelligence aide. At the height of the operation Iyad privately confirmed to a reporter that the CIA-PLO links had been vital to the success of the operation.

According to Iyad, the PLO had been "bringing in scores of defectors from the Nidal group," creating a situation that had left the ANO "very vulnerable around the world." Three of the most important defectors from the ANO were Abdulrahman Issa, Atef Abu Bakr, and Sobhia Murad, the widow of the ANO's second-in-command. Their eyewitness accounts of the bloody conflict inside Nidal's organization provided evidence that the CIA's program to divide the ANO was succeeding. In one particularly brutal incident that they reported to the CIA, Nidal had personally gunned down half of his ruling "politburo." Two of these murdered associates, the defectors said, were buried by Nidal inside the concrete walls of his home. Nidal later threatened to murder Abu Iyad, after calling him the person most responsible for the ANO's internal problems.

At several points during the two-year campaign against Nidal, the struggle between the PLO and ANO devolved into open warfare, as ANO-sponsored militias engaged in battles against PLO forces in southern Lebanon. A series of mysterious murders in Beirut in late 1988 was also attributed by ANO members to Arafat and Iyad.

The CIA had also secretly tracked ANO operations since 1986 by gathering information from officials at the notorious Bank of Credit and Commerce International in London, where the ANO maintained several covert accounts. The CIA was able to determine that Nidal, using the pseudonym Shakir Farhan, had deposited millions of dollars of operating capital in the bank. Nidal frequently used an intermediary based in London to make these deposits and to act as his financial agent. Documents from BCCI that were obtained by the CIA helped identify ANO operatives in England, France, and Germany.

The PLO also was able to provide the agency with a wealth of documents on Abu Nidal's extensive European network. The information included details of his Austrian and Swiss bank accounts, his recruiting techniques, his arms deals, and how he purchased weapons through front companies he had established in Germany and the Netherlands. The agency used these documents to uncover ANO operations in the Far East.

By the end of the CIA's operation nearly three hundred ANO operatives—the heart of the organization's European and Middle Eastern wings—had fled the group. Some of these Palestinians made their way to Tunis, where they were debriefed, retrained, and then recruited as security officers for Fatah, the PLO's mainline faction. "We took the ANO apart," remarks Vince Cannistraro. "When we were done with that operation, Abu Nidal could not even pick up the pieces."

* * *

Few of Casey's other programs had as much sustained influence as the counterterrorism center—with one exception. In early 1982, Casey unexpectedly decided that the CIA should expand the work of the Soviet Collection Division, to cover the whole world. For many years, this unit was a legendary, elite group of Russian experts and operations officers who gathered intelligence from American business executives working in the USSR. Casey ordered that the division's assets and expertise be consolidated into the Operations Directorate's modest National Collection Division (NCD). This restructuring would make the NCD the primary collection unit inside the DO. The new NCD's mandate would be to amass intelligence on the entire international community, with an emphasis on interviewing American business leaders working in foreign countries besides the Soviet Union.

Casey wasn't finished. He then married this newly enlarged, hybrid organization with the Domestic Contact Division, which had an extensive network of academics who were internationally acknowledged experts in their fields. The NCD's new mandate, as a kind of internal superagency, was to interview well-known American industrialists who had gained intimate knowledge of foreign businesses and governments. The idea was to extend the DO's capabilities to reflect what Casey viewed as a changing world order; the Soviet Union would be just one of many intelligence targets, still important, to be sure, but not key.

Like the creation of the CTC, Casey's edict gave the National Collection Division enormous new power inside the DO and caused immediate controversy among clandestine service officers. The head of the Soviet Collection Division, Ted Carlson, a six-foot careerist who sports a thick blond mustache (and is well known at the agency as one of the mainstays of those who've made the Soviet bloc their life's work), was especially suspicious of Casey's proposal, telling colleagues that the DCI was diluting more than four decades of work on the USSR. Carlson, who had helped recruit some of the first American businessmen to negotiate contracts with the Soviet Union in the late 1960s, doubted that his work could be effectively extended to other parts of the world; the one factor that made his division such a success was that its officers had a special Soviet expertise.

Carlson's skepticism was seconded by a number of the service's senior espionage officials. What the CIA needed, they said, was a smaller, more focused effort at targeting American businessmen, not a large internal superagency. Casey dismissed the complaints. Intelligence requirements were changing so quickly, he argued, that the CIA could ill afford to train a new generation of regional analysts whose sole purpose was to chart economic and business trends around the world. The CIA didn't need regional experts, he argued, so much as it needed good operations officers; recruiting agents, gathering information, and running operations weren't any different in Jordan, say, than in the Soviet Union.

Casey had the final word. The NCD's new mandate would be to provide a detailed survey of technological advances, industrial, productive, and manufacturing output, and insights into the personalities of foreign business leaders. The intelligence, Casey maintained, could provide some of the best strategic information the United States could find on foreign capabilities.

Casey's grand plan for the National Collection Division should not have come as a surprise to the CIA's top managers, especially considering that he was a former New York lawyer with a lifelong interest in business. Casey felt at ease among American industrialists, and he often leaped at any opportunity to speak to business groups. He had a special knack for making them think that their judgments were given great weight by the national security establishment and that they could turn a profit at the same time that they spied for their country. Invariably he made his audiences feel as if they were sharing something that he would tell no one else, and on more than one occasion he melodramatically entertained business groups with a harmless anecdote that he paraded as insider information, a ploy he used that was designed both to disarm and to flatter. He often made sure to repeat one of his favorite phrases, that the CIA was involved in "the business of intelligence" and that the agency had much to learn from the business world; he pumped business people for information at the same time that he impressed them with his performance as a master spy. (He usually followed such theatrical presentations with a scathing attack on the press for leaking classified information, as if to say that he knew that business executives would never be so incautious.)

Despite internal agency opposition to his creation of a National Collection Division, Casey's determination to emphasize CIA contacts with the business community did not necessarily mark a revolutionary change in CIA policy—at least not at first. Gathering material from friendly American entrepreneurs was a standard practice that dated from the agency's first days and was institutionalized as one of the most productive means of assessing Soviet intentions by the Intelligence Directorate's Office of Soviet Analysis, where many of the DO's debriefings were studied with great care. But according to a former head of clandestine operations, John McMahon, the process had always been hit-or-miss, in large part because operations officers tended to recoil from anything that even suggested the CIA was involved in industrial spying. In addition, the agency traditionally treated information from American business sources cautiously. As McMahon told one reporter, "...these damn fools always wanted to go out and play cloak-and-dagger. They were always taking more risks than they were worth."

Casey understood the drawbacks of his new policy, but he was convinced its benefits outweighed any potential for harm. In defending his decision, he often pointed to the numerous intelligence coups scored by the old Soviet Collection Division, arguing that if they could be duplicated elsewhere, the CIA would be more prepared for the odd and unusual than ever before. "Bill Casey hated surprises," his former special assistant Herbert Meyer explains. "He wanted the CIA to have as much notice on something as possible; he saw that as its primary responsibility. American businessmen couldn't do that alone, but they could help."

For Casey, then, the newly revamped NCD was like an early-warning system, a way for the CIA to overtly measure threats to American security at the same time that it enhanced the agency's reputation in the American business community. Casey even told one top assistant that the CIA might indirectly benefit from the program's expansion by exposing the agency to the sound management policies practiced by a number of "modern Horatio Algers."

Whatever Casey's ultimate intention, there's little doubt that his initiative gave the new National Collection Division its start; by mid-decade the NCD was one of the fastest-growing and most important offices of the clandestine service. Its overt collection capabilities were upgraded, and its network of business contacts in the United States was expanded to include executives working in China, North Africa, and the Middle East. By 1984 the agency's two dozen domestic offices established to gain more ready access to American entrepreneurs were enlarged to meet Casey's new requirements. At Langley, meanwhile, the NCD was tying itself more closely to the espionage tradition of the clandestine service, where it had always been viewed as simply an adjunct to espionage operations. Casey's new emphasis on using American business executives as information sources permeated every level of the CIA.

The agency's ties to the international business community were expanded in other ways: By mid-1984 more than 150 American corporations were providing cover for CIA officers overseas, an increase of nearly 40 percent from twenty-four months earlier. But at the end of 1984, just as the controversy over Casey's decision to expand the NCD was finally dying down, he added another twist that raised concerns. He promoted James Kelly, the deputy chief of the Near East Division (who was in charge of South Asia operations), to initiate an NCD program that came dangerously close to *recruiting* American entrepreneurs to provide information to the CIA.

Casey appointed Kelly to head this new division because of his expertise in Near Eastern affairs and because he was convinced the appointment would make it clear that the program was a top agency priority. "It was a straightforward espionage operation," contends one CIA officer. "Casey's appointments made the division very, very aggressive. Casey wanted this done in the worst way. His idea was that you recruit businessmen who are working overseas to report for you. The idea was to take the information and turn it into missions for the DO."

In other words, the NCD was no longer charged with simply collecting intelligence; it was now involved in espionage. By early 1985 eight CIA case officers were training and recruiting businessmen as sources of information in foreign nations, and soon after, the head of the division went to Cairo to recruit business executives operating in Egypt as clandestine sources.

In a July 1986 speech to a group of Denver, Colorado, business executives, Casey openly hinted at the CIA's new commitment to using Americans as intelligence sources: "In addition to the commercial information services we subscribe to, the publications we purchase, the databases we receive or compile, and our own people overseas, we listen closely to what the business community has to tell us. We find U.S. businessmen—whether they be manufactures, bankers, or commodity dealers—ready and willing to share their insights with us on subjects ranging from high-technology developments in Europe and Japan, to Third World debt problems, to Soviet grain purchase, and many more."

Casey's remarks sounded innocuous enough, but it was clear what he had in mind when he unexpectedly acknowledged that the agency had begun a new program that would enhance its contacts with American businesses. "We have reorganized our component responsible for being in touch with the business community and we are devoting some of our best talent—and a lot of it—to the endeavor," Casey said. ". . . we view this relationship as essential to our mission and we want to ensure that it remains a strong one."

In late 1986 the NCD expanded its mandate once more. This time Casey directed the division to recruit foreign businessmen to gather information on technological advances made by foreign industries. The CIA's first target was Egypt. "This step was very controversial," recalls a CIA officer. "The head of Arab operations was opposed to it, and Clair George was opposed to it. Most of the more moderate people in the CIA thought that it went too far, way beyond our mandate. The argument was that we had given our station chief in Cairo the right to spy on foreign companies that our American corporations were competing against. It was off the reservation."

This private dispute over the NCD's mission eventually resulted in a scaling back of Casey's original plan. The division reverted instead to its more traditional program of questioning American business executives returning from overseas. The division's mandate was once more overt, and uncontroversial. But in the short time that it was allowed to actively recruit American and foreign business executives as CIA agents, the NCD had a remarkable effect on agency operations. Ironically, the program did not create results until after Casey had died, and it was William Webster who eventually benefited the most from the policy.

On the afternoon of June 24, 1988, U.S. Customs Service officials intercepted a 432-pound consignment of carbon-carbon fiber matting bound for Cairo. The high-tech substance is used to coat long-range warheads and rocket motor nozzles and is employed as an absorbent material in the outer layers of "stealth" radar-evading aircraft. The packages were being loaded aboard an Egyptian military C-130 at Baltimore-Washington International Airport. Their destination, called Cairo-South by NE Division officers, was the main transit point for arms shipments into and out of the Middle East. Because the material is essential in developing long-range ballistic missiles, it is stringently controlled by U.S. export laws.

Twenty-four hours before the seizure of the carbon-carbon material, a criminal complaint was filed in the U.S. district court in Sacramento, California, alleging that two Egyptian military officers had conspired with an Egyptian-born rocket scientist to export high-tech equipment to Cairo. The investigation culminated in the arrest of three suspects: James Huffman, an American marketing representative for Teledyne; Abdelkader Helmy, an Egyptian-American who is a recognized expert in the field of rocket propulsion, and Helmy's wife.

While the Customs Service trumpeted its operation as a major victory in its continuing effort to stem the illegal transfer of American technology to foreign countries, its investigation could not have been successfully completed without intelligence gathered by Casey's expanded National Collection Division. In a wide-ranging operation that spanned four continents, the NCD learned that high-ranking Egyptian, Argentine, and Iraqi officials, purportedly including Egypt's defense minister, Abdel Halim Abu Ghazala, were involved in an international conspiracy to purchase and, if necessary, steal sophisticated rocket components. Even more disturbing, the information implicated a number of Western corporations that had conspired to defy bans on the export of advanced materials to third world countries for military application. The evidence was as detailed as it was stunning: Using agents in Washington, Paris, Buenos Aires, Cairo, Moscow, and Baghdad, Egyptian and Iraqi officials succeeded in gathering the materials necessary to build an Arab missile capable of placing a warhead in any capital in the Middle East. "It was going to be one hell of a missile, and it was going to change everything," an NE Division officer says.

According to information gathered by the NCD, this scheme to build an Arab missile actually began in late 1982 in South America, shortly after the Argentine military was routed by Britain in the Falklands War. Humiliated by its defeat, the Argentine government established a modestly funded missile development program whose goal was to build a weapon that could be used to attack the British navy in the South Atlantic. But Argentina was unable to fund the project fully because of its crippling balance of payments crisis, and the program fell on hard times. The scheme was given a badly needed boost in October 1984, however, after Egyptian military officers quietly visited Buenos Aires and signed a secret protocol that made Argentina, Egypt, and Iraq partners in a plan to design, manufacture, and deploy an Arab equivalent to the American Pershing II medium-range ballistic missile. (These weapons were called the Condor II by the Argentineans and the Badr 2000 by the Egyptians.) The development program was given a jump start by the infusion of $3.2 billion in funding from Iraq. As part of the plan, the two Middle Eastern nations agreed to purchase from Argentina hundreds of millions of dollars of solid-fuel rocket motors and rocket fuel, thereby repaying the Argentines for providing the program's technological know-how. At the same time, the partners would be helping Argentina deal with its severe economic problems.

The CIA was first tipped off to this illegal operation in the mid-1980s by an American businessman working in the Middle East who had befriended several high-level officials in Egypt's defense industry. (This case turned out to be the first major test of the newly reorganized National Collection Division's expanded mission.) It was clear initially that the business executive's information was too vague to be of much value. At the NCD's urging, the businessman returned on visits to Cairo during the next two years to gather more information on the program. The intelligence he obtained showed that Arab nations were working "frantically" to develop a medium-range ballistic missile, which was "nearing completion." The businessman's Egyptian sources confirmed that the end user of this stolen technology was Iraq.

After signing the secret agreement in Argentina, Egypt and Iraq set out to purchase advanced European technology that would provide the three countries with a missile infrastructure. In Europe, Egyptian agents approached scientists from West Germany's largest aerospace firm, Messerschmitt-Boelkow-Blohm (MBB), to provide overall guidance for the project. The lucrative agreement eventually earned the company more than $250 million, most of it paid by the Iraqi government. Another West German company, Consen, reportedly agreed to supply two hundred technicians to help train Iraqi scientists. More than a dozen senior missile experts from MBB were also hired for the program. An MBB subsidiary company, Transtechnia, helped Egyptian and Argentine technicians redesign their primitive rocket motors. Transtechnia also initiated plans to ship laboratory equipment to a secret Iraqi research facility, Saad-16, near the northern Iraqi city of Mosul. Meanwhile, Egyptian agents also approached SNIA-BPD, a subsidiary of the Italian giant

Fiat, which channeled equipment and technicians to Iraq, and CFF Thompson, a French firm, was enlisted to develop the missile's guidance system.

By 1986 the Argentine-Arab missile program was one of the fastest-growing and most dangerous military projects in the world. "There was quite a bit of fear in the agency that the Arabs could do this very successfully and really pose a threat to the Israelis," recalls an NE Division officer. "They were doing it by piecing together different kinds of technology from different countries. They were using CFF Thompson [for] doing the guidance system. Messerschmitt of Germany was doing the propellant and the rest of it. This thing was going to have a longer range and a bigger payload than anything else the Arabs had ever possessed."

The program's goal was to build two hundred missiles for both Egypt and Iraq with a range of at least six hundred miles. Both Egypt and Iraq had earlier purchased Soviet Scud-B missiles—Iraq even toyed with the idea of somehow rigging a sophisticated Argentine-developed nose cone onto the more primitive Soviet-manufactured Scud-B. The Badr 2000 would be the first weapon of its kind deployed in the Middle East. When combined with a nuclear warhead, it would transform the region's fragile balance of power.

The National Collection Division put the final pieces of the conspiracy together by early 1988, after additional reports reached the CIA from American businessmen working in Cairo about Egypt's role in the three-nation missile pact. The most alarming news was that Egypt was building a pharmaceutical facility in a Cairo suburb that could be easily converted to the manufacture of chemical munitions. The detailed accounts provided to the NCD by several American business executives indicated that scientists and chemical substances were making their way to Abu Zabal, a city on the Nile River north of Cairo. (According to government officials who later traced the flow of these chemical substances, equipment for the facility was provided by a Swiss firm, Krebs, A.G.) The new site was easily detected because it was near several American manufacturing facilities—including a maintenance and repair plant for American M-1 tanks operated by General Dynamics and a joint venture factory operated by Johnson & Johnson.

Based on these reports, The Customs Service began tracking Egyptian officials working in Washington and California. In June, Customs agents decided that the Egyptian-American team was attempting to smuggle sophisticated nose cone technology out of the United States.

After the June 1988 arrests, officers from the National Collection Division (as well as Near East experts in the clandestine service) realized that the international conspiracy they'd uncovered had created an extremely volatile situation that threatened to shatter the fragile understanding reached by Egypt and Israel during the Carter administration.

They had busted more than a simple conspiracy to export controlled products illegally; this was a massive undertaking aimed at altering the Middle East's balance of power. Egyptian military officers involved in the conspiracy were known opponents of their government's opening to Tel Aviv. They had long been arguing that Egypt needed to acquire its own missile capability to offset Israel's production of its highly accurate Jericho II missile, an offensive weapon that could easily reach Cairo.

For its part, Israel was also secretly plotting to frustrate Egyptian efforts to produce such a missile. CIA officers concluded, for instance, that the failed car bomb assassination of Ekkehard Schrotz (the CEO of a Swiss company that helped finance the Egyptian rocket program) was probably carried out by Israeli intelligence agents. (An unknown pro-Iranian group, Guardians of Islam, took credit for the incident, but agency officers could never discover anything about them. The claim made by the group—that it was punishing business executives for helping Iraq—was dismissed.)

The information developed by the NCD confirmed that the Arab missile program was being directed at the highest levels of the Egyptian and Iraqi governments. The evidence indicated that President Hosni Mubarak undoubtedly knew about the plot. "Mubarak knew it was going on; sure he did," asserts a former CIA officer. "We really put pressure on him to stop the whole thing. The Israelis were also really upset about it. I heard they came to us and said, 'Hey, what the hell happened to Camp David? We're not supposed to have crazy people on our border.' " This veteran CIA officer adds: "We said we were going to do something about it, and we did."

Both Egyptian and Argentine officials denied their countries were involved in developing the Condor II as an offensive weapon. The Egyptians, in an official press statement, passed off the attempt to export the materials as "nothing more than a procedural mistake of neglecting to obtain export licenses for a material that can be purchased on the open market in the United States, and which is used in nonmilitary fields..." Argentina claimed it was developing the Condor II in order to give South America its first satellite.

The June 1988 arrests were only the beginning of the CIA's interest in tracking the international missile cartel. Throughout that summer of 1988 the National Collection Division continued to investigate technology transfers from several countries to Egypt and Iraq. The evidence the NCD uncovered convinced a number of CIA analysts that Saddam Hussein was attempting to build a missile infrastructure so sophisticated that it would make him the most powerful leader in the Middle East. The agency discovered, for instance, that a West German firm, Messerschmitt, was providing Iraq with simulation laboratories and mission control units, and advanced technical know-how—everything, in short, that could be used to construct a formidable missile launch capability. "Our number one concern during the summer of 1988 was the Arab missile," confirms a CIA officer. "We were really tracking developments. That was one of our collection priorities."

By the end of 1988 the CIA had determined that Iraq had nearly fifty Scud-B mobile launchers ready for deployment against any threat, with Israel being the obvious target.

It was not until more than two years later, during the Gulf War, that the world learned that Saddam Hussein's missile program was not an idle threat. But in 1988 his possible future intentions were overshadowed by the immediate scandal sparked by the Customs Service's arrests. The public and press were then far more concerned about the emerging international conspiracy that was being run out of the Egyptian Embassy in Washington, and involved high-ranking Egyptian officials. Despite Egypt's adamant denials and Argentina's insistence that it was only developing a satellite capability, the U.S. government privately presented a demarche to President Mubarak that demanded the resignation of his defense minister. Mubarak reluctantly complied. Iraq, on the other hand, did not respond publicly to the allegations that it was involved in importing sophisticated missile technology; nor were any of Iraq's top overseas officials directly implicated in the plot. A knowledgeable CIA officer is adamant, however, about Iraq's crucial role. "The Egyptians were only the intermediaries for Iraq," he says. "Saddam Hussein paid the entire bill."

The arrests of June 1988 vindicated the late William Casey's belief that the CIA's diligent pursuit of information from business executives— which had worked so well for so long in the Soviet Division—could be productively applied to international problems. The arrests ended all remaining doubts about the NCD's role as a valuable intelligence-gathering arm of the clandestine service. And even more important than the way this program expanded the CIA's information collection capacity was the clear shift it signaled in the agency's mission and priorities, as laid out by Casey and continued by Webster.

The CIA was changing from a bureaucracy dedicated to assessing America's primary cold war threat, the Soviet Union, to a mission that was at once diverse and controversial. The agency was attempting to become a center for activities and areas of specialization that it would have eschewed just a few years earlier: most especially in economic intelligence, counterterrorism, and narcotics. This difficult transformation caused continued grumbling among many of the agency's mid-level employees. It seemed to them that Webster's background as a law enforcement officer was now being imposed upon the CIA. The fact that it was Casey, not Webster, who had opened the door for agency cooperation with other parts of the U.S. bureaucracy did not seem to matter. Casey was a legend; Webster, a former head of the FBI.

Nor did many of Webster's closest associates escape the broad-brush criticism. In December 1988 the newly appointed head of the clandestine service, longtime Soviet Division veteran Richard Stolz, was widely viewed as well-meaning but ineffective. Unlike Clair George before him, Stolz was perceived as an operations chief who would take few risks. He was thought to be more interested in the agency's ability to survive in Washington than in how it would make its mark as an activist arm of the executive branch. Thomas Twetten, his deputy, was seen in much the same light, as a headquarters desk jockey whose minimal field experience tarred him as a to-get-ahead, go-along bureaucrat. The real powers of the clandestine service, the career branch officers and division chiefs, believed they were being hamstrung by Webster's reforms. The third-generation CIA officers who'd led the agency through the difficult Turner years and stood by their fallen chief, Bill Casey, were not able to reverse the trend, especially since the most famous among them (Dewey Clarridge, George Cave, John McMahon, George Lauder, and Ed Juchniewicz) were recently departed.

All of these circumstances seemed to have created a feeling that the power of the clandestine service, its sense of its own elitism, its reputation and its capabilities, was flowing away from the CIA. There was no longer any doubt that the clandestine service was under attack: from the Pentagon's clique of high-ranking military officers (who wanted to strip the agency of its control over paramilitary assets) to the Congress—who wanted to cripple CIA proposals in a welter of regulations and laws—to the White House, where political expediency often played havoc with agency analysts. The belief that the agency had lost its influence was reinforced by a number of unforeseen factors, the demise of the Soviet Union as a primary threat to American security being the most important.

It was that perception, that there was a widening gulf between what the CIA did and what it needed to do, that best symbolized what ailed the agency in the late 1988. This lack of direction came at just the wrong time: The organization was as insulated as it had been at any previous time in its history. Nor did the agency seem capable of change. The one thing that had made the CIA so valuable for four decades—its ability to keep secrets and conduct operations far from the public's gaze—was the one thing that was now undermining its influence. The sad irony of the agency's status on the eve of George Bush's inauguration was that its operations were so "compartmented" and its secrets so closely held that it was nearly paralyzed. Or as one former CIA officer put it: "I can't tell you why sources and methods are so secret, because to do so would be to tell you about sources and methods. And I can't do that."

As a result, the general impression in Washington was that the agency was accumulating intelligence for its own sake. "The CIA was scared to death to share anything it had," a congressional intelligence aide says, "because that would be revealing secrets, and the CIA doesn't want to do that." Even inside the executive branch the CIA's intelligence product was viewed with disdain. The agency's primary cachet—that it could provide timely and accurate intelligence to the President—was in disrepute. A former senior Reagan administration official remembers the typical frustration that NSC officers felt when confronted with agency papers. "We could never get a clear answer," he says. "Everything was always watered down, the CIA was playing politics with itself. No one was willing to stick his neck out and say, 'This is what's going to happen.'" The consequences for the agency were fearsome: Important government officials were starting to believe that agency experts knew no more than anyone else.

Surprisingly, a large number of CIA officers, especially at the higher, senior-management level, agreed with these assessments. In an attempt to resolve the problem, a team of employees fanned out through the bureaucracy near the end of Casey's term to find out what kind of intelligence the government wanted. That the question needed to be asked in the first place was an indication of just how tenuous the CIA's position inside the executive branch had become; the agency knew that it was supposed to be collecting intelligence, but it didn't know what kind. The inquiry proved to be a dispiriting exercise. "We sent our people out to talk to the consumers [of intelligence] because we thought we could better define what people wanted," a retired former senior officer reflects. "It was real simple, we wanted to see if we were doing our job. So we would ask, 'What kind of intelligence do you want us to collect?' Well, the CIA found that a lot of the time the government doesn't know what it wants the agency to collect. They just don't have any idea what their requirements are. They will take whatever you give them. And then they live on it, and they say, 'Give me more of this; please keep collecting this.' When they don't really need it. And they don't even know that they don't need it. What the Christ are we collecting information for if we can't use it?"

Casey's solution to this crisis was to begin tearing down the walls that separated the CIA from the rest of the government and to streamline internal intelligence units. Recasting the mission of the National Collection Division and establishing the Counterterrorism Center were two such changes. Despite its earliest success, the NCD program was modest in comparison with what Casey really had in mind: He wanted to establish an intelligence unit that could someday conduct international business espionage. "The Japanese did it from day one," a Casey defender says. "The Kampetei was always a commercial intelligence service. That's what they did best. So now we say, 'Well, we broke up the Kampetei after World War Two, so they don't have an intelligence service.' But that's just not true. All they did was relocate it; it's now based in their companies. They have the best foreign intelligence service in the world."

The CTC was the model for the new program that Casey envisioned would stem the CIA's loss of power and resuscitate its reputation inside the executive branch. He foresaw a series of cooperative multiagency intelligence units whose purpose would be to more effectively use the information that the CIA so diligently collected. The real purpose of the CTC was also political: Casey wanted to dismantle the wall of mistrust that had been built up around the agency from four decades of self-imposed bureaucratic isolation. He also wanted to rearrange Langley's power centers.

On the eve of Bush's inauguration the CIA remained rudderless. It was unable to wield the kind of power it once had; it was demoralized by resignations, frightened by the requirements of a changing world, divided over the question of intelligence sharing, and led by a relatively inexperienced director who was increasingly isolated from the most important officers in the clandestine service. For George Bush it must have looked a lot like 1976; he had once again inherited an agency in crisis.

8
★ ★ ★
A Man for This Season

*B*ush's reappointment of Webster seemed to reinvigorate the DCI. Over the month leading up to the January 1989 inauguration, Webster appeared in more public forums than at any other time in his tenure. Webster was raising his profile in order to make himself look more valuable to the new Bush team and to emphasize his grasp of intelligence issues. The strategy worked: Webster seemed more confident and more capable than before and more willing to take on the responsibilities of leading the CIA. But this higher profile did little to change rank-and-file opinions of him. "There were jokes circulating all the time," a CIA officer recalls. "Whenever we heard that he did really well at something, we realized that this accomplishment brought him up to just about average when you compared him with someone like Dulles or McCone."

This remark seems especially uncharitable when weighed against the enormous pressures that were being brought to bear on Webster during the period just before Bush took office. Especially demanding was the death of Matt Gannon and the urgency to find the terrorists who bombed Pan Am 103. The CIA was also working overtime to sort through increasingly worrisome intelligence reports that indicated that Muammar Qaddafi's program to complete a chemical weapons facility in Libya was nearing completion. The Rabta plant, named for the crossroads town where it was being built, had the capability of producing weapons-grade chemicals and unidentified poison gases. Reports about the Rabta facility had been causing great anxiety with the soon-to-be-departing Reagan administration since October 1988.

In one of the rare instances in recent history, the CIA was tipped off about the chemical facility by a human intelligence source inside a foreign government. In this case a CIA officer serving in Italy was told about the plant by a Libyan asset inside the Qaddafi government. When the Reagan administration first publicized the information several months later, to put pressure on Qaddafi to shut down the facility, the Libyan leader protested by sending his foreign minister to Rome to complain about the presence of American bases in Italy, which were within striking distance of Tripoli. According to an eyewitness account from the CIA's source, the Libyan foreign minister "lambasted" his Italian counterpart and announced that Libya was declaring a "day of mourning in remembrance of Italy's colonization. ..." The Libyans also announced that a planned rapprochement between Tripoli and Rome was being put on hold. This was a mild response to the pressures being brought against Qaddafi by the United States, but the simmering crisis was bound to get worse.

On October 28, 1988, just as President Reagan's eight years in office were ending, the CIA monitored a Libyan television address by Qaddafi having to do with the Rabta facility. Qaddafi categorically denied that Libya was engaged in producing chemical weapons, saying the facility was a "medicine manufacturing plant."

That same week the State Department sent a report to the CIA that indicated that Qaddafi was willing to once again chance a military showdown with the United States in order to increase his stature and influence in the Arab world. The NE Division's top officers decided that the situation involved much more than just a matter of Qaddafi's engaging in diplomatic appearances; photographs from KH-11 satellites trained on the Rabta facility at the end of October showed unmistakably that the Libyan leader was earnestly pressing forward in producing a large chemical weapons stockpile.

A chilling State Department intelligence report sent to the CIA on October 28 showed just how important the plant was for the Libyan leader. "Qaddafi has the jitters over U.S. charges on his CW plant," the top secret report said. "The Libyan Air Force has declared Rabta an air exclusion zone and advised that all aircraft overflying the area would be fired upon. According to Special Intelligence, his turnaround on Italy seems self-defeating though he may believe [Prime Minister Bettino] Craxi and Foreign Minister [Giulio] Andreotti intend to postpone planned visits."

Starting in early November, the CIA moved purposefully to recruit as many Libyan nationals in Europe, Canada, and the United States as they could to gather more information on the plant. CIA officers also flooded into Malta, the only transit point into and out of Tripoli. By the end of the month, according to an NE Division officer, the agency had obtained enough information to confirm that the plant would become operational "by midsummer, 1989." That schedule gave the agency enough time to come up with a plan to destroy the facility.

To heighten the pressure on Qaddafi, President Reagan—then in his last weeks in office—called Webster and a group of Near East Division officers to the White House on December 18 to discuss measures he could take to disarm the plant. During the briefing Webster assured Reagan that the CIA had "unimpeachable human sources" in Libya who had given it "the best information" available about the plant's status. However, Webster conceded that the agency had not yet concocted a feasible plan to deal with the Libyan threat—short of military action.

Reagan then contacted European leaders to determine whether they would support an air strike against the plant. Only Britain unconditionally agreed and as in the case of the April 1986 bombing of Libya, Margaret Thatcher told the President the United States could make use of its British bases for the strike. On December 21, the same day that Pan Am 103 was destroyed, Reagan told ABC's David Brinkley that he was conferring with U.S. allies on a possible strike.

During the next month both Reagan and President-elect Bush continued to put pressure on European allies to come up with a plan to stop further exports of chemicals to Libya and to support a program to destroy the Rabta plant. The greatest pressure was brought against West Germany, which was identified as the government most responsible for failing to monitor chemical exports to Tripoli. At first the Germans denied responsibility. But under pressure from Secretary of State George Shultz and later his successor, James Baker, the Germans admitted that the chemical capabilities at Rabta had indeed resulted from their technology. The CIA identified three German companies in a secret report on the Rabta plant issued on the eve of Bush's inauguration and implicated a fourth owned by an Iraqi businessman in London.

It wasn't until two months after Bush became President that the CIA reported that Qaddafi had ceased chemical weapons production at the plant, at least for the time being. Even so, the Rabta crisis raised fears at Langley about other chemical technology exports from European companies. These concerns became the subject of a series of public speeches made by William Webster in early 1989. What the DCI did not tell his audiences was that such exports were occurring every day from U.S. plants—right under the noses of CIA officers.

In mid-January, Webster, Stolz, Kerr, and Twetten put in place a plan designed to heighten the agency's importance in the new administration. Their initial objective was to make sure the incoming President was fully briefed on the CIA's worldwide operations. They prepared a detailed paper summarizing U.S. intelligence programs that was to be given to Bush within hours of his inauguration. It was important the briefing go well. Because of the new President's network of unofficial ties to the agency and his experience with intelligence issues, Bush would examine the CIA's assessments more critically than any of his predecessors. So Webster told Stolz in mid-December, "we have to be more than ready." Stolz needed little prodding. As he told a now-retired colleague, Langley's performance during the transition period would set the stage for Bush's treatment of the agency in the year that followed. Stolz realized it was crucial that the CIA impress the new President.

The briefings were conducted both prior to and immediately following Bush's inauguration, but they did not have the impact that everyone predicted. Bush was serious but relaxed during many of the agency's most important presentations and seemed not to use the meetings to pass judgment on the CIA's, or Webster's, work. Agency officers were relieved.

The CIA's senior officer caste was well aware of Webster's drawbacks as DCI but considered it important that he stay on to lead the agency. He provided continuity and the critically important imprimatur of honesty. He was unlikely to get the agency involved in public scandals. But these same officers were divided over the question of whether Webster could survive very long in the new administration. On the one hand, they knew Webster was friendly with Bush and had his confidence. After all, Bush was responsible for his 1987 appointment. They knew that Webster was viewed as a weak DCI in administration circles, which actually played to his advantage. James Baker, the new secretary of state, did not want a foreign policy competitor at the CIA.

On the other hand, the agency's senior management was concerned by continuing rumors that Webster would soon be replaced, supposedly because Bush wanted to start his administration with a clean slate. Webster would have to go, according to this theory, because he was identified in the public mind with the stain of the Iran-contra affair—even though he was put in place for the express purpose of cleaning up the agency. There was also speculation that Bush might want to run the agency through an intermediary because of his close identification with the institution. Webster, they also argued, would inevitably be replaced because he was perceived as a transitional figure, not an intelligence professional. More critically, Webster's value to the administration would likely be judged on his ability to get close to Bush. That was a problem since the DCI had said that, unlike Casey, he would not participate in Cabinet meetings. Such a policy might inevitably lead to his exclusion from the President's inner circle.

These views were reinforced just prior to the inauguration when a report spread through the CIA that Bush had offered the DCI's post job to two other officials before deciding to retain Webster. The two, Brent Scowcroft (whom Bush decided to name as his national security adviser) and General Colin Powell, who elected to remain as head of U.S. Forces Command in Atlanta, declined the position. Nevertheless, it was now clear that Bush was definitely interested in making a change at Langley. If that was his position in December, it would likely be his position throughout his presidency. It seemed obvious that the only reason Webster remained as DCI is that Bush could find no one else more suitable who wanted the job.

The view that Bush wanted to manage the agency himself was ameliorated to some degree by his personal assurance to Webster that he would not interfere in his work. This promise came during a telephone conversation the two had the night before he announced Webster would stay on as DCI; Bush told him to "keep up the good work" and pledged his full cooperation. As he spoke, Bush sounded comfortable with his decision to retain Webster and sympathized about the challenges that he knew Webster still faced as DCI. Bush reaffirmed that Webster had been the right man for the job in 1987; he stressed that he had no plans to replace Webster in the immediate future. The conversation was short but reassuring. It was the vote of confidence that Webster felt he needed to impose his own style on the CIA.

Despite receiving this blessing directly from the President-elect, rumors of Webster's imminent departure continued to circulate in Washington. To put a halt to this speculation, the agency's Public Affairs Office decided in December that it was important to highlight Bush's continued confidence in Webster's abilities. (This was an odd sort of maneuver, since such praise should have come, rightly, from the White House.) The Public Affairs Office continually emphasized Webster's long hours and stellar performance as DCI; more important, the spokesman stressed that he remained a valued part of Bush's most trusted circle of advisers. This closeness to Bush, it soon became clear, was the new administration's litmus test of effectiveness. CIA public affairs officer James Greenleaf, for instance, repudiated reports that Webster was about to be replaced dozens of times over the next two years with the same words. "The judge continues to have the trust of the President," he would repeat again and again. To buttress this statement, he invariably added, "You know, they're good friends."

As events were to show, it was not even so much a question of whether Webster was Bush's friend (that was never in doubt) but whether he was as close a friend as Brent Scowcroft, Colin Powell, Robert Gates, Richard Cheney, or any of the half dozen or so officials in the President's immediate circle. Each of these insiders knew that the closer they were able to get to Bush, the better their chance of survival. Over the next four years those closest to the President would even make flagrant attempts to push others away. The question was not, then, whether Webster was a good DCI, or the President's friend, but whether he was a member of George Bush's club.

This jockeying for position was a key reason for Webster's angry reaction to a *Washington Post* article that appeared on New Year's Day, 1989. The report, headlined CIA AIDE ACTS TO LIFT REPRIMAND, was the first evidence of what would become a vicious feud between Bush's aides and Webster over his status inside the new administration. The article outlined a little-known private spat that had been simmering between Webster and Charles Allen, a highly respected but controversial veteran CIA official. Their argument was over Webster's decision to discipline Allen for his role in the Iran-contra affair. Allen was outraged by Webster's decision and had initiated steps to get it reversed. Allen had first tried to appeal the reprimand by using internal agency channels. When that failed, he hired well-known Washington lawyer R. James Woolsey, one of the city's most highly touted political street fighters. Woolsey happened to be a good friend of Brent Scowcroft, the nation's NSC director-designate. Webster knew that in fighting Allen, he was also confronting one of the new administration's most powerful figures.

It was not something he wanted to do.

The Allen-Webster controversy was the talk of the agency. Allen, whom reporter Michael Wines called "a tall, graying man given to sober suits and precise grammar," was generally viewed as an eccentric workaholic who often picked fights with superiors. Herb Meyer, a former special assistant to DCI Casey, describes Allen as a "brilliant man" with "a yen for controversy. He is a highly respected but outspoken career officer." Another senior CIA officer adds that Allen was viewed as "more than just a little weird; it was hard to know just where he was coming from." At times during his career Allen seemed almost out of control as he often spent all night at his office and made unreasonable demands on his secretarial staff. A former colleague remembers "a remarkable seventy-two-hour marathon" during which Allen closeted himself in a CIA office and emerged with a new study on Soviet foreign policy that, Allen believed, would virtually recast agency thinking on changes in Eastern Europe.

Allen was known for his offbeat views, and his detractors said he had a huge ego. He regularly challenged CIA intelligence assessments and virtually appointed himself the agency's unofficial watchdog and resident skeptic. It's difficult to find a CIA official about whom there is such divided opinion—he is viewed as "brainy" by some; a "complete political creature" by others—but few doubt his formidable talent as an agency infighter. Allen had been consistently able to fend off critics while he rose to some of the CIA's top slots.

Allen's reprimand stemmed from his failure to cooperate with the internal investigation conducted by Webster's man, Russ Bruemmer, into the CIA's involvement with Oliver North. When Webster's decision was issued, in December 1988, Allen was outraged, as were a number of his supporters both inside the agency and among the extensive network of retired CIA officers. Over the next several months Allen built a defense that rested on this support and on his bulldoglike faith in the rightness of his own position. (He went so far as to tell one colleague that if his reprimand wasn't lifted, he would quit the agency, "which would leave the nation virtually defenseless".) What angered Allen's supporters the most was Webster's apparent disregard for Allen's warning to CIA leaders that Colonel North was diverting profits from Iranian arms sales to support the contras. Allen's colleagues claimed that he was the most prescient CIA officer they'd ever encountered and they recited his Iran-contra warning to prove this contention.

Allen first became involved in the Iran-contra affair in late 1985 when Casey ordered him to meet with Iranian arms dealer Manucher Ghorbanifar. Allen was aware of Ghorbanifar's reputation, but he accepted the assignment as a challenge. After several conversations with the Iranian, Allen concluded that Ghorbanifar was a man of some talent, but he was disturbed by his willingness to exaggerate his prowess as an intelligence officer. Here was a man, Allen thought, who was titillated by the opportunity of working with the CIA.

Allen's fears were heightened when Ghorbanifar proposed an elaborate "scam" to fleece Muammar Qaddafi of ten million dollars. The amount was the price that Qaddafi had put on the life of a London-based Libyan opposition leader named Mohammed al-Mugharief. Ghorbanifar's proposal was that he and the CIA would fake Mugharief's murder and funeral and then they would collect Qaddafi's reward and split it. Oliver North was fascinated by the proposal, but Allen and Casey had doubts that it would work. Allen remained the most skeptical; he joked to one colleague that Ghorbanifar was "loony." Based on this scheme, and similar incidents, Allen reported back to Casey that Ghorbanifar was "flamboyant," "clever," "cunning," and a "con man."

Allen did not urge Casey to shut the door on Ghorbanifar. Allen believed that Ghorbanifar could still prove valuable to the CIA just as long as he was nurtured carefully. He was also willing to ignore the warning signs that Ghorbanifar was untrustworthy, because there was strong evidence that the arms dealer had some high-level contacts inside the Iranian government. Allen, who was then serving as the CIA's national intelligence officer for counterterrorism, also found Ghorbanifar attractive for another reason: The Iranian said he could ferret out terrorist plots aimed at Persian Gulf leaders, which was Allen's area of responsibility.

As the Iran arms sales operation proceeded in secret, Allen effectively became Ghorbanifar's CIA "case officer." At the same time, Allen also remained one of the agency's main contacts to Oliver North. At key points as the operation continued, Allen came close to confronting North with his suspicions that profits from the Iran arms sales—the "residuals," as North called them—were being diverted, but he never did. Instead, Allen took his worries up the CIA's chain of command.

In late August 1986 Allen told Deputy Director of Intelligence Richard Kerr that there was something about the North operation that bothered him and that might cause problems for the CIA. Allen suspected that North was running a secret program funded by the profits from purposely overpriced American military hardware that had been sold to Iran. Allen's warning was not categorical, since he was not yet fully aware of North's commitment to the contra cause or his abhorrence of congressional restrictions on U.S. aid. Allen told Kerr that he was worried. "It's going to be extremely messy if there is something amiss about the operation," he warned. Kerr listened carefully and then passed Allen's report to Deputy DCI Robert Gates during the first week of September 1986. Kerr was unimpressed with Gates's reaction. Kerr reported back to Allen that he did not think Gates believed him.

Allen took the next step by expressing his feelings directly to Gates. During an October 1 meeting Allen emphasized that he thought the Iran operation might become public. He warned that unpaid arms dealers were threatening to go to the newspapers with their story unless they were given their money. "I can't prove it," he added ominously, "but based just on the indicators, I've come to sort of an analytical judgment that money is perhaps being diverted" to the contras in Central America. "This thing has all the makings of a disaster." Allen later recalled that Gates was startled by the revelation and "started to laugh because it sounded absurd, but then he became very serious and said, 'Well, that would be a very serious thing.'"

Gates took Allen to see Casey on October 7. Allen repeated his warning at this meeting and volunteered to write out a memo of his "troubles." That summary was produced on October 14 and was then followed by a second paper in November, which stated that Canadian businessmen "believe that they have been swindled and that the money paid by Iran for the arms may have been siphoned off to support the contras."

The two Canadians were well-known international arms dealers Ernest Miller and Donald Fraser, who claimed they had lent Saudi businessman Adnan Khashoggi ten million dollars on a promise of eight million dollars in profits for arms sales to Teheran. The money was used to underwrite Ghorbanifar's purchase of U.S. weapons and spare parts, which would then be shipped to Iran. The millions of dollars in anticipated profits from the sales would benefit everyone—Ghorbanifar, Khashoggi, Fraser, and Miller. But Iran refused to pay because the arms were overpriced. This left Ghorbanifar (and Khashoggi) ten million dollars in debt. On October 7, Fraser's and Miller's business partner, Roy Furmark, an old business associate of Casey's from his New York days, came to see the DCI about the money. He said that Khashoggi was threatening to make the Iran arms operation public unless he was paid and that Fraser and Miller had probably already approached members of the Senate Select Committee on Intelligence with their information.

This bald attempt to extort money from the CIA was the development that most bothered Allen. It was a main reason why he so insistently pressed his fears on Robert Gates. The key, Allen stressed, was the flow of money from Iran to the contras. Those transactions involved the CIA in an illegal operation. Gates responded to Allen's warning by asking the CIA's general counsel to review the Iran operation. Gates later told Congress that the counsel's finished report found no substantiation of Allen's claim. Gates insisted that he knew nothing of the details of the Iran-contra operation outside of this one incident because he had never been briefed about it by Casey or by the head of clandestine service, Clair George.

Although Allen was unable to get Casey and Gates to act on his warning, he became an instant hero inside the clandestine service when the Iran-contra scandal exploded into public view. From then on he was widely perceived as an officer willing to put the agency ahead of his own career. His well-documented warnings that the Iran operation was "spinning out of control" made Webster's reprimand two years later appear ungracious at best and a witch-hunt at worst.

Webster's handling of the entire matter was so poorly implemented that when the story of Allen's appeal reached *The Washington Post,* it further isolated the DCI from the agency's most powerful career officers. Allen was well known by almost everyone of consequence in Langley's upper echelons and by many powerful Washington officials as well. During his three decades as a CIA officer he had served in nearly every major part of the agency, though he was never appointed to head a major directorate. During the early 1980s he had been a valued adviser to William Casey and was credited with upgrading the agency's antiterrorism and counternarcotics capabilities.

Allen's work was so valued that in 1986 Casey appointed him the CIA's representative to a supersecret interagency project to study how to ensure the survival of the U.S. government and its leaders during a nuclear conflagration. This continuity of government (COG) project bolstered Allen's reputation as one of the most outspoken figures in the intelligence community and identified him as one of the rising powers at the CIA. Through it all, Allen maintained his reputation as an argumentative and irreverent officer whose disarming comments often bordered on insubordination. "Let me see now," one colleague quotes Allen as saying during a COG meeting, "our job is to throw the Constitution out the window." But his service as the project's deputy director also sharpened his already refined sense of impending disaster. The assignment brought him in contact with Oliver North, who was delegated to monitor COG's findings by National Security Adviser Robert McFarlane.

For many officers, Allen was viewed as the DI's Dewey Clarridge, the first in a strange new breed of analyst-operators who were familiar with both sides of the CIA. Allen, they believed, was well on his way to becoming a member of the CIA's pantheon of great intelligence officers.

The enthusiastic opinion of Allen was not much in evidence, however, in the DI, where a number of outspoken analysts bitterly criticized him for bending his views to political expediency during the Iran initiative. Allen, they said, took advantage of his access to Casey to promote a political line—that an opening could be made to Iranian moderates—that could not be supported by the information they had gathered on Iran's internal politics. Allen played the White House game, these critics claimed, by using contrived information provided by CIA consultant George Cave to support the Iran program. "Charlie Allen briefed the NSC on the basis of Cave's disinformation," a senior CIA analyst explains. "The DI [Kerr] was cut out of this process. The senior Iranian analyst . . . had no knowledge in the beginning that this activity was taking place." The divergence of views about Allen inside the CIA intensified the traditional divisions between the clandestine service and the DI at the same time that it, paradoxically, added to Allen's reputation as a hard-driving agency loyalist.

By slapping down a bona fide intelligence hero, Webster found himself involved in a mud-slinging contest not only with a number of influential former CIA officers but also, at least potentially, with Brent Scowcroft. "They circled the wagons inside the clandestine service," a DO official says. "It was like they were defending one of their own." The controversy started on the day that Webster issued a reprimand to Allen for his role in the Iran-contra affair and escalated throughout the following year. Allen protested vehemently, but when it became clear that Webster was standing his ground, Allen went outside the agency for relief. In the wake of the *Post* article, it appeared that Allen was willing to slug it out with Webster in public, no matter how embarrassing that might prove. Webster realized that Allen was not bluffing. Given Allen's almost neurotic aversion to authority figures, he had Webster trapped. "Charlie knew that Judge Webster would never, never, never make public the reason for his reprimand," emphasizes a veteran CIA officer. "So Allen was willing to go head to head with Webster if necessary."

Ironically, Allen's attack on Webster was as unjustified as Webster's reprimand, though only a few CIA officers knew that in January 1989. According to several of Webster's allies, Allen deserved the reprimand since he failed to comply with the DCI's request for "full cooperation" with the agency's internal investigation of the Iran-contra scandal. In the midst of the Bruemmer inquiry a set of missing papers that contained information on the arms-for-hostages operation were found in Allen's office. Allen claimed that he had inadvertently forgotten about these files. (CIA officers have quipped to New York Times reporter Michael Wines that Allen's office "looks like the La Brea tar pits.") Despite the normal disarray on Allen's desk, high-ranking CIA officials dismissed Allen's assertion; Webster's instructions, they believed, had been pointedly ignored, and it was time that Allen stopped thumbing his nose at senior agency officials. To his defenders, however, Allen's was a minor indiscretion in comparison with the service he'd done the agency. "Allen warned Casey, warned Gates, and warned Kerr about Oliver North," says a CIA officer, in his defense, "and then Webster came in and started investigating him." Another officer puts forth a different version: "Allen wasn't about to be intimidated by Webster; he just didn't have much respect for him."

Senior officials hoped that Allen's current position—as the national intelligence officer (NIO) for warning—would moderate his natural tendency to court controversy. His job was to assess the possibility of an imminent Soviet attack and to provide warnings on other coming crises. That particular NIO slot, though very important, is also effectively removed from the day-to-day activities of the agency. Webster enjoyed the prospect of keeping Allen in this outpost. "The idea was to keep Allen out of the way, to put him somewhere where he couldn't do any damage and Webster wouldn't have to come in contact with him," as a Webster aide confirms. Former FAA official and terrorism expert Billie Vincent, a close personal friend and colleague of Allen's, suggests that the NIO job may have been a way of keeping him out of the limelight. "They probably thought he was going to just go to sleep in that job," Vincent says, "imprisoned by Soviet experts with thick glasses who sit around and count missiles."

A CIA colleague who closely follows Allen's career agrees that his exile to the post of NIO for warning was tailor-made for Allen's personality. "Charlie got the hang of his new job in about three seconds," this co-worker notes. "There was no way the Russians were going to attack us, and he knew it. But he wasn't going to get stuck doing nothing. He was interested in studying everything."

Allen redefined his job and upgraded his small staff to incorporate officers from every important CIA division and then expanded his mission so that it included issuing warning notices on every part of the world. Eventually he began to warn his superiors and other executive department branches about a host of threats to U.S. interests—warnings that included everything from lone terrorists to backwater third world liberation movements. By the end of 1988 Allen was giving a detailed twice-a-month briefing on worldwide threats against American security to White House, State Department, and CIA officials.

Although Allen's supporters use nearly reverential tones to describe him, as NIO he also made a number of powerful enemies in the intelligence community—even among activists in the clandestine service, who point out that he was as often wrong about his warnings as he was right. The critics say he was too harsh in his presentations to be effective. He became a lightning rod for discontent inside the CIA and a symbol of its arrogant elitism. "The military hated his guts and did everything they could to undermine him," a CIA officer explains.

Allen's constant need to skirmish with his superiors was also becoming a tiresome eccentricity. But of all the criticisms, his penchant for issuing "the sky is falling" warnings was by far the most serious. Allen was starting to be viewed, in the words of reporter Michael Wines, as a "Cassandra-like character" whose shrill polemics were undercutting his effectiveness. "Warning is a process, not an event like 'I predict,' " Wines quotes a Bush administration official as saying. "Holding one's fire and getting it right is important. Firing a lot, and getting it right occasionally, is not."

For Allen's Washington lawyer, R. James Woolsey, however, his client was a man of "ability and integrity," whose reprimand was an injustice that needed to be put aright. Considering Allen's connection through Woolsey to the Bush administration's hierarchy, and the dangers inherent in further publicity on the case, Webster was forced to agree. Allen was not a figure to be taken lightly, in view of his highly touted reputation. It was no use punishing a symbol; Webster knew that if he was to have any chance of gaining the confidence of the CIA's rank-and-file activists, he needed Allen on his side. However, the public pressure brought to bear by Allen—and the clear threat that the CIA would be publicly sued—were clearly the most important factors that Webster took into account. A few short weeks after *The Washington Post* reported about the controversy, Allen's reprimand was quietly dropped from his record. As far as Webster was concerned, the resolution of the Allen case brought a belated end to a sad chapter in CIA history—the

Iran-contra scandal. With this ending Webster felt he had been left free to make a new beginning, by running the agency as the Bush administration's director of central intelligence.

George Bush established one of the most tightly knit foreign policy teams in modern American history. This small group of friends who constituted a close corps of advisers at the very center of the administration virtually dictated every aspect of international relations. The administration's most powerful senior official was Secretary of State James A. Baker III, Bush's former campaign director, fellow Texan, and lifelong friend. Baker was Bush's first appointment, made within hours after the election. Baker loomed as an important figure in the CIA's future because of his enormous influence as architect of Bush's foreign policy and because he was particularly sensitive to interagency feuds of the kind that he believed had caused the Iran-contra affair. That scandal would not have happened, Baker believed, if Secretary of State George Shultz and Secretary of Defense Caspar Weinberger had spent more time promoting President Reagan's policies instead of arguing with each other; their feud had paralyzed the administration and allowed Casey the chance to promote the disastrous opening with Iran. Baker wanted to make sure that it did not happen again and that no one at the CIA would be able to challenge his supremacy as the nation's chief foreign policy architect.

Another key Bush adviser stationed outside the White House was Congressman Dick Cheney, who was named secretary of defense after John Tower had failed to win Senate confirmation. Cheney was not initially viewed as part of Bush's inner circle, but the new President soon came to rely on his understated advice. Cheney was appointed largely because of his good congressional relations and well-known conservatism on defense issues. As time went on, his power grew inside the administration, although he posed no immediate challenge to Baker's position as first among equals among Bush's advisers. Cheney was a hard-liner on U.S.-Soviet relations and was loath to undertake the kinds of defense budget cuts being called for in Congress. Any potential problem with Cheney's uncompromising conservatism was more than offset, however, by his reputation as a hardworking and knowledgeable expert on military affairs.

Inside the White House, Bush appointed retired Air Force General Brent Scowcroft as his national security adviser. Scowcroft was a powerful voice at the center of the administration, and like Cheney, he was a hard-liner on U.S. relations with the Soviet Union. Scowcroft also served as a bridge to the old-line Republican foreign policy establishment, including the retinue of experts surrounding former Secretary of

State Henry Kissinger (who had most recently been Scowcroft's partner in a lucrative international consulting firm). Because of Scowcroft's prior experience as NSC adviser under President Gerald Ford, he was viewed in early press reports as a potentially powerful competitor to Secretary Baker. But within days after the inauguration Bush approved National Security Directive 1, which established a new process for making vital foreign policy decisions. The directive stipulated that Scowcroft would play a diminished role as NSC adviser. He would be a policy coordinator and an "honest broker" between any competing positions during administration debates.

Former New Hampshire governor John Sununu was appointed to be the President's chief of staff. He was given the task of being the administration's tough guy, a "pussycat with claws" as *The Washington Post* called him. Sununu took pride in his assigned role; from his first day in office he was perceived as Bush's gatekeeper, with the same kind of abrasive personality made famous by Nixon's chief of staff H. R. Haldeman. Sununu quickly gained a reputation as a partisan infighter, who put adherence to White House policy and loyalty to George Bush above all else. In his arrogant and self-centered manner, he was an indispensable aide who was willing to do the political dirty work that Bush found unpleasant. Part of Sununu's job was to make sure that the blame for White House policy gaffes was passed off to scapegoats on the Bush team, like William Webster, whom Sununu viewed as the administration's weak link. Webster, who had few supporters among Bush's inner circle, was perceived by Sununu as a tainted holdover from the Reagan years.

The surprise White House nomination during the administration's first days was Robert Gates, a Georgetown University Ph.D. and former lifelong CIA employee specializing in Soviet analysis. Gates had an impressive foreign policy résumé that compared favorably with any of the others in the close group around Bush. A native of Kansas, Gates entered the agency in 1968 and served his first five years as a junior analyst. In 1973 he was named assistant national intelligence officer for strategic programs. Gates first met Bush in 1976 and became one of his admirers and defenders during Bush's year as DCI. In 1977 Gates transferred temporarily to the NSC staff; in 1979 he became director of the CIA's strategic evaluation center. In 1981 Gates became the director of the CIA's Office of Policy and Planning; he was also named by Casey to be the agency's national intelligence officer for the Soviet Union and Eastern Europe. In 1982 he was named deputy director of intelligence. In 1983 he became chairman of the prestigious National Intelligence Council. He then became executive assistant to the DCI, and in 1986 deputy DCI. After Casey's death he became acting director of the CIA but was not confirmed by the Senate to win the job full-time. He then served loyally as Webster's deputy for nineteen months before Bush chose him as deputy national security adviser.

Casey's former special assistant, Herb Meyer, was one of Gates's earliest supporters at the CIA. Meyer went out of his way to tell Casey that Gates was an intelligent, acerbic, and outspoken analyst—a loyal admirer whom Casey could count on. Gates was just the kind of official that Casey was looking for in the DI to promote to a top position. "I'm a very big Gates fan," Meyer told a clandestine service officer in the early 1980s. "That guy is going places." While Gates already had established a large fan club at the NSC, Meyer's patronage helped keep him on the fast track in the intelligence community and made him an important figure inside Casey's small circle of advisers. Casey understood, however, that Gates was mistrusted inside the clandestine service, so he made sure to separate him as much as possible from senior DO officers, like Dewey Clarridge and Clair George, both of whom viewed Gates with suspicion. The continuing support of Casey and Meyer through the 1980s helped propel Gates to the top of the agency.

Gates's appointment to the Bush White House was initially perceived around Washington as a reward for his sacrifice during the final, scandal-ridden days of the Reagan presidency, when he graciously took himself out of the running as DCI. But the NSC assignment made more sense than most observers realized at the time, since Gates was one of the nation's leading Sovietologists. When Brent Scowcroft served as Gerald Ford's NSC director in the mid-seventies, Gates was his leading adviser on Soviet policy. He had impressed Scowcroft with his remarkable breadth of knowledge of Soviet affairs and his savvy political sense. President Bush also remembered Gates's loyalty in 1976, when he was DCI. Gates's gracious exit from consideration as DCI during the Reagan years had left an added feeling of goodwill. He seemed a perfect choice to be Scowcroft's deputy, since his selection was a signal that Bush's foreign policy would be centered on winning a series of sweeping arms control compromises with the USSR.

Gates's first assignment at the NSC was to bring order to the bureaucratic wreckage left behind by the Reagan team in the wake of the Iran-contra affair. He was named to head the NSC's Deputies Committee, comprised of the top aides to each of the major foreign policy bodies of the executive branch. It was an enormously powerful position that assured that Gates's views would gain the routine attention of the President. Gates set to work immediately after the inauguration to fashion a series of papers on key foreign policy questions. He was soon dabbling in every aspect of American foreign policy—from the opening of talks with the PLO in Tunis (initiated in the last months of the Reagan presidency) to monitoring the increasingly savage fighting between U.S.-

supported mujaheddin guerrillas and the remaining Soviet troops in Afghanistan. Gates was also instructed by Scowcroft to oversee covert operations. He was told to produce an internal paper providing Bush with guidance on which of the CIA's foreign operations should be retained and which scrapped.

Gates worked tirelessly to put his stamp on the new Bush team. His control of the Deputies Committee allowed him to exercise enormous power at the heart of the national security establishment. During the first months of the new administration Gates's two decades of experience at the CIA were given great weight during NSC discussions about foreign policy and intelligence issues. His influence was also reflected by his place in the White House pecking order. During the President's off-the-cuff press conferences Gates was often seen standing beside Scowcroft and Sununu, as part of the powerful new White House troika. From such visible signals it was soon obvious that Gates was serving as more than just Scowcroft's deputy. He was actually in virtual control of the day-to-day operations of the NSC staff, leaving Scowcroft to serve as a kind of deputy president for international relations, and as Bush's "official friend." At no other time since the beginning of the NSC system was a deputy given such public exposure. Although Gates rarely gave speeches or spoke to the press on the record—that was left to Scowcroft or Baker— it was clear that Bush prized his advice and viewed him as a gifted foreign policy thinker.

Ironically, Bush's opinion was not shared by many of Gates's former colleagues at the CIA. A large number of career officers had privately criticized Casey years earlier for appointing Gates as deputy director. While it was not uncommon to appoint an analyst, like Gates, to the CIA's second slot, his previous association with the NSC and his controversial views about mixing the work of analysts and operations officers riled high-ranking DO officials. For them, Gates was a "self-promoter" who was "out to make a name for himself." One CIA officer, who views him as "incredibly ambitious," says that this description is the only way to explain his meteoric rise from a mid-level position in the Intelligence Directorate ("he was just another Ph.D. down there," a CIA officer says) to the second most important position at the agency. Nor was Gates extolled as the Soviet expert that both Scowcroft and Bush thought he was. But those dissenting views mattered little, since Gates had won the backing of William Casey—who mattered the most. One DI analyst remembers a briefing where Casey sat "flap-mouthed" as Gates "recited the names of every Politburo member, their constituency, education, and party background, all without notes. It was like he had been living with these guys."

Gates's critics in the DI reply that this anecdote is misleading. His meteoric rise at the CIA is more the result of pure accident, they say.

In the early 1970s, they recall, Gates's otherwise undistinguished career as a Soviet analyst was given a major boost by confidential reports from a secret Russian agent code-named Trigon. This information from Trigon—about the USSR's border conflict with China—represented some of the best raw intelligence the CIA had ever been given. Gates, then still a junior analyst in the Office of Current Intelligence, was given responsibility for synthesizing the materials and passing his reports on them to NSC Adviser Henry Kissinger at the White House.

Kissinger was impressed with the value of this intelligence—it fit well with President Nixon's ongoing strategy of détente. He was even more electrified by Gates's insights, which were absolutely critical to Kissinger's decision to find an opening to China as a way of putting pressure on the Soviet Union. From that point on Gates's future sponsorship by both Kissinger and Scowcroft was assured. But, it turned out later, Gates's breathtaking rise through the CIA from then on had actually been based on a mistake. CIA officers later discovered that the Trigon reports were entirely fabricated Soviet disinformation. They had been passed to the CIA in order to convince American intelligence officials that the USSR was militarily stronger than it appeared. In 1977, when that fact was finally revealed (after the CIA cut off all communications with Trigon), it was too late. Robert Gates was already speeding on his way to the top.

The most negative views of Gates resulted from his discomforting self-confidence and innate conservatism. CIA officers thought he had a negative effect on Casey, because he refused to rein in Casey's visceral reaction to anything that even hinted at Soviet influence. "Casey would see the Russian bear behind every tree, and we needed someone to calm him down," a CIA veteran remembers. "What we got instead was this guy who gave Casey's bear added substance. They were of the same ilk."

Former CIA officer David Whipple has a different explanation. "I've always liked Bob Gates," Whipple says, "but he comes from a different side of the house. He has a different view of things than someone who's been in operations all his life. There's a prejudice in the operations directorate against a guy who doesn't have those kinds of experience."

Whipple's view actually understates the almost reflexive mistrust that CIA operations officers had for Bush's new national security deputy. At Langley, Bush's increasing reliance on the former deputy DCI went so far as to raise doubts about the President's loyalty to the intelligence community. Gates's appointment seemed to be a signal to the CIA's leadership that the President was going to depend on Gates to run the agency from his White House office.

At first Gates was careful to be anything but intrusive. During one of the administration's first national security briefings he went out of his way to praise Webster's grasp of intelligence issues. During subsequent

CIA briefings Gates always deferred to the DCI. Webster noticed Gates's respectful treatment and returned the favor by publicly dismissing rumors that Gates had been put in place to oversee him. Webster called such allegations "complete nonsense."

In spite of such denials, the Washington media establishment remained convinced during the first months of the Bush administration that Gates was running the CIA from his NSC office or was at least secretly keeping Bush up-to-date about activities on the agency's seventh floor. These rumors fueled other press reports that speculated about Webster's imminent departure as DCI. These articles, in turn, provided grist for more stories about White House-CIA skirmishes and criticisms of Webster's performance. These stories became a journalistic cottage industry during the next four years. Eventually, this slow drip-drip-drip of political gossip amounted to a kind of bureaucratic water torture. As a result, Webster aides had to spend much of their time buttressing his image as a competent, take-charge DCI.

To make matters more difficult for Webster's public relations team, during the first two years of the Bush administration reporters consistently exaggerated Gates's influence at the agency. In reality, Gates had only a handful of allies inside the DI and even fewer in the clandestine service. "If he'd called over here to ask what was going on, I doubt anyone would tell him," a CIA officer says. Nor was Gates particularly well liked in Webster's immediate circle. Richard Stolz privately dismissed reports of Gates's influence in the intelligence community. Stolz told colleagues that Gates's performance during his confirmation hearings had buried forever his chances for the CIA's top job. Stolz, like most others from the clandestine service, disliked the fact that Gates had spent part of his career at the NSC and had prospered during Casey's reign. Richard Kerr, appointed deputy DCI by Bush on the same day that Gates was given his NSC job, also remained unbowed by rumors about a Gates pipeline. "I don't pay attention to any of that," Kerr once told Webster. Even though Kerr was originally a protégé of Gates's, he was far more concerned with the day-to-day management of the flood of intelligence reports from around the world than with gossip that Gates was Bush's surrogate DCI.

Kerr, a career officer with a fondness for precision and details, appreciated Webster's stringent insistence that the CIA's intelligence product remain untainted by political considerations, a belief that he once described to an associate as "the only thing that really makes us an intelligence agency." He was also very sensitive to critics who believed the CIA spent most of its time watering down its foreign intelligence summaries. "It was always this 'well, if this happens—but it might not— then there's a small chance this will happen, unless this other thing happens,'" one well-known congressional CIA critic says. "It's clear the

CIA wasn't interested in sticking its neck out on anything because if they were wrong, then we'd say, 'Well, what do we need them for?' "

Kerr decided he would change that attitude. He spent his time as head of the DI making certain that papers not only were clearly written, but gave the CIA's best estimate of what the intelligence meant. A former analyst remembers one of Kerr's most dismissive comments, made after Kerr had read a précis of a paper on a minor aspect of Soviet agricultural production. "He didn't even look up from his desk," the analyst recalls. "He just said, 'Anyone can read this in the newspaper. Tell me what it means.' "

Kerr's greatest fear was that DI assessments would be polluted by political prejudices, and he knew that no matter how sensitive analysts were to his insistence on intellectual integrity, there was always a chance that reports would be crafted to satisfy their intended audience. "It's anathema," former DI head Ray Cline says, "for an analyst to produce something because he thinks it will go down better at the White House or State Department. It's worse than plagiarism. To twist a report, a paper, an assessment of any kind to fit the needs of conventional wisdom, to trim your sails, so to speak, well . . . it's just not done." Kerr worried that there would be another Iran-contra scandal, but that this time it would go unnoticed because it wouldn't involve shipments of arms or diversions of funds, and that the DI, where the bulk of the agency's most important work was done, would peg its bureaucratic survival to prevailing political beliefs in the face of incontrovertible facts. The implications of such an event, Kerr told an associate, were chilling. It would mean the end of the CIA. "We can pack our bags and go home," he said.

This was the most serious charge made against Gates: that he skewed intelligence estimates to curry political favor. Kerr did not want to believe the reports, but he realized that Gates's well-aired conservatism on U.S.-Soviet relations raised questions about his objectivity. Gates had toned down his anti-Soviet views during the more liberal Carter years and then, just as quickly, had become outspoken when Ronald Reagan was elected President. The changes in Gates's political views did not go unnoticed. "Anyone who can get along with both Stansfield Turner and then William Casey is suspect in my eyes," a recently retired clandestine service officer notes. "Bob isn't exactly a man for all seasons; he's a man for this season and then a different man for the next one."

What made these reports especially disturbing to Kerr was that he liked Gates and owed much of his own recent success to Gates's promotions. When Gates became William Casey's deputy, Kerr filled Gates's empty spot as deputy director of intelligence, and when Gates left to serve as Scowcroft's NSC deputy, he told Bush that Kerr should succeed him as deputy DCI.

However, Kerr believed that Gates had made a number of avoidable mistakes as director of intelligence that sparked an undercurrent of dissatisfaction with Gates's leadership. In his first day on the job, back in January 1982, for instance, Gates called a meeting of DI senior officers in the agency's bubble. After he was introduced as the directorate's newest head, he was given a resounding welcome; for analysts in the Office of Soviet Analysis, his appointment was viewed as a triumph. Their opinion of him changed, however, after hearing what he had to say about CIA assessments. "Gates disappointed us," an analyst present that day remembers. "We were just stunned by what he said. The first words out of his mouth were 'You're doing a lousy job.' We knew then that things were going to change."

Several of those who were present in the auditorium or watched his remarks on closed-circuit television describe Gates's presentation as "unforgettable," "astonishing," and a "betrayal of everything we stood for." While the new DI had intended only to make it clear that there would be changes at the CIA, the speech made him more enemies than friends.

"My assignments," Gates began, "to the NSC and the White House under three Presidents of both parties and close association with two DCIs have shown me our senior readers' side of the fence, the perspective of the policy maker. And there I have seen analysis that was irrelevant or untimely or unfocused or both, all three; failure by analysts to foresee important developments or events; close-minded, smug, arrogant responses to legitimate questions and constructive criticism; analysts pretending to be experts who did not read the language of the country they covered, who have spent little if any time there, who were oblivious to academic or private-sector research on the country and who argued that none of that mattered; flabby, complacent thinking and questionable assumptions combined with an intolerance of others' views... a predilection to write history, as opposed to looking ahead; poor, verbose writing; a pronounced tendency to confuse objectivity and independence with avoidance of issues germane to the United States and policy makers...."

On and on it went, for twenty breathtaking minutes, as Gates laid out a litany of charges of malfeasance, incompetence, incompleteness, tardiness, prejudice, stupidity, and isolation mixed with accusations of frivolity and outright laziness. "I intend to insure," he said, "that the primary focus of you and your managers is kept on the single purpose for our existence: Produce the best-quality intelligence available anywhere. That is my only goal." Gates's words stood as a ringing declaration from the early Casey years that the Directorate of Intelligence would change and things would be run the way that he wanted them run.

One of Gates's subsequent controversial decisions turned the intelligence directorate upside down. For thirty-five years the line separating analysts from operations officers was inviolate; the two directorates worked as distinct entities and cooperated only through reports officers. There was even a time when armed guards separated the offices of the clandestine service from those of the intelligence directorate. Fraternization was strictly forbidden and considered as heinous a crime as original sin. The reason behind the division was straightforward: The clandestine service was a policy-making organization and an arm of the President, while the DI was supposed to serve the truth, reporting it as objectively and completely as humanly possible. To mix the two would be like deploying the 82nd Airborne to Harvard Yard. The policy was set in stone; the separation of analysis from espionage was part of the agency's iconography. "The two never mesh," David Whipple says. "The DI would never disagree with an espionage operation because we would never know about it."

After telling DI officers they were doing a lousy job, Gates proposed a revolutionary change: Starting with his tenure as DI, analysts would be required to spend three to four weeks in overseas stations with CIA field officers. The policy established Gates as a powerful, and widely hated figure inside the CIA.

Robert Gates was only forty-five years old when President Bush appointed him Scowcroft's deputy, but despite his comparative youth, he was very much a foreign policy hard-liner—one of the many Russian scholars whose opinions on U.S.-Soviet relations were formed during the heart of the cold war. His mistrust of Soviet motives was an article of faith. In 1983, for instance, Gates described the Soviet threat as "the lineal descendant of the same threat Western civilizations have faced for three and a half thousand years; it is the threat posed by despotisms against the more or less steadily developing concept that the highest goal of the state is to protect and foster the creative capabilities and the liberties of the individual." Gates refused to change his views even after CIA assessments started to point out that Gorbachev's sweeping reforms were substantive and likely to be long-lasting. To his critics, Gates was not just out of step with significant changes in the USSR, he was ignoring the best intelligence estimates the CIA could provide.

Many CIA officials assumed that Gates's views inevitably would come in conflict with those held by his former protégé, Richard Kerr, even though Kerr was hardly a foreign policy liberal. As a recognized expert on Soviet military affairs, Kerr had access to the same reports as Gates. Unlike Gates, however, he believed them. Kerr was heavily influenced by Gorbachev's domestic initiatives and believed that they portended credible attempts to recast the U.S.-USSR relationship. Kerr wanted the United States to take advantage of the opportunities afforded by *perestroika*. His differences with Gates over Soviet reforms were not a matter of degree: Kerr believed the Soviet leadership was faced with an unprecedented economic and political crisis. He attempted to impress this view upon the chief of the Office of Soviet Analysis (SOVA), George Kolt, a strong Gates partisan. Kerr argued that Gorbachev's announcement that the Soviets would unilaterally cut their forces in Eastern Europe was a reflection of massive political changes inside the USSR that were little understood in the West. Gates's protégés inside SOVA disagreed. They held strictly to the Gates-Kolt line; they maintained that Russia's history was littered with the wreckage of reform movements that were inevitably followed by a xenophobic reaction. The current move to reform would end, they warned, and the Soviet Union would remain an implacable enemy of Western democracy.

The outlines of this heated debate inside the CIA were hinted at on February 28, 1989, when Kerr appeared before the Senate Intelligence Committee to be confirmed as deputy DCI. While Kerr had prepared well for this Senate hearing, he was caught unawares by the depth of concern among committee members that the CIA had failed to predict Gorbachev's startling announcement of unilateral military cuts. So, ironically, Kerr, who was inclined to see Soviet reforms as an opportunity, was forced to defend the views of CIA skeptics, the most prominent of them being Robert Gates. In this case Kerr fell back on a well-worn agency canard: that it was not the CIA's job to predict specific foreign policy moves. "Sometimes the people that are making the decisions have not yet made the decision that you're trying to predict," he said.

Kerr attempted to draw a distinction between the CIA's analysis of Soviet military moves—for which he was responsible—and the agency's views of Soviet internal reforms. He defended his own work, but without drawing attention to what he perceived as the narrow viewpoint of Gates's SOVA protégés. He said that several of his own assessments warned of specific Soviet initiatives on military reductions. Kerr admitted that he had misjudged the "magnitude" of the Soviet reform movement and that the agency faced a number of built-in problems in predicting Soviet behavior, but he defended the agency's overall product. There were enormous changes going on in the USSR, he testified, and the CIA was successfully reporting on them.

None of the senators who listened to Kerr missed his indirect criticism of the CIA's Gates-influenced assessments. But nearly all of them failed to understand the depth of feeling that Gates's views engendered. At the end of February 1989, the debate taking place inside the CIA about what was happening in the USSR was mirrored by the administration's own uncertainty. But just when this battle at Langley seemed primed to explode into public view, the agency was confronted with its first major intelligence crisis of the Bush years. As fate would have it, this sudden problem had nothing to do with the USSR.

9

★ ★ ★

Lao Pengyou

*T*he three men who made their way to the presidential cabin at Camp David on a cold morning in mid-February 1989 were old friends. They talked and smiled as they walked slowly, three abreast, over the wintry ground. On the right was James Lilley, the recently returned U.S. ambassador to South Korea. Lilley was a genteel, Yale-educated China analyst whose reputation was firmly established among the small group of top U.S. government experts on Asia. Next to him, walking in the middle with a distinctive rolling gait, was the more publicly well-known Professor Michael Oksenberg of the University of Michigan, the nation's leading expert on China. He was consumed by the subject of China and could talk about it for hours. The man on the far left was Harry Harding of the Brookings Institution. Harding, as gentlemanly as Lilley, if less outspoken, was fast becoming the elder statesman of Asia analysts—his name was repeated with reverence and his judgments on China were given great weight in government circles.

These three men were to be joined at the lodge by the President and two of the CIA's top East Asia officers, who had been flown to Camp David via helicopter. The special Camp David briefing was scheduled after President Bush announced that he would make relations with China a major part of his foreign policy agenda and would visit Beijing as his first overseas trip as President—a symbolic starting point for his four-year journey as President. For Bush's political advisers, the China trip was viewed as a chance for the new President to show off his foreign policy expertise and activist international plans with a high-profile entrance on the world stage. His arrival in Beijing would be nothing less than a triumphant return to a city where he had launched his quest for the White House. Bush had served as head of the U.S. liaison office in Beijing during the mid-1970s, at the beginning of China's opening to the West.

Bush took enormous pride in his China experience. He enjoyed telling the story of how he was slated originally to become an ambassador to either England or France until he pushed President Ford for the China job. "An important, coveted post like London or Paris would be good for the résumé," Bush wrote in *Looking Forward,* his political autobiography, "but Beijing was a challenge, a journey into the unknown." As Bush also knew, the Beijing assignment would look better on his résumé than nearly any other diplomatic appointment. Bush served only thirteen months in Beijing, but afterward he thought of himself as an authority on China's political structure and on the aspirations of the Chinese people. He had gotten close to the Chinese, Bush believed, soon after arriving in Beijing in September 1974, when he purposely shunned the trappings of his new office and took to the streets of the city as a native, pedaling his bicycle among the admiring crowds who called him, as he later noted, "Busher, who ride the bicycle, just as the Chinese do."

Bush's major contacts to the Chinese population actually involved a half dozen of the nation's increasingly powerful industrialists. This group of young entrepreneurs, centered in Beijing, later formed the core of the nation's new business class in the post-Mao era. Bush also got to know many of China's political leaders, including Vice Premier Deng Xiaoping, who later led China's modernization efforts. Bush's most significant and lasting friendships from his days in Beijing were to the network of leading American experts on China he met as a result of his tour of duty. The most important of these experts was James Roderick Lilley, one of the group of men who made their way to Camp David in February 1989.

Before Lilley began his diplomatic career, he had been a celebrated figure in the CIA's clandestine service, where he had served for over twenty-five years. Fluent in Mandarin, Lilley was described by CIA associates as a "thoughtful, intelligent, good professional" with a legacy as a cerebral, but argumentative operations officer. He took pride in his reputation as one of the few egghead activists on China ever produced by the CIA. If his well-known knack for making enemies inside CIA headquarters bothered him, he did not show it. In the 1960s—an era when the Near East Division was producing a corps of mythic figures, like Dewey Clarridge, the East Asia Division likewise could point to Lilley as its young, rising star. Lilley was the benighted competitor of Clarridge for the eventual leadership of the Operations Directorate.

There was little doubt that Lilley had the experience necessary to do the job: He began his CIA career in 1951 after graduating from Yale and served as an operations officer in Japan, Taiwan, the Philippines, Cambodia, Laos, and Thailand. He was named deputy chief of station in Laos in 1965; he took the same post in Hong Kong in 1968. When Bush arrived in Beijing, Lilley was already serving there as the first CIA chief of station ever posted to China. After Bush left Beijing to direct the CIA, Lilley also returned to Langley as the agency's national intelligence officer on China. That assignment made him the intelligence community's leading expert on Chinese affairs. Like Clarridge, Lilley remained one of Bush's most trusted aides during his nine months as DCI. Lilley retired from the CIA in 1978 and then served as a consultant for a number of U.S. corporations (including the Hunt Oil Company in Dallas). He returned to public service in 1980 as a late addition to the Reagan presidential campaign.

Because of his secret CIA background, Lilley was virtually unknown inside candidate Reagan's close circle of advisers until Richard Allen, a top foreign policy aide to the Reagan-Bush ticket, included him on a campaign team named to travel to China in August 1980. The trip was put together at the last minute to help repair the damage done to Sino-American relations in the wake of Reagan's controversial announcement that he thought the United States should recognize Taiwan as "the real China." The statement caused enormous problems, especially for Bush, who was worried that the statement might hurt the GOP's election chances.

Richard Allen vividly recalls the incident: "We needed to put to rest some of the bad publicity Reagan was getting about his views toward China, so I suggested to him that Bush and I should take a trip to Beijing and issue a statement on what we'd found. Bush and I decided that we would meet first at Kennebunkport, where he introduced me to Lilley. Bush asked if I minded if Jim went along on the trip to China, because he could serve as interpreter. I said that was fine with me."

Allen says that their three-man team put an end to the Taiwan controversy "in pretty short order, largely because we were tough with Deng Xiaoping. We just weren't going to throw our relationship with Taiwan away."

But that was not the whole story. During the 1980 trip to China, Bush and Lilley tried to reassure Deng and his colleagues that U.S. policy toward China wouldn't change—no matter what Reagan said about "two Chinas." But their arrival in the Chinese capital was chilly: Deng subjected them to a grueling questioning on U.S.-China relations in the Great Hall of the People. "He kept asking us: 'What do you think you're doing?' " Lilley remembers. "He was very upset, very angry. At one point he asked: 'Doesn't our friendship mean anything? Are you just going to throw us away?' We did our best to reassure him that Reagan wouldn't change U.S. policy toward China, but he just didn't believe us."

When the three Americans finally returned to the United States, they brought back a five-point program, written by Allen with Lilley's help, that recast Reagan's cold war views. The position paper was a bald attempt to slip a new program past Reagan, hoping he would agree with the views they had outlined without really realizing what they had proposed. But after they touched down in Los Angeles, the three unofficial envoys discovered that Reagan was intent on continuing his anti-China tirade. Their meeting with Reagan at a Los Angeles hotel was cooler even than Deng's greeting in Beijing. Reagan said that he not only was unconcerned by the public debate his China remarks had sparked but was going to give a new speech that would end the controversy. The address, which Reagan had written on yellow legal paper, terrified Allen and Lilley. As Lilley later explained: "If Reagan had read that speech on TV, we would have been at war. That's how bad it was."

Reagan's trusted adviser and future attorney general, Edwin Meese, intervened to head off the disaster. Bush brought Meese into the Los Angeles meeting with the express purpose of calming down Reagan; Meese was the one person who could do it. Meese first studied the speech in silence; then he coaxed Reagan into reading the carefully crafted Allen-Lilley document. Meese insisted that there really was not much difference between the two documents. With Reagan's top advisers looking on, the candidate reviewed the new five-point program. After a long pause Reagan nodded his head. He stared at Meese for a moment with a look of resignation on his face. "It was very emotional in a way because Reagan was just caught," recalls a former campaign official. "Reagan knew he had to rely on Meese, because, you know, he didn't have the vaguest. Allen and Lilley were a nervous wreck waiting for his answer. Finally, Reagan asked: 'Is this what you want me to say to the press?' Meese nodded. Reagan finally said: 'Well, ah'—you know the way he talks—and he said a couple more times, 'Well, ah . . .' and then he finally looked up and he was defeated. He knew it, and he said: 'Well, all right, if this is what you want me to read to them then I'll do it, I guess,' And he had a press conference and the issue just died."

Lilley's 1980 trip to China marked his initiation into the world of politics and transformed him from one of the CIA's former top East Asia experts to a formidable figure inside the Reagan White House. The metamorphosis, based on his continued backing from Bush and Allen, was swift and meteoric. After the China trip, Lilley was perceived as an administration partisan whose future success as a Reagan insider was assured. After Reagan's election Lilley was asked to serve as one of the transition team's key foreign policy advisers; after Reagan's inauguration Lilley became one of Richard Allen's leading East Asia experts on the National Security Council staff.

Six months later, when President Reagan needed someone to head the American Institute in Taiwan (the unofficial U.S. liaison office in Taipei), Lilley got the job. It was a surprising selection, Allen explains, in view of the fact that "it was very unusual for CIA people to be named to ambassadorial posts—it was taboo."

Lilley's nomination also surprised his former colleagues at the CIA. "He was one of the first former CIA officials, I believe, who were given that kind of post in any administration," notes a senior agency officer.

The Taiwan appointment should have marked Lilley's final transition from the world of spies to the world of diplomats. However, his selection sparked bitter resentment among State Department officers, who viewed him as "an interloper" and "a made-up diplomat." A State Department officer adds: "There also was quite a bit of opposition to the appointment because Lilley just wasn't liked at State."

This feeling grew more widespread in 1984, when Lilley returned to Washington to serve as a consultant to the Defense Department's bureau of International Security Affairs. The following year, he became deputy assistant secretary of state for East Asian and Pacific affairs, an assignment that was again bitterly opposed among the hierarchy at Foggy Bottom—where veteran diplomats traditionally mistrusted anyone transplanted from "across the river [at the CIA]." In 1986 President Reagan appointed Lilley to be U.S. ambassador to South Korea. After serving in Seoul for three years, Lilley returned to Washington in time to attend the inauguration of his good friend, George Bush. During the first days of the new administration Lilley's name was mentioned publicly in connection with several administration posts, including his old position as the State Department's assistant secretary of state for East Asian and Pacific affairs.

But this time senior State Department officials were so opposed to his presence that his appointment was effectively blocked. Deputy Secretary of State Lawrence Eagleburger, James Baker's second-in-command, was most often mentioned as the one official who quietly opposed Lilley's elevation and succeeded in derailing it. However, according to a high-level State Department officer, "Eagleburger and Baker didn't openly oppose him; they knew better than that. You just can't do that around George Bush." Eagleburger privately believed that Lilley was too conservative for the State Department post because he was thought to be "part of the pro-Taiwan clique." Eagleburger's opposition to Lilley also reflected the deep mistrust in the diplomatic community of transplanted former CIA officers. And it was a reminder that

Secretary Baker thought of himself as the dominant architect of Bush's foreign policy. "Baker didn't want any competition," observes a State Department official, "and that meant Lilley had to be pushed aside."

But President Bush could not ignore Lilley's claim to an important job in the new administration. The former national intelligence officer for China was a good friend and longtime political supporter who had been generous when it counted. Bush remembered Lilley's patient tutoring when he was the new, inexperienced U.S. envoy in Beijing. As a respected CIA insider Lilley had also helped smooth Bush's first days at the agency by reassuring his colleagues in the clandestine service that he thought the new DCI would do a good job. After privately conferring with Baker about Lilley's future in the days after the inauguration, Bush hit on a formula that would keep Lilley at an important post in the administration without offending the sensibilities of the State Department's career cadre: Lilley would be named U.S. ambassador to China, succeeding Winston Lord.

Bush was especially pleased with this solution because it meant that he would have his own man in Beijing. The only worry that remained was whether Lilley would become engaged in a test of wills with Baker over U.S. policy in the Far East.

But as Lilley made his way to the Camp David briefing a few weeks later, that possibility seemed especially remote. Prior to this February 1989 session Lilley and Baker had met privately to discuss the China job and to iron out any potential differences. Lilley was already aware of the hesitation from State Department officials that greeted his appointment. He told Baker that he considered himself a loyal foreign service officer, and pledged that he only wanted to stay on as ambassador in China for two years, instead of the usual three. Baker could not have been happier—the United States would be represented by a diplomat who was well known to the Chinese leadership, and his own position as the administration's leading foreign policy spokesman would be protected. He had Lilley's promise.

In many ways the subsequent Camp David briefing was a model of how Bush would handle foreign policy matters during his administration. After a round of pleasantries the two CIA officers began their presentation with a standard, fact-filled analysis of U.S.-China relations. (One administration official described this introduction as "a mélange of boiler plate statistics.") The CIA report specifically noted that "trade with China stood at $14 billion, the U.S. was China's third largest trading partner, 40,000 students were studying in the U.S. and the largest bilateral programs involved technical and scientific cooperation." The CIA briefing was followed by the personal assessments of Michael Oksenberg and Harry Harding on Chinese political developments. When they had finished, Bush turned to listen to Lilley's views on South Korea.

After listening to the three experts for the allotted two hours, Bush again turned to the CIA's officers and asked for a political rundown on changes in the Chinese politburo. The CIA's assessment was sanguine: The only threat to the Communist party's primacy, the officers said, came from a group of urban intellectual reformers with ties to the overseas Chinese community; the nation itself seemed free of internal dissent. In addition, the long-running power struggle over who would succeed Deng Xiaoping as China's paramount leader was winding down—with a group of conservatives led by politburo member Li Peng emerging as the winners. Therefore, the CIA's East Asia analysts concluded, the possibility of a major political crisis in China seemed remote.

When Lilley left Camp David, he was pleased with Bush's decision to make China the destination of his first foreign trip. Such an official visit would show that the new administration viewed its relations in the Far East on a par with those of the Soviet Union. Lilley knew that America's relations with China would become even more important in the years ahead, as the Chinese leadership began to look outward. Not everyone in the Chinese Communist party agreed with that strategy, but so far Deng had been able to keep these differences out of the public eye. The CIA was right. The chance that there would be a revolution from below in China seemed remote. But as Lilley himself had warned on more than one occasion, anything was possible.

The first report that a brutal massacre was under way in the western district of Beijing, more than a mile from Tiananmen Square, came late in the evening on June 3 (Chinese time), four months to the day after Lilley's name appeared in newspaper accounts as Bush's choice to be ambassador to China. From their vantage point on one of the upper floors of the Yanjing Hotel, U.S. intelligence officers looked down at a crowd of at least one thousand protesters facing off against a brigade of soldiers, tanks, and armored personnel carriers from China's 27th Army, which was pushing the crowd east toward the square. As the students chanted their defiance, several of the soldiers randomly opened fire, bringing forth screams from those packed into the middle of the street. Undaunted, the crowd continued to surge forward. As soldiers knelt and raised their weapons to their shoulders, a second, coordinated volley cut down more of the demonstrators. Behind the riflemen, a tank sprayed machine-gun rounds into the stores along the avenue. The crowd moved back to a barricade erected near a bridge leading into central Beijing, leaving half a dozen bleeding bodies in their wake. Stunned by the brutality of what they had just witnessed, CIA officers inside the hotel contacted the U.S. Embassy using their secure radios. The first report was transmitted at precisely 10:03 P.M.

Several minutes later, these CIA officers reported a new development: Chinese soldiers had sprayed the Yanjing Hotel with bullets and then turned their guns once again at the protesters. Several minutes later, with the crowd re-formed and standing its ground, a third volley of intense automatic weapons fire left even more bodies on the street. The crowd then responded with a new tactic: The demonstrators sang "The East Is Red" and the "Internationale." Meanwhile, groups of students manned barricades along the streets, from which they made forays against the tanks and personnel carriers behind the line of soldiers. Within two hours after the first attack, student commandos had successfully disabled and set ablaze a dozen army trucks. Four trolley cars— part of the barricades along the western extension of Chang'an Avenue, which led directly to the square—were burned by the army. The battle raged, without letup, for nearly four hours.

These opening moments of the massacre of pro-democracy demonstrators in central Beijing were later vividly described by reporter Peter Thompson. Thompson, in another part of Beijing, listened in horror to the distant sounds of combat. "We could hear popping sounds," he said, "and we thought that they must be tear gas, but then the sound became a quicker pop-pop, and we knew that that had to be automatic rifles. What was shocking was that we heard the roar of crowds and then the firing of machine guns, and the roar would die away but not the firing." It was later reported the "Internationale" was sung by Beijing Normal Teachers College students, "who linked arms and marched forward in an insane and terribly courageous attempt" to stop the advance of the tanks making their way toward the square.

From his office inside the American Embassy nearly three miles to the east of the battle raging along Chang'an Avenue, U.S. Ambassador Lilley heard the same distinct sounds and knew that what he had feared the most over the last several days had finally begun. "The demonstrators will be removed from Tiananmen," he had told the CIA's Beijing chief of station four days before the start of the crackdown. "The army is committed to ending the protests, by force if necessary."

The station chief had shaken his head in disagreement. He told Lilley that the agency's best information was that China's leaders would not move to break up the demonstrations anytime soon. He was confident of this assessment. He dismissed Lilley's warning with a wave and a shrug. As if to underscore these assurances, the station chief left China two days later on the long trip back to CIA headquarters in Langley, Virginia, for routine consultations. No one was bothered by his absence until the massacre began; then they all remembered what he had said before he departed: Don't worry, nothing will happen while I'm away; if the Chinese Army was going to attack, it would have done so already.

The COS's decision had disastrous consequences: His departure left the CIA's secret network of agents and other sources inside China in disarray. To make matters worse, other key members of the U.S. Embassy staff chose to flee Beijing out of fear for their personal safety within days of the Tiananmen crackdown. Half a dozen State Department officials and even a small number of CIA employees returned to the United States. Only five major embassy officers, including Ambassador Lilley and the State Department's chief of intelligence, were left behind to deal with the growing chaos of a huge nation that appeared to be on the edge of civil war. On the basis of his rank and experience—and the coincidental absence of the COS—Lilley became America's de facto chief intelligence officer in Beijing for the first time in fourteen years. Fortunately, he had predicted almost to the hour when the Chinese politburo would order the attack, so he was able to dispatch a number of surveillance teams to monitor the crackdown. One of these teams was in the Yanjing Hotel, one was in the Beijing Hotel to the east of Tiananmen Square while another was posted inside the square itself. Two other teams were posted in the Beijing Toronto Hotel and in the Friendship Hotel, just to the south of the square. Late on the afternoon of June 3 the command post at the Yanjing reported skirmishes between the army and student protesters. But it wasn't until 10:03 that the real battle started.

As the battle moved from west to east down Chang'an Avenue toward Tiananmen, Lilley received reports from his other command posts. While a massacre was under way in western Beijing, things were relatively quiet to the east of the square, though a second contingent of troops were visibly confronting crowds of people near the foreign diplomatic compound. Other soldiers had also taken up positions outside the Beijing Hotel just outside the east rim of the square. Small skirmishes were reported east of the embassy. Inside Tiananmen Square itself, Lilley was informed, a large number of students continued to rally around the "Goddess of Democracy" statue, which had been erected by demonstrators a month earlier.

At the Beijing Toronto Hotel, where Lilley and his staff had decided to house American students who wanted to leave China, a confrontation between protesters and troops was just getting under way. Later in the early morning the soldiers were told that there were Americans in the hotel, and they shot out their windows. For nine hours after the first fighting began, Lilley diligently reported all this news to the White House and State Department via an open phone line. The next morning, after the crescendo of violence had peaked and then subsided, he signed off, finally overcome by emotional exhaustion and deeply embittered by what he had witnessed. His last report noted that soldiers were still shooting onlookers near the square, including one woman who was shot in the back. In all, at least one thousand (and perhaps many more) pro-democracy demonstrators and their sympathizers died on the streets of Beijing on June 3 and 4.

By far the most interesting report Lilley had received during the early-morning hours of June 4 came in to him just before 2:00 A.M. from an American intelligence team posted inside Tiananmen Square. The report said that Chinese security officers were circulating among the remaining encamped students and urging them to leave. "The army is coming," one officer told a protester. "They're going to kill you." The assessment from the U.S. observers included a detailed description of "negotiations" between student protesters and security officers. The discussions were puzzling; they led the American intelligence team to speculate that a special security unit had been sent into the square in advance of the army with the express purpose of averting bloodshed. If true, it meant that not everyone in the Chinese leadership wanted to bring a violent end to the demonstrations. There was division and disagreement among China's leaders—there seemed to be no other explanation.

According to CIA monitors, the Chinese security teams had also set up loudspeakers, which then broadcast warnings that the students should leave the square peacefully. Security officers on buildings surrounding the square looked down at the students, some motioning them to leave and pointing west, in the direction of Muxidi. At 4:00 A.M. the lights in the square were extinguished as a warning. Finally, the handful of pro-democracy leaders still inside Tiananmen agreed to leave, but only if they could retrieve a semblance of victory. They would march out of the square together, they said, singing the "Internationale" as they left. At approximately 5:00 A.M. the students inside the square—their ranks swollen by demonstrators who had fled the bloodshed in other parts of the city—marched out of Tienanmen, heading east toward the Beijing Hotel.

It was then, just as dawn was breaking, that the worst bloodshed of June 4 occurred. As the large crowd of students passed in front of the Beijing Hotel, they collided with another huge crowd of demonstrators retreating in their direction as soldiers from the 27th Army pursued them from the east, pushing them toward the square. Through a tragic coincidence in timing, these battling protesters retreating westward had bumped into the large group streaming out of the square itself. In the resulting chaos, the soldiers coming from the east opened fire and kept shooting. The slaughter lasted for nearly one hour. The bodies of those killed were stacked three deep outside the hotel lobby.

The evidence that the CIA has since compiled on the Tienanmen massacre indicates that military commander Yang Shangkun (China's ceremonial president) sent the 27th Army into Beijing to strengthen his position inside the politburo. The vicious slaughter was purposely planned by President Yang himself, even though he had not obtained the unreserved approval of the top man in the party, paramount leader Deng Xiaoping. While Deng had agreed that units of the People's Liberation Army (PLA) should be deployed to Beijing to suppress the prodemocracy movement, he was shocked by the violence that resulted. Another key politburo member who opposed the violence in the streets was China's internal security chief, Qiao Shi. The CIA and several leading American experts on China concluded that a significant struggle took place in the midst of the Tiananmen attack between Yang and Qiao. That's why Qiao's security officers attempted to clear the square without bloodshed. They thought Yang was trying to take over the government.

Lilley was horrified by the slaughter and, in a meeting of embassy personnel on the day after the attack, referred to the Chinese leadership as "bankrupt." Upon reflection two years later, he was still emotionally shaken and even more enraged by what he had seen. His voice filling with anger, he referred to the Chinese leadership as "those greaseballs, those thugs," and when reminded that Deng Xiaoping, the most powerful man in China, often referred to him as *Lao Pengyou*—an almost affectionate Mandarin term that means "old friend"—Lilley laughed bitterly. "Not anymore," he replied. He was also deeply scarred by the controversy that followed in the United States—when the American press criticized him for not moving quickly enough to draw up plans for the evacuation of American dependents.

In the aftermath of Tienanmen, Lilley and other American experts on China had agonized over whether they should have anticipated the crisis better. Lilley readily admits that no one who briefed George Bush at Camp David in February 1989 was able to predict the tumultuous events that occurred in the streets of Beijing four months later. While Lilley told Bush at one point during the Camp David briefing that he thought "a leadership struggle" was under way in China, he had advised that the battle was nearly resolved. (Conservatives inside the Chinese politburo had successfully blocked reformer Zhao Ziyang's attempts to enhance his chances to succeed Deng as paramount leader, Lilley said, and in doing so, the conservatives had turned China even more decisively away from the West and democracy.)

Nor had President Bush's triumphant return to Beijing in February 1989 resulted in any new thinking about what was going on inside China's political institutions. It was noted in Washington that the death in April of well-known Chinese reformer Hu Yaobang had given China's reformers new life. But there were few, if any, voices inside the CIA or elsewhere in the U.S. government that believed that China's slumbering pro-democracy forces would suddenly arise in his memory. Nevertheless, considering the CIA's massive recruiting efforts in China during and after the Cultural Revolution, the events of June should not have come as such a surprise.

For more than twenty years China had remained the CIA's greatest puzzle. After the collapse of Chiang Kai-shek's Nationalist Army in 1948, the agency was left without any appreciable human intelligence sources inside the new revolutionary Communist government. During the first years of the People's Republic the CIA relied almost exclusively on a dwindling number of nationalist agents who either remained behind after the Communist triumph or were brought into China from Taiwan. In those years CIA operations in China paralleled the current activities being run in the Soviet Union, though with even less success; as in Eastern Europe, the United States attempted to recruit émigrés as intelligence agents, but also as in Eastern Europe, the networks the CIA established proved ephemeral. In the mid-1950s the agency changed its strategy and attempted to recruit Chinese bureaucrats at the People's Republic embassies in Africa, Asia, and South America. However, the few successes of these early years were more than offset by a number of stunning intelligence embarrassments: The CIA failed to predict the Chinese Army's intervention in Korea; the CIA failed again to foresee China's detonation of an atomic weapon, and, perhaps most embarrassing of all, the CIA was itself penetrated by the Tewu, China's foreign intelligence agency.

Long before this penetration was discovered, the most notorious Chinese spy case of the 1950s involved a woman whom the Chinese code-named Lily Petal. She had arrived in the United States posing as Min Chiau-sen, an American who had actually drowned off the China coast when the ship she was on sank during a journey to her native land. The Chinese recovered the body and immediately sent Lily Petal in her place to New York to set up a spy network. Her team continued functioning productively for the next thirteen years. The CIA suffered a more serious setback in that decade, however, when, in late 1952, one of its spy planes was shot down over northeastern China. The pilot, Jack Downey, alias John Donovan, and his CIA passenger, Richard Fecteau, were captured, tried, and convicted of espionage by a Chinese military tribunal.

Another incident in that same year had a shattering impact on the CIA for over three decades. In 1952 the Chinese recruited Jin Wudai, known at the agency as Larry Wu-Tai Chin, in Okinawa, where the CIA was establishing a series of electronic listening posts to spy on the mainland. Chin spent thirty-four years at the CIA passing details of its most secret programs back to his handlers in Beijing.

The head of the CIA's East Asia operations during the 1950s and early 1960s was Desmond FitzGerald, a charming, wealthy, and well-connected Bostonian who later went on to run the entire operations directorate. From Langley, FitzGerald ran covert programs against China that were based in Taiwan, where paramilitary units trained for operations against the mainland. Fitzgerald's second-in-command was Ray Cline, a Harvard and Oxford graduate who became the CIA's chief in Taipei and later rose to be deputy director of intelligence. (For a time Cline was even considered the DI's first real candidate to become CIA director, though as he now acknowledges, "it just wasn't in the cards.") FitzGerald and Cline commanded some of the most talented, and controversial, groups of espionage officers in the American intelligence community. Although they recruited few really valuable human sources inside China itself, they enjoyed several notable successes against Chinese stationed in other countries, especially in operations against Tewu units based in Africa. The most important of these successes, which has been publicized, occurred later, in 1966, when the CIA engineered the overthrow of Ghana's Kwame Nkrumah and replaced him with a government that quickly expelled three hundred Tewu advisers.

The CIA's most significant triumphs against Mao Zedong's regime were scored during the Cultural Revolution (from 1965–1973), which sparked a virtual civil war in China and inside its overseas embassies. In September 1966 the Central Committee's Investigation Bureau (the Diaochabu) dispatched special security officials to Chinese embassies to purge "traitors, revisionists, and CIA agents." The internal investigations and firings that followed split the Chinese diplomatic community and resulted in a windfall of agents for the CIA. The Chinese witch-hunt even resulted in summary executions. In Holland, for instance, an engineer named Xu Zicai was rushed to a hospital after he was found beaten and tortured along a road near the residence of the Chinese diplomatic staff. He told Dutch authorities that he had been accused of working for the CIA. Within days he was kidnapped from the hospital by a Chinese commando unit and returned to the embassy, where he later died of his wounds. Similar incidents involving Chinese nationals occurred throughout the world. According to one CIA officer, who graduated from the agency's China Operations Course, the purges were unusually vicious in Africa, where CIA operations had been particularly effective in blocking China's efforts to penetrate the continent's most viable liberation movements.

"Anybody with any brains could see that the Chinese had big problems coming after the Cultural Revolution" explains this same CIA officer. "Their overseas operations were in chaos because of the splits that the movement caused. Their important program to penetrate and liaise with liberation movements in Africa fell apart by the late 1960s." The CIA's most intensive, and successful, recruiting efforts took place during those years. According to a former East Asia division officer, the Cultural Revolution split Chinese embassies into three factions. "The hard-liners," he explained, "were mostly at the top. The rehabilitated Cultural Revolution people were right in the middle. The rest were radicals of the revolution. So we got into the mid-level and identified the people who had been hurt by the Cultural Revolution. Then we tried to recruit them."

Among the most valuable Chinese agents that were recruited during the Cultural Revolution was a large group of China's most respected scientists, writers, and diplomats. "Their security and intelligence officers treated these scientific and technical people like shit," a former East Asia Division veteran recalls. "The embassies were just blowing up. These people would do anything to change things in their country. We discovered that they were the most dedicated agents we had ever had. They gave us whatever we wanted."

One of these windfalls included detailed information on China's secret science and technology program. In the mid-1970s officers from the East Asia Division recruited one of China's top missile scientists, who gave the CIA precise intelligence on Chinese nuclear capabilities. This information documented that the Chinese had made greater progress in developing nuclear weapons and missile delivery systems than CIA analysts had previously realized. The disclosure should have tipped off the CIA to the presence of Larry Wu-Tai Chin, who by then had been passing U.S. nuclear secrets to the Chinese government for more than twenty years.

"We were shocked to learn that the Chinese had a small, sophisticated, but significant intercontinental [missile] delivery system," another former CIA officer says. "They had technically proficient computer systems which they had some help on. Apparently some of the plans for these systems were stolen from the United States."

In 1971, when President Nixon and Henry Kissinger orchestrated the U.S. opening to China, few U.S. officials could have guessed that one of the results of the normalization would eventually be cooperation between the CIA and Tewu in a series of joint ventures aimed at deterring Soviet expansion in Asia and Africa. In 1974, for instance, CIA analysts concluded that the Soviets were secretly arming the Popular Movement for the Liberation of Angola (MPLA) in an effort to make the newly freed Portuguese colony a pro-Soviet ally in southern Africa. In response the CIA created an Angolan Task Force that distributed nearly twenty-five million dollars in covert aid to anti-MPLA groups during the next year. The Chinese joined in this effort by providing small arms to anti-MPLA fighters through CIA stations in South Africa, Zambia, and Zaire. The Chinese continued the anti-Soviet operation even after the CIA was barred by Congress from supplying the rebels with any more aid.

By far the most successful of these joint operations took place in Afghanistan, where Sino-American interests coincided to help arm and train mujaheddin guerrillas fighting the Soviet army. The Chinese supplied the guerrillas with weapons (paid for by CIA funds), which were transported overland from China to Pakistan along the Karakoram road, a seven-hundred-mile mountainous link between the two countries. In late 1988 the CIA also helped fund a massive construction project that paved this China–Pakistan road all the way to the Pakistani border. The CIA and Tewu set up joint training camps for thousands of mujaheddin warriors along the Pakistan-Afghan border, in Peshawar, and in southwestern China, where they received machine guns, rocket launchers, and antiaircraft missiles.

CIA-Chinese cooperation in several large-scale intelligence programs also provided the agency with a window on Chinese military capabilities—something it had never before had. This was especially true in the Afghan operation, which provided new insight into the difficulty China had in arming its troops. According to a former CIA officer, mammoth logistical problems plagued the joint Sino-American operation in Afghanistan during its first year. Afghan guerrilla leaders complained that many of their weapons did not match, while others simply didn't work. The Chinese have a significant small-arms industry, but their inability to supply sufficient amounts of shells for their weapons led CIA analysts to conclude that the Chinese probably had difficulty keeping their own army units supplied with ammunition. A number of CIA analysts and operations officers involved in the program also concluded that the Chinese were dumping some of their outdated weapons in Afghanistan and using American funds to purchase modern weapons for their own army. The Afghan Task Force debated whether to ask U.S. officials to complain about the dumping but decided to simply note the information without comment.

The unforeseen benefits of Sino-American cooperation in Afghanistan resulted in a number of startling new conclusions about the state of the People's Liberation Army (PLA). In one report CIA researchers observed that some Chinese Army units were better supplied than others, apparently because they were more trustworthy. The conclusion (that there were moderate and hard-line elements inside the Chinese military) seemed to prove a long-held assumption among China watchers—that there were deep disagreements over national policy inside the Chinese elite. It was quite possible, CIA analysts concluded, that in times of crisis (especially during a battle over party leadership) the PLA might not be as loyal to the government as the party's politburo believed. A top secret intelligence paper prepared at the end of 1988, entitled "Chinese Military Modernization—Looking at the 1990s," hinted at possible divisions in the army resulting from the leadership's inability to provide adequate training and weaponry. The report noted that China was selling its "antiquated weaponry"—some of it, still, to Afghan guerrillas—to fund a new modernization program. "Group armies in the northeast will probably continue to get the best available personnel and equipment," the report concluded.

The short legacy of Sino-American cooperation in many areas was not present in Cambodia, however, where authorities from the two large powers backed different factions of anti-Vietnam rebels. The Chinese provided massive shipments of small arms, mortars, and tanks to the Khmer Rouge. The arms, funneled through corporations owned by high-ranking Thai military officers, caused political embarrassment for successive American administrations and fed rumors that the CIA was also secretly supplying Pol Pot's guerrillas. (The agency has consistently condemned these reports as "fabrications.") Yet, these charges undermined American diplomatic efforts to resolve the Cambodian civil war and led to an undercurrent of tension between the United States and China in the waning days of the Reagan administration. Still, it was the common opposition to the USSR that kept the alliance together.

Fear of Soviet expansionism in Africa and Asia was so intense that nine years after Henry Kissinger's trip to Beijing, American and Chinese intelligence officials agreed to a joint technical collection program, a cooperative Sino-American intelligence-sharing operation that targeted Soviet nuclear and missile test sites in eastern Asia. The resulting mammoth and expensive construction project established two listening stations in Qitai and Korla in the desolate Xinjiang Autonomous Region in western China. These two posts are manned by tandem intelligence teams of Chinese and American technical experts under control of the NSA. The technical materials obtained by the stations are transported daily to the U.S. Embassy in Beijing by a Chinese intelligence team (and are shared with Chinese military officers). The CIA also runs two other intelligence-gathering posts in cooperation with the Chinese, a radar installation code-named Cobra Dane and an intelligence collection ship, code-named Cobra Judy.

The weight that the United States placed on the value of CIA-Chinese intelligence cooperation became clear in the immediate aftermath of the June massacre. While the administration took a number of highly publicized steps to signal American displeasure with the Chinese government, it was clear that President Bush was unwilling to go so far that he would sacrifice the nation's twenty-year intelligence accomodation with the Chinese. The brunt of the criticism against the Bush administration—for being soft on the Chinese actions—was leveled at Ambassador James Lilley, who was already under fire in the American press for his alleged reluctance to tongue-lash Chinese leaders for sending the 27th Army into central Beijing. During a trip back to the United States to confer with Bush after the Tiananmen massacre, Lilley was heckled by human rights activists during a stopover at the airport in Seattle. He lost his cool. "You don't know what you're talking about," he angrily shouted at them. After a videotape of this embarrassing incident was broadcast on national television, Bush was forced to defend the actions of his ambassador. When public pressure mounted on Bush to recall him, the President praised Lilley as "one of the best listening posts we have in China."

But that was not what Lilley's detractors inside the NSC and State Department were saying. At the same time that Lilley was being subjected to criticism in public for his "soft stance" on China, he was being disparaged in private by officials at the White House and Foggy Bottom for being too tough. At the heart of the conflict was Lilley's belief that U.S.-Chinese relations were too dependent on their mutual suspicions of the Soviet Union. Once the Soviet threat disappeared, Lilley argued, so too would the underpinnings of America's relationship with China. Lilley diligently conveyed his controversial views to Bush in two separate Oval Office meetings, in July and December 1989. The United States was being blackmailed by the Chinese, he warned. The American government should stand up to China's leaders and —as he said—"call their bluff." He also reiterated that America's policy in China was "reactive" and "too dependent on Soviet actions."

Lilley's strategy of "decoupling" the U.S.-China relationship from its dependence on a common enemy gained adherents in the CIA, where China analysts had been busy recasting their previous thinking since the June massacre. The pro-Lilley faction at the agency argued that the Tiananmen crisis showed that China's military and the internal security service were engaged in a bitter battle over Chinese domestic policy. They cited numerous intelligence reports to buttress their claims. During the days leading up to the crackdown, they pointed out, more than two thousand Chinese Army officers were dismissed for their support of the pro-democracy movement and for openly calling on the regime to meet the students' demands. Some soldiers were even executed. The purges continued well after the events of June, as army units of questionable loyalty were transferred and downgraded. There was also widespread dissension in the ranks of the Chinese security service, which produced a windfall of new agents for the China branch of the CIA's East Asia Division. In addition, the democracy movement had made inroads inside the security organs, whose officials mistrusted China's military leaders.

The President's top advisers, however, were more intent on criticizing the CIA after Tienanmen than in pushing it to take advantage of the new leverage the incident would give to U.S. foreign policy in East

Asia and the Pacific. William Webster was castigated in administration circles for showing himself to be a weak and ineffective leader of the intelligence community, and for failing to provide adequate warning of the crackdown. The criticism was especially intense among those who saw China as the linchpin of America's anti-Soviet world strategy. If the United States had been able to predict the problems of late May and early June, the critics said, it might have been able to head off the final reckoning. While Lilley and others privately dismissed the criticism, their position was consistently undermined by the CIA's inarguably poor performance, symbolized by the return of the chief of station to his post, three days after the 27th Army moved into Beijing.

The Bush administration's view of China as a strategic counter to Soviet influence in Asia had a powerful impact on U.S. policy in the region. In the wake of the Tiananmen massacre, this policy had an even more critical effect on one of the agency's most dangerous covert programs. It was for this reason that Operation Yellow Bird—the unofficial name for the clandestine rescue from China of the most important pro-democracy leaders—remains one of the Bush administration's most closely guarded secrets. Bush's principal foreign policy advisers—Brent Scowcroft, James Baker, and Robert Gates—feared that the program would enrage China's leaders, and perhaps even throw them into the arms of the Soviets. Nevertheless, the broad-ranging covert rescue effort gained Bush's full support. "Let's put it this way," says a former CIA official, "the agency would have never done what they did in China after the massacre if they didn't have approval from the White House. There was a presidential finding."

For a six-month period following the June 4 crackdown, a network of dozens of the CIA's most valued agents in China, Hong Kong, and Macao provided a safe haven and a means of escape for the most important organizers of the pro-democracy movement. Bush and the CIA actually had little choice in endorsing this CIA program: They knew that the agency's extensive network of contacts on the mainland made a presidential finding redundant, since an underground rescue effort would be launched by U.S. agents no matter what Washington said. In fact, Bush's finding had endorsed a program that was already well under way; it had actually started on the day of the massacre.

The shadow of Langley's hand can be discerned in several little-publicized incidents that took place in China following the bloodshed in June. On the morning of the massacre, for instance, two of the pro-democracy movement's most important leaders, Wuer Kaixi, of Beijing Normal University, and Li Lu, a fellow student from Nanjing University, mysteriously disappeared despite the best efforts of China's security apparatus to find them. By the last week of June two other leading dissidents, Wan Runnan, a leading scientist, and Yan Jiaqi, an adviser to pro-democracy politburo member Zhao, made it to the West. The escape of all four was made possible by a network of supporters who supplied them with ready-made identity cards, large amounts of cash, phony train tickets, and a series of safe houses along an "underground railway" that led from Beijing to the southeast, where the dissidents were smuggled aboard boats for the treacherous open-sea journey to Macao or overland to Hong Kong. Such a sophisticated operation could not have been conducted without at least the tacit cooperation of the CIA.

An indication of the CIA's role was foreshadowed by Lilley's decision to help the most endangered pro-democracy leaders make it to the West in the days preceding the crackdown. During the last week of May, Lilley had blithely handed out U.S. visas to more than two hundred Chinese intellectuals, scientists, and students and on several occasions even lent money (from the embassy's special contingency fund) for train and airline tickets to Hong Kong and safety. In the immediate aftermath of the slaughter Lilley also provided logistical support for U.S. intelligence assets searching for a way out of China. It was, in the words of one of his colleagues, "reminiscent of our retreat from Saigon, though this time we weren't going to leave our friends behind." In several other instances Lilley's successful appeal for the release of arrested students was followed by their "arranged disappearance" from Beijing. Many of these young people later made their way to the West. In the absence of credible agency leadership in China, Lilley was once again the CIA's Beijing chief of station.

All this was done "under the nose of the Chinese security police," a CIA East Asia officer notes, but it was not done without their connivance—at least in some few cases. The Chinese Communist party had a well-established web of millions of informers spread throughout the country, which created a huge obstacle. But the security apparatus was in some cases paralyzed by the events of June 4, in large part because of the perception that President Yang Shangkun and his relatives, the so-called Yang Dynasty, had subverted public order in an attempt to wrest control of the party apparatus from China's leading reformers.

Because of these feelings against Yang and the army, some security officials were persuaded to cooperate in the escape of students and other dissidents. On the day following the Tiananmen massacre, Chinese astrophysicist Feng Lizhi made his way to the U.S. Embassy escorted by a group of journalists. Feng knew how to use the press for protection; he had once even hidden in the hotel room of a noted American reporter. According to a serving CIA officer, Feng's escape to the embassy was so easy that it would not have been possible "without the cooperation of the Chinese security organs." Ambassador Lilley, still eager to protect sources and methods, offers only a vague explanation. "China is not the most competent totalitarian government," he observes. No matter how Feng arranged his escape to the embassy, it is evident in several other instances that pro-democracy leaders could not have made their way to the West without the tacit assistance of Chinese security officials. Some of these officials may have even worked with CIA agents in Beijing and in other parts of the country.

In the vast majority of cases, however, the Communist party network and the Chinese security police diligently stalked the fleeing dissidents. Large numbers of these protesters were eventually arrested, tortured, and then executed. During the first week after June 4, thousands of students were detained. Within two weeks a list of the twenty-one "most wanted" pro-democracy leaders was publicized throughout the country. As the Communist party reestablished its power over the nation (the Beijing massacre sparked major disturbances in seventy Chinese cities), it became more and more difficult for the large network of pro-democracy sympathizers to organize and conduct their operation successfully. It was during this most critical period, from the beginning of July to the end of December 1989, that a large group of agents, recruited in the years that followed the Cultural Revolution, turned to the agency for assistance.

Operation Yellow Bird, though initially organized by pro-democracy sympathizers based overseas, soon came under the watchful eye of the British consul general in Hong Kong and of high-ranking French overseas intelligence officers in Macao. The CIA station in Hong Kong initially maintained an "arm's length" relationship with these pro-democracy sympathizers. Within a short time, however, the station began to provide advice and support to the rescue effort through a large group of American recruits on the mainland. Fortunately, the CIA was well positioned to help the operation. The credit was due to the remarkable work of CIA East Asia expert John Gilhooley, whose unprecedented recruitment of Chinese agents in the early and mid-1980s provided the contacts necessary to make the operation a success. Although Gilhooley had died before the Tiananmen crackdown, his most important networks on the mainland were still intact, and they provided the first contacts between the rescue underground and the groups in Hong Kong and Macao.

The CIA's most significant contacts in Beijing, meanwhile, came from the small groups of students who had provided security for the demonstrators in the square. One of these units, the "Dare to Die Brigade," was especially vital, since it contained some of the most fearless and dedicated members of the pro-democracy movement. Agents previously recruited by Gilhooley in Hong Kong and on the mainland made contact with the Dare to Die Brigade in mid-May, during the height of the demonstrations, in order to assess the composition of the movement's

leadership and to evaluate the chances for its eventual success. These
initial contacts proved to be even more valuable in the months following
the Tiananmen massacre, when brigade members formed the core of
the rescue effort.

The close ties between the network of Hong Kong and Macao sympathizers and what became the Beijing to Shenzhen "underground railway" grew throughout July and August. As the operation expanded, it
adopted more sophisticated methods to avoid detection, including the
use of disguises, scrambler phones, night-vision gunsights, infrared sig-
nalers, and speedboats and weapons for offshore operations. A CIA
officer confirms that "most of the high-tech equipment was supplied by
the agency" through front organizations set up for that specific purpose
in Hong Kong. But the program was "never a full-blown" or "solely
sanctioned" CIA operation, even though many of the agency's most
important contacts inside China were involved. A number of Western
intelligence agencies played significant roles in the success of the underground—particularly the British, French, and Americans—which accomplished the remarkable feat of rescuing fifteen of the twenty-one
students and organizers on China's "most wanted" list.

Several weeks after the Tienanmen massacre, a group of students,
dissidents, and intellectuals smuggled out of China appeared before the
press in Paris to announce the formation of a Chinese democracy movement in exile. The establishment of such a group was the crowning
achievement for Operation Yellow Bird (which continued to secretly
transport dissidents to the West). Even so, CIA officers refused to acknowledge their role in the operation; the agency silently followed the
lead of the beaming U.S. Secretary of State Baker, who publicly thanked
the French government for "cutting the red tape" and allowing those
who escaped China to take refuge in France. For all the world knew, it
was the French who had masterminded the rescue operation.

Six months after the rescue effort began, near the end of President
Bush's first year in office, the wall of secrecy surrounding Yellow Bird
began to crack with the first public disclosures. Privately, CIA officers
expressed genuine surprise that the American public accepted the cover
story that the U.S. government had not assisted the French rescue effort.
CIA officers remained quietly bitter that they did not receive any of the
credit. But the Bush White House did not want to crow about Operation
Yellow Bird, again because of their obsessive fear that China would be
driven into the hands of the Soviet Union if the full extent of CIA
activities were exposed. The CIA thought there was no such risk—a
reinvigorated Sino-Soviet alliance was just not possible.

CIA officers involved in the rescue operation believed that the White
House preoccupation with Sino-Soviet relations was reflected in President Bush's decision to send Brent Scowcroft on a secret mission to

China just months after the Tienanmen massacre. The NSC adviser arrived in Beijing at the very moment when CIA agents were involved in high-seas gun battles with the same force that had brutally suppressed the pro-democracy movement on June 4. The unpublicized Scowcroft mission was an extremely bitter pill for those CIA officers who had recruited young Chinese dissidents who were risking their lives to bring democratic government to their country. Two of these dissidents (who still cannot be identified) were among the most important CIA agents ever recruited in China. They were captured after the Tienanmen massacre and then disappeared, silently, into China's gulag, where they were presumably executed. While Scowcroft was shaking hands with the Chinese leadership, the fate of these two brave Chinese citizens remained unknown.

10
★★★
Negligent Homicide

The China crackdown faded from the headlines by midsummer, only to be replaced by the troubles in Panama, where a sexually driven pockmarked general with a fascination for voodoo provided strong evidence that the United States prized anticommunism above all else, even if it meant supporting a dictator whose hatreds were psychotic. The CIA recruited, nurtured, paid, praised, and defended Manuel Noriega for three decades as a way to demonstrate its promise to win the costly twilight struggle with the Soviet Union. But, by mid-1989, the price it was paying for clinging to Noriega was proving to be too steep.

America's mishandling of Panama was seen as the CIA's failure. In the public's mind, Langley's support for Noriega was, at best, an example of its incompetence; at worst, it was a reason to believe that the agency wanted to strangle democracy in Central America. Customarily the CIA did not respond to such allegations in public. In private CIA officers argued that they were just following orders that originated in the White House. The CIA's defenders protested that the agency should not be held accountable for the Panama debacle any more than they should be blamed for the murders in central Beijing. Noriega, they said, was the collective responsibility of every President from Eisenhower to Reagan, all of whom tended to view Panama as a pleasant backwater—a Graham Greene–like country of wide-brimmed hats where anti-Castro zealots could still purchase humidors of Cuban cigars.

The most vocal critics of the agency and Noriega were dismissed by CIA professionals, who argued that America's political ideals could be firmly established only in societies that were stable (meaning anti-Communist). The superpower conflict made people like Noriega possible, even necessary. Even a case officer as respected as Alan Fiers, the former head of the Central America Task Force and once one of the rising stars in the Directorate for Operations, later admitted that the battered Latin American Division was brimming with people who ached for a victory, "just one victory, somewhere," against the spread of Soviet influence.

Noriega was perceived in the intelligence community, therefore, as much less of an embarrassment than the public considered him to be, and far from the satanic figure presented by the press. In the words of one CIA officer, Noriega was "a son of a bitch, but he was our son of a bitch." The dictator's constant anti-Americanisms and his humiliating and arrogant bullbaiting were irritating, to be sure, but he had provided an island of certainty in Central America at a time when the agency desperately needed one. Noriega was an avowed supporter of American efforts to overthrow the Sandinista government in Nicaragua. For those veterans of the L.A. Division's quiet wars—who lived every day with the fact of their past failures against Fidel Castro—Noriega's help was the only thing that mattered.

From a different perspective, the CIA's longtime support for Noriega helps to set straight much of the conventional wisdom about how the American intelligence community operates. The commitment to the principle of intellectual integrity is a notion so powerful inside the CIA that it has become its unofficial creed: No intelligence assessment should be tilted by political considerations, no raw information should be tarnished by partisan predilections or personal ambitions, and no estimate should be corrupted by prejudice. The truth itself must be reported, no matter how embarrassing or dangerous.

This unassailable creed, a solid first principle of intelligence, has enabled the CIA to promote unpopular and controversial positions. The agency's warnings on Vietnam, for instance, have taken on heroic proportions: Retired CIA officers take great pleasure in pointing out that they consistently warned President Johnson that the United States would be defeated in Southeast Asia. But what these officers fail to add is that in choosing whichever intelligence they collect, they have already *made* a political choice, whether they want to admit it or not. And such choices often influence the conclusions they draw.

This was the case with Manuel Noriega and helps to explain, at least in part, why the CIA seemed so willing to defend him. As long as the agency refused to investigate (or, more important, chose to ignore) Noriega's ties to international drug traffickers, his common friendships with arms merchants, his association with international terrorists, his money-laundering schemes, and his crude murders, then CIA officials could claim that they did not actually *know* at all. This is what drove Senators John Kerry and Jesse Helms to rage: that CIA officers could listen to the allegations, claims, and arguments of members of Congress, journalists, and foreign policy experts and blandly respond that they could not say for certain whether the charges were true or even really important. Up until 1989 these evasions were routine because the overarching concern of the CIA was not really Panama at all but the Soviet Union. Central America was considered critically important mainly because it was one of the CIA's battlegrounds with the USSR.

Once the U.S. government decided after World War II that the Soviet Union was the single most significant threat to American freedom and democracy, all of the CIA's subsequent moves had followed from that premise: the Mossadegh coup, the overthrow of Arbenz, the civil war in the Congo, the Bay of Pigs, the Cuban missile crisis, the massacre of Communists in Indonesia, the disaster in Vietnam, the murder of Allende, and support for the contras. The very raison d'être of the CIA as a special instrument of foreign policy was predicated on the belief that the Soviet Union might triumph if the agency did not exist. The CIA's effectiveness was largely measured by how well it thwarted, or failed to thwart, Soviet designs.

The difference in the winter of 1989 was that the Soviet threat was disappearing, which gave Noriega a new prominence. The CIA was forced to redefine its thinking and reformulate its intelligence targeting; in many ways, Noriega was the agency's first post–cold war challenge, a dictator who was a non-Communist threat to the United States. Noriega had become more than just an embarrassment; he was now an intelligence target and an enemy of the Bush administration. The new assessment had a remarkable effect on the CIA. When told to gather intelligence on Noriega's transgressions, the agency was able to comply with unusual speed (since much of the information was already at hand). In approximately eight months leading up to February 1989, Langley was able to put together an intelligence portfolio cataloging Noriega's sins that went beyond anything that either Senators Kerry or Helms could have hoped for. Suddenly CIA officials were Noriega's biggest critics.

The Pentagon's enthusiasm lagged well behind this bandwagon for two main reasons. First, military intelligence officers, who were barely able to conceal their disdain for the CIA's past tutelage of the Central American dictator, were now disgusted by the agency's swift conversion; they had been reporting for years on Noriega's transgressions while Langley maintained a diligent silence. More important, the nation's highest-ranking military officers were looking out for their own interests.

They feared that they would be called upon to resolve the Panama mess with a military operation that would likely be both controversial and bloody. The most powerful proponent of this view was the chairman of the Joint Chiefs of Staff, Admiral William Crowe, who had long opposed using force in Panama. Crowe was simply unwilling to jeopardize America's standing in the Canal Zone, where thousands of U.S. dependents remained as potential hostages to Noriega's violent whims.

The CIA and Pentagon clashed over what to do about Noriega for half a year before Bush became President in early 1989. This struggle, primarily waged as a paper war—fought out through conflicting intelligence reports—sometimes ignited into vitriolic battles between the anti-Noriega group centered in the CIA's Latin America Division and a large group of military officers serving in the upper echelons of the DIA and Defense Department. (The CIA's station chief in Panama, in particular, was convinced Noriega could be removed with little trouble while the Pentagon dismissed such optimistic predictions.) These battles illustrated the differing views in Washington about how to shape American intelligence policy in the post–cold war era. The debate showed that the traditional conflict between the CIA and Pentagon continued even though the Soviet monster was being exorcised. In the end the two bureaucracies were even accused of using the fate of an American intelligence officer for their own purposes.

February 26, 1989, was a fairly typical day in Panama. It rained in the morning, then cleared and rained again, and then cleared for good in the early afternoon. At the American base at Fort Clayton, the military routine that began at the turn of the century, when the United States claimed a thin stretch of land to build a canal from the newly independent nation of Panama, seemed outwardly unaffected by the Noriega dictatorship. After a series of nasty confrontations, American citizens, Zonians, as they were called, shied away from contact with the Panama Defense Forces. But there was no overt sense of crisis. Noriega was looked upon by the Zonians as a crazy man, who would have to be dealt with by his own people.

At about midday on the twenty-sixth Colonel Gerald E. Clark—America's foremost soldier-diplomat in Central America—drove out of Fort Clayton and headed for a meeting with an American intelligence officer. He laid a briefcase of important documents on the seat next to him. Two hours later, at about twenty minutes after two in the afternoon, Clark returned along the same route—what the Panamanians refer to as Omar Torrijos Avenue and the Americans call the Gaillard Highway. Suddenly an oncoming car filled the lane in front of him. The crash that followed was catastrophic. Clark's car was thrown across the highway, coming to rest on the roadway's shoulder. The small car that struck him head-on then hit another car and ended up just a few feet away from Clark, on the same side of the road.

The subsequent report from the Department of the Army's Criminal Investigation Division (CID) noted: "Victim: 1. Clark, Gerald Edmund (Deceased); COL; 387-50-3398; 27 May 42, San Juan PR; M; White; Headquarters, United States Army South (USARSO), Ft. Clayton, RP, Violation of Article 133, Panama Penal Cod (PPC); Negligent Homicide (as a result of a tragic accident)."

According to a medical report filed later, Gerry Clark died of severe injuries (multiple trauma, laceration of the spinal cord, and a severed aorta) sustained "secondary to a car accident." His death, which had been nearly instantaneous, occurred after an automobile driven by a Panamanian national inexplicably swerved into his lane and struck his car head-on; the front end of Clark's small Toyota sedan was almost totally destroyed and the tires were blown out in succession from front to back. A third car in the lane opposite Clark was also involved; one of its passengers, a middle-aged Panamanian housewife on her way to buy vegetables, suffered multiple fractures and a concussion. Her husband, who was driving, wept openly at the side of the road, believing his wife was going to die. Across the road Clark sat motionless, slumped over his steering wheel.

Photographs of the accident provided by the CID's Panama Field Office reflect the near-total destruction caused by the impact of the crash. Almost miraculously the two passengers in the oncoming automobile, which had been obtained from a nearby International Rent-a-Car office, were not fatally harmed. The twenty-five-year-old driver, an unemployed and propertyless Panamanian, suffered a concussion and loosened teeth and was hospitalized for a number of days. His companion, a nineteen-year-old Panamanian student, suffered only facial bruises and was released the day after the accident. Neither of them had been drinking; both of them were accomplished drivers who were wearing safety belts. (Clark, as was his habit, was not strapped in.) The accident occurred during the daylight hours on a straight stretch of road that was not particularly hazardous, (although witnesses confirmed that there were often accidents on the three-lane highway as the result of illegal passing).

There never seemed to be any real initial doubt that Colonel Clark had died as the result of an unforeseen and tragic accident. Military police officers who arrived minutes after the crash testified that it would have been almost impossible to stage the incident. Nor was there any evidence to suggest that any of the Panamanians involved were employed in any official capacity with the Noriega regime or worked for any intelligence agency. (Military intelligence officers even checked to make certain that no one had been secretly communicating by way of walkie-talkie near the scene of the crash.) The sudden accident was so startling that none of the survivors were able to reveal the exact chronology of circumstances that led to it. When asked how many vehicles were involved in the accident, for instance, the driver of the third car said he could not remember because the crash "was so unexpected that I could not see what happened."

Despite these initial judgments, the Pentagon immediately dispatched a special three-man investigative team to Panama City to find out if Clark had been murdered. A second team, comprised of officials from the State Department's Office of Diplomatic Security, traveled to Panama to follow up on the military's investigation. Clark's DIA colleagues and CIA officers have privately confided that the agency also sent a special team of investigators to Panama to conduct their own inquiry. Before any of these investigators had filed a preliminary report, the Pentagon sought to lessen public speculation by forcefully insisting that Clark's death was "an unfortunate mishap." A senior Army officer was assigned to make certain that all press inquiries were handled quickly and categorically. "Gerry Clark died in an automobile accident," he stressed. "It was an accident. There is no story here."

Such quick and absolute denials were enough to raise anyone's suspicion. From his DIA office in Washington, Colonel James Coniglio, part of the triumvirate of officers who served as defense attachés with Clark in Central America, was particularly disturbed by the circumstances of his colleague's death. "It just seemed so odd at the time," he recalls, "so I started to ask questions. We were all very upset by this." Coniglio was eventually satisfied with the answers he received. "I went to people who would know," he says, "and they told me that they were certain that it was an accident. I'm satisfied in my own mind."

Coniglio accepted the official version of Clark's death because it also fitted what he fondly called "the profile" of one of America's "most competitive, most dedicated" intelligence officers. "Anyone who thinks that this was staged has just got it all wrong," Coniglio adds. "If you had ever driven with Clark you would know what I mean. This accident was certainly not beyond explanation." According to Coniglio, Clark lived a fast life in Panama and took risks every day that others found unacceptable—both at work and behind the wheel of his car.

Suspicions about Clark's death lingered anyway because of the dangerous nature of his secret work. Not only was Clark a topflight DIA officer schooled in the back-alley politics of Latin America, but he was also engaged in Panama in what had to be considered one of the most harrowing missions he had ever undertaken. Officially Clark was on assignment to the 470th Military Intelligence Brigade located in the Canal Zone, but he was actually conducting a survey of the viability of the opposition forces arrayed against Noriega. Where possible, he was also supposed to help their efforts. According to two Pentagon intelligence officers, it was a closely held secret that Clark's assignment was not given to him by the Defense Department but rather by the CIA, which specifically had requested his services to run its anti-Noriega campaign in Panama.

Clark's mission certainly was not lost on the group of military investigators charged with determining the cause of his death. At the time of the accident the colonel was carrying a briefcase packed with classified papers and had just returned from a meeting with a U.S. official who was also in contact with Panamanian opposition figures. A day earlier Clark had attended several meetings with leaders of Panama's "Herrera Group" and was helping to coordinate their opposition efforts.

Clark was well suited for this job. He not only had encountered Noriega several times during the previous five years, but was the officer who had escorted Colonel Herrera Hassan from Israel to Washington when the U.S. government had sought to gain his cooperation in the anti-Noriega effort. Despite State Department doubts about Herrera Hassan's abilities and heavy pressures from a pro-Noriega faction at the Pentagon and CIA, Clark pushed for the establishment of an opposition group with the Panamanian colonel as its leader. In the words of one DIA officer, Clark "vouched" for Herrera Hassan; while Clark acknowledged that Herrera Hassan might not be the perfect choice for the job, he was dedicated and fearless. In the end Clark's experiences in Panama proved to be frustrating. "Gerry just didn't think we were doing enough," says a former DIA colleague. "The Herrera Group was a mess; the propaganda effort just wasn't serious. Noriega was more entrenched than ever."

For Clark, Noriega represented the worst of Latin America—he was a stereotypical pseudo strong man who had gained popularity by playing on the traditional anti-American sentiments of the population. Clark thought Noriega was "a schoolyard bully" and "a snarling dog," a true enemy of the United States. According to opposition figure José Blandón, who was visibly shaken by the news of Clark's death, Clark "despised Noriega, and the feeling was mutual." U.S. Army Colonel John Cash, who served with Clark in Central America, agrees: "For him, Noriega was an embarrassment." Clark understood from experience that Noriega could not be removed from power through negotiation or simple political manipulation. (Clark had witnessed the vain attempts by State Department officer Michael Kozak to coax Noriega out of office a year earlier.) Clark told his colleagues that the only thing that Noriega really respected was raw power. At every opportunity, therefore, he pushed for an escalation of America's anti-Noriega program.

Clark's almost legendary hatred of Noriega was a key reason why the official explanation of his death began to erode in the months that followed. The first sign of discomfort among U.S. investigators occurred in mid-March, when Panamanian officials privately claimed that they had exposed the unreleased negatives of the photos taken during Clark's autopsy. The incident remains unexplained and puzzling—especially because Panamanian authorities had promised to turn over their autopsy conclusions to the U.S. Army but then always refused to do so. In April journalists familiar with Clark's work in Panama began to hear rumors that he might well have been the victim of a purposeful attack. These suspicions were heightened when the U.S. government refused to turn over to the public its own findings on Clark's death; the doubts were then compounded by the unwillingness of Panamanian officials to respond to routine questions about the accident. A number of Clark's friends believed that his death at least deserved something more than a pro forma investigation.

The first break came in mid-April, after Senator D'Amato learned about the doubts surrounding Clark's death. Then a new member of the Senate Intelligence Committee and an outspoken critic of the Reagan and Bush administration's ineffectual efforts to remove Noriega, D'Amato was enraged that the U.S. colonel might have been murdered. "That son of a bitch," D'Amato said in describing Noriega, and then, for emphasis, repeated the epithet. He ordered his staff to conduct a separate investigation of the incident. The day after the outburst D'Amato questioned Secretary of the Army John Marsh about Clark. Marsh replied that a further investigation of the accident was under way but that there were no indications so far of any foul play. D'Amato thereafter received official assurances that there was no reason to suspect Clark was murdered. While D'Amato's own staff investigators eventually came to agree with that conclusion, the senator's continuing skepticism on the events surrounding Clark's death reopened the case, and a second official team was sent to Panama, in May 1989, by the Pentagon.

These investigators, however, had enormous difficulty in obtaining permission from the Noriega government to look into the Clark case. They were thwarted by the authorities at every turn. Panamanian police officials were uncooperative, even insulting, about the American investigation. They failed to show up for appointments or turn over any of their evidence. Even something as simple as obtaining permission to photograph Clark's vehicle met with resistance. It was as if they purposely wanted to feed the rumors about Clark's death.

Even more startling to U.S. investigators was the refusal of Panamanian officials to cite the driver of the car that had caused Clark's death with any criminal misconduct. Nothing had been done despite the fact that the driver of the car that had swerved in front of Clark's vehicle did not have a valid driver's license. It was not until late May, at U.S.

insistence, that the young Panamanian driver was officially charged with negligent homicide.

The man's subsequent explanation of the events preceding the accident is vague on details, full of inconsistencies, and more than a little suspicious. On the night before the incident, he said he had been at a party where he was asked "by an acquaintance of mine" named "Pocho"—whom he had never met before and could not identify to investigators—to meet him at a hotel the next day to help him pick up a car that would then be delivered to an unknown location for an unknown purpose.

"Well, Pocho showed up," the driver said, "and told me to go pick up the car that was being lent to him and that the automobile was located by San Miguel. Pocho gave me a note which authorized me to pick up the vehicle. Upon arriving [in] the San Miguel [area] by the Nueva Gloria Bar...stood a young man whom I had never seen before and whose name was unknown to me. I gave him the note and said to him: 'Pocho says that you are to give me the car.' He did not want to give it to me, so he began to call [over the phone] to I don't know whom and since his call could not get through, he decided to give it [the car] to me, [even though] he would not trust me as to what I was telling him."

Prior to the accident, the driver added, he had been visiting his girl friend, "whose name I do not remember."

Neither could the man remember anything about the car—who had told him to get it, the name of the rental agent, or where it was to be delivered. U.S. military intelligence investigators obtained a copy of the rental agreement, but it was almost incomprehensible. A knowledgeable Pentagon official claims that CID officers could not find witnesses to the accident either during March or April, and they discovered that key parts of the witnesses' previous testimony were contradictory. But the most suspicious stumbling-block remained the driver, since he could not even remember some simple facts about his own life. And at no time during the investigation did the driver show any remorse whatsoever about his role in Clark's death, even though he was indisputably responsible for the accident.

In the end the Pentagon could do nothing with these suspicions. Colonel A. T. Rossi, the head of the preliminary U.S. investigation, wrote in April that the evidence they found was persuasive that "the death of Col. Gerald E. Clark...was just an unfortunate highway accident." Three weeks later the second group of American investigators dispatched to Panama came to the same conclusion. Their report noted: "Further investigation into the circumstance surrounding the death of Col. Clark has been accomplished due to new allegations that he was intentionally murdered.... The accident in which Col. Clark died occurred on a well-travelled road on which drivers frequently pass illegally and unsafely. It is nearly inconceivable that an accident which would require split-second timing and a driver willing to risk his own life in a head-on collision could be successfully orchestrated."

Questions about Clark's death were supposed to be laid to rest with this final report. Yet Clark's DIA colleagues remained strangely embittered by the way the investigation of the February 26 traffic accident was handled. If Clark had been murdered, only one man might have ordered it. Under those circumstances, General Noriega's life would surely be forfeit; at the very least the United States would have been forced to act against him.

The highly political nature of Clark's death had been evident since three days after the accident, when he was buried with full military honors at Arlington National Cemetery. It was clear from the throng that attended the memorial service that Clark was a popular officer. One of those in attendance, Panama opposition figure José Blandón, remembers: "All the people who were interested in Central America were there at the funeral—good Panamanians, bad Panamanians, people from the CIA and the contras, Ambassador William Walker from El Salvador, Bob Pastorino [from the NSC], Elliott Abrams, and Nestor Sanchez. It was dead quiet."

As the service was about to begin, Colonel Oliver North arrived to pay his respects. Everyone knew that North had been Clark's contentious competitor and an officer he blamed for many of the problems he had confronted earlier in Honduras. North's appearance caused a murmur to run through the crowd. "I was surprised Ollie showed up," a Clark partisan says. "It was a little much, very inappropriate really. This [the service] was for Clark's friends. I don't see how North could claim that."

Inevitably, Clark's death became a subject of widespread concern in the intelligence community. In effect, those officials who raised questions about the Pentagon's investigation of the accident essentially formed the heart of the anti-Noriega group that had gained prominence inside the CIA. For them, Clark's death (even if it was accidental) came to symbolize the ambiguities of the crisis in Panama; the very fact that Noriega was even mentioned as the possible mastermind behind an assassination was cause enough to accelerate a program to overthrow the Panamanian dictator. DIA officials, on the other hand, were willing to take a more moderate view. They conceded that Clark was an important U.S. military intelligence officer, but they maintained that his role in assisting the Noriega opposition would not have made him a target for murder.

The controversy over Clark's death unveiled a larger and more serious debate in the intelligence community over the Noriega problem—it bared the distrust and suspicions that characterized the CIA and Pentagon's views on what to do in Panama. Colonel James Coniglio, who knew Clark as well as anyone, said it best: "I would be very, very careful if I were a reporter about printing allegations of Clark's murder. I know that there are people in this government who would like it known that Colonel Clark was killed by Noriega. They need a reason to get him."

During the first six months of 1989, Manuel Noriega purposely incited a program of intimidation against Americans living in Panama in an arrogant attempt to win the support of his own people. The often violent incidents threatened civilian lives and tweaked American claims to superpower status. In January three PDF soldiers assaulted an American woman; in February a U.S. Army sergeant was attacked by Noriega soldiers; and a few weeks later Panamanian police ordered twenty-one school buses full of hundreds of American children stopped for license plate violations (this incident turned out to be a nerve-jangling warning of what might happen to American dependents if the United States pressed its campaign against him).

A DIA intelligence summary issued in the midst of these episodes reported that there were "almost 1000 total harassment incidents in the past 13 months" aimed solely at terrifying Americans. Another summary written at the time detailed U.S. vulnerability. "The incidents involving the Panama Defense Forces range from treaty violations and intrusion on U.S. installations to detentions without charge and severe beating," the military intelligence report concluded. "Detentions without charge are prevalent; 292 such incidents were logged from February 1988 through the end of February 1989." The memo added that there were "20 cases of U.S. personnel physically attacked by the PDF."

It is no wonder, then, that President Bush's top advisers were convinced that the crisis in Panama was one of his most pressing concerns. This was certainly the view of Secretary of State Baker, whose first week in office was consumed by a series of detailed briefings on the increasingly dangerous situation. At one of these meetings Baker was handed a thick folder of sensitive CIA reports that documented that Noriega had become more than just a potentially fatal political embarrassment for George Bush; he was a full-blown threat to American security. One CIA memo, in particular, gave a blunt assessment of the danger the United States faced; the agency reported that Noriega had received well over twenty million dollars from Muammar al-Qaddafi, ostensibly to keep his government alive in the face of previously imposed U.S. economic sanctions. "We didn't have to state the obvious," an intelligence analyst familiar with the briefings says. "It was clear from our reports that Noriega had aligned himself with terrorists." Another special intelligence summary sent to Baker in February explained that the Noriega-Qaddafi connection had started in September 1988, when the CIA first confidently reported that U.S. financial penalties were having an effect. "The economic sanctions have now taken serious hold," the CIA reported. "Noriega has run through his Libyan money."

Baker also received classified reports on a number of mysterious incidents in which U.S. and Panamanian soldiers had clashed in open fire fights near American bases—episodes that had been kept quiet up until that time. U.S. intelligence agencies believed one incident may have actually involved Cuban military commandos, who engaged in a raid on an American tank farm in the Canal Zone. The raid began in the darkness of early morning, when Marines guarding the tank farm were fired upon by unidentified soldiers wearing "black camouflage uniforms using assault rifles and mortars." The fighting continued for "2½ hours," but miraculously the Americans suffered no casualties. Similar incidents, the CIA told Baker, were not only possible, but likely.

On the basis of such CIA reports, it was evident that the internal agency dispute over what to do about Noriega had ended—with at least a partial victory scored by his opponents inside the CIA's Latin America Division of the DO. In retrospect, the agency's leadership clearly concluded that something had to be done, if for no other reason than to show that it was distancing itself from its past relationship with the Panamanian dictator. After the consulting study by the GAMA Corporation was completed, the CIA inaugurated a special espionage program recommended by senior officers in the clandestine service. Using foreign agents as its primary reporting source, the agency established a complex and highly sensitive program that targeted Noriega's funding sources in Europe, Asia, and South America. A special task force on Panama was also created inside the DO to review the raw intelligence data received from sources in banks in England, Switzerland, South America, the Cayman Islands, and Panama itself.

Perhaps the most valuable intelligence was obtained in Switzerland, where the DO was passed revealing documents on Noriega transactions from a high-level executive of the Discount Bank and Trust Company of Geneva, in which the Noriega government and several Panama corporations had large deposits. Throughout the last days of 1988 and the early part of 1989, the CIA reported, both Noriega's personal money and Panamanian corporate funds were surreptitiously transferred from Geneva to a bank in the Cayman Islands, to bring them closer to Panama. While some intelligence analysts speculated the transfers might represent "capital flight" by Panamanian businessmen, CIA officers were more inclined to view the transactions as evidence that Noriega feared the United States might gain access to his funds.

The CIA's data on these transfers were given to the State Department in the form of a top secret memo written by the Bureau of Intelligence and Research: "The Panamanian branch of Switzerland's Discount Bank and Trust Company on July 5 [1988] transferred over

U.S. dols 236 million to the books of a bank in Grand Cayman, according to Special Intelligence."

None of this information was a salve to Baker, who was convinced that Noriega could survive the economic pressures by ruthlessly stripping Panama of its remaining assets. This view reflected the conventional wisdom inside the Bush administration, which viewed the value of the sanctions suspiciously. Four months after the CIA's espionage program began, administration officials were arguing that sanctions alone could not remove Noriega—regardless of the assurances Langley had previously given. The administration pointed out that its position was reinforced by the CIA's own intelligence: Noriega could obtain funds from any number of sources, including foreign banks, confiscated property, and allies like Qaddafi.

In early 1989 the CIA's view of sanctions began to change. Previously, throughout 1988, the agency had blithely assured President Reagan that the sanctions had "taken serious hold." But CIA officials were unwilling to make the same claim to President Bush six months later. Nagging doubts about the sanctions' effectiveness and worrisome reports that U.S. corporations were ignoring the administration's barriers had undermined Bush's efforts to use economic pressure to force Noriega from office. But Bush had painted himself into a corner regarding what his administration would do about Noriega; during the fall campaign he promised the American electorate that he would not engage in negotiations with the dictator about his voluntary retirement, while CIA officers involved in the internal debate over what to do about Noriega insist that the agency continued to give the White House "accurate and timely intelligence" on the political situation in Panama. After February 1989, it is clear that Langley slowly shifted its position to reflect President Bush's own thinking: The only way to get rid of Noriega was to remove him forcibly from power. The sanctions, the CIA conceded, were just not working.

Military intelligence officers, on the other hand, remained just as convinced that the sanctions would eventually work, since the Pentagon wanted to avoid military action in Panama. To back up the military's position, the Pentagon launched a broad attack that called into question every claim made by the CIA to Secretary Baker in February. The most outspoken anti-CIA critiques were circulated by DIA officials. In one defense intelligence summary, Pentagon officers openly scoffed at the CIA's breathless reports of Qaddafi's efforts to bankroll Noriega. "Suggestions have been made that cash could be obtained from outside sources such as drug traffickers or Libya," the widely circulated DITSUM noted, "but few tangible developments concerning these sources have been reported." This initial slap set the stage for a bareknuckle battle between the DIA and CIA over how to handle Noriega.

The opening shot of this interagency fight was fired when the CIA recirculated a top secret intelligence report that had first made the rounds during President Reagan's last year in office. It was titled "Hawari operatives travel to Panama to mount operations against U.S. interests," and the CIA noted that the head of the Hawari/Special Operations Group—the intelligence and security arm of the PLO—was planning a major terrorist attack against U.S. assets in Panama. The CIA memo was unusually detailed. "Three Lebanese Palestinians, traveling on genuine, true name passports, have departed Lebanon for Panama where they intend to mount terrorist operations against U.S.-registered ships in the Canal Zone. Following this, they plan to travel to the U.S." The report added: "A second team of three Palestinian operatives departed Beirut for Panama in early September. While in Panama, the six operatives also will attempt to infiltrate other operatives into the U.S. by stowing them away on ships headed for U.S. ports."

This report and a subsequent high-level briefing by counterterrorism officers on Noriega's ties to a variety of radical Palestinian groups brought the equivalent of loud guffaws from the DIA. "Several factors challenge the credibility of this report," a tone-deaf DIA memorandum argued several days after the CIA's hysterical call to arms. "If Arafat had foreknowledge of a Hawari operation against U.S. interests, he would probably block the action on the basis that it would be destructive to the interest of the Palestinian movement at this time." The DIA report then took on a dismissive tone: "Gen. Noriega would probably disapprove . . . terrorism on Panamanian soil, fearing that an attack threatening the security of the canal or U.S. interests in Panama would provide Washington with a good reason for a military move against him. Thus far, the actions of Noriega strongly underscore his desire to avoid providing the U.S. with such a justification."

That statement summed up the *official* position of the DIA; in private, military intelligence officers were even more caustic in their criticism of the CIA. One officer pointed out that the agency "was certainly aware" of Israeli intelligence cooperation with Noriega and suggested that the CIA's warning was "Israeli-inspired." The DIA had some basis for floating this suspicion since one of Noriega's closest friends was former Mossad agent Mike Harari. He had gained notoriety in 1974 for mistakenly identifying an innocent Moroccan waiter working in Norway as the Palestinian mastermind of the massacre at the Munich Olympic Games. After Harari ordered the Moroccan murdered, he was dismissed from the Mossad. He later traveled to Panama, where he offered his services first to General Torrijos and then, after his death, to Noriega. PDF antiriot squads subsequently bore the marks of his training: Small units would wade into crowds as a means of intimidation and then use swift, certain, and overwhelming force, with an emphasis on bloody physical beatings. Harari became so important to Noriega that he was put in charge of keeping a close eye on defectors from the PDF, and he identified Herrera Hassan as a probable troublemaker after the colonel returned from his frustrating trip to Washington. Harari dismissed Herrera Hassan as Panamanian ambassador to Israel on Noriega's orders.

Despite Harari's influence on Noriega, it is doubtful the CIA's report on Palestinian hit teams originated in a pro-Israeli cabal at the agency. A more modest explanation of the warning is put forward by a veteran DIA official, who says: "They don't run their raw intelligence data on terrorism through the divisions. If they had, it would have never seen the light of day."

The CIA chose not to fire back at the Pentagon's criticism. The agency decided to let its warning about hit teams stand as reported. "There was a lot at stake in the Noriega situation," explains a retired CIA officer. "If we have good information, detailed information, we have to report it. We can't come to the conclusion that it's false just because it doesn't fit the model. If a U.S. ship had been attacked in the Canal, the DIA would be screaming that we hadn't done our job."

It is not unusual for the DIA and Langley to disagree, but their acrimonious exchange of 1989 was unique. It was almost as if the two bureaucracies had shifted roles: The CIA's previous conservative recommendations on Noriega, its go-slow approach, and its belief that his successor might become a "Manuel II" were abandoned in favor of a tougher strategy. Sanctions, the CIA decided, would not force Noriega from office; he was confident, well funded, and supported by a network of international terrorists. The DIA, however, viewed the same intelligence reports in a completely different light: Noriega was running out of money, his government was nearing collapse, and reports of his ties to Libyan hit men were based on flimsy evidence.

Noriega was the equivalent of an intelligence hot potato. The CIA was telling the White House that the crisis in Panama was reaching a critical stage that called for direct action and hinted at military intervention. That view enraged military officers, who privately castigated the CIA for wanting the Pentagon to bail them out. "They created the mess," one DIA officer complained, "and now they want us to clean it up for them."

The battle between the CIA and Pentagon became so intense that, by March, Latin America experts were beginning to take sides in the debate. Former Assistant Secretary of State for Inter-American Affairs Elliott Abrams, for example, told reporters that JCS Chairman Crowe was purposely ignoring reports of attacks on U.S. citizens in Panama. Crowe struck back. "The Chairman has chosen to deal with [the reports of violence in Panama] in a more private way through [the Southern Command]. That's his style," Crowe spokesman William Smullen told the *Army Times*. "He's not one to take his case to the public or press."

Colonel Ronald T. Sconyers, the public affairs director for the Southern Command, defended the military in a letter to *The Washington Post* in which he denied that there was a "cover up or downplaying" of any harassment incidents in Panama. "On the contrary," Sconyers wrote, "the U.S. Southern Command has made every attempt to publicize all incidents that do not compromise security or an ongoing investigation."

Sconyers's explanation was accurate but incomplete. What he could not reveal was that American intelligence officers were under routine scrutiny by Noriega's security service. The CIA had told Secretary Baker that a number of Americans had been detained. CIA officials also admitted that Noriega had succeeded in penetrating certain Panamanian opposition forces; a number of Herrera Hassan's operatives had been "rolled up." A public admission of their arrest would have exposed both the administration's impotence in developing an effective plan to force Noriega from office and the bitter Pentagon-CIA feud.

Put simply, the intelligence war that was waged throughout early 1989 paralyzed the Bush administration: The Pentagon stridently opposed military intervention against Noriega, while the CIA continued to have difficulty mounting a coup to topple him.

While Noriega baited the Americans and heckled their attempts to remove him, he never took any decisive action that might force an open confrontation. CIA analysts predicted that he would emphasize a strategy that played on Latin sensitivities about "Yankee aggression." By aiming his propaganda at the average Panamanian citizen, Noriega apparently hoped that he could restore his popularity as a nationalist.

The CIA was helpless in the face of such tactics. While the agency's chief of station in Panama City worked hard to build a strong opposition force in the Canal Zone, he offered little hope that Colonel Eduardo Herrera Hassan could establish a credible threat to Noriega's rule. Meanwhile, the station chief, who was an activist from the Dewey Clarridge school, became frustrated by Washington's inability to take tough measures against Noriega and criticized the U.S. program in a number of reports that were circulated among senior agency managers. Eventually his complaints became so shrill that he was cautioned against overstepping his instructions.

"[The CIA station chief] wanted to push Noriega into doing something stupid by keeping the pressure on," a CIA colleague explains. "He recommended that we take some action, not just by showing support for Herrera but by actually arming [the opposition]. He thought the temperature was rising in Panama and we could put that to use."

At the heart of the station chief's proposal was a plan to spark an internal PDF revolt that could be used as a pretext for intervention; under some circumstances in this scenario PDF officers might even turn Noriega over to the Americans for trial. The recommendations were immediately rejected. The President's finding called for support of opposition forces, and the CIA's policy was to follow his instructions to the letter.

In view of the mood at the CIA, the head of the clandestine service, Richard Stolz, did not seriously consider urging a more active agency role in Panama for two main reasons. First, Noriega was Langley's most public controversy; the CIA was taking a beating in the American press with nearly every mention of his name. Too many reporters were closely watching what the CIA was doing. Second, the station chief's proposal also cut too close to the edge of the law: The agency was not only barred from assassinating foreign leaders, it was prohibited from aiding coups whose avowed purpose was assassination. No CIA officer stationed overseas wanted to be implicated in an Allende-style murder. The restriction was viewed so seriously, in fact, that CIA officers involved in politically volatile incidents in Africa, Asia, and Latin America often refused to communicate with pro-American dissidents for fear that their actions would be misinterpreted. Neither Stolz, Webster, nor Twetten were willing to take any chances; the CIA would help opposition forces, but the success of their operation was in their own hands.

By early May, however, it was clear the CIA's efforts were failing. Panamanian dissidents had failed to build a credible counter to Noriega. In one instance the agency had difficulty finding Panamanians willing to expand the clandestine radio network that was put in place during the previous year. Nor could they persuade anyone to mount a psychological operations campaign to increase domestic discontent with the Noriega regime.

These psychological operations, or psyops, programs were approved at a high-level meeting at the White House in mid-February, when Bush, Baker, Gates, Webster, and Stolz decided to give opposition forces ten million dollars to help in the upcoming May elections. The finding, the fourth such clandestine CIA program on Panama approved during the Reagan-Bush years, was intended to see whether the hatred for Noriega among opposition figures could be translated into a grass-roots movement among Panama's citizens. It was not until mid-March, however, that the CIA officers who were dispatched to Panama to run the program were able to begin disbursing the American funds.

In spite of the commitment of resources that was planned and the strong views of the Panama station chief, the CIA's heart was not really in the program. While the agency was now eager to publicly highlight, and even exaggerate, Noriega's criminality, its lack of direct action in Panama was a clear reflection of the take-no-risks attitude of both Webster and Stolz. Much like the agency's unsuccessful clandestine radio network in 1988, the CIA's psyops program of 1989 proved to be a modest and ineffective means of tapping into Panamanian disgust with Noriega. The final campaign amounted to no more than the distribution of pamphlets run off by a small press in the Canal Zone. It was hardly surprising that these papers were nearly useless in bringing Panamanians into the streets to defy Noriega. In light of this failure, questions are still raised as to whether the ten million dollars earmarked by President Bush was actually ever spent.

The CIA's efforts to help the opposition actually became a public embarrassment, since opposition leaders routinely told reporters that they had never seen any of the American money. For this and other public relations reasons, the CIA eventually took full credit for an efficient, but independent clandestine operation that gave Noriega's intelligence service fits. This other program had all the hallmarks of a successful covert operation: It was well conceived, expertly run, security-conscious, very effective, and highly embarrassing to the PDF.

The only problem was that the CIA had absolutely nothing to do with it.

The program grew out of an otherwise innocent conversation at Panama's Rotary Club between Kurt Frederick Muse, a thirty-nine-year-old U.S. businessman and radio enthusiast, and a group of fellow club members who were civic-minded American entrepreneurs. During a club luncheon in Panama City in early 1988, Muse excitedly mentioned to his friends that he had been secretly listening to PDF communications on his police scanner. He explained that he had even been able to monitor the regime's police operations and had taken copious notes on its tactics against anti-Noriega demonstrators. Another Rotarian, Muse discovered, was doing the same thing.

Muse soon recruited several other amateur radio buffs who opposed Noriega to monitor PDF communications. Within a short time there was a group of about half a dozen American businessmen tapping into the regime's communications network. After a few months, as Muse's network became more sophisticated, the group communicated its findings to one another every day (including a list of frequencies used by the PDF). The group even intercepted calls made from cellular phones by high-level PDF officers, during which the speakers described the sexual acrobatics of Panama's highest-ranking soldiers. Muse and the other radio hobbyists took notes on PDF drug deals and the arrest of opposition activists.

Eventually Muse and his volunteers compiled a massive data bank of information on Noriega's nefarious activities and the tactics used by the PDF in breaking up antigovernment demonstrations. They were even able to listen in on the PDF plans to arrest opposition President Eric Arturo Delvalle. Muse was able to warn Delvalle about Noriega's plan and help his vice-president, Roderick Esquivel, elude PDF officers and leave the country.

The next step in Muse's escalating involvement in Panamanian politics evolved naturally: He figured out a way to block out PDF transmissions and break in on them with messages of his own. Using directional antennas, transmitters, and microphones, Muse and his cohorts succeeded in overriding the signal of Radio Nacional, the government-run station. Muse was both shocked and pleased by his success.

So was the CIA. It monitored Radio Nacional from a small base inside the Canal Zone and provided daily transcripts of the programming to Langley. When the station unexpectedly went off the air, CIA officers knew that someone was purposely interfering with the signal. They were ecstatic; it was their first indication that a native opposition had taken up the struggle against Noriega.

Muse recorded and aired a three-minute anti-Noriega message that called upon the dictator to allow the Panamanian people to hold free elections. Noriega's forces were stunned by the message and by their inability to pinpoint who was behind it. Noriega blamed the United States and the CIA for invading his sovereign airwaves. The agency had no idea what he was talking about. After Muse's first three-minute message was transmitted he made it even more difficult for the PDF to identify him or his colleagues: He bought timers, tapes, and other sophisticated radio equipment to make broadcasts automatically. He also moved his equipment into a vacant apartment, so even if the PDF was able to pinpoint the source of the messages, it would not be able to arrest the culprits. Muse also diversified his radio holdings, so that if one station was shut down, another would provide backup broadcasts.

In one typical message broadcast three times each day, Muse urged the PDF to overthrow Noriega. He used stark, nationalist language, as if he were a Panamanian citizen: "You're ashamed of your profession because it has been denigrated by the trash that leads you." Muse also took advantage of his abilities to monitor police and PDF broadcasts with his simple scanner. He and his team used this information to transmit conflicting orders to Noriega's supporters who spilled into the streets to put down demonstrations.

By mid-March 1989 Muse was running eight radio stations from eight different locations inside Panama. Just as Noriega's police picked up the signal from one station, another would become operational; Noriega's internal security police were hot on his trail, as was the CIA.

The CIA got to Muse and his fellow conspirators first, that same month. After an initial meeting the agency provided the American businessmen with sophisticated radio equipment that they could not purchase over the counter. Muse was also approached by CIA-backed intermediaries in the Panamanian opposition, who gave him a high-powered transmitter to make sure his broadcasts reached the widest possible audience. To the CIA's credit, it did little to interfere with his operation. It diligently refrained from giving him advice or providing him with pro-American broadcast information; he was doing fine by himself. The agency even provided a television transmitter. Eventually Bosco Vallarino, one of the opposition group's most optimistic and outspoken figures in Miami, provided Muse with tapes from the opposition and suggested programming subjects.

Vallarino, who was a nationally known radio and television personality before leaving Panama under pressure from Noriega in the mid-1980s, admired Muse's "creativity and courage" and said that the American businessman, "the accidental spy," as he called him, "did more in two months [in February and March 1989] than we [in the opposition] were able to do in two years." From Florida, Vallarino continually suggested new ways to thwart the PDF and advised Muse on broadcasts that "would really get to Noriega." The CIA had enormous confidence in Muse. Case officers who monitored his operations and provided reports on his activities were surprised that he had no formal training in deception, countersurveillance, or operational security, and had been able to elude the PDF troops arrayed against him for so long.

Despite the informality of Muse's network, it was one of the most well-conceived, well-protected, and effective anti-Noriega operations being run in Panama. In terms of its impact on the Panamanian people, it was actually better than anything the CIA had put in the field.

The success lasted for only a few more weeks. After a series of close calls the PDF finally identified Muse and tracked down his radio network. Muse fell into the hands of Noriega's soldiers on April 5, along with a number of Panamanian opposition figures and $350,000 worth of radio equipment. Bundled off to a security cell where he was kept in isolation, he waited for his expected execution.

Two weeks later, Webster and Defense Secretary Cheney met in Washington to discuss the Muse situation. Webster made the most of the opportunity by hinting that Muse was an important agency asset and that his rescue was a matter of honor in the clandestine service, which had stood by helplessly as first Buckley and then Gannon were killed by terrorists. This must not happen again, Webster told the secretary of defense; the CIA could not allow one of its "agents," as he called Muse, to be killed. Cheney undoubtedly knew that Muse was hardly a CIA case officer or agent, but he agreed that his rescue would be made a part of the Pentagon's military plan to intervene in Panama. After the meeting Cheney ordered that a new military operation be added to SOUTH-

COM's overall military plan for the invasion of Panama: If, and when, U.S. forces intervened, a specially trained Delta rescue team would be designated to break into Modelo Prison and retrieve the CIA's agent. But the CIA was not the only part of the U.S. government having problems.

Two weeks after Muse's arrest, on April 21, the mistrust inherent in the relationship between the United States and the Panamanian opposition movement was worsened by an unprecedented White House decision to leak information to the press about the intelligence finding that Bush had signed in February. The information originally appeared in *U.S. News & World Report,* which disclosed that the opposition would receive funds for anti-Noriega projects and to offset costs of "printing, advertising, transportation and communications." President Bush intended to send Noriega a message, via the leak, that active measures were being taken against him. Opposition officials, however, charged that the leak placed a number of their operatives in Panama in grave danger. They were so shocked that the *U.S. News* article was allowed to appear that they were convinced that a pro-Noriega cell was still active in Washington. Several opposition leaders even attributed the leak to a cabal of Bush allies inside the U.S. government headed by Nestor Sanchez, who they believed was the real culprit behind the story.

The real reason the White House approved the leak actually had nothing to do with either Noriega or the opposition; it was intended solely for domestic consumption. The leak occurred on a Friday night, after the White House learned that *The Washington Post* was going to print a negative story that Bush had been consistently "outfoxed" by the wily Noriega and that the White House was being tightfisted with funds earmarked for the opposition. The White House hoped that the timing of the leak would both embarrass the *Post* and help convince the American people that Bush was doing everything he could to force Noriega from power—including turning over $10 million for a secret program to oust him.

But this strategy turned sour. Within twenty-four hours of the leak Noriega lambasted Bush and the CIA by plastering anti-American headlines across the top of Panama's newspapers. THEY SOLD THEIR COUNTRY FOR $10 MILLION, one such headline read.

The only good news in the spring of 1989 was that the administration would no longer have to deal with the colorless and acquisitive Eric Arturo Delvalle, who was ending his term as Panama's president. The new opposition candidate in the upcoming May elections would be fifty-two-year-old Guillermo Endara, a soft-spoken, rotund, and otherwise unimpressive lawyer who specialized in labor relations. In fact, despite his appearance (he was short and weighed well over two hundred pounds), Endara was an intelligent and courageous political leader who many believed would make a good president. Unlike Delvalle, Endara had a clear sense of the kind of president Panama needed and was committed to democratic principles. He was also a nationalist who was sensitive to claims that he was an American puppet.

Endara joined an opposition ticket comprised of two coequal vice-presidents, who were well-known opposition politicians: Guillermo "Billy" Ford, a bouncing, robust, and fiery public speaker, and Ricardo Arias Calderón, a hesitant and cerebral professor whose political organization had deep roots among the committed democrats of Panama. Surprisingly, their three-man campaign was formally approved by Noriega, who wanted to show that his own candidates could win an election against a pro-American ticket. It was a vast miscalculation: Endara, Ford, and Arias Calderón took their campaign to the people in the midst of a vast international team of election observers, which included former President Jimmy Carter, his wife, and nearly two dozen other Americans.

It was clear from the outset of the polling on May 7 that Noriega was on the verge of suffering an electoral humiliation—a defeat of landslide proportions that would be a repudiation of his government. During the day, however, the announced returns favored Noriega. Carter denounced the results. "The government is taking the election by fraud," he said. "It's robbing the people of Panama of their legitimate rights." After the voting, Carter flew back to Washington to report personally to Bush. He told the President that Endara, Ford, and Arias Calderón had clearly won the election. But Carter cautioned against military intervention, suggesting instead that the President seek coordinated pressure with Latin American countries. Bush was circumspect but firm. "The Panamanian people have spoken," he announced to the press, "and I call on General Noriega to respect the voice of the people. And I call on all foreign leaders to urge General Noriega to honor the clear results of the election."

In the midst of this turmoil Noriega took what might well have been his most decisive step on the road to disaster.

On May 10 Endara, Ford, and Arias Calderón took to the streets of Panama City to rally support for their victory in an attempt to force Noriega from office. The rally started calmly enough, as the three opposition leaders paraded through the city with a throng of chanting boosters. The mood was jubilant—as if the people of Panama believed that all they had to do to remove the dictatorship was to show their unity. Endara, Ford, and Arias Calderón shared the general mood even though they correctly sensed they were in great danger. That morning Noriega decided he would make an example of their arrogance and break up their march by sending in the PDF along with a group of paramilitary pro-Noriega thugs, who were members of his Dignity Battalions.

The first confrontation with the crowd took place on the Vía España, where Panamanian soldiers fired buckshot and liquefied tear gas at the marchers. As the large throng made its way toward the center of the city, they were blocked by heavily armed PDF battalions. After a tense, thirty-minute standoff the crowd suddenly dispersed into the side streets and alleys, and then reemerged en masse near the cathedral. This time the nervous tension of the day was shattered when PDF troops sprinted into the crowd and began to single out and brutally beat opposition figures. As the opposition candidates tried to flee, they were assaulted by Noriega partisans wearing Dignity Battalion T-shirts. Arias Calderón was clubbed half a dozen times by PDF soldiers before he managed his escape, a hasty retreat that turned into a sprint for the safety of a group of automobiles parked several blocks away.

Endara and Ford were not so lucky. Endara was beaten bloody as he stooped to pick up his glasses. His head snapped several times from the blows of two soldiers that surrounded him. He was eventually carried off by his bodyguards, leaving his supporters to wonder if he had been killed.

The most inhuman incident of the day took place when Billy Ford's bodyguard, Manuel Guerra, attempted to shield Ford from a murderous attack by a PDF soldier. Guerra was shot in the head at powder-burn range and died within seconds. The PDF soldiers then turned on Ford, clubbing him again and again, so that his face cracked open and blood spewed over his already red-stained shirt. This horrifying scene of Panama's elected vice-president being beaten was broadcast that evening on national television in the United States. He was shoved into the back of a PDF van and driven to a nearby prison.

The violent images of Ford being clubbed shocked America and were the subject of an avalanche of CIA cables. Within hours of the incident a full report was on President Bush's desk. This time Bush reacted quickly. The next day he announced that he agreed with Carter's assessment that the May 7 election had been stolen. Two days later, during a commencement address at Mississippi State University, he was even more blunt, by calling on the PDF to launch a coup. "I would love to see them get him out," he said. Later, aboard Air Force One, the President expanded on his comments: "They ought to just do everything to get Mr. Noriega out of there," he told reporters.

Despite Bush's obvious anger, he had yet to determine just exactly what the United States should do in Panama. The continuing intelligence war being waged inside the government was at least part of the reason for his hesitation.

It took Bush more than four months to break the logjam—to separate the warring parties in his own administration long enough to design a strategy that would remove Noriega at the same time that it would reassert American power and prestige. The first step was quietly taken in June, when the Justice Department gave the President the authority to order the FBI to seize a fugitive living abroad for violating U.S. laws, thereby making Noriega a target for a Matta-like seizure. The second step took place in July, when Bush replaced General Fred Woerner, the head of the U.S. Southern Command, with General Maxwell Thurman, known among his colleagues as a tough fighting soldier.

Bush then made one of the most fateful decisions of his administration, one that virtually guaranteed the United States would use force to remove Noriega from power: He replaced retiring JCS Chairman William Crowe with Colin Powell. At first glance Powell seemed no more willing to use force in Panama than Crowe: He was viewed by fellow officers as a steady administrator whose combat experience dampened his enthusiasm for using the U.S. military to solve political problems. Powell, a former NSC adviser under President Reagan, was a consummate politician and had a healthy respect for the pitfalls of military intervention against small countries, but when compared with Crowe—whose mistrust of military force seemed inborn—he looked, acted, and talked like a warrior. More significantly, he was personally intent on erasing the residue of the Vietnam failure from the military's record. After Powell's appointment the Joint Chiefs were headed by a hawk rather than a dove.

By late September everything was nearly in place. From the Pentagon, Powell ordered General Thurman to reevaluate American plans for intervention in Panama, where opposition forces, still in retreat from the bloody incidents of May, continued to push their CIA contacts for weapons that would make a successful coup possible. The CIA and Pentagon continued their internecine sniping, but their previously bitter war had subsided.

In the midst of this lull, DCI Webster boarded a specially designed military intelligence aircraft for a journey to a high-level European conference of CIA officers stationed in Europe and the Near East. The meeting was the result of twelve months of complex planning; it was no easy task to bring together so many officers in one place from so many different stations. It was absolutely essential that Webster attend. He had been briefed on the meetings by special groups of analysts and operations officers who gave him a full rundown on agency operations. His staff had spent many hours familiarizing him with the pressing issues he would deal with. Little did he know that in his absence George Bush's Panama predicament would become a crisis, nor would he have ever guessed that the crisis, when it had passed, would serve as an excuse for the White House to launch its first all-out assault on his performance as DCI.

11

★ ★ ★

The Blame Business

*L*ate on the afternoon of Sunday, October 1, 1989, an unexpected call came into the U.S. military headquarters in the Panama Canal Zone. Major Moisés Giroldi, one of General Noriega's confidants, wanted to talk to "high-level American officials" about a plan to launch a coup. The request was quickly passed up the line, first to the military headquarters of Max Thurman and then to the CIA station chief in Panama City. The message was then transmitted to Langley, first to the desk of the chief of the DO's Latin America Division, then to ADDO Twetten, and finally to his boss, DDO Richard Stolz. Within one hour, the CIA leadership had decided to meet with Giroldi to see what he had in mind.

It was not an easy decision. As far as anyone in the agency knew, the Panamanian major was committed to the continuation of the Noriega regime. The military head of the CIA-funded opposition group in Panama, Colonel Eduardo Herrera Hassan, had previously reported that of all the officers at the upper levels of the PDF, Giroldi was the least likely to take part in an anti-Noriega coup. Giroldi was so devoted to Noriega that a number of DO officers believed he viewed him with near adoration. Giroldi's wife was also tied in to the Noriega clique as a key member of a group of young officers' wives, most of whom had grown up in the slums of Panama City. Giroldi, his wife, their children, and their friends all owed their position and status to Manuel Noriega.

Despite these misgivings, DO senior managers gave approval for two CIA officers to visit Giroldi to find out what he had to say. It was standard procedure to listen to dissidents, even if they were not initially trusted. The officers were given precise instructions: Their primary job was to listen to Giroldi without making a commitment of American help in any way, at any time. A U.S. policy decision would be made only after hearing from Giroldi, and not before informing the President. In no way, CIA headquarters stressed, were the officers to give any indication of how the United States would respond to his actions.

Two hours after the initial phone call, two CIA officers arrived at the agreed meeting site, the home of one of Giroldi's friends. As the two Americans sat across from the PDF major, they appeared neutral, unsmiling, and only minimally cordial. In a rambling opening statement that amounted to an apology, Giroldi began by saying that he wanted the Americans to understand that he was a Panamanian patriot. He said he had decided to take action against Noriega only in order to save Panama. Events were slipping out of control, he explained; Noriega was becoming more intransigent and the people more dissatisfied. Giroldi added that he still had the utmost respect for Noriega and wanted to make sure that the general's retirement from Panamanian politics was completed without harming his reputation. The CIA officers remained silent as the major got around to his specific plan.

Giroldi said that he wanted to persuade Noriega to retire by seizing him the next morning at the Comandancia, the headquarters of the PDF. He maintained that his actions were backed by some of the most important PDF officers. Once Noriega was denied the support of his most loyal troops and was unable to communicate with his top officers, Giroldi said, he would voluntarily resign from office. Giroldi explained that he would announce on a national broadcast to the Panamanian people that Noriega had been relieved of his duties and would be allowed to stay in the country. Still, the CIA officers did not respond.

Giroldi continued by asking for some assurances from the Americans. He said that he wanted his family to be taken into American custody for their own protection. He also wanted U.S. troops to seal off Fort Amador and the main route into the city that would be used by Noriega's most loyal troops in Rio Hato.

When Giroldi had finished, one of the CIA officers responded with a carefully worded, deliberate statement. The plotters must know, he said, that the U.S. government could not support a coup that resulted in Noriega's death. To stress this point he repeated himself. It was American policy and a specific requirement of American law, he said, that U.S. officials could not participate in a foreign coup that involved bloodshed or an assassination. The CIA officer then asked if Giroldi's coup would involve Noriega's murder. Giroldi replied that his intention was not to harm Noriega; rather, the general would be peacefully retired from the PDF. Apparently satisfied by this answer, the two CIA officers gave Giroldi a telephone number where they could be reached and assured him that his family would be protected if they turned themselves over to the Americans. They then returned to the Canal Zone and filed their report.

At Langley, suspicions about Giroldi's motives had already set in. A special group of analysts and operations officers met in an informal session to review the report from Panama and study his proposals. After a short discussion they concluded there was little that the CIA could do to verify what the PDF major had said. They simply did not know whether he was serious about launching a coup or, as a number of LA division experts remarked, he was "sandbagging" the Americans by wrapping them into a false coup after which they would embarrass the United States by broadcasting American military moves to the world. It was as likely, they warned, that Giroldi was the feared "Manuel II" as it was that he was a credible, democratically minded, Panamanian nationalist. A number of CIA officers were especially leery of Giroldi's request that American troops should block key intersections in Panama City to keep Noriega's loyalists from coming to the dictator's aid. The plan just didn't smell right, one CIA officer later explained, because it showed that Giroldi was more interested in preserving Noriega's feelings than in overthrowing him. It was hard to believe that having spent years with Noriega, Giroldi would assume that he would "retire" quietly; it was far more likely that Noriega would react swiftly, brutally, and with every weapon he had.

William Webster, then thousands of miles away in Europe, later explained that the agency's officers in Panama gave Giroldi "a less-than-even chance of succeeding because his plan wasn't well thought out." Webster was being kind: The CIA actually concluded that Giroldi was planning what has been called "a tender coup" that significantly underestimated Noriega's desperate need to survive. Coups that succeeded, experienced clandestine service officers noted, were single-minded and violent and left no doubt of the outcome. An older generation of clandestine officers who had ringside seats for a number of third world rebellions would say that the first order of business was to murder the strong man, to show that there was no going back. But that outcome seemed to be the farthest thing from Giroldi's mind.

In spite of these doubts, the agency scrambled to put together information on Giroldi and the officers who supported him. Searching through daily intelligence reports from more than fifty human intelligence sources in Panama, Europe, Israel, and even Africa, the CIA was able to construct a working model of the coup plotters' organization and probable plan. It was only an outline, since the agency had very little firsthand information that was either reliable or detailed enough to give it a complete picture of what might happen in Panama in the next twenty-four hours. Among the plotters was Captain Nicasio Lorenzo, the head of counterintelligence in the PDF. The CIA concluded that Lorenzo and Giroldi probably counted on the support of a group of officers educated at Nicaragua's military academy, most of whom had graduated in 1974. Many in this class became part of a contingent of progressive officers who served in a UN peacekeeping force that was sent to Namibia the previous April—Major Agustín de García, Captain León Tejada, and Captain Juan Arza. (Colonel Guillermo Wong, Colonel Julio Ow Young, and Captain Javier Licona, some of Noriega's most trusted subordinates, were also involved in the plot, though the agency didn't know this at first.)

At least part of the reason that Giroldi and his followers wanted to get rid of Noriega, agency officials believed on October 1, was the top-heavy structure of the PDF. The long tradition of upward movement in the Panamanian military was dependent on the retirement of its top officers. Their departure guaranteed that nearly everyone below them eventually received an increase in pay. But when Noriega refused to retire, such promotions became stymied, causing grumbling in the senior officer corps. Still, this problem did not seem enough reason to launch a coup, especially considering the other benefits that Noriega supporters were getting from his regime. Over the next twenty-four to forty-eight hours the CIA worked overtime in a vain attempt to find out what really motivated Giroldi. Their failure to come up with a good answer increased the natural suspicions about his motives—they just did not trust him.

Neither did Max Thurman, the new SOUTHCOM commander, who was convinced that Noriega would go out of his way to embarrass the United States. A proposed coup by one of his top lieutenants seemed just the way to do it. After all, Thurman was aware that Giroldi had been instrumental in helping save Noriega in March 1987, when the regime was threatened by the sunrise coup launched by Major Augusto Villalaz. During that attempt, Giroldi had shown almost unbelievable courage and loyalty to Noriega by rallying a PDF battalion in the face of overwhelming force. After Giroldi was arrested and had a pistol put to his temple by Villalaz cohort Major Jaime Benitez, Giroldi agreed that he would attempt to convince his troops to surrender. But when he faced them, he ordered Benitez arrested and fired a clip of shells from a nearby seven-millimeter machine gun to wake up pro-Noriega soldiers who were still asleep. His quick action saved the Noriega regime.

Thurman's instincts proved to be right on target, at least initially: Giroldi sent word on Monday morning that he had postponed the coup to the following day because Noriega had not reported to the Comandancia as planned. Giroldi said that he would launch the coup early the next morning. On Monday night Giroldi's wife, three children, and father-in-law showed up at Fort Clayton asking for U.S. protection, as

Giroldi said they would. Still, Thurman continued to believe that the Giroldi coup was a setup and that the United States should take no overt action to support the major until it was sure he was serious. As a precaution, however, President Bush (who had been informed of Giroldi's planned actions on Monday morning) directed Thurman to move a number of American units into positions closer to the intersections that Giroldi said should be blocked.

The CIA also got ready, by placing a number of opposition agents in key positions to watch the coup unfold and by putting its high-tech intelligence-gathering network on alert. It also dispatched several opposition agents into downtown Panama City to monitor public reaction to Giroldi's move. The two CIA officers who had interviewed Giroldi a day earlier reported to Langley that they were now convinced that the Panamanian major was committed to carrying out his plan. If he was bluffing and was in collusion with Noriega, they noted, the coup would have taken place on Monday, as he had originally said.

Senior CIA officials, however, remained agnostic. They reasoned that there was little they could do to help Giroldi if he ran into trouble. One CIA officer, since retired, recalls that many experts at the agency were convinced that Giroldi's attempt to remove Noriega would be transformed by the course of unexpected events and problems. The major would soon realize that he would have to use force and that the inevitable confrontation would almost certainly result in PDF units facing off against each other.

From his meeting in Germany, Webster was kept informed of the events in Central America through hourly updates that he received from Langley via a secure phone link. Immediately after hearing of Giroldi's plan, Webster asked both Stolz and Twetten whether it was necessary for him to return to Washington. They both agreed that he did not need to, since there was little that he could do at agency headquarters. The response to Giroldi's coup, if it took place, would have to come from the White House.

The attempt was over almost as soon as it started—or so it would seem in the days that followed. At about eight on the morning of Tuesday, October 3, Noriega arrived at the Comandancia and was greeted by the rattle of light arms fire. His Mercedes swerved recklessly before coming to a stop in front of his headquarters, where he emerged, shielded by two bodyguards, and sprinted up a stairway to his second-floor office. Visibly sweating and emotionally shaken by the near-misses in the courtyard below, Noriega telephoned his girl friend, Vicki Amado, and directed her to get in touch with his loyal commanders at Río Hato military base while he ordered troops stationed nearby to come to the Comandancia. A confident Giroldi, posted down the hall and around a corner from Noriega, called out that he should give himself up. Giroldi was apparently convinced that his coup had already succeeded; he'd arrested most of the dictator's personal staff and was satisfied that U.S. troops were in position, blocking any pro-Noriega reinforcements. Thirty minutes later, after several more frantic phone calls, Noriega followed Giroldi's advice. He was marched out of his room, down a short hallway, and into a room where he was seated in a chair as if on trial, and subjected to an unofficial court of inquiry.

A number of the coup plotters argued that Noriega should be immediately executed for crimes against the people of Panama. Hearing these alarming threats, Noriega began to sob and pleaded with Giroldi that he deserved to live. It was a pathetic scene. Noriega begged Giroldi to spare his life. Another group of plotters contended that the only way to get rid of Noriega was to turn him over to the Americans, who would then be forced to intervene on the side of Giroldi and his lieutenants. Giroldi brought the debate to an end by giving orders to his soldiers to escort the dictator to a nearby building. He reassured Noriega that he would not be executed, but cautioned that he must agree to resign his post as head of the Panamanian military. Noriega, shaken by his experience, recovered himself and nodded his agreement. Then, once he was locked alone in the other room, he continued plotting a countercoup by using a telephone that Giroldi had failed to disconnect.

The action at the Comandancia attracted the attention of the Americans in Fort Clayton, who were informed that a fire fight had broken out between loyalist and opposition troops at just before eight o'clock. They could not tell whether Noriega had been killed in the exchange of fire, but they assumed that he was still alive, since the shooting started again and continued for thirty minutes. Approximately five hundred yards from Noriega's headquarters, in a building outfitted as a military prison, Kurt Muse also heard the gunfire. At first he thought the Americans had finally invaded Panama and his rescue was at hand.

Three thousand miles away in Washington, Senate aide Deborah DeMoss received a phone call fifteen minutes after the initial shooting started from one of the leaders of the anti-Noriega political groups, who said that he had heard that a coup was under way. He added that he was in touch with rebel forces inside the Comandancia and that Major Moisés Giroldi was the organizer of the effort.

Minutes later DeMoss received another call, this time from the Comandancia itself, where one of Giroldi's confederates told her that it was essential for U.S. forces to block the roads leading to PDF headquarters so that Noriega could not be rescued. DeMoss, now an aide to the Senate Foreign Relations Committee, called Senator Jesse Helms to tell him the news. Helms immediately called the State Department for more information and then directly telephoned SOUTHCOM headquarters to see if Giroldi's request for American help was being heeded. Helms and DeMoss were almost jubilant, even though both realized that the first hours of any coup were dangerous and unpredictable. They were well aware that Noriega had been able to survive a number of close calls before, and that Giroldi did not seem to have much of a plan to get rid of him. DeMoss was informed by one of the plotters that Noriega was alone in a bedroom, thinking about what he should do next. The plotter said he was convinced that Noriega would agree to resign without a fight. DeMoss was doubtful.

DeMoss's information about the situation in Panama was incredibly accurate; she seemed to know more about what was going on inside the Comandancia and on the streets of Panama City than the CIA did. She was in touch with the plotters, SOUTHCOM headquarters, the State Department, and Panamanian opposition figures. As she gathered information, she diligently forwarded it to Foggy Bottom's command center. But the more involved she became, the more convinced she was that the Bush administration was doing nothing to support Giroldi. She was surprised to learn that Thurman was still somehow convinced that Giroldi was trying to set him up, while the State Department, White House, Pentagon, and CIA all seemed to agree: The decision on whether Giroldi was really trying to depose Noriega was in Thurman's hands, not theirs. Compared with the din of activity coming into DeMoss from the Comandancia and the American military headquarters in Panama, the silence from official Washington was chilling.

Meanwhile, back at the Comandancia, Giroldi had dispatched his key lieutenant, Javier Licona, and three other rebels to make contact with the Americans at Fort Clayton in order to turn over Noriega to them. This Panamanian delegation then had to wait for another hour before it was allowed to meet with Thurman's second-in-command, Major General Marc Cizneros. Not surprisingly, considering Thurman's doubts about Giroldi, the four men received a chilly reception from Cizneros, which grew even more somber when Licona suggested that Noriega be taken into custody by the U.S. Army. They could come to get him, "right now," Licona offered hopefully. Cizneros, a respected Spanish-speaking officer familiar with Panamanian customs, shook his head no. The United States was more than willing to arrest Noriega and bring him to trial, he said, but he had to be delivered to the Americans at Fort Clayton. The American military would *not* come to get him.

As these discussions were continuing, Noriega's rescuers were moving quickly to bring pressure on the coup plotters to release the dictator and end their occupation of the Comandancia. A special PDF unit that backed Noriega was being flown into the capital from Río Hato with the objective of surrounding the Comandancia. Another unit, acting under orders that were telephoned to them by Noriega from his bedroom "cell," was seizing the plotters' families. Members of the frightened families called Giroldi to tell him they were being held hostage. They were convinced they would be murdered unless he surrendered. At 11:00 A.M., three hours after Noriega was seized, the battalions of elite troops summoned from Río Hato opened fire on the Comandancia, blasting out windows and sending shards of concrete hurtling through the air. Within minutes, the pro-Noriega troops arrested earlier by Giroldi were released and ran out of the building to join the counterattack.

This turn of events marked the most critical time for the coup plotters and the CIA. For several hours the agency's intelligence network in Panama had been receiving indications of PDF troop movements along major highways. The network also monitored the air transport of troops into Panama City. Most significantly, the agency's sophisticated high-tech electronic warning system showed that PDF units had left their billets and been placed on alert. The intercepted messages were evidence of one of two possibilities: Either Noriega was in touch with PDF reinforcements or the coup leaders had gained the allegiance of key military units. The CIA systems were working well, but there was still no way to find out exactly what was happening inside the Comandancia.

For Giroldi, the news had all turned sour as he went from desperation to resignation. Surrounded and outnumbered by Noriega's troops, spooked by the calls from the captured families, and convinced that the Americans would not come to his aid, he decided to give up. The decision caused no heated arguments among his fellow officers; they could see that the coup had been betrayed and that it was only a matter of time before Noriega's forces attacked. At 12:30 P.M. Giroldi surrendered himself to Noriega, who was already dealing harshly with those involved in the coup; a soldier who had roughly shoved him hours before had his hands cut off before he was executed on Noriega's orders. Giroldi was arrested and escorted away, but it was clear that he too would be summarily executed.

Throughout the morning, as all of these events unfolded, Thurman moved slowly and indecisively to support Giroldi. Two hours after the coup began, Thurman ordered American troops to surround Fort Amador, but they had strict orders not to do anything else. Cizneros's cold response to the Giroldi delegation, at 11:00 A.M., was an obvious reflection of Thurman's personal mistrust; negotiations for Noriega's arrest and transport to the United States were not even under way when they were undermined by Thurman's insistence that Noriega be brought to Fort Clayton. Most significantly, Thurman had failed to move quickly to seal off the Comandancia from Noriega's rescuers, and by the time that he did—sending Marines to block the road to Río Hato—it was too late. In Thurman's defense, he was acting under certain inflexible constraints: Washington's instructions prohibited him from taking any action that would be interpreted as U.S. intervention or that would bring American troops into conflict with the PDF. So he did nothing at all.

In Washington, Bush huddled throughout the morning with his senior foreign policy advisers, Baker, Scowcroft, Gates, Powell, and Sununu, trying to decide what they should do about the situation in Panama. They remained largely uninformed about events in the Comandancia and suspicious of the plotters' motives. They were relying heavily on updates from Thurman, who told them again and again that he believed Giroldi might be staging the coup to embarrass the United States. Even after it became apparent that Giroldi was serious and that the plotters had exchanged fire with PDF units, the President refused to order Thurman to support the coup. Amazingly, no high-level Bush administration official was willing to believe that here, finally, was a heaven-sent opportunity to end the Panama crisis.

In Panama events were coming to a brutal end. Noriega was giddy with power and was more convinced than ever that he was a leader of destiny: A coup that was almost guaranteed to succeed just hours before had effortlessly fallen into his hands. It was a personal victory; he had kept his head at the darkest hour and emerged triumphant. His retribution was swift, sure, and inhuman. Giroldi was trundled off to a nearby Comandancia interrogation center, where he was savagely tortured, shot in the elbows and kneecaps, kicked in the ribs, had his leg broken, and was finally executed the next morning.

Back in Washington, the White House sensed that it had made a terrible mistake but adamantly refused to acknowledge that it might have done things differently. Press spokesman Marlin Fitzwater flatly denied that the administration had been told in advance about the coup. "If we were [told]," he said, "the President doesn't know about it, and the secretary of defense doesn't know about it."

Within minutes, as reporters pressed their questions, Fitzwater contradicted himself. "We do not know who's involved here," he said. "We had some rumblings. We had rumors that this might occur, but there have been numerous rumors over the past few months...." As officials on Capitol Hill began to ask questions and obtain more information, the White House story began to crumble. Jesse Helms, for one, was outraged by the administration's lack of action in Panama. Taking to the Senate floor, he compared White House officials to "Keystone Kops." Marshaling all the outrage he could, Helms then laid out a minute-by-minute chronology of the coup. He attacked the administration for failing to take custody of Noriega when it was offered.

The White House fired back. The administration never had a chance to arrest Noriega, Fitzwater replied. He added that Helms was "full of it." John Sununu phoned Helms's top foreign policy aide and demanded that the senator immediately produce proof of his allegations. "Where is your evidence?" Sununu shouted. "Prove it. Show us anything." After that telephone conversation, a confident Fitzwater felt vindicated. "They couldn't produce anything," he told the press corps.

Pressure mounted on the administration, however, during the next few days as it was revealed that Helm's charge was accurate and after Capitol Hill sources charted administration actions on the day of the coup. By October 7 key congressional leaders were openly questioning Bush's explanation that there was no advance warning. Even less satisfying was the Pentagon's explanation of who knew what and when. American military forces in Panama "never had any intention of going in to get Noriega," a military source told one journalist. "It was not our coup. For us to go in would have been a mission beyond the scope of U.S. policy." Clearly flustered, the official added: "That was not part of our planning process."

Defense Secretary Cheney's response was to blame the Congress for clogging up the phone lines. "We had situations here where members of Congress were literally calling agencies downtown, or even people in Panama, as these events unfolded, demanding information," he said. "That creates all kinds of problems." (The press later learned that Cheney had been in no position to know this; he had been off in Gettysburg, touring the battlefield with the head of the Soviet military.)

As criticism mounted, administration officials became more defensive about their inaction and less successful in deflecting allegations of incompetence that seemed to grow with every passing day. To rebut charges of a "lights-out" attitude at the Defense Department, the Pentagon told reporters that it had convened a special command group on the day before the coup to monitor events in Panama. Spokesman Pete Williams even held a press conference to explain the Pentagon's stance, but his statement was baldly inaccurate. "We have found absolutely nothing to indicate that at any time there was any request to the United States to come and get Noriega," he said, "or any position that they would be willing to offer him to us." Rebel leaders, who had been transported by the U.S. military to Miami in the wake of the coup, strongly disagreed with Williams and responded in public. They told newsmen that Cizneros had been noncommittal about using U.S. troops and had expressed concern about how the world would view American intervention.

The controversy became so hot by the second week of October that President Bush was prompted to strike back at his critics with unusually harsh words. He accused his congressional critics of being "instant hawks" who were making "stupid arguments" that the United States should have intervened, and he reiterated that the administration did not have enough information on Giroldi or his fellow plotters to have supported them. "I have not seen any fact in all the reports that have come out that would make me have done something different in terms of use of force," he said. Bush added that his administration's failure to act was not due to any concern for Noriega. "I want to see him out of there, and I want to see him brought to justice." Still uncertain that he had done enough to stanch the fires, Bush fell back on a well-worn canard from the Reagan days: "The American people," he said," are strongly supporting the position I took."

Sensing that his arguments were becoming more and more shrill and less believable, Bush advised White House aides to stop talking about the events in Panama. It was advice he should have taken himself. After he was told that administration sources were busy leaking information on what the White House knew on the day of the coup, he blew a gasket and lectured a number of advisers to "put a lid on it." When even *that* comment was passed to the press and appeared in an article that said Bush was angry over administration leaks on Panama, it got the best of him. Bush's reaction was as close as he ever came to a tantrum in public. "I didn't get angry," he told a group of reporters. "I didn't get angry. What I did say is: 'I don't want to see any blame coming out of the Oval Office or attributed to the Oval Office in the face of criticism.' I'm not in the blame business! Blame, if there's some to be assigned, it comes in there. And that's where it belongs."

Bush's next remark, made off the cuff, seemed to come out of nowhere. "There has not been an intelligence gap that would make me act in a different way," he said—thereby suggesting that there indeed was one. Bush made this statement nearly two weeks after Moisés Giroldi had tried to topple Noriega. By then, with the White House under siege from Congress and the press, it was clear that the administration's previous good grace about the Panama foul-up had vanished and that the solid front of camaraderie that was so highly prized by Bush, Baker, Cheney, and Sununu was beginning to fray. "The boys," as they were called by NSC staffers, were even starting to bicker among themselves. Bush's odd statement—that there had not been "an intelligence gap" on October 3—was the cue for the administration to begin a public relations offensive designed to take the pressure off Bush. The administration's first strategy was to deny that it had done anything wrong, the second to deny that it knew of the coup beforehand. The third was to blame someone else. The victim of choice was the CIA.

The administration's strategy to change the nature of the Panama debate surfaced on October 16, on page one of *The Washington Post,* after a White House official spoke to reporters David Ottaway and Ann Devroy in a desperate attempt to focus attention away from the President and his advisers. Ignoring Bush's statement that the administration should not be "in the blame business," the unidentified White House source

said that the real reason the administration had failed to act in Panama
was that the CIA had not given it up-to-date information on Giroldi or
the other plotters.

William Webster was singled out by the anonymous White House
official as the real culprit of the Panama crisis. He was an "ineffective"
CIA director, the source charged, and the White House was "frustrated"
by his continuing foreign policy gaffes. The source criticized Webster's
performance as DCI in a number of other crises. He claimed that the
agency had also failed in China and Afghanistan (which was the subject
of a bitter internal administration debate several weeks earlier).

But the part of the story that really caught everyone's attention was
the almost needless backbiting about the Panama failure and the insulting references to Webster that were becoming commonplace in the
Bush administration. The *Post* story noted chief of staff Sununu's quip
from a White House staff meeting that "he had learned more about the
attempted coup in Panama from watching Cable News Network than
from Webster's Central Intelligence Agency." The venom in Sununu's
attack showed that the White House was scapegoating its own failures,
and the President's principal aide had obviously chosen Webster as the
administration's fall guy. A Senate Intelligence Committee source added
fuel to the *Post* report by noting that Webster had been out of the country
during the attempted coup. The implication was that the DCI was off
playing tennis when he should have been manning the phones at the
CIA.

The *Post* further reported that the White House believed Webster
was too chummy with Congress. "One knowledgeable source," the story
noted, "said Webster is considered 'too captive of Congress,' too lax in
day-to-day management of intelligence and lacking a broad strategic
overview of foreign policy and the intelligence community's role." Another anonymous source was quoted as saying: "There is a sense that
the institution [the CIA] is not being very energetically or effectively led.
...There is unhappiness with the intelligence being provided overall
and with the conclusions based on that intelligence." This source added:
"[Webster] is not close to Bush. He's not close to Baker. He's not close
to Scowcroft. There's no reason for him to be treated with any great
weight."

When the Ottaway-Devroy article hit the newsstands on the morning
of October 16, the public response from Langley was understated and
confident. "We have no reason to believe that the President is in any
way dissatisfied with Judge Webster's performance as head of the CIA,"
an agency spokesman said. For a moment, the CIA tried to act as if the
wizard himself, William Casey, were back on the scene, waving his hand
disparagingly at the group of reporters who wanted the real story. Webster was tough, the CIA spin doctors were saying; he could take it. "You

know, Judge Webster really doesn't pay much attention to this sort of thing," a CIA public affairs spokesman said in a whispered, just-between-us response to the *Post* piece. "It just doesn't bother him."

Nothing could have been further from the truth. Webster was not Casey; he did not have Casey's self-confidence or the discernible air of being above it all that had come so easily to his predecessor. The *Post* story had hit its target, wounding Webster's public reputation and, more importantly, his stature inside agency headquarters at Langley. Whatever confidence that CIA officers had in Webster—buoyed most recently by his adept handling of questions from Congress about a number of covert programs—was dealt a blow by the White House leaker. If Webster had lost the confidence of the administration, then the CIA's status as an arm of the executive department was in jeopardy. Also harmed was Webster's much-touted ability to calm public fears about CIA excesses and failures, which was the primary reason he had been appointed DCI. The one thing he had in common with Casey was his ability to work with Congress to gain needed budget increases. Now that, too, would be in doubt.

For all these reasons, Webster's private reaction to the *Post* story was intense, and his denial was categorical. "The judge is very angry that this type of thing would make it into the newspaper," a senior CIA official explained. "It's just not true. It's hard to believe something like this from unidentified sources."

This last comment was pure Washington boiler plate since Webster and his CIA allies had figured out exactly whom Ottaway or Devroy had talked to. They knew who had it in for the DCI at the White House. They were convinced it was John Sununu.

According to officials close to Webster, the DCI also had good reason to be angry with the *Post* for the way the newspaper presented the story. For one thing, CIA officials point out that Ottaway and Devroy knew that Webster was in Europe on a business trip. The CIA people thought that the reporters could have at least mentioned that fact in their article. Ottaway and Devroy were just causing trouble, CIA officials believed—they were stirring up the Panama pot. "This is how the *Post* gets its jollies," one CIA official said. There was also anger at the way that the two reporters had "blindsided" the CIA by not giving Webster "a heads-up"—a warning about when the article would appear.

"The *Post* story had been in the works for many months, but there was always an understanding that Webster would have the last word," explains a CIA colleague, "that he would be allowed a chance to respond. We cooperated and attempted to answer questions about Webster and his role in the decision-making process at the White House. We made it clear that the CIA had come through for Bush, that we provided the White House the intelligence we thought was necessary. But then the

Post story came out. It just shocked the hell out of us. We still don't know why we weren't allowed to have a say-so in this, at least to be warned."

David Ottaway, a veteran reporter, passes off the criticism. "They knew it was coming," he responds. Then he adds: "It really wasn't up to me. The editors decide when to run a story, not me." (When Ottaway passed Webster in a hallway at the CIA the morning after the article appeared, the DCI greeted him as if nothing had happened. "I would have slapped him," a Webster aide says.)

Not surprisingly, Webster had few sympathizers among senior and mid-level officers in the clandestine service, which was the the heartland of the CIA's conservatism and the wellspring of its numinous mistrust of the public press. Many of these CIA veterans felt that Webster had gotten what he deserved for thinking that he would somehow get the last word in the *Post* article. The *Post* enjoyed a good fight and always had. Experienced CIA officers had known this all along. They believed the best thing the Public Affairs Office could do was pack up its press releases and Rolodexes and go back to the work of intelligence.

On the morning of October 16, Webster had come into his seventh-floor suite without saying a word and had retreated angrily behind a closed door. Seated at his desk, with pictures of his family behind him—including one of his daughter holding the Bible as he took his oath as DCI (one of his proudest possessions)—Webster studied *The Washington Post* article in mounting rage. His secretary, who had been with him since he had first come to Washington as a virtual unknown to head the FBI more than a decade earlier, knew enough to leave him alone. She diverted all calls and waved off entreaties from his aides who wanted to begin the day's business. "Not yet," she said, "the judge is busy just now." One telephone message, however, she decided to pass along. It was Robert Gates on the line from the White House. Webster gave his approval for the call to be put through.

Gates was apologetic and embarrassed by the *Post* story. He assured Webster that he was not the source of the report. The President, he said, was not responsible for the article either and was as surprised and angered by it as everyone else. Gates stressed that Webster had Bush's full confidence. Webster listened silently. Gates went on to reconfirm his loyalty to Webster with a single sentence. We work well together, he said; he didn't want that to change.

But if Gates wasn't the source of the report, then who was? Webster later told his top assistants that he already knew. "This is Sununu's work," he said, confirming what they had already guessed. Webster waited for Sununu to call with an apology. The call finally came just after midday. After Sununu greeted Webster in his usual gruff tones, he dismissed the story as a fabrication, and reassured him in easy, bantering tones that he never talked to reporters about what was going on in the White

House. Webster interpreted the comment as a backhanded confirmation that Sununu was the source for the Ottaway-Devroy report; even if he thought Webster was incompetent, he'd never say so publicly—on the record.

During the week that followed the article, the Washington journalism community debated the identity of the *Post*'s White House source. Conventional wisdom settled on Gates as the likely culprit because everyone assumed that he still coveted the DCI job he had been forced to relinquish. To repair his image on Capitol Hill, he had been diligently working to prove his commitment to openness through frequent briefings of the Senate Intelligence Committee. He had already won a number of converts; Democrats and Republicans alike were impressed by his breadth of knowledge and his immediate attention to their questions. The rumors of a Gates comeback were given new life by the Ottaway-Devroy story, which quoted White House sources as implying that Gates indirectly controlled the agency. "Some Bush presidential aides have suggested," the *Post* reported, "that Bush is relying on Robert M. Gates, Scowcroft's deputy, as his chief intelligence adviser and is, in effect, 'working around' Webster." Webster's aides dismissed this part of the story. One of these senior CIA officials later explained that anyone who made the claim "doesn't understand how the CIA works; it's sheer bullshit." There was, of course, another explanation: that Gates could not have had the kind of influence at the agency attributed to him by the *Post*'s sources at the White House because, quite simply, he was not trusted by many of Langley's senior officers.

Webster had spoken to Gates for two hours that morning, covering a broad range of topics: the Panama crisis, the CIA, and White House handling of the press. He talked to Sununu for fifteen minutes. But in all that time neither Gates nor Sununu was able to give him a clear sense of what the President thought of him or whether Bush believed that the CIA had actually failed in Panama. Then, in the early afternoon of the sixteenth, Bush himself called to invite Webster "to stop by for a talk" at the White House. Twenty minutes later Webster was seated on a couch across from Bush in the Oval Office.

Later that afternoon Webster returned to his office at Langley to brief his top aides. In attendance were four men: DDO Richard Stolz, Deputy Director Richard Kerr, DDI John Helgerson, and the head of public affairs, James Greenleaf. Webster recounted for them what Bush had said: that he could stay as long as he wanted at the agency and that he had the President's full support. *The Washington Post* story was an unfortunate incident and the result of a crisis that had gone badly for the administration. Webster should not take it personally. Bush added that he did not want officials in his administration taking shots at each other in the public press. But he notably omitted saying that he would punish the leaker or even attempt to find out who it was. Webster, in turn, assured Bush that any future mistakes made by the agency should be brought to his attention; he could take it. Bush nodded approval; Webster's job was not in danger, Bush reemphasized.

The result of all the October 16 meetings was an unprecedented high-profile effort to bring the agency into the public eye and paint the director as a hands-on leader with formidable foreign policy skills. The campaign also would be Langley's response to complaints that the agency was not providing adequate intelligence guidance for policymakers. For those astute observers who tried to monitor the labyrinthine ways of the CIA, Webster's unusual public prominence following the *Post* article showed just how deeply Sununu's criticism of the agency had struck and how bitterly it was resented.

Webster's offensive began on the same day the White House skewered him in public, when he called upon Congress to give the CIA "greater latitude" to support coups. Ironically, Webster's response to his critics was essentially the same as that voiced by clandestine service officers to William Casey, many years before: If you want us to deal with the likes of Noriega, Webster said, then the law should be changed to allow the CIA to do so. Webster outlined this position in an interview with *The New York Times,* in which he specifically argued for a "reinterpretation" of Executive Order 12333, which barred the CIA from assassinating or assisting in the assassination of foreign leaders. The executive order was being interpreted literally in the DO, where the actions of operations officers were under close scrutiny in the wake of the Iran-contra scandal. Although Webster had now put the onus for liberalizing this order on Congress, a number of CIA officers later pointed out that he had been personally to blame for at least some of the chill on agency actions and on the constant questioning of what case officers were, and were not, allowed to do.

Despite his past position, Webster was now indicating that he was more than willing to ease up on the reins, rather than being personally blamed for being an ineffective DCI.

There were several other, even more salient reasons why he took a high profile after October 16. According to one CIA official, Webster was "under pressure from the DO to make changes in the agency's rules of engagement." It was in Webster's interest to do this so he could win back the allegiance of the agency's elite. An ally of Webster's was even more specific. "The judge is isolated here," this CIA official explained, soon after the public controversy was sparked by the *Post* article. "He's done his best to win the confidence of these people [in the DO], but that's a very hard thing to do. He's up there on the seventh floor, and it's almost impossible to find out what's going on in the building."

Within hours of his meeting with President Bush, Webster was trying to end that isolation and reassert his control over an agency that was somehow slowly slipping through his fingers. He told *The New York Times* that the Congress and President needed to address the ambiguities in the executive order. "When you have deliberate blurring," Webster said, "it puts a terrible and I think unacceptable pressure on the people who have [to] do the work." Webster then implied that new rules might not have made a difference in the Panama situation, but could "very well make a difference in the next one." He indicated that there was a "like-lihood" that the next plotter in Panama would, "probably," have to mur-der Noriega. As for the October 3 attempt, Webster refused to take the blame for the administration's failure to judge Colonel Giroldi's motives successfully. Rather, he carefully took a swipe at his White House de-tractors. "There's always a lot of fallout and temptation to finger-point if things didn't go exactly the way they should," he said, "and I suppose my turn has come up."

The day after the *Times* story appeared, Webster continued his of-fensive. He directed the CIA's Public Affairs Office to be more aggressive in publicizing his views on American intelligence and his performance as CIA chief. The Public Affairs Office quickly scheduled a number of interviews with journalists whom Webster probably would not even have considered meeting prior to October 16. When the CIA's public affairs staff spoke to reporters themselves, they strongly supported Webster and expressed their anger at reports that he was not doing a good job. They uniformly blamed the Bush White House for spreading that mes-sage and for making Webster the scapegoat for White House mistakes. But both they and Webster refused to be drawn into an obvious public confrontation.

"We're just not going to be diverted by the political machinations of this situation," the public affairs chief, James Greenleaf, explained on the eighteenth. "I know that it looks like we are playing politics, but we're not. We were just in the planning stages of how to handle a new interpretation of the executive order when the Ottaway story broke. But we didn't plan it that way."

Greenleaf's denial obscures the persistent quality of Webster's self-defense in the month that followed. Over the next thirty days Webster transformed the criticism over the Panama debacle into a public forum to review his tenure as DCI. After the President defended Webster in public on October 17, the DCI had an "editorial luncheon" with top editors at *The Washington Post*. According to a *Post* reporter, it was "an amazing performance"—a wide-ranging interview on a dozen topics dur-ing which Webster appeared well briefed and amazingly conversant with intelligence policy.

One outcome of this session was that Ottaway wrote an article that was a near paean to Webster's abilities. Titled COMING OUT OF THE COLD, the story opened with a bow to the problems he faced in taking over for Casey. Ottaway noted: "Webster, who had won a reputation for unimpeachable rectitude as director of the Federal Bureau of Investigation, set out on that task with a vengeance, in many cases making sure to do the opposite of things his discredited predecessor, William J. Casey, had done."

The article reviewed the charges made by the White House on October 16, but then signaled the reader that there was far more behind the attack on Webster than simple dissatisfaction with his performance as DCI. Ottaway wrote: "Whether Webster can persuade the White House that he is 'a team player' and ready to do its political bidding remains to be seen. It is also far from clear how well he will adapt to the new politically 'activist' role the White House is apparently calling upon him to play by helping more directly to shape and assure the success of its foreign policy."

The article presented universal acclamation for Webster's performance as director from ranking CIA officials, including Deputy Director Richard Kerr and DDO Richard Stolz. Not only was it unusual for such serving CIA officials to be quoted in print, but it was unheard of for someone in their position to even be identified.

Yet there they were, praising Webster and defending the CIA in the *Post* and several other newspapers. It was a full court press from the agency that also amounted to a subtle attack on the Bush administration's criticism that Webster was not "a team player." For Kerr, Stolz, and others, the real issue was whether the CIA would be allowed to retain its independence, or whether President Bush and his advisers would succeed in using the agency to promote their own political agenda.

For Stolz especially, the issue of the CIA's political independence was paramount. It was the one issue that had forced his retirement during the Casey years and the one assurance he had gained from Webster that spurred his return. Without an absolute guarantee of such independence, he realized, the agency would inevitably repeat the mistakes of the Iran-contra affair.

The paradox was that in order for Webster to be effective, he *had* to be part of the Bush team. For a President who prized staff loyalty to the exclusion of almost everything else, continuous demonstrations of teamwork and sacrifice were the *only* way to win favor for the agency. This made the events of October 1989 all the more devastating. For CIA officers with a yen for reading Washington's political tea leaves—which included just about everyone at Langley—it seemed eminently clear that George Bush was less interested in the views of an independent intelligence agency than in making sure that he received unquestioned support for his political program. A number of senior agency officials were beginning to suspect that a man whom most viewed as having been an interim CIA director, and who had used his agency position to further his personal ambitions, would now use it to guarantee his political success as President.

That is not to say that Bush did not have his supporters at the agency; he did, and in large numbers. Most of his admirers were veterans of the clandestine service, normally conservative officers who had spent a lifetime in combat against America's cold war foes. For them, Bush's ascendence to the presidency was the ultimate expression of their faithful service to America. Despite their traditionally cynical view of politicians, Bush represented the tough-minded, hard-nosed attitudes they prized. They believed that Bush's short time as DCI provided him with a knowledge of the agency and its worth that was not shared by any previous President. He understood the need for clandestine operations and elevated the need for secrecy—perhaps the most important part of the DO's distinctive character—as an essential part of his presidency.

These two contending views of Bush's presidency set the stage for the next eighteen months—from the last part of 1989, which saw the triumph of democratic revolutions in Europe, to the summer of 1991, which brought the retirement of William Webster. In those eighteen months the divisions between the clandestine service and the Directorate of Intelligence were more starkly drawn than at any time in the previous forty years.

By mid-1991 the conflict between the two directorates, and within each, had become so intense that it finally burst into public view during Senate hearings held to confirm Bush's choice as Webster's successor. In that forum, the forty-year battle between the agency's moderates and militants came down to a question of whether CIA officers could serve both the President and the truth.

The first indication Kurt Muse had that his liberation might be at hand occurred when he heard gunfire outside his prison cell just a few minutes before one on the morning of December 20, 1989. The shooting which was directed at the Comandancia was accompanied by the sound of helicopters moving in from overhead. It was a moment of hope for the modest American businessman, whose nearly nine months inside Modelo Prison had not dimmed his faith in his country. He was certain that he would be rescued; his only question was whether the team sent to carry him to safety would arrive before he was shot by one of Noriega's handpicked executioners who were stationed just down the hall at a simple metal desk. As Muse stood pondering this dilemma, looking out over the darkened grounds between the prison and PDF headquarters, "all hell broke loose." Outside in the hall, as agitated PDF soldiers shouted to their leaders for orders, U.S. helicopter gunships fired thousands of rounds into the Comandancia. It was only seconds before Noriega's headquarters was totally demolished. By then Muse realized that a U.S. attack on Panama—called Operation Just Cause—was in full swing.

Bush invaded Panama because he had no choice. The CIA was either unwilling or unable to spark a full-scale coup—or both—while opposition forces were poorly equipped to overthrow the dictator. Nor could the President chance another Giroldi-like embarrassment. He committed U.S. troops in strength for a quick, though bloody, fight against the Noriega regime. Bush knew that an overwhelming military victory not only would boost his political support at home, it would also rid his administration of an embarrassing problem.

None of that mattered to Kurt Muse, however, who was watching the American attack on the Comandancia from his prison cell. He moved away from his prison window, fearful that he might be inadvertently wounded by ricocheting shells. A moment later a blinding flash and the loud rush of air from an explosion sent Muse onto his back. He noticed his cell door was still intact; he eyed it fretfully, convinced these were the last moments of his life. From a distance, then coming closer, he could hear the sound of rifle fire. Suddenly, someone yelled out his name from the hallway. "Stay down," the voice called, "I'm going to blow the door!" Muse dived for the floor, heard the blast, and then saw a Special Forces officer kneeling beside him to help him up. In a few moments he was aboard a helicopter bound for a waiting jet, which was to take him to the United States. The next several minutes became a haze, as the helicopter was hit, gyrated madly out of control, and then crashed. Muse was rescued yet again. Put aboard another helicopter, he finally made it to safety and was flown north. A few weeks later he and his family met with President Bush in the Oval Office. He learned that Bush had made his rescue a personal goal, as had William Webster.

Muse was a hero in every sense of the word. He had been elevated from simple citizen to agency contract agent, from small entrepreneur with an abiding interest in the Rotary Club to America's most important and public opposition voice in Panama. This ceremony at the White House was surely the most important and memorable milestone of his life. He was given a medal, shook hands with the President, and was even lionized by the director of central intelligence. He had become "our man in Panama."

But like many agents before him, Muse's services were soon forgotten. He set up residence with his family in Burke, Virginia, and began to look for work. The CIA had better things to do than look after him; he was, after all, somewhat of an embarrassment, living proof that rank amateurs could do a better job of embarrassing foreign dictators than it could. Then, too, the CIA had other worries.

The agency participated fully in Operation Just Cause. It hastily set up a Panama Task Force that worked with a special liaison committee at the Defense Department. The CIA's jobs were among the most important: to draw up targets, recruit new agents inside Panama, review on-site changes in the PDF order of battle, and debrief Panamanian immigrants on the habits and schedules of Noriega and his assistants. Their operations centered on psychological warfare, to grind away at the PDF in the days and hours leading up to American intervention. In this they succeeded; Noriega was unprepared for the invasion and unable to respond to it. In the midst of the battle the CIA was required to give judgments on the effectiveness of U.S. weapons and tactics and to usher the new leaders of the nation through their first day in office. Yet, the CIA's important role in Just Cause was overshadowed by the attention it was soon giving to the major event of that December.

Just as one crisis was finally ending—in Panama—another was beginning once again inside the CIA. In the weeks before the U.S. invasion of Panama, a unique and unexpected revolution swept through Eastern Europe. The effects of these monumental changes were felt by every government and every intelligence agency. But for the CIA, the fall of communism and the rise of democratic movements in the old Soviet bloc marked the beginning of a reassessment that was to shake the very foundations of the intelligence community. The resulting skirmishes over just who was responsible for the agency's failure to predict the earthshaking events of the winter of 1989 and 1990 would take on immense importance in the months ahead until, inevitably, the conflicts that had been kept under cover in the CIA for forty years—and most especially during the previous ten—broke into public view.

★

December 1986: Oliver North is sworn in before the House Foreign Affairs Committee to answer questions concerning arms sales to Iran.

★

William Casey waves to reporters on December 10, 1986, after leaving a hearing on arms sales to Iran. Two days after this picture was taken Casey collapsed in his office at the CIA.

★

George Bush and Manuel Noriega during their 1983 meeting at the Panama City airport.

William Webster's Amherst friend and Clair George's replacement as DO, Richard Stolz. This picture was taken in 1965, just after Stolz was expelled from the Soviet Union, in retaliation for the U.S. expulsion of a Soviet spy.

A smirking Manuel Noriega emerges from the Comandancia after the October 1989 coup led by Moises Giroldi has failed.

New U.S. Ambassador to China James Lilley presents his credentials to Chinese President Yang Shangkun in May 1989. Lilley later became a hero to Chinese dissidents, whom Shangkun ordered slaughtered.

The nose section of Pan Am flight 103 lies in a field three miles from Lockerbie on the morning of December 22, 1988.

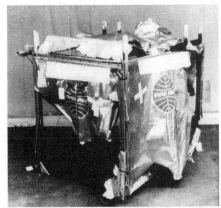

★ Cargo container 14L.

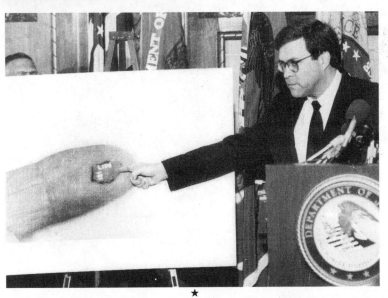

Attorney General William Barr points to the fragment of the circuit board found at Lockerbie. The piece of the circuit board was from a timing device hidden inside a radio that was secreted aboard the aircraft. The evidence changed the CIA's mindset on who bombed Pan Am 103.

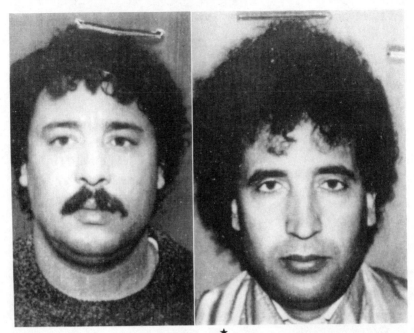

The perpetrators: Libyans Lamen Fhimah and Abdel al-Megrahi.

In the wake of Iraq's invasion of Kuwait, CIA Director William Webster briefs President George Bush at Camp David. *From left to right:* Secretary of Defense Richard Cheney, President Bush, Vice President Dan Quayle, Chief of Staff John Sununu (partially hidden), and Webster. Standing in the back is Paul Wolfowitz.

★
Ninety-six hours into Operation Desert Storm, Bush confers by phone with General Norman Schwarzkopf. John Sununu, Robert Gates, and Brent Scowcroft agreed with Bush's view that the war should be brought to an end.

Howard Teicher after resigning from the NSC. In 1979, he predicted that the United ★States would someday have to face Saddam Hussein.

★
The Gang of Eight during the Gulf War: (*left to right*) JCS Chairman Colin Powell, White House Chief of Staff John Sununu, Defense Secretary Richard Cheney, Vice President Dan Quayle, President Bush, Secretary of State James Baker, National Security Adviser Brent Scowcroft, and Deputy National Security Adviser Robert Gates. William Webster was not invited.

The Agency's Cassandra, Charlie Allen: As National Intelligence Officer for Warning, Allen told the White House that Iraq would invade Kuwait. Bush disagreed.

March 1991: Saddam Hussein appears on Iraqi television to announce that he has suppressed revolts aimed at overthrowing his government.

Robert Gates testifying before the Senate Select Committee on Intelligence during his confirmation hearings in September 1991.

We're going to miss ya, Pal: George Bush announces William Webster's retirement as CIA Director.

Friends and enemies: (*from left*) CIA officials Hal Ford, Larry Gershwin, Jennifer Glaudemans, and Douglas MacEachin. Of the four, MacEachin defended Gates.

Senators Howard Metzenbaum and Senate Intelligence Committee Chairman David Boren confer during Gates's confirmation hearings.

★

One happy family: Robert Gates; his wife, Becky; President Bush; and Supreme Court Justice Sandra Day O'Connor on November 12, 1991.

Part III
★★★
The Sorcerer's Apprentice

12
★★★
Earthquake

*T*he day after Kurt Muse was rescued from his prison in Panama, Romanian troops opened fire on a crowd of demonstrators in Bucharest. Over the next forty-eight hours the nation teetered on the edge of civil war as the Romanian Army, which sided with the people, fought a series of vicious gun battles with the Communist party's secret police, the Securitate. Within three days the issue was decided. On Christmas Day 1989, Romania's Communist dictator, Nicolae Ceausescu, and his wife were hastily tried and executed by a firing squad. A new government promising basic freedoms and democratic elections took power. It was the last and bloodiest revolution in a year of revolutions.

Eleven months before the execution of the Ceausescus, in January 1989, the Hungarian government signed a human rights agreement recognizing a citizen's right to travel abroad. Five days later Poland announced it would legalize the Solidarity trade union movement. The move to reform in the Soviet bloc was temporarily stymied in February, however, when Czechoslovakia arrested eight hundred human rights activists. In spite of this attempted crackdown, protests against Communist regimes continued to mount in Eastern Europe in the months that followed.

In May, Hungary opened its border with Austria and its Communist leader, János Kádár, was forced into retirement. In June, in the first democratic election held in Eastern Europe since the end of World War II, Solidarity candidates won ninety-nine of one hundred seats in a new Polish Senate and all the seats in a lower house of parliament. In Romania, the suppression of the minority Hungarian population sparked the first open defiance of Ceausescu's regime. The reformist tide was felt even in East Germany, the most tightly controlled Communist nation of Eastern Europe. Thousands of East Germans began to make their way to Hungary and then to freedom in Austria. The beginning of the final act in this historic drama took place in East Berlin on October 7, when Mikhail Gorbachev informed East German leaders that the USSR could no longer support its Warsaw Pact allies. Over the next ninety days the world watched with amazement as the Soviet empire in Europe dissolved with stunning speed.

The end of the old order in Europe sparked a period of recrimination, second-guessing, and self-doubt among the CIA's Soviet analysts, who were well aware that they had utterly failed to predict Gorbachev's stunning retreat. In fact, the breakdown was total in the DI over the four years that Gorbachev was head of the USSR: CIA analysts simply had no idea that the Soviet Union was on the verge of a major social and political revolution. For an institution that spent 50 percent of its resources trying to discern the intentions of Soviet leaders, an expenditure of tens of billions of dollars over forty years, the depth of the failure beggars credulity. The performance of the Office of Soviet Analysis, in particular, was inexcusable; its intelligence assessments significantly underestimated the power of Gorbachev's reforms and seriously overestimated the health of Soviet society. Senator Daniel Patrick Moynihan, the most outspoken critic of the agency's failure, called its performance "shameful."

The collapse of the Romanian police state stands as a symbol of the intelligence failure. During the previous ten years the CIA had purchased Soviet military secrets of "incalculable" value from Ceausescu's brothers in order to develop U.S. countermeasures to Warsaw Pact technology. It was a high-level, closely held, and extremely successful covert operation, and one that effectively allowed the CIA to penetrate important parts of Ceausescu's intelligence apparatus. Given this unprecedented access, Langley should have been able to monitor the riptide of discontent that eventually overwhelmed the Bucharest regime. But that was not what happened. The swiftness and stunning success of the revolution in Romania came as a distinct shock to the CIA. In the month leading up to Ceausescu's execution, CIA analysts issued no warnings that his life might be in jeopardy. They simply had no idea that what had transpired earlier, in Hungary and Czechoslovakia, might also happen in Romania. Much of the DI's thinking on the Romanian Revolution actually seemed to be influenced by a predisposition *against* the possibility that Ceausescu could be overthrown. It was as if such events were totally outside the CIA's understanding.

The depth of the agency's failure in all the revolutions of that year was mind-boggling; the CIA didn't even come close. The trail is littered with statistics that were compiled to show that such revolutions were out of the question. In 1986, for instance, the CIA estimated that East Germany's per capita gross national product (GNP) was $220 *higher* than West Germany's. The same mistakes were made when the agency examined other Warsaw Pact countries and then were repeated for the Soviet Union, whose economic growth rates had been described in increasingly glowing terms by the CIA for forty years.

In 1959, for example, Allen Dulles told the Congress that the increasing rate of Soviet industrial growth would mean that the gap between the economies of the USSR and the United States would be "dangerously narrowed" by the early 1970s. The claim was ludicrous, but it remained unquestioned. The CIA later predicted that the Soviet Union's economic power, by the late 1970s, would be two thirds that of the United States; in fact, it was not even one third. The CIA has defended these estimates to the present day. Agency officials maintain publicly that they had been right all along; they claim they knew the Soviet Union was going to collapse and had said so. George Kolt, the head of the DI's Office of Soviet Analysis, has been the agency's chief defender on this issue. "I plan to review for you our methodology..." he told Congress in 1990, "[and] cite previous public testimony that I believe will show that essentially we were right in our descriptions of the Soviet economy over time and in its prospects."

Kolt offered a detailed explanation of how the CIA uses its methodology to estimate Soviet GNP according to a complex formula that compared the economies of many nations. His discourse was thoroughly confusing. An economist later referred to the explanation as a "scam" since agency analysts called their methodology a Soviet Cost Analysis Model. A CIA officer has a better explanation for the confusion, saying that the agency was always measuring the wrong thing. "GNP simply measures how much crap they [the Soviets] produce. The fact that it is crap is a qualitative measure." But neither this rationale, nor Kolt's defense of it, could explain how the agency could have been so wrong.

Highly respected American economists (who did not work for the CIA) were embarrassed by Langley's estimates on Soviet economic strength and they said so. The criticism fell on deaf ears; the agency was simply unwilling to admit it had made a mistake—and not a small one at that. It was a colossal mistake, one that, according to a noted economist, ranked with economists' failures to predict the Great Depression. Or worse: One CIA analyst says the agency's failure to assess adequately the USSR's economic capacity (and inevitable collapse) was perhaps the worst failure in U.S. intelligence since the bombing of Pearl Harbor.

"We should not gloss over the enormity of this failure to forecast the magnitude of the Soviet crisis..." former CIA Director Stansfield Turner has since written. But that was exactly what happened. In one earlier study the CIA said the Soviet Union's economic output would surpass U.S. production by 1993—an unbelievable miscalculation, since by 1991 it was an open question whether the USSR would last that long.

A better explanation is that the CIA did not really make a mistake after all. After the U.S. government concluded in the late 1940s that the Soviet Union was a serious threat to American interests, CIA analysts had no choice but to make it so. No wonder, then, that the agency had little to say about the 1989–1990 revolutions—they invalidated forty years of work. The analysts decided instead to stake their credibility on Webster's accurate forecast that the Soviet Union would undertake massive cuts in military expenditures. The events of 1990 proved Webster right, but it seemed a minor victory amid the rubble of the CIA's failure to foresee the dissolution of Gorbachev's empire. As Turner later succinctly wrote, the CIA "missed by a mile."

How could DI analysts so blithely misread the political and economic trends that marked the end of the cold war? At least part of the answer lies in a series of incidents that shook the CIA during the 1980s and had a powerful effect on how agency analysts viewed their work. During a nine-year period (from early 1981 to December 1989) the Directorate of Intelligence suffered a critical loss of brainpower, a drain so acute that many key offices were left without enough experienced analysts to provide credible assessments. Even during Webster's years, the agency had difficulty attracting the kinds of specialists who had traditionally staffed its most important analytical positions.

The crisis of the 1980s was most keenly felt among mid-level analysts, who believed they had little chance of having their ideas accepted by the agency's senior managers. The crisis took the shape of a bell curve: The DI's power was enhanced at first in the early 1980s after Casey arrived and increased its stable of experts. But these same experts, and many of their veteran mentors, then resigned in disgust as a result of the Iran-contra scandal. The departures accelerated as the decade passed; nearly 20 percent of all analysts in the Office of Soviet Analysis left the CIA between 1984 and the end of 1987. The figure represented a progressive evaporation of the agency's professional capabilities. "The attrition was very high in the agency at the end of Casey's term," former analyst John Gentry confirms. "You had a clear cultural desire to serve in the early to mid-1980s that was changed markedly in the senior offices. We were decimated."

Nothing changed during the two years following Casey's death, although Webster, Kerr, Helgerson, and many other senior officials tried to stem the flood of retirements, transfers, and resignations. The veteran analysts who stayed were deeply troubled by the nearly total collapse of the DI's abilities to provide meaningful and well-focused intelligence reports and by its failure to attract and keep dedicated and well-trained professional analysts. It was particularly difficult to explain why such a mass flight took place in an institution that had been the recipient of enormous congressional largess over the previous years. Nor can the mass departures be blamed solely on the embarrassment of the Iran-contra affair; other scandals had racked the agency, but none had sparked this kind of exodus.

The real reason for the steady disintegration was a little-known, bitterly fought contest that festered inside the Directorate of Intelligence. In some respects, this battle was more important than any dispute that had ever taken place inside Langley's walls. It went to the heart of the CIA's commitment to provide objective intelligence assessments that were untainted by political considerations. According to former Deputy DCI Bobby Ray Inman, the struggle centered on a small number of analysts inside the Office of Soviet Analysis, where a sharp division existed between experts who believed that the USSR was economically incapable of maintaining an expansionist foreign policy and a group who believed the Soviets were unreconstructed imperialists.

According to Admiral Inman, this in-house intelligence war was first ignited by America's humiliating retreat from South Vietnam in April 1975, an event that effectively destroyed the CIA's preconception of American prestige and shattered, perhaps forever, the fundamental belief of its employees that America's leaders have, in analyst Thomas Barksdale's poignant phrase, "an informed awareness of the forces that motivate other countries and deal with these forces with a thoughtful blend of its moral, military, and economic resources." If, as Inman puts it, the fall of Saigon "was like an earthquake," then the battles inside the DI during the next fifteen years were its aftershocks.

Mel Goodman, an opinionated, sometimes overly loud, but nonetheless brilliant specialist in Soviet affairs, joined the CIA in 1966 and was immediately assigned to the Office of Current Intelligence as a junior analyst. From early in his career, Goodman was singled out for swift promotion as one of the agency's most promising Sovietologists. Soon after arriving at Langley, he was designated to take a position inside SFP—the CIA's prestigious Soviet Foreign Policy Division. Over the next two decades Goodman held "every major analytical and managerial position in the DI" as an expert on Soviet foreign policy and third world relations. He eventually rose to head a division in the Office of Soviet Analysis—a job that was considered a fitting achievement for his long and dedicated service to the intelligence community. Goodman, it was thought, could someday become chief of the CIA's intelligence arm; some colleagues hoped that he might be selected as the first DCI to come from the DI. He was an intense and gifted man with piercing eyes who retained a fierce commitment to the ideals of the CIA.

Goodman was perfectly suited for his profession: He worked long hours and his papers were uniformly "concise, well argued, and insightful," while his understanding of Soviet foreign policy was considered unmatched by any other expert at the agency. Goodman made it his business to grill clandestine service officers on their knowledge of KGB and GRU tradecraft, thinking it might come in handy in the future. He became the DI's unofficial expert on what the Soviets could and could not do. On occasion, he even served as a filter for DO knowledge on the tradecraft of the Soviet intelligence service. In one memorable incident recalled by a colleague, Goodman dismissed a DO report because it contradicted his own conclusions about the way in which the Soviet internal security system actually worked. At one point he reminded operations officers that the study of the KGB's tradecraft might consume an enormous amount of time, but it was essential to master it. Such blunt remarks might have been insulting coming from anyone else, but for Goodman they were simple statements of fact.

SFP was known for its often controversial papers on Soviet policy and for its very sharp, skilled arguments on Communist expansionist policies in the third world. Throughout the 1970s, a CIA colleague explains, Goodman built a reputation as "an immensely talented and intellectually charismatic analyst," who "made a name for himself by his prescient views on what was going on in the Kremlin." For instance, his research papers on Kremlin leaders, which were used by the DI to compose overwhelmingly detailed biographies, were nothing less than dazzling. Goodman also gained adherents to his compelling findings about the Soviet Union's views on the emerging nations in Africa, Asia, and Latin America. At a very young age he was considered the agency's resident expert on Communist intrigues in the third world and was sought out by agency leaders for his views. Considering the superheated competition among the tightly knit clan of Soviet experts, the praise Goodman earned was unusual. Compliments are not readily handed out by SOVA veterans.

The world of Soviet analysis was built from scratch after World War II by men who were considered giants at the CIA. These trail blazers, who served as mentors to its junior analysts during the seventies, were led by Sherman Kent, the controversial head of the agency's Office of National Estimates; Abbott Smith, his successor; Ambassador Llewellyn Thompson; and William Hyland (once considered a candidate for DCI). This older generation of intelligence analysts strictly adhered to a code of integrity and firmly believed that the future of the nation depended on their honesty. Kent had an especially profound influence on Goodman. It was people like Kent and Thompson who built the agency's reputation among Washington policy makers, and it was because of them that the CIA's Soviet experts knew their views were given enormous weight in the councils of government.

The CIA's analytical tradition was built in the 1950s on the foundation of Sherman Kent's philosophy of competing viewpoints. Instead of one umbrella research organization, as the DI became after 1975, Kent decided the CIA needed three independent intelligence branches that produced their own work. No single official was given overall responsibility for producing political intelligence. The structure rewarded disagreement and, some have argued, actually prevented the CIA from being undermined by the kinds of witch-hunts that characterized the McCarthy era. "We were basically untouchable," a retired analyst explains, "because no one could claim that we were a cabal. We argued, sometimes endlessly, about the simplest problems. We presented divergent views. It was a wide open process."

By the mid-1960s Kent's three institutions—the Office of National Estimates, the Senior Research Staff, and the Office of Current Intelligence—comprised the brain of the CIA. Anyone who presented a unique insight was valued, sometimes even lionized. It was that way for Goodman, who received increasing deference by senior officials for his work. They appreciated his abilities and tolerated his intellectual eccentricities, his sometimes discomforting habit of holding on to a position in the face of overwhelming disagreement. It was also clear to his colleagues that he was highly principled and demanded solid evidentiary material to back up any claims.

Goodman had joined the CIA several months before another fresh-faced Soviet analyst, Robert Gates, arrived on the scene after graduating from William and Mary. The two men became friends and shared a common bond: They both wanted to make the CIA a career, and they both were intensely interested in foreign policy questions, especially those involving the USSR. But eventually they took different paths. Goodman stayed on a straight career track, up the ladder through the various pay grades, rising steadily from office to office and assignment to assignment. Gates, on the other hand, left the agency and eventually became an intelligence aide on the National Security Council, where he met Brent Scowcroft.

The fall of Saigon had a profound effect on both Goodman and Gates. For Goodman, the U.S. adventure in Vietnam was a human tragedy and a foreign policy disaster. He was deeply affected by what he saw as America's failure to understand the aspirations of the Vietnamese people, and he became convinced that Vietnam's revolution was inspired by a nationalist and anticolonialist movement in Indochina. He argued that the war was not part of the Soviet Union's quest for world domination.

Gates disagreed: Vietnam's leaders were inspired by Communist ideas, he believed, and its revolution was given impetus by the expansionist policies of the Soviet Union, which was Vietnam's major arms supplier. His argument was based on prima facie evidence: America was compelled to support South Vietnam because of Soviet support for the North.

The differences reflected a deepening disagreement at the CIA over the ability of the Soviet government to promote and finance anti-American revolutions in the third world. One group, led by the increasingly opinionated Goodman, believed that the USSR was economically incapable of supporting and maintaining an expansionist third world policy. The opposing group, whose intellectual guru was Gates, believed that the humiliating U.S. withdrawal from Vietnam gave the Soviets an unprecedented opportunity to take advantage of America's weakness. This view was built on the well-established credo that U.S. strength deterred Communist aggression, while American military weakness provided an incentive for Soviet expansion

In the years following the fall of Saigon, a series of jolting aftershocks rolled through the intelligence directorate. The first event occurred within a year of America's withdrawal from Southeast Asia, when a civil war broke out in Angola. The controversy over the nature of Soviet designs on southern Africa caused the DI to lose its well-established reputation for comity and academic reserve. The argument intensified when the Ford administration decided the CIA should covertly ship arms to support Angola's antigovernment forces in their burgeoning struggle. Fearing further American involvement in a losing cause and concerned about the downturn in the U.S. economy, Congress barred the President from promoting this secret war, effectively shutting down the CIA's program.

The CIA's internal debate about the U.S. role in Angola was even more rancorous, with Goodman and Gates serving as advocates for the opposing points of view. It became increasingly obvious that the activist versus minimalist divisions that marked earlier disagreements between the DI and the clandestine service now divided Soviet analysts. The fundamental creed of American foreign policy was being attacked by a small but vocal group—led by Goodman—who questioned the ability of the Soviet Union to support an overseas adventure for an extended period. One CIA report even pointed to a debate about Angola then occurring inside the Soviet government, where a clique of reformers were arguing that the USSR could no longer afford such large-scale foreign interventions. This view gained more adherents when the Soviets decided to use Cuban troops as their surrogates in Angola; this was evidence, it was thought, of a compromise between the adventurers and their detractors in Moscow. Gates and his adherents believed that viewpoint played into the Soviets' hands; the Kremlin would like nothing more than for the CIA to believe the USSR was growing weak.

The mistrust sparked by the Angola operation began to permeate every debate in the DI over Soviet intentions. The breakdown, now more bitter and caustic than ever, was occurring along partisan lines, between liberal and conservative groups of analysts. Put simply, the protagonists were at one another's throats, disagreements and academic arguments that traditionally characterized such DI debates were replaced by an unprecedented political intensity that bordered on ideological fervor. These Soviet analysts knew the positions they supported could have a profound effect on American foreign policy; some were convinced that the future of the nation depended on their conclusions.

This ideological controversy was sharpened in 1979 by the invasion of Afghanistan, which seemed to support the hard-line position that Soviet expansionism was the natural result of American weakness. It was not a matter of resurrecting discredited analytical judgments—the DI's commitment to America's cold war creed still held sway among the vast majority of analysts inside the Directorate of Intelligence. But Soviet analysis had undergone a revolutionary change, primarily because Mel Goodman and the Soviet experts surrounding him had an enormous effect on the CIA's thinking. They viewed the Soviet Union as a society in crisis, with divided loyalties, and uncertain of its future. The fault lines were becoming apparent at the very top of the Communist bureaucracy, where a group of reformers were becoming more outspoken in opposing the leadership's ideological commitment to world revolution.

CIA analyst Douglas MacEachin, who served on a number of research task forces during his twenty-four years at the agency, remembers that a KGB defector gave the United States intelligence about the Afghan invasion that supported Goodman's general claim. "I had a chance in the late 1980s," MacEachin recalls, "to read a raw debrief of that Soviet officer, who was the highest-ranking KGB defector we've had. He was discussing the internal debate in the Soviet Union before the invasion of Afghanistan. The KGB opposed it, and the Foreign Ministry opposed it. And he gave their arguments. Those were exactly our arguments for saying why they wouldn't do it. 'But,' he said, 'those gorillas in the Central Committee, those ideologues, they won the day.'"

Goodman and other Soviet experts believed their views were supported by economic data they had compiled on the Soviet empire. This point was made by one of Goodman's disciples, Jennifer Glaudemans, during congressional testimony many years later. "The Soviets themselves were keenly aware that they could no longer sustain the burdens of their empire," she said. "They saw their own weaknesses and vulnerabilities, and that is why we got new thinking in Soviet foreign policy in the mid-eighties. As *glasnost* proved, the Soviets saw much of their foreign policy as a net loss. Not worth the benefits they were getting. The decisions to deploy SS20s [missiles] in Europe, to invade Afghanistan, and to subsidize other discredited regimes in the third world were publicly criticized in the Soviet media and in the parliament."

The debate was transformed in November 1980, after Ronald Reagan was elected President, in part as a result of his promise to rebuild the weakened national security state. He was convinced that the Soviet Union was an evil empire bent on world domination and inherently incapable of any internal changes. The Soviet Union was a monolith, he thought—a government without debate that ruthlessly suppressed dissent and marshaled enormous resources for a final, apocalyptic confrontation with the United States. His views were reinforced by a dedicated group of pro-defense advocates, known for their hard-line views on Soviet intentions. Their spiritual leader was Paul Nitze, who had headed the Team B effort on estimating Soviet military expenditures back in 1976. He had concluded the USSR was building a military machine bent on developing a first-strike nuclear capability to destroy the United States. His views were bitterly opposed by a growing number of Soviet analysts.

The special committee on the Reagan transition team that addressed questions about the future of the CIA included members of the Committee on the Present Danger—containing Team B members—and the conservative Madison Group (so named for its meetings at Washington's Madison Hotel). While Nitze was the formal head of these antiagency conservatives, the actual transition mechanism fell into the hands of Lieutenant General Edward Rowny, who had resigned from the Army in protest over the Carter administration's moderate negotiating position on SALT II. These CIA analysts grouped around Goodman believed Rowny would do anything he could to dampen the impact of their arguments regarding the estimates process. Rowny's teammates, who were also viewed as being anti-CIA, included three conservative members of the staff of the Senate Intelligence Committee: Angelo Codevilla, Mark Schneider, and Kenneth deGraffenreid. Codevilla, in particular, was singled out as "an agency hater" who would "do anything to take us apart."

The opening statement of the Reagan transition team's final report sparked deep animosity among the liberal-to-moderate wing of Soviet analysts and gave rise to fears of a purge of the unofficial Goodman caucus: "The fundamental problem confronting American security is the current dangerous condition of the Central Intelligence Agency and of national intelligence collection generally. The failure of American intelligence collection has been at the heart of faulty defense planning and a vacillating and misdirected foreign policy." Paradoxically, the report criticized the CIA for being "politicized" and dismissed arguments that the CIA provided objective intelligence as being "arrant nonsense." Singled out for special rebuke was the agency's legislative counsel, Fred Hitz, who was blasted for his role in attempting to gain congressional approval for the Carter administration's SALT II agreement. Hitz, the report said, should be fired.

The report alleged there were twelve CIA failures during the Carter years, most of which involved underestimating the Soviet threat. The list included "the abject failure" to forecast the massive Soviet buildup of strategic weapons, "the failure to predict" the improved accuracy of Soviet ballistic missiles, "the wholesale failure" to understand or counter Soviet propaganda, and "the general failure to explain" the characteristics of Soviet conventional weapons systems. In sum, the Reagan transition team charged that the CIA had been captured by a band of liberals who consistently underestimated the Soviet Union's commitment to world domination. The agency was an ossified, bureaucratic, un-American institution. "These failures are of such enormity," the report charged, "that they cannot help but suggest to any objective observer that the agency itself is compromised to an unprecedented extent and that its paralysis is attributable to causes more sinister than incompetence."

Veteran analyst Douglas MacEachin offers a different view of what was happening in the CIA in late 1980. Far from seeing the DI's position in a "sinister" light, MacEachin attributes the agency's deep divisions to the kind of ideological mind-set reflected in the transition team's report. "I think that very often the debates in the intelligence community over Soviet actions and intentions ended up in two camps," he says. "The one camp saw itself as rational and understanding real political decisions, and the other camp was viewed by them as a bunch of knuckle-dragging ideologues and commie bashers. On the other side, the group saw itself as hard-nosed realists and the other guys were wimpy com-symps [Communist sympathizers]. That's colorful language, but I think people, if you can find honest people out where we work, they will tell you that's not too far off. In the early 1980s, the hard-nosed realists were after the pinko-commie wimps and com-symps. That was the case publicly, and that was the case everywhere we read." What MacEachin fails to note is that the leader of each group was well known inside the agency. The leader of the Com-symps was Mel Goodman, and the leader of the hard-liners was Robert Gates.

Within weeks of being confirmed as DCI, William Casey dismissed the transition team and began distancing himself from its conclusions.

He promised his top managers that decentralizing the agency—"taking it apart," in Codevilla's phrase—was the last thing he wanted to do. Casey wanted to be director of the Central Intelligence Agency; he did not want to oversee a massive reorganization. The shock of the transition team's conclusions continued to reverberate through the Directorate of Intelligence anyway, since it was feared that Casey would have to appease administration conservatives. That intuition proved to be correct; within his first year, Casey punished SOVA for its decidedly moderate views on the Soviet threat. In essence, Casey sent the Soviet analysts into a kind of internal exile, an analyst's Siberia. It was a warning that their dissents were not welcome.

The punishment was actually initiated prior to Reagan's inauguration by the DDI, John McMahon, who approved the most massive reorganization of the agency's analytic structure in history. Of course, McMahon's motivation was far different from either Reagan's or Casey's: He had no intention of punishing SOVA; he simply wanted to streamline procedures by breaking up parts of the various offices inside the DI to allow for more integration of intelligence expertise. It was left to the new DDI and Casey's first deputy director, Bobby Ray Inman, to put the changes into effect.

After Gates and Inman tinkered with McMahon's suggestions, other "far-reaching changes," as Gates himself later termed them, were put in place in early 1982: "It was a period of great turbulence," Gates later admitted, that caused "predictable great disruption." In the end the Office of Soviet Analysis was separated from the rest of the agency and split off from its Eastern European component. "Not only did most people find themselves in different offices with different colleagues and different supervisors in 1982," Gates explained, but "they now found changes in the analytic process itself. All of this meant there were a number of unhappy analysts early in my tenure."

That was a considerable understatement; the 1982 reorganization was actually a devastating blow to CIA morale.

A later internal review summarized the demoralization caused by the reorganization and described the crippling blow it dealt to SOVA's traditionally excellent intelligence papers. The report noted that the reorganization "created problems" because it physically separated Soviet analysts from the rest of the agency. The move also led to rumors that senior SOVA analysts were being put on notice that their moderate positions on the USSR's overseas intentions were being closely scrutinized.

These suspicions built up resentment and hostility toward the Reagan administration, the new DCI, William Casey, and especially Gates. After his opening remarks to DI officials on January 7, 1982, the new DDI and the agency's moderate Soviet experts were inexorably set on a collision course. According to former agency analyst Harold Ford, Gates was viewed as a man with "a very strong personality" who "challenged positions very heavily" and "held views in rough agreement with top officials." In other words, Gates was widely considered to be the administration's hatchet man—appointed to bring the DI's Soviet office to heel.

Ford's characterization of Gates was based on his firsthand knowledge; they served together on the National Intelligence Council. But Ford's on-the-record description was actually an understatement of SOVA attitudes. Privately, other analysts viewed Gates as "smug, condescending, and callous" and characterized him as "very politically motivated." Ford later added to his own description a summary of attitudes inside the DI during Gates's term: "He has always been good at winning people to his cause, and he's always been good at ingratiating himself." The already sober mood inside SOVA was further darkened in 1982 by Gates's insistence that its intelligence papers had to be "sharpened and refocused" in order to be more useful to policy makers. The moderate analysts thought they knew what that meant: Gates wanted the CIA's most important national intelligence estimates changed, so that their conclusions reflected his own conservative views on the USSR.

These instructions from Gates were the culmination of a year of battling between him and Mel Goodman. The first open clash between them came in early 1981, when Gates was still the national intelligence officer (NIO) for the Soviet Union. Predictably, the fight was over Casey's insistence that the Soviet Union surreptitiously supported international terrorism. Gates enthusiastically supported these views even though Casey's other top assistants struggled to soften their boss's public statements on Claire Sterling's headline-grabbing claim. The CIA's liaison officers to Congress continued to valiantly sweep up after his astonishing remarks on terrorism during Senate hearings. When Casey ordered the DI to draft a Special National Intelligence Estimate, Gates (as NIO) was given responsibility for producing the final conclusions.

The project began during the month after Reagan's inauguration. When the first draft was finished, it gave only a lukewarm endorsement of the claims made by Sterling and Casey. This outcome was actually a courageous attempt by the moderates to undermine the DCI's views. The estimate stated: "The Soviets have opposed international terrorist activity in public and, in private, have urged their own clients to avoid its use. Neither the Soviets nor Eastern Europeans directly sponsor or coordinate terrorist groups; they do not provide direct assistance to groups which are primarily terrorist; and they do not encourage the use of terror by their third-world clients." Gates was dissatisfied and demanded that the paper be reworked. To make sure that his orders were followed, he assigned the work to junior analysts in the newly created Office of Global Intelligence (OGI).

"This [the terrorism estimate] was done in this case by a writer," Goodman later told the Senate Intelligence Committee, "who had arrived at the CIA only weeks before he was given the assignment, and the manager of the product was an official who had arrived at the agency maybe several months before he was given that assignment." During the next four months the initial low-key assessment was transformed into one of the shrillest and most controversial intelligence documents of the cold war. It contradicted almost every piece of original research done on the Soviet Union complied since 1948. The findings horrified SOVA analysts, who were powerless to stop Casey and Gates from turning it over to the White House.

The final SNIE concluded: "The Soviets are deeply engaged in support of revolutionary violence worldwide. Such involvement is a basic tenet of Soviet policy, pursued in the interests of weakening unfriendly societies, destabilizing hostile regimes, and advancing Soviet interests. . . ." The paper went on to detail Soviet terrorist operations that included "hijackings, assassinations, kidnapings, bombings and the victimization of innocent civilians."

SOVA moderates could hardly believe their eyes. Goodman was convinced that Gates had plotted a "manipulation of the system" to satisfy Casey.

After the SNIE was presented, Goodman and Soviet analyst Lyn Ekedahl wrote a response to Casey that directly challenged Gates. They routed their memo through the upper levels of the CIA, thereby making sure that everyone who mattered saw their complaints, and were prepared for later conflicts between SOVA and Gates. "The Soviets do not instigate, coordinate, or control terrorist activity," they reported. "There is no direct collaboration between the USSR and such purely terrorist organizations as Baader-Meinhof, the Red Brigades, PIRA, and the Japanese Red Army. The Soviets do not supply them directly with military assistance or training."

In the end their memo had little impact because Casey's views were ignored by other senior officials in the Reagan administration, particularly Secretary of State George Shultz, who refused to include the SNIE in his briefing book. ("The estimate outraged him," Goodman later remarked.) Casey's reaction, on the other hand, was predictable: He dismissed the conclusions of Goodman and Ekedahl out of hand. Neither Casey nor Gates even bothered to respond formally.

With the furor over the Soviet terrorism assessment still simmering, Goodman's next, and most important, battle with Gates took place in February 1982. At issue was a draft of a national intelligence estimate (NIE) on Soviet intentions in the third world that had been written by experts in Goodman's division. In many ways this estimate was intended to be a unique, precedent-setting document; for the first time in forty years the CIA was outlining a significant shift in Soviet foreign policy. SOVA's major conclusion was that the leadership in Moscow was reluctantly undertaking withdrawal from the third world. Goodman was arguing that the Soviets had, in effect, "blinked" and were beginning an international retreat. The NIE stressed that the USSR was confronted by mounting problems as it tried to support its discredited third world allies, while suffering from growing economic burdens at home and facing the sobering realization of America's willingness to counter any such expansion. Goodman considered his assessment to be based on sound reporting from a wide variety of sources, including interviews with Soviet defectors who confirmed that there had been a rethinking of the USSR's world view inside the Communist leadership.

Gates rejected Goodman's estimate with a four-page response. "I have read the attached draft," he wrote, "and, unhappily, find it to be rather dry and lacking any sense of the dynamics of Soviet involvement in the Third World and why involvement in the Third World is important to the Soviet Union." He castigated Goodman for failing to give the study a historical introduction that put Soviet expansion in the third world in perspective. But what was most shocking about Gates's response was that he failed to attack the estimate on the basis of its sourcing; he seemed concerned only about changing its conclusions. Gates ended his response by ordering the draft to be sent back to Goodman with a suggestion on how to redraw its findings: "In short, I see a lot more trouble for us in the Third World in the years ahead because it's easier to make trouble than it is to solve it." Once Goodman read that passage, he knew that Gates wanted a paper that would reflect his personal position, not the truth.

Goodman was also very angry about another passage in the Gates memo—one they had previously fought over. Gates charged that Goodman's draft failed "to take adequate account of recent information" the CIA had acquired "on the nature and extent of Soviet active measures in the Third World in Africa, the Islamic world, and elsewhere." Gates wrote that these reports should have been thoroughly discussed in the NIE "in my view."

Goodman was dumbfounded by this instruction. He remembered that this "recent information" Gates was now citing on Africa had been discredited in an internal DI debate that had taken place several months earlier. In late 1981, while Gates was still the NIO for the Soviet Union, he had instructed a senior analyst to prepare an assessment on Soviet activities in Africa. The resulting draft report was a glowing account of Soviet opportunities in the Third World. Goodman, who was the SOVA representative to the meeting that discussed the assessment, found the conclusion to be "outrageous." He felt it was "only fair" to approach the author of the study in advance to warn him that he had "problems" with the conclusions and that he was going to be raising these questions at the final meeting on the assessment. When Goodman confronted this senior analyst, the man replied: "Your problem isn't with me. . . . I am just a hired pen in this enterprise."

"Who hired you?" Goodman asked.

"Bob Gates," the embarrassed analyst responded.

Goodman was outraged when he finally attended the meeting presided over by Gates to assess the final Soviet-Africa estimate. After about thirty minutes of discussion around the table, with Goodman raising all the problems that had troubled him, Gates became uncomfortably impatient. As Goodman recalled: "[Gates] looked at me—but I think the message was for everyone in the room; I didn't take it personally—'Look,' he said, 'this is the assessment Casey wants, and this is the assessment that Casey is going to get.' "

In effect, Gates had criticized Goodman's 1982 NIE on "Soviets and the Third World," for its failure to reflect his own and William Casey's views, which were contained in a paper that Gates had personally commissioned. "What Casey and Gates did was to introduce unprecedented measures to change the system," Goodman later explained. "For the first time we had to clear terms of reference and drafts before they were coordinated with the DCI." For the professional analyst, it was a major change from the days of Sherman Kent. "Essentially all intelligence was filtered through Bob Gates," Goodman added.

The ongoing Goodman and Gates feud had a crippling effect on the DI, but especially on SOVA, where the group around Goodman fought a losing battle with the CIA's leadership over a series of controversial assessments that significantly influenced the Reagan administration's foreign policy. To review the most important intelligence papers issued during this fight is to stroll through the ideological minefields of the era: regarding Afghanistan, a paper on the limitations of the mujaheddin was rejected (by Gates); regarding Nicaragua, Casey was enraged when analysts questioned whether the Soviets would actually send MiG fighters to the Sandinistas (they did not); and finally, regarding alleged Soviet involvement in the attempted assassination of Pope John Paul II, Gates helped engineer a secret study that argued the case *for* Soviet complicity, when his critics said there was little or no evidence to support the view. (This study was secret, but Gates made sure that Vice President Bush received a copy.)

The warfare between Goodman and Gates carried over to the first year of Webster's tenure, when the DI was hit with a new round of resignations and transfers. Analysts were simply not convinced that the new DCI would protect them from the continuing politicization of their intelligence product. Reports that Gates was secretly running the CIA from the White House made matters worse—Webster was considered neither a strong leader nor politically astute enough to stand up to Bush or his NSC protégé. Subsequent events seemed to support their view. During Webster's tenure Gates was more outspoken in private and public about his anti-Soviet views than ever before, even in the face of clear evidence that enormous reforms were under way in the USSR. In published articles and speeches he made claims about the findings of U.S. intelligence that had not been cleared with the DI (a normal practice before he and Casey took control of the analyst in 1981). In several of his prepared remarks, he dismissed the impact of Gorbachev's reforms.

It was predictable that the Reagan administration's initial distrust of the CIA in 1981 would have a lasting effect on many careers. The circulation of the Reagan transition report sparked a mass exodus inside the DI that was still under way in 1989. While Casey had tried his best to heal these wounds and to hire qualified replacements, his own political prejudices undercut whatever gains he made. By 1989 the war inside the CIA had resulted in a clear-cut victory for conservatives; they had manipulated the CIA's intelligence product to such a degree that they were incapable of understanding the enormous changes in the Soviet society or predicting the revolutions that swept through Eastern Europe at the end of the decade. The more accurate views of the moderates and nonideologues were simply not welcome.

"Senior analysts began to leave," Goodman has explained. "They began to look for a way out. You know, you can deal with this kind of abuse just so much.... If you take it seriously, you get weary. And you wonder about the waste and abuse in terms of government resources that went into training these senior people.... I believe there is [only] one analyst left in the Soviet foreign policy shop. Everyone else has either left the Soviet area completely, left the CIA completely, or in my case, I resigned because of the politicization...."

If William Webster, Richard Kerr, Richard Stolz, Thomas Twetten, John Helgerson, or any other senior CIA manager was embarrassed by his agency's inability to predict the collapse of the Soviet empire, he did not show it. Instead Webster continued his public campaign to restructure the agency by shifting its focus away from the superpower conflict and toward a new emphasis on combating terrorism, narcotics trafficking, and arms and chemical weapons proliferation. Webster was proud of the changes he had instituted; he emphasized them at every opportunity as a way of taking public attention away from the agency's obvious failures.

But Webster's problem was not public, it was private. At the beginning of 1990, his isolation from the clandestine service was complete and his alienation from important analysts inside the intelligence directorate was an established fact. He was being continually criticized for his lack of foreign affairs expertise.

No one understood this better than he did, so he spent long hours trying to grasp basic foreign policy issues. It was not a subject that he was particularly interested in, a fact that never ceased to amaze other CIA officials who were consumed by such topics. Admiral Inman, who believed Webster was doing a good job, had cautioned him against this lack of interest back in 1987, when Webster first called him to discuss the CIA job. "Foreign policy wasn't his strong suit, and everyone understood that," Inman says. "And it took him a long time to pick it up. That was certainly frustrating for some people. But I think that he mastered it finally and grew to enjoy it."

Webster's eventual proficiency with a number of these issues was due largely to the counsel he received from Helgerson and Kerr, both respected foreign policy experts with unlimited open-door access to his office. The DCI needed them, desperately. "We would have these round tables over lunch on the seventh floor, and we would try to explain some issues to the judge, and he would nod and agree with everything we said," a senior analyst remembers, "but after we would leave and he was all alone, he'd call in his top aides. They would come in and see Webster sitting there with this blank look on his face. They would know what had happened and would sit down and explain things to him. They'd go over and over it."

Webster also depended on a number of other analysts who shared his belief that the agency needed to continue emphasizing its relations with the public and Congress. One of them was Joseph De Trani, a career operations officer whom Webster eventually recruited to take over the Public Affairs Office. Webster was hypnotized by De Trani's infectious exuberance, which came complete with a New Jersey accent and a rah-rah view of the CIA that Webster especially prized. During background briefings with reporters, De Trani acted as the agency cheerleader, taking a soft approach to traditional press-agency tensions and always promoting CIA's successes. "This is an exciting, exciting place," De Trani would say during a typical interview. "And these are exciting times. Great things are happening here. Great, great things."

De Trani, Kerr, Stolz, Twetten, and Helgerson were the mainstays of Webster's inner circle. By Webster's third year as DCI, a second, outer circle of officials also started to form around him: a group of clandestine service officers and analysts who began to appreciate his vaunted political abilities, his deft handling of Congress, and, perhaps most important, his ability to hold on to his job in spite of the White House's mistrust that he was not a team player. That last accomplishment, in particular, seemed to work in his favor. For all his blind spots, at least Webster would not sit in silence and allow the Bush administration to disparage the agency.

Nor would he allow Congress to attack the CIA without putting up a defense. In late 1989, for instance, Webster unceremoniously thumbed his nose at complaints from Capitol Hill that the agency was purposely pulling support away from guerrilla groups engaged in what was thought to be the final stages of the war in Afghanistan. The controversy had begun months earlier, when Soviet military forces withdrew from Afghanistan, and had reached its peak when Congress complained about the poor performance of the head of the Afghan Task Force. In rising to defend the agency, Webster was faced with yet another unexpected crisis of confidence.

When the Soviet Union withdrew the last of its troops from Afghanistan on February 15, 1989, the mood inside the clandestine service was euphoric. For the first time in forty years a covert CIA program had succeeded in forcing a Soviet withdrawal from a third world country. To mark the victory, Webster held a unique celebration in his office, to which he invited members of the Afghan Task Force and senior officers from the NE Division. He even gave a little speech, during which he toasted the head of the task force and outlined the covert program's ten-year history. "This is a victory for America," he said, "but it is also a victory for the CIA." As he turned to the officers of the task force, he added: "Most of all, this is a victory for you." When he had finished, the top CIA officials who were present applauded heartily for the task force representatives. According to one officer, this truly emotional moment helped create a special bond between Webster and the task force officers.

The Soviet Union's defeat in Afghanistan was well worth celebrating. The CIA had spent three billion dollars providing rifles, mines, mortars, rocket launchers, and eventually, shoulder-held ground-to-air missiles—Stingers—to the mujaheddin. Through this massive effort, the agency had succeeded in establishing its first complete battlefield covert operation. From a corridor of offices at Langley, the task force ran a war by proxy by plotting strategy, purchasing arms, and designing exotic new weapons systems that were "Afghan-friendly." The CIA even purchased hundreds of Tennessee mules to transport the arms overland from Pakistan to rebel groups. The result was a complete rout. After the first Stinger missiles were successfully fired at Soviet helicopters on September 26, 1986—downing three of four Hind Mi24 gunships above the Jalalabad airport—a thousand more of the weapons were sent overland from Pakistan. The mujaheddin forced the Soviets to fight on their terms, on the ground, in a fruitless slugging match that exhausted the USSR's military capabilities.

The Soviet Union left Afghanistan in a ruined condition after ten years of war and so weakened that few believed it could survive a guerrilla offensive. The American press reported that it was only a matter of time before the ruling People's Democratic Party in Kabul was overthrown. This view was a mirror of America's own experience in Vietnam, where the U.S. withdrawal had been followed within two years by a decisive North Vietnamese military offensive. CIA analysts who studied Afghanistan's political and military balance came to the same conclusion. They published an intelligence report that said it would take six to twelve months—but no more—before rebel forces gained a total victory. Agency analysts also concluded that the USSR was so spiritually and economically fatigued by the conflict that Gorbachev would soon abandon support for the struggle.

There were a handful of dissenting voices to this view, including members of the Afghan Task Force who were convinced that the seven major mujaheddin groups operating inside the country were too politically and ideologically divided to agree on a common military program. A number of CIA operations officers also worried that anti-Western Islamic fundamentalism remained a major motivating philosophy inside the resistance, which could cripple further U.S. efforts to control guerrilla strategy. They pointed out that the major guerrilla army was controlled by the Islamic party led by Gulbuddin Hekmatyar, who was suspected of promoting anti-Western sentiments. Hekmatyar received most of his supplies through the Pakistan intelligence service, which had in-country responsibility for disbursing the CIA's largess. Other groups received a fraction of the materials. In other words, unlike North Vietnam, where a unified political party and a well-trained, conventional army acted as a single unit to conquer the South, Afghan resistance leaders were divided on the question of what a new government should look like.

In sum, even though there was good cause to celebrate a CIA triumph on February 15, there was no reason to believe yet that the victory was final. In a few months, task force officers knew, Afghanistan could end up looking like Lebanon.

If there were doubts at the CIA that the Afghan resistance could merge into a united front, few people questioned what the Soviets would do: They were considered to be gone from Afghanistan for good. Because of this consensus, there was no reason to continue the massive shipments of arms to South Asia. Accordingly, the agency cut back on its support for the mujaheddin during the first three months following the Soviet withdrawal. The decision proved to be a mistake: Gorbachev's commitment to supporting his client state, the Najibullah regime, was more than just talk; it was a major concession to the Kremlin's powerful Afghan lobby, undertaken in order to win its support for the withdrawal.

During the next six months after the Soviet retreat, a massive resupply effort from Moscow sent $1.4 billion in aid to support the Kabul regime.

The first sign that the agency's assumptions were wrong about what would happen in Afghanistan did not come until early July 1989, when Afghan guerrillas failed to pull off a coordinated attack on government outposts near Jalalabad. From then until the autumn, mujaheddin military operations were poorly coordinated and widely dispersed. Worse yet, a group of thirty guerrilla leaders returning home from a strategy session were assassinated by a rival resistance faction. The massacred group was part of the Jamiat-i-Islami, which operated in the northern part of the country. Jamiat members blamed the Islamic party and Hekmatyar for the attack and said that one of Hekmatyar's field commanders, Sayad Jamal, was responsible. The incident presaged a full-fledged civil war inside the country that could only strengthen the Kabul regime.

Controversy over the CIA's failure to predict the Soviet resupply, second-quessing about the agency's cutback of arms to the mujaheddin, and fears that the once united rebel groups could not be brought together boiled over on August 3, during a luncheon meeting at Langley between Webster and congressional leaders. The members of Congress were the Afghan resistance's most outspoken supporters on Capitol Hill. Among these members of Congress were some of the same voices that had argued for the deployment of Stingers in 1986. The luncheon erupted into a bitter exchange between Webster and Senator Gordon Humphrey (R-NH), who headed a special task force on Afghanistan in the Senate. Humphrey told Webster that it appeared the agency had "forgotten about Afghanistan," and he accused the CIA of underestimating the Soviet's commitment to the Kabul regime. Humphrey insisted that a leadership change was necessary inside the CIA's Afghan Task Force, which, he said, had "seriously mismanaged" the covert program. Florida Republican Representative Bill McCollum chimed in, saying that the agency's "scandalous" performance had "squandered a certain victory" by cutting back on arms supplies.

Webster vigorously defended the agency program, but was forced to admit that internal assessments that resistance forces could win the war in six to twelve months had been optimistic. It now appeared, he said, that it would take much longer and that the mujaheddin's internal strife had to be resolved before a victory would be possible. Webster carefully did not mention that the CIA had purposely drawn down weapons stockpiles on the basis of the agency's prediction and that it didn't want highly sophisticated weapons systems falling into rebel hands or, worse yet, ending up in the hands of international terrorists. The congressional leaders left dissatisfied; Webster refused to agree that the task force's chief should be replaced by a more activist official.

This confrontation had been building for some time. A week before the luncheon, Webster had received a copy of a letter sent to the Senate Intelligence Committee by Senators Humphrey and Orrin Hatch (R-UT), that underscored their concern over the agency's failures in Afghanistan. The senators urged that the issue be studied in a special closed session. Hatch produced his own report on the controversy several months later. He concluded that mid-level CIA officers were not to blame for the program's mismanagement. "It's the president's fault and Webster's fault," he said. The Intelligence Committee complied with Humphrey's and Hatch's request by calling Undersecretary of State Robert Kimmitt to testify, and the House complemented the Senate investigation by holding its own session and inviting a resistance leader to appear.

The result of all this congressional scrutiny was that enormous pressures were brought to bear on the CIA to increase the Afghan weapons flow via Pakistan. To counter the growing controversy, the White House and State Department launched a campaign to reunite the feuding Afghan groups. Finally, Webster gave in to congressional pressure to remove the head of the Afghan Task Force, Daniel Webster—a popular and respected career clandestine service officer. He was assigned to a temporary position in another part of the DO.

Task force officers were enraged by Webster's decision; it seemed he had squandered whatever alliances he had formed with them in February. No amount of argument could change his mind. Stolz attempted to ameliorate the bitterness among DO officers by arguing that Webster's move was made only to keep the agency's program out of the public eye and to ensure that the guerrilla forces it supported would win an eventual victory.

Stolz's mediation failed. Task force officers remained unconvinced that Webster understood the significance of his action. Privately, however, Webster realized he could not remain an effective DCI and throw away what little support he had gained in the DO as a result of the victory in Afghanistan. He had gotten his job because of his reputation of being able to handle the Congress, by ensuring both Bush and the CIA that he could be an open and honest arbiter of agency concerns. Now it looked as if the politicians were handling him. By mid-December 1989— four months after Dan Webster was removed—the DCI was ready to undo the damage caused by the Afghan controversy. To the surprise of his detractors he quietly reassigned Dan Webster as head of the task force. The DCI's actions immediately helped solidify his support inside the CIA. It was just this backing that he desperately needed when White House attacks on his performance were renewed during the next eighteen months.

13
★★★
Mind-sets

On March 7, 1990, eighteen months after the CIA first received reports that Libya was manufacturing chemical warfare agents at Rabta, the Bush administration charged that the North African government was resuming production at the plant and demanded it be closed. One week later a mysterious fire destroyed most of the facility; eyewitness accounts given to journalists indicated that the destruction was nearly total, though the fire's origin was unknown. The inferno had burned through the plant's large main production area and spread a thick cloud of potentially dangerous gases over the Libyan desert.

American intelligence officials refused to comment on the Rabta "accident," except to deny they had any role in the blaze. President Bush also issued a denial which was backed by anonymous White House sources who confided that the United States had not used satellite intelligence capabilities to monitor the fire's progress, and that even if it had, the thick cloud cover over North Africa made producing such photographs impossible. On March 15 White House press secretary Marlin Fitzwater repeated Bush's denial. "The origins of the fire are unknown," he said simply. "The United States had no involvement."

Fitzwater added that the incident was not mentioned during a telephone conversation that morning between Bush and West German Chancellor Helmut Kohl. Members of the White House press corps were surprised by this statement because West German firms had been implicated in designing the Rabta facility and exporting chemicals to start production.

When pressed by reporters, Fitzwater conceded that the United States could be credited at least indirectly with the plant's destruction. "We get an assist out of this," he reluctantly admitted. "You get that on defense or on offense."

Even though this last statement contradicted his earlier denial, Fitzwater was implying that the United States knew more than it was willing to admit. He even went further. He hinted that the CIA had known about the plant for some time.

In answering a question about the possibility of West Germany's role in designing the facility, Fitzwater indirectly acknowledged that the CIA had been monitoring the Rabta danger. "We have had a number of contacts with our allies concerning this plant," Fitzwater admitted, "discussing issues of how [the plant] gets experts and . . . chemicals. . . ."

In fact, the Bush administration secretly pressured the West German government to do something to make sure that Libya's chemical weapons capability never became operational.

There are a lot of clues that seem to point to West Germany's responsibility for setting the fire. First, the fire occurred at a uniquely opportune time: The plant had not yet become fully operational; it was just beginning to produce mustard gas as well as Sarin and Somin, two other toxic materials. Second, the fire was set where it could do the most damage: in a number of key locations inside the plant's huge main production facility. A separate fire was also set in a primary storage warehouse nearby, where the most volatile chemicals were kept. Third, the fire was set carefully: In the first hours of the blaze, nothing burned in the structure around the unroofed part of the plant (purposely constructed that way in order to allow the mixing of chemicals for mustard gas). The absence of fire at this spot allowed for the maximum dispersal of chemicals that were burning in the nearby main production facility. Finally, the fire was set off just the right way to ensure that chemical agents were not loosed on the environment.

The State Department did not deny that the West Germans started the fire. The department's official statement also signaled that the United States was not surprised or unhappy about it. "The chemical agents that we know of at the plant would not present a danger to neighboring people when burned," State Department spokeswoman Margaret Tutwiler dryly informed the press. She then obliquely confirmed that the plant's destruction was not an accident. "The preferred method of destroying mustard gas is, in fact, an open fire," she added, matter-of-factly.

For its part, the West German government denied involvement in the plant's destruction. ("The idea . . . is completely baseless, plucked from the air," a spokesman said.) In all likelihood, these denials were deliberately misleading. But if West Germany *was* responsible for the

Rabta fire, it could not have acted without the assistance of the CIA. There were several reasons that pointed to an American role. The agency had recruited anti-Qaddafi dissidents and anyone else with knowledge of the Rabta facility for nearly eighteen months prior to the incident. The CIA had compiled a voluminous amount of detailed information on the plant from chemical weapons experts and executives from European import-export companies that did business with Libya. The CIA also provided evidence to the White House to rebut West German claims that they had nothing to do with constructing the plant. That information was passed by the U.S. government to West German intelligence officers.

After receiving this information, one week after the Rabta fire, West German government officials charged Jürgen Hippenstiel-Imhausen, the head of Imhausen-Chemie, AG, a large chemical export firm, with illegally shipping plans and equipment to Libya. The indictment was filed three days after Libya announced that it had ceased payments on West German imports and had canceled all Libyan oil deliveries to West Germany.

In the meantime, Qaddafi had accused West Germany of setting the Rabta fire by using "very sophisticated means," perhaps a timing device, "to make it appear that the sabotage was actually an accident." Qaddafi said he had arrested two West Germans for setting the fire.

Despite his denials, Fitzwater's remarks of March 15 signaled an important victory for the intelligence community, though that victory would have unforeseen ramifications in the year ahead.

March 15, 1990, stands out as one of the most important days of the Bush administration, though not simply because of the incident in Libya. In Israel the conservative government of Prime Minister Yitzhak Shamir fell after losing a vote of confidence in the Knesset. The defeat came after Shamir announced that Israel would not participate in peace talks, which he had first proposed, with Palestinians in the occupied territories. That same day in Baghdad thirty-one-year-old British journalist Farzad Bazoft was hanged by the government of Saddam Hussein on charges that he'd spied for Israel and Britain. The stunning news of Bazoft's execution was widely condemned by the international community—but not at the White House.

The two events, in Jerusalem and Baghdad, were more closely related than they first appeared and had a significant impact on U.S. foreign and intelligence policy. On the one hand, President Bush's role in the fall of the Shamir government marked a significant departure from the pro-Israel stance of the Reagan years. On the other hand, the muted U.S. reaction to the Bazoft execution reflected the administration's hands-off attitude when it came to dealing with Hussein.

The events leading up to the Shamir government's sudden collapse were set in motion on the evening of February 22, during an overseas telephone conversation between Bush and Shamir. Sitting in the Oval Office listening to Bush's end of the conversation were his two top NSC advisers, Brent Scowcroft and Robert Gates. At several important points during the call the President turned to them for advice. Bush expressed his strong concern to Shamir that Soviet immigrants would be settled in large numbers in newly constructed towns in the occupied territories and that this building program could derail Israeli-Palestinian talks on self-rule. As the discussion became particularly contentious, Bush implied that Shamir was purposely attempting to undermine any chance for an Israeli-Palestinian understanding. Bush then cited Israeli housing figures as evidence that Shamir was deliberately increasing the number of settlements in the occupied territories—"creating facts," as the Israelis say—at just the wrong time.

Shamir politely disagreed; he promised Bush that no more than 10 percent of Soviet Jews would end up in new settlements in the occupied territories. Bush said he was pleased.

After the call and after Gates had studied the numbers, Bush discovered that Shamir's arithmetic was only partly accurate. Gates told the President that Shamir had conveniently forgotten to mention that large numbers of Soviet Jews also would be settled in East Jerusalem, which Shamir did not view as an occupied territory. When those figures were added, the total came to much more than 10 percent. Shamir's claim was intentionally subtle; if the United States agreed with his figure of 10 percent, then the administration would recognize Israeli sovereignty over all of Jerusalem. Bush was enraged. He believed Shamir had purposely misled him, even lied to him. After consulting with Scowcroft, Gates, and Secretary of State Baker, Bush decided to pressure Shamir publicly on the settlements issue.

The culmination of the strategy took place during a press conference in Palm Springs, California, on March 3, when Bush took a verbal slap at Israel for its policy of building new settlements in the West Bank, in Gaza, and, as he purposely added, "in occupied East Jerusalem." Bush's remark, which spurred little initial comment in the U.S. press, made big headlines in Israel. Shamir struck back by dismissing Defense Minister Shimon Peres from the Cabinet, which sparked a government crisis. On March 15 Shamir lost a 60–55 vote of confidence in the Knesset and was forced to call for new elections. The fall of Israel's government and the subsequent political crisis postponed Mideast peace talks indefinitely. Meanwhile, the building of new Israeli settlements accelerated in East Jerusalem and elsewhere. Strangely, however, the Israeli political crisis had little discernible impact on White House officials. They viewed the no-confidence vote philosophically: It meant that the less intransigent

Labor party would have a new chance at leading the government, *if* it won the election.

It is now clear that, in fact, Bush's comment backfired; in a fit of anger he had derailed the most viable Middle East peace offensive in nearly a decade. Shamir called Bush's bluff on Jerusalem, thereby signaling Washington that he would do anything to hold on to the formerly divided city. So instead of coaxing Shamir to the peace table, Bush pushed him away; it was another two months before a new government in Israel was strong enough to begin dealing with the peace issue and another sixteen months after that before Shamir actually met his antagonists face-to-face.

Iraq's execution of Bazoft also caused enormous problems for the White House, which had been trying to kick-start a more substantive relationship with Saddam Hussein during the previous fourteen months. The administration's policy was based on a little-known State Department study on Iraq issued at the end of the Reagan years. This paper, completed with the help of CIA Middle East experts, had reached four general conclusions: that the Persian Gulf "is a geo-strategic entity" key to the survival of the United States, that Gulf regimes (particularly the governments of the Gulf Cooperation Council—Kuwait, Qatar, United Arab Emirates, and Bahrain) are politically unstable and need long-term U.S. military and political support, that the Gulf states are "West leaning" (a tendency, the paper said, that must be "reinforced"), and that Saddam Hussein was a rational leader who would not follow a failed policy.

The State Department study was buttressed by a similar White House document issued shortly after Bush took office. That three-page report, approved as National Security Directive 26, said that the United States would pursue improved relations with Iraq through a long-term policy of limited cooperation that was driven by the perceived Soviet threat to "vital" American security interests. NSD 26 urged a program of economic reconstruction in Iraq and hinted that other initiatives could take place that would help moderate the revolutionary nature of the Iraqi regime. Saddam Hussein, the paper implied, would be responsive to these economic and political incentives.

Even though there were strong warnings and objections to NSD 26 from a number of administration experts and members of Congress, senior officials at the White House and State Department believed that Hussein's hatred of Israel and mistrust of the United States could be effectively reined in. From the moment the new President took office until he initialed NSD 26, the Bush administration endorsed the 1988 State-CIA study: Hussein was a "ruthless, but pragmatic" leader.

That spring, however, the Iraqi dictator was being ruthless. On March 15, 1990, five days after Farzad Bazoft was convicted by a revolutionary court, he was executed for spying on Iraq. The British journalist was originally arrested in September 1989, after entering an off-limits military-industrial complex at al-Hillel, which he believed contained technology for producing chemical weapons. (A massive explosion had occurred at the plant the week before his visit.) Iraq conducted a show trial: Bazoft was denied counsel, and the only evidence produced against him was a thin test tube of soil confiscated from his suitcase. He admitted that he had taken the sample to test it for traces of chemicals, and he signed a confession, but he later vehemently argued that he had made the statement under duress. He denied he was a spy.

The execution was carried out in spite of the international outcry that descended on Iraq after his arrest. British Prime Minister Margaret Thatcher called the execution "an act of barbarism which is deeply repugnant to all civilized people." In Washington, however, spokesman Fitzwater issued a lukewarm response for President Bush.

During the morning White House press briefing, a reporter asked: "Iraq has hung a journalist working for a British newspaper ... and you seem to be ambivalent at best about his hanging. We don't condemn the hanging by Iraq?"

"We don't have any information on the case," Fitzwater replied.

"Do you suspect he was a spy, as Iraq says?"

"We don't have any judgment on the case," Fitzwater answered.

"... After you get more information, are we going to have a more definitive reaction to the hanging of the journalist?"

"I would not expect so," Fitzwater said. "This was a British citizen. It is a matter where international clemency was asked for, and we regret that that wasn't granted. But ... it was not a U.S. citizen. And we don't have any judgment on the case itself."

The seeds of the coming U.S.-Iraq conflict were planted with that official comment from the White House press room on March 15. The Bush administration not only refused to condemn Hussein, it also seemed intent on proving that its policy of playing to his pragmatic side could work. Bush was signaling the world that the American government believed it could successfully convert a Middle Eastern radical into an Arab moderate. That Hussein later interpreted Washington's silence as assent—on this issue and a whole host of other matters—is now part of the historical record. But the events of March 15 and its immediate aftermath also betrayed another peculiar mind-set on the part of administration policy makers: They saw little hypocrisy in condemning Muammar al-Qaddafi for producing chemical weapons at the same time that they ignored a much greater threat from Iraq.

The fall of the Israeli government and the Bush administration's response to the Bazoft hanging left the clear impression that the White House had either failed to master the subtle signals of Middle East politics or was so convinced of the rightness of its views that its officials were incapable of imagining how they might fail. This second factor was the key. Having decided that Hussein was a pragmatic leader, the Bush administration ignored repeated CIA warnings that he continued to import materials for chemical and nuclear weapons and to harbor terrorists. In sum, the CIA had documented that his leadership of Iraq was little different from Qaddafi's rule in Libya. As the CIA soon found out, the two Arab strong men shared more than just the same hatred for the West—they also shared the same terrorist.

The Pan Am 103 investigation was stalled. After interviewing thousands of people in dozens of countries, police officials, terrorism analysts and forensic specialists were no closer to solving the crime in March 1990 than they had been fifteen months earlier. In Lockerbie, otherwise patient intelligence officers were beginning to question if they would ever find out who killed the 270 victims of the disaster. While millions of dollars had been poured into the investigation, it seemed possible that the bombing would forever remain a mystery. There was no longer any doubt that the victims aboard the aircraft and in the small village below had been murdered by terrorists, but no one could say for certain just who these killers were. Nor was the evidence good enough to indict the leading suspect in the case, Ahmed Jabril, the leader of the Popular Front for the Liberation of Palestine—General Command. The investigators in Lockerbie and Washington were missing a key piece of evidence which they needed to tie Jabril to the Pan Am bombing; they were missing the bomb itself.

That changed suddenly on a misty morning in early April when a Scottish worker discovered a nondescript fingernail-sized charred brass plate during a sweep of a field near Lockerbie. The worker gingerly placed the tiny plate, and an attached fragment of an electronic chip, inside a plastic bag and returned it to the evidence center, where such discoveries were studied, identified, and cataloged. The plate was a mystery. During the next several weeks, despite the best efforts of bomb experts and 747 construction engineers to identify its origin, no one could say for sure that it was part of the mechanism that brought down the Pan Am flight. There was only a hunch, a general feeling among several experts, that the plate was very important, perhaps the best clue they had yet discovered on the identity of the bombers. As these bomb experts continued to work on identifying the plate, a team of terrorism analysts scoured both CIA and MI5 intelligence files in the hope of discovering a link between the plate and other bombs.

The first tentative identification came in June, when a veteran CIA analyst recognized that the brass plate was "actually a tiny piece of the circuit board of a timing device." This startling conclusion transformed the paralyzed investigation. It meant that the *Maid of the Seas* was destroyed not by a bomb containing an altimeter-triggered mechanism (a sophisticated barometer set to go off at thirty thousand feet) but by a bomb detonated by a primitive chip-driven timer. This timing device indicated that the bomb could have exploded at Heathrow Airport or Frankfurt or Malta or any place in between if the aircraft had been delayed for any length of time. The immediate significance of the Lockerbie discovery slowly dawned on investigators: It meant that the PFLP—GC's bomb maker, Marwan Kreeshat, was not a suspect in the Pan Am 103 case. It also probably eliminated Jabril as a primary suspect since his European terrorist network was caught by the Germans with far more sophisticated detonation devices; all of them used altimeters, not timers.

That summer Kreeshat repeated his denial that he had anything to do with the Pan Am bombing during a follow-up interview conducted by CIA officers in Amman. "This is not a very good bomb," he said. "I would never have made it."

By eliminating Kreeshat and Jabril as suspects, the major intelligence organizations responsible for solving the Pan Am crime (the CIA, FBI, Scottish police, and MI5) were forced to discard fifteen months of carefully constructed theories and their most promising working hypothesis. As they restudied their evidence, they were left with a number of basic facts: the simple timer mechanism was housed in a nonworking radio, a form of Semtex called RDX was the explosive agent, the power source of the bomb was two AA batteries, and the radio was wrapped in clothing bought at Mary's House in Malta. Everything else—who planted the bomb and why—was still unknown.

The plate's discovery also destroyed the usefulness of detailed information on Jabril's operative based in Europe, Hafez al-Dalkamouni. (Dalkamouni's visit to the headquarters of the Iranian Revolutionary Guards contingent in Lebanon prior to the bombing no longer mattered.) Nor was there any link between the bombing and the cache of explosives found by the German police in Neuss. Information that PFLP—GC operatives surveilled cafés regularly frequented by Americans in Germany, and were photographed at the Pan Am airline counter in Frankfurt, now also seemed far less important than it first had appeared.

In the wake of the April discovery, investigators from the CIA's Counterterrorism Center realized that their inquiry had been propelled by a number of premises that had remained largely unquestioned for sixteen months: that Kreeshat was involved in some way, that the breakup of Jabril's European terrorist network implicated him as the leader of the plot, and that behind it all was a group of master planners in Iran. Some CTC investigators concluded that the CIA and its sister intelligence organizations were perhaps too willing to blame the bombing on the PFLP—GC when other evidence tended to discount Jabril's involvement. Because the evidence against Jabril seemed so overwhelming, everyone had failed to follow up to the same degree on reports that pointed in other directions. In particular, they had discounted the view that other terrorists, like agents from Libya, had as much of a motive to act against the United States as Jabril, other groups of radical Palestinians, Syria, or Iran.

Former CTC official Vince Cannistraro admits that investigators of the Pan Am case "didn't see the whole picture," although he still vigorously defends the agency's overall performance. "There was very convincing evidence and patterns that pointed to PFLP—GC involvement," he says. "The CIA didn't ignore other evidence, but there was a tendency to discount it once a preliminary conclusion was reached. It was a very intense investigation, but by its very nature some reports had to be given less priority in favor of others that were more convincing."

This tortured defense, cited by other CIA officers as well, shows that the CIA could be easily victimized by the legacies of its past. "We may have been overanxious in the Pan Am case," a retired CTC officer concedes, "but the Iranians and the PFLP—GC had strong reasons to retaliate against a U.S. airline. We'd brought down the [Iran Airways] Airbus, accidentally, to be sure, and they vowed revenge." In the wake of secret U.S. dealings with Iran during the Iran-contra scandal, CIA officials also may have been quite eager to accept a conclusion that pinned the blame for the bombing on Iran; it fitted well with their commitment to showing that the agency was mending its ways. Having been wrong once, it was almost as if the CIA were trying to pay penance for its past sin by transforming allegedly pro-Western, moderate Iranians, once thought of as possible friends, into terrorist beasts.

Having discarded their previous hypothesis, the CTC stepped up its review of evidence it had earlier dismissed. One interesting lead was the short transcript of an anonymous telephone call to a Rome news agency from an unidentified person who claimed that Pan Am 103 was destroyed in retaliation for the U.S. bombing of Libya in 1986. Another lead, which came from a suspicious West German intelligence report, was the text of an intercepted communication from the "Head of the Libyan Office" in London to the Libyan Foreign Liaison in Tripoli. A number of CTC officers had dismissed this report earlier because it seemed to exonerate the PFLP—GC in the bombing, and it let the Germans off the hook for releasing a number of PFLP—GC members from German jails—including Kreesat. With both of those factors now downgraded, the intercept took on added importance. "Greetings of the Revolution," the intercept read. "We take this opportunity to wish to you 'Praise to God' our revenge has been taken for our martyr of the American aggression by the slaughter of the American & British imperialists. The American plane which crashed included some of the savage American forces departing from Frankfurt to New York via London. In my name & that of my fellows we congratulate the heroes who did this."

As the possible Libyan connection was given new attention, CTC analysts traced the origin of the brass plate (which investigators now indentified as a small part of a computer chip), and bomb experts in Lockerbie and Washington redrafted the bomb's exact specifications. The object was to try to determine what possible link the chip might have with other bombs confiscated by the CIA or other intelligence services. When this key work was completed in early July, investigators were still puzzled about the bomb's origin. Its specifications failed to match any technology previously used by Palestinian fringe groups, nor did it match the known operational profile of any major international terrorist organizations.

An essential piece of the puzzle was put in place four months later, however, by American investigators who identified the computer chip's manufacturer as a Dutch firm, which had sold the devices to a Swiss corporation that used them to produce the timers. The Zurich-based firm, Meister et Bollier, Ltd. (known as MEBO AG), sold the timers to a Libyan company, ABH, which sublet offices from MEBO AG in Zurich. A close business relationship also was maintained between MEBO AG and senior officials from the Libyan military command and intelligence service. In 1985, MEBO AG sold twenty prototype digital electric timers, Model MST-13, to Izzel Din al-Hinshiri, a high-level Libyan government official. That transaction was the first solid lead the CTC uncovered about the hitherto mysterious chip.

In the end, however, the mystery of the bomb was not solved by terrorism experts from the CIA, but by a young forensics expert from the Scottish police who, acting on a hunch, asked to see specifications for a number of similar timing devices confiscated in western Africa in 1988.

Ten months before the Pan Am disaster, two Libyan intelligence officers were taken into custody by Senegalese authorities as they stepped off an Air Afrique flight in Dakar. The two Libyans, later identified as Mohammed al-Naydi (alias Mohammed al-Marzouk), and "Mansour Omran Saber" (whose true identity is still unknown), were suspected of being involved in terrorist activities. They were arrested after the Senegalese were tipped off by a CIA officer, who identified them by checking their names against a "watch list" of alleged terrorists compiled at Langley. (The CIA had been tracking the two men since August 1986, when the agency uncovered a Libyan-backed plot in the West African nation of Togo to blow up the American Embassy in Lomé; the Semtex-based explosives seized in that aborted operation were provided by Libyan intelligence agents in Benin, which had close ties to Qaddafi.)

The arrests in Dakar initially amounted to a minor incident, a small unit action in the continuing undeclared war between the United States and Libya. Over the previous five years the CIA had made increased efforts to gather information on Qaddafi's intelligence strategy in the sub-Saharan Muslim states and had gained some minor but significant penetrations of a number of Libyan intelligence cells. Western Africa was viewed as particularly fertile ground for Libyan terrorist teams; airport security was lax in the nations that bordered the eastern Atlantic, and the United States had only recently begun training antiterrorist units in the region.

When Senegalese officials checked the Libyans' bags, they discovered a virtual mother lode of terrorist accessories: a pistol and silencer, twenty-five rounds of ammunition, nineteen pounds of a Semtex type of explosive, and, most important of all, ten electronic bomb timers. Naydi and "Saber" were detained and interrogated by the Senegalese but then, four months later, unexpectedly released. They immediately left for Tripoli. The State Department expressed its outrage: "We are extremely disappointed by Senegal's action, which raises questions about that country's commitment to the struggle against international terrorism."

Senior CIA officers later concluded that the two Libyans were freed as a result of a secret Senegalese-Libyan agreement that included restoration of diplomatic relations between the two countries (broken off eight years earlier). A former CIA officer adds that the deal also involved "the suborning of a Senegalese official who is now living in high style in Provence. We have pictures of this bribed official in France," the former officer says bitterly. "We know who he is, how he got his money, and exactly what happened."

Fortunately, a French magistrate in Dakar obtained permission from Senegalese police officials to photograph the contents of the Libyans' suitcases before they were released. Detailed black-and-white photographs of the Semtex and timing devices confiscated at the Dakar airport were passed by the judge to the French intelligence service (the actual explosives then mysteriously disappeared, along with the timing devices; a former CTC official presumes that all of this evidence probably ended up back in Libya). French officers then "very quietly" slipped the photographs to the grateful Americans. CIA officers in Senegal also surreptitiously photographed Naydi and "Saber" at the jail in Dakar and as they were being put aboard an airliner bound for Tripoli. These photographs were added to the growing CTC files on Libyan operations in Africa.

Twenty-eight months after the two Libyans were released, the

French photographs of the Libyan Semtex and the timing devices made their way to the desk of a young Scottish forensics expert at Lockerbie. The investigator compared the Dakar photos with both the actual timing devices obtained from the Swiss firm and with a timer reconstructed from the chip recovered near Lockerbie.

The match was perfect.

A final, essential piece of evidence implicating Libya in the bombing was soon provided by the French. On September 19, 1989, one year after the release of Naydi and "Saber" and ten months after the destruction of Pan Am 103, UTA flight 772 was destroyed by a bomb after leaving N'Djamena, the capital of Chad. As in the case of Pan Am 103, the destructive force of the explosion spread parts of the DC-10 aircraft across hundreds of square miles. The flight had originated in Brazzaville, Congo, and was on its way to Paris via N'Djamena, with a stopover scheduled for Marseilles. The jet blew up some four hundred miles into its journey, over the desolate Ténéré desert in southern Niger. All 171 people on board were killed.

It took three days for French and American investigators to reach the distant crash site. (The United States dispatched a team of investigators to the scene because the aircraft was manufactured by the McDonnell Douglas Corporation.) After viewing the charred remains, air safety experts almost immediately concluded that sabotage had caused the disaster. Several days later the authorities announced that UTA 772 was destroyed by terrorists in "a Lockerbie-type explosion." French investigators said they found traces of Semtex on material taken from one of the aircraft's cargo holds.

Like the Americans before them, French officials initially blamed Iran for the incident; they disclosed that Iranian-backed terrorist groups in Lebanon had warned that France was the target of terrorist attacks because it had failed to keep promises it made during hostage release negotiations in 1988. As with the Pan Am 103 case, however, French officials changed their view after gathering startling new information about Libya's responsibility for the attack.

The evidence tying Libya to both the UTA and Pan Am bombings was obtained in March 1990, when French authorities arrested a Congolese man in Paris for heroin trafficking and questioned him about his ties to a West African drug network. In exchange for a lenient sentence the trafficker offered to lead the French to the bombers of UTA 772. He revealed that the UTA bombing was carried out by a specially trained cell of Congolese opposition leaders on behalf of the Libyan People's Bureau in Brazzaville. The Congolese dissidents, the informer said, received their training in Libya after making contact with the clandestine

"Mathaba network," a group established to recruit sympathetic Africans by the Libyan vice minister of foreign affairs, Moussa Koussa.

The informer named two other Mathaba operatives from the Congo who were members of the terrorist group: Bernard Yanga, then being held in a Brazzaville jail, and Jean N'Galina, being held in Kinshasa, Zaire. When French officials interrogated Yanga, he filled in many details about the Libyan network and then mentioned that N'Galina had even better information. N'Galina told the French an interesting story. In September 1988, he said, he attended a meeting in Tripoli where high-level Libyan officials laid out a plan to bomb both an American and a French airliner; Pan Am 103 and UTA 772 were specified as targets. N'Galina named both Moussa Koussa and Abdullah Senoussi, Qaddafi's brother-in-law and the de facto head of Libyan intelligence, as key participants in the meeting and the masterminds of the two terrorist attacks. According to U.S. officials, a third Congolese operative hired by the Libyans, Apollonaire Majatany, actually brought the bomb aboard the UTA flight, but got off the aircraft in N'Djamena before it exploded.

French and American intelligence officers later speculated that the Libyans targeted the UTA plane in the mistaken belief that Mohammed al-Mugharief, the high-profile leader of the CIA-backed National Front for the Salvation of Libya, was on board. A former Libyan auditor general, Mugharief was high on Qaddafi's hit list.

By the autumn of 1990 investigators from Langley and Lockerbie had resolved most of the more puzzling questions that surrounded the destruction of Pan Am 103. They believed the aircraft was destroyed as part of a plot among high-level Libyan intelligence officers and several leading figures in the Qaddafi government. The bomb itself was hidden inside a Toshiba radio and was detonated by the same kind of timer as those confiscated by Senegalese authorities in 1988. The evidence against Libya was overwhelming: CIA investigators found Naydi's name on a purchase order for the timers in Switzerland. The evidence was soon to be supported by startling new information obtained by the CIA—a member of Naydi's network bought the clothes in Malta that were found in the debris in Lockerbie. The only question still to be answered was how the bomb got on board the airplane. The CIA knew who planned the attack but did not know yet who carried it out.

The investigation into the Pan Am bombing uncovered the most complex and intriguing terrorist story the CIA ever handled. It may take many more years to unwrap the almost unbelievable coincidences that marked the trail of evidence in the case. For instance, at the same time that Libyan agents were purchasing clothes in Malta, so too were members of the PFLP—GC. CIA officers have difficulty explaining away this coincidence, but some speculate that Libyan intelligence agents became aware of Jabril's planned terrorist spectacular and undertook an operation that would throw blame on his organization. Others speculate that the Libyans and Jabril cooperated in the bombings; they point to unconfirmed reports that Qaddafi and Jabril met on September 3, just days before Senoussi, Moussa, and the Mathaba network met to put the finishing touches on their plans.

Another coincidence, which *did* have a payoff, involved evidence linking the Pan Am bombing to Abu Ibrahim, the Middle East's terrorist guru based in Baghdad, whose leading pupil, Mohammed Rashid, was still in an Athens jail. The remnants of the suitcase recovered by French investigators in 1989 from the Ténéré desert were later identified as one of five such devices purchased by the Libyans from Ibrahim in the mid-1980s, when Rashid was on the loose. This typical Rashid-type mechanism was very simple, with the Semtex hidden in the suitcase lining. But since there was not one whit of evidence of cooperation between Qaddafi and Ibrahim, CTC officials and terrorism experts found such a link difficult to believe.

In the days immediately after the Lockerbie disaster, CTC officers had indeed speculated that Ibrahim might somehow be involved in the Pan Am bombing or that, at the very least, the network left behind by Rashid could have planted the explosive. By January 1989 the CIA had compiled a list of suspects who might have the means and motive to carry out the attack. This list included Ibrahim and terrorists with ties to him, but most of them were discounted after the CTC concluded that the best evidence pointed to Ahmed Jabril.

In autumn 1990, eighteen months later, after the CIA analyst matched the tiny brass plate found near Lockerbie with the timing devices confiscated in Dakar, CTC officers reviewed the original suspect list. This time it was winnowed down to a handful of candidates, all with known connections to the Libyans.

One of them was a former Libyan diplomat named Muftah Abdulwanis el-Abbar, who also had been a well-known Libyan intelligence officer and maintained connections to international arms traffickers. The problem for CIA officers was that Abbar had been recruited by a Libyan opposition group controlled by the agency.

It is a curious tale. Muftah Abdulwanis el-Abbar was born on March 23, 1947, in Labiar, Libya, to one of the nation's leading families. Yet his later success was not based solely on his family ties, for in every respect he was intelligent, hardworking, tall, handsome, worldly, and creative. In 1967 he supported Qaddafi's coup against King Idris and soon became an important figure in the new government. A graduate of Libya's military academy, Abbar set out on a career as an Army officer but resigned his commission in the mid-1970s and entered the Libyan foreign service, which assigned him to postings in Madrid and Geneva, where he also presumably served as an intelligence officer. Abbar parlayed his diplomatic and intelligence career into a small fortune; he became a businessman in the late 1970s and invested millions of dollars in a wide variety of enterprises in Europe, Canada, and the United States. By 1980, he had established residence in Canada, and the suave, gentlemanly, and polished Libyan later married a strikingly beautiful model from Vancouver named Heather Goodall.

Abbar apparently never broke with Qaddafi after he left government service, even though he later claimed otherwise. Instead the evidence suggests that he was deliberately transferred to the Libyan diplomatic service to carry out special intelligence assignments. He even retained this relationship after he became a businessman. By 1985, he was well known in Germany and Geneva at a time when international weapons traders were attempting to conclude a secret deal between Qaddafi and the Soviet Union. "We all knew what Abbar was trying to do," recalls one arms dealer. "During his time in Germany he was involved in shipping Soviet ground-to-air missile systems through various front companies to Tripoli. I saw him in the company of Manucher Ghorbanifar. I got the impression that they were friends. But I thought Muftah was a real asshole, so I didn't really get close to him."

Abbar was also noticed by American intelligence officers, who tracked him from the early 1980s, when he was first admitted to Canada. Later, after the Iran-contra affair was made public in 1986, the FBI sent a team of investigators to question him on several occasions about a number of still-classified topics, according to a former intelligence officer. He was also questioned by the Royal Canadian Mounted Police about his business dealings in Canada, which included associations with Ernie Miller, Donald Fraser, and Adnan Khashoggi, all of whom were implicated at one time or another in aspects of the Iran-contra affair. By then, Abbar was rich; he had purchased a luxury condominium in Toronto, owned three Rolls-Royces, and kept accounts in the Crédit Suisse Bank. A confidential report on him from the U.S. embassy in Toronto sums up the doubts about his activities: "There is no doubt el-Abbar is into arms dealing of some sort, perhaps for the Libyan government," it reads. "The amount of his wealth also raises the possibility that it is nothing more than Libyan Government funds used by el-Abbar as a 'front man' to deal in Western business circles."

Abbar's shadowy business dealings had brought him in contact with an array of large and small enterprises in a number of industries. He became a principal officer in several corporations and was friendly with a number of bankers with suspicious international dealings. Back in 1982, an officer at one of these banks, Pan American National Bank in New Jersey, allegedly approached him for a loan of five hundred thousand dollars to cover the bank's losses. Abbar agreed to lend the bank money, but only if he could use Pan American's contacts to obtain a U.S. passport—since the phony American papers he had been using were confiscated by U.S. officials in Canada several months earlier. The agreement was made through the bank's contacts at the passport office in Puerto Rico, and in late 1982 Abbar obtained the document by posing as a businessman working for the Sparatec Corporation, a defense contractor located in New Jersey. In 1983 Pan American Bank went belly up.

The passport scheme was bound to fall apart. Not only had U.S. law enforcement and intelligence officials been tracking Abbar's movements, but federal investigators were also following the trail of money he had paid to Pan American. Abbar was indicted on charges of fraudulently receiving a U.S. passport in 1986. A judge in Puerto Rico then issued a warrant for his arrest.

There is reason to believe that Abbar was targeted for recruitment by the CIA long before the Puerto Rico indictment was unsealed. The agency was well aware of his ties to Fraser, Miller, and Khashoggi and his vulnerability to arrest should he ever enter the United States. One investigative report indicates that the State Department wanted to help Abbar iron out his problems as a way of getting him into the United States. When he set out on a personal trip from Montreal to New York on October 4, 1988, therefore, American officials were waiting to greet him as he got off the plane at La Guardia Airport.

Abbar was arrested by U.S. customs officers on charges of possessing a fraudulently obtained passport. He was bound over to the Puerto Rico court for trial. While in New York, his lawyer asked for his release on five hundred thousand dollars bail. Abbar was granted permission to move to Palm Beach, Florida, where he took up residence in a palatial hotel. Within the month, he asked for permission to travel to Springfield, Virginia, a suburb of Washington.

Abbar went to Virginia in late November 1988. Intelligence officers say that he met there with Aly Abuzaakouk, the North American chief of the National Front for the Salvation of Libya, which was the CIA front group led by Mohammed al-Mugharief whose military wing was then conducting a secret war against Qaddafi from inside Chad. According to intelligence sources, Abbar told Abuzaakouk that he was in trouble with American authorities and that he wanted to offer his services to the NFSL. Abuzaakouk took Abbar to meet with CIA officers, who tried to convince him to work for them. The outcome of this meeting has never been officially disclosed, but Abbar's subsequent actions offer clues to what happened.

After visiting Virginia, Abbar returned to Puerto Rico, where he pleaded guilty to a single charge of passport fraud. He also filed an extensive affidavit with the court. He claimed that he was alienated from the Libyan Revolution, disliked Qaddafi, and wanted to make the United States his home. He described himself as a simple businessman and asked that he be given a chance to prove that he could be a good citizen. After this plea, the judge in the case was stunned by the prosecution's apparent inability, or unwillingness, to present a case against Abbar. The judge had no recourse but to give Abbar a light sentence: a thousand-dollar fine and a one-year suspended sentence. He was not even deported, a standard sentence for all those charged with a felony. For whatever reason, the U.S. government was simply not interested in prosecuting Abbar.

After his release on bond, Abbar petitioned the court again, this time for permission to travel to Britain. His request was granted, and the Libyan left Miami sometime during the second week of December.

He immediately dropped out of sight.

A week later, on December 21, Pan Am 103 fell from the sky.

Abbar was one of the original suspects in the Lockerbie bombing. His name appeared on two intelligence documents that tied him to Mohammed Rashid's network in Europe; he was "a Rashid lieutenant," a counterterrorism expert says. Abbar fit the agency's profile of the bomber they were seeking: He was a known arms trafficker, was well known inside Qaddafi's inner circle, and was still suspected of being a Qaddafi loyalist.

While the CIA was willing to believe Abbar's story that he had finally and absolutely recanted his loyalty to Qaddafi, other intelligence services were not. He was especially mistrusted by Britain's MI5, whose counterterrorism officers were angered by the CIA's decision to use him as an agent. When he arrived in London in December, therefore, he was closely watched. An unverified rumor contended that he was detained temporarily at Heathrow by angry MI5 officers who questioned him about his plans for his stay in London. What happened after that is unknown, since Abbar was able to elude British surveillance.

British officials had good reason to resent CIA requests that Abbar be allowed to come to England without being harassed. They knew him as a former diplomat at the Libyan People's Bureau in London and as a notorious arms trafficker who often used Malta as a transit point for his frequent trips to Tripoli. There was little doubt among the British that he was using the Americans to slip out of a serious criminal charge that could have put him in jail for a long time. The refusal to prosecute him was seen as a contemptible way to gather information on a short-term problem (the British believed Abbar had been recruited to provide insight on the Rabta plant). The cards were not worth the bet: the British were convinced that Abbar was in Qaddafi's pay.

Their convictions were so strongly held that British intelligence officers were willing to circulate rumors after the Pan Am bombing about Abbar's movements that later proved to be false. One British intelligence source, for instance, claimed that Abbar and his Canadian wife had traveled to Malta before the bombing and were actually seen purchasing clothing at Mary's House—in light of evidence later uncovered by CTC officers, that claim seems suspect. "The Brits invented the game, and play it for keeps," says a former CIA officer. In other words—if British claims about Abbar were true, the leading intelligence agency of the United States would be implicated in bombing one of its country's own aircraft. No wonder the CTC had not found the bomber, these British rumors implied; the Americans never wanted to find him at all; it would be too embarrassing.

British intelligence officers also claimed that Abbar and his wife may have been the couple spotted in Sliema, Malta, by Christine and Geoffrey Middleton, British vacationers who told investigators about a mysterious incident at a local restaurant. According to the Middletons, a couple matching the general descriptions of Abbar and his wife entered the open-air cafe and solicited patrons who planned to leave the island to carry a suitcase back to London. The couple claimed that the bag contained toys for their children. A friend was supposed to carry the bag for them, they said, but had left Malta without taking it. The couple approached three likely travelers with the request, but they all refused. Lockerbie investigators later followed up the Middleton's story but were never able to make much of it. While it seemed possible that the episode could prove that Abbar and his wife were involved in the bombing, a simple check of dates casts doubt on the identification: the CTC determined that Abbar was not in Malta on the specific day in question, so he simply could not have been the man spotted by the Middletons.

The CTC remained suspicious of Abbar, however, because they could not determine his whereabouts on other days between December 9, when he arrived in London, and December 21. He was also a CTC target because his brother was a Libyan Arab Airways pilot on the Tripoli to Malta route and was himself a suspected intelligence officer. In November 1990—in the aftermath of the computer chip discovery and the identification of Libya as a probable suspect in the bombing—CTC officials visited Tony Gauci in Malta with their latest piece of evidence, a detailed physical description of Abbar. Gauci identified him as the man who bought the clothes at his shop in December 1988. But according to an informed intelligence officer, the identification was only tentative; it was based solely on a verbal description, not an actual photograph. During a second visit, intelligence officers presented Gauci with a photograph of Abbar provided by an allied intelligence service. Again, Gauci believed that the CIA had found the man who bought the clothes in his store, but he still insisted that he was not *absolutely* certain. He said he needed to see more. In the end, intelligence officers say, Gauci refused to give the certainty the investigators needed. Abbar was much taller than the man who had purchased the clothes, he said. He simply was not the man.

Gauci eventually identified another Libyan, Abdel Basset, as the man who purchased the clothes found in the unidentified bag at Lockerbie. Scottish, English, and American investigators linked Basset with Lamen Fhimah, an employee of Libyan Arab Airlines. Basset and Fhimah flew from Tripoli to Malta on December 7, 1988. Basset then flew to Zurich. Both later returned to Libya. Two weeks later, on December 20, they flew back to Malta, where Fhimah put the brown Samsonite suitcase with stolen airline tags that contained the bomb aboard Air Malta Flight KM-180 to Frankfurt.

Muftah Abdulwanis el-Abbar currently lives a quiet life of luxury in a mansion near London that once belonged to pop singer Tom Jones. He has told reporters that allegations that he was somehow linked to the bombing of the 747 are "ludicrous." Officials at Langley refuse to talk on-the-record about the Pan Am 103 investigation and refer all questions to the FBI's Washington field office, which is coordinating the CTC inquiry. Occasional leaks to the press about the investigation have fueled speculation that the CIA may be covering up some unexplained role in the Pan Am tragedy. Foreign intelligence officers who cooperated in providing the CIA with information on Abbar, for one, remain convinced that the agency's Libyan recruit helped plot the tragedy in some still unknown way. But in spite of the fog that surrounds the incident and the international sniping it sparked, there is now no doubt that Libya bears responsibility for the murder of 270 people.

In France a magistrate has charged four Libyans, including Mohammed al-Naydi, with being involved in the bombing of UTA 772. The French jurist is also deciding whether to bring charges against those Libyan officials who, as the evidence clearly indicates, might be responsible for the crime for planning the bombing of Pan Am 103, including Naydi, Abdel Basset, Lamen Fhimeh, Senoussi, and perhaps Moussa Koussa. It is not expected that Qaddafi will be named in any indictment. Neither has it been determined whether Abbar will be implicated as part of a larger network of plotters. The only thing that *is* certain is that the worst crime in U.S. and British aviation history was not an accident or part of a strange conspiracy that involved a CIA-DEA–run sting operation—as claimed by Pan Am and its chief investigators.

By the early autumn of 1990 the mystery of the destruction of Pan Am 103 was finally resolved. As Salmon Rushdie would say, it was like "a seed pod giving up its spores, an egg yielding its mysteries." Even as international condemnation was mounting against Libya, the initial conclusion reached by investigators within days of the tragedy was still the most compelling. The murder of 270 innocent men, women, and children was a satanic act of revenge.

14
★ ★ ★
Ruthless but Pragmatic

*T*he CIA watched Saddam Hussein with mounting apprehension for many months—all through the winter of 1990 and into the next spring. Iraq's ruler seemed intent on causing a violent conflict somewhere, whether it was by helping Lebanese-Christian leader Michel Aoun fight the Syrians or by rattling his own saber against Iran. The first *public* hint that there was a major crisis brewing in the Middle East came on April 1, 1990, during a speech Hussein gave to a group of Iraqi Army officers. Dressed in the khaki combat uniform of Iraq's Republican Guards and sporting a general's insignia, he boisterously bragged of Iraq's chemical weapons capability and lashed out at Israel as the most likely aggressor in any future war. His boiler plate rhetoric was not unusual; he styled himself an Iraqi Nasser, the only leader in the Middle East capable of returning the Arab people to greatness.

But his speech went beyond anything that he had said before: "By God, if the Israelis try anything against us, we'll see to it that half their country is destroyed by fire," he proclaimed. ". . . whoever threatens us with atomic bombs will be exterminated with chemical weapons." The speech had immediate resonance in the Middle East, where it struck a chord with the Arab masses. To them, Hussein appeared to be a leader the Arab world was looking for; someone who could stand up to the United States and Israel.

President Bush reacted strongly to Hussein's threat. "I think these statements are very bad," he told the press. "I'm asking Iraq very strongly to immediately reject the use of chemical weapons."

Secretary of State Baker was also disturbed by Hussein's speech, so much so that he believed the United States should take steps to punish Iraq. In a meeting with Assistant Secretary of State John Kelly, Baker considered a broad range of sanctions that would signal U.S. displeasure, including the suspension of funds from the Export-Import Bank. The plan met with approval from Baker's inner circle of advisers: Kelly; Dennis Ross, the director of the State Department policy planning staff; and Robert Kimmitt, the undersecretary of state for political affairs.

But the State Department's program went much too far. Both Brent Scowcroft and his deputy, Robert Gates, thought that Baker's response would be counterproductive, pushing the United States into an unwanted confrontation with Iraq. Hussein, they reasoned, would be enraged by economic sanctions and would view U.S. actions as confirmation of a plot against him. Scowcroft and Gates believed the Iraqi strongman could be persuaded to moderate his opinions through a good-faith effort of cooperation with the West, and they pointed out that their view was in keeping with overall American policy. The President agreed and endorsed this go-slow approach. Bush, Scowcroft, and Gates were convinced that Iraq was in no position to fund, let alone fight, a major regional conflict. They were persuaded that sanctions would do little to moderate Hussein's language; history showed that economic pressures rarely worked. The primary basis for the Bush policy was to maintain normal relations with Iraq in order to provide stability in the Persian Gulf region.

This restrained response was underlined by a carefully worded letter Bush sent to Baghdad in April, which was read to Hussein by a group of five influential U.S. senators, including Republican heavyweights Robert Dole and Alan Simpson. Dressed in a tailored gray business suit, Hussein cordially met the American delegation in the Iraqi city of Mosul and listened intently to what they had to say.

Bush's letter criticized Hussein's threat against Israel and counseled him to work for peace in the region: "... your desire to equip yourself with chemical and biological weapons, far from strengthening your country's security, exposes it to serious dangers," the letter read. "Your recent statements, in which you threatened to use chemical weapons against Israel, have caused a stir around the world, and it would be a good thing for you and for peace in the Middle East if you reconsidered such dangerous projects and such provocative statements and acts."

Hussein was unmoved by the appeal. He denounced America's Middle East policy and accused the United States of launching a propaganda campaign against him. The five senators uniformly expressed their disagreement.

"Let me point out to you that twelve hours ago President Bush told me that he and his government were hoping to improve relations with

Iraq," Dole responded. "I can even assure you that President Bush will oppose sanctions. He could even veto any such decision, unless any provocative act should occur." Dole's demeanor was matter-of-fact, but his words were pointed and carried weight; it was obvious that he was speaking for the President. Hussein nodded, apparently satisfied with the answer.

Ambassador April Glaspie, who accompanied the group, seconded Dole's statement: "As American Ambassador, I can assure you, Mr. President, that this is indeed the policy of the United States government."

When Dole left Iraq, he was convinced that Hussein was someone with whom the United States could deal—a tough man but a realist. To build on this new conciliatory mood, Bush sent a telegram to Hussein marking the end of Ramadan, saying he hoped for better ties between the United States and Iraq.

Soothing words about the Iraqi threat also were heard in other quarters in Washington. Assistant Secretary of State Kelly told the Senate Foreign Relations Committee that the government opposed placing sanctions on Iraq. "This administration continues to oppose the imposition of sanctions," he told the committee, "which would penalize American exporters and worsen our balance-of-payments deficit." He added: "Furthermore, I fail to see how sanctions could increase the possibility of our exercising a moderating influence on the actions of Iraq." This last statement was the exact opposite of the conclusion that Kelly had drawn earlier in the month during his long meeting with Baker. While many on the Senate committee strongly disagreed with Kelly's statement, the initial outrage over Hussein's threat against Israel was beginning to die down, and the move to impose sanctions was losing steam.

As the White House and State Department were hammering out their moderate line on Iraq, the CIA was continuing to gather chilling information about Hussein's war machine. If anything, CIA analysts decided, intelligence reports showed that Iraq was accelerating its attempts to obtain sophisticated and dangerous new military technology. Immediately after the Bazoft hanging in mid-March, for example, British customs agents, running a complex sting operation in London, arrested two Iraqis and seized a shipment of U.S.-manufactured high-speed electronic capacitors known as kytrons, used to trigger nuclear detonators. At the end of March, classified U.S. intelligence reports, based on satellite reconnaissance photos, revealed that Iraq had built launchers that could fire missiles on Tel Aviv, Damascus, or Riyadh. In mid-April British authorities seized a shipment of eight steel cylinders, which they said could be used to construct 130-foot artillery barrels, or superguns.

The CIA also developed a list of U.S. corporations that were believed to be involved in both legal and illegal transfers of American-manufactured technology to the Middle East. The agency's National Collection Division worked overtime adding to its already extensive files on Iraqi military projects. The NCD's final list included firms that had shipped everything from high-speed computers to microwave communications (or "relay") systems, all with military applications to Baghdad. In many instances, the transfers were backed by export licenses issued by the Commerce Department and cleared by the White House. The CIA also monitored a number of Iraqi tests of its newest missiles, including one reportedly fired at a test range in Mauritania, which had close ties to Hussein's government. The intelligence report sent to President Bush about this test firing was based on satellite images taken over the West African nation.

The CIA issued its first warning on possible Iraqi designs on Kuwait in early May 1990. The warning was based on firsthand reports from a number of Middle Eastern sources. The information was greeted with skepticism at the White House, however, because administration officials believed the evidence was flimsy: Hussein had threatened Israel, not Kuwait. Even so, the CIA report was a sign that a Middle East war might be brewing; the authors noted that Hussein had issued a clear threat against two of his southern neighbors, Kuwait and the United Arab Emirates, by accusing them of taking part in a plot "inspired by America" to restrict Iraqi oil revenues. The allegation was backed by a letter, sent to the Arab League by Iraqi Foreign Minister Tariq Aziz, which accused Kuwait of stealing Iraqi oil, building military installations on Iraqi territory, and cooperating in an "imperialist Zionist plan" to depress world oil prices.

One week later, during a meeting in Baghdad with Ambassador Glaspie, Hussein denounced the United States for waging an economic war. "The Gulf states' policy of forcing down the price of oil is undermining Iraq's survival," he added.

Speaking under specific instructions from President Bush and Secretary Baker, Glaspie sympathized with Hussein's problems. "I admire your extraordinary efforts to rebuild your country," she replied. "I know you need funds. Not only do I say that President Bush wants better and deeper relations with Iraq, but he also wants an Iraq contribution to peace and prosperity in the Middle East." Glaspie then reassured her host that the United States would stay clear of any inter-Arab disputes, a point later publicly reemphasized by State Department spokeswoman Margaret Tutwiler.

CIA analysts were divided over the meaning of all this activity. On the one hand, they knew Hussein had been engaged in an increasingly strident debate with Kuwaiti leaders on a number of topics: the price of oil, a port on the Persian Gulf, and relief from debts owed to the Kuwaiti government. On the other hand, they knew that an invasion of Kuwait would be suicide for Hussein. After eight years of war with Iran, Iraq could not afford a massive military push anywhere in the Middle East: the country was nearly forty billion dollars in debt, its elite attack formations had been shredded, and its population was only just now beginning to mount a significant economic recovery. Despite this, nearly all high-ranking CIA officials agreed that Hussein's buildup needed to be very closely monitored.

In May and June, therefore, the U.S. intelligence community shifted its massive technological resources to target Iraq. By July the CIA's satellite network had deployed more reconnaissance equipment in orbit above the Iraq-Kuwait border than had ever been focused on any single target before. In all, the CIA had access to four KH-11s in an adjustable polar orbit, and a Lacrosse imaging radar satellite, launched by the space shuttle in 1988. The agency's imaging laboratories were working overtime to process the information the platforms produced on the Iraqi buildup. By mid-July CIA analysts had become convinced that Saddam Hussein was planning much more than just a show of force against Kuwait.

One of the most important agency warnings about possible Iraqi aggression was sent to the White House on July 17. The agency reported that U.S. reconnaissance satellites had photographed upward of thirty thousand Iraqi soldiers moving south, toward Kuwait's northern border. Additional evidence of this military buildup continued to emerge during the next week. Finally, on July 27—the same day that Glaspie spoke privately with Hussein in Baghdad—the Pentagon's Central Command secretly requested an American show of force in the Persian Gulf as a warning that the United States would respond to an invasion of Kuwait. Like their CIA counterparts, DIA officers were alarmed by what they were seeing on satellite reconnaissance photos. But both the White House and State Department vetoed the Pentagon's request; the United States would continue taking its moderate stance on the Baghdad regime.

The veto did not mean that the CIA stopped watching what was going on in southern Iraq. CIA imaging experts continued to work around the clock to track Iraqi troop movements. They noticed, for instance, that Iraq had reactivated a key radar facility that had remained largely silent since the end of the Iran-Iraq War—an important sign that Hussein was planning to invade Kuwait.

The most convincing piece of evidence that Hussein was bent on an invasion, however, was obtained by CIA analysts from aerial photographs taken on the night of July 27, some three hours before dawn broke over the Middle East. Using an infrared system that magnifies starlight, a KH-11 satellite showed Iraqi trucks hauling ammunition, fuel, and water to troops poised on Kuwait's northern border. The photographs meant that Iraq would move quickly, almost certainly in the next few days, and that the attack would be more than just a border "raid"—there was no other way to explain the presence of the Iraqi military's overly long logistical "tail." According to one published report both William Webster and Joint Chiefs of Staff Chairman Colin Powell thought this evidence was the most solid and convincing they had yet seen. It was now "probable," they believed, that the Iraqis were going to invade Kuwait. The attack was imminent.

On the morning of July 28, a contingent of grim-faced CIA officials arrived at the White House to deliver a crucial early-morning briefing to the nation's chief executive. The group included DCI Webster, DDO Stolz, the CIA's top Near East expert, and two satellite-imaging analysts. A last-minute addition was Langley gadfly Charlie Allen, the national intelligence officer for warning. The CIA officials carried highly sensitive data gleaned from the far-flung U.S. technical networks, as well as a file of intelligence reports and assessments. The KH-11 satellite photographs taken the night before were contained in a thick manila envelope. They provided the primary evidence that Webster was to present to the President. The CIA had also prepared a report for Bush from Langley's Political Psychology Division, which was responsible for trying to assess Hussein's attitudes and intentions.

The information Webster was about to put on Bush's desk was exhaustive and detailed, but it lacked one important component—no one in the group could say for *certain* whether Hussein would invade Kuwait or exactly when the attack would come. CIA analysts themselves were divided; those who argued that the Iraqi leader was intent on a full-scale assault based their opinion on the conviction that he was irrational, while those who once claimed that an Iraqi invasion would be suicidal now argued that Hussein was planning only a punitive military raid on Kuwait's oil fields, perhaps as a bargaining chip to be used for later negotiations. But no one knew for sure. Information on his intention was impossible to come by. The CIA did not have convincing eavesdropping evidence from high-level Iraqi planning meetings and did not have a human intelligence source inside the Iraqi dictator's inner circle.

Bush listened silently to the CIA presentation, but after it was over, he said he still was not convinced that an invasion was imminent. He pointed out that the agency's warning was based exclusively on information gathered through technical means, and while this evidence was impressive—some of the photographs were so detailed he could read the markings on the side of Iraqi tanks as they moved down the Basra–Zubair road toward the Kuwaiti border—he did not want to overreact. He noted that he had discussed the problem with numerous officials in the Middle East and they had assured him that Hussein was attempting to extort concessions from Kuwait.

Bush's human intelligence sources were inarguably the best in the world. Over the previous weeks he had personally spoken with Egyptian President Hosni Mubarak and Jordan's King Hussein in an attempt to ascertain just what Iraq was likely to do. In one of these conversations, Mubarak had assured Bush that Hussein would not use force if he could win concessions through intimidation; the Iraqi strong man had told him that himself, Mubarak added. According to a Middle Eastern official who was privy to the Mubarak-Hussein exchange, the Iraqi leader had promised that he would not take action against Kuwait until after he had talked with its leader, Prince Jabir al-Ahmal al-Jabir al-Sabah, during a meeting with him in Jidda, Saudi Arabia. Mubarak had interpreted this pledge to mean that the Iraqi was bluffing, and that was what he told Bush. The same assurance was repeated by King Hussein.

With these messages in mind, Bush told Webster that he needed more evidence. In the meantime, he assured CIA officials he would continue to monitor events in the Middle East by conferring on the phone with his own, high-level, foreign intelligence sources. After ninety minutes the meeting broke up.

The immediate fallout over the July 28 meeting is difficult to discern, especially in light of the puzzling charges that surfaced later that the CIA had failed to warn the White House of Saddam Hussein's true intentions in Kuwait. Members of Congress were Langley's chief critics; they pointed out that if the agency had adequately alerted Bush to the impending catastrophe, he certainly would have taken steps to warn Hussein that his actions would bring an immediate response from the United States. CIA officials defended the agency by pointing to Bush's lack of action in the immediate wake of the actual invasion. They cite that muted reaction as indirect evidence that their earlier good-faith efforts to convince him of Hussein's intentions had been ignored. They argued that Bush consistently overestimated his own intelligence prowess. Since he was the first President to have served as DCI, he believed that he was as capable of making sound intelligence judgments as the CIA's experts.

To senior officials at Langley, this was the President's most disturbing quality. Bush relied almost exclusively on personal contacts for his information. While he closely read official CIA assessments and important intelligence documents, he rarely relied on them as the basis for his foreign policy decisions. He also prided himself on his ability to read "raw" CIA reports, for instance, even though experienced analysts knew that these background documents often could be misleading; their credibility needed to be assessed in the light of other information before they were passed on to policy makers. By short-circuiting that process, CIA officials believed that Bush signaled his disdain for the opinions of agency experts. Bush's personal style of diplomacy, his reliance on the friendships he had struck up with international leaders, and his presumed expertise on intelligence matters often became a substitute for accepting hard-nosed analysis from CIA veterans.

Bush's defenders reject this harsh judgment. "Intelligence officers always believe their views aren't taken into consideration," remarks Middle East expert Graham Fuller. "Frankly, I think we have to be delighted that we finally have a President who knows what intelligence is; that's always been the CIA's biggest concern. In my opinion, Bush uses the CIA's information well. But he has his own views which are independent, and frankly that's his prerogative and not much different than what past Presidents have done. We don't need an automaton in the Oval Office."

Did the Bush administration miscalculate Hussein's intentions? "By invading Kuwait," Fuller replies, "Saddam threw away all he had won. We were astonished that he invaded. In the end, you can't predict poor decisions, and Saddam's decision to invade Kuwait was a terrible mistake on his part."

Former Assistant Secretary of State Richard Murphy also defends Bush, saying that it was impossible for the President, or anyone else, to predict the Iraqi invasion at the end of July. "We were just predisposed to think this wasn't going to happen," Murphy says. "Even the Kuwaitis didn't think it would happen."

Despite this, when agency officials returned to their desks at Langley after the July 28 meeting, they were exasperated by Bush's attitude toward their warnings. They believed the intelligence information they had obtained was among the most detailed they had ever presented to a President in such a situation. While they knew that Bush could pick and choose what to believe, they were sure of Iraqi intentions: While it wasn't *absolutely* certain Hussein's forces would invade Kuwait, it now seemed assured beyond any reasonable doubt. One CIA official recalls that analysts in the DI were particularly upset that the President did not send a tough warning to Iraq, but opted for a telegram to Hussein that reemphasized the need to improve relations between the two countries. Bush told the Iraqi that his threats against his neighbors were "unacceptable," but there was no promise of retaliation should his army move across the border with Kuwait.

On Wednesday morning, August 1, Webster hand delivered another package of intelligence briefings and the latest satellite photos to Brent Scowcroft at the White House. The material contained startling new information on Hussein's intentions; CIA analysts were now saying they believed there was absolute evidence that he was going to war. When Bush looked at the photos he saw an overwhelming military force arrayed along Iraq's southern border. Some eight divisions in all, including three of the elite Republican Guard units, were poised to strike at the center of Kuwait's oil fields and the capital city beyond. Webster advised that the CIA was convinced that the invasion would take place sometime in the next twenty-four hours.

Included among the CIA reports was an assessment from analyst Charles Allen, who wrote that the agency's warning officers now believed that the invasion was likely to be a full-fledged takeover of Kuwait. "This was as clear a warning as Charlie could give," an intelligence officer explains. "It was stated bluntly and clearly. I thought he was putting himself on the line." Allen predicted that the onslaught would have as its goal the total destruction of the emirate. He used the agency's technical information to back up his claim, and he repeated what he, Webster, and others had told Bush just days before—there would be no reason for a military buildup as massive as the one aimed at Kuwait unless Hussein meant business.

Allen's report was passed on that morning to other senior policy makers, including Robert Kimmitt at the State Department, who was stunned by what he read; he'd rarely seen such a blunt prediction. In the absence of Gates, who was on vacation, Kimmitt decided to call together the Deputies Committee later that afternoon. At that meeting, with the CIA assessment on everyone's mind, Deputy Director Richard Kerr was asked about his conclusions. While Kerr did not back down from Allen's prediction, he acknowledged that many others at the agency remained uncertain about the extent of the Iraqi attack. He, for one, was convinced it would take place.

After this session President Bush met with White House officials to discuss the CIA's new information. Brent Scowcroft seemed to be the most concerned. If Iraq invaded Kuwait, he said, the United States would have few clear options. As was his custom, Bush allowed others to present their views before he stated his. In this instance, he gave a rambling discourse on his contacts with other Arab leaders. But he still was not convinced that Saddam Hussein would send his military units into Kuwait.

Kimmitt, however, decided to take a number of steps to deal with the predicted crisis. Even before the Deputies Committee met, he passed the CIA's information on to Secretary of State Baker in Siberia, where he was meeting with Soviet Foreign Minister Eduard Shevardnadze. Baker was silent as he listened to Kimmitt's roundabout description of the agency's warning (they were speaking over an unsecured telephone line) and then said that he would find out if Shevardnadze knew anything about Hussein's plans. After a luncheon with the Soviet foreign minister, Baker broached the subject; he told Shevardnadze that the U.S. intelligence community was reporting that Iraqi forces were massing on the

Kuwaiti border and might invade. The foreign minister was noncommittal. "We hope you'll try to restrain these guys," Baker said. Shevardnadze waved off the remark. Hussein was bluffing, he argued, just as he had many times before. The Iraqi had no intention of invading Kuwait. Certainly, he said, the Soviet Union had no such information. "I trust him," Shevardnadze added.

A strange paralysis seemed to grip official Washington over the next few hours. Even among the nation's top policy makers there seemed to be little open concern about what might be about to happen in the Middle East. George Bush was still convinced that Saddam Hussein was bluffing, that the buildup was a prelude to new demands on Kuwaiti oil reserves or, at most, that Iraq was planning a raid to gain a new oil terminal on the Persian Gulf.

By the evening of August 1 many senior U.S. officials were preparing to go on vacation or spend a long weekend at the beach. Brent Scowcroft left the White House a little after 5:00 P.M. It was one of the rare days that he could be home in time for dinner with his family. President Bush and Secretary of Defense Cheney were preparing to fly to Aspen, Colorado, the following day to meet British Prime Minister Thatcher, who was attending a foreign policy conference there. At the Pentagon, one of the administration's foremost international experts, Paul Wolfowitz, was putting the finishing touches on a major paper that he had spent months preparing. He knew that Thatcher would be in the audience at Aspen when he presented it. Wolfowitz did not know it yet, but his speech would have to wait.

At eight-thirty that evening—four o'clock the next morning in the Persian Gulf—Iraqi troops stormed across the border of Kuwait. The tiny emirate's military formations melted before the Iraqi tank formations. Knowing that resistance was futile, Kuwaiti soldiers surrendered en masse. There was some opposition in Kuwait City, but inside six hours the capital was under the control of Iraqi soldiers. What was left of the Kuwaiti Air Force (which was swept from the skies in just minutes by the Iraqis) was fleeing to bases in Saudi Arabia. In Washington, officials from the NSC, CIA, State Department, and Pentagon scurried back to their offices, stunned by the swift turn of events. Brent Scowcroft heard about the invasion at his home in suburban Maryland and returned immediately to the White House. He decided the best thing to do was call a meeting of the Deputies Committee and chair it himself. Within a few hours the committee drafted a statement for the President to read the next morning and recommended that the administration immediately freeze all Iraqi assets in the United States. Bush called a meeting of the National Security Council for the following morning.

Early the next day the administration's major foreign and domestic policy advisers, including the Central Command's General Norman Schwarzkopf, gathered in the White House Cabinet Room to help plan the American response. Photographers snapped pictures of the session while reporters shouted questions at Bush. "We're not discussing intervention," he said. After a few moments the doors were closed. Bush then called on Webster to give an update on the situation in Kuwait. This presentation was perhaps Webster's most critical performance as DCI. He did well; his information was detailed, and his tone was somber: The Iraqi army was in full control of Kuwait City, he said, and what little resistance it was meeting was being quickly overcome. More than one hundred thousand Iraqi troops were already in the country, with more on the way. The CIA's most recent reconnaissance photos indicated that Iraqi armored units were within ten miles of the Kuwait-Saudi border. Webster added that the CIA could not predict Hussein's next move. A large portion of the Iraqi army was headed south, but there was no way to tell whether it would actually invade Saudi Arabia.

Other officials then spoke. Robert Kimmitt talked about the U.S. diplomatic response to the invasion. Bush's top domestic advisers discussed sanctions. Finally Schwarzkopf outlined U.S. military options. The NSC meeting adjourned with no discernible U.S. policy in place. To some participants it looked as if Bush were uncertain how to respond.

After the meeting Bush cornered Cheney outside the Cabinet Room to discuss his trip to Aspen. Cheney had already begged off; he was needed at the Pentagon to study U.S. readiness and decide on what military steps were feasible. Bush also wanted to stay in Washington; he wasn't looking forward to meeting Thatcher. Unlike Reagan, he had never felt close to her. Just the thought of the long flight to Colorado now seemed insurmountably daunting. Bush said it felt like the wrong thing to do, especially in light of the crisis in the Persian Gulf. "Do you think I have to go?" he asked. "Yes, Mr. President," Cheney replied. Bush rolled his eyes.

Bush's uncertainty about the Colorado trip carried over into his public remarks. During a morning press conference, he said that the administration was not contemplating a military response to the invasion, but his statement was convoluted and contradictory. For perhaps the first time since he was elected President, Bush seemed to show the pressure. When he boarded Air Force One, he was still mulling over the new Persian Gulf crisis.

Mrs. Thatcher was less circumspect. She greeted the President affably—"It's *so* good to see you again, Mr. President," she said—and then, still staring him straight in the eye, she added a bit of personal advice, as if they were sharing a secret: "You must know, George, he's not going to stop." She let the matter drop there and walked with him into the Aspen Center conference room. Two hours later, after the President had finished his speech, the two emerged and walked a short distance to the Colorado home of the U.S. ambassador to Great Britain, where they closeted themselves with their top aides for a brief discussion.

Thatcher came right to the point. "Now, then, what are you planning to do about the Iraqis?" she asked.

Bush was momentarily taken aback. He responded as he often did to such difficult, yet direct questions, by laughing slightly, smiling, and nodding. Then, still clearly off-balance, he bungled the answer. "Well, I don't know," he replied. He shook his head uncomfortably as Thatcher waited for him to go on. "We have many options," he added.

Thatcher was shocked by Bush's uncertainty. "You have to respond, right now, immediately!" she declared. The look of horror on her face was genuine. "We will stand behind you, Mr. President," she stressed. Her right hand was balled into a tight fist on her lap. She was adamant, talking in a low voice, peering intently straight at Bush, and leaning just a bit forward in her chair. "We will stand behind you, but you must do something, you must, you must," she repeated. "You have to stand up to this man." She was lost in her own words, her mouth a line of grim determination. She was mad—mad at Saddam Hussein, but madder still at Bush. "I know what Ronald Reagan would have done," she said, her jaw set firmly. "Yes, yes, I know. Our friend, my friend, President Reagan, he would stand up to this, this ..."

Flustered, she leaned back, and then moved forward decisively, reaching out with her right hand to grasp Bush by his arm. He was startled by her vehemence. "This man is Hitler," she insisted. "We have stood together before. We have met men like this. We can do it again. We *must* do it again."

Bush nodded vigorously, suddenly steeled by her words. "We will," he replied.

But she had not heard. Seemingly exhausted by her own arguments, her last words were a plea. "George," she said, "this isn't the time to go all wobbly." (An aide to Thatcher later explained her intensity to a shocked American official. "We let you blokes retreat once in this century from your responsibilities," he said, referring to the first part of World War II, "and we paid a terrible price. We can't allow that again now, can we?")

From that moment forward President Bush was committed to the use of American power in the Persian Gulf. The press noticed it immediately; there was a new hardness in his voice, as if he had tapped into some unseen reservoir of determination. It seemed that he was spoiling for a fight. He was transformed by Thatcher's words. It was as if he suddenly realized he personally had been offended, lied to, led on, and snookered by Saddam Hussein. "Just watch and learn," he told reporters. Standing next to Thatcher, he looked and acted as if he were the leader of the free world. He looked as if he were the President of the United States.

The next afternoon Webster returned to Langley with a set of new instructions. The President, he informed his aides, wanted the CIA to come up with a plan to topple Hussein's government. Bush had arrived at this decision in the midst of an NSC brainstorming session earlier in the day. During a comment by Scowcroft about the need to hit Hussein at home, Bush suddenly turned to Webster and said he wanted a covert program that would destabilize the Iraqi regime. "Anything that will undermine his government" or "cause him trouble" would be helpful, Bush remarked, whether the pressure came from internal resistance groups or exiled leaders. The program, he stressed, should be an all-out effort. Bush wanted to show Hussein that the invasion was not going to go unanswered, and this was one way to do it.

Webster was surprised. Until then the discussion had focused on a hastily prepared CIA assessment about how the Iraqi invasion would affect American security. According to the report, Iraq now controlled access to almost 25 percent of the world's oil resources. The effect of such a weapon could be devastating. Webster was immediately struck by the immensity of the task: The agency had a massive amount of information on Iraq, but outside of a few poorly placed and closely watched Iraqi diplomats, it had little useful intelligence from the top of the Baghdad government. Nor could the agency do much to get inside Hussein's head. CIA officials were embarrassed by the paucity of information on him and on what might bring him down. According to a former CIA analyst, the agency's psychological profile of the Iraqi was "one of the thinnest documents the CIA had on any world leader." The agency could not rely on its past assessments, since what few conclusions it had come to about Hussein had turned out to be wrong—he was far from the pragmatic leader they viewed him as back in 1988.

The agency knew it could not count on a restive native Iraqi population to act against him. Contrary to Western public perceptions, Iraq was a largely modern, industrialized society, and Hussein had taken great pains to provide a wide range of benefits to the Iraqi population. As a result, Iraqis generally supported the government and viewed Hussein as a homegrown hero. There was virtually no political life in Iraq; the regime was repressive, omnipresent, and insulated. Any sign of dissent was brutally and unhesitatingly eliminated. It was almost impossible to infiltrate or recruit CIA agents inside the country; the system was just too closed. "Knowing the intention of world leaders requires the knowledge that comes from human intelligence," Webster later ruefully admitted in public, "[and this is] often very difficult to acquire—and frankly, difficult to acquire in that type of autocratic environment [i.e., Iraq]."

Webster was reassured that something could be done to help shake up the Baghdad regime by Richard Stolz and Dick Kerr, who had already established an Iraq Task Force (ITF) to deal with the crisis. The task force brought together the agency's leading experts in a wide variety of areas: politics, psychology, covert and paramilitary operations, economics, communications and signals interception, satellite reconnaissance, counterintelligence, and terrorism. Leading the ITF was the top specialist on the Middle East, a clandestine service officer with two decades of field experience. He was an Arabist by training and inclination who had run some of the agency's most successful espionage operations; even ADDO Thomas Twetten deferred to him. Within hours of Webster's return from the White House, the task force chief sent out new intelligence requirements to the London chief of station, who was instructed to make contact with a broad spectrum of Iraqi exiles, including former Baath party officials.

The hastily assembled ITF was split into three sections: one in the clandestine service, one in the DI, and one in the Directorate for Science and Technology. Special coordinating officers linked the three groups, and liaison officials from other federal agencies were given desks in the ITF offices.

The major task force components were up and running within twenty-four hours of the invasion. "We just basically went into some offices in the DO," a CIA officer explains, "and started rearranging things. We just set it up from scratch and brought people in that we needed. We stripped other sections bare. Everything was put aside for this. Everything."

The work was intense, nerve-jangling, and demanding, with 50 to 60 support officers assigned to each task force. Within a few weeks, the clandestine service's contingent had grown to 150 officers. By the end of August nearly seven hundred CIA employees were involved in assisting ITF operations in some way.

"It's exciting because you're in the middle of it all," says a senior Pentagon official who served on a number of such task forces. "You know everything before it's in the press. It's also a pressure cooker that builds rapidly. People want answers yesterday. The jobs can involve almost anything: sifting intelligence reports, answering the phone, preparing briefings, putting together maps, attending meetings, setting up operations. There are also specific sections set up inside the task force to handle specific problems and to prepare position papers and reports."

The burden of predicting what was going to happen fell to the DI's task force. Its job was to assess Iraqi military capabilities, the probable performance of U.S. allies, the effects of economic pressures on Baghdad, and the likelihood of political disagreements inside Hussein's inner circle.

By far the largest and most important ITF group was assembled to monitor, coordinate, process, and assess communications intercepts, signals intelligence, and photo intelligence. This huge task force worked closely with satellite offices at the NSA, NRO, and DIA. A special interagency hookup allowed ITF officers in Washington and at key stations overseas to view and discuss high-resolution photographs of Iraq culled from the thousands of such images taken from U.S. satellite platforms above the Middle East. The group analyzed signals intelligence intercepts obtained by NSA listening posts at Iraklion Air Base in Greece, and at Sinop and Pirimik air bases in Turkey (the closest site to Iraq). The NSA also supplied material from joint U.S.-British ground stations in Oman and Cyprus that listened in on overseas telephone calls. This entire high-tech setup was a chance for the CIA to show its stuff. Each of the major ITF offices was hooked into a teleconferencing system that had been perfected by the CIA over a period of two years. The system was electronically tied to both agency stations overseas and other federal offices outside the CIA.

Webster felt more self-assured after the NSC meeting of August 3. He had become comfortable with his job and more at ease around senior CIA officers who, just months before, felt that they had to hold his hand through the tough spots. That was not the case now, where the former judge and FBI chief could take control of what was essentially a political situation. He didn't need to know the intricacies of foreign policy; he had to be a leader, the agency's primary representative to Bush. More important, he had to exude confidence, a clear sense that he knew what the administration was going to do and agreed with it. That was why he seemed especially eager and positive when he returned to Langley. This was an opportunity, he told his aides, for the CIA to shine. The President was counting on them to come up with some answers. Take your time, he cautioned key DI analysts who were inundated with volumes of new material, take your time and get it right; from now on they all would be working longer hours. He directed his personal staff to set up a cot in his office and start preparing his remarks for the next morning, when he was due at Camp David to give yet another briefing to the President.

August 4 was a red-letter day for the CIA. The dejection of July 28 was replaced by a feeling that bordered on euphoria. Everything the agency had sought to establish over the previous forty years had come to pass. The agency got it right; it had made a risky prediction that had stood up in the face of widespread skepticism from the President and Middle Eastern leaders. After all, that was why the CIA had been established in the first place: to be able to precisely forecast when American interests would be in danger, when the nation was about to be attacked. When the President should be warned.

The exultant mood on the seventh floor on the late afternoon of August 4 was the natural result of having "called the shot" on Kuwait. But this elation was soon mixed with a somber response to the most recent batch of satellite photographs received from the NRO. After an initial analysis (the photos were first examined by experts at a secret location—"Building 16"—in Washington), the prints were spread out on the conference table in a room adjoining the director's office. Webster, who had just returned from a morning meeting with Bush at Camp David, was given an assessment by his top analysts: If Saddam Hussein was planning to pull out of Kuwait, as he had promised during the last twenty-four hours, then he had better start moving soon. The photos taken by a KH-11 satellite perched over the Kuwaiti desert showed that Iraqi troops continued to pour into the immediate area above the Saudi border. There were already nearly as many men there as had invaded Kuwait forty-eight hours earlier. It even appeared that the Iraqi army had entered the neutral zone between Kuwait and Saudi Arabia. The analysts pointed out five such incursions. They feared that Hussein might move into Saudi Arabia's oil-rich eastern province at any moment.

Webster nodded his head with concern. It now looked as if the information he had given Bush that morning might be wrong. The DCI had been the first to speak during the special session, and it had been a proud moment. Nearly everyone in the room had realized that the CIA's warnings during the previous week had been uncannily accurate. His voice was even and unemotional as he summarized the most recent technical information on Iraq's military deployment. One hundred thousand Iraqi troops were massing just north of the Kuwait-Saudi border, he said, but none of the units had actually gone south beyond that line. Directly across the border a Saudi force of one thousand men faced three Iraqi armored divisions (the same number Charlie Allen had seen on the night of July 27, poised to strike at Kuwait). The Saudi Royal Army, well equipped but small and poorly trained, would put up little resistance if Hussein decided to invade. The Iraqis could lop off one third of the oil-rich kingdom in something less than three days. It was a conservative estimate. Webster then repeated his major point to the President and his advisers: Iraqi forces had not crossed the border, and there was no reason, yet, to suppose that they would.

Now, back in the conference room near his office, Webster feared that he might have misled Bush; Hussein might invade Saudi Arabia after all. Kerr agreed. This was "pure Soviet doctrine"—the massing of independent tank formations for a lightning strike deep into enemy territory, the intent not so much to surround and strangle as to smother and overwhelm. The Saudis would be helpless in the face of such strength. So far as Kerr could make out, the Iraqis were planning to continue their roll southward.

Webster studied the photos once again, but he decided not to tell Bush that the CIA believed the United States should be prepared to stop Hussein's elite Republican Guards somewhere on the outskirts of Riyadh. Not only was that still uncertain (Saddam might pull back, it might be a mistake), but Bush could decide what to do without Webster's telling him. Besides, Webster knew that the President had probably already seen the intelligence photographs. The DCI wanted more information. He instructed Kerr to send him hourly reports on what the Iraqis were doing. He then reminded his top assistants that they shouldn't forget that Hussein had promised to pull out of Kuwait after a few days; he wanted to be informed immediately of any sign that such a withdrawal was happening.

At Camp David, Bush had already made his decision. Before adjourning the special session with his top advisers, he informed them that he was initiating Pentagon Plan 90-1002. U.S. forces, he said, should be prepared to take up positions to defend Saudi Arabia; the greatest military armada since the American intervention in Vietnam would be deployed. The only thing Bush needed to do was convince the Saudi government, so at 1:00 P.M. he placed a call to King Fahd. The connection was clear. After greeting the king, the President repeated what Thatcher had told him at Aspen: "Your Majesty, you know, he's not going to stop."

The top analysts at the CIA could not have said it better. Although the President had no certain information that Iraqi forces would continue past Kuwait's southern border, there was also no reason to assume that they would not. Bush was using his discretion by warning the Saudi king of his concern. At the same time he was convinced that he was not overstating the case. The President mentioned to Fahd that he wanted to send a special emissary to discuss with him a possible response to the invasion. Fahd replied that he would not commit himself to an American troop presence, but he seemed uncertain about what to do next. He was waffling; receiving a high-level American official might commit him to accept overt American help. He finally agreed to the meeting, but added a condition: "Don't send the diplomat," he said firmly. Bush agreed. Cheney would make the journey. Not Baker.

Later that afternoon, Cheney, accompanied by Schwarzkopf, Gates, and a CIA photographic expert, boarded a specially equipped Boeing 707 aircraft at Andrews Air Force Base on the outskirts of Washington for the trip to Saudi Arabia. In hand were the CIA's latest intelligence estimates. But the most important information Cheney needed arrived by way of a digitized readout while the plane was somewhere over the Atlantic. The CIA's latest photographs showed that two columns of Iraqi tanks had actually entered Saudi Arabia. It might have been a mistake on their part—the border was a poorly marked wilderness—but Cheney couldn't take any chances. He would show the photos to King Fahd when he arrived in Riyadh.

It was a long presentation, but purposely short on technical details. Cheney did not want to confuse the Saudi king with a complicated analysis. He wanted only to emphasize that the threat was there and the United States was prepared to meet it. When the threat had disappeared, the Americans would go home. They would leave equipment behind so that the Saudis could more adequately defend themselves in the future. Most of all, they would keep their pledge and do what they had said they would. They would not back down.

Cheney repeated the President's promise that the United States was committed to the defense of Saudi Arabia. "We want to work with you," he stressed. He then pushed for the immediate deployment of American forces. Cheney showed Fahd the photos he had received on board the 707. The king was clearly angry, as he passed the photos to his brother, the crown prince, seated behind him.

Fahd was impressed with the American evidence. He said that Saudi Arabia had no ulterior motives; he believed the United States. After agreeing to the deployment, he rose to shake Cheney's hand: "The only thing I want to know," he said, "is whether, at the end of this, Saddam Hussein will be able to pick himself up off the floor."

Cheney responded quickly. "No," he said.

On August 7, CIA officials played host when President Bush paid a rare visit to agency headquarters. His drive out to Langley was an act of gratitude, a stunning semiapology, on the part of the President. It was his way of acknowledging that the CIA had been right in July. When Bush made his entrance, the central lobby was packed with more than a thousand officers, analysts, and support staff. It was a triumphant return to his former office. He was clearly pleased. "You've done a great job," he told the group of officers who greeted him.

As he walked through the crowd, he reached out to shake the hands of as many employees as he could, while an official photographer snapped picture after picture. Within hours these photographs appeared in a glass case in the hallway leading to the agency cafeteria, where they remained on view for the next month. "It was a real morale booster for us over here," recalls CIA spokesman Mark Mansfield.

Bush was so gratified by his welcome that he commented on it at length during his private session with Webster and the CIA's top Middle

East analysts that followed his arrival. He added that his every return visit to Langley brought back good memories of his time as DCI.

A very strange thing happened in the weeks following Bush's good will trip to Langley. As with the coup in Panama, ten months earlier, administration officials began to look around for someone to blame when the press, and the Congress began to ask questions about preinvasion U.S. policy toward Iraq. Why was the White House caught so unprepared, so flat-footed? Why had the United States failed to respond at the first threat of Iraqi aggression? At least some administration officials were willing to blame the CIA. The most noticeable leak appeared on the newsstands on August 13, in the August 20 edition of *Newsweek*, in its "Conventional Wisdom Watch" column, which presents a brutally direct thumbs-up or thumbs-down view of the world. Next to the entry "CIA," *Newsweek* editors put a red "down" arrow and the following tag line: "Told everyone before invasion it was OK to go on vacation. Good work, guys."

The widely read column brought anything but chortles to the agency's Public Affairs Office. "We have no idea where that one came from," spokesman Mansfield remarked. "I can't even begin to comment on it."

"My understanding is that public affairs didn't respond," a CIA officer recalls. "But Webster noticed. It looked like a cheap shot to him."

Another CIA officer told a reporter at the time that the CIA was not interested in getting into a "pissing match with the White House." Insisting that the conversation be "kept out of the papers," this officer added: "Our information on Iraq was among the most timely and detailed we ever had. We were right on the money. There were no surprises. The word on that has to get out, but I suppose that this isn't the best time for it. Maybe later."

Other officers were not as low-key. "This is typical White House crap," one said. "Just pure baloney." Another officer was more specific. "*Newsweek* is the publication of choice for John Sununu, who blames the CIA for every administration screwup. Maybe he ought to clean up his own house first."

Bush did his best to defend the agency from the anonymous sniping. "We had good intelligence," he told reporters, "and our intelligence [on Iraq] has had me concerned [about the Persian Gulf situation] for some time now." Senator Boren also said he gave the agency "very high marks" for its July and August intelligence assessments.

Most congressional leaders agreed. "This is a case where the collection of data from the intelligence community probably got ahead of the formulation of policy," Congressman Robert G. Torricelli (D-NJ) bluntly told *The Washington Post*. "There may have been a better understanding of the intelligence situation than a comprehension by policy makers of the implications of what was taking place."

The *Newsweek* article eventually passed into history, assuaged by Bush's August mea culpa, but it still left a bitter taste among Webster's top assistants. "It doesn't matter what we do," one said. "We're going to get blindsided by the White House. This is just the way that politics is played in this administration, I guess."

The explanation was far more complicated than that. There was no doubt among senior officers at the CIA that President Bush was looking for someone to take Webster's place as DCI. He was easing him out. It was not that Bush disliked Webster; he just felt more comfortable with a close group of aides who understood his own views on things. Somehow, even after Panama, Bush never felt wholly at ease with Webster as DCI, despite their continuing friendship and Webster's clear claim to personal integrity and loyalty. He had done everything Reagan, and now Bush, had wanted him to do. He had improved relations with Congress and increased public confidence in the intelligence community at the same time that he had kept the agency free of scandal and unwanted negative publicity. But that never seemed to be enough.

"Bill Webster just didn't fit in," an administration official admits. "When it came down to it, the President just wanted someone with more hands-on experience at the agency."

In his nineteen months in office Bush had become closer to his top circle of White House aides than most recent presidents. They had formed a distinctly cohesive group. Bush often made his top aides share in his entertainment, much to the chagrin of Brent Scowcroft—a man who mowed his suburban Washington lawn dressed in Bermuda shorts and black socks—whose distinctive frown aboard Bush's power-boat off the Maine coast was an unmistakable sign of his own preferences. At times Bush seemed more the leader of a fraternity than President of the United States. (Bush's top assistants, led by Scowcroft, affectionately called him the skipper—something Webster would never do.) The DCI, whose own tastes included frequent appearances at Washington social events (which Bush disliked) seemed out of place in Kennebunkport.

By August 1990 Bush also had come to store great confidence in Robert Gates, whose role as the leading foreign policy administrator and intelligence expert was growing. Gates was an integral part of what came to be called the Gang of Eight—Bush, Quayle, Baker, Powell, Cheney, Sununu, Scowcroft, and Gates. This team was put in charge of the day-to-day management of the Iraq crisis. During the tense months that followed, this group would meet often to make decisions and plan strategy. Webster was rarely present.

Many CIA officers contend that Webster's absence from the inner circle had as much to do with how the agency's managers viewed their job as it did with Bush's clubbish leadership style. It almost seemed as if Webster, Kerr, Stolz, Helgerson, Twetten, and De Trani had made a distinct decision to stay away from Bush, to maintain their isolation, even when important foreign policy decisions were being made. That was just the way that Webster had said he wanted it, a view he had made clear after the White House criticized him the previous October in the wake of the failed Giroldi coup in Panama, when he was accused of being an ineffective CIA director.

During one interview Webster wrestled with the question of the role of intelligence in formulating policy. It is the job of the CIA, he stressed, to present the facts as well as it can and not to engage in policy. The fact that the DCI is not a member of the President's Cabinet, he said, was purposeful; the CIA is not a policy-making body. It gathers intelligence for the President and his government and then stands aside, to let them act. The worst thing that can happen, he said, is for the line between intelligence and policy to be blurred; that is when the agency's objectivity is most often questioned. The CIA serves the President, he said, but above all, it serves the facts.

But what happens, he was asked, if the President misinterprets the evidence? What happens if, after all the hard data have been presented, the President and his top advisers refuse to acknowledge what has been presented?

Webster did not hesitate before replying. "You tell them," he said, "that they have not read the intelligence closely enough."

The question was whether Webster actually did this in July or whether, when faced with Bush's doubts, he remained silent—instead of saying forcefully: "Excuse me, Mr. President, but you're apparently not reading what we've shown you here. Please study it again." Somehow, considering his personality, it seems unlikely that Webster would be so blunt with Bush, a man who spent many hours in his own career reading the kinds of intelligence reports that the DCI presented on the morning of July 28. Webster may have answered that question himself during a public speech on September 18, when he implied that the failure of that past summer should be laid at the door of the Oval Office. It was the closest he ever came to criticizing anything the administration did.

Webster was almost embarrassed for Bush. "I don't always understand our policy," he said, "and sometimes—even in the best-run administration—we haven't really gotten around to having one, because something has not been foreseen."

The simple truth was that Bush had not believed the CIA because he could not; to do so would have meant rejecting the advice of his top foreign policy advisers and turning a deaf ear to his most trusted Middle East sources. And it would have meant that the Reagan/Bush policy had been wrong about Iraq for nearly eight years.

* * *

During the days and weeks after Iraq's invasion of Kuwait, the agency dedicated massive resources to providing detailed intelligence assessments to Bush, his White House staff, the State Department, and the Pentagon. Behind the scenes, administration officials were nearly unanimous in praising the CIA's intelligence product. The joint CIA-NRO-NSA satellite and signals coverage of the Middle East was constant and exhaustive, and constituted the single most important and effective weapon in the U.S. intelligence arsenal. The CIA also established a senior interagency group to track international terrorists. Special intelligence notes on terrorist threats were included in the President's Daily Brief.

Within the first two weeks after Hussein's invasion, the CIA secretly landed two special paramilitary units inside Kuwait City to gather information on Iraq's defense and to make contact with the nascent Kuwaiti resistance. By the end of August, CIA-directed Green Beret units operating from a secret base inside Saudi Arabia were helping organize, train, and support Kuwaiti resistance efforts and plan strikes into their country.

The destabilization campaign against Hussein garnered the most attention. The CIA recruited a number of Iraqi exiles who knew the inner workings of his government and infiltrated two top intelligence teams into the center of Baghdad. On two separate occasions CIA officers were able to carry out dangerous rescues of important agency sources working in the country. But Webster later underplayed the value of the Iraqi dissidents whom the CIA recruited in London and Riyadh. "I think those closest to Hussein present his greatest threat," he remarked in a public speech, "more so than those who wish they were in positions of power and are on the outskirts in terms of dissident activity."

Soon after the invasion the CIA conducted a special Oval Office briefing on Iraq's nuclear capabilities and reported that Hussein was only two years away from developing a nuclear weapon. This intensive session was a milestone for administration officials: "This briefing changed the way the president and his men had been looking at the Gulf crisis," *The Times* of London reported. "It was no longer enough to free Kuwait. Saddam also had to be overthrown."

The CIA also handled all intelligence liaison operations with the Soviet Union, Iraq's former ally, and induced a high-ranking Soviet officer to show his nation's military transfer agreements with Iraq to the Department of Defense. Escorted by two CIA security officers, this Soviet official quietly sneaked into the Pentagon at the end of August.

The agency's work in Europe was also extremely valuable. CIA investigators interviewed hundreds of engineers, scientists, architects, contractors, and businessmen who had worked inside Iraq. German business firms provided most of the information, including blueprints of major Iraqi installations. In Egypt, CIA officers tracked down one of their most important business contacts, who provided them with the plans for the Iraqi Defense Ministry. (The key thing to do, he told them, is to set off a bomb on the ministry's fourth floor, where the command computers are housed.) The ministry became one of the first targets for American attack planes in the opening hours of the war.

Within two months CIA officials had catalogued Iraqi weak points and were confident they had identified how Hussein planned to maintain command and control of his forces during the war. The CIA's work went forward under the assumption that the start of any battle would feature a massive aerial bombardment of Iraqi military resources; while targeting decisions would be made by the U.S. military, the basis for those decisions would come from the CIA's data. "One of the advantages that we have over there, I'm convinced, a major advantage, is that we have very, very effective intelligence capabilities to support targeting," explained General Leonard Perroots, the former head of the DIA. "I don't believe that there's a major target that we don't already have targeted in a fixed sense."

In order to prepare for Iraq's defenses, CIA officers were dispatched to France to ask Iraq's second most important weapons supplier for precise information on Iraqi weapons, proficiency, and placement. The French gave the United States detailed information on Mirage F-1 aircraft, Exocet missile radar systems, and French-manufactured attack helicopters. CIA technicians also helped position U.S. satellites to watch key Iraqi military formations and bases in order to provide an accurate count of Hussein's major weapons. By November, CIA analysts believed they had a good idea of Iraqi chemical and biological weapons capabilities; they targeted plants and marshaling yards that, if destroyed, would neutralize the effect of the weapons in the war's opening stages. CIA technicians helped the NSA deploy the most important, and secret, radar installations to help track the Iraqi leadership. They used three highly sensitive receivers called elephant ears (each is the size of a football field) to identify Iraqi command "nodes" and intercept signals transmissions from Baghdad to field commanders.

The CIA's performance overseas was decisive and significant, but in Washington its public actions seemed to be tentative and uncertain. This apparent lack of enthusiasm spelled trouble for the agency in the Oval Office, where a premium was placed on the need for the administration to speak with one voice. This problem was no more apparent than in early December, at the height of the public controversy over future actions in the Persian Gulf. There were reports that President Bush had decided that the economic sanctions placed on Iraq in August would not force Hussein out of Kuwait. The CIA put itself at the center of the debate when Webster testified before the House Armed Services Committee during a series of hearings on the Persian Gulf crisis. Over time, Webster confidently predicted, the sanctions would force the Iraqi military machine to disintegrate. Webster presented a detailed statistical analysis drawn up by the ITF of the impact of sanctions, including anecdotal information that foodstuffs and petroleum stores in Iraq were being hit hard.

Both Webster's public and closed-door testimony on the effect of sanctions seemed so optimistic that it spurred the committee chairman, Representative Les Aspin (D-WI), to conclude that the CIA was convinced that the U.S. economic embargo might force Hussein from Kuwait if given enough time to work. "The embargo on Iraq's trade is essentially total," Aspin wrote in a report issued on December 21. "The Director of Central Intelligence, Judge William Webster, told the committee that sanctions have shut off more than 90 percent of imports and more than 97 percent of exports."

Less than one month later, on the eve of the Senate's historic debate on the war, Webster's testimony became the focus of intense scrutiny when Democrats charged that he had reversed his position on sanctions. Just twenty-four hours before the Senate arguments began, Webster wrote a letter to Aspin that "clarified" the CIA's earlier position. "Sanctions alone," the DCI wrote, "will not" force Hussein's withdrawal from Kuwait. Members of Congress were enraged by the timing of the response; Webster, the critics charged, was politicizing intelligence.

The CIA's Public Affairs Office struck back at the critics. "You have to take a look at the original testimony," CIA spokesman Mansfield responded. "The judge never said that sanctions alone would do the job." Mansfield was right, but only to a point, since Webster's "clarification" was badly timed. It was released three weeks after Aspin had published his own conclusions. Whether Webster intended to do so or not, it seemed as if the CIA were intent on backing the President and as if Langley were a captive of the White House.

The sanctions controversy had a demoralizing effect on the CIA, where analysts questioned Webster's ability to function as a credible and independent DCI. They believed that he had bungled the one thing that he was supposed to do well; his highly touted ability to maneuver through Washington's political shoals was now in doubt. Among his major detractors was Fritz Ermath, the head of the agency's National Intelligence Council. Ermath, an officer of enormous status, was horrified by Webster's reversal. Why couldn't the DCI have told Aspin that he stood by his earlier testimony? he asked a colleague. Ermath spoke from personal knowledge since he was the key official in the internal CIA debate about Webster's original testimony to Aspin. Throughout December, Ermath had steadfastly maintained that sanctions would *not* work and tried several times to convince Webster of that fact, but had failed. The paradox of the subsequent disaster in January was that it need not have happened at all, if only the DCI had listened to the agency's top experts.

"Webster misread the intelligence at first and needed to be corrected," a high-level State Department official said at the time. "His credibility has been very seriously damaged. And the CIA, regardless of how it's bearing up under this crisis, regardless of its performance, is very badly demoralized."

A few days after Representative Aspin published his report on sanctions, Ambassador James Lilley visited his old friend George Bush at the White House. It was a social call, with a little business mixed in. The meeting took place in the Oval Office on a late winter afternoon. Bush greeted Lilley cordially and motioned him to a chair. As they discussed the situation in the Persian Gulf, Lilley reported that the Chinese had been very cooperative in supporting U.S. actions against Iraq. Bush smiled and nodded approvingly. When Lilley finished, Bush asked if he still enjoyed being ambassador. After taking a deep breath, Lilley made his pitch. He wanted to be reassigned to Washington by the end of April, he said, since that would mark the end of his second year in China. For his next job, he wanted either a high-level CIA position or a top spot at the NSC. Bush nodded, with a twinkle in his eye. "You ought to pay a visit to Chase Untermeyer," he said, his smile growing broader. "I think we have something for you."

Lilley was puzzled by Bush's vague reply. After leaving the Oval Office, he walked down the hall to Untermeyer's office. As the White House chief of personnel, Untermeyer seemed overly busy, but on this day he was happy to see his unexpected visitor as he rose to greet him. "What are *you* doing here?" he asked in surprise. Lilley explained that he was in Washington for only a short time and thought he would stop by to see the President. He then recounted what Bush had said. "Do you know what he's talking about?" Lilley asked. Untermeyer was genuinely mystified that Lilley had to ask him such a question after speaking to the President and chuckled briefly as he returned to his desk. "You're going to get a job at a much higher pay grade than me," he replied.

Lilley left the White House intrigued by the challenge of taking on the top spot of the CIA. He had been in touch with several of his former colleagues at Langley and knew that Webster was having some problems. There was now no doubt in his mind: Bush wanted to change directors, and he believed Lilley could do the job. But Lilley's own feelings were mixed. He had spent many years as a government employee, and the pressure-filled CIA job would take him away from his wife and grown children to an even greater degree than before. The job was nothing but work. He shook his head to clear the doubts; he would love to be DCI.

A few days later Lilley returned to China, where he resumed his responsibilities as ambassador. Three weeks after that, on the night of January 16, the United States launched Operation Desert Storm.

It was a time of great excitement in Washington. But for many, the war's opening moments must have brought back bitter memories of lost opportunities. A number of former Reagan administration officials, for instance, were angered that the United States now found itself facing Saddam Hussein's forces along the border with Kuwait. They were convinced that the current crisis need not have happened at all—if only Ronald Reagan, George Bush, and many other foreign policy officials had heeded their warnings about the Iraqi dictator's true intentions back in 1982.

15
★ ★ ★
Baghdad Station

On a windswept day in February 1982 a private airliner from Paris landed at Amman's International Airport and taxied to a spot just a hundred yards from the modern main terminal. A number of officials waited as the passengers disembarked, then escorted them to a group of waiting limousines for the trip into the city to meet with Jordan's King Hussein. The most important passenger on the flight was William Casey, who carried his own brown briefcase as he crossed the tarmac. There were no reporters present to shout questions at him; it was a classified visit, one of the most secret ever launched in the short history of the new Reagan administration.

Casey met privately with King Hussein within minutes after his touchdown and then was ushered into an ornate room where he shook hands with a large, gray-suited Iraqi official named Barzan Ibrahim Hassan al-Tikriti. He was the head of the General Intelligence Directorate (Iraq's CIA) and happened to be the half brother of Saddam Hussein. Their discussion was polite, though without any hint of outright cordiality. Casey's presentation was animated: The United States was concerned about Iraq's military campaign against Iran, which had begun in 1979. The United States wanted to open up an intelligence liaison relationship with the Iraqis, Casey said, in order to make certain that Baghdad could defend itself against Iranian attacks. He sketched out the details of the plan.

Casey was particularly concerned with the military situation on Iraq's southern front, where Iranian tank formations were poised to take advantage of key Iraqi weaknesses. He displayed hand-drawn CIA maps of Iranian and Iraqi deployments and explained how U.S. experts believed that Iranian forces would counter Iraqi moves. His presentation was factual and unemotional, but the impact of his words was clear: The United States feared that Iraq was on the verge of a major military defeat, that its defensive lines were badly overextended, and that Iranian infantry divisions could punch through them all the way to Basra. The resulting chaos would be disastrous for the Baghdad regime.

In Washington, intelligence officers and foreign policy experts waited for news about the outcome of the meeting. Casey's mission had been put together at the last minute, in an atmosphere of growing crisis. The intelligence community had only recently obtained evidence of a possible Iranian military victory and had a difficult time convincing its friends in the Middle East that Saddam Hussein was in grave danger. Even so, Casey spent a week in Paris waiting for word to come that Hussein would send a representative to meet with him. The negotiations had not been easy. The intermediaries for the planned visit, including King Hussein of Jordan and King Fahd of Saudi Arabia, had assured the Iraqi leader that the United States had important information that he should listen to. But after initially agreeing to see the U.S. representative, Hussein drew back. He told King Hussein and King Fahd that he just did not trust the Americans. There followed a week of reassurances. Finally, the visit went forward and Barzan was dispatched to Amman.

It was an unusual and dangerous journey for Casey, especially since the United States and Iraq did not have diplomatic relations. For thirteen years, ever since the 1967 Arab-Israeli conflict, the two nations had spoken to each other across a gulf of misunderstanding and mistrust. In the meantime, Iraq had become the Soviet Union's most important ally in the region; the USSR shipped weapons and technology in ever-increasing amounts to Baghdad and sent military advisers to help the regime plan its strategy against the Iranians. But the Soviets did not have the technology the Americans did and apparently had little idea that Iraq was facing a political and military disaster.

Casey's talk with Tikriti lasted two hours. The Iraqi intelligence official then flew off to Baghdad to inform his leader of its results: The United States and Iraq had a new agreement. They would share intelligence on Iran, and the CIA would send a group of experts to Baghdad to help in the war effort.

Less than two hours after the end of the meeting, Casey reported via secure communications link to Washington that his mission was successful. Several months later, two more officials, including a high-ranking CIA officer, made a second trip to the Middle East. This time they went directly to Baghdad. The Americans carried a new set of drawings of

Iraqi and Iranian military deployments, meticulously drawn to scale by a group of intelligence community military experts. In addition to Barzan, the two met with Saddam Hussein, who still doubted the American wanted to help him. But after seeing the CIA maps he changed his mind. Several hours later, the officials returned to Baghdad's airport for the trip back to Amman. CIA officers monitoring the operation were overjoyed. The CIA's new intelligence liaison relationship with Iraq was going according to plan.

At the Reagan White House, however, several experts on the National Security Council staff were worried. These critics feared the United States was helping create a new monster in the Middle East, which would inevitably turn on its masters with the very weapons it had been given. America was playing with fire, they thought. One of these strong-willed analysts was Howard Teicher.

Until the publicity surrounding the Iran-contra affair forced him out of the government, Teicher was considered one of Washington's leading experts on the Middle East. Prior to taking a job on the Reagan NSC, he had made a name for himself as an opinionated commentator on the region's affairs while serving in a number of posts at Foggy Bottom and the Pentagon. His quiet, cerebral, self-assured style made him a particularly attractive figure inside the Reagan administration, where conservatives dominated policy discussions by pushing their particular viewpoints to extremes. He became a welcome figure at the NSC, where his barely audible presentations brought the room to silence. Teicher was a brake on the process, a reflective intellectual whose commitment to the conservative agenda was tempered by his conviction that policies were more the result of political necessity than ideology. "Conservative, yes, he was conservative," a colleague says, "but he wasn't an ideologue in the normal sense of that word. Howard's a single-issue guy. He was totally focused on the Middle East."

His detractors have a different view. For them, the short, balding, intense, and often impatient Middle East expert was one of the leaders of a distinct pro-Israel faction inside the Reagan administration. A former CIA officer observes: "Teicher was convinced the Israelis were the only friend we had in the region and we had to do as much as we could to support them. He tended to view any threat to Israel as a threat to the United States. That's how he saw the world."

Teicher's reputation as a hard-line anti-Hussein partisan and an advocate for strong American-Israeli ties was made apparent in 1979, when he wrote a controversial fifty-page assessment on Iraq for the Pentagon. The still-classified study was, in Teicher's words, "filled with facts and analysis." His closest associates, however, say that it was a startling, controversial, and refreshingly prescient view of U.S.-Iraqi relations. In a key part of the narrative, Teicher predicted that Hussein would start a war with Iran "in nine months" in order to make Iraq the most powerful Middle Eastern oil-producing nation. Teicher laid out his views in disarmingly persuasive terms. The paper was so impressive, in fact, that it ended up on the desk of Secretary of Defense Harold Brown, who read it closely but rejected its conclusions. Teicher later characterized Brown's comments in matter-of-fact, but poignant, terms. "They [the Iraqis] are not the nasty guys you claim they are," he quotes Brown as saying. Brown was right in at least one respect: Teicher's report did not mince words. "Howard said that Saddam was a madman who had to be stopped at almost any cost," a Pentagon analyst recalls.

"I argued that Iraq was deceiving us as to their true intentions," Teicher responds. "They were becoming involved in a confrontation with Iran, ostensibly to curb the radicalism of the Khomeini regime. In my opinion, everything they were doing seemed to indicate that they were attempting to establish themselves as the major Arab power in the Middle East."

Teicher's paper was filled with statistics that suggested Iraq was engaged in a breakneck program of military expansion whose purpose was not so much to threaten Iran as it was to intimidate Israel and eventually break the back of American influence in the Middle East. In many respects, Teicher thought, the rise of Iraq could lead only to a confrontation between Saddam Hussein and the United States. "There were a number of us in the national security establishment who could see this coming," he says. "We knew that sooner or later Saddam would confront us."

When Teicher joined the Reagan team as an expert on the Near East and South Asia, he found a number of like-minded analysts, including Donald Fortier, the NSC's director of political and military affairs. Teicher and Fortier formed an alliance with several mid-level support officers, most significantly Oliver North, who viewed Iraq as an unreconstructed terrorist state that would stop at nothing to humiliate the United States. North viewed Israel as a bulwark against Iraqi autocracy and extolled its virtues to anyone who would listen. His admiration for the Israelis was deepened by his close cooperation with them in planning a number of counterterrorism initiatives. North's worshipful stance on Israel was paralleled by his views of State Department and CIA Arabists, part of what he called a "corporate culture" that "relished any antagonism that could be fostered between us and the Israelis." Some of this, he says, "came from a long-standing and barely hidden pro-Arab tilt at State, which I'm hardly the first to notice. Another large chunk, I believe, is the result of an ingrained streak of anti-Semitism in our government. Many mid-level government officials—and not only at the

State Department—are the sons and grandsons of the great elite American families, where a genteel, discreet anti-Jewish prejudice was often taken for granted."

Israel was clearly Iraq's chief enemy in the region and Hussein's most outspoken critic in the world community. Soon after the Reagan administration took office, Israel's arguments about Iraqi intentions held sway in the State Department and White House, but only because then-Secretary of State Alexander Haig pushed Israel's position. He persuaded Reagan to allow Israel to ship high-tech weapons to the Iranian port of Bandar Abbas, knowing full well that they would end up on the battlefields of the Iran-Iraq War. Haig's influence also was responsible for the United States' muted response to Israel's June 1981 strike at Iraq's nuclear reactor at Osirik, using U.S.-manufactured F-16s.

By early 1982, as Iraq's military position deteriorated, Teicher's, Fortier's, and North's views on Iraq were ignored inside the Reagan White House. The national security staff eventually came to be dominated by officials who believed that the major threat to American interests in the region came from Iran, where the Islamic fundamentalist revolution of 1979 had succeeded in unseating the pro-American government in Teheran. The United States had good reason to fear Iran, which held fifty-two Americans hostages for 444 days at the end of the Carter administration and continued to label the American government as "the Great Satan." NSC officers were especially fearful that the Iran-Iraq War, waged without letup since Hussein's invasion in 1980, would result in the defeat of the Baghdad regime and the establishment of a Shiite fundamentalist state on the Persian Gulf. At first the United States had nothing to worry about—the Iraqi military performed well in a series of battles throughout 1981—but by early February 1982 the tide was turning.

DCI Casey received a series of briefings that month on the Iran-Iraq war that sent a chill through the upper levels of Washington's foreign policy establishment. According to CIA military experts, Iraq's attacks in southern Iran had ground to a halt, and its military formations were overextended and poorly led. The war was turning into a slaughter. Casey was told that Iraq's attempts to unify Kurdish forces against Teheran in the north also were failing. Simply put, Iraq had lost the initiative in the war. After nearly one year of fighting on the defensive, Iran was ready to counterattack. Saddam Hussein was in trouble.

Acting swiftly, Casey proposed that the United States establish an intelligence liaison with Baghdad that would be inaugurated by the visit of a high-level American official to the Iraqi capital to meet with Hussein. He won quick acceptance of the proposal from Ronald Reagan. The Iraqis were a different matter. Hussein said he didn't want the meeting and didn't trust the United States. It was only after a series of telephone conferences with King Hussein of Jordan and Saudi Arabia's King Fahd that he relented. It was then that Casey met with Tikriti in Amman. The subsequent mission to Baghdad, intelligence officers now say, was conducted by National Security Adviser William Clark and CIA officer Bert Dunn (then chief of the Near East Division).

But the success of the two CIA missions did little to alter the military facts, and the gloomy February predictions by CIA analysts turned out to be tragically accurate. An Iranian offensive in mid-March resulted in a major defeat for Hussein's army: Ten thousand Iraqi soldiers were killed, fifteen thousand wounded and another fifteen thousand taken prisoner. Two Iraqi armored divisions were decimated; 320 Iraqi tanks were destroyed and 350 captured. A large number of Hussein's forces were pushed back across the Shatt al-Arab. Iran lost four thousand dead. The fighting was the most brutal of the war, but most important of all, the Iranians fought hard and well, reversing a series of demoralizing defeats they had suffered in the first year.

The bad news continued: Iraqi formations continued to be vulnerable to Iranian attacks in spite of the CIA's best efforts to warn Hussein that he needed to muster a more effective defense. Saddam Hussein's personal leadership of the war—countermanding his own military commanders' decisions and ordering hasty and ill-prepared attacks—was having a terrible effect. In April, CIA analysts told Casey that a large portion of Iraq's military was in danger of complete disintegration. The primary evidence was a series of satellite photographs of Iraqi troop deployments near the strategic city of Khorramshahr, just miles from the Iran-Iraq border. Outside the city, thirty-five thousand Iraqi troops were nearly surrounded by Iranian formations, some seventy thousand soldiers in all, backed by two hundred tanks and massed formations of artillery. The fall of Khorramshahr would open Iraq's Shiite-dominated southern provinces to a general Iranian offensive, which could then sweep all the way to Baghdad. Iran would easily tap the anti-Hussein feelings of Iraq's Shiite majority, turning them against the Sunni-dominated government.

The CIA overestimated the impact of the Iranian offensive, but not by much. Iraq lost twelve thousand to fifteen thousand troops in the battle for Khorramshahr. While most of its units were able to make a hasty but organized withdrawal to the north, their defensive lines remained shaken. The Baghdad regime was edging closer to defeat: Iranian troops were thirteen miles from Basra, and the Iraqi war effort was having a debilitating impact on its society. Fully 40 percent of the male population was being poured down a single road to Basra, and industrial and manufacturing capacity was grinding to a halt. Sensing that Iraq's troops were stretched thin and that if they gave a little push somewhere the regime would crack, Kurdish insurgents launched commando raids on Hussein's forces in the north.

The continuing military disaster on Iraq's southern front had serious repercussions throughout the Arab world and in the United States. During June Saudi Arabia and Syria attempted to broker a negotiated settlement of the war that included the replacement of Hussein with a council representing all of Iraq's major political factions. Meanwhile, in Washington, the Reagan administration started considering what final steps it might take to save the Baghdad regime from defeat. Intelligence and foreign policy officials believed the efforts they had already made— not just the opening of February but removing Iraq from the list of states supporting terrorists (thereby allowing American high-tech firms to trade with Iraq)—came too late to reverse the massive defeats of the winter and spring.

In the late spring of 1982, Casey and his top assistants decided to expand the formal liaison relationship with Hussein in the hope that it could influence his government to take radical new steps to retrieve his nearly impossible military position. The initiative was prompted by a series of new assessments on Iraqi military vulnerabilities that was given to Casey in early June. CIA experts once again predicted the imminent collapse of the Baghdad government, through either a direct military defeat by Khomeini's Revolutionary Guards or an internal Shiite rebellion. The situation was worse than ever. Units of Iranian soldiers had blown huge holes in Iraq's defenses, and to make matters worse, Shiite uprisings were raging in Karbala, Basra, Hilleh, and Nasiriya. The agency's top analysts reported that the road to Baghdad was virtually open. Hussein's military commanders either were purposely placing the regime in danger or were too incompetent to provide an adequate defense.

Once again, Casey and Reagan acted to reverse the crisis and save Iraq. They approved an expanded intelligence relationship that included supplying Hussein with information on Iranian troop positions obtained from AWACS surveillance planes that had been sold to Saudi Arabia in October 1980. The CIA also sent a special squad of intelligence officers to help Hussein plan his military defense, and a secret agency station was established close to the presidential palace in Baghdad. This time the Iraqi leader listened to his American friends, turning over the conduct of the war to his military professionals and moving to patch up relations with his Kurdish enemies.

According to a number of CIA officers, Robert Gates, Richard Kerr, and Thomas Twetten were put in charge of overseeing the program, though its day-to-day operation was placed firmly in the hands of Bert Dunn. The original arrangements between the United States and Iraq stayed in place: The leaders of Jordan and Saudi Arabia continued to guarantee America's good-faith efforts and pledged renewed support to the Baghdad regime. Hussein was helped in other ways: Trade barriers that had been in place since 1967 were eased, and work was done to gain acceptance of Iraqi requests for loans from other nations. Reagan administration officials later claimed that this was a true "exchange": In return for U.S. help in the war, Hussein provided the Americans with information on Middle East terrorists, expelled Abu Nidal from Baghdad, provided information on Soviet influence in the region, and shared intelligence reports on Iran.

To emphasize America's good faith, CIA officers recommended ways in which the Iraqi military could best counter Iranian moves. Their information startled Hussein: America's intelligence was shockingly accurate and detailed. It appeared that the United States knew more than he did about the status of the battlefield and what was going on inside his country. U.S. information on southern Shiite rebellions was also excellent. The CIA's program was a sucess. By June 1982, Hussein embarked on a major overhaul of his regime and reshuffled a number of key Cabinet positions, replacing sycophants with economic and political experts. He also replaced a number of military commanders and ordered a strategic withdrawal of most of his forces from Iran, shoring up his defensive lines around Basra. From then on Iraq would fight a defensive war, on its own territory. Hussein's government also stopped announcing war casualties—it was too demoralizing.

During separate Iranian offensives in the summer of 1982, Iraqi forces beat back massed Iranian ground attacks whose success would have spelled disaster for Baghdad. The most dangerous thrust brought the Revolutionary Guards to a point five miles north of Basra, on the Basra to Baghdad road. But each time their attack was stopped by well-deployed Iraqi infantry divisions. Iranian troops were virtually slaughtered by the suddenly well-coordinated fire of Iraqi artillery batteries. They lost seven thousand soldiers each day for three weeks. Iraqi losses were less than one tenth that total. The Iranians never broke through. By early August, dispirited and exhausted by the heavy toll of the attacks, they retreated. They were left with a small strip of Iraqi territory, ten miles long and three miles wide. For the next two years the war remained at a standstill.

Soon after being reelected for a second term as President, Ronald Reagan expanded the United States–Iraqi relationship. The President extended diplomatic relations and received Iraqi foreign minister Tariq Aziz in Washington. Baghdad sent its own ambassador, Nizar Hamdoon, a confidant of the Iraqi president, to Washington. He soon became a familiar figure on the Washington social circuit. Hamdoon became an important source of information for the Baghdad regime on Reagan administration fears that the Iranians would defeat Hussein in the Iran-Iraq war and was a trusted intermediary in the U.S.-Iraq intelligence exchange. At one point in the relationship, Hamdoon even gave a dinner to honor then-U.N. Ambassador Jeane Kirkpatrick, and an unofficial Iraqi lobby was started in Washington. It gained a significant following.

The White House accommodated Saddam in other ways, putting Iran on the list of states sponsoring terrorism and browbeating American allies to cease all weapons shipments to Teheran as part of Operation Staunch. But the most important step was the reopening of the U.S. Embassy in Baghdad, which was the heart of the CIA's covert program to assure Hussein's survival. For a number of White House officials who opposed the policy, this was the last straw.

"This wasn't an intelligence relationship," Howard Teicher says bitterly. "This was an intelligence dump. We gave Iraq what they wanted to prevent their defeat by the Iranians. We saw key vulnerabilities in their defensive lines, and we knew that Iran could roll all the way into Baghdad. We could see the establishment of a fundamentalist Shiite state in southern Iraq, and it scared us to death. So we told Saddam, 'Wake up, there's a sieve in your lines.' That's exactly what we said. We gave them strategic advice. We saved them."

Teicher confirms that in 1982 the CIA secretly engineered a "tilt" to Iraq in its bloody war with Iran, but his claims go even further. "We sent them information through Jordan and Saudi Arabia to establish our bona fides," he explains. "We gave them overhead and electronic information—a treasure—that disclosed to Saddam the nature of our intelligence capabilities."

Teicher argues that the United States did for Saddam Hussein what it had never done for even its closest allies: It bared sources and methods of intelligence collection and reporting—Langley's secret of secrets. "Casey and his top assistants were involved," he reveals, "at first through a representative that was sent out there to give Saddam the information and then by liaison officials from the station in Baghdad."

Teicher believes the entire American government shared the blame for propping up Hussein. "The bureaucracy at the State Department was dominated by Arabists," he reflects, "and when we opened to Iraq, they were like pigs in shit. The opening looked like bad news for the Syrians, so the Arabists thought that now we had a lever on them, too. They thought that [Syrian President] Assad would want better relations with us as a result."

Teicher, Fortier, and North blamed Secretary of State Shultz and Secretary of Defense Weinberger for the tilt. North has since written: "The American tilt toward Iraq and antipathy toward Iran were two of the few things that Shultz and Weinberger ever agreed on." He singles out Shultz for particular condemnation by quoting the secretary as saying: " 'We wouldn't want to see,' an Iranian victory ... we have been deliberately working to improve our relationship with Iraq." Teicher adds: "Shultz let his views on terrorism run our Iraq policy; as soon as Saddam said that he had expelled Abu Nidal, that was okay with him."

By 1985, Teicher, Fortier, and North had been joined at the NSC by Robert McFarlane, the President's new national security adviser, who brought to his job the same unerring support for Israel characteristic of his three other colleagues. McFarlane also had deep doubts about the U.S. opening to Iraq that was coupled with an almost deplorable lack of knowledge of Arab affairs. He was fearful that the United States had picked the wrong ally in the region. His views were buttressed by an old friend, David Kimche, the former deputy director of Mossad and the director general of the Israeli Foreign Ministry.

Teicher's memory of the opening to Iran is vivid. "It was in 1985," he recalls, "when Bob [McFarlane] was first approached by the Israelis, by David Kimche. He pointed out to us what we already knew, that Iran was the key to the region, the strategic linchpin. But this opening to Iran was not an Israeli program; this was our program. Anyone who looks at a map can see how important Iran is."

McFarlane delegated the task of reviewing U.S.-Iranian relations to Fortier and Teicher, who then approached the CIA's national intelligence officer for the Near East, Graham Fuller, to draft a special national intelligence estimate, titled "Toward a Policy on Iran." The final estimate claimed there was evidence of a power struggle inside Iran and urged the United States to help Iranian moderates gain power.

Graham Fuller's 1985 SNIE is one of the most curious documents in CIA history. It was based on little direct on-the-ground intelligence from Teheran and was put forth without cooperation from the clandestine service. One month later the follow-up National Security Decision Directive, which established official U.S. policy, expanded on many of the SNIE's arguments: It revived Washington's forty-year fear that the Soviet Union was gaining influence in Iran and even proposed increased weapons trades "on a case-by-case basis," should the regime moderate its views. What was even more strange was that the program was proposed with little or no reliance on any credible intelligence information. It was the result of belief—not fact. Not only were there no moderates inside the Iranian government, but the Soviet Union's influence on Iran was negligible. The USSR's political organization inside the country, the Tudeh party, was nonexistent; it had been unceremoniously slaughtered by the mullahs, after the CIA secretly gave them a list of its members.

Despite these obvious failings, Teicher still defends the SNIE and admires its author. "Fuller felt that our policy was very asymmetrical," he says, choosing his words carefully. "He was a strategic thinker. He knew how important Iran could be."

What Teicher does not mention is that Fuller was an open critic of the pro-Iraqi sentiment inside the U.S. government. At the same time, Fuller dismissed CIA and White House fears of resurgent Islamic fundamentalism. "There was a genuine visceral fear of Islam in Washington," Fuller says. "It was a force that was utterly alien to American thinking, and that really scared us."

Fuller goes on to suggest that pro-Iraq policy makers may have been suffering from some kind of political neurosis. "Senior people at the Pentagon and elsewhere were much more concerned with Islam than communism," he explains. "It was almost an obsessive fear, leading to a mentality on our part that you should use any stick to beat a dog—to stop the advance of Islamic fundamentalism."

A number of Fuller's CIA colleagues remain critical of his role in the Iran-contra affair and privately question whether he really knew what he was doing. "Graham would believe the last thing that someone told him that sounded right," one former CIA officer remarks dismissively. "When Teicher approached him with the Iran idea, he loved it. It was a big canvas for him. It was exciting. That's Graham for you; he was always trying to come up with the one theory that could solve all the problems, that could explain everything."

The May 1985 SNIE is the most convincing evidence available that the Iran opening was initiated to counter the CIA program with Iraq and not, as was proposed later, to provide a basis for releasing American hostages held by Iranian surrogates in Lebanon. It had nothing to do with the Soviet Union or moderates. "Myself and a lot of others were concerned that this intelligence exchange with Iraq was a slippery slope," Teicher explains. "We were giving Saddam strategic information that told him what he needed to do to fool us. We had to come up with a counter to that." Was the Iran opening a reaction to the CIA's dealings with Iraq? "You said that, I didn't," Teicher responds. "The American people have to draw their own conclusions. All I'm saying is take a look at the facts."

Teicher's conclusion draws a strong negative reaction from retired CIA officials familiar with the agency's secret opening to Hussein. "It's hogwash," says one. "This man [Teicher] stereotypes Arabs, and his boss [McFarlane] routinely killed them [a reference to the bombing of Druze strongholds in Lebanon in 1983]. They're people of mediocre intelligence. They have no understanding of the Middle East. Their common view of the world is that Israel can do no wrong and Iraq can do no right. Perhaps they would have liked it better if we'd had a bunch of screaming Shiites in southern Iraq instead of Saddam Hussein."

Another intelligence official is more specific: "The two programs ran along different tracks. The point is that we would have tried to stop the Iranian initiative if we'd known of it sooner. That's why it was run out of the NSC."

The CIA's secret tilt to Iraq, meanwhile, was expanded even as the NSC pursued its fruitless overtures to Iran. In August 1986 the CIA established a secure and highly sophisticated electronic communications system that linked Washington directly with Baghdad. For two months Hussein's regime received direct cable traffic via the Baghdad station on Iranian military deployments. The link also transmitted CIA assessments of Iraqi bombing raids on Iranian installations. Much of the analysis was performed by a special unit inside the Baghdad station, which was able to provide Iraq's military commanders with real-time intelligence that was detailed, incredibly accurate and designed to give Hussein a decided advantage over Iran. According to a 1986 account published in *The Washington Post,* Casey even met with Iraqi officials in Washington to make sure that the link was functioning properly and "to encourage more attacks on Iranian installations." While the White House described the information provided to Baghdad as "purely defensive," an administration source said that the CIA program was "a cynical attempt to engineer a stalemate" in the Iran-Iraq War. The fact that an administration source would make such a comment shows the deep divisions the program was causing in the administration.

The notion that the United States was involved in an "attempt to engineer a stalemate" has rarely been questioned since the *Post* published its 1986 story. In fact, that was never the case. Pro-Iraqi factions inside the Reagan administration, and pro-Arab CIA and State Department officials, were not interested in an endless war in the Persian Gulf—they were committed to an Iraqi victory and were doing everything they could to ensure it. In comparison with the U.S.-Iraq intelligence deal, the "arms-for-hostages" scheme was a very modest program. It could never have assured an Iranian victory. History provides the final proof.

In early 1988, Iraqi units overwhelmed Iranian forces on the strategic Fao Peninsula in a well-planned and complex military maneuver that was designed and managed with the help of the United States. American military experts provided by the CIA mapped out the routes Iraqi forces used in the offensive, and Iraqi commanders trained for the onslaught for one year under the watchful eye of American intelligence officers. The peninsula was reconquered in only thirty-six hours. The Iraqi victory undermined Iranian morale and brought a virtual end to the war.

The devastating Iraqi victory was made possible by an upgrade of intelligence being supplied to Baghdad that went far beyond simply providing Hussein and his military commanders with hand-drawn maps of Iranian troop deployments. According to senior intelligence officials, the material included "narrative text reports derived from highly sensitive electronic intercepts and photoreconnaissance of Iranian targets." In at least one case, actual satellite photos of Iranian positions were shown to Hussein and his strategic planners with CIA officers present. While none of these photographs was actually turned over to the Iraqis, the action was unprecedented. The materials carried the highest U.S. government intelligence classification.

"Our intelligence dump was made so that Iraq could win," Teicher says. "The CIA gave Saddam the best stuff it had. And when they saved his regime, they gave him more. People who were opposed to us on Iran said the United States was better off tilting to Iraq."

Teicher suggests that the U.S. intelligence material was so sensitive that Iraq may have been able to "reverse engineer" its military defenses, to defend its own troops from the systems the United States was using to spy on Iran. After 1988, the Iraqis undertook a massive military program to harden and hide their command, control, and communications systems. Teicher's fear, that the CIA had shared "sources and methods," had come to pass. "The key was the secure landlines, used for communications," Teicher says.

The picture painted by Teicher and others is of an administration bitterly divided over the CIA's role in Iraq and of a marionette President who was manipulated first by one set of foreign policy partisans and then by another. The bare outlines of the full story are only not being made public—but at least for Teicher and North the final judgment is in: The CIA's relationship with the Baghdad regime convinced American policy makers that Iraq could eventually become a long-term U.S. ally and reinforced Saddam Hussein's belief that the United States would stand aside as he accumulated more power in the Arab world. Far more than U.S. relations with Iran or Iraq was at stake, however, Teicher now implies. In effect, America's entire Middle East policy, including its strategic relationship with Israel, was coming under attack.

Former Reagan administration officials play down suggestions that the CIA's opening to Iraq resulted in the disaster of August 1990. For example, former Deputy Assistant Secretary for Near East and South Asian Affairs Edward W. Gnehm defends the Reagan-Bush policy. "As a powerful nation with a global outlook," he says, "we are obliged to develop as close relationships as possible with countries in these positions. There was a reasonable expectation that Saddam Hussein might well want to develop closer ties to the West." NSC official Richard Armitage also rejects Teicher's thesis. "We knew this wasn't the League of Women Voters," he told *The New York Times.*

The fact remains that from 1988 until the opening round of the Persian Gulf War, the Iraqi military underwent a massive program to make sure that its major communications links would remain unsevered in the case of war. By then Teicher was out of the government, his career short-circuited by his role in the Iran-contra affair. His former colleagues say he was purged.

* * *

Whatever hopes the Bush administration had of moderating Saddam Hussein's radical regime ended on August 2. Once the realization set in of what Iraq had done, the White House seemed committed to the path of war and consistently opposed attempts to negotiate a solution to the crisis. The CIA monitored a number of back-channel attempts to mediate the confrontation by private, and not so private, messengers. One of these messengers was a former high-level CIA official whose experience in the Middle East was used by Iraqi moderates in an attempt to mediate a face-saving withdrawal from Kuwait. At the end of August the message, in the form of a memorandum, was relayed to Brent Scowcroft. The deal offered an Iraqi withdrawal in exchange for an end to sanctions, access to two islands in the Persian Gulf, and alleviation of Baghdad's financial crisis. It was clear that the proposal came from Hussein himself. But because the White House demanded an unconditional withdrawal, Bush rejected the overture.

A much more serious effort was made several weeks later in a letter sent by Hussein (he called himself "The Giant in the Country of the Two Rivers") to Imam Sheikh Dr. Shamseddine al-Fasi, the spiritual leader of the Middle East's large mystical Muslim sect, the Sufis, and a man with enormous regional influence. This letter was a bold attempt by Hussein to split the U.S.-Saudi military relationship and included an offer of Iraqi withdrawal from Kuwait in exchange for Saudi Arabia's pledge to expel American forces. The Saudis, however, never took the proposal seriously, in large part because of its vitriolic language (Hussein referred to President Mubarak of Egypt as "Hosni the liar") and because they feared Iraqi military power. The message was so offensive and one-sided that it embarrassed the Saudi royal family.

The most important Iraq-U.S. back channel was handled by U.S. intelligence officers and officials of the Palestine Liberation Organization in North Africa and Europe. The Palestinians became perhaps the most serious negotiators during the crisis, even though Hussein's invasion divided the PLO's leadership. Their internal squabble was over what one senior PLO official called Yasir Arafat's "premature" support for the invasion. Arafat was castigated by a number of his closest colleagues, including Salah Khalaf (Abu Iyad), who remained one of the agency's major points of contact inside the PLO. "I don't want my own cause associated with the destruction of the Arab region," Iyad told an Algerian reporter. "We are really caught between two fires." Supporters of Arafat's position, on the other hand, were convinced that the United States had "tricked" Hussein into his August conquest. They too feared a Persian Gulf bloodbath, which could forever end any hopes for a Palestinian homeland. "These men in Saddam's army, they kill people like you eat chicken," PLO spokesman Bassam Abu Sharif remarked at the height of the crisis. Sharif was perhaps the most articulate spokesman for an Arab solution to the impasse; he appeared several times on American television to plead that the United States should allow time for Arab leaders to negotiate an Iraqi withdrawal, but his public efforts failed.

Privately, the major points of contact between the Iraqis, the Americans, and the Palestinians were a European businessman with strong ties to Baghdad; his friend, Secretary of State James Baker; and Abu Iyad, who hoped that Hussein would unconditionally quit Kuwait. A number of meetings were held between the Palestinians and the European businessman in Europe in December 1990 and January 1991, with notes of the meetings passed to State Department officials. "We have done our best," Iyad said, in describing the talks, "but we have not yet found a common ground." As in the previous attempts at negotiation, Hussein wanted something in return for his withdrawal, a position unacceptable to the White House.

Even when it appeared that the Iraqis would not withdraw prior to an American attack, Iyad held out hope that this Palestinian back channel would succeed. "Let me just say that Mr. Baker seems to appreciate our work in this area," he confided. "You never know."

All attempts at mediation through this channel, however, finally came to an end in mid-January, when Abu Iyad was murdered in Tunis by a gunman planted in his security detail by Abu Nidal, whose own terrorist organization was virtually destroyed by a joint PLO-CIA program. Nidal had gotten his revenge against his nemesis, just as he had said he would. It was a bloody time.

With the failure of all negotiations, CIA operations reemphasized support for the primary American mission—the military defeat of Iraq. As of January, Webster remained an outsider in these policy discussions; he was still attempting to retrieve the high standing that he had gained inside the White House in August but that had been diminished by his crippling statements in December on the effect of U.S. sanctions. As the January 15 deadline approached, Webster seemed adrift, uncertain about his next moves and worried about his position inside the Bush national security establishment. Not only was he excluded from the Gang of Eight, he was also viewed as being increasingly irrelevant inside the CIA.

The worst thing that could have happened to him took place in late August when DDO Richard Stolz, his loyal ally, guide, and messenger to the clandestine staff, announced that he would be retiring at the end of the year. The move had been a long time in coming, but it was still a shock. The announcement also surprised members of the Senate and House intelligence committees who viewed Stolz as Webster's right-hand man. During a special meeting on Capitol Hill, Webster admitted to the two committee chairmen that Stolz's plans "come as a real blow" and

390 Eclipse

were "a real loss for us [at the CIA]." Inside the clandestine service the announcement was greeted more philosophically. Operations officers said that Stolz looked visibly exhausted; he was putting in backbreaking hours because of the Iraq crisis, and his family life was suffering as a result. A number of his colleagues recall that he was tired of the CIA and add that he had told Webster at the beginning of his tenure that he would not stay on much past two years.

Stolz was confident that Webster could handle the DCI's job without him and was satisfied with the impressive work of his own assistant, Thomas Twetten, who capably handled the DO's day-to-day activities. Over the previous two years, Twetten's advice to Webster had been invaluable, and he had taken his place as one of his most loyal supporters inside the agency. Like Stolz, Twetten was not interested in taking risks and was viewed as a conservative operations man. Unlike Stolz, however, Twetten was a Middle East expert, just what the agency needed in the months ahead. Stolz believed it was time for a new generation to take its place on the seventh floor; he was ready to pass the baton.

During his retirement party in December, Stolz seemed particularly affected by the toasts raised in his honor by his colleagues. It was not simply that he was ending a career of great usefulness; there was also a sense that somehow the CIA itself was changing. The old guard was fading away. The young men and women recruited in the salad days of the 1950s and 1960s, who had formed the core of the agency's second generation, were coming to the end of their careers. Stolz, Clarridge, George, and scores of others had provided a necessary bridge from the old "oh so social" OSS set, which had led the agency in its early years, to a new, more strident generation of experts who prided themselves as much on their political savvy as they did on their experience as field officers. It was as if the agency itself were retiring. Stolz was a symbol of the spy wars against "the target"—a throwback to the days when the CIA focused primarily on the Soviet threat. Now those days were gone.

The new generation of CIA officials reflected the attitudes of the agency's new senior triumvirate—Thomas Twetten, Richard Kerr, and Hugh E. "Ted" Price, who had earlier succeeded Gus Hathaway as head of counterintelligence and was slated to become Twetten's assistant, the ADDO. Twetten's ascension was proof that a CIA employee did not need to be a great station chief or espionage officer to become head of the clandestine service. Twetten was the agency's premier survivor, a man who had tenaciously outlasted his competition to become one of the CIA's most important voices. Perhaps the primary reason he was named Stolz's successor, however, was his absolute commitment to the DO's ideals. Twetten had not only remained untainted by the Iran-contra affair, he had tried to distance Langley from its effects.

Price, by comparison, was viewed as an agency infighter with a cold bureaucratic heart. Now that he had made it to the top, he apparently felt he no longer had to treat the retiring generation of officers with deference, as he had on so many previous occasions. During the retirement party of one operations officer, Price didn't even emerge from his office, even though the ceremony was being held in an adjoining room. It was a sign of the chasm that had opened between the older generation and their younger successors.

Price's manner epitomized this new breed. They styled themselves as much more "professional" than their predecessors, who, they said, had involved themselves in romantic flights of fancy—tracking KGB officers through Europe, Africa, and Asia and generally "mucking about" with nefarious characters. As often as not, this younger group claimed, such goings-on had ended in disaster, precisely because the older generation tended to see the world in simple terms—as a contest between good and evil. The agency had paid a high price for these past performances and had lost the confidence of a large part of the Washington bureaucracy as a result.

The veterans, on the other hand, often criticized the younger officers as bureaucratic paper pushers who ignored time-tested traditions. But even they conceded that the CIA was forced to operate in a more open environment precisely because of their past mistakes. Change was inevitable, even if it was not welcomed.

For many retired CIA officers from the first and second generations, Price's open slights to their former colleagues who were still serving were not simply a sign that he lacked courtesy, but were a sign that the agency's tightly knit way of doing things, its sense of being an elite, was eroding. These new leaders were no longer genteel, baggy-trousered intellectuals motivated by patriotism and a fear of communism, but technocrats and organizers whose tradecraft was suspect and who owed their rise in prominence to their ability to step over the bodies of their associates. As one veteran complained, "These new people are woefully ill prepared to deal with the realities of the nineties. If they think we had it easy with just one international enemy, let's see how they do with a whole host of them."

At least in 1991, however, there was only one.

The Pentagon called its new military doctrine the strategy of invincible force, but there was nothing "new" about it: Generals Ulysses S. Grant and William T. Sherman had used the same tactics in the Civil War, when they pummeled the undermanned Confederate forces in Richmond and Atlanta with crashing waves of blue-clad soldiers who sometimes pinned their names to their uniforms in anticipation of their deaths. The attacks were typically preceded by massive artillery bombardments that sometimes lasted several hours. When Grant's army finally launched an all-along-the-line assault against the Confederate capital, it found empty trenches. The main difference in the coalition's preparation for the Persian Gulf War was that the final offensive was preceded by a month-long aerial bombardment that was perhaps the most devastating in human history. In twenty-four hours, the allied air force virtually swept the Iraqi war machine from the skies.

The Pentagon's doctrine placed unique requirements on the CIA, which was given the task of assessing the effects of the coalition's ceaseless aerial sorties on everything from Iraqi troop and civilian morale to the actual count of destroyed or damaged military vehicles. Everything that moved in Kuwait and southern Iraq was counted, then re-counted, and reassessed yet again. Anything that moved was bombed, and if it moved again, it was bombed again. The primary targets were nuclear and chemical facilities, airfields, command and control bunkers, and finally, Iraqi troops themselves. Secondary targets included electrical power stations, sewage treatment plants, telephone systems, communications towers, bridges, and railroad lines. But by far the most important task given the CIA was assessing the numbers and quality of Iraq's warmaking machine—the actual troop carriers and tanks at Hussein's disposal.

For the most part the CIA provided the most conservative estimates of bomb damage of any government agency. By the beginning of February, agency estimates placed the total number of Iraqi military vehicles damaged by the bombardment at 14 percent—which was low by Pentagon standards. The joke that circulated in the Defense Department was that if CIA bomb damage assessment officers saw a photograph of a tank turret on one side of the river and the tank's body on the other side, they reported that the vehicle was damaged—since some of it was left. According to one DIA intelligence officer, the CIA's "goofs" were "constant and legendary," because "they didn't want to get blamed if we went in there and found tough resistance." Intelligence community analysts responded to the charges by saying that Pentagon planners often chose the wrong targets, destroying Iraq's capability of waging war, its electrical and petroleum plants, instead of its actual military formations. By the time of the invasion, they argued, almost 70 percent of Iraq's electrical power was destroyed, along with nearly 90 percent of its petroleum-producing capabilities, while the Republican Guard, Iraq's frontline troops, suffered far fewer casualties than Pentagon planners were claiming.

High-ranking military officers became involved in the conflict over bomb damage assessments from the first day of the war; they complained that the CIA's reports were so vague that they were useless. "There were caveats all over the place," a senior Pentagon official recalls. "Because the CIA could not be certain, its reports really didn't tell us anything at all." The assessments conflict was not unlike the struggle over intelligence that was waged during the Vietnam War, when CIA analysts routinely accused their Pentagon counterparts of giving an optimistic outlook when none was warranted. In Southeast Asia the CIA turned out to be right, and the Pentagon wrong. Now, in the Persian Gulf, CIA analysts apparently remembered that earlier lesson and acted accordingly. They steadfastly argued that it was better to be on the safe side, and more certain, than to waste valuable American lives finding out otherwise.

By any objective standard, however, it was undeniable that the CIA seriously miscalculated Iraq's ability to hide and fire its mobile Scud missiles. After the first Scud attack on Israel, launched just after the allied air assault began, the Pentagon became so frustrated at Langley's inability to spot Scud locations by high-tech means that it sent hunter-killer teams into southern and western Iraq to find the missiles themselves. The CIA's failure to pick up electronic traces of missile launch sites was considered a breakdown of the U.S. signals intercept capability. Part of the problem was that the agency undercounted the number of missiles that Iraq could deploy in the first place ("by a factor of some three hundred," one intelligence analyst says). It also underestimated Iraq's ability to construct crude, but deadly, missile launchers on the backs of trucks. Military officers grumbled to the press that the hunt for the Scuds took air assets away from other targets, notably the elite Republican Guard units south of Basra.

In the most critical incident, CIA, DIA, and intelligence officers on the staff of General Norman Schwarzkopf engaged in what one officer describes as "a long distance shouting match" over bomb assessments. Schwarzkopf himself became engaged in the contest, criticizing agency intelligence officers in Saudi Arabia for failing to give his commanders timely intelligence reports. His major complaint (repeated during congressional testimony after the war) was that the agency was not providing anything useful, and that when it finally did, the information was outmoded. The CIA resented the outburst, and refused to change its conservative policies. Schwarzkopf's own military intelligence officers thereafter relied on their own "gunsight" intelligence reports, studying films of bombings to determine whether they had knocked out specific targets.

The CIA also failed to estimate Iraqi chemical and nuclear capabilities properly, both before and after the war. The numerous reports and assessments on these dangerous Iraqi programs were often confusing and ambiguous—a sure sign that the CIA did not know the full extent of Hussein's capabilities. While officials from Langley presented a major briefing on the topic at the White House in the weeks following the invasion, they were forced to review their statistics in January, on the eve of the American bombing campaign, and again in February. But the most embarrassing incident occurred shortly after the war ended when an Iraqi scientist who defected to the West brought reports of several hidden Iraqi nuclear installations. His testimony clearly proved that the CIA had underestimated Iraq's nuclear development program.

Perhaps the worst intelligence failure of the war took place in the early-morning hours of February 13 (Baghdad time), when American fighter-bombers suddenly attacked what they believed was a command bunker at Amariya, in a suburb of Baghdad. Two radar-evading stealth F-117As each dropped a heavy, laser-guided bomb that penetrated thick concrete walls and exploded in darkened underground rooms, killing hundreds of innocent men, women, and children in their sleep. Intelligence for the targeting had come directly from CIA interviews with Iraqi exiles and foreign engineers who said they had been hired by the Iraqi government to modify the shelter for military use. The Bush administration responded to the worldwide outcry that greeted the disaster by saying that Hussein may well have used civilians to "further his war aims." The White House and Pentagon defended the bombing by insisting that there was no doubt that the shelter was used as a military command center.

But Lieutenant General Perroots, the former head of the DIA who served as a consultant to the Pentagon during the Gulf War, later revealed to BBC-TV reporter Tom Mangold that the bombing was a terrible misjudgment that was based on outdated U.S. information. "It was old intelligence," he confirmed uncomfortably and emotionally. "We should never have bombed it." Perroots had nothing but scorn for the CIA's performance in the Gulf War. "Oh, hell," he remarked. "The CIA has never had a good war. William Webster is absolutely on the ropes over there."

Just twenty-four hours before General Norman Schwarzkopf launched Operation Desert Storm, an unknown official inside the Bush White House launched a new broadside against Webster and the CIA. This criticism was more vitriolic than any previous attack and had the sting of authenticity; it was as if Webster were being publicly rebuked. The remarks attributed to this anonymous source appeared in *The Philadelphia Inquirer* on February 22. The article went well beyond the accusations of ineffectiveness and incompetence that had plagued Webster over the previous two years. "He's pathetic and weak," the official sniped, referring to the DCI's performance in briefings on the Gulf Crisis. "He has a hard time completing a thought. He doesn't know what to do with the agency." The article also quoted Senator Arlen Specter (R-PA), a longtime member of the Senate Intelligence Committee, who complained: "The intelligence community is virtually rudderless." The *Inquirer* reported that Webster was "under attack" for his poor showing and that he was purposely excluded from White House meetings on the war.

The criticisms had the feel of a well-orchestrated campaign to force Webster's resignation. A senior administration official and close confidant of the President's believes that the negative comments were issued by Robert Gates. Unlike the situation in the October attack, however, this time no one at the White House reacted with a statement supporting the DCI. Webster's phone remained silent. For once CIA officials did not specifically rule out either Sununu or Gates as the author of the criticism, though privately they were convinced that Gates was responsible for the *Inquirer*'s attack. The official response was laconic. "The President has expressed full confidence in Judge Webster," CIA spokesman Mark Mansfield said. He stressed that Webster was "fully in charge," that he had "briefed the President daily" during the Persian Gulf crisis, and he adamantly denied that the CIA's performance during the crisis had been lacking. Perhaps sensing that this time his boss was in real trouble, Mansfield added his own unflinching views: "Judge Webster is one of the great public servants of the last quarter century." Off the record, Webster's supporters were livid and characterized the *Inquirer* report as "pusillanimous drivel" that was "astonishingly uninformed and filled with pejorative quotes. The anonymous 'weak and pathetic' quote was absolute nonsense."

The aggressive response was a signal for some that Webster's time as DCI was coming to a swift conclusion. "The handwriting is on the wall," a CIA officer admitted. He privately speculated that James Lilley had already been anointed by Bush as Webster's successor.

Webster was especially disturbed by the story and worked throughout February to gather a defense. Unfortunately, however, he found that he could not count on support from those who'd defended him in the past. Even Senate Intelligence Committee Chairman David Boren, one of Webster's biggest Capitol Hill boosters, and a man who could take credit for his having been confirmed as DCI in the first place, issued a startling about-face on his performance. Most recently Boren had given Webster "the highest marks for personal integrity, character, rule of law ... perhaps the highest of any the agency ever had." But now, in February 1991, Boren implied that Webster's management during the Persian Gulf crisis was unacceptable. "I don't think we had good strategic intelligence at all," he remarked.

Choosing his words with care, Boren added that his committee "didn't want to micromanage the CIA, but it's clear we're going to have to look at the agency in the next six to twelve months." The senator also confided to aides that Webster's handling of the DCI's job was a case study in why the intelligence community needed to be reorganized.

Boren was joined in this effort by the new leader of the House Select Committee on Intelligence, Representative Dave McCurdy, who pledged that he would be an aggressive chairman. "I intend to reestablish our credibility as an oversight committee," he said. "We are not going to be shrinking violets." Then he issued a personal warning to the DCI. "I intend to stand up to Judge Webster," he declared. McCurdy represented a new attitude among House committee members, who were convinced the agency had botched its role as the nation's premier intelligence organization during the Persian Gulf crisis. McCurdy believed that a top-to-bottom reorganization of the intelligence community was the best solution to the problems. "It is not going to be enough just to change the names on the doors or the blocks on the organization chart," he argued. "There are so many additional areas that need attention. The number of Arabic speakers [at the CIA] is abysmal. The number of area specialists for the next decade is equally abysmal. That's disgraceful."

Several senators had similar plans. One month before American soldiers liberated Kuwait, New York Senator Moynihan introduced S. 236, "A Bill to Repeal Certain Cold War Legislation." He called for the virtual dismantling of the CIA and the transfer of its major functions to the State Department and Pentagon. His bill was actually a stalking horse for more serious reorganization proposals, but it gave voice to a growing consensus that there should be a major shift in American intelligence priorities now that the cold war was over. Nor, apparently, had the Senate forgotten about the Iran-contra affair, despite Webster's persistent effort to wipe the stain from the agency. "This bill will reassert a most important principle which was also lost in the fog of the cold war," Moynihan stated on the floor of the Senate, "that the executive branch may not resort to extralegal devices to evade the laws in national security cases."

To Webster it must have seemed that the roof was caving in. Not only was he suddenly deprived of his considerable powers as a politician, but he had to rely for advice on a group of assistants who were intelligence professionals and much less familiar with the ways of Capitol Hill. Unlike the departed Richard Stolz, Bill Baker, and Jim Greenleaf, the new team did not know him well and had not served alongside him when he was under attack. Webster was well liked by Twetten, Kerr, Price, and De Trani, but it was clear they would not circle the wagons as Stolz had done during the dark days of the Giroldi coup. Throughout the rest of February and March the CIA rumor mill circulated a number of interesting possibilities: that Webster would suddenly announce his retirement and leave the CIA quickly, that he would somehow salvage his position, that he would strike back at his detractors via the press. For those who knew him best, however, there was never any doubt that

Webster would remain Bush's loyal soldier to the end. He would retire gracefully and graciously, praising Bush and the handpicked successor Bush would choose and quietly return to the more private life of a lawyer who enjoyed tennis, collected autographed books, and made the rounds of the Washington social scene. Like Clarridge, Cave, George, and a host of others before him, he had actually survived longer than anyone had predicted.

The U.S. victory in the Persian Gulf was an astonishing display of military planning, small-unit training, and sheer power. From the opening moments of the battle there was never any doubt about who would win. "It's not even going to be close," a confident DIA officer predicted in early January. "You'll see."

On the night of February 23, 1991, Saudi troops and American Marines assaulted the main Iraqi lines in southern Kuwait. It was a feint designed to pin the Iraqi infantry in place. Farther west, an entire American corps leapfrogged to the north, deep into southern Iraq, then swung quickly east, surrounding Kuwait and cutting off thousands of Iraqi soldiers. The bold maneuver outstripped its projections: Iraqi soldiers surrendered by divisions. Ninety hours into the battle, the war was virtually over and pan-Arab forces began entering the southern suburbs of Kuwait City. Farther north, remnants of the still-intact Republican Guard walked slowly back toward the Shiite-dominated cities of Safwan, Nasiriya, and Basra. In a final spasm, American aircraft butchered Iraqi troops retreating along a single highway north of Kuwait City.

It was President Bush who ultimately decided to stop the fighting. He told his top assistants that he wanted to "end the killing," but he was reflecting the advice given to him by Brent Scowcroft and Robert Gates, who both steadfastly insisted that the job was done once Kuwait was liberated. They counseled that U.S. troops should stay in Iraq until there was a full accounting of American prisoners and a formal armistice was signed by Iraqi field commanders. But no longer. Gates, in particular, held out hope that Hussein was so weakened that he would be toppled by his own officers. Clearly the effort to destabilize the Baghdad regime had not succeeded: Hussein's regime was teetering, but no one had yet launched the final coup.

Gates expressed his concerns to Bush in the final hours of the war. He feared that Hussein would be replaced by an even more radical anti-American leader and that a Shiite from the dictator's inner circle could take over the Iraqi government. Gates seemed to imply that it might be better if Hussein survived. But when Bush asked him if he thought there would be a Shiite uprising in Iraq, Gates said he did not think so.

Gates was wrong. After the Iraqi surrender, Iranian-backed Shiite rebels seized Nasiriya and Basra. The fighting was bloody and brutal, in some cases outstripping the catastrophic American invasion in late February. Over five hundred thousand Iraqi citizens became refugees, and nearly one hundred thousand were killed. The fighting in Nasiriya was particularly bitter, as elite Republican Guard units fired artillery shells point-blank into houses and businesses that sheltered Shiite fighters. There were countless executions on both sides. The Bush administration decided not to intervene. "We are banking on the military or Baath leaders to pull him [Hussein] out of power as the unrest worsens," an administration official explained.

When the spreading rebellion sparked a revolt among Iraq's large Kurdish population, a debate on whether the United States should intervene erupted in the White House. At first the interventionists—a group that included Pentagon officials and even Bush himself—had the upper hand. On March 13, Bush announced that U.S. aircraft would shoot down any helicopters being used to suppress the revolts. A week later two Iraqi jet fighters were shot out of the sky. But on March 26 Bush decided to let the revolts run their course without American help.

The exact details of White House discussions about the uprisings are not known, but the circumstantial evidence indicates that the administration purposely decided to allow Hussein to slaughter his opponents in the south. The murderous response to the Shiite uprisings was fine-tuned; the White House allowed Hussein free rein in southern Iraq, drawing the line at his use of chemical weapons and fixed-wing aircraft. What protests there were in the United States against this policy were muted by the celebration of the overwhelming American victory. Nor did any of America's allies in the Middle East disapprove of Washington's decision. The fear of a Shiite state on Saudi Arabia's northern border was simply too great. Even Egypt, which was not directly threatened by the uprisings, expressed concern about Iraq's "territorial integrity," a code phrase that meant Iran should not be allowed to take advantage of the devastation in southern Iraq. On March 28, Saddam Hussein launched a major counteroffensive, using his still-intact Republican Guard. The southern revolt was crushed inside one week, and when Hussein later shifted his forces to the north, the Kurds were also subjected to a ceaseless punishment.

As the fighting raged in early April, a specially trained eleven-man CIA paramilitary team was dropped into northern Iraq. There was still a hope that the Kurds might somehow score a major victory and establish a semi-independent Kurdish state. They might even spark a revolt among Hussein's inner circle. This was the last chance for such a change of leadership. By the beginning of April, the CIA team had successfully made contact with Kurdish rebel leaders. A short time later, however, the team's chief political officer came to a tentative conclusion that proved to be all too accurate—the Kurdish revolt would fail.

What a spectacular victory it had been: American forces killed thousands of Iraqi soldiers, burying some of them alive in their trenches in southern Kuwait. The loss of life was matched by the horrific toll that the air campaign took on Iraq's infrastructure; the UN secretary-general said that the country had been relegated to "a pre-industrial age." Another report warned that 170,000 children under the age of five would die in Iraq unless immediate steps were taken to repair the nation's water purification facilities. In Washington, meanwhile, these troubling figures did little to dim popular acclaim for George Bush's victory. The nation's attention quickly turned to other matters.

16

— ★ ★ ★ —

Gatesgate

The 1980s were dubbed "the decade of the spy": In 1982 renegade CIA officer Edwin Wilson was arrested for selling arms to Libya; in 1985 Jonathan Pollard was charged with passing classified documents to Israel, and John Walker was arrested for selling secrets to the Soviets. That same year Edward Lee Howard defected to the Soviet Union, and KGB defector Vitaly Yurchenko became "the spy who got away." Finally, in 1986, revelations about America's secret opening to Iran and its not-so-secret war in Nicaragua placed the CIA under new scrutiny, and then led to hearings on the Iran-contra scandal in 1987, which bared massive amounts of information on how the agency conducted its operations. When William Webster succeeded William Casey as DCI, the CIA was battered and bleeding.

Nothing during the previous ten years, however, compared with the startling revelations of 1991. Although no one was arrested for supplying weapons to terrorists or spying for a foreign government, the secrets uncovered in the third year of George Bush's presidency were, nevertheless, astounding. For the first time in four decades, the American people got a behind-the-scenes look at the CIA and learned that the men and women who worked there were at war with themselves— and had been for many years.

The first hint that 1991 would be "the year of the CIA" surfaced in November 1990, when twelve-year veteran analyst John Gentry resigned his position in the Office of Resources, Trade, and Technology, the successor to the Office of Global Issues. His letter of resignation to

DDI John Helgerson was widely circulated in the intelligence community and on Capitol Hill in early 1991. Gentry's letter gave a hint of things to come:

> I can no longer work in an organization in which satisfaction of bureaucratic superiors is more important than superior analysis, in which the key analytic question often is "what does the boss really want?" rather than "what is really of significance to US foreign policy and national security?" in which subservience of intellectual integrity to the wants of superiors is essential to bureaucratic success; in which analysts' fear of "managers" has created an analytical corps of "scared rabbits," in which analysts ... are relegated to the role of research assistant or propagandist in the service of de facto senior analysts up the review chain who inject personal political opinions and desires into Directorate products, regardless of fact or analysts' judgments.

Gentry was not the first analyst to resign from the agency, but unlike many of his predecessors, Gentry's political motives were above question. To all appearances the forty-one-year-old former Army Special Forces officer and Phi Beta Kappa economist was a level-headed conservative—a military officer by training and an intellectual by choice. He was hardly the type to make outlandish or unsupported claims. Tall, thin and intense, a man whose long strides perfectly matched his military training, Gentry appeared stripped of any personal ambition. "I don't expect to become rich or famous," he said several months after his resignation, "and I don't want to hurt anyone or the CIA." He steered clear of personal attacks after resigning, not only in order to keep his promise to CIA security officials but also to give his claims greater credibility. He typically shook his head at reporters who wanted to know how he felt about Helgerson, Kerr, Gates, or SOVA head George Kolt. "I can't mention names," he replied.

Even so, it was clear that all four men, especially George Kolt, were his targets. In his letter of resignation Gentry told Helgerson:

> It has been genuinely distasteful to have worked for a division chief who ordered a politically pointed current intelligence article based on a press clipping despite numerous hard facts to the contrary, my judgment to the contrary, and the opposition of other DI components. In discussions about the issue, my branch chief questioned my loyalty to the Office of European Analysis, but not to honesty, the Agency, or the Nation. These men repeatedly made clear that they intended to serve a political constituency and to choose their data selectively—often picking

information scraps specifically refuted by numerous, more reliable reports.

The division chief Gentry referred to could only be Kolt. "I can't name anyone," Gentry later repeated. "But I will say that the head of the Office of Soviet Analysis is a big part of this problem."

Other charges in Gentry's letter were even more explosive. He claimed that (during one debate) a "division chief ... threatened to kill an analyst," a supervisor "admitted to having neuroses, acted like it in my view, and permitted regular lies by a staff member about US intelligence capabilities to visiting foreign intelligence officers...." In another case, a branch chief "repeatedly, purposely, altered the facts contained in articles ... in the alleged interest of making sentences and paragraphs more readable." Another branch chief "stole my personal property from my desk." Still another high-level official "rummaged through analysts' desks to discover [as he said] 'what kind of analysts' he had in his branch."

Gentry was equally outspoken in person, singling out Gates—though, carefully, not by name—as the one person most responsible for "the current culture" at Langley. "What I have seen is the bureaucratization of the CIA," he explained several months after leaving the agency. "And it started with the guy at the White House who used to be Casey's deputy."

Gentry's sweeping criticisms touched every part of the CIA. He indicted not only Kolt and Gates but also Kerr and Helgerson as "the leaders most responsible for the lack of integrity, [which is] the agency's [chief] crisis." Momentarily forgetting his promise never to name CIA officers, Gentry confirmed that "Helgerson was stunned by my resignation. His attitude was 'This just can't be true.' As if he'd never heard that there were any problems. The tone of his voice was that 'You're just not level-headed.' " On the other hand, Kerr—or rather, as Gentry calls him, the "deputy director"—was "personable enough, all right," but a man "given to excuses." Gentry says he was not alone in his feelings. At one point in early 1990, he recalls, a group of DI analysts urged him to present their complaints to Kerr. After many attempts he finally cornered the deputy director at an agency reception. Gentry told him that the DI was demoralized and that a large number of analysts believed that its intelligence product was being polluted by political concerns. Kerr listened politely, but shrugged off the complaints. "If these people have problems with the way the agency is run," Gentry remembers him saying, "then the solution for them is to leave."

Within two months of Gentry's resignation several important DI officers decided to follow Kerr's advice. The most significant of these resignations was of a senior economist who had been with the agency for more than twenty years; it was a demoralizing loss that the agency could not afford. But those vacancies were only the beginning of its most recent problems: In the year leading up to Iraq's invasion of Kuwait, nearly "50 percent" of all Persian Gulf experts in the DI left the agency because they were "fed up" with the way their division and the DI were being managed. According to this source, three key Near East and South Asia office analysts departed in the midst of the Persian Gulf crisis, despite the pleas of DI officials for them to stay. Their resignations placed an enormous strain on the agency's intelligence capabilities. The reasons they gave for leaving were unerringly the same: poor management, lack of integrity, and a straitjacket approach to analysis. "Much of the blame for the erosion of analytical expertise can be traced directly to a lack of leadership within the DI," a knowledgeable analyst later complained.

Since all these quiet departures went unnoticed by the general public, the problem was largely ignored by the agency's senior managers, who continued to describe the CIA's intelligence assessments as "well reasoned and well written, carefully argued and meaningful." Gentry insists the DI's output was anything but. "The desire to serve has become the desire to satisfy," he points out. "The responsibility for producing good work has become the responsibility for satisfying people up the line." The agency's response to such grievances was muted, following the standards set during much of Webster's term: The CIA served the President, who had no complaints about its intelligence product. Its defenders, meanwhile, dismissed the resignations as being the result of "general disgruntlement over the stress that the job causes. A lot of these people just can't take it." These same arguments, however, could not be used to deflect public criticisms leveled by younger analysts whose careers were just starting to fulfill their promise.

One of these relative newcomers was Stephen A. Emerson, who had served as a mid-level analyst at the CIA for only eight years before resigning. Like Gentry, Emerson tried to air his criticisms internally before deciding to leave, but was constantly rebuffed by the DI's senior managers. He left his job five months after the Gulf War ended, and only after he had exhausted all attempts to spark internal reform. "It is pathetic to see what passes for 'analysis' in DI publications today," Emerson wrote in his resignation letter to Helgerson. "Solid, insightful, and expert analysis is all too often shunned in favor of the alarmist, the glitzy and the wishes of senior managers in the production feeding chain." Among the most disturbing trends that forced his decision, Emerson noted, was the "all too common practice of altering analysis (and even factual information) to conform with the views of senior Agency or U.S. policymakers." In other words, Emerson was resuscitating the litany of charges that marked the worst moments of Casey's tenure as DCI: that the agency's product was "politicized" and that senior analysts were writing estimates in disregard of the facts.

Emerson claimed the CIA had learned little from the lessons of the Iran-contra scandal:

> One of the most disturbing trends ... has been the subtle, but distinct, disregard for the rule of law within the Agency. Despite the Congressional investigations of the 1970s and the lessons of the 1980s, there remains a pervasive belief by many senior officials that the Agency is above the law. Moreover, Agency and DI officials are all too willing to exceed the limits of their authority and substitute their judgment for that of the Executive and Congress. In fact, a senior official in the Office of General Counsel once told me that "the Agency doesn't have to obey the law; it can do whatever it wants."

Emerson saved his sharpest words for Helgerson himself: "My discussions with you on this topic have been less than comforting; you apparently would rather believe that the situation simply does not exist."

Webster continued to defend the agency's product in the face of these mounting internal criticisms, even though he had ordered half a dozen studies of the problem during his four years as DCI. None of them had helped. While he insisted that the agency's papers reflected the opinions of some of its most dedicated and outspoken experts, his closest aides say that he continually agonized over how he should deal with the hemorrhage of the CIA's brightest minds. He belatedly concluded that the system of producing estimates needed a complete overhaul, but then decided it was too late for him to begin the reforms.

Gentry believes that Webster missed a chance to have a real impact. "The coordination process is very, very bad, and what you end up with is the lowest common denominator paper," he says. "That's a common experience in the DI. A dissent is never, never, never put out. The organization speaks with one voice. That's very important to them."

Webster had failed to act because he was being squeezed by competing forces. On the one hand, the White House demanded that he take a greater hand in managing the agency, which meant that he was expected to quiet its most outspoken dissenters. On the other hand, he was being pressured by a group of mid-level career officers to initiate a broad reform of policies, especially inside the Directorate of Intelligence. The problem was that Webster's lack of foreign policy experience forced him to rely on senior officials (like Kerr, Helgerson, and Kolt) who were, in many instances, beholden to Gates for their positions.

By the end of the Persian Gulf War, Webster was a crippled DCI, whose status as head of the intelligence community had been called into question so many times that he could not have put in place the reforms necessary to bring the agency into a new era—even if he had wanted to. In the wake of *The Philadelphia Inquirer* article, Webster was more isolated from the agency's middle echelon officers than ever. He was also in the uncomfortable position of being a top administration official whose opinions were ignored inside the White House and who could not even get an audience with the President to promote his viewpoints. "The handwriting's on the wall," a CIA officer observed in April. "The President wants him gone."

During the last week of April, after one of Webster's daily intelligence briefings, he mentioned to a group of his top aides that he was considering reentering private life. It was an offhand remark, but Webster knew that his statement would make its way to the Oval Office. In previous incarnations, such a rumor would have been met by an instant vote of confidence from the President in the form of a return telephone call or a public statement. This time there was silence. During the next few days, anxious calls were made from the CIA on Webster's behalf to high-level administration officials asking for information about White House plans for the DCI. This discreet polling did not go well. "It looks like it might be Lilley," a strong Webster ally grumbled to a reporter. In desperation, he added: "Is there anything the press has on him? Anything we can use against him?"

During the first week of May, Webster decided to act without any further delay. He informed the White House directly that he was thinking about leaving the agency—in order to give the President one last chance to try to dissuade him. Again there was no response. On the evening of May 7 Webster called Bush with his final decision; he said it was time to leave. At Webster's request the press conference announcing his departure was scheduled for early the next morning.

Webster arrived alone in his chauffeur-driven limousine from his home in suburban Maryland in time for a short conversation with the President, who greeted him with a broad smile and a long handshake. Standing in the long hallway outside the White House press room, Bush took the opportunity to thank Webster personally for his years of government service. In an unusual outward show of affection, Bush put his arm around the retiring director and called him "old friend." Robert Gates and Brent Scowcroft looked on, smiling and nodding their approval, then joined President Bush in his fulsome praise.

Bush escorted Webster down the hall and into the brightly lighted room, where the major networks were interrupting their morning news shows for a special report from the President. Then, with a live, worldwide television audience looking on and with Webster standing by his side, Bush began: "It is with a great sense of pride—genuine pride in his accomplishments—and long years of dedicated service to his country, that I announce that Bill Webster has informed me of his intention to retire as the Director of Central Intelligence. Bill has brought an integrity, and effectiveness, and an insight to the many intelligence-gathering operations of this nation. He has done a superb job."

It was an overly formal statement, delivered by a clearly uncomfortable President who realized that the announcement surprised no one at all. Bush sensed the lack of drama; he repeated several times that this was "his [Webster's] decision" and that no one had forced him out. The most depressing moment of the morning occurred when Bush, searching for a list of Webster's accomplishments as DCI, said that his major triumph was his ability to follow "the guidelines that I set down at the beginning of this Administration . . ."—in other words, his ability to follow orders.

In the next breath Bush unintentionally uttered a truth that revealed what little impact the CIA actually had on his administration. What he meant to say was that unlike William Casey, Webster had not involved himself in policy *decisions*. But what he really said—in garbled fashion—was that information from the CIA had no influence on White House *actions*. The hallmark of Webster's years, Bush remarked, was that "Intelligence is not trying to shape policy." Catching the slip, Webster issued a wry smile.

That was exactly the problem, and Webster's greatest failure. As DCI he had excused himself from the administration's most important discussions by insisting that the CIA should stay clear of policy making. In so doing, he hoped to keep the intelligence product untrammeled by political considerations. That well-intended principle, however, remains one of his most confusing legacies. In excusing himself from policy discussions, Webster was never able to tell the President that the decisions he made were not supported by the facts, as he once promised he would do. And in the one chance he did have to do this, in the week before Iraq's invasion of Kuwait, he was ignored; George Bush said he had better sources of information than the CIA. No one knows what might have happened had Webster told Bush that he was ignoring clear signs of an impending catastrophe—the results could not possibly have been worse and would have been the same had the United States had no CIA at all. Bush was right: CIA assessments had little to do with shaping administration policies, if indeed they had any effect at all.

William Webster is a man of enormous goodwill and personal integrity. He is intelligent and articulate, with a highly refined sense of humor. But he was never able to overcome the enormous obstacles placed in his path by either White House officials or those rank-and-file careerists whose loyalty he desperately sought. In the end both groups abandoned him. For four years Bush's top aides undermined his hold on the CIA, questioned his effectiveness and leadership and casually blamed him for their own failures. The attacks were mean, petty, narrow-minded, and vicious. At Langley, the large group of reformers might have recruited Webster to serve their yearning for change or to insist that a White House bent on its own program listen to what they had to say. Instead, those who needed him most in both the clandestine service and the Directorate of Intelligence cracked jokes at his expense, passed around rumors about his night life, traded gossip on his latest overseas exploits, and dismissed his insistence on honesty as if it were some kind of middle-class affectation.

The press and Congress joined the clamor. Reporters complained that Webster enjoyed the Washington social scene, got a casual thumbs-down in weekly newsmagazines, was *too* open with Congress, and played too much tennis. Moreover, he didn't look the part; he was a lightweight, not close to the President, wasn't listened to in the councils of government, and made commonplace mistakes; he was merely an "interim" director. It was almost as if everyone were afraid that in the wake of Casey's leadership the nation would snooze off in the middle of some international crisis. On Capitol Hill, Senator Boren and most of the members of the Intelligence Committee had initially praised him for his openness and then turned on him when they claimed the agency had failed to perform up to standards during the Persian Gulf crisis. Bush administration officials called Webster "ineffective" and "pathetic" behind his back, but he had come closer to predicting the enormous changes facing the nation than any other senior government spokesman. At the same time that Gates and Cheney were arguing that *glasnost* and *perestroika* were passing fads, the man who once wondered where Morocco was located was telling everyone that Gorbachev's reforms were revolutionary.

He was right, and they were wrong.

Webster's CIA was caught flat-footed in China and Eastern Europe, failed to bring the Afghan civil war to an end, and bungled its attempts to unseat Manuel Noriega, but it scored impressive victories on other fronts. Webster, Kerr, and other CIA officials consistently argued that worldwide nuclear and chemical weapons proliferation would be the most important issues of the coming decade, that the United States needed to inaugurate a program of economic espionage, that Yugoslavia would be plunged into civil war, that the Soviet Union's economic conditions would worsen to the point of international crisis, that Iraq would invade Kuwait, that Gorbachev faced a threat from his own government, that North Korea was developing nuclear weapons, and that China's dissidents could be saved and were worth saving. There are many adjectives that might be used to describe this record, but "ineffective" and "pathetic" are not among them.

For all that, it also was clear that Webster contributed to his own downfall. His attempts to cultivate reporters were amazingly inept, and at a time when agency officers were engaged in a long-term debate about openness, he transformed the CIA's Public Affairs Office into a virtual den of flacks. They could barely contain their glee when they spoke about him. They pushed Webster's "hands-on" control of the CIA, his "enormous abilities" and "long work hours," argued over and over that he retained "the confidence of the President," and ended up by spending much of their time seeking out friendly journalists to write favorable stories on his life and accomplishments.

These spokesmen expended little effort, if any, in explaining the real work of the agency or detailing the more mundane programs of gathering intelligence. For instance, they completely bungled the nearly unanimously accepted view that the CIA should inaugurate a program of international intelligence gathering on the economic policies of foreign trade competitors, with the consequence that most Americans think that the agency wants to begin a program of industrial sabotage at the behest of corporate moguls intent on some kind of "hooliganism." As a result, the CIA remained more vulnerable to calls that it should be dismantled at the end of Webster's term than at almost any time in its history.

Webster sensed this problem during the last few weeks at Langley. When he was not consumed by reading White House tea leaves on his own fate, he spent much of his time responding to congressional calls for agency reform and defending Langley against claims that its intelligence capabilities had not measured up during the Persian Gulf War. He was alternately combative and exhausted by the exchanges, and in the end he was simply unwilling to wage a costly fight over his performance with his White House enemies. He probably would not have won the battle in any event. Agency arguments that he was not nudged aside—that Bush was surprised that he wanted to leave Langley and that he could have stayed on as DCI as long as he wanted—were pure nonsense. By May it was clear to both Webster and his top assistants that the constant attacks were fatally undermining his status inside the administration.

"Director, we're going to miss you, pal . . ." Bush said on the morning of May 8.

Webster then stepped to the microphone. He admitted that he had had difficulty in making the decision to leave the CIA and that there was "never an easy time to go." He paid homage to the agency and its fine people, and then turned to Bush. "It's been an extraordinary experience to have worked with you, Mr. President," Webster said. (While this statement later caused loud guffaws at Langley, no one in the White House press room laughed.) Webster went on to emphasize that the agency had positioned itself well for "the challenges of the nineties." He specifically defended the work of the last months. "I'm very proud of the performance that the entire community rendered during the Persian Gulf [War]. . . ." he said. Then, his voice trailing off, he suddenly confronted his decision to reenter private life. "You hate to leave," he said, "but something tells you that it's a good time to leave."

Bush was smiling, seemingly proud of the man he had chosen to head the CIA all the way back in 1987. But the President was already looking toward the future. "We haven't talked successor," he replied to a question. "Haven't got anyone in mind."

There were four contenders for the job: James Lilley, Robert Gates, former deputy director Bobby Ray Inman, and New Hampshire Senator Warren Rudman. This short list was narrowed down quickly to just two names—Lilley and Gates. It seemed for several days that the choice would be Lilley. Bush trusted him, had worked closely with him, and respected his credentials—he was a CIA veteran with nearly three decades of experience in the clandestine service. That long service in the DO gave him an inside track over Gates, since no one had ever been appointed DCI from the Directorate of Intelligence, in the belief that the head of Central Intelligence had to have more than a passing knowledge of how espionage and covert operations were conducted. The day after Webster resigned, Lilley's name was floated to ranking members of the Senate Intelligence Committee, where it was greeted with tentative approval. Outside of a few questions about his outspoken views on China, the word came back that Lilley would have little trouble getting confirmed.

Still, he was far from the odds-on favorite for the job. Secretary of State Baker, for one, was disturbed by reports that Bush was considering the ambassador and opposed his selection for much the same reason that he had vetoed his candidacy for a State Department position just over two years earlier: Articulate and outspoken, Lilley was a competitor, a feisty debater, and a knowledgeable foreign policy expert. But he was not a member of Bush's inner circle, so no one in the White House knew how he would fit in, and that was an extremely important consideration. As a State Department official recalls: "Baker preferred a known quantity, someone who was a little less fiery. He waved the bloody red shirt a bit, you know, and ended up telling Bush, 'Listen, we don't need another Bill Casey.' "

Scowcroft agreed with Baker's judgment. He preferred that Bush name his personal favorite, Gates. Scowcroft and Gates got along very well and were in sync on nearly every important foreign policy issue. Scowcroft was convinced that Gates had successfully restored his tarnished reputation from the Iran-contra affair. John Sununu, Bush's chief of staff, seconded this opinion. Gates had done well in every job he had held, Sununu contended.

Sununu was convinced that Gates's past would not prove to be an obstacle to Senate approval. While there were a number of certain no votes against Gates on the Intelligence Committee—Senators Howard Metzenbaum (D-OH) and Bill Bradley (D-NJ) were two committed opponents—Sununu was reassured by fellow New Hampshirite Senator Warren Rudman that Gates had more than enough friends on the committee to win confirmation. Sununu informed Bush that Rudman could usher the candidate through the process and act as his chief defender. Sununu's arguments had enormous influence, especially in light of the advice Bush received from other top political aides, who did not see much difference between Gates and Lilley. They said it didn't matter who Bush nominated—he had stored up enough goodwill in the Congress and among the American people as a result of the war that he could select whomever he chose.

What caused optimism at 1600 Pennsylvania Avenue sparked pessimism on Capitol Hill. Republicans on the Senate Intelligence Committee had no preference for DCI, and were ready to defend either nominee. Warren Rudman, however, firmly believed that Lilley would be Bush's choice—even after the White House asked him whether nominating Gates would cause problems for congressional Republicans. Howard Metzenbaum agreed with Rudman, and believed that Bush would not dare nominate someone as controversial as the former deputy director—the President would not chance exhuming the Iran-contra corpse, which could bring to light his rumored complicity in the affair. Metzenbaum's staff, however, knew that the scandal was "all history" on the Hill, where Iran-contra prosecutor Lawrence Walsh's investigation of the matter was being criticized as "glacially slow" and "a fishing expedition." The President was in a perfect position: "After what Bush did to Saddam," one of Metzenbaum's aides said, "he could get Adolf Hitler confirmed."

Bush's decision was not made until the evening of Friday, May 10, when he huddled with his top political advisers in the White House. In the end, the arguments of Baker, Scowcroft, and Sununu had the most influence. Gates could win confirmation, Bush was told; he was a trusted and loyal aide and had the experience necessary to bring the CIA into the post–cold war world. Lilley's experience was also valuable, but Gates was clearly the President's man. His nomination would show the country that Bush had nothing to fear from a rehash of the Iran-contra scandal.

There were a number of other less obvious, though extremely important reasons why Bush turned to Gates instead of Lilley. For one, Gates would be the first DCI nominated from the DI, a clear signal that Bush would place greater reliance on analysts than on clandestine operators. Second, Gates styled himself as a reformer—a DCI who, in the words of one administration official, "would shake things up over there [at Langley]." Finally, unlike Lilley, who was vacationing in California during the weekend that Bush made his decision, Gates was in Washington and made it known that he wanted the job.

Perhaps most important of all, Gates was the choice of a number of highly regarded CIA veterans close to the President. One of these men, former agency deputy director Bobby Ray Inman, argued that Gates had been identified as a possible future DCI as early as the late 1970s and been pushed into increasingly important positions with the express purpose of grooming him for the job. "Bob Gates is an enormously talented individual," Inman told one reporter at the time. "Of all the people in the DI in the late seventies and eighties who were capable of taking on the position as director, Bob was the one guy that I thought could really do the job. There were a lot of people who agreed."

Ray Cline, another Bush supporter and former senior CIA analyst, also became an outspoken Gates backer. "I think it's finally time now to look to the DI for leadership in the intelligence community," Cline said. "It's been a long time coming. Bob Gates will be an excellent director."

The White House took additional soundings from members of the Senate Intelligence Committee over the weekend of May 11 to determine whether Gates would face any unforeseen concerns. They were satisfied with the results. Chairman Boren was the key. The powerful Democrat told White House officials that he had a high opinion of Gates and was impressed with his performance at the NSC during the previous two years.

With this support in hand, on the following Tuesday Bush announced to the public that Gates was his choice. Bush added that he did not believe that questions about Gates's role in the Iran-contra scandal would present a problem. "All will be well," Bush confidently remarked. "This man has my full trust. He's honest, and he's a man of total integrity."

As expected, Boren implied that Gates would have smooth sailing during the confirmation process. He commended Bush's nominee for being "extremely able and nonpartisan." Everything was going according to plan.

The Gates nomination was greeted with a sense of palpable disbelief in the clandestine service, whose officers could barely bring themselves to accept that an analyst would now lead the agency. But that reaction was nothing compared with the response inside the Directorate of Intelligence, where Bush's announcement caused a fire storm. "This is an outrage," one analyst growled. "This guy is hated here, absolutely hated. The perception is that he will do anything the President asks him to." An operations officer agreed. "The entire DO is opposed to the Gates nomination—both all the retired officers and the people in there now," he noted. "They don't want him. He doesn't know operations. They are afraid that he will be so ineffective as a leader of operations that the DO will come to a total standstill." These negative feelings were informally documented by a group of retired officers shortly after the nomination. During a weekly luncheon of former high-ranking CIA officials, a straw poll taken on the Gates nomination showed that he lacked support among some of the most influential opinion leaders in the intelligence community: Eight voted against Gates, four voted in his favor, and four abstained.

The small number of CIA professionals who welcomed the Gates nomination tried to play down the hostile reports that were rippling through the government. "There is some skepticism in the DI over Gates," retired CIA official David Whipple admitted, "but that's only because they know that Bob will make some changes, some necessary changes. On the other hand, I think there's a lot less concern inside the clandestine service. They don't really expect him to come in and change things wholesale; that's just not his way. They know that he will have to rely on experts, and they're confident that he will." Whipple, the executive director of the Association of Former Intelligence Officers, serves as an unofficial ombudsman for the CIA to the Washington press corps and is widely quoted on intelligence issues. "This isn't a unanimously welcomed nomination," he acknowledged, "and I'd be less than honest if I said it was. But that's not what the agency needs. The President wants to put his stamp on the agency, to say that we need better analysis in the future, and Bob Gates is the nation's top analyst."

It was not unusual for veteran officers to criticize a new nominee— that certainly had been the case when President Reagan nominated Webster as DCI—but such controversies usually die out in a few weeks. That was not the case with Gates. In the weeks that followed Bush's announcement, CIA officers continued to react very negatively to his appointment. Their views were filtered up to ADDO Ted Price, who was given the task of calming fears and rebutting claims that the nomination meant there would be a "housecleaning" at Langley. Price reassured the clandestine service that little was likely to change under the new DCI and that he and Twetten would still be given full responsibility for espionage operations. The same guarantees were given by Deputy Director Kerr and DDI Helgerson, though with far less favorable results; both were considered among Gates's closest protégés.

Because the anger and resentment was so strongly felt among serv-

ing officers, however, an unprecedented number of CIA employees quietly made their way to Capitol Hill on their own during the next month
to give their views on Gates. Many of them felt betrayed by Bush, who,
as the first former DCI to become President, should have been more
sensitive to their opinions. Bush, they contended, knew exactly what
many at the CIA thought of Gates and nominated him anyway. At a
time when the agency desperately needed a leader who could be trusted
he had given them the one previously tainted official many mistrusted
the most. Bush did not care what they thought; he was the in-your-face
President. "There is a lot of opposition to this choice," a Senate aide said
at the time. "There are people coming out of the woodwork. It's amazing
to see. We're not talking about just a handful of people."

Gates attempted to short-circuit this opposition by initiating a number of well-planned visits to his most intransigent opponents, including
Howard Metzenbaum. The strategy was to appear to be the easygoing
supplicant, a man who realized he had made mistakes in the past but
was now willing to go out of his way to make up for them. Gates greeted
the aging Ohio Democrat cordially, with an open smile on his face, as
he followed him into his office. They sat uneasily across from each other,
exchanging pleasantries, before falling silent. Gates then explained that
he knew Metzenbaum opposed his appointment, but he hoped he could
change his mind. He stressed that he knew little about the Iran-contra
affair and that he would not allow such shenanigans during his term as
DCI. Metzenbaum remained impassive during this display, except to
slightly nod his approval at key moments during Gates's presentation.
But when Gates had finished, he frowned and shook his head. "You
know," he bluntly replied, "I just don't believe you." The exchange that
followed gave Gates's opponents their first hint of a possible weakness
that might bring him down: Taken aback, Gates was stunned and objected angrily and loudly to the Ohio senator's lack of confidence. The
meeting ended with Gates storming from the office. "He went off the
deep end," a Senate aide recalls.

In many ways Gates actually had a winsome personality. He had a
ready smile and an infectious, volcanic laugh that he knew how to use
to his benefit. The other side of the coin, however, was that he was just
as quick to anger; it was as if he had difficulty controlling the extremes
of his emotions, as his meeting with Metzenbaum showed. If Gates was
pushed, he would crack, spilling out his barely concealed disdain for his
detractors. Gates was ambitious and temperamental, and, when
crossed, he could be meanspirited and vindictive. A strategy emerged
to take advantage of Gates's flaws. His opponents wanted to question
him again and again about the details of the Iran-contra affair while
presenting convincing testimony about his own problems at the agency
during the 1980s. They hoped he would blow up under the strain.

In response, Gates's supporters marshaled as many resources as they could on his behalf and counseled him to lock in his charming smile and hold his fire.

An official CIA task force was assigned to research Gates's successes and present a convincing case for his confirmation. This group compiled a sheaf of materials that included testimonials on his effectiveness as DDI and deputy director. According to a Senate investigator, more than thirty senior CIA officers were enlisted to produce background materials Gates would use to explain his plans for the intelligence community in the 1990s and to respond to charges that he had suffered a lapse in judgment during the Iran-contra scandal. The task force focused primarily on questions it believed would be raised by the committee's key swing votes: Senators Sam Nunn (D-GA) and Dennis DeConcini (D-AZ). When the final vote was tallied, they believed that most Senate Democrats would look to Nunn for guidance.

The one vote that could be counted on came from David Boren, the committee's chairman, and an open Gates supporter. Few committee members were able to adequately explain this tie. They speculated that Gates cultivated Boren by sharing important classified information with him that he would not share with anyone else—thereby winning the Oklahoma senator's trust and confidence. Whatever the reason, there was little doubt that Boren's views were deeply held, and had been for quite some time. At the height of the Iran-contra investigation, committee staff knew, Boren intervened whenever possible to defend Gates from harsh questioning on his own role in the scandal. At times, his efforts were embarrassing.

The most pointed example of Boren's defense of Gates occurred on July 31, 1987, when Gates was called to give a deposition on his role in the scandal. When Boren heard that Gates would be deposed, he was enraged—he told Democratic Congressman Louis Stokes, a member of the House Intelligence Committee, and Republican Senator William Cohen that he objected to the questioning. Gates had already appeared as an intelligence committee witness, Boren said, and told everything he knew. To emphasize his outrage, Boren walked over to the Hart Senate Office Building to put his feelings on the record on the day Gates was being questioned. He burst in on the session nearly forty-five minutes after it had begun and interrupted committee lawyer Paul Barbadoro. He was noticeably winded by his walk from Capitol Hill.

"Let me interject," Boren said. ". . . It has been our understanding— and Mr. Gates has not entered any objection to this—but it has been our understanding when we had a Members meeting of the [Intelligence] Committee that it was not necessary to call Mr. Gates to testify. The members of the Committee, I had thought, decided it and that if he were asked he would be asked [only] to give his policy feelings about oversight. We have been through all of this under sworn testimony in his confirmation hearings and we, the elected members of the [Intelligence] Committee, if we have any rights in this matter, felt that it would be unnecessary to go over these matters again." He was just warming up. "I'd like to have my feelings entered into the record," he continued, "as an elected Member of the [Intelligence] Committee under the Constitution of the Senate, that the members of the Committee, I had thought, had some rights in this, and Chairman Stokes of the House Intelligence Committee authorized me to convey a similar feeling about this. . . . But I don't see any point in going back over this, because I think our committee has delivered to this Committee the full transcript of the sworn testimony of Mr. Gates on these matters."

Barbadoro, amazed that Boren had burst in, responded angrily: "Well, Senator, if there's one thing I didn't need to learn from these hearings, it is that elected and accountable officials make the important decisions."

"I thought that was what we were investigating," Boren snapped. "I think it's a little ironic that while we're investigating that matter that our own Committee seems to be functioning to the contrary."

In simple terms, Boren was accusing Barbadoro of acting beyond his mandate. The counsel was a hired gun, not a senator. He was supposed to obey orders; no one had told him he could question Gates.

"If I have misinterpreted my instructions from the Committee, I apologize," Barbadoro icily replied. He then explained that he had spoken with Gates during an earlier meeting at Langley and had offered to give him a chance to respond to allegations made about him by Oliver North. "I understood that Mr. Gates was in agreement with that," Barbadoro added, "but I, of course, defer to the elected members of the Committee."

Boren was caught. It appeared that Gates, who was sitting right there, had actually agreed to the deposition, hoping to clear his name.

Barbadoro pressed his point. "You're the boss," he told Boren. "You tell me what to do."

Boren hesitated for a moment. He finally replied that he only wanted to make sure that Gates was asked questions on new material, not on issues that he had discussed "ad nauseam" during his confirmation hearings.

Barbadoro was not impressed. "Well, you're the boss," he repeated. "In fact, I'll defer to you. You can ask him any questions you want."

Barbadoro leaned back in his chair and waited.

After thinking it over, Boren backed down. "I want to make it clear that I'm not expressing any feeling that counsel here [Barbadoro] who is conducting this questioning is acting in bad faith," he said. "I think he is a person who always conducts himself in good faith and there has simply been a misunderstanding. It could as easily have been on our side as on his, and I certainly know Mr. Gates is anxious to answer any questions that are relevant that need to be asked."

The deposition finally went forward, but with Boren remaining in attendance to guard Gates's interests. Gates's opponents believed that this kind of coddling was exactly what Boren would do during the 1991 confirmation process. The only real possibility that the Gates nomination could be derailed, they figured, would be if some major new revelation on the Iran-contra scandal was made public before the hearings began. They were scheduled for late June.

Unrestrained warfare over the Gates nomination became public on June 23, when former CIA operations officer Thomas Polgar, who had served as an Iran-contra investigator for Congress, censured Bush's nominee in a widely read opinion piece in *The Washington Post*. "My objections to Gates center on his performance during the Iran-contra affair," Polgar wrote, "which tarnished Reagan's presidency more than any other single episode of his two administrations. Throughout it, Gates acted as if he was in a complete fog or was interested primarily in keeping the truth from being aired in public or, indeed, from reaching Congress."

Polgar was not alone in doubting Gates's story. For more than a month, committee investigators had been searching for evidence that could impeach his claim that he had heard little about the Iran-contra affair, from either Casey or anyone else. There was actually little to go on: Gates's enemies at the CIA were legion, but they had little firsthand information on the former deputy director's participation in the affair. The main sources who might shed light on his exact role were three officers with direct knowledge of the operation in 1986 and 1987—the chief of the Central America Task Force, Alan Fiers, former DDO Clair George, and Dewey Clarridge—but they weren't talking.

That deadlock changed suddenly on July 9, 1991, when Fiers pleaded guilty in federal court in Washington to two misdemeanor charges of withholding information from Congress on the diversion of funds for the contras. "In 1986, I was faced with some very difficult decisions," Fiers told the press after his court appearance. "At that time, I did what I thought was in the best interests of the country. Today I was faced with equally difficult decisions and today I have done what I think is in the best interests of the country and not only that, but what the Constitution requires of me." Fiers admitted that he had known about the diversion months before but had purposely misled Congress on his role in the affair. He agreed to cooperate fully with federal prosecutors and to give them information on other CIA officials, including Clair George. Fiers said that George told him to lie about the agency's secret program because it would put a "spotlight" on the White House's own role in the operation.

It was clear from Fiers's plea that George, former State Department official Elliott Abrams, Dewey Clarridge, and Donald Gregg, then-Vice President Bush's chief national security adviser, were targets of independent counsel Lawrence Walsh's probe and would probably be indicated in the weeks and months ahead. Walsh's investigators even hoped that they might be able to work out a plea agreement with Clair George in exchange for information on who else knew about the program. George's closest associates, however, dismissed this possiblility. "Clair George will never talk," one said. "Never, never, never." In fact, Walsh was less close to breaking open the CIA's full role in the case than anyone at the time quessed—most of those called as witnesses, one Washington lawyer familiar with the probe related, "were very uncooperative. They didn't remember anything. They were saying, you know, 'Iran-contra, what the hell is that?'"

Fiers's plea cast immediate doubt on Gates's claims that he knew nothing of the Iran-contra operation. As a result, the White House was barraged with questions about whether Bush's nominee was in danger of being indicted. After all, his critics pointed out, Gates's immediate superior, Casey, knew of the operation, and George, who was immediately beneath Gates in the CIA chain of command, probably did as well. Gates had also met with Oliver North and John Poindexter at the White House. Bush spokesmen responded to the questions by pointing out that Gates was a "subject" of the Walsh investigation, not a "target," and that it was unlikely that he would be indicted. Gates's defenders further argued that as a deputy director he had almost no operations responsibilities and that Casey wanted to keep it that way. This meant that Gates did not know the full details of the Iran-contra affair. "The fact of the matter is that Casey didn't trust Gates," a former senior CIA official explains. "Nor did George or Clarridge. They didn't respect him. Why should they tell him what was going on?" The current evidence seems to bear out that argument.

Whether Gates knew the full details of the Iran-contra operation or not, both George and Clarridge *did*, in fact, view him as an amateurish upstart, and regularly denigrated his abilities to a number of their colleagues. One of them remembers George referring to Gates as "that puppy," and recalls that Clarridge dismissed Gates's abilities with a simple negative shake of his head. "Clarridge just hated Bob Gates," this officer recalls. "That he [Gates] had anything to offer at all was just laughable. No one paid too much attention to him. I can't think of one instance where either of these guys asked Gates for his opinion on anything." A number of former high-level officers agree with the judgment, going so far as to claim that Gates reciprocated the feelings, though in a far different way. "Whenever Bob saw Clair coming, he would just turn and go the other way," one says. "I got the distinct impression that he was scared of George. You know, Clair George could be very intimidating—he could just stare you down in a meeting if you crossed him."

The Fiers plea raised enough questions during the summer of 1991, however, that the Senate Intelligence Committee considered postponing the Gates hearings until after Labor Day. President Bush denounced this plan during an informal session with reporters at his vacation home in Kennebunkport. He complained that the committee should not accept "rumor" or "run like a covey of quail." His face flushed with anger, Bush turned on his questioners and accused the press of contributing to the public doubts about Gates. "I just don't think it's the American way to bring a good man down by rumor and insinuation," he said. "That's not the system." Bush went on emphatically: "What we're entitled to in this country is fair play, innocence until guilty. Don't leave a person twisting out there... it just distresses me to hear hypotheses raised that throw questions on his integrity."

Bush had good reason to want to rush the Gates confirmation process. The White House had received information in early July that George, who could answer all the questions about Gates's role in the scandal, would be indicted by the end of August and that Walsh had developed strong cases against Clarridge, Abrams, and Gregg as well. Gregg, then serving as U.S. ambassador to South Korea, had even quietly returned to Washington at the beginning of July to look for a defense counsel. Abrams remained unruffled, but was opening negotiations with Walsh's office to dispose of his case through a plea bargain. Not surprisingly, Clarridge was the calmest of all. He spent part of the summer in the Middle East on behalf of his corporate employer.

In the midst of this flurry of activity, on the evening of July 16, the Senate Intelligence Committee decided that it had little choice but to ignore the President's pleas on behalf of his nominee for a speedy confirmation. They decided to postpone the hearings until September 16. The decision was agreed to by Gates himself, who met with Boren and Vice Chairman Frank Murkowski on Capitol Hill the night before the delay was announced. The two senators told Gates they had little choice; they had to allow Walsh a chance to finish his investigation. "They didn't want it to look like they were rushing the nomination," a committee staff aide later confirmed, "hoping to get Gates confirmed before George was indicted." According to this staffer, Gates agreed to the postponement because "he said he was confident that nothing new would come out of the Walsh investigation." When the meeting adjourned, Gates telephoned Scowcroft to tell him the news.

Boren thought the postponement would actually help Gates. The committee had already interviewed a number of top CIA officials about the nominee's role in the scandal and had turned up nothing new. Gates's supporters on the committee were also privately reassured that other CIA officials, including former Latin America Division chief Jerry Gruner (Alan Fiers's former boss), would tell committee investigators that they doubted Gates had any role in the Iran-contra operation. Boren and Murkowski had been told that Gruner's testimony would be seconded by DDO Thomas Twetten (also a subject of Walsh's investigation) and Charlie Allen, the NIO for warning, who had first told Gates of his fears of a diversion in 1987. From all of these indications, Boren remained confident that Gates would be cleared of any wrongdoing and confirmed as CIA chief.

Gates's opponents on the committee were beginning to agree. They had originally expected Charlie Allen to provide incriminating details on Casey's dealings with Gates. They were convinced that Allen—who personally disliked the former deputy director—would say that Gates must have known of the diversion. But Allen was not cooperating. Nor was Alan Fiers, whose indictment added little to the committee's knowledge of what Gates knew and when he knew it. As far as the staffs of Senators Bradley and Metzenbaum were concerned, the CIA had circled the wagons and was working full time to get Gates confirmed, despite fears of what he might do once he became DCI. In August, Metzenbaum's staff decided to look elsewhere for ammunition; these aides devised a strategy that targeted former DI officers who claimed that Gates had politicized the agency's intelligence product.

By early September the opponents of Gates had given up hope that any new indictments would sidetrack his confirmation. Their view was bolstered by the ho-hum attitude that greeted Clair George's indictment, one week before Gates was to face the Senate committee. George made it clear to Walsh that he would not cooperate in his investigation and described himself as "a pawn in a continuous drama of political exploitation." The bandy-legged former clandestine service officer played cat and mouse with the press outside his home in suburban Maryland, appearing to be more intent on the placement of his garden implements than on the prospect of spending a few years in jail. He regaled journalists with his own rough opinions of the world and reminded them that he had faced tougher times than they could provide.

Without testimony from George, which was now out of the question, the one man left who might impeach Gates's claim that he was qualified to be DCI was a former senior analyst then unknown to the public, none other than Mel Goodman, Gates's old adversary. Goodman did not relish this role—he did not hold a grudge against the CIA—but he was convinced that the agency, and Gates, had betrayed their legacy as an objective, nonpartisan intelligence organization. He agreed to tell committee investigators what he knew about Gates's career inside the DI and then to appear in public as a witness against the nominee. In case he had any illusions about what might happen, he was warned that his testimony would be ferociously attacked by Gates's allies on the committee. The questioning of his motives, the staff cautioned, would be long, bloody, and personal. Everything would be open to scrutiny. Goodman said he understood.

The administration, meanwhile, was doing everything it could to prepare for the hearings, including hosting a series of White House meetings with Senate Republicans to chart the confirmation strategy. Gates reassured his Senate backers at these discussions that he would candidly admit he had made mistakes during Casey's tenure. He said he was ready to face this delicate issue squarely, in order to disarm his critics. He had even drafted an apology that acknowledged he had not realized the seriousness of the Iran-contra scandal while he was at the CIA. The weekend before the hearings the campaign for Gates went into full swing: Brent Scowcroft appeared on national news programs as his primary public defender; a three-man team, led by White House deputy chief of staff Andrew Card, was put on call to manage the confirmation process; and Senator Rudman became a roving one-man "truth squad." Rudman's job was simple: he would rebut major accusations and make sure Gates did not lose his temper.

Gates was more than ready. He entered the Senate Hart Office Building on the morning of September 16 looking confident and determined. There was an air of self-assurance about him, a clear knowledge that his future was in his own hands. He smiled on cue for the cameras. He nodded to acquaintances who were seated in the press table directly behind him, then sat quietly waiting for the session to begin. His only sign of discomfort came from the crowd of photographers who sat on the floor in front of him, snapping his picture. He seemed somewhat diminished for a moment, but when Senator Boren began his opening remarks, he sat in apparent rapt attention.

Even when Senator Metzenbaum criticized him during his opening statement, Gates appeared unruffled and stared back at the Ohio liberal, as if he believed he could change his mind in the days ahead. There were no surprises during these early jabs, and if Gates was nervous it did not show; his hand was steady when he rose to take the oath to "tell the truth, the whole truth, and nothing but the truth." The packed hearing room fell silent as he began his testimony.

Gates was calm, polished, and plainspoken; his opening remarks were personal, understated, and, in parts, almost endearing. He portrayed himself as a simple man unwilling to do battle with his detractors. He had arrived in Washington in 1965, with everything he owned "in a 1965 Mustang and no money," he said. "The Mustang is long gone, sold before it became a collector's item, and I still have no money." He briefly sketched the outline of his career at the CIA, emphasizing his commitment to the institution and the ideals that it represented. He described himself as a patriot-servant with a "deep conviction in the greatness of this country... and in its mission as a force for good in the world." He said he was committed to change and well aware that the collapse of the Soviet Union would transform the face of American intelligence. He declared that he was ready for the challenge.

He then addressed the question of his role in the Iran-contra scandal. It was a moment of high drama. He hesitated briefly and took a deep breath. He then laid aside his prepared remarks and reached for a single yellow sheet of legal paper that he had laid down separately on the table. "Because of the great interest that this committee has and the centrality of Iran-contra to these proceedings," he said, "I wanted to add some additional, personal thoughts on this subject at the end, that I wrote down last night.

"I've just referred to a commitment about trust and confidence," Gates continued. "I don't make that commitment lightly; it is a direct outgrowth of watching the constant crises, primarily over covert action in CIA-Congressional relations between 1981 and 1986 culminating in Iran-contra. I suspect few people have reflected more than I have on the Iran-contra affair; what went wrong, why CIA played by rules not of its own making, and what might have been done to prevent or at least stop this tragic affair. CIA has already paid a fearful price and learned costly lessons. But today I want to speak about the misjudgments that I made and the lessons I learned. First, in retrospect, I should have taken more seriously... the possibility of impropriety or even wrongdoing in the government and pursued this possibility more aggressively. I should have pressed the issue of possible diversion more strenuously with Director Casey and Admiral Poindexter. I should have done more.... Second, I should have been more skeptical about what I was told. I should have asked more questions and I should have been less satisfied with the answers I received, especially from Director Casey. Third, I should have pressed harder for reversing the provisions in the January finding prohibiting informing Congress.... Clearly, if I could relive October 1986... I would do things differently. I learned the lessons of Iran-contra."

He then put aside his handwritten text and faced the committee.

It was a solemn and heartfelt mea culpa. Despite subsequent news reports that Gates's comments had been prepared well in advance—and were therefore less extemporaneous than he led the committee to believe—his straight-from-the-shoulder confession was impressive. Gates's testimony was "a solid performance," in the words of *The Washington*

Post, that when added to the character references from former deputy
directors John McMahon and Bobby Inman, brought the anti-Gates
movement to a standstill. Senator DeConcini symbolized the effect that
the confession had on committee members who were still up in the air.
"I thought you were just going to say, 'I don't remember, I don't remember,' but you've gone way beyond that," DeConcini told Gates, "and
I want you to know that I appreciate that." Even Metzenbaum grudgingly
agreed that "in all probability, he will be confirmed." Senator Rudman
was ecstatic. He praised Gates for his honesty.

Warren Rudman provided Gates's first line of defense, continually
interrupting questioning by Howard Metzenbaum, who took aim at Gates
immediately following his presentation. It was clear that Rudman was
making sure that Gates had time to compose his answers and, even more
important, that Gates did not repeat the explosive exchange he had had
with the Ohio senator back in July.

Over the next week the pro-Gates forces on the committee were
aided by several witnesses who were previously thought to oppose the
nomination, most prominently Alan Fiers. The now-indicted and very
public operations officer refused to comment on Gates's fitness for the
job. His sole words of praise were that Gates was "an exceptionally gifted
analyst ... and exceptionally gifted operator within the bureaucratic
structure and one that ... had a meteoric rise within the agency." Fiers's
only criticism was that Gates was viewed inside the CIA as a man who
was "sort of on the make" and not "the kind of person you get chummy
with." This was far from the hard-hitting condemnation that Gates's
opponents thought Fiers would land. It deflated one of their last prospects of stopping the nomination.

Even Charlie Allen would not impeach Gates's credibility. Allen and
Gates had separate accounts of who said what to whom during the Iran-
contra diversion, but like Fiers, Allen was circumspect about Gates's role.
He even said that the former deputy director was "startled and disturbed" by rumors of White House involvement in mixing the Iran and
contra operations and confirmed Gates's testimony that he, Allen, took
evidence of the diversion directly to the DCI. There were sharp differences between Allen's and Gates's testimony on when Gates knew of the
diversion and what he proposed to do about it, but the differences were
neither stark enough or certain enough to cause anyone on the committee to change their minds on Bush's nominee.

Even though Gates seemed assured of confirmation, Mel Goodman's
commitment to testify was unshaken. He and two other former analysts—
Jennifer Glaudemans and Hal Ford—remained convinced that if Gates
were allowed to become DCI, he would ruin the agency's ability to provide fair and objective analysis to the executive branch. Their dramatic

testimony was presented in a closed-door committee session on the evening of September 25. If what they said was true—that Gates had corrupted the intelligence product and purposely slanted CIA studies in order to curry political favor with the White House—not only would he fail to win confirmation, but his public career would also end in humiliation.

Goodman's charges were specific: Gates and Casey had purposely manipulated the Directorate of Intelligence in order to support the opening to Iran in 1985; they had consistently underestimated evidence of economic problems in the Soviet empire because the data did not accord with their own beliefs; they had suppressed and derailed intelligence estimates that called into question Soviet sponsorship of international terrorism; they had dictated a study that showed Soviet complicity in the attempted assassination of Pope John Paul II when no such evidence existed; and finally, they had restructured the agency's counterterrorism efforts with the express purpose of providing a platform for their own views. Goodman revealed that Webster had tried to undo the damage by launching an investigation of Casey's and Gates's attempts to politicize the agency's intelligence product.

"But I guess what I find most important and most offensive is that Casey and Gates arrogated to themselves the power to make intelligence judgments," Goodman said, "that they had contempt for a process that was designed to allow independent analysis; that they damaged the integrity of that process and the credibility of the Central Intelligence Agency where I have spent 24 years; that they ignored the long established ethics and morality of an intelligence officer; and that even the President of the United States was given falsified reports and uncoordinated analysis. I worry about the signal that would be sent in returning Gates to the environment he created. But I guess what shocks me more than that is that so few people at the CIA could create such an environment, and they do that—and they did that, so easily. And I think it is for that reason that I have a sense of shame."

Despite Goodman's shocking allegations, Jennifer Glaudemans was by far the most credible witness put forward by Gates's opponents. To a neutral observer, it was entirely conceivable, for instance, that Goodman might be overstating his case, or that he had a special, personal reason for opposing Gates's nomination and attacking the Bush administration. Goodman understood this all too well. He even later admitted to close friends that he might have been too shrill in his attack. That problem was clearly not the case with Glaudemans, a young and obviously intelligent former CIA analyst. She openly disdained the political battle over the nomination. "I take no satisfaction," she said, "in sharing with you the basis of my conviction that Mr. Gates politicized intelligence analysis and is responsible for an overall degradation of the analytical process."

With the exception of Rudman—who dismissed her testimony as something akin to the rantings of a whining adolescent—even those closest to Gates thought her testimony was credible and heartfelt. While the CIA might be able to afford the loss of a person like Goodman, there was a sense that it could not afford to alienate its young recruits, like Glaudemans, who left her job at Langley in disgust after serving for only six years, primarily in the Office of Soviet Analysis.

She provided the second dramatic moment of the hearings. "Let me be clear," she stressed. "I am here today at your request. As you may know, I walked away from this mess nearly two years ago.... I find the reexamination of old scars and the publicity surrounding these hearings personally difficult. Until several weeks ago, I had expected someone else would be testifying in this seat. So I hope you understand that I am not motivated by some overwhelming desire to bad mouth the Central Intelligence Agency or anyone personally. When I left the agency, I did not write a book, or go to the media, nor did I solicit this committee. And I do not intend to talk to the media after these hearings."

Glaudemans outlined what she called the "careless and perhaps potentially deliberate inattention to the maintenance of a culture devoted to truth" over the previous ten years. "There was, and apparently still is, an atmosphere of intimidation in the Office of Soviet Analysis," she said. "Many, including myself, hold the view that Mr. Gates had certain people removed because of their consistent unwillingness to comply with his analytical line. Even today, I am aware of a perception in SOVA that managers could risk their positions if they are not sufficiently pliant.

"I believe that the atmosphere has worsened over the last couple of years," Glaudemans went on to say. "The nature of politicization has become more blatant and I think the analysts more cynical. As bad as things might have been in the old third world division, I do not believe I have ever heard such a bitter cry for greater integrity than I have heard recently coming out of my colleagues in SOVA. And here I would urge you to consult some of the recent managerial advisory group surveys, they are nicknamed MAG surveys, on the Office of Soviet Analysis. And I can relay one anecdote to you, that there is a perception that maybe the office would do better to hire more secretaries and get rid of the analysts, because secretaries take better dictation."

Glaudemans was clearly enraged by Gates's claim that many of the complaints against him were sparked by junior analysts who were frustrated at not being higher up in the process. Gates had told the committee that he, too had many of these same feelings when he first began working at the CIA. "Senators," Glaudemans responded, "I think that answer is the most smug, condescending, and callous answer to such a sensitive question I could possibly imagine. And I believe it offers an insight into Mr. Gates's managerial style. I shudder to think what he might do if he is confirmed."

Following Glaudemans was Hal Ford, at age seventy still one of the CIA's most articulate and respected spokesmen. His testimony also came as a shock. Ford had been asked first to appear on behalf of Gates, but had changed his mind over a period of two weeks of contemplation and conversations with numerous agency employees. "I welcome the opportunity to modify my prepared statement which you have," he began. "In fact, I'm going to depart quite a bit from it, so you can tear it up."

Ford briefly described how he knew Gates and admired his attempts to make intelligence estimates "shorter, sharper and more relevant to the needs of our policymaking consumers." But then all of Ford's comments about Gates turned sour. "In brief," he remarked, "my message is that I think it will be a mistake to confirm Bob Gates as DCI." Ford explained that the main reasons he was changing his mind were the ground swell of opposition to Gates from people he respected and Gates's own testimony. "For me, the word that captures his testimony is 'clever.' The forgetfulness of this brilliant officer—he, a photographic memory— does not to me wholly instill confidence."

Goodman's, Glaudemans's, and Ford's testimonies—especially that of Glaudemans—raised serious doubts about Gates's integrity and his willingness to provide objective assessments. The charges were stated so convincingly that they provided a distinct challenge to Senator Rudman's hope that Gates could move through the confirmation process without harming his ability to lead the intelligence community. Rudman's solution to this problem was simple: He ignored Glaudemans and Ford and attacked Goodman.

During a public session of the committee on October 1, Rudman called into question Goodman's recollection of specific instances in which he said Gates had skewed the intelligence product. The senator even produced a recent letter from William Webster on a key incident in 1987, when Webster's top assistant, Mark Matthews, interviewed CIA analysts about the issue of politicization. Matthews's interviews of CIA analysts were neither secret nor kept from Gates (as Goodman claimed), Rudman argued. In fact, Rudman charged, they had nothing at all to do with Gates; Goodman was lying. "You are entitled to your own opinions," Rudman angrily snapped at Goodman, "but you are not entitled to your own facts."

Committee staff assistants now claim that Matthews inexplicably changed his testimony against Gates. During private sessions with committee investigators, they charge, Matthews backed up everything that Goodman said about the investigation of Gates. Later, they allege, he changed his story after getting political pressure from the White House. A staff assistant for Warren Rudman denies the charge, calling it "just a fabrication."

Behind the scenes, meanwhile, White House pressure on committee Republicans to defend Gates was growing, even though the testimony of the anti-Gates triumvirate had done little to change the committee's support for Bush's nominee. On the evening of October 2, Gates huddled with the President's top political advisers and CIA officials at the White House to come up with a response to the charges leveled against him. They decided he should respond with a full frontal assault against his accusers, taking on each claim in turn and knocking it down. That's just what he did. On the morning of October 3 Gates made a final appearance before the committee. He was the most combative anyone remembered having seen him. His testimony was bitter, personal, and, in parts, vindictive. He even implied that his lack of popularity at Langley was one of the reasons he should be confirmed, since it would send a message to employees that the changes he proposed would be put in place in spite of their opposition.

"It has caused me some real pain that old friends like Hal Ford and Mel Goodman have come forward," Gates remarked. But, he added, being nominated DCI was "not a popularity contest. I sure as hell wouldn't win one at CIA." He then presented a detailed twenty-point response to his critics, and lashed out at Goodman's most serious charges. Gates claimed that "a careful review of the record of what was published and sent to policy makers demonstrates that the integrity of the process was preserved." He recited much of his 1982 speech to the DI, which he freely admitted had made him many enemies. He ended his testimony by reminding the committee that he enjoyed the full confidence and support of President Bush. "This uncommon relationship between us and his expectations, having himself been Director, offers a unique opportunity to remake American intelligence, and to do so while preserving and promoting the integrity of the intelligence process in a strong and positive relationship with the Congress," he said.

More than one week after Gates defended himself, the Senate Select Committee on Intelligence met in its final session on his confirmation. There were no surprises. Metzenbaum and Bradley said they would vote against him; they were joined by DeConcini and South Carolinia Democrat Ernest Hollings. Hollings had proved to be one of the most articulate of Gates's critics and at one point at the end of the hearings startled him with a blunt assessment of his nomination. "You're a bright fella," he said, "but you're part of the problem being put up to solve the problem.... You're a very valuable fellow at the

White House. If I were Bush, I'd get you in and I'd be in clover." When Gates defended himself, saying he was "nobody's toady," Hollings responded testily: "The director of CIA doesn't belong to Congress or the president. . . . That crowd over there, Sununu and the president, think they own you."

But the most important votes on the committee—from Boren and Sam Nunn—were in Gates's favor. The final vote was 11–4. The final Senate vote, tallied in the first week of November, was predictable: 64–31 in Gates's favor. No one was at all surprised, especially after Sam Nunn said he would vote for the nominee; nor was there really any doubt Gates would be confirmed after the vote of the Intelligence Committee.

Robert Gates was sworn in as William Webster's successor by Sandra Day O'Connor with George Bush and Gates's wife, Becky, looking on, on November 12, 1991. He was the fifteenth director of central intelligence. It was a proud moment for Gates, whose strong views on intelligence and on how the CIA ought to be run marked him as a man who would take immediate action to punish those who opposed his nomination. "Charlie Allen and all the rest of them thought they could ingratiate themselves by coming out for him," a Senate Intelligence Committee aide said. "But they won't save themselves. Allen, Kerr, the rest of that crew. He'll get rid of them. He'll clean house."

Gates promised that wouldn't happen. He was a changed man from 1985, he'd said at a key point in his confirmation hearings, and had learned how to handle people by watching how William Webster did it. He made a promise to David Boren: There would be no retribution, no purges, no mass firings. He would conduct an open and honest administration and, in the best traditions of the CIA, see to it that everyone felt he or she had a role. Dissenters would be honored and defended.

Now, in his acceptance speech, he attempted to calm agency fears. He said that the people of the CIA were its greatest asset. The people at Langley, he said, were more than a team; they were a *family.*

He emphasized the word. "I hope this sense of family, with all that that implies," he concluded, "can be strengthened in the time ahead."

— ★ ★ ★ —
Epilogue

Villiam Webster reentered private life as he had entered the CIA, as a newcomer who needed all the help he could get. Everyday chores took on a new seriousness. After more than a decade as head of the FBI and CIA he had never had to drive himself anywhere. One week after he left his job as DCI, he bought a map of downtown Washington so that he could find his way around.

Paradoxically, Webster was now less willing to answer questions about his own term as DCI than he had been when he was inside the agency. He seemed to enjoy his privacy as a collector of autographed books. He was seen less frequently on the Washington social circuit. Webster did not harbor any ill feelings about his time as head of the most powerful intelligence agency in the world. The former DCI continued to support George Bush as President and Robert Gates as head of the CIA.

Webster took on a new job as a partner in a well-known Washington law firm. On some mornings he could be spotted, briefcase in hand, walking anonymously along K Street on his way to work. His good friends, however, say that the former chief of spies for the most powerful nation on earth had difficulty acclimating himself to his new job. He had not been a practicing lawyer for nearly two decades.

Robert Gates had different problems. The bitterness and rancor sparked by his appointment continued well after he was sworn in as the fifteenth director of central intelligence. Gates dealt with the controversy by assuring those who opposed his appointment that there would be no recriminations for their past actions. Everywhere he went inside the CIA he exuded an attitude of quiet competence, sprinkling his normally chilly professional demeanor with a newfound sense of camaraderie.

There were changes. After the divisive debate that marked his confirmation, Gates decided to lower the agency's public profile. The Public Affairs Office, for example, was not nearly as cooperative with reporters as it had been under Webster, even though Gates publicly promised a new openness from senior officials at Langley. Gates also made certain that the caveats that marked many of the CIA's views were left out of his public statements.

Just two months into his tenure as DCI, Gates appointed several internal task forces to study the CIA's role in the post–cold war world. He kept the Senate Intelligence Committee informed of their proceedings and testified on the agency's attempts to increase its coverage of a new set of issues: proliferation, terrorism, counternarcotics, and the makeup of the emerging republics of the former Soviet Union.

Gates's steady hand trembled only once or twice. During one appearance on Capitol Hill shortly after his confirmation, for instance, the new DCI flatly rejected the notion that the agency had predicted Iraq's invasion of Kuwait back in August 1990. Gates's statement was widely interpreted inside Langley as the first signal that his confirmation as DCI had not changed his previous habits; he was not about to embarrass President Bush by dredging up one of the CIA's proudest moments.

Four months after his nomination a long-awaited study on the politicization of intelligence reports concluded that the problem was not "pervasive" and "had much to do with poor people-management skills. . . ." The review of the issue was ordered by Gates and carried out by former Deputy Director of Intelligence Edward Proctor. Many disgruntled analysts inside the Office of Soviet Analysis dismissed the paper's conclusions as too "cautious." One mid-level Near East analyst joked that Proctor's conclusions proved that the era of objectivity at the agency was over forever; even Proctor's report, he said, read as if it had come from Gates.

But some things did change. At the end of 1991 Richard Kerr retired as deputy director. Close friends of his said that he was happy to leave and pleased by the success he had attained. He had never expected to become deputy DCI, they said, and looked on his continual promotions inside the agency's bureaucracy with barely concealed wonder.

Thomas Twetten remained as deputy director for operations, but the tightly knit community of senior CIA officials inside the clandestine service did not believe that would last very long. Twetten was still viewed with suspicion as little more than a bureaucrat by mid-level operations officers. They also believed that Gates would eventually choose a new DDO more to his liking.

After appearing on Gates's behalf during the DCI's confirmation hearings, Charles Allen returned to his desk at the CIA to continue his job as national intelligence officer for warning. But as with Twetten, no one believed that he would survive Gates's tenure. Even his closest associates, who viewed him as a man of principle, criticized him for supporting Gates's nomination. When told that Allen would be forced to retire, a former senior CIA officer expressed the opinion of many at agency headquarters. "If that is true," he said bitterly, "it is *richly* deserved."

Long since retired, Richard Stolz jealously guarded his own privacy. He consistently refused to grant press interviews and led a life of apparent contentment as one of the CIA's most secretive former officials.

Dewey Clarridge and Clair George continued their long and indecisive court battles over their own role in the Iran-contra scandal. Both remained unbowed by their troubles. By early 1992 many retired intelligence community officials looked on them as martyrs and took up a collection to support their legal defense.

The agency itself was a far different institution from the one it had been four years before. Gone forever were the days of constant crisis, when the world was filled with agents of an uncompromising enemy whose stated purpose was the destruction of the free world. The CIA—once one of the most powerful and secretive institutions in the world—was now a much diminished bureaucracy; its mythic hold on the American people was slowly, and finally, being stripped of its mystery.

———★★★———
Author's Note

This book is the result of three years of research and writing. In that time I have interviewed scores of U.S. government officials. In some cases I conducted multiple interviews. In a few significant instances I have checked the narrative of this book with former government officials to make certain that I have reflected their words accurately. This book was not reviewed by serving CIA officers or by officials of the CIA prior to its publication.

The handful of serving CIA officers who agreed to provide material for *Eclipse* would do so only on condition that they remain anonymous. Even retired officers with special knowledge of key incidents or events would not allow me to identify them by name. I have done everything I can in the book to give the reader a clear idea of the former or current status of the source but without giving away his or her identity. In some, small number of cases, I have used dialogue from meetings. In each case the dialogue has been verified with the participants or by third parties who are privy to the information and in a position to know what was said.

There is simply no way to tell, with certainty, exactly what happened in each and every instance. Memories are faulty; scenes fade; individuals' personal perceptions are colored by beliefs. This is certainly true in the case of those who work for or with the CIA. It is incumbent on every author, therefore, to take great care with the perceptions of others. I have tried to do so here.

A request for confidentiality places an enormous burden on an author—but even more so when the subject is as sensitive as the one covered in this book. Therefore, while I have used material from interviews conducted "on background"—which means that source gave me the information only with the understanding that he or she would not be identified—I used the material only when it could be confirmed by other primary sources, from classified documents, or from other named officials.

The simple truth is that it is nearly impossible to obtain information on this topic without a promise of confidentiality.

In the course of my researches I was very fortunate to have access (with one other reporter) to an unprecedented amount of classified material from a source inside the executive branch of the U.S. government. These documents are referred to in the Notes by the description "confidential document in the possession of the author."

It is *not,* however, impossible to know what to disclose and what not to disclose—what is truly a secret and what is not. My access to sensitive government documents gave me a much greater insight into this difficult problem than I might otherwise have. The CIA keeps secrets for good reason; the lives of foreign nationals who help this country depend on their ability to do so. But I have found that many of the CIA's other secrets are kept from public view because agency officials are afraid of being embarrassed or because publicizing such secrets would cause political harm to specific agency patrons on Capitol Hill or in the White House. The debate over what to disclose and what not to, therefore, was much less agonizing than I thought it would be.

The end of the cold war will, I trust, lead to the release of thousands of documents on the conduct of American foreign policy over the last forty years. That is as it should be. An informed and educated populace is the pillar of democracy. But the true secrets of the American intelligence community—the names of those foreign nationals who provided critically important information to the U.S. government—must remain forever unknown.

Notes

PROLOGUE

29 Richard Helms attempted to strike a delicate balance: In *The Man Who Kept the Secrets*, Thomas Powers provides some valuable insights into President Lyndon Johnson's relationship with Helms. "... Johnson never asked Helms for his private opinion [of the war], and Helms never volunteered it," Powers writes. He describes the DCI in the following terms: "Helms was not a man who brought his fist down on the table and raised his voice, who pressed opponents with debaters' questions or answered criticism with sarcasm. He was the coolest of advocates, presenting his Agency's views on paper, defending them on paper, a paper general in a paper war."

PART I: THE WIZARD

One: Rashid's Revenge

35 Casey came into his office: Joseph E. Persico, *Casey* (New York: Viking, 1990), pp. 550–51. See also Bob Woodward, *Veil* (New York: Simon and Schuster, 1987), p. 504.

35 The first medical report: *Veil*, p. 504.

36 he was always on the move: Author interviews with former CIA officials Herbert Meyer, Thomas Polgar, and Raymond Cline. See also *Casey*, p. 266.

36 Casey was independently wealthy: *Casey,* pp. 267–69. Persico skill-fully tells the complex story of the revelations of Casey's questionable financial dealings that were raised when he was President Reagan's campaign chairman and during his first months as DCI.

37 It would have surprised many: *Casey,* p. 552.

37 Preparations for Casey's burial: Confidential interview. Some of the details of the funeral were provided by national newspaper reporters who were in attendance, including *Newsday*'s Saul Friedman.

37 The seating of official Washington: Ibid. Some of Casey's closest friends from the intelligence community were absent, including Dewey Clarridge, the cosmopolitan clandestine service officer whom Casey had befriended and confided in. Also absent was Oliver North. Both Clarridge and North, as well as a number of the most prominent among Casey's friends at the CIA, attended a wake in his honor the night before, what they described as "the true me-morial to Casey." Richard Secord also stayed in Washington but was not invited to the wake. Secord appeared to give testimony to the congressional committee convened to investigate the Iran-contra scandal on the day before the funeral and named Casey as the Iran-contra operation's chief planner.

37 The only controversy of the day: Mary Thornton, "Casey Criticized at Funeral," *The Washington Post,* May 10, 1987.

38 "These men and their comments...": Ibid.

39 Feeling betrayed and deceived: Confidential interview. According to a CIA officer, Casey would "sometimes go into a dark funk" over the inability of the clandestine service to follow his instructions.

39 The CIA's terrorism experts knew all about Rashid: Confidential interview.

39 "Born in Jordan on April 24...": According to a confidential doc-ument in the possession of the author.

40 With the help of the Palestinian bomb maker Abu Ibrahim: "Ter-rorist Group Profiles," U.S. Department of State, November 1988. See also Steven A. Emerson and Cristinia Del Sesto, *Terrorist* (New York: Villard Books, 1991).

40 The bomb killed a sixteen-year-old: According to a document in the possession of the author. FAA bomb expert Walter Korsgaard says that U.S. intelligence officials tested and retested the bomb in a mock-up of the Pan Am seating arrangement in order to help determine where the bomb was originally planted.

40 "individuals traveling as a Moroccan family...": According to a confidential document in the possession of the author. A number of State Department documents say that Rashid "is a prominent Palestinian terrorist associated with the Hawari organization (Colo-

nel Hawari is chief of Fatah special operations)...." The report is incorrect. Rashid was never a member of the Hawari organization. The Hawari organization comprises the personal security team for PLO Chairman Yasir Arafat and provides security for other organizational leaders. They deny having any association with Rashid.

41 a Palestinian businessman known to the agency as "MJ Holiday": Confidential interview. See also Denny L. Kline (supervisory special agent), "Airline Bombings," Forensic Science Research and Training Center, FBI Academy, Quantico, Virginia. Kline gives further details of the operation without identifying the individuals involved by their CIA code names.

41 "Holiday" provided the agency: Confidential interview.

42 The carnage might have caused hundreds of casualties: At first the Swiss couldn't find the bomb. The agency told them to look again and sent out a specialist to help them. This time the Swiss carefully dismembered the suitcase and searched its lining. They found several small strips of Semtex sewn into the upper lining of the suitcase; it was nearly undetectable. Because of the way that Rashid had built the bomb, the CIA concluded, the courier's inability to go through with the bombing probably saved his life. The trigger on the bomb doubled as its detonator. Having been given clear instructions on how to "set" the bomb, the courier was told he had plenty of time to make his escape. That was a lie; the timer-detonator mechanism was "matched," according to a U.S. counterterrorism expert. This meant that when the courier set the trigger, he would have blown himself into unidentifiable pieces, what CIA officers dryly refer to as "mystery meat."

42 Sartawi had not been a U.S. agent: Confidential interview. See also Patrick Seale, *Abu Nidal: A Gun for Hire* (New York: Random House, 1992), pp. 172–76. Seale gives some interesting clues to why Sartawi was gunned down and thereby indirectly ties Abu Ibrahim into the Abu Nidal organization.

42 The officer broke in: Confidential interview.

43 During one briefing Casey had vehemently argued: Ibid.

43 the apartment of the accused terrorist's girl friend: Ibid. One senior CIA operations officer says that the chief of station in Athens was not expelled for this reason but rather because the agency ran a successful "black bag job" on the headquarters of the Greek intelligence service. The goal was to retrieve the bomb maker's materials left in his girl friend's apartment. The stolen bomb was quickly put aboard an American flight bound for Washington's Dulles International Airport, where it was turned over to CIA officials. "The Greeks were just too embarrassed to admit that we could get right

inside their government," this former agency officer says. Former
FAA officer Walter Korsgaard will not comment on a report that
he was the courier who returned the bomb to the United States.

43 Casey bellowed his way onto the seventh floor: Confidential
interview.

44 The CIA's younger officers: Ibid.

44 The DCI's most important intelligence advisers: Ibid.

45 The French had adroitly stood by in 1979: Ibid.

45 CIA officers discovered the French weren't as interested in kidnapping Rashid: Ibid. Confusion exists over when and where the kidnapping was to take place. One retired agency officer says it was to
take place in Tunis. A former NSC staff intelligence officer, however, says that it was definitely planned for the Sudan. Considering
the placement of high-level State Department intelligence officials
at the time of Rashid's arrest (they were in Sudan, expecting Rashid's
imminent arrival) in Greece, it is clear the operation was to take
place in Khartoum. Most of the evidence supports this conclusion.
An executive branch document indicates that SIRO (Special Intelligence Reporting Office, the name the State Department uses to
identify the CIA) was tracking Rashid through Sudan and North
Africa.

45 At the last minute, however, a full-scale internal skirmish: Ibid. An
executive branch memo notes: "SIRO [Special Intelligence Reporting Office] has details of Rashid's whereabouts and has informed
their counterparts that Rashid is expected to board KLM flight to
Khartoum at Athens Airport 1600 hours Athens time Monday, May
31, 1988.... In delivering note, however, you should advise GOG
[government of Greece] that we suspect that Rashid was involved
in the bombing of TWA Flight 840 in April of 1986 in which three
Greek Americans and one other U.S. Citizen were killed...." The
CIA was pulling out all the stops to get Rashid.

46 It had proved to be one of the most frustrating experiences: Interview with retired CIA officer David Whipple.

47 Secretary of State Alexander Haig obtained a galley proof of the
book: John Ranelagh, *The Agency: The Rise and Decline of the CIA*
(New York: Simon and Schuster, 1986), pp. 697–98.

47 The SNIE even presented evidence that the USSR: "Draft SNIE
11/2–81" (Soviets & Terrorism), memorandum of Helene L. Boatner, April 27, 1981. This memorandum summarizes each of the
draft SNIEs on the Soviet Union and international terrorism and
was released during the 1991 confirmation hearings on Robert Gates
to be director of central intelligence.

48 Casey had become convinced the agency was crippled by a fear:
Confidential interview.

48 Although Casey came to the CIA with few illusions: Ibid.

48 "I will tell you that [it] is . . .": *Report of the Congressional Committees Investigating the Iran-Contra Affair* (hereafter *Iran-Contra*), Appendix B, vol. 5, depositions, p. 861.

49 George . . . had developed a basic mistrust of: Confidential interview. According to this senior intelligence official, George's hesitations over many of Casey's programs "did not keep George from carrying out Casey's wishes. Clair was a good soldier."

49 The appointment was a disaster: Ibid. See also *Casey*, pp. 300–01.

49 "a cheat and a crook and totally dishonest": *Iran-Contra*, Appendix B, vol. 3, pp. 569–70.

49 the Mossad . . . also presented him as a source: Theodore Draper, *A Very Thin Line* (New York: Hill and Wang, 1991), pp. 133–34. Cave later said in a deposition (*Iran-Contra Affair*, Appendix B, vol. 3, pp. 574–75): "One of the most interesting things about Ghorbanifar is up to the time of the Iran initiative he never told us about his Israeli connections. We knew about him because he had been with Star Shipping. He was the Iranian Director of Star Shipping which was a joint Iranian-Israeli concern with heavy intelligence overtones." After the conclusion of the Gates confirmation hearings, at the end of 1991, CIA officer Charles Allen sent a long, rambling letter on the Iran-contra affair to the Senate Select Committee on Intelligence blaming the scandal on Israel, which had set up the United States with Ghorbanifar in the first place. There is now little doubt that Ghorbanifar was working for Israel.

49 The test showed that he lied on all but one question: *Iran-Contra*, Appendix B, vol. 3, pp. 572–73.

50 The CIA's file on Hakim, kept in the agency's military liaison branch: Confidential interview. This senior CIA official says that the reason this file was kept in the military liaison branch, rather than in the files of the Near East Division, is that Hakim once worked in some capacity for U.S. military intelligence.

50 "a businessman with broad . . .": Ibid. See also *A Very Thin Line*, p. 37.

50 Clarridge and North were friends: Oliver North, *Under Fire* (New York: Simon and Schuster, 1991), pp. 221–22. North gives a glowing description of Clarridge, using Clarridge's relations with Congress as a symbol of his hard-nosed attitude. North later adopted the same approach during his hearings before congressional committees investigating the Iran-contra scandal.

50 Clarridge, a flamboyant: *Veil*, p. 168. When Clarridge was later indicted for lying to Congress during hearings on the Iran-contra affair, he appeared in front of the federal courthouse in Washington

in fatigues and said that he was ready to do battle with the special prosecutor.

50 Casey trusted Clarridge: Confidential interview. According to this source, the trust wasn't automatic. "He [Casey] had real doubts about him right when he first met him [in Europe]."

51 he gave Richard Secord the name of a CIA airline: *A Very Thin Line*, pp. 192–93.

51 As punishment for his gaffe: Confidential interview. There is disagreement on this point. One CIA official says that "Clarridge's transfer was planned" by Casey long before the Iran-contra affair. Clarridge was also asked about the coincidental timing of his "transfer" by a number of close colleagues but denied he was being punished by Casey. It was, he told them, "just time to move on." Considering the timing of the assignment, however, I have chosen what I think is the most likely scenario. Clarridge was transferred to a different job to get him out of the line of fire.

51 "We figured he wouldn't...": Ibid.

52 he befriended Ashraf Marwan: Ibid. Ashraf Marwan refused to be interviewed for this book.

52 One of these reports, which the agency viewed as authoritative: John Barron, *KGB* (New York: 1974), Reader's Digest Press, pp. 58–9.

53 It took Twetten three hours: Confidential interview. It is not known if Twetten related one of the CIA's most protected secrets: that the Russians knew that Israel would launch a surprise attack on Egypt in 1967 but purposely failed to inform their Egyptian allies. If Egypt was defeated in the war, the Soviets thought, they would be forced into even closer ties with the USSR.

53 Thanks to Sakharov's information: Vladimir Sakharov with Umberto Tosi, *High Treason: Revelations of a Double Agent* (New York: G. P. Putnam's Sons, 1980), pp. 224–36. Sakharov's defection from Kuwait is legendary. He walked into the desert, where he found a preplaced radio with a directional antenna that was to guide him to a jeep. His instructions were relayed by walkie-talkie: He was to drive for two hours and "be met" by an agency officer. Within twenty-four hours he was in the United States, being debriefed, and after several months was given a new identity and residence. The CIA feared for his safety, but Sakharov apparently didn't; eleven years later he wrote of his adventures.

54 In the late 1970s he became chief of station in Amman, Jordan: Confidential interview.

54 In Amman, Twetten inherited a divided and demoralized station: Ibid.

54 Returning with North from a meeting in West Germany: *Iran-Contra*, Appendix B, vol. 5, depositions, p. 93.

55 "I am not one who presses frontally": Ibid., p. 95.

55 Cave was a born skeptic with a bad back: Ibid., Appendix B, vol. 3, depositions, pp. 655–56.

56 "After I heard about the initiative ...": Ibid., p. 825. According to agency analysts, Cave began publishing intelligence claims about the need for an opening with Iran in the President's Daily Brief (PDB), the most closely held of all the CIA's publications at the time of his involvement in the Iran opening. His PDB work gave the operation an imprimatur of credibility that it did not deserve, these critics say. This allegation later resurfaced as an all-out attack on the clandestine service by DI officers, who said that Cave "produced exclusive dissemination...DO reports that were misrepresented. The misrepresentation was simple. The source line said that these reports came from a moderate Iranian with good access. There was no such moderate Iranian with good access. These were George Cave's reports. George Cave's thinking. And George Cave's analysis...he was allowed to prepare articles...on the basis of his reports without coordination in the DI, without reference to sourcing."

57 "He did what he thought was right": Author interview with former senior CIA officer Thomas Polgar.

57 "He had terrible administrative problems": Author interview with former DDI Raymond Cline.

58 "Did you contribute...": Mary Thornton, "Casey Criticized at Funeral," *The Washington Post,* May 10, 1987.

Two: Our Man in Teheran

59 When Baker mentioned the idea to Tower: Confidential interview. See also "The CIA: A Straight Arrow for Director," *Newsweek,* March 16, 1987.

59 Gates believed that his CIA colleagues: Confidential interview.

60 Tower called the White House to say: "The CIA: A Straight Arrow for Director," *Newsweek,* March 16, 1987.

61 At this point Vice President George Bush: Confidential interview. See also "Tilting with Intelligence," *National Journal,* May 9, 1987.

61 Webster was intrigued with the idea: Author interview with William H. Webster. See also Jeff McConnell, "Coups, Wars, and the CIA," *The Boston Globe Magazine,* May 13, 1990.

61 He had actually planned to leave the FBI in 1985: Ibid.

62 "The FBI's one thing...": Ibid.

62 That night Webster made a second call: Author interviews with William H. Webster and Admiral Bobby Ray Inman.

62 Inman reassured Webster that he could: Ibid.

62 Webster made his decision early the next afternoon: Ibid.

63 he was also not without his detractors: Nat Hentoff, "Saint for Our Time," *The Village Voice,* April 7, 1987.

63 While Operation ABSCAM resulted in a number: Peter Hernon, "Strong Sense of History Drives Webster," *St. Louis Post-Dispatch,* March 16, 1987.

63 In Operation Corkscrew: Ibid.

64 The sting operation the FBI attempted: Ibid.

64 He was "complimented and honored": Author interview with William H. Webster.

65 Senator David Boren, the articulate Oklahoma Democrat: Confidential interview.

65 Senator William Cohen: Ibid.

66 What bothered him most: Author interview with Senator William Cohen.

66 At Langley, Reagan's announcement was greeted: Ibid. See also "Tilting with Intelligence," *National Journal,* May 9, 1987.

66 The Near East Division's leading counterterrorism expert: Confidential interview.

67 "I won't be staying here long now": Ibid. Clarridge later told friends that he was planning to leave the CIA in any event and that he never had any desire to serve as its director for operations.

67 Webster publicly opposed lifting restrictions: "Tilting with Intelligence," *National Journal,* May 9, 1987. See also Blaine Harden, "Super Cop," *Washingtonian,* April 1984.

67 Webster had tipped his hand: Ibid.

67 "in a later, more sober time...": Ibid.

68 Webster had opposed a White House plan: Ibid.

69 "I never confuse movement with action": Author interview with William H. Webster.

69 "Ever since I can remember...": Interview with CIA public affairs chief James Greenleaf. See also Blaine Harden, "Super Cop," *Washingtonian,* April 1984. Webster says "that [statement] is true, but I didn't think I said it all that much."

70 "There were closed door meetings...": Confidential interview.

70 In 1982 they heard unverified rumors that: Ibid.

70 The CIA also discovered that the Iranians: Ibid.

71 Larkin set the tone for the meeting: Ibid.

72 Dead drops were considered primitive: Ibid. For an exhaustive study of recent intelligence community tradecraft—and some failures— see Tom Mangold, *Cold Warrior* (New York: Simon and Schuster, 1991), pp. 227–36.

73 The agency's Teheran station in exile: Confidential interview. Iran-contra documents in *United States of America* v. *Oliver L. North* make mention of a TEFRAN, the meaning of which was made clear to

me by a former CIA officer. The officer detailed the responsibilities of what he called "our station in exile."

75 On a quiet morning in late April 1987: Ibid.

75 Within days the Senate Intelligence Committee had arrived at its own ready explanation: Ibid.

76 "We can't say whether the story was true or not": Interview with SSCI staff investigator. The FBI's agent stopped reporting to the bureau in 1987 and afterward left Iran. It isn't known what he reported on, how the bureau used the material, or if his reports were shared with the CIA. The agency has refused comment on the issue, though detailed reports of it made their way into the public press. In April 1990 a congressional staff investigator, Jim Curry, told the author that the SSCI conducted a review of the incident and concluded that the allegations based on the report "cannot be proved." Does that mean that the allegations are true? "Not necessarily," Curry said to the author. "The allegations might be true, but we'll never know." Another committee aide said that there were "certain parts of the story that seem to hang together. The story is certainly plausible." But then he added: "We have to conclude this never happened." A similar report was publicized by columnist Jack Anderson, but it, too, was denied by Senate Intelligence Committee aides. The story has since disappeared from view.

77 "The first knowledge I had of any possible activity . . .": "William H. Webster, Director to Honorable David L. Boren, Chairman, Select Committee on Intelligence" (letter), April 6, 1987. A copy of the letter is in the author's possession.

77 "They asked him the same question . . .": Confidential interview.

78 under pressure, he agreed: "Affidavit of William H. Webster," director, Federal Bureau of Investigation, April 6, 1987. A copy of the document is in the author's possession.

78 His daughter held the Bible for him: Author interview with William H. Webster.

Three: Just Off the Boat from the FBI

79 In Southeast Asia the CIA was engaged: Don Oberdorfer, "U.S. Weighs Arms for Cambodian Resistance," *The Washington Post*, April 30, 1989; and Don Oberdorfer and Valerie Strauss, "Cambodian Resistance Seeks U.S. Military Aid," *The Washington Post*, April 19, 1989. Three different factions opposed the Hun Sen (People's Republic of Kampuchea, now State of Cambodia) regime in Phnom Penh: the Communist Khmer Rouge, which ruled the country through a policy of terror until the intervention of the Vietnamese in 1979; the Khmer People's National Liberation Front; and a weak

faction headed by the former Cambodian head of state Norodom Sihanouk, who also served as the titular chief of state in the American-backed Coalition Government of Democratic Kampuchea. America's support for the coalition government was, in effect, viewed for many years by much of the world community as de facto recognition of the Khmer Rouge. Until recently the coalition was the official representative of Cambodia and had a seat at the United Nations largely because of the pressures brought on UN members by the United States, despite the fact that all three factions control a fraction of the population of the central government and enjoy little support. Since 1988 the five permanent members of the UN Security Council have been trying to engineer the establishment of a government of reconciliation in Phnom Penh.

80 The agency was also involved in an important military campaign in Afghanistan: *Casey*, pp. 225–26. See also *Veil*, pp. 78–9; Michael Dobbs, "Soviets Complete Pullout from War in Afghanistan," *The Washington Post*, February 16, 1989; and Michael Dobbs, "Afghan Pullout Marks Historic Reversal for Soviets," *The Washington Post*, February 13, 1989.

80 the agency gave fifteen million dollars: *Veil*, p. 426, and David B. Ottaway, "Zaire Is Said to Cut CIA Arms Flow to Angolan Rebels," *The Washington Post*, October 4, 1989. Woodward places the total covert funding at thirteen million dollars. My sources indicated it was "two to three million dollars higher."

80 In Central America the CIA provided the anti-Sandinista contra forces: David Hoffman and Helen Dewar, "Baker Rules Out Early Bid to Aid Contras Militarily," *The Washington Post*, December 21, 1988. The Reagan administration had originally asked for more than sixteen million dollars in military aid to the contras, but the funds had not been voted by Congress. The nonmilitary aid was nearly double that amount.

81 In Lebanon the CIA had installed a small: According to a confidential document in the possession of the author.

81 The U.S. policy of refusing to provide: The Reagan administration's prohibition against trading for hostages was put back in place in 1986 in the wake of the Iran-contra revelations, and CIA officers were under orders to turn down offers of money or arms for hostages. They were, however, strictly instructed to report all such offers for consideration of the agency's hostage locating and rescue task force. Because of this, the administration's prohibition left the door open for negotiations with hostage holders, in an attempt to win their release without any kind of payment in return. Nor did the prohibition stop CIA officers or their assets from conducting

surveillance of hostage locations or from trying to locate hostages, in the words of a DO officer, "by other means." Because of this, the CIA was able to identify clearly the location of a number of hostages in 1989 and again in 1990 and could have launched a rescue operation to retrieve them. But all such plans were eventually vetoed by the agency, the NSC staff, or the Pentagon.

81 the agency had successfully penetrated Lebanon's small intelligence service: Confidential interview.

81 Not even the head of Syrian intelligence was informed: Ibid. Details on this operation are also in a confidential document in the possession of the author. Other information about U.S. cooperation with Syria in locating hostages has since become public. The information clearly indicates there are deep disagreements in the Syrian intelligence service about any program of cooperation with the United States.

82 In Thailand, for example: Ibid. See also Mark Perry and Scott Malone, "How Scandal Almost Sank Our Secret Cambodia War," *The Washington Post,* October 30, 1988.

82 Senior officers working in Langley's Afghan Task Force: Confidential interview.

82 There were plenty of theories: Ibid.

82 Just as U.S. funds threatened the stability of Pakistan: Graham E. Fuller, "Let's Not Blow It in Afghanistan," *The Washington Post,* November 27, 1988, and David B. Ottaway, "U.S., Pakistan Agree to Continue Afghan Rebel Aid," *The Washington Post,* June 11, 1989.

83 Nabih Berri's Amal militia: Confidential interview. Berri's name and organization are mentioned specifically in State Department papers on the hostage crisis that were leaked to the author by a Reagan administration source.

83 the CIA suffered the loss: *Veil,* pp. 244–45.

83 In one instance a Lebanese employee: According to a confidential document in the possession of the author.

84 Noriega was not only a former CIA asset: John Dinges, *Our Man in Panama* (New York: Random House, 1990), pp. 292–94.

86 At the center of these controversial reviews: Ibid. See also David Wise, *The Spy Who Got Away* (New York: Random House, 1988), pp. 19–20. The best, and most complete, account of the Howard case appears in *The Spy Who Got Away.* Wise interviewed Howard in Budapest, where the former CIA officer all but admitted that he had been spying for the Soviets prior to his defection. The Soviet official whom the CIA suspects that Howard betrayed was Adolf Tolkachev, a defense researcher who had been arrested by the KGB. Wise gives an anecdotal account of Howard's training that turns out to be

typical for most CIA officers: During one training session FBI agents faked an arrest of Howard to determine how he would act under pressure. He was extraordinarily calm. He knew it was a test, he later said, because he could see that the FBI agent who drew his gun didn't have it loaded.

86 the striking Virginia patrician: Ibid., pp. 12–14.

86 But in that exam: Ibid., pp. 85–90.

87 Yurchenko's sudden and stunning defection: Ronald Kessler, *Escape from the CIA* (New York: Pocket Books, 1991), p. 5.

88 The DO was rife with gossip: Confidential interview.

90 He began his remarks by mentioning William Casey's tenure: "Remarks by William Webster upon His Swearing-in as Director at Central Intelligence," May 26, 1987.

90 "There are some today...": Ibid.

90 Following the ceremony, a muted reception: Confidential interview.

91 In the CIA's "bubble": Ibid.

91 "I've worked with many of you...": Ibid.

91 Webster moved swiftly to rebuild: Ibid. See also "Speech of William M. Baker," assistant director, Criminal Investigation Division, Federal Bureau of Investigation, before the Harvard Lecture Series, Boston, Massachusetts, July 27, 1989.

92 and widely viewed at the CIA as a perfect agency spokesman: *Veil*, p. 265.

92 "He was a tool of the DO": Confidential interview.

92 Lauder, a tall, thin-smiling man: Lauder had a distinguished career overseas that was matched by his administrative skills at Langley and his ability to initiate new officers into the agency's program. That is perhaps the best explanation of why Casey decided to appoint him to the public affairs job. He served as a member of the clandestine service for nearly three decades before his retirement, which occurred in the immediate aftermath of Baker's appointment. The CIA denies that it uses members of the press for information and vehemently rejects the notion that it uses them as unofficial CIA officers. The latter claim is correct; the CIA would never hire a reporter to gather information. Nevertheless, the agency provides background briefings for reporters who are going overseas and says that they should feel free to share information with the agency should they choose to do so. A number have.

92 "Most people are afraid...": Author interview with former CIA officer David Whipple.

93 He was proud that he learned: "Speech of William M. Baker," assistant director, Criminal Investigation Division, Federal Bureau of Investigation, before the Harvard Lecture Series, Boston, Massachusetts, July 27, 1989.

93 "We didn't even give him...": Confidential interview.

93 "That day, I entered an auditorium...": "Speech of William M. Baker," assistant director, Criminal Investigation Division, Federal Bureau of Investigation, before the Harvard Lecture Series, Boston, Massachusetts, July 27, 1989.

93 "Never lie...": Author interview with William H. Webster.

94 "This is a mistake...": Confidential interview.

95 But he was under the greatest pressure: Ibid.

95 "Fire Fernandez," one urged. "Get rid of him": Ibid.

96 The appearance of fairness: Ibid.

96 Webster's early schedule was taken up: Ibid. During an interview with former CIA public affairs officer James Greenleaf in October 1989, I was told that "it is pretty standard that a new director show the flag" and confirmed that Webster took several overseas trips during his first months as DCI.

96 "Morocco," he said aloud to himself. "Let me see now": Ibid.

96 "We have to make ourselves welcome...": Ibid. One of Webster's top assistants dismisses criticism of his boss's foreign policy abilities: "No one ever thought he was going to be a foreign policy genius. I would say Webster did a fair job."

97 "Do you really mean to tell me...": Ibid.

97 Fuller suggested that the United States ease: "The US-Soviet Struggle for Influence in Tehran," memorandum from Graham E. Fuller, May 7, 1985, and "Toward a Policy on Iran," memorandum from Graham E. Fuller, May 17, 1985.

98 Webster learned that Fuller's: Ibid. Throughout the writing of this book Graham Fuller refused to discuss his role in the Iran-contra affair or his authorship of the SNIE that did so much to change American policy toward Iran. He had no such hesitation when it came to discussing the Middle East or South Asia in general, however.

98 Webster called in Mark Matthews: Ibid. Matthews later vehemently denied that his investigation was a secret or that it was aimed at specific CIA officers or senior analysts. The claims and counterclaims about his findings are still a subject of controversy inside the CIA. In spite of Matthews's later statements to the contrary, senior analysts at Langley hold firm to their position that Webster called Matthews in to investigate reports of politicization against high-level CIA managers, including Robert Gates.

99 "I obviously have not conducted a poll of my colleagues...": "The Iranian Imbroglio: Implications for the Intelligence Process," memorandum from Thomas M. Barksdale, December 2, 1986.

99 The combination of the Matthews review of the Fuller SNIE: Fuller mounted a defense of his paper only during the 1991 confirmation

hearings of Robert Gates and has consistently refused to speak of it in conversations with reporters. In the wake of the scandal, he quietly left the CIA for a position at the Rand Corporation, a California-based government think tank, where he has maintained a distinguished public profile as a Near East specialist. In private discussions with his colleagues, Fuller maintains that the SNIE was based on solid intelligence information and took note of the fact that Iran was strategically significant. In addition, he correctly points out that the paper on Iran was approved by William Casey. Webster heard these arguments in Fuller's defense but would not shift his opinion of the damage caused by the 1985 SNIE. Fuller served as the CIA's national intelligence officer for the Middle East and was deputy chairman of the CIA's powerful National Intelligence Council (NIC). The NIC is a committee of the agency's sixteen NIOs and is responsible for preparing the agency's major intelligence reports, which are then passed on to policy makers at the White House. According to one CIA officer, however, the NIC is "virtually powerless, like a group of wise old men. They study a problem and lay out how we [in the clandestine service] should handle the problem. We study what they have sent us and then we throw it in the basket and do whatever we damn well please."

99 A well-known Washington lawyer: Author interview with William H. Webster.

100 While Bruemmer did not single out: Confidential interview.

100 Finally, on November 13, the day: Ibid.

100 George recommended that the CIA: Ibid. Civilian support for sending the mujaheddin high-tech weapons centered on Undersecretary of Defense for Policy Fred C. Iklé and State Department intelligence chief Morton Abramowitz, according to published reports. They were joined on the Hill by Senator Gordon J. Humphrey (R-NH) and Representative Charles Wilson (D-TX), who visited rebel-held territory. Wilson, Humphrey, and a group of congressmen pressed the CIA on their hesitations to send Stingers to the mujaheddin. After the program was approved, congressional aide Vaughn Forrest became a Capitol Hill gadfly on the program and the agency's chief critic. "There were as many divisions inside the CIA as there were up here in Congress," he says, "so we had to sort those out, too."

101 nearly seven hundred Stingers were shipped: Some commentators cite different figures for the total number of Stingers sent to Afghanistan. Ottaway ("Stingers Were Key Weapon in Afghan War, Army Finds," The Washington Post, July 5, 1989) cites an Army report that says the Afghan guerrillas scored an impressive 79 percent hit ratio against Soviet targets. Between September 1986 and February

1989, Ottaway says, an estimated nine hundred to one thousand Stingers were sent to Afghanistan. The discrepancy of the above figure with Ottaway's may result from the fact that at the time of the interview the number of Stingers in Afghanistan was, in fact, much lower.

101 The toll exacted on the Soviet military by George's program: David B. Ottaway, "Stingers Were Key Weapon in Afghan War, Army Finds," *The Washington Post,* July 5, 1989.

102 "He [Stolz] was used to guide": Confidential interview.

102 Admiral Turner passed over Stolz: Author interview with Stansfield Turner. See also Stephen Engelberg, "Webster Names Ex-Agent to Top CIA Post," *The New York Times,* December 9, 1987, and Ann Devroy and Walter Pincus, "Deputy CIA Head Chosen for National Security Post," *The Washington Post,* December 29, 1988.

102 Nothing could compare, however, to the bitterness that Stolz felt: Confidential source.

102 He had served most of his career: Stephen Engelberg, "Webster Names Ex-Agent to Top CIA Post," *The New York Times,* December 9, 1987.

103 One surprising name on this list was Charles Allen: Bob Woodward and Walter Pincus, "CIA's Webster Disciplines 7 Employes over Iran Affair," *The Washington Post,* December 18, 1987. See also Walter Pincus, "CIA Aide Acts to Lift Reprimand," *The Washington Post,* January 1, 1989.

Four: Senator, Soldier, Dictator . . . Spy

104 The struggle between them had started back in 1977: Frederick Kempe, "The Noriega Files," *Newsweek,* January 15, 1990. See also Jim McGee and David Hoffman, "Rivals Hint Bush Understates Knowledge of Noriega Ties," *The Washington Post,* May 8, 1988, and "Drugs, Money and Death," *Newsweek,* February 15, 1988.

104 Seven years later: Joe Pichirallo, "U.S. Probes Panama Strongman on Drug Ties," *The Washington Post,* November 11, 1987.

105 Spadafora told Helms: Author interview with Deborah DeMoss.

105 "The people of Panama...": "Situation in Panama," testimony of Elliott Abrams before the House Subcommittee on Western Hemisphere Affairs, March 10, 1986. Abrams did not respond to a request for an interview for this book.

105 "Jesse was just overcome...": Author interview with Deborah DeMoss.

106 Hersh's report: Seymour Hersh, "Panama Strongman Said to Trade in Drugs, Arms and Illicit Money," *The New York Times,* June 13, 1986.

106 his ties to the Reagan administration: Kevin Buckley, *Panama: The Whole Story* (New York: Simon and Schuster, 1991), pp. 53–54.

106 This session was Noriega's third such meeting: Frederick Kempe, *Divorcing the Dictator* (New York: G. P. Putnam's Sons, 1990), pp. 178–79.

107 In a number of late-night: Confidential interview.

108 At a meeting in his office: Ibid. Senator Kerry's chief investigators were never able to identify the two CIA officers who attended the meeting, who would not give their names. "They sat stone-faced through the whole thing, except to tell us that what we were saying just wasn't true," a Kerry staff assistant says.

108 The CIA delegate was the most outspoken: Ibid.

109 "He was running for the Senate...": Ibid.

109 "I would like you to tell the committee...": "Statement of Jorge Morales," hearings before the Subcommittee on Terrorism, Narcotics, and International Communications, May 27, 1987 (part 1), pp. 46–47.

110 Manuel Antonio Noriega was recruited: *Divorcing the Dictator*, pp. 44, 50.

110 In 1969 Noriega was appointed: Ibid., pp. 64–65.

110 code-named Operation Canton Song: Ibid., pp. 27–32.

110 Bush decided that the CIA would take no action: Ibid., p. 28.

111 three terrorist bombings in Panama: Ibid., p. 29.

112 "He was always wondering...": Confidential interview.

113 at a reported salary of: Ibid. Reporter Frederick Kempe puts the figure at closer to two hundred thousand dollars.

113 "a kind of superspy for Latin America": Ibid. Sanchez says he was first introduced to Noriega in 1975 and admits that he opposed a number of actions to displace him as leader of Panama. He claims that his opposition was born of his view that the Panamanian people should be responsible for their own government, that Noriega was a minor irritant, that there wasn't anyone better to replace him, and that if he were replaced, a Communist takeover would probably follow. But Sanchez's congressional critics say that he "based his analysis of the PDF officer corps [that it had been penetrated by Communists] on Noriega's own files."

113 offers to help the United States fight Nicaragua: *Our Man in Panama*, p. 147. The depth of Casey's support of Noriega was made plain by former Deputy Assistant Secretary of State for Intelligence and Research (INR) Francis J. McNeil. "Noriega came to Washington to meet with Director Casey on, I believe, November 1, 1985," he told a congressional committee. "Mr. Casey's memcon [memorandum of conversation] made clear that he let Noriega off the hook. He scolded Noriega only for letting the Cubans use Panama to evade

the trade embargo, but never mentioned narcotics nor, if I recall correctly, democracy. Mr. Casey's memcon noted that Noriega had been nervous when he came to [the] meeting, but departed reassured, or words to that effect."

113 a number of reporters were dispatched: According to a reporter at *The Washington Post,* Lally Weymouth was dispatched to Panama for this express purpose but was unable to locate a tape.

113 "Don't sit on this evidence...": Confidential interview.

114 During a 1983 stopover in Panama: *Divorcing the Dictator,* p. 162.

114 "You could draw a line...": Confidential source.

114 "There were all these questions...": Author interview with Jack Blum.

114 "Bush is in the government during...": *Divorcing the Dictator,* p. 29.

114 Stolz believed the CIA could not: Confidential interview.

115 "The CIA's information was useless...": Author interview with the assistant federal prosecutor Richard Gregorie.

115 "Sooner or later Kerry...": Confidential interview.

115 "I will always have a hard time...": Author interview with the assistant federal prosecutor Richard Gregorie.

116 the State Department decided to launch: According to a confidential document in the possession of the author. See also Stephen Engelberg, "Panamanian's Tale: '87 Plan for a Coup," *The New York Times,* October 29, 1989.

116 In late March Herrera Hassan was spirited out of Israel: *Divorcing the Dictator,* pp. 289–93.

116 The real opponents of the plan: Confidential interview.

116 The chief of station was caught flat-footed: Ibid.

117 the State Department's lack of concern: *Divorcing the Dictator,* p. 292.

117 "During a Saturday meeting...": Confidential interview.

117 D'Amato remains convinced that Sanchez: Author interview with Senator Alfonse D'Amato.

117 "I have no business relationship...": "Statement of Nestor D. Sanchez," hearings before the Subcommittee on Terrorism, Narcotics and International Communications (part 4), p. 202.

119 Abrams's programs began when Ronald Reagan: *Divorcing the Dictator,* p. 289.

119 Abrams resuscitated the threat of: Ibid., p. 290.

119 The Joint Chiefs of Staff stridently reiterated their opposition: According to a confidential document in the possession of the author.

119 an embarrassing spendthrift: Ibid.

119 In April Reagan signed: William Scott Malone (with reporters Tony Kimery and Mark Perry), "The Panama Debacle—Uncle Sam Wimps Out," *The Washington Post,* April 23, 1989.

120 "I could have found...": Confidential interview.

120 "a legal golden parachute": *The Congressional Record,* May 17, 1988, vol. 134, no. 69.

120 Clark had been given the task: Confidential interview. According to *Divorcing the Dictator,* p. 292, Herrera Hassan was escorted during his stay in Washington by Clark.

121 Born in Puerto Rico in 1944: Author interview with James V. Coniglio. For other background on Clark, see *Divorcing the Dictator,* pp. 316–17.

122 "Gerry told me they were...": Author interview with Deborah DeMoss.

122 "Ollie didn't like Gerry...": Ibid.

122 "Clark was the best...": Author interview with José Blandón.

122 One of the most notorious of these firms was SETCO: SETCO stands for Servicios Ejecutivos Turistas Commander. DEA documents name Matta as head of the corporation. Another government report says SETCO was "a corporation formed by American businessmen who are dealing with Matta and are smuggling narcotics into the United States." SETCO was widely known inside the U.S. government as a corrupt corporation engaged in drug trafficking, and DEA agents in Central America were put on notice about Matta and SETCO as early as 1983. A U.S. Customs report dated May 9, 1983, says SETCO "provided cargo transport services for contras based in Honduras." The DEA report says Matta owned "three DC-4 type aircraft." A retired DEA official says "the planes were used for two purposes: arms in, drugs out."

122 Juan Matta Ballesteros: Stephen Engelberg, "Suspect in Murder of Drug Agent Is Seized in U.S. Trap in Honduras," *The New York Times,* April 6, 1988; Larry Rohter, "Military Infighting Seen Behind Honduran's Arrest," *The New York Times,* April 15, 1988; and Larry Rohter, "Seized Honduran: Drug Baron or a Robin Hood?" *The New York Times,* April 16, 1988.

123 On the morning of April 5: Confidential information. Details of the actual arrest of Matta were obtained in interviews with officers of the U.S. Marshals Service and U.S. Customs Service and confirmed in reports at the time. See also Stephen Engelberg, "Suspect in Murder of Drug Agent Is Seized in U.S. Trap in Honduras," *The New York Times,* April 6, 1988, and Bill McAllister, "Trap Set as Honduran Suspect Jogged," *The Washington Post,* April 7, 1988.

123 DEA and U.S. Marshals officers: Confidential interview.

124 "This [operation] was ours...": Author interview with Howard Safer.

124 the CIA was willing to tolerate drug corruption: Agency officials have consistently, fervently, and, I believe, justifiably denied any

involvement in drug trafficking. Reports that they are involved in the trade are exaggerated at best, fabricated at worst. These denials notwithstanding, there is little doubt that agency officers serving in overseas posts have looked the other way when confronted with the fact that some of their agents are involved in criminal activities, including trafficking. Faced with such clear ties as those that existed between SETCO and the drug trade, agency officials answer that they can neither confirm nor deny, nor in any way discuss, CIA operations. These public denials are matched in private conversations with retired officers who are usually more open about "past" agency policies. The same vehement denials are repeated, but the sentence "The CIA is not a law enforcement agency and has no power to arrest" is added. It's an interesting caveat.

124 The CIA's officer in Tegucigalpa: Confidential interview.

124 On the night of April 7: Loren Jenkins, "Honduran Riot Poses Setback for U.S.," *The Washington Post,* April 16, 1988.

125 High-level agency officers argued: Confidential interview. The Marshals Service is still very sensitive about its role in the Matta kidnapping. Steven Boyle, a spokesman for the service, vehemently denied that Matta was "kidnapped" or "extradited" from Honduras but refused to explain exactly what happened on the morning of April 5. Howard Safer, the former head of operations at the Marshals Service, admits that the operation is hard to categorize. "Let's just call it a policy of prerendering," he says. Rendering is a legal policy set down by the U.S. government that allows its law enforcement officers to pursue fugitives and lawbreakers, even if they are foreign nationals, in foreign countries and bring them to the United States for trial. The word "render" is, however, at best a quasi-legal explanation for seizing a foreign national on foreign soil. Boyle refused to explain the difference between "render" and "kidnap," except to say that one was legal and one was not.

125 Stolz won approval: Ibid.

125 The group he established reviewed all findings: "The CIA Under Judge William H. Webster's Leadership," CIA paper, in author's possession.

125 "Except," he added, "for one": Author interview with William Webster. Webster would not specify which operation he disapproved of, but the timing of the interview (October 18, 1989) led me to believe that it involved Manuel Noriega. Information that Webster disapproved of a covert program to seize Noriega was confirmed by a number of his top associates.

125 "Webster was against this thing...": Confidential interview.

125 "The CIA wanted to show...": Ibid. News of Webster's opposition

to the operation became general knowledge in the Directorate for Operations just before the CIA presented the plan to the Senate Intelligence Committee.

126 "Your [Senator Daniel] Inouye testimony...": According to a confidential document in the possession of the author.

126 "Dick Stolz, Rich Armitage...": Ibid.

126 The committee was also concerned: Confidential interview.

127 "We have 15,000 Americans...": Ibid.

127 "I'm surprised they didn't list...": Ibid.

127 In September the CIA's chief of station: According to a confidential document in the possession of the author.

127 "This was a joke.": Confidential interview.

127 "The CIA and military...": Ibid.

127 "My first reaction...": Author interview with Jack Blum.

128 The study was conducted: Confidential interview. A copy of the GAMA Corporation study is in the possession of the author.

128 "Jay Grunin": According to a confidential document in the possession of the author.

128 The Green Team: Ibid.

128 included Major Mark Inniss: Ibid. I telephoned Inniss at his number at the Defense Intelligence Agency. I asked him if he knew Gerry Clark. "Never heard of him," he said. I asked him if he was ever part of the GAMA Corporation study. "Never heard of it," he said. I asked him if he was head of the Panama desk at the DIA. "I can't talk about that," he said. That was the end of the interview.

128 "chances of Noriega leaving...": Ibid.

129 "I was Noriega in the game...": Author interview with Colonel James V. Coniglio. Unlike Inniss, Coniglio provided what information he could on Clark, Central America, and the GAMA Corporation study. But he would not discuss any matters pertaining to intelligence operations on Central America in general or Panama in particular. He was outspoken in his view that Clark died as the result of an accident, saying he had investigated it thoroughly.

Five: 354 days

130 Dole had publicly demanded: *Divorcing the Dictator,* p. 335.

130 "Part of what I don't do...": Ibid.

130 Bailey suggested that: "Statement of Dr. Norman A. Bailey," House Select Committee on Narcotics Abuse and Control, March 29, 1988.

131 Gregg explained that Bush: Joe Pichirallo, "Gregg Says Envoy Told Bush Noriega Was a Problem," *The Washington Post,* May 21, 1988;

"Bush Broadens Noriega Explanation," *The Washington Post,* May 10, 1988.

131 "In terms of drugs...": At the urging of his top campaign aides, Bush became more outspoken about Noriega as the campaign wore on. The more outspoken he became, the better he did in the polls. In fact, he distanced himself from the perceived do-nothing strategy of the Reagan administration. Noriega did not respond to any of his statements, which became more strident and categorical: "Drug dealers are domestic terrorists, killing kids and cops, and they should be treated as such. I won't bargain with terrorists, and I won't bargain with drug dealers either, whether they're on U.S. or foreign soil."

131 "Available to me as an officer...": "Statement of Dr. Norman A. Bailey," House Select Committee on Narcotics Abuse and Control, March 29, 1988.

131 The first authoritative report about: The decade-long case made against Noriega in the national press is discussed in "Thank You, Gen. Noriega," *The Washington Post,* May 27, 1988.

132 "It's hard to believe...": Confidential interview.

132 Among these skeptics: Author interview with Jesse Helms and Deborah DeMoss.

132 "You're not doing enough...": Confidential interview.

132 Bush aide Sam Watson: According to a confidential document in the possession of the author.

133 "[The CIA] has not been back...": Ibid.

133 The CIA had recruited a number of other Panamanians: Confidential interview.

133 Villalaz had participated in: Author interview with Augusto Villalaz. Villalaz tells of the time he piloted Omar Torrijos on a special visit to see Colonel Muammar al-Qaddafi of Libya. The three-day visit, he says, was very uneventful, except that the Panamanians were "treated like kings." Torrijos was greeted with all the pomp accorded a foreign leader, Villalaz says, "including a red carpet. I mean, they actually rolled one out. I couldn't believe it." Qaddafi apparently hoped that he could recruit Torrijos as a potential anti-American ally, but his plan didn't work. After Villalaz closed the aircraft door in preparation for takeoff, he remembers, Torrijos turned to him and said: "That man is crazy." Later DIA terrorism summaries noted the possibility that Libyan-hired terrorist teams were reported on their way to Panama, a residue of fears in the American government that both Torrijos and Noriega were willing to engage in trade with anyone, despite their ties to the United States.

134 Captain Moisés Giroldi: *Divorcing the Dictator,* p. 279.

134 "The American government seemed to think...": Author interview with Augusto Villalaz.
135 many CIA officials thought Bush should be retained: Confidential interview.
135 "a quick study": Ibid.
136 Bush accepted Ford's offer: George Bush, *Looking Forward* (New York: Doubleday, 1987), p. 130. See also Richard Ben Cramer, "How Bush Made It," *Esquire,* June 1991; Dan Goodgame, "What If We Do Nothing?," *Time,* January 7, 1991; Marci McDonald, "Power Tennis, Anyone?," *The Washington Post Magazine,* July 18, 1989, and Bob Woodward and Walter Pincus, "At CIA, a Rebuilder 'Goes with the Flow,'" *The Washington Post,* August 10, 1988.
136 Bush believed he was a logical choice: *Looking Forward,* p. 164.
136 Bush was acutely aware that being confirmed: Ibid., p. 163.
136 "Having lost out to Rockefeller...": Ibid., p. 129.
136 Less important was the actual: Confidential interview. Not only did Bush take "far less interest in the CIA" than many thought he would, according to this source, but he "had the good sense" not to try to make himself an intelligence expert. Despite this, it is also clear that Bush later used his CIA experience to lay claim to a special knowledge of intelligence work, an attitude CIA officers later found irksome.
137 "The CIA has been through...": Ibid.
138 "I met with the President...": Ibid.
138 he always made sure he never...: Ibid.
139 Veteran officer Angus Thuermer, who attended many of Bush's daily meetings: Author interview with former CIA officer Angus Thuermer.
139 "He understands that part of the world...": Confidential interview.
139 capable of producing digitized photographs despite clouds or darkness: The revolution in technical intelligence gathering that began under Bush was expanded under Turner and Casey. Bush's budget called for the construction and deployment of four KH-11 satellites to replace several older systems. Phasing out aging satellites saved the CIA some four hundred million dollars, thereby making the purchase of the KH-11s possible. But almost immediately after winning approval for this addition to the agency's budget, Bush ordered the CIA's Directorate for Science and Technology to begin planning a new generation of successors to the KH-11. The development of all-weather satellites was a much more difficult proposition, however, because of the sophisticated technology involved. While money for these Lacrosse satellites was appropriated in 1976, it was many years before one was launched. Some CIA officers are less than impressed by Bush's innovations. They say that the technical "rev-

olution" taking place during his term was actually planned long beforehand by William Colby.

139 four overseas ground stations: Only three of the four ground stations Bush asked for in 1976 were actually built. They are referred to now by their rather unsophisticated names as elephant cages—football-length arrays of multiprongs that are so sensitive that they can pick up communications hundreds of miles away. The technology is extremely valuable since intelligence analysts can not only tune in on private conversations but identify their location.

140 This criticism of Bush arose: Confidential interview. There is a great deal of disagreement on whether Bush was popular with the agency's career officers. John Ranelagh characterizes Bush as a "popular" DCI, a view that was nearly universally held until recently. The myth of Bush's popularity was increased by a number of widely quoted articles from CIA veterans who supported Bush's presidential candidacy, including Miles Copeland's "Old Spooks for Bush," which was printed in the *National Review* in March 1988. A more careful portrait is drawn in a five-part *Washington Post* series by Walter Pincus and Bob Woodward that appeared in August 1988. While confirming that Bush was popular at the CIA, Pincus and Woodward note the controversy over his appointment of Knoche and defense of the Team B study. They conclude that Bush successfully "tiptoed through the minefield." Interviews with scores of his former associates, however, lead me to believe that he has many detractors. After an interview with a former official who unstintingly praised Bush's tenure at Langley one of the official's children caught up with me at a Washington social event. "You interviewed my father," this person said. "You know, he despises George Bush."

140 Colby had provided the initial impetus: *The Agency,* pp. 622–25.

141 "Why have outside experts?": Author interview with former CIA Director for Intelligence Ray Cline. Team B was made up of conservative officials and Soviet experts. In addition to Pipes, other members of the team included DIA head Daniel Graham, Air Force General John Vogt, SALT negotiator William R. Van Cleave, Rand Corporation analyst Colonel Thomas Wolfe, USAF systems analyst General Jasper A. Welch, Jr., Paul Wolfowitz from the Arms Control and Disarmament Agency, and Paul Nitze, who was renowned for writing one of the most sobering national security assessments in cold war history. General Vogt dismisses concerns that the team's report was slanted: "We did an honest assessment, as kind of a standard for the agency. The controversy that developed should have never happened."

143 "Bush lurched from controversy to controversy...": Confidential interview.

143 an internal CIA auditing team: According to a confidential document in the possession of the author.

144 These problems were particularly true at the very top of the Thai military: Confidential interview. See also Mark Perry and Scott Malone, "How Scandal Almost Sank Our Secret Cambodia War," *The Washington Post*, October 30, 1988.

144 there was never any question of withholding the news: Confidential interview. An initial report given to me suggested that there was talk of a "cover-up" until it was decided that the Senate Intelligence Committee would "probably find out anyway." I choose to believe a much more authoritative account of a very senior CIA official who said that it was generally agreed the theft would not endanger the program. That seems most likely; Richard Stolz had his hand on the pulse of the agency at every minute and would have been privy to field reports on the operation.

145 Stolz told Senator David Boren: According to a confidential document in the possession of the author.

145 This team spent nearly a month: Confidential interview. A CIA-Senate team later made the same trip, according to documents in the author's possession.

145 Five Democrats on the: Confidential interview.

145 "Can you give us a good reason...": Ibid.

146 In exchange for keeping: According to a confidential document in the possession of the author.

146 nearly eight million dollars was set aside: Mark Perry and Scott Malone, "How Scandal Almost Sank Our Secret Cambodia War," *The Washington Post*, October 30, 1988. The incident is fully documented in a classified paper in the author's possession: "While agreeing to continue the program, the SSCI cut the FY 89 funding from $12 million to $8 million. Moreover, there will be quarterly reprogramming of approximately two million dollars for the program which will provide the opportunity for periodic Congressional review to ensure that funds are being properly expended and that control mechanisms now being put into place are working."

146 *The Washington Post*, which disclosed: Concern about the leak within the State Department bordered on the hysterical. A cable sent to the U.S. Embassy in Bangkok also showed that the government was taking steps to make certain the controversy did not grow: "We understand that *The Washington Post* plans to run a story... in the Sunday 'Outlook' section on corruption in the covert assistance program to the Cambodian NCR. It appears that they may have gotten access to authoritative documents on this issue, perhaps including the SSCI staff report. On October 28 David Ignatius, editor of

'Outlook,' called [Assistant Secretary of State Morton] Abramowitz who refused to comment. We are considering, however, whether to invite Ignatius in to go over the story with a view to making it the least damaging possible." In fact, Ignatius was called in but refused to soften the story, and it was published as scheduled. The leak did not come from the Senate Intelligence Committee, even though the CIA and State Department sent a team to its chairman, David Boren, accusing the committee members of releasing the audit. Boren went through the roof. State Department, CIA, and White House officials were chagrined when they realized that one of their own officers had leaked the document. They conducted a major internal executive department investigation to determine who he was. While they had several suspects, they were never able to prove who the leaker was. That gave Boren enormous satisfaction.

147 the front page of *The Bangkok Post*: "U.S. Urged to Retract Charge Against Military," *The Bangkok Post*, November 11, 1988. "Chavalit: Name Names or Go to Hell," *The Bangkok Post*, November 10, 1988. See also Nayan Chanda, "A Lethal Boost," *The Far Eastern Economic Review* (October 27, 1988).

147 Within days of the initial report: *Washington Post* foreign editor David Ignatius kiddingly claimed to Bradlee that he was the one burned in effigy.

147 "The President and the judge . . .": Author interview with former CIA officer James Greenleaf.

149 Within several weeks of the election: George Lardner, Jr., "Webster: Not Lobbying to Keep Job," *The Washington Post*, November 18, 1989. See also Don Oberdorfer, "Scowcroft Provides Policy Anchor," *The Washington Post*, November 24, 1988, and Don Oberdorfer, "Bush Urged to Select Strong Security Adviser," *The Washington Post*, November 12, 1988.

149 Webster said as much to his three top assistants: Confidential interview.

149 "slim and none": Ibid.

150 Stolz told Webster: Ibid.

150 "against every instinct I have": Ibid. Richard Stolz refused an interview with the author on this subject. While Webster was not usually so self-effacing, he often had difficulty promoting himself with elected officials, according to a close associate. He had maintained a low profile in the Reagan White House during his FBI years—a strategy that did not work in the Bush administration.

150 "We live in a dirty and dangerous . . .": Quoted in "Speech of William M. Baker," assistant director, Criminal Investigation Division, Federal Bureau of Investigation, before the Harvard Lecture Series, Boston, Massachusetts, July 27, 1989.

151 "[W]hat [Webster] wants is a smooth . . .": Author interview with CIA public affairs officer Mark Mansfield.
151 A report of the conversation: George Lardner, Jr., "Webster: Not Lobbying to Keep Job," *The Washington Post,* November 18, 1989.
151 James Baker was convinced that it would be a mistake: Confidential interview.
151 the last thing the CIA needed now: Ibid.

Six: Out of a Clear Sky

153 "Just before dawn . . .": Salman Rushdie, *The Satanic Verses* (New York: Viking, 1988), p. 3.
154 a cruising altitude: David Leppard and Nich Rufford, "Lockerbie: The Final Reckoning," *The Sunday Times* (London), December 17, 1989.
154 luggage container 14L: Ibid.
154 eighteen inches by twelve inches: Ibid.
154 Up to two years later: Author interview with former CIA and CTC officer Vincent Cannistraro.
154 ("like the ripping of . . ."): Author interview with FAA official Walter Korsgaard.
155 put aboard by a drug-toting dupe: Author interview with Pan Am investigator Daniel D'Ahroni. A copy of Pan Am's private report (the Interfors Report) is in the author's possession.
155 a CIA officer traveling on the aircraft: Confidential interview. This view was commonly held up to one year after the bombing and was being exhaustively investigated by a number of reporters. The view was reinforced by the fact that the luggage of State Department regional security officer Daniel O'Connor showed up on a carousel in New York two days after the explosion. Considering the difficulty of a bag switch, CIA investigators soon eliminated the possibility. The possibility was also investigated by Pan Am's New York and Washington lawyers, who were interviewed for this book. The rumor was fueled by an initial report, put out by the AP wire service ("CIA Beirut Chief Is Among the Dead") on December 25, 1988, that the CIA station chief had been aboard the aircraft.
155 an agency sting operation: Author interview with Pan Am investigator Daniel D'Ahroni.
155 a "showcase," as one report said: Michael Wines, "An Inquiry in Hot Pursuit," *The New York Times,* January 1, 1989.
155 The man in overall charge: Confidential interview. The director of the interagency Counterterrorism Center is Michael Gallagher of the Federal Bureau of Investigation. Gallagher would not agree to

an interview for this book. The FBI's team of investigators worked out of the bureau's Washington field office.

155 Dewey Clarridge had recommended him: Ibid.

156 a system known to the intelligence community as DESIST: Ibid.

156 "We could get information...": Ibid.

156 The Pan Am Task Force investigation: Ibid. A number of CIA officers sketched out the CTC's organization chart for this author, as well as details on how the Pan Am Task Force inside the center operated.

157 investigators had determined by then: Author interview with FAA official Walter Korsgaard.

158 He had an office at the White House: Author interview with former CIA and CTC officer Vincent Cannistraro.

158 In February 1987 he became a: Ibid.

158 "You just don't turn down...": Confidential interview. Confirmed by author interview with Vincent Cannistraro.

158 "probably wasn't the best thing...": Author interview with former CIA and CTC officer Vincent Cannistraro.

159 Korsgaard was dispatched to Karachi: Author interview with former FAA official Billy Vincent and former FAA official Walter Korsgaard.

159 "This was very unusual...": Confidential interview.

159 "Oh, yes," he replies when prompted, "I was in Athens ...": Author interview with former FAA official Walter Korsgaard.

159 During another overseas trip: Ibid.

159 "Walt had a hell of a time...": Confidential interview. Confirmed by author interview with former FAA official Walter Korsgaard.

160 On several occasions: Confidential interview.

160 On the morning of the second day: Author interview with former FAA official Walter Korsgaard.

160 "That's it," he said: Ibid.

160 In Tunis the CIA dispatched: Confidential interview.

160 As far away as Bangkok a CIA officer: Ibid.

161 Even in Jordan: Ibid.

161 McKee, who had been dispatched: Copies of Charles D. McKee's personal fitness reports dated from January 1975 to April 1986 are in the author's possession. See also Richard Gazarik, "Flight 103 victim on sensitive mission," and "McKee excelled in career," *Greensburg (Pa.) Tribune Review.*

161 Pan Am Clipper Club lounge: Airline documents, including itineraries, schedules, and documents from overseas travel bureaus that detail the travel plans of all the principals, are in the author's possession.

161 "There was a tragic sense of loss...": Author interview with former CIA and CTC officer Vincent Cannistraro.

162 Gannon was actually one of the graduates: Confidential interview.

162 Prior to being sent to Beirut: Ibid.

162 Newspaper articles published in the days: "CIA Beirut Chief Is Among the Dead," Associated Press, December 25, 1989.

163 he was involved in espionage operations: Confidential interview.

163 "Six temporary duty assignments...": Ibid.

163 The problem was exacerbated: Ibid.

163 Twetten and Turco were blamed: Ibid. The CIA was able to find where Buckley was being held but, for some reason, was unable to effect his rescue. One of Buckley's closest friends makes a very strong case that while some in the agency were intent on retrieving him at almost any cost, rescue attempts were hampered by red tape. One CIA officer states that the agency was actually able to get a picture of the building Buckley was being held in, a photograph that was immediately brought out of Lebanon and shipped to the United States. The agency was also able to interrogate Lebanese citizens who had seen Buckley in captivity. These reports were also passed on to the CIA. What is not known is why the agency was unable to rescue him if it had such precise information on his location.

163 "Buckley wasn't liked...": Ibid. See also Mark Perry, "The Secret Life of an American Spy," *Regardies,* February 1989.

164 Buckley's legacy was based on the physical courage: Author interview with Lieutenant Commander Chip Beck (USN). Beck was a close Buckley associate, worked diligently for his release, spoke at his memorial service, and gave the eulogy when Buckley's body was returned, in 1991, to the United States. He had served with Buckley in Vietnam and Beirut.

164 Through surrogates, secret agents: "What Can Be Done About Kaddafi?," *Newsweek,* December 3, 1984.

164 the NE division established links: Confidential interview.

164 headed by Libyan exile leader Aly Abuzaakouk: Ibid.

165 Operation Early Call: "What Can Be Done About Kaddafi?," *Newsweek,* December 3, 1984.

165 Libya Task Force chief Vince Cannistraro: David C. Martin and John Walcott, *Best Laid Plans* (New York: Harper & Row, 1988), pp. 315–16.

165 "redraw the map of North Africa": Ibid., p. 265. Bob Woodward and Don Oberdorfer were the first to report on a U.S.-Egyptian covert plan aimed at overthrowing the Qaddafi government.

165 The CIA's top adviser in Chad's capital: Confidential interview. In the course of my research on former CIA officer William Buckley,

I was allowed access to a number of classified documents on his career, as well as photographs of him on assignment in both Beirut and Chad.

166 The CIA determined that both the TWA bombing: Ibid.

166 A month before the bombing: Confidential interview. See also Youssef M. Ibrahim, "Libya Denies Link to Airline Blasts," *The Los Angeles Times,* June 28, 1991.

166 This Libyan army in exile: Clifford Krauss, "Failed Anti-Qaddafi Effort Leaves U.S. Picking Up the Pieces," *The New York Times,* March 12, 1991; Jack Anderson and Dale Van Atta, "CIA Backed Qaddafi Assassination Try," *The Washington Post,* June 12, 1985; and "Have Rebels Will Travel," *Newsweek,* March 25, 1991.

167 "Matt's death took a lot out...": Confidential interview.

167 at the last minute he changed: Copies of Gannon's itinerary and travel voucher are in the author's possession.

167 The guard was also a former member: According to a confidential document in the possession of the author.

168 Polhill was being held: Ibid.

168 A secret cable from the American Embassy in Beirut: Ibid.

168 "RSO [regional security officer] stated that...": Ibid.

168 "In my view, 'rescue money'": Ibid.

168 McKee, a six-foot-five-inch, 270-pound: From copies of Charles D. McKee's personal fitness reports dated January 1975 to April 1986.

169 "I said 'Where are you?' ": Richard Gazarik, "Flight 103 Victim on Sensitive Mission," and "McKee Excelled in Career," *Greensburg (Pa.) Tribune Review.*

169 "Maj. McKee continues to perform...": "Charles D. McKee Evaluation Report," U.S. Army, April 1986.

169 Among the personal effects: Copies of McKee's notebooks are in the possession of the author.

170 "was either assigned to or worked for the CIA": Confidential interview. Officially McKee was an officer serving with the Army's Intelligence and Security Command, though there is some doubt that he ever served with the DIA. According to one report, McKee served as assistant defense attaché in Lebanon and was a counterintelligence officer in Saudi Arabia. Another report says that he helped train the Saudi National Guard (a 1982 fitness report notes that McKee served as "Executive Officer for the Commanding General of the U.S. Military Training Mission to Saudi Arabia"); this is perhaps the best-documented evidence available that McKee performed the same job in Lebanon. Another fitness report describes him as "One of the U.S. Army's best."

170 a colleague remembers seeing him: Confidential interview.

170 Rashid was listed just below: Ibid.

171 Jabril headed a small, but dangerous: A February 1989 request to the DIA on information about the PFLP—GC and Ahmad Jabril was filed by reporter William C. Triplett and shared with this writer. It showed that DIA files contained 200 documents; 173 originated with other agencies and were referred to those agencies for response. The DIA released 8 documents and withheld 19. The CIA released 10, which were all unclassified FBIS reports. The NSA did not release documents, although the denying letter indicates the agency kept an extensive file on the organization. The State Department released 3 documents and withheld 6. The Army's Intelligence and Security Command had 5 documents on the group, all of which were listed as exempt from release. Clearly the U.S. government had a long history of investigating both Jabril and the PFLP—GC.

171 "All you have to do...": Author interview with former FAA official Billie Vincent.

171 For three months prior: According to a confidential document in the possession of the author. The Federal Aviation Administration issued no fewer than six separate bulletins on foreign threats to U.S. carriers in the months preceding the bombing of Pan Am 103. The most important bulletins were released in November and early December. There was a veritable flurry of intelligence activity on possible terrorist events right up until the night of December 21 and in the immediate aftermath of the Pan Am bombing.

171 "As of mid-November 1988...": Ibid.

172 they acted without U.S. knowledge: Confidential interview.

172 A top secret U.S. intelligence document: According to a confidential document in the possession of the author.

172 "Police raids on October 26...": Ibid.

172 Hafez Machmed Kassem al-Dalkamouni: "On the Trail of Terror," *U.S. News & World Report,* November 13, 1989, and John Walcott, "Jet-Bomb Probe Points at Radical Palestinian Unit," *The Wall Street Journal,* February 3, 1989.

173 "Preliminary analyses [have been completed] by West German authorities...": According to a confidential document in the possession of the author.

173 CTC officers also believed the Germans had bungled: Confidential interview. See also Gavin Hewitt, "Did German Bungling Lead to Pan Am 103?," *The Washington Post,* September 24, 1989.

173 CTC investigators discovered: Confidential inteview.

174 "Turco basically asked...": Ibid.

174 in a message to the U.S. Embassy in Helsinki: Edward Cody and David B. Ottaway, "Pan Am Bomb Probe Focuses on Palestinian Held in Sweden," *The Washington Post,* November 12, 1989.

174 "We knew something was going on...": Confidential interview.

174 Members of the Stockholm group: David Leppard and Nick Rufford, "Police Close In on Lockerbie Killers," *The Sunday Times* (London), December 17, 1989.

174 the suspects often traveled to Malta: Ibid.

175 The owner of Mary's House: Confidential interview.

175 "If you show me the picture of the man...": Ibid.

175 "That the Stockholm suspects...": Author interview with former CIA and CTC officer Vincent Cannistraro.

176 "It took us two months...": Ibid.

176 "That took us a little longer...": Ibid. Though CIA investigators eliminated the possibility that Gannon (or O'Connor's) bags were switched with one carrying the bomb, that was not the same as eliminating Gannon as a target.

176 "At one point in the investigation...": Ibid.

176 "I did not make the bomb...": Confidential interview.

177 Webster shielded Twetten: Ibid.

PART II: THE ANALYST

Seven: The Crisis of the CIA

183 the "militarization of intelligence": Confidential interview. See also George Lardner, Jr., "In a Changing World, CIA Reorganizing to Do More with Less," *The Washington Post,* July 5, 1991.

184 "filled with guys in uniform": Ibid.

184 National Photo Interpretation Center: Ibid. The first intelligence photo interpretation laboratory was established inside the CIA in 1953 as the Photographic Interpretation Division (PID), according to Jeffrey T. Richelson, a noted author on the subject. The NPIC was an outgrowth of this first office, which was enlarged throughout the 1950s. The DS&T also operates an Office of Development and Engineering, an Office of SIGINT Operations, and an Office of Research and Development.

184 the National Security Agency: The growth of the NSA and NRO are accurately charted in *Blank Check,* by *Philadelphia Inquirer* reporter Tim Weiner (New York: Warner Books, 1990). See also George Lardner, Jr., "In a Changing World, CIA Reorganizing to Do More with Less," *The Washington Post,* July 5, 1991.

185 The NSA is responsible for: Jeffrey T. Richelson, *The U.S. Intelligence Community* (Cambridge, Mass.: Ballinger, 1989), pp. 21–6.

185 over $850 million in total funding: Confidential information. The most recent, most accurate figure for total military intelligence spending was published in *The U.S. Intelligence Community*. Richelson

says the DIA has a budget (in 1989) of $450 million. Each of the other major services has a budget of at least $410 million. The $850 million above—for the total of the four services—is a very conservative estimate.

185 The DIA spends: *The U.S. Intelligence Community,* p. 42.

186 according to one authoritative estimate: Author interview with William H. Webster. No one agrees on any of the figures. One CIA officer goes so far as to say that "only a few people at the top of the agency really know." Webster's statement accords with estimates made by John Ranelagh in *The Agency.* Ranelagh puts the total yearly budget for the agency at one billion dollars and for the NSA at ten billion.

186 a budget estimated at: *The Agency,* p. 677.

186 a hundred million dollars on espionage programs: Author interview with William H. Webster. Webster never cited an exact figure, saying only that the espionage budget was a hundred million dollars. He obviously meant that hundred million was for covert operations, a much more narrowly defined activity.

186 While officers of the clandestine service: Confidential interview.

186 nearly 20 percent of all officers: Ibid. Accounts vary on the percentage of officers who have resigned, sought reassignment, or retired from the CIA from 1980 to 1990. Sometimes the figures overestimate, or underestimate, the numbers that have left—depending on the speaker's point of view. Even conservative estimators, however, admit that the agency was critically damaged because of Casey's reign and by the Iran-contra revelations.

187 The most important corps: Ibid.

187 One of the best young officers: Ibid. The name of this person is generally known in the intelligence community but cannot be printed here.

188 on an autumn night in 1986: Ibid.

189 Casey wanted to create: Ibid. Did Casey actually foresee the collapse of the Soviet Union? It is doubtful. Instead, as Bobby Ray Inman noted, "it's more likely that he was hypothesizing from a position of pure faith. No one ever thought the cold war would go on forever."

189 "one of the most controversial...": Author interview with former CIA and CTC officer Vincent Cannistraro.

190 "The CTC was the model...": Ibid.

190 "At the time of the TWA hijacking...": Confidential interview.

190 "We damn near had a civil war...": Ibid.

191 the CTC circumvented: Ibid.

191 "There's a very dangerous trend...": "Sworn Testimony of Mel

Goodman before the Senate Select Committee on Intelligence," September 25, 1991.

191 "We gave them the lead...": Author interview with former CIA and CTC official Vincent Cannistraro.

191 *City of Poros*: Confidential interview. This CIA officer says that "the *City of Poros* operation was the last straw for the agency; after they killed all those people in Greece, we had to break them up." The implication of the statement was that the CIA had been gathering information on the Abu Nidal organization for some time (another source says since the early 1980s) but had taken no steps to break it up. As this book was going to press, reporter Patrick Seale published *Abu Nidal: A Gun for Hire*, giving other details of the incident itself. His account does not differ from mine.

192 Using moderate Palestinian: Ibid.

192 the agency's close cooperation: Author interview in Tunis with Abu Iyad (Salah Khalaf), second-in-command of the PLO.

193 "bringing in scores of defectors...": Ibid.

193 Three of the most important defectors: Youssef M. Ibrahim, "Arabs Say Deadly Power Struggle Has Split Abu Nidal Terror Group," *The New York Times*, November 12, 1989.

193 Nidal later threatened: Author interview in Tunis with Abu Iyad (Salah Khalaf), second-in-command of the PLO.

193 the struggle between the PLO and ANO: Ibid.

193 The CIA had also secretly tracked ANO operations: Confidential interview. The operation continued well into 1990, when the arm's length CIA-PLO cooperation became much closer. According to reporter Jonathan Randall of *The Washington Post,* the PLO regularly turned over to the CIA ANO documents obtained by defectors from Nidal's Tripoli-based organization. Included in the documents was "a wealth of details about his [Nidal's] recruiting techniques, Swiss and Austrian bank accounts, multimillion-dollar arms deals, safe houses and a network of cells—active and dormant—in Eastern and Western Europe, the Arab world, Southeast Asia and the Indian subcontinent...." During a personal interview PLO official Abu Iyad confirmed much of this information, adding that the PLO's fight with Nidal was "to the death, but we will win."

193 nearly three hundred ANO operatives: Confidential interview.

193 "We took the ANO apart...": Author interview with former CIA and CTC officer Vincent Cannistraro.

194 Casey unexpectedly decided that the CIA should expand: Confidential interview.

194 the head of the Soviet Collection Division, Ted Carlson: Ibid.

195 Casey felt at ease: Author interview with Herbert Meyer.

195 "...these damn fools always wanted...": *Casey*, p. 456.

196 "Bill Casey hated surprises...": Author interview with Herbert Meyer.

196 more than 150 American corporations: Confidential interview.

196 Casey appointed Kelly: Ibid.

196 "It was a straightforward espionage operation...": Ibid.

197 "In addition to the commercial information...": William Casey, "Address to the Denver Chief Executive Officers," Denver, Colorado, July 30, 1986.

197 "We have reorganized our component...": Ibid.

197 "This step was very controversial...": Confidential interview.

198 On the afternoon of June 24, 1988: Patrick E. Tyler, "High Link Seen in Cairo Spy Case," *The Washington Post*, August 20, 1988. See also Adel Darwish and Gregory Alexander, *Unholy Babylon* (New York: St. Martin's Press, 1991), pp. 171–72.

198 Their destination, called Cairo-South: Confidential interview.

198 a criminal complaint was filed: Robert Gillette, "Third World Missiles Linked to German Firm, Italian Firms," *The Los Angeles Times*, March 11, 1989.

198 the arrest of three suspects: *Unholy Babylon*, pp. 171–72.

198 including Egypt's defense minister: Patrick E. Tyler, "High Link Seen in Cairo Spy Case," *The Washington Post*, August 20, 1988.

198 "It was going to be one hell of a missile...": Confidential interview.

198 this scheme to build an Arab missile: Ibid.

199 The CIA was first tipped: Ibid.

199 Egyptian agents approached scientists: Ibid.

199 Another West German company, Consen: Robert Gillette, "Third World Missiles Linked to German Firm, Italian Firms," *The Los Angeles Times*, March 11, 1989.

199 An MBB subsidiary company: Kenneth R. Timmerman, *The Death Lobby* (Boston: Houghton Mifflin, 1991), pp. 151–54. The fourth suspect in the attempt to export American high-tech products illegally was Colonel Hussam Yossef, who was, according to one official, "in overall command of the illegal export operation from his base in Austria." Helmy later pleaded guilty to a reduced charge of exporting materials without a license and cooperated with American officials in the investigation.

199 Egyptian agents approached SNIA-BPD: Ibid.

200 "They were doing it by piecing together...": Confidential interview.

201 Ekkehard Schrotz: Ibid.

202 a West German firm, Messerschmitt: *The Death Lobby*, pp. 151–54.

202 nearly fifty Scud-B mobile launchers: Confidential interview.

202 "The Egyptians were the intermediaries...": Ibid. In addition to the NCD, independent investigations by the Customs Service linked

Egypt's defense minister, Field Marshal Abdul Halim Abu Ghazala, with the conspiracy. According to published reports, Ghazala approved the illegal export operation during a trip to Washington to sign a ten-year "memorandum of understanding" giving Egypt special status as a strategic ally. Evidence of his involvement was also shown by transcripts of intercepted telephone conversations in which his name was mentioned by Egyptian military officers. During Ghazala's Washington visit one of his entourage, carrying a diplomatic passport with the name Fouad Mohamed, traveled to California to meet with Helmy. They returned to Washington bearing two heavy boxes containing the carbon-carbon materials. The unknown Egyptian officer, later identified as Brigadier General Yehye Almagal, was a member of Ghazala's headquarters staff specializing in procurement.

203 There was no longer any doubt that the clandestine service was under attack: Confidential interview.

204 "The CIA was scared to death...": Ibid.

204 "We could never get a clear answer...": Ibid.

204 "We sent our people out to talk to...": Ibid.

205 "The Japanese did it from day one...": Ibid.

Eight: A Man for This Season

206 "There were jokes circulating...": Confidential interview.

207 the State Department sent a report: According to a confidential document in the possession of the author.

207 "Qaddafi has the jitters...": Ibid.

208 To heighten the pressure on Qaddafi: Confidential interview.

208 secret report ... identified three German companies: Ibid.

209 "we have to be more than ready": Ibid.

210 This promise came during a private telephone conversation: Ibid.

210 The Public Affairs Office continually emphasized: Author interview with Mark Mansfield and other CIA public affairs officers.

210 "The judge continues to have the...": Ibid.

211 headlined CIA AIDE ACTS TO LIFT REPRIMAND: Walter Pincus, "CIA Aide Acts to Lift Reprimand," *The Washington Post*, January 1, 1989.

211 a "brilliant man": Author interview with Herbert Meyer.

211 "more than just a little weird...": Confidential interview.

211 "a remarkable seventy-two-hour marathon": Ibid.

212 Allen first became involved: *Iran-Contra*, Appendix B, vol. 12, pp. 105–06. See also *A Very Thin Line*, p. 268. Allen was also present, earlier, when Dewey Clarridge tried to find a carrier for arms bound to Iran.

212 Allen's fears were heightened: *Iran-Contra*, Appendix B, vol. 1, pp. 992–1000.
213 Allen told Deputy Director of Intelligence: *A Very Thin Line*, p. 437.
213 During an October 1 meeting: Ibid., p. 437.
213 "I can't prove it...": Ibid., p. 438.
213 Ernest Miller and Donald Fraser: Ibid., pp. 438–40, 510. In fact, Furmark's report to Casey was a lie: Khashoggi invented the scheme and had Furmark carry it out in order to get his payment; there was no group of angry Canadian investors involved in the Iran-contra affair. Fraser knew Khashoggi, as did Miller, but they did not lend him any money having to do with shipments of arms to Iran. Khashoggi later said that the money actually came from a Saudi business associate. Theodore Draper, in *A Very Thin Line*, notes: "The deception practiced by Khashoggi about his mythical Canadian creditors did not reflect well on CIA Director Casey's acumen in this final phase of his life." To make it plain, it seems that Casey was allowing the nation's leading intelligence agency to be threatened with blackmail.
214 Gates responded to Allen's warning: Ibid., p. 446.
214 He had been a valued adviser to DCI Casey: Confidential interview.
215 Allen, they said, took advantage of his access: "Sworn Testimony of Mel Goodman before the Senate Select Committee on Intelligence," September 25, 1991. Allen had a fascinating career, as a briefer to the NSC, a writer of classified biographies, and a trusted adviser to several heads of the CIA. In the early years of the Reagan administration he came to know Oliver North as a member of the continuity of government project. COG was put together to plan for a post-nuclear America. See "The Doomsday Government," Cable News Network, Mary Whittington, Producer, November 17, 1991. See also Eric Schmitt, "Nuclear War Plan in 80's Skirted the Constitution," *The New York Times*, November 18, 1991.
215 "They circled the wagons...": Confidential interview.
216 "Charlie knew that Judge Webster...": Ibid.
216 In the midst of the Bruemmer inquiry: Ibid.
216 "Allen warned Casey, warned Gates...": Ibid.
216 "The idea was to keep Allen out of the way...": Ibid.
216 "They probably thought he was going to...": Author interview with former FAA official Billie Vincent.
217 "The military hated his guts...": Confidential interview.
217 "Warning is a process...": Michael Wines, "CIA Sidelines Its Gulf Cassandra," *The New York Times*, January 24, 1991.
217 a man of "ability and integrity": Ibid.
218 That scandal would not have happened, Baker believed: Confidential interview.

218 well-known conservatism on defense issues: Ibid. See also Molly Moore, "Cheney Predicts Gorbachev Will Fail, Be Replaced," *The Washington Post,* April 29, 1989.

218 Scowcroft was a powerful voice: Don Oberdorfer, "Scowcroft Provides Policy Anchor," *The Washington Post,* November 24, 1988.

219 "pussycat with claws": Mark Rezendas, "A 'Pussycat' with Claws, Sununu Leaving Mark in Home State," *The Washington Post,* December 24, 1988.

219 In 1973 he was named: Patrick E. Tyler, "Skeptic with Strong Views," *The New York Times,* May 15, 1991.

219 Gates first met Bush: Confidential interview.

219 In 1983 he became chairman: "The New Spy Wars," *U.S. News & World Report,* June 3, 1991.

220 Casey's former special assistant: Ibid.

220 "I'm a very big Gates fan": Author interview with Herbert Meyer.

220 Gates set to work immediately after Bush's inauguration: Confidential interview.

221 He was actually in virtual control: Ibid. See also Patrick E. Tyler, "Skeptic with Strong Views," *The New York Times,* May 15, 1991, and Andrew Rosenthal, "Bush Picks Deputy for U.S. Security to Head the CIA," *The New York Times,* May 15, 1991.

221 One CIA officer, who views him: Confidential interview.

221 Nor was Gates extolled as the Soviet Expert: Ibid. See also Don Oberdorfer, "Baker Blocked Speech by NSC Deputy on Gorbachev Reforms," *The Washington Post,* October 28, 1989.

222 a Russian agent code-named Trigon: "The New Spy Wars," *U.S. News & World Report,* June 3, 1991.

222 CIA officers later discovered: Ibid.

222 "Casey would see the Russian bear...": Confidential interview.

222 "I've always liked Bob Gates...": Author interview with David Whipple.

222 he went out of his way to praise Webster's grasp: Confidential interview.

223 "complete nonsense": Author interview with William Webster.

223 "If he'd called over here...": Confidential interview.

223 "I don't pay attention...": Ibid.

223 "It was always this 'well, if this happens ...' ": Ibid.

223 "It's anathema": Author interview with former CIA Director of Intelligence Ray Cline.

224 "Anyone who can get along...": Confidential interview.

225 Kerr believed that Gates had made a number of: Ibid.

225 "Gates disappointed us...": Ibid.

225 "My assignments to the NSC...": "Statement of Robert M. Gates,"

SSCI nomination of Robert M. Gates to be director of central intelligence, October 3, 1991.

225 "I intend to insure...": Ibid.
226 For thirty-five years the line separating: Confidential interview.
226 There was even a time: Ibid.
226 "The two never mesh...": Author interview with former CIA officer David Whipple.
226 "the lineal descendant of the same threat...": Patrick E. Tyler, "Skeptic with Strong Views," *The New York Times,* May 15, 1991.
227 Kerr was heavily influenced by Gorbachev's: Confidential interview. See also Jeffrey R. Smith, "CIA Assesses Effect of Gorbachev Cuts," *The Washington Post,* December 13, 1988, and Patrick E. Tyler and Molly Moore, "Soviet Defense Spending Cut as Promised, CIA Reports," *The Washington Post,* November 15, 1989.
227 Kerr argued that Gorbachev's announcement: David B. Ottaway, "CIA Defends Reports on Soviet Moves," *The Washington Post,* March 1, 1989.
227 "Sometimes the people that are making the decisions..." Ibid.

Nine: Lao Pengyou

229 The three men who: Author interview with James Lilley.
230 "An important, coveted post...": *Looking Forward,* p. 130.
230 "Busher, who ride the bicycle...": Ibid., p. 139.
230 Before Lilley began his diplomatic career: Confidential interview. In an interview with the author, China scholar Michael Oksenberg called Lilley "one of the most creative thinkers on China that I have ever met."
230 "thoughtful, intelligent, good professional": Confidential interview. In an interview with the author, China scholar Robert Ross said that he views Lilley as "one of the CIA's best resources ever" and "a man who can be trusted in China."
231 he began his CIA career: Mark Perry and Jeff Goldberg, "Will Judge Webster Be Benched?" *The Nation* (April 15, 1991).
231 Lilley also returned to Langley: Author interview with James Lilley. See also Charles Bremner, "Asia Hand Holding Steady," *The Times* (London), June 14, 1989.
231 Lilley retired from the CIA in 1978: Ibid.
231 The trip was put together: Author interview with Richard Allen.
231 "We needed to put to rest...": Ibid.
231 "He kept asking us...": Author interview with James Lilley.
232 "If Reagan had read that speech...": Confidential interview.
232 future attorney general, Edwin Meese: Ibid.

233 "it was very unusual for CIA people...": Author interview with Richard Allen.

234 "trade with China stood...": According to a confidential document in the personal possession of the author.

235 the long-running power struggle: Confidential interview.

235 From their vantage point: Ibid. Former Ambassador Lilley confirmed that the United States had several "listening posts" throughout the city during the night of the massacre.

236 Within two hours after the first attack: Fred Shapiro, "Letter from Beijing," *The New Yorker*, June 19, 1989.

236 "We could hear popping sounds...": Ibid.

236 "The demonstrators will be removed...": Author interview with James Lilley.

237 Only five major embassy officers: Ibid.

237 Small skirmishes were reported: Fred Shapiro, "Letter from Beijing," *The New Yorker*, June 19, 1989.

237 While the massacre continued: Daniel Southerland, "Troops Roll Through Beijing to Crush Protesters; Hundreds Feared Killed as Chinese Fight Back," *The Washington Post*, June 4, 1989.

238 By far the most interesting report: Confidential interview.

238 According to CIA monitors: Interview with Michael Oksenberg. See also Jesse Birnbaum and Howard G. Chua Eoan, "Despair and Death in a Beijing Square," *Time*, June 12, 1989.

238 in front of the Beijing Hotel: Fred Shapiro, "Letter from Beijing," *The New Yorker*, June 19, 1989. According to American intelligence officers who witnessed these events, the army's actions at the Beijing Hotel provide evidence that the 27th Army commander Chi Hoatian and his uncle Yang Shangkun (a prominent member of the politburo and China's president) purposely decided to wipe out all pro-democracy resistance with an overwhelming show of force. "I think the evidence is very strong for the belief that the events around Tienanmen reflected an intraparty power play by Yang," China expert Michael Oksenberg says. Professor Oksenberg also agrees with intelligence interpretations of the role of the People's Security units in the events of June 4. In the days after the Tienanmen incident, Oksenberg began to study the thesis that the People's Security units opposed the military's violent suppression of the pro-democracy movement: "In my study I've found that at no time during the Tienanmen incident is there evidence that the state security apparatus was involved in any way. Nor can I find any evidence that they took part, any part whatsoever, in suppressing the rebellion."

238 The bodies of those killed: Nicholas D. Kristof, "Tiananmen Crackdown, Students Account Questioned on Major Points," *The New York*

Times, June 13, 1989. There was no shooting inside the square itself. The first reporter to note this was Kristof of *The New York Times,* who says that Chinese student accounts of a slaughter in the square were incorrect. Instead, as reflected here, most of the killing took place in the Muxidi district to the west of the square (along Chang'an Avenue) and then, later, north of the square. According to Kristof, "While troops were shooting in all areas around the square, they did not attack the students who were then clustered around the monument [in Tiananmen]. Instead, the students . . . were negotiating with the troops and decided to leave at dawn, between 5 A.M. and 6 A.M." My account of the events in Beijing disagrees with Kristof's in this instance: The students were negotiating with units of the People's Security apparatus at the time that Chinese military units were battling students in western Beijing and moving in from the East. Kristof does not mention the negotiations.

239 Lilley was horrified: Author interview with James Lilley.

239 "those greaseballs, those thugs": Ibid.

240 attempted to recruit Chinese bureaucrats: Confidential interview.

240 a woman code-named Lily Petal: Roger Faligot and Remi Kauffer, *The Chinese Secret Service* (New York: William Morrow, 1987), pp. 226–27.

240 Jack Downey, alias John Donovan: Ibid., p. 226.

240 known at the agency by the name Larry Wu-Tai Chin: Ibid., pp. 226, 240.

241 (For a time Cline was even considered the DI's . . .): Author interview with former CIA Director of Intelligence Ray Cline.

241 "It just wasn't in the cards": Ibid.

241 the CIA engineered the overthrow of Ghana's Kwame Nkrumah: Confidential interview. Agency operations that targeted China often involved a variety of colorful CIA officers in other divisions. The Kwame Nkrumah coup is a case in point. Howard Bane, who fought the Chinese in Thailand in the mid–1950s, was the CIA's chief of station in Accra, Ghana's capital, in 1966, when orders came for him to help a group of Ghana's military officers overthrow Nkrumah. Bane's plan to "attack the embassy with rocket launchers . . . spray it with machine-gun fire, and sprinkle it with grenades" was vetoed by his superiors at Langley, who laconically cabled him instructions: "Just overthrow Nkrumah!" The coup took place on February 24, 1966, but Bane, according to one colleague, was sorely disappointed that his plan for dealing with the Chinese, to "blow the whole lot up with dynamite," was rejected.

241 The Chinese witch-hunt: *The Chinese Secret Service,* p. 361–62. See also John Byron and Robert Pack, *The Claws of the Dragon* (New York: Simon and Schuster, 1992), pp. 301–03.

241 "Anybody with any brains . . .": Confidential interview.

242 Among the most valuable Chinese agents: Ibid.

242 "Their security and intelligence officers . . .": Ibid. The CIA's recruiting program was indirectly helped by China's disenchantment with the USSR. A portent of this division was first posited by agency analysts in 1955, when Ray Cline (then head of the Office of Current Intelligence) demanded "the application of rigorous common standards of political and economic analysis to all parts of this vast totalitarian empire, which I was certain could not be the monolith of which it was then fashionable to speak." The ideological rivalry was made public in 1960, when the USSR withdrew its scientific teams from China. The CIA continued to push its view that the Sino-Soviet split was a fact of life that could be creatively used by the United States to enhance its position in Asia, but it did so against increasingly strident critics whose own world view could not accord to different versions of communism.

242 "We were shocked to learn . . .": Ibid.

242 In 1971, when President Nixon and Henry Kissinger: One of Kissinger's first requests during his secret 1971 visit to Beijing was the release of CIA spies Downey and Fecteau. Kissinger proposed an exchange: "You have recently tried to infiltrate the CIA using one of your agents in Europe who defected to us. We immediately saw through it. We are going to return him to you. And you have men whom we would like to recover. Let us hope that such incidents are not repeated in the future." The Chinese mole was Liao Heshu, a "defector" from Holland who turned himself into the Dutch police with the words "I want to defect to the West, put me in contact with the CIA." Liao was responsible for kidnapping Chinese engineer Xu Zicai, and after an intensive interrogation it was clear that he was a Chinese double agent. He was thereafter given a job at the CIA translations department, while the CIA hierarchy decided what to do with him. In 1971 the swap was made.

243 The Chinese supplied the guerrillas: Chinese intelligence officials and their CIA counterparts had to go through some tense and even comic incidents before they were able to cooperate completely. According to a report published in The Chinese Secret Service, "American narcotics agents based in Pakistan mistook the first Chinese [mujaheddin] instructors for drug-traffickers from Hong Kong and had them arrested by the local authorities."

243 the CIA also helped fund: George Lardner and R. Jeffrey Smith, "Intelligence Ties Endure Despite U.S.-China Strain," The Washington Post, June 25, 1989.

243 CIA researchers observed that some Chinese Army: Confidential interview. See also "The Chinese Army's Uneasy Truce with Itself,"

Newsweek (June 19, 1989); Robert Delfs, "Repression and Reprisal," *The Far Eastern Economic Review,* June 22, 1989. Dr. Robert Ross of the Brookings Institution gave a number of useful insights on the Chinese Army during an interview in June 1989.

243 A top secret CIA study: According to a confidential document in the possession of the author.

244 The Chinese provided massive shipments: George Lardner and R. Jeffrey Smith, "Intelligence Ties Endure Despite U.S.-China Strain," *The Washington Post,* June 25, 1989.

244 the resulting mammoth and expensive construction project: Ibid.

244 Cobra Dane and Cobra Judy: Ibid.

245 "One of the best listening posts...": Mark Perry and Jeff Goldberg, "Will Judge Webster Be Benched?," *The Nation,* April 15, 1991.

245 Lilley diligently conveyed: Confidential interview.

246 Webster was castigated: Ibid.

246 Operation Yellow Bird: Gavin Hewitt, "The Great Escape from China," *The Washington Post,* June 2, 1991.

246 "Let's put it this way...": Confidential interview.

246 On the morning of the massacre: Ibid. In an interview with the author Michael Oksenburg laid out a very similar thesis for CIA-Chinese cooperation in the wake of Tienanmen. "I personally believe that the Tienanmen massacre was a reflection of an intraparty struggle," he said. "I don't think that they intended it to be that violent, and when it was, a part of the party just rejected it. There's strong evidence to suggest that they helped some of the students get out of the square alive, and there's at least reason to believe that some elements in the Chinese security apparatus continued that program for quite some time afterward."

247 The escape of all four: Associated Press, "Activists in Hong Kong Assist 4 Chinese Dissidents to Escape," *The Washington Post,* June 27, 1989.

247 During the last week of May: Confidential interview.

247 Chinese astrophysicist Feng Lizhi: Author interview with James Lilley.

247 "China is not the most...": Ibid.

248 initially organized by pro-democracy sympathizers: "Activists Determined to Continue Fight," Hong Kong AFP (reporting service), December 27, 1989; "Prodemocracy Activist Rejects Accusations," Hong Kong AFP, December 27, 1989.

248 the British consul general there: Confidential interview.

248 CIA East Asia expert John Gilhooley: Ibid.

248 the "Dare to Die Brigade": "Hong Kong, Macao Stowaway Helpers Arrested," Xinhua Domestic Service, December 25, 1989.

249 it adopted more sophisticated methods: Gavin Hewitt, "The Great Escape from China," *The Washington Post,* June 2, 1991.

Ten: Negligent Homicide

252 "just one victory, somewhere": "Statement of Alan Fiers," Senate Select Committee on Intelligence, September 19, 1991.

252 Noriega was "a son of a bitch": Confidential interview.

253 Langley was able to put together: Ibid.

254 The most powerful proponent of this view: Ibid.

254 At about midday on the twenty-sixth: "CID Report of Investigation [Final]," U.S. Army Criminal Investigation Command, June 29, 1989.

254 at about twenty minutes after two: Ibid.

254 Clark's car was thrown across the highway: Ibid.

255 the Department of the Army's: Ibid.

255 "secondary to a car accident": Ibid.

256 the crash "was so unexpected...": Ibid.

256 the Pentagon immediately dispatched: Confidential interview.

256 A second team, comprised of officials: Ibid. The confidential source said that the second team of investigators was secretly dispatched from the CIA, but this could not be confirmed. A reinvestigation, however, was conducted after a number of senators urged the Pentagon to review the findings. New York Republican Senator Alfonse D'Amato was most instrumental in calling for a new investigation. An official report filed by the U.S. Army's Criminal Investigations Division (CID), on the other hand, notes that no other investigative teams were dispatched to Panama, but both CIA and State Department sources say otherwise. "They [at the CIA] didn't treat this as a normal incident," a former CIA official said, while an employee of the State Department remembers accidentally seeing "diplomatic security cables" on a "separate State Department investigation; there were a lot of questions about what happened to Gerry Clark."

256 "Gerry Clark died in an automobile accident...": Author interview with General Patrick Black, U.S. Army. Black made a number of telephone calls on the Clark accident, all of them to reporters covering the story. *Newsday* reporter Knut Royce, for instance, remembers Black calling him and saying, "There's no story here," the exact words he used with me. In all, a Pentagon official says, General Black made more than thirty calls to reporters. General Black reached me after hearing from his own sources on Capitol Hill that I was following up on Clark's death. He initiated the call.

256 "It just seemed so odd...": Author interview with Colonel James V. Coniglio.

256 "Anyone who thinks that this...": Ibid.

256 Officially Clark was on assignment: Ibid.

257 the colonel was carrying a briefcase packed with: Confidential interview.

257 "Gerry just didn't think...": Ibid.

257 "a schoolyard bully" and "a snarling dog": Ibid. Clark's disdain for Noriega was well known to congressional committee aides as well as to his colleagues in the intelligence community.

257 "despised Noriega, and the feeling was mutual": Author interview with José Blandón.

258 "That son of a bitch": Author interview with Senator Alfonse D'Amato.

258 It was not until late May: Confidential interview.

259 where he was asked "by an acquaintance...": "CID Report of Investigation [Final]," U.S. Army Criminal Investigation Command, June 29, 1989.

259 "Well, Pocho showed up...": Ibid.

259 U.S. military intelligence investigators obtained: The copy of the rental agreement is in the author's possession.

259 "the death of Col. Gerald E. Clark ... was just an unfortunate: "CID Report of Investigation [Final]," U.S. Army Criminal Investigation Command, June 29, 1989.

260 "All the people who were interested...": Author interview with José Blandón.

260 "I was surprised Ollie showed up": Confidential interview.

261 "I would be very, very careful...": Author interview with Colonel James V. Coniglio.

261 three PDF soldiers assaulted: Tom Donnelly, "Terror in Panama," *Army Times*, March 20, 1989. See also William Branigin, "Americans in Panama Complain of Harassment," *The Washington Post*, April 11, 1989.

261 A U.S. Army sergeant was attacked: Ibid.

261 "almost 1000 total harassment incidents...": According to a confidential document in the possession of the author.

261 "The incidents involving the Panama Defense Forces...'": Ibid.

261 the agency reported that: Ibid.

261 Another special intelligence summary sent to Baker: Confidential interview. The intelligence document used to brief the secretary of state is in the author's possession.

261 "The economic sanctions have now taken...": According to a confidential document in the possession of the author.

262 U.S. intelligence agencies believed one incident: Ibid.

262 from a high-level executive of the Discount Bank and Trust Company of Geneva: Ibid.

263 "Suggestions have been made that...": Ibid.

264 "Hawari operatives travel to Panama...": Ibid.

264 "Three Lebanese Palestinians...": Ibid.

264 "Several factors challenge...": Ibid.

264 the agency "was certainly aware": Confidential interview.

265 "They don't run their raw intelligence...": Ibid.

265 "There was a lot at stake...": Ibid.

265 "They created the mess...": Ibid.

265 Former Assistant Secretary of State: Tom Donnelly, "Terror in Panama," *Army Times,* March 20, 1989.

265 "The Chairman has chosen to deal with...": Ibid.

266 "[The CIA station chief] wanted to push Noriega...": Confidential interview.

268 The program grew out of: William Scott Malone (reported with Mark Perry and Tony Kimery), "The Panama Debacle—Uncle Sam Wimps Out," *The Washington Post,* April 23, 1989.

268 Muse soon recruited: Neil C. Livingstone, "Danger in the Air," *Washingtonian,* June 1990. See also *Panama: The Whole Story,* p. 176.

269 When the station unexpectedly went off the air: Ibid.

269 "You're ashamed of your profession...": Ibid.

269 Muse was running eight radio stations: Ibid.

270 Muse was also approached: Confidential interview.

270 provided Muse with tapes: Author interview with Bosco Vallarino.

270 admired Muse's "creativity and courage": Neil C. Livingstone, "Danger in the Air," *Washingtonian,* June 1990. See also "U.S. Move in Panama Called Inept," *The Washington Post,* April 28, 1989; News service report, "Panama Arrests American," *Washington Post,* April 8, 1989.

270 Two weeks later Webster: Ibid.

270 After the meeting Cheney: Confidential interview.

271 disclosed that the opposition would receive funds: Ibid.

271 THEY SOLD THEIR COUNTRY FOR $10 MILLION: *Panama: The Whole Story,* p. 176. See also William Branigin, "The Mean Season," *The Washington Post,* April 29, 1989, and William Branigin, "Opponents of Noriega Warn of Electoral Fraud," *The Washington Post,* April 19, 1989.

271 The new opposition candidate: Ibid., p. 173. The three opposition candidates were opposed in the campaign by Carlos Duque, an obese crony of the dictator's who had profited from his rule by heading Transit, SA, a Noriega-linked business. Duque's two vice-presidential running mates were Major Ramón Sieiro (Noriega's brother-in-law) and Aquilino Boyd, Panama's version of Harold Stassen and a member of one of the nation's leading families. Boyd, it was said, would do anything to be president, while Duque wanted

nothing more than to guard his own lucrative business interests. All three realized they owed their positions and their pending election to Noriega, and they ran on a nationalist campaign filled with anti-American invective.

272 "The government is taking the election by fraud": *Panama: The Whole Story*, p. 179.
272 "The Panamanian people have spoken...": Ibid.
272 as the three opposition leaders paraded: Ann Devroy and Molly Moore, "Noriega's Forces Attack, Club Opposition Candidates," *The Washington Post*, May 11, 1989.
273 Arias Calderón was clubbed: Ibid.
273 His head snapped several times: Ibid.
273 "I would love to see them..." *Panama: The Whole Story*, p. 183.
274 The second step took place in July: Ibid., pp. 189–90.
274 boarded a specially designed military intelligence aircraft: Confidential interview.

Eleven: The Blame Business

275 Late on the afternoon of October 1: *Panama: The Whole Story*, p. 198.
275 The request was quickly passed up the line: Confidential interview.
275 Giroldi was the least likely: *Panama: The Whole Story*, p. 197.
276 Two hours after the initial phone call: Ibid., p. 198.
276 Still, the CIA officers did not respond: Confidential interview.
276 The plotters must know, he said: Ibid.
276 Giroldi replied that his intention: *Panama: The Whole Story*, p. 198.
277 A number of CIA officers were especially leery: Confidential interview.
277 "a less-than-even chance of...": *Panama: The Whole Story*, p. 199. See also John M. Goshko, "Left Alone by Plotters, Noriega Phoned Rescuers, Webster Says," *The Washington Post*, November 4, 1989.
278 Among the plotters: *Divorcing the Dictator*, p. 386.
278 (Colonel Guillermo Wong ...): Confidential interview.
278 Thurman ... was convinced that Noriega: David Hoffman and Ann Devroy, "U.S. Was Caught Off Guard by Coup Attempt," *The Washington Post*, October 6, 1989.
278 Giroldi had shown almost unbelievable courage: *Divorcing the Dictator*, p. 279.
278 Giroldi sent word on Monday morning: William Branigin, "Rebel Ignored Plea to Delay Coup," *The Washington Post*, October 14, 1989.
279 The CIA also got ready by: Confidential interview.
279 many experts at the agency: Ibid.
279 At about eight: *Divorcing the Dictator*, p. 382.

279 Visibly sweating and emotionally shaken: Ibid., p. 383.

279 A confident Giroldi, posted down the hall: Ibid., p. 384.

280 A number of the coup plotters argued: Ibid., p. 386.

280 Approximately five hundred yards from: Neil C. Livingstone, "Danger in the Air," *Washingtonian*, June 1990.

280 Deborah DeMoss received a phone call: *Panama: The Whole Story*, pp. 203–05.

281 Meanwhile, back at the Comandancia: Ibid., 205.

281 come to get him, "right now": David Hoffman and Joe Pichirallo, "Rebels Held Noriega for Hours," *The Washington Post*, October 5, 1989.

282 For several hours the agency's intelligence network: Confidential interview.

282 At 12:30 P.M. Giroldi surrendered himself: John M. Goshko, "Left Alone by Plotters, Noriega Phoned Rescuers, Webster Says," *The Washington Post*, November 4, 1989.

282 Two hours after the coup: Don Podesta, "Coup Attempt Against Noriega by Rebel Troops Fails in Panama," *The Washington Post*, October 4, 1989. See also William Branigin, "Panamanian Captain Arrested in Coup Attempt Dies in Custody," *The Washington Post*, October 11, 1989, and Ann Devroy, "U.S. Keeps Troops on Sidelines," *The Washington Post*, October 4, 1989.

283 In Washington Bush huddled: Confidential interview. See also George C. Wilson, "Lack of Information Hampered U.S. Response to Panama Coup Attempt," *The Washington Post*, October 15, 1989.

283 Giroldi was trundled off to: *Divorcing the Dictator*, p. 392.

283 "If we were [told]" he said: Ibid., p. 393.

283 "Keystone Kops": *Panama: The Whole Story*, p. 212.

283 Helms was "full of it": John Sununu and Brent Scowcroft later called Deborah DeMoss and a number of Helms's aides to the White House for a discussion of the coup. But Sununu and Scowcroft weren't interested in hearing DeMoss's side of the story. They were enraged that Helms was going public with his information.

284 "Where is your evidence?": Molly Moore and Joe Pichirallo, "Cheney: U.S. Willing to Take Custody," *The Washington Post*, October 6, 1989.

284 "never had any intention of going...": "Panama: The Official Word," *Washington Post*, October 10, 1989.

284 "We had situations here...": Ibid.

284 "We have found absolutely nothing to indicate...": Ibid.

284 He accused his congressional critics: David Hoffman, "Bush Attacks Critics of Response to Coup," *The Washington Post*, October 11, 1989.

284 "I have not seen any fact...": Ibid.

286 he was an "ineffective" CIA head: Ann Devroy and David B. Ot-

taway, "CIA Director Under Fire," *The Washington Post,* October 16, 1989.

286 "he had learned more about ...": Ibid.

286 "One knowledgeable source said Webster": Ibid.

286 "There is a sense that the institution ...": Ibid.

286 "We have no reason to believe ...": Author interview with Mark Mansfield and other CIA public affairs officers.

286 "You know, Judge Webster really doesn't pay ...": Confidential interview.

287 "The judge is very angry ...": Ibid.

287 Ottaway and Devroy knew that Webster was in Europe: Ibid.

287 "This is how the *Post* gets its jollies": Ibid.

287 "The *Post* story has been in the works ...": Ibid.

288 "They knew it was coming ...": Author interview with David Ottaway.

288 "I would have slapped him": Confidential interview.

288 studied *The Washington Post* article in mounting rage: Ibid.

288 "Not yet," she said ...: Ibid.

288 Gates was apologetic: Ibid.

288 "This is Sununu's work": Ibid.

289 "Some Bush presidential aides ...": Ann Devroy and David B. Ottaway, "CIA Director Under Fire," *The Washington Post,* October 16, 1989.

289 Webster had spoken to Gates: Author interview with William Webster.

289 Twenty minutes later: Ibid.

290 in an interview in *The New York Times:* Stephen Engelberg, "CIA Seeks Looser Rules on Killings During Coups," *The New York Times,* October 17, 1989. The executive order on assassinations was signed by President Gerald Ford. It said: "No employee of the United States Government shall engage in, or conspire to engage in, political assassination." The order was strengthened by Jimmy Carter to say that "no person employed by or acting on behalf of the United States Government shall engage, or conspire to engage, in assassination." Every President since Ford has reiterated the policy.

290 "under pressure from the DO ...": Confidential interview.

290 "The judge is isolated here": Confidential interview.

291 "When you have a deliberate blurring ...": Stephen Engelberg, "CIA Seeks Looser Rules on Killings During Coups," *The New York Times,* October 17, 1989.

291 "There's always a lot of fallout ...": Ibid.

291 "We're just not going to be diverted by ...": Author interview with James Greenleaf.

292 "Webster, who had won a reputation…": David B. Ottaway, "Coming Out of the Cold," *The Washington Post,* October 22, 1989.

292 "Whether Webster can persuade…": Ibid.

293 The first indication Kurt Muse had: Neil C. Livingstone, "Danger in the Air," *Washingtonian,* June 1990.

294 "Stay down…": Ibid.

PART III: THE SORCERER'S APPRENTICE

Twelve: Earthquake

307 The day after Kurt Muse: "Upheaval in Eastern Europe, The Turning Points," *The Washington Post,* January 14, 1990.

307 on Christmas Day: Ibid.

307 the Hungarian government signed a human rights: "Refugees Force a Fateful Choice," *The Washington Post,* January 14, 1990.

307 Five days later Poland: "The Communists Lost Control of the Process," *The Washington Post,* January 14, 1990.

307 In May Hungary opened its border: "Upheaval in Eastern Europe, the Turning Points," *The Washington Post,* January 14, 1990.

308 its intelligence assessments significantly: Confidential interview.

308 had purchased Soviet military secrets: Ibid.

309 East Germany's per capita gross national product: "Statement of Sen. Daniel Patrick Moynihan," Senate Select Committee on Intelligence, September 16, 1991.

309 Allen Dulles told the Congress: Ibid.

309 "I plan to review for you…": Ibid.

309 "We should not gloss over…" Ibid.

310 a critical loss of brainpower: Confidential interview.

310 "The attrition was very high…": Author interview with John Gentry.

311 The veteran analysts who stayed: Confidential interview.

311 the struggle centered on a small number: Author interview with former Deputy DCI Admiral Bobby Ray Inman.

311 "an informed awareness…": "The Iranian Imbroglio: Implications for the Intelligence Process," memorandum from Thomas M. Barksdale, December 2, 1986.

311 "was like an earthquake": Author interview with former Deputy DCI Admiral Bobby Ray Inman.

311 "every major analytical and managerial…": "Sworn Testimony of Mel Goodman Before the Senate Select Committee on Intelligence," September 25, 1991.

312 "concise, well argued, and insightful": Confidential interview.

312 "an immensely talented...": Ibid.
313 "We were basically untouchable...": Ibid.
313 Kent's three institutions: A number of confusing reorganizations have occurred at the CIA over the last forty years. The major sections referred to as offices in the DI are called divisions in the DO. The counterpart to the DO's Soviet Division is called the Office of Soviet Analysis in the DI. Until 1981 Soviet analysts were grouped with experts on Eastern Europe. The Office of National Estimates— one of the three institutional precursors of the DI—was also eliminated during the reorganization of 1975, when the three separate organizations became the Directorate of Intelligence. Mel Goodman began his career as an analyst in the Office of Current Intelligence (OCI), which didn't exist in 1981. The DI's 1982 internal reorganization integrated country experts with political and economic analysts grouped under geographic regions, thereby bringing the DI into line with the rest of the agency. In addition to the Office of Soviet Analysis, the DI contains an Office of European Analysis (EUR), an Office of Africa and Latin America Analysis (ALA), an Office of Near East and South Asian Analysis (NESA), an Office of East Asian Analysis (EAA), an Office of Global Issues, and a Senior Review Panel. It also contains offices for special assistants on specific topics and support offices on imagery analysis and directorate production capabilities.
313 The fall of Saigon had a profound effect: Author interview with former Deputy DCI Admiral Bobby Ray Inman.
314 a small but vocal group: Confidential interview.
314 One CIA report even pointed to a debate: "Sworn Testimony of Mel Goodman Before the Senate Select Committee on Intelligence," September 25, 1991.
315 This ideological controversy was sharpened: Confidential interview.
315 the Soviet Union as a society in crisis: Ibid.
315 "I had a chance...": "Sworn Testimony of Douglas MacEachin," Senate Select Committee on Intelligence, September 25, 1991.
315 "The Soviets themselves were keenly aware...": "Sworn Testimony of Jennifer Glaudemans," Senate Select Committee on Intelligence, September 25, 1991. See also David Ignatius, "Why Bob Gates Is the Eeyore of Sovietology," The Washington Post, May 28, 1989.
316 The special committee on the Reagan transition team: The Agency, pp. 662–63.
316 Lieutenant General Edward Rowny: Ibid., pp. 659–60.
316 "an agency hater": Confidential interview.
317 Singled out for special rebuke: The Agency, p. 661.
317 "These failures are of such enormity..." Ibid., p. 665.
317 "I think that very often...": "Sworn Testimony of Douglas

MacEachin," Senate Select Committee on Intelligence, October 2, 1991.

317 Casey dismissed the transition team: *The Agency,* pp. 670–71.

318 Casey "punished SOVA": Confidential interview.

318 "It was a period of great turbulence": "Statement of Robert M. Gates," SSCI nomination of Robert M. Gates to be director of central intelligence, October 3, 1991.

318 A later internal review: Papal Task Force, "Note to Deputy Director for Intelligence," July 12, 1985 (CIA internal document).

319 "a very strong personality": "Sworn Statement of Hal Ford," Senate Select Committee on Intelligence, October 2, 1991.

319 "smug, condescending and callous": "Sworn Testimony of Jennifer Glaudemans," Senate Select Committee on Intelligence, September 25, 1991.

319 "sharpened and refocused": "Statement of Robert M. Gates," SSCI nomination of Robert M. Gates to be director of central intelligence, October 3, 1991.

319 "The Soviets have opposed international...": "Draft SNIE 11/2–81" [Soviets & Terrorism], memorandum of Helene L. Boatner, April 27, 1981.

319 "This [the terrorism estimate] was done...": "Sworn Testimony of Mel Goodman Before the Senate Select Committee on Intelligence," September 25, 1991.

320 "The Soviet are deeply...": "Draft SNIE 11/2–81" [Soviets & Terrorism], memorandum of Helene L. Boatner, April 27, 1981. The Boatner memo summarizes the positions of a number of papers on the Soviets and terrorism. It includes a series of SNIE drafts, beginning with one that says there is little or no evidence of Soviet funding of terrorist activities and ending with one that says that they are "deeply involved" in such activities.

320 "The Soviets do not instigate...": Ibid.

321 "I have read the attached draft...": "NIE on Soviets and the Third World," memorandum from Robert M. Gates, February 14, 1982 (CIA internal document).

321 "In 1981, when Gates was the NIO...": "Sworn Testimony of Mel Goodman Before the Senate Select Committee on Intelligence," September 25, 1991.

322 After about thirty minutes: Ibid.

323 "Senior analysts began to leave...": "Sworn Testimony of Mel Goodman Before the Senate Select Committee on Intelligence," October 2, 1991.

324 "Foreign policy wasn't his strong suit...": Author interview with former Deputy DCI Admiral Bobby Ray Inman.

324 "We would have these round tables...": Confidential interview.

324 "This is an exciting, exciting place . . .": Author interview with former public affairs official Joseph De Trani.

325 Webster held a celebration: Confidential interview.

325 "This is a victory . . .": Ibid.

325 the CIA even purchased hundreds of Tennessee mules: David B. Ottaway, "What Is 'Afghan Lesson' for Superpowers?" *The Washington Post,* February 12, 1989.

326 Hekmatyar received most of his supplies: Confidential interview. See also Lally Weymouth, "An Afghan Rebel Chief Tells America 'No Deal,' " *The Washington Post,* September 17, 1989.

327 During the next six months: David B. Ottaway, "CIA Removes Afghan Rebel Aid Director," *The Washington Post,* October 2, 1989. See also David B. Ottaway, "U.S. Increasing Arms Flow to Afghan Resistance," *The Washington Post,* July 16, 1989.

327 a group of thirty guerrilla leaders: Steve Coll, "Afghan Rebel Faction Decries Attack by Rivals," *The Washington Post,* July 20, 1989.

327 Controversy over the CIA's failure: Representative Bill McCollum, "The CIA Has Bungled It," *The Washington Post,* September 10, 1989.

327 The luncheon erupted into a bitter exchange: David B. Ottaway, "CIA Removes Afghan Rebel Aid Director," *The Washington Post,* October 2, 1989.

328 Webster gave in to congressional demands: Ibid.

328 he quietly reassigned Dan Webster: Confidential interview.

Thirteen: Mind-sets

329 the CIA first received reports: According to a confidential document in the possession of the author.

329 a mysterious fire destroyed: R. Jeffrey Smith and Patrick E. Tyler, "Fire Strikes Chemical Plant in Libya," *The Washington Post,* March 15, 1990.

329 "The origins of the fire . . .": "Regular White House Briefing," Reuters News Service, March 15, 1990.

330 "We get an assist . . .": Ibid.

330 "The chemical agents . . .": "Regular State Department Briefing," March 15, 1990.

330 (The idea . . . is completely . . ."): R. Jeffrey Smith and Patrick E. Tyler, "Fire Strikes Chemical Plant in Libya," *The Washington Post,* March 15, 1990.

331 one week after the Rabta fire: Serge Schmemann, "German Is Charged in Libyan Case," *The New York Times,* March 22, 1990.

331 Qaddafi had accused West Germany: Jennifer Parmelee, "Libya

Holds Suspects in Fire Probe," *The Washington Post,* March 28, 1990. One theory to emerge in U.S. intelligence circles is that the Libyan government ordered the plant to be set ablaze in order to stave off a U.S. military strike. The way that the fire was set and the fact that there were no casualties lent much credence to this belief. Well after the incident a number of articles appeared in national newspapers saying that high-resolution American satellite photographs indicated that the plant had not been destroyed after all, that Qaddafi had staged the destruction, *but without actually burning the plant.* According to these reports, the Libyans painted burn marks on the top of the plant and even dismantled other parts. But the reports are unconfirmed, and intelligence officials say that the Rabta plant is not in operation.

332 during an overseas telephone conversation: Confidential interview.

332 Bush said he was pleased: Ibid.

332 Bush was enraged: Ibid.

332 Shamir lost a 60–55 vote: "Israeli Government Falls over Refusal to Begin Peace Talks," Reuters News Service, March 15, 1990.

333 *if* it won the election: The Shamir peace proposal for limited Palestinian self-rule was, at the time, universally judged as a ploy, that Shamir put it forward in the belief that it would prove unacceptable to Palestinians. When his proposal was accepted, Shamir had to find a way out. Shamir's defenders strongly disagree with this view, however, and accuse Bush of purposely causing Israel's government crisis in March 1990. The foundation of Bush's policy was suggested by a paper written by Graham Fuller, who had left the CIA after the Iran-contra scandal to join the Rand Corporation. Fuller's paper, completed the previous August, said that creation of a Palestinian state was "inevitable." Fuller said that Palestinians in the occupied territories "can and probably will remain committed to the struggle over the long haul—and perhaps for decades—regardless of the punishment meted out [by the Israelis]." The paper had a powerful effect on the administration.

333 This paper, completed with the help: According to a confidential document in the possession of the author.

333 improved relations with Iraq through a long-term policy: NSD 26 reads, in part: "The United States remains committed to defend its vital interests in the region, if necessary and appropriate through the use of U.S. military force, against the Soviet Union or any other regional power with interests inimical to our own."

333 "ruthless, but pragmatic": According to a confidential document in the possession of the author.

333 Farzad Bazoft: *Unholy Babylon,* pp. 248–50.

334 Bazoft was denied counsel: Ibid.

334 "Iraq has hung a journalist...": "Regular White House Briefing," Reuters News Service, March 15, 1990.

335 they were missing the bomb itself: Confidential interview.

335 on a misty morning in early April: Michael Wines, "Libya Now Linked to Pan Am Blast," *The New York Times,* October 10, 1990, and Youssef M. Ibrahim, "Libya Denies Link to Airline Blasts," *The New York Times,* June 28, 1991.

335 The plate was a mystery: Author interview with former CIA and CTC officer Vincent Cannistraro.

335 "actually a tiny piece of the circuit board...": Ibid.

336 "This is not a very good bomb": Confidential interview.

336 surveilled cafés regularly frequented: Ibid.

336 were photographed at the Pan Am airline counter: Ibid.

336 a group of master planners in Iran: One month after the discovery of the brass plate at Lockerbie, the seven-member Presidential Commission on Aviation Security and Terrorism completed its study of the Pan Am attack. It focused almost exclusively on lax security measures that might have contributed to the air disaster. The report criticized Pan Am for failing to follow security guidelines and said the airline's security arrangements at Heathrow and Frankfurt were deplorable. The commission also recommended the U.S. government consider launching "preemptive or retaliatory military strikes against terrorist enclaves in nations that harbor them." If these recommendations had been followed, American warplanes would have bombed Iran, or Syria, or PFLP—GC headquarters in Damascus— which was not responsible for the crime. The author interviewed the chief investigators of the commission.

337 "didn't see the whole picture": Author interview with former CIA and CTC officer Vincent Cannistraro.

337 "We may have been overanxious...": Confidential interview.

337 the short transcript of an anonymous telephone call: According to a confidential document in the possession of the author.

337 "Greetings of the Revolution": Ibid.

338 The Zurich-based firm: Copies of sales documents have been shown to the author.

338 The two Libyans, later identified as: Michael Sheridan, Rupert Cornwell, et al., "Libya Blamed for Lockerbie," *The Independent,* November 15, 1991.

338 the CIA had been tracking: Confidential interview. See also Elaine Sciolino, "U.S. Accuses Benin of Abetting Libyan Terrorism," *The New York Times,* May 20, 1988; Lally Weymouth, "The Business of Terrorism in Libya," *The Washington Post,* November 20, 1991; and

UPI, "Togo Thwarts Bomb Plot," *The Washington Post*, August 12, 1986.

339 When Senegalese officials checked: Author interview with former CIA and CTC officer Vincent Cannistraro. See also William Drozdiak, "French Super-Magistrate Pursued Libyan Link," *The Washington Post*, November 15, 1991.

339 "We have pictures of him [in France]...": Confidential interview.

339 "very quietly" slipped the photographs: Ibid.

340 The flight had originated in Brazzaville: "Terror at 30,000 Feet," *Newsweek*, October 2, 1989.

340 French officials initially blamed Iran for the incident: Youssef M. Ibrahim, "Investigators Reach Wreckage of French Jet," *The New York Times*, September 22, 1989.

340 The evidence tying Libya: Confidential information.

341 The informer named two other Mathaba operatives: "Mathaba" is shorthand for Mathabah al Thauriya al Alamiya, also known as Mathaba International, Libya's highly compartmented external security organization, according to *Africa Confidential*, a well-respected newsletter on American foreign policy in the region. Mathaba is housed in Tripoli, in the offices of the "Higher Institute for Agriculture." The institute hosts thousands of exchange students from West Africa and Latin America. After training at the institute, the students are sent to Libyan field centers, which are overseen by Khouildy Hamidi, who is responsible for Tripoli's extensive overseas education program. Hamidi was among the original group of officers who helped Qaddafi take power in the late 1960s. The African desk is divided into three geographic areas. The desk overseeing operations in West Africa is headed by Abdul Salem Zadmeh, who was allegedly involved in the planning of the UTA bombing. The European desk is headed by Sayed Gadafadam, Qaddafi's first cousin. Mathaba officials regularly travel in Africa using Lebanese passports. The Tripoli host for the Mathaba network is Moussa Koussa, who books rooms for visiting dignitaries at the Damanta Hotel, which he owns. Koussa is the financial wizard of the Qaddafi regime and the son of a wealthy Libyan family.

342 This typical Rashid-type mechanism: Confidential interview.

342 Muftah Abdulwanis el-Abbar: Ibid. Material on Abbar, his relationship to the CIA and to the National Front for the Salvation of Libya, was the result of an investigation conducted with *Newsday* reporter Knut Royce. Royce interviewed Abbar, who denied having anything to do with the bombing of Pan Am 103. Royce also interviewed officials of the National Front for the Salvation of Libya and CIA,

FBI, and foreign intelligence officers for material on this story. Confidential documents on Abbar's past and documents on his court appearance in Puerto Rico were also made available. Copies of foreign intelligence documents on Abbar are in the personal possession of the author.

342 he supported Qaddafi's coup against: Ibid.

343 Abbar apparently never broke with Qaddafi: Ibid.

343 He was well known: Ibid.

343 "We all knew what Abbar was...": Ibid.

343 the FBI sent a team of: Confidential interview.

343 He was also questioned: Confidential interview.

343 He became a principal officer: Ibid.

344 Abbar was arrested: According to an arrest warrant.

344 Abbar went to Virginia: Confidential interview.

345 an extensive affidavit with the court: According to a court affidavit.

345 Abbar was one of the original suspects: Confidential interview.

345 he was especially mistrusted by Britain's MI5: Ibid.

346 Geoffrey and Christine Middleton: Steven Emerson and Brian Duffy, *The Fall of Pan Am 103* (New York: G. P. Putnam's Sons, 1990), p. 235.

346 his brother was a Libyan Arab Airways: Confidential interview.

346 Gauci identified him as the man: Ibid.

347 Gauci eventually identified another Libyan: Ibid.

347 Lamen Fhimah: *United States of America* v. *Abdel Basset Ali al-Megrahi, Lamen Khalifa Fhimah,* United States District Court for the District of Columbia, November 14, 1991. The mind-set that infected agency investigators looking into the Lockerbie disaster seemed to spread to members of the press. Any number of journalists claimed to have resolved the crime, at the same time that the CTC, MI5, FBI, and Scottish investigators hadn't. Among the theories: that there was a DEA-CIA foul-up in Frankfurt (the favorite theory of Pan Am's lawyers), that Khalid Jaafar, a Lebanese Arab living in Detroit, either was duped into bringing a suitcase with the bomb aboard or did so on purpose (he was completely innocent), and finally, that the bomb was smuggled aboard by disenchanted ramp rats in Great Britain. In many instances the reporters were given these stories by investigators who were merely speculating. In the aftermath of the Pan Am 103 indictments many of the reporters who were certain they had cracked the crime stuck by their story that the U.S. government was covering up Syria's involvement in the terrorist act for political reasons. A large number of the families of the victims also took this view. Aside from speculation of a parallel operation conducted by the PFLP—GC (based in Damascus), there is no evidence of any Syrian, PFLP—GC, or Iranian involvement. Walter Korsgaard says:

"If the Libyans really did it, it means an Iranian bomb is still out there somewhere."

347 In France a magistrate has charged: William Drozdiak and George Lardner, Jr., "French Seek 4 Libyans in Jet Bombing," *The Washington Post*, October 31, 1991.

Fourteen: Ruthless But Pragmatic

349 a speech Hussein gave to a group of: *Unholy Babylon*, p. 252, and Christopher Dobson and Simon O'Dwyer-Russell, "Iraqi Leader Threatens to Gas Israel," *The London Daily Telegraph*, April 3, 1990.

349 "By God, if the Israelis try anything...": Ibid.

350 In a meeting with Assistant Secretary of State John Kelly: Don Oberdorfer, "Was War Inevitable?," *The Washington Post Magazine*, March 17, 1991.

350 The NSC advisers believed Hussein: Confidential interview. For more details on the views of the White House prior to the crisis, see Don Oberdorfer, "Was War Inevitable?," *The Washington Post Magazine*, March 17, 1991.

350 a carefully worded letter: *Unholy Babylon*, p. 270.

350 "...your desire to equip yourself with...": Pierre Salinger and Eric Laurent, *Secret Dossier: The Hidden Agenda Behind the Gulf War* (New York: Penguin Books, 1991), p. 23.

350 "Let me point out to you...": Ibid., p. 24.

351 "As American Ambassador, I can assure you...": Ibid., p. 24.

351 "This administration continues to oppose...": Ibid., p. 24.

351 classified U.S. intelligence reports, based on: Confidential interview.

352 The CIA also monitored a number of Iraqi tests: *Unholy Babylon*, p. 96.

352 The CIA issued its first warning: Confidential interview.

352 The allegation was backed by a letter: *Unholy Babylon*, p. 262.

352 "The Gulf states' policy of forcing down...": Ibid., p. 270.

352 "I admire your extraordinary efforts to rebuild...": Mark Perry and Jeff Goldberg, "The CIA's Secret Plot to Oust Saddam Hussein," *Regardies*, November 1990. The transcript of the Glaspie-Hussein meeting was released by the Iraqis and remains undisputed by the State Department.

353 shifted its massive technological resources: Confidential interview.

353 access to four KH-11s: Ibid.

353 The agency reported that U.S. reconnaissance satellites: Ibid.

353 showed Iraqi trucks hauling ammunition: Ibid.

354 On the morning of July 28: Ibid.

354 He pointed out that the CIA's warning: Ibid.

356 "Intelligence officers always believe their view . . .": Author interview with Graham Fuller.

356 "By invading Kuwait, Saddam threw away . . .": Ibid.

356 "We were just predisposed . . .": Author interview with Richard Murphy.

356 Webster hand delivered another package: Confidential interview.

357 "This was as clear a warning . . .": Ibid.

358 "I trust him": "The Moscow Connection," *Newsweek,* September 17, 1990.

358 many senior U.S. officials were preparing to go: Confidential interview.

358 At eight-thirty that evening: Mark Perry and Jeff Goldberg, "The CIA's Secret Plot to Oust Saddam Hussein," *Regardies,* November 1990.

358 Early the next day: Bob Woodward, *The Commanders* (New York: Simon and Schuster, 1991), p. 225.

359 "We're not discussing intervention": Ibid.

359 Bush cornered Cheney outside the Cabinet Room: Confidential interview.

359 "You must know, George . . .": Ibid.

361 The next afternoon Webster returned: Confidential interview.

361 "Anything that will undermine his government . . .": Confidential interview. See also *The Commanders,* p. 237.

361 "one of the thinnest documents . . .": Confidential interview. The country's leading expert in the field of developing psychological profiles of political figures is Dr. Jerrold Post, a psychiatrist and now a professor at George Washington University. Dr. Post served in the U.S. government for seventeen years and is recognized as the leading expert in the field of psychological assessments of world leaders. He is the father of the CIA's program on political psychology, having established the intellectual framework under which it still operates. Post's government experience included briefing Presidents Carter, Reagan, and Bush on how to deal with various world figures—from Israel's Begin to Libya's Qaddafi. In assessing Hussein, Dr. Post told *The New York Times:* "This is no psychotic megalomaniac. He is a highly rational man—dangerous but well focused. . . . This is a man who waits very patiently, uses time as a weapon, to get what he wants. If he sees a way out of this, with a fig leaf, he'll take it, and then two years from now, or five years from now, his appetite will be undiminished and he'll strike again somewhere." British reporter Tom Mangold conducted the first on-the-record interview with Post.

361 It was almost impossible to infiltrate: Ibid. See also Stephen Kurkjian,

"CIA Wages Quiet War on Iraq," *The Boston Globe,* February 11, 1991.

362 Leading the ITF: Confidential interview. This officer cannot be named in this book.

362 "We just basically went into some offices...": Ibid. The confidential interviews on American intelligence operations against Iraq and descriptions of the CIA task force in this chapter were conducted, in most cases, by BBC producer Tom Mangold, BBC Washington correspondent Jeff Goldberg, and the author, for a program entitled "America's Secret Intelligence War In Iraq," which aired on the BBC's news program *Panorama.* The material was also used by reporter Jeff Goldberg and me for a piece entitled "The CIA's Secret Plot to Oust Saddam Hussein," which appeared in *Regardies* in November 1990. See also Steve Kurkjian, "CIA Economists Are Key Players in Crisis Analysis," *The Boston Globe,* September 6, 1990.

364 Webster, who had just returned: Confidential interview. According to one former CIA officer, "the photo analysis division is run out of Building Sixteen.... All the photo interpretation stuff is done there. It's a huge operation, mostly scientists. They get the material over a special wire that's hooked into both the DoD [Department of Defense] and the NSA. It's very impressive stuff that they do. They can take thousands of pictures every day. If they get anything useful, they study it by committee to determine whether to take it to the DCI."

364 Kerr agreed. This was "pure Soviet doctrine": Ibid.

365 "Don't send the diplomat": Mark Perry and Jeff Goldberg, "The CIA's Secret Plot to Oust Saddam Hussein," *Regardies,* November 1990.

366 "We want to work with you": Ibid.

366 "The only thing I want to know...": Ibid.

366 "It was a real morale booster for us...": Author interview with CIA public affairs officer Mark Mansfield.

368 "It doesn't matter what we do...": Confidential interview.

369 It is the job of the CIA, he stressed: Author interview with William Webster.

369 The worst thing that can happen, he said, is for: Confidential interview.

370 Within the first two weeks: Ibid.

370 CIA-directed Green Beret units: Ibid. See also Bill Gertz, "U.S. Commandos Steal into Iraq to Spot Mobile Missiles," *The Washington Times,* January 25, 1991.

370 "I think those closest to [Hussein] present his...": Confidential interview. See also Laurie Mylroie, "How We Helped Saddam Sur-

vive," *Commentary*, July 1991. One of the key Iraqi opposition leaders in direct contact with CIA officials was Saad Jabr, the leader of the New Umma (Nation) party, based in London. Jabr is the son of an Iraqi prime minister under the monarchy that was overthrown in 1958 by military officers supported by the Baath party. The New Umma is dominated by Western-educated Iraqi exiles. Jabr concedes that it will be nearly impossible to overthrow Hussein. "There is no opposition to Saddam inside Iraq," Jabr explains. "If someone tells you he has an organization or cells inside Iraq, he is lying ... or being too optimistic." The CIA also recruited a high-level dissident in Riyadh, Saudi Arabia, and drew up tentative plans to smuggle him into Baghdad so that he could spark a revolt. This official was Salah Omar Ali al-Takriti, a former minister of culture in the Baath party in Baghdad. He was codirector of the CIA-sponsored *Voice of Free Iraq*, which broadcast ineffectual dissident messages into the country throughout the war. Middle Eastern officials familiar with his background scoff at any suggestion that he might have provided a credible alternative to Hussein's leadership. Takriti was in charge of the executions of fourteen dissidents soon after Hussein took power and won favor for staging a public hanging of them in downtown Baghdad.

370 CIA officers tracked down one of their: Confidential interview.

371 "One of the advantages that we have over there ...": BBC interview with General Leonard Perroots.

371 CIA officers were dispatched to France: Confidential interview.

371 They used three highly sensitive receivers: Ibid.

372 Webster confidently predicted: R. Jeffrey Smith and George Lardner, Jr., "Iraq Sanctions Seen Working Slowly," *The Washington Post*, November 24, 1990.

372 "The embargo on Iraq's trade is essentially ...": "Securing U.S. Interests in the Persian Gulf Through Diplomacy," Committee on Armed Services, U.S. House of Representatives, December 28, 1990. See also Sidney Blumenthal, "Whose Agents? The CIA and the War Debate," *The New Republic*, February 11, 1990.

372 "You have to take a look at ...": Author interview with Mark Mansfield.

372 Ermath ... was horrified by Webster's reversal: Confidential interview.

373 "Webster misread the intelligence ...": Ibid.

373 Lilley made his pitch ...: Mark Perry and Jeff Goldberg, "Will Judge Webster Be Benched?," *The Nation* (April 15, 1991).

373 "You ought to pay a visit ...": Ibid.

373 "What are *you* doing here?": Ibid.

373 "You're going to get a job ...": Ibid.

Fifteen: Baghdad Station

375 in February 1982 an airliner landed at: Confidential interview. See also Elaine Sciolino, *The Outlaw State* (New York: John Wiley & Sons, Inc., 1991), pp. 163–66; *The Death Lobby*, pp. 242–43; Laurie Mylroie, "How We Helped Saddam Survive," *Commentary*, July 1991; and Paul Gigot, "Iraq: An American Screw-Up," *The National Interest*, Winter 1990.

375 Their discussion was polite: Confidential interview.

375 He sketched out the details: Ibid. There is growing debate over who first went to Amman and when. The evidence indicates that it was Casey himself. He did not travel to Baghdad. One report says that the CIA chief of station in Amman at the time was Thomas Twetten and that he was the intermediary who helped set up these meetings. That is not the case.

376 He displayed hand-drawn CIA maps: Ibid.

376 including King Hussein of Jordan and King Fahd: Ibid.

376 Several months later two other U.S officials: Ibid. See also "Nomination of Robert M. Gates to Be Director of Central Intelligence," Senate Select Committee on Intelligence, committee report, October 24, 1991, pp. 179–83.

377 "filled with facts and analysis": Author interview with Howard Teicher.

378 "I argued that Iraq...": Ibid.

378 "There were a number of us...": Ibid.

378 North viewed Israel as a bulwark: *Under Fire*, pp. 153–55.

378 a "corporate culture" that "relished any antagonism...": Ibid., p. 154.

378 "...an ingrained streak of anti-Semitism...": Ibid., p. 155.

379 The war was turning into a slaughter: Dilip Hiro, *The Longest War* (New York: Routledge, 1991), p. 89.

380 a series of telephone conferences: Confidential interview.

380 An Iranian offensive in mid-March: *The Longest War*, p. 59.

380 Iraq's military was in danger of complete disintegration: Confidential interview.

380 in the battle for Khorramshahr: *The Longest War*, p. 59.

381 Saudi Arabia and Syria attempted to broker: Ibid., p. 62.

381 approving an expanded intelligence relationship: Confidential interview.

381 placed firmly in Dunn's hands: Ibid.

382 Hussein embarked on a major overhaul: *The Longest War*, p. 67.

382 Nizar Hamdoon, a confidant of Hussein's: *The Death Lobby*, pp. 221–22.

383 He even gave a dinner: Confidential interview. That she was lionized by Hamdoon doesn't bother Kirkpatrick. In one of her occasional foreign policy op-ed pieces she accused the State Department of "self-deception" for ignoring warnings on the Kuwait invasion from the CIA. "It is the famous 'Arabist' mind set that is common in the State Department's Bureau of Near Eastern Affairs (NEA) and in the foreign offices of Europe," she wrote in a *Washington Post* opinion piece. "The NEA is peopled by intelligent, industrious specialists on the language, culture, history and politics of the Arab world. Many of them have learned to view the world through the eyes of those whom they have studied and all too often have come to feel a unique indulgence toward Arab strongmen, a special irritation with Israel and a sense that U.S. concerns with democracy and human rights are not quite relevant to their area. This 'clientism,' often the other side of the coin of area expertise, distorts U.S. policy, especially with regard to Iraq, Syria, the PLO and Israel."

383 "This wasn't an intelligence relationship": Author interview with Howard Teicher.

383 "We gave them strategic advice": Ibid.

383 "Casey and his top assistants . . .": Ibid.

383 "The bureaucracy at the State Department . . .": Ibid.

383 "The American tilt toward Iraq . . .": *Under Fire*, p. 287.

384 "It was in 1985 . . .": Author interview with Howard Teicher. McFarlane first considered a new U.S. policy on Iran as early as August 1984, when he convened an interagency group to study the problem. The group published its findings in October, saying that the United States could resume arms shipments to Iran if the regime was willing to restore normal relations. An NSDD on the subject was drafted in December, but to no effect. McFarlane dropped the effort until May 1985.

384 "Fuller felt that our policy . . .": Author interview with Howard Teicher.

385 "There was a genuine visceral fear . . .": Author interview with Graham Fuller.

385 "Graham would believe the last thing . . .": Confidential interview.

385 "Myself and a lot of others . . .": Author interview with Howard Teicher.

385 "It's hogwash. This man . . .": Confidential interview.

386 the CIA established a secure and highly sophisticated: Ibid.

386 "narrative text reports derived from . . .": Ibid.

387 "Our intelligence dump was made so that . . .": Author interview with Howard Teicher.

387 "The key was the secure landlines . . .": Ibid. A CIA officer responds

angrily to this claim: "If the Iraqis figured out that they needed to bury their landlines because they just discovered we had satellites, then Saddam is dumber than anyone ever thought. This is like Standard Defense. Saddam didn't need our photographs to figure out that we had satellites looking at him, all he needed to do was watch CNN."

Teicher admits that even the Israelis may have been hoodwinked by Hussein. Teicher claims that during his trip to Israel, in 1984, Prime Minister Yitzhak Shamir told special Middle East envoy Donald Rumsfeld that Israel considered Iran—not Iraq—its greatest enemy, and he proposed the construction of an oil pipeline from Iraq through Israel to the Mediterranean to help Hussein's economy. The report flabbergasted Teicher, who remembered that Israel had bombed the Iraqi nuclear plant at Osirik in 1981. He concluded that Israel had undergone a change of heart about the Iraqi strong man. According to Teicher, the pipeline offer was passed on to the Iraqis, but Foreign Minister Tariq Aziz said that he was too frightened to tell Hussein about it. "The president [Hussein] will kill me on the spot," he reportedly said.

388 "The Giant in the Country of the Two Rivers": According to a confidential document in the possession of the author.

388 "These men in Saddam's army, they kill people...": Author interview with PLO official Bassam Abu Sharif.

389 "We have done our best...": Author interview with PLO official Abu Iyad.

389 when Abu Iyad was murdered in Tunis: Sharon Waxman, "PLO Says Arab Once Linked to Iraqi-Backed Group Killed 3," *The Washington Post,* January 14, 1991.

389 Webster admitted to the two committee chairmen: Confidential interview.

390 During the retirement party of one: Ibid.

391 "these new people are woefully ill prepared to deal...": Ibid.

392 its estimates placed the total number: "CIA Counts More Iraqi Tanks Left Than Does Pentagon," AP wire service, February 21, 1991.

392 "constant and legendary": Confidential interview.

392 "There were caveats all over the place": Ibid. See also Tim Weiner, "Targeting of Iraq Is Complex and Inexact, Experts Say," *The Philadelphia Inquirer,* February 14, 1991.

393 the hunt for the Scuds took air assets away: U.S. commando teams carried with them into Iraq specially constructed communications equipment as well as special spotter guns that could not be seen from the ground. When the teams spotted a Scud, they figuratively "shined" a beam on the target, which could be seen by a high-tech electronic "eye" in a nearby American fighter. The fighter then

homed in on the beam and destroyed the target. The teams also took part in covert sabotage of Iraqi installations, intelligence collection on the status of Iraqi forces, and search and rescue operations to find downed American and allied pilots. A specially trained CIA team also was smuggled into Baghdad at the beginning of the air war to report on conditions in the Iraqi capital and was surreptitiously removed after the allied ground offensive began.

394 the worst intelligence failure of the war: Rick Atkinson and Dan Balz, "Bomb Strike Kills Scores of Civilians in Building Called Military Bunker by U.S., Shelter by Iraq," *The Washington Post*, February 14, 1991.

394 "It was old intelligence": BBC interview with General Perroots.

394 "He's pathetic and weak": Tim Weiner and Owen Ullmann, "CIA's Webster Criticized as Ineffective," *The Philadelphia Inquirer*, February 22, 1991.

394 "The intelligence community is virtually...": Ibid.

395 "The President has expressed full confidence...": Author interview with Mark Mansfield.

395 "Judge Webster is one of the great...": Ibid.

395 "The handwriting is on the wall": Confidential interview.

395 "I don't think we had good...": Tim Weiner and Owen Ullmann, "CIA's Webster Criticized as Ineffective," *The Philadelphia Inquirer*, February 22, 1991.

396 He called for the virtual dismantling: "A Bill to Repeal Certain Cold War Legislation," *The Congressional Record*, U.S. Senate, January 17, 1991. See also Daniel Patrick Moynihan, "How America Blew It," *Newsweek*, December 10, 1990.

396 "This bill will reassert a most important...": Ibid.

397 "It's not even going to be close": Confidential interview.

397 he was reflecting the advice given to him by Scowcroft and Gates: Ibid. See also Andrew Rosenthal, "Scowcroft and Gates: A Team Rivals Baker," *The New York Times*, February 21, 1991.

398 "We are banking on the military...": Ibid.

398 Bush announced that U.S. aircraft: Laurie Mylroie, "How We Helped Saddam Survive," *Commentary*, July 1991.

398 a specially trained eleven-man CIA paramilitary team: Ibid.

398 the CIA team made contact with Kurdish rebel leaders: Ibid.

Sixteen: Gatesgate

401 "I can no longer work in an organization...": Resignation letter of John Gentry, a copy of which is in the author's possession.

401 "I don't expect to become rich or famous...": Author interview with John Gentry.

401 "I can't mention names": Ibid.
401 "It has been genuinely distasteful...": Resignation letter of John Gentry, a copy of which is in the author's possession.
402 "What I have seen is the bureaucratization...": Author interview with John Gentry.
402 "the leaders most responsible for the lack...": Ibid.
403 the most significant of these resignations: Confidential interview.
403 "Much of the blame for the erosion...": Resignation letter of Stephen Emerson, a copy of which is in the author's possession.
403 "The desire to serve has become the desire...": Author interview with John Gentry.
403 "It is pathetic to see what passes...": Resignation letter of Stephen Emerson, a copy of which is in the author's possession.
404 "One of the most disturbing trends...": Ibid.
404 "The coordination process is very, very bad...": Author interview with John Gentry.
405 "Is there anything the press has on him?": Confidential interview.
405 "It is with a great sense of pride...": Andrew Rosenthal, "Webster Leaving as CIA Director; Ex-Deputy in Line," *The New York Times,* May 9, 1991.
406 "Intelligence is not trying to shape policy": Ibid.
408 "Director, we're going to miss you, pal...": Ibid.
408 "never an easy time to go": Ibid.
409 Lilley's name was floated to ranking members: Confidential interview.
410 "After what Bush did to Saddam...": Ibid.
411 "would shake things up over there...": Ibid.
411 "Bob Gates is an enormously talented individual...": Author interview with former Deputy DCI Admiral Bobby Ray Inman.
411 "I think it's finally time now...": Author interview with former CIA Director of Intelligence Ray Cline.
412 "This is an outrage": Confidential interview. See also Tom Polgar, "The See-No-Evil CIA Nominee," *The Washington Post,* June 23, 1991.
412 a straw poll taken on the Gates nomination: Ibid.
412 "There is some skepticism in the DI...": Author interview with former CIA officer David Whipple.
412 Price reassured the clandestine service: Confidential interview.
413 CIA employees quietly made their way to Capitol Hill: Ibid.
413 "You know ... I just don't believe you.": Ibid.
414 objected to the questioning: *Iran-Contra,* Appendix B, vol. 11, pp. 1001–06.
414 "Let me interject," Boren began: Ibid.
415 "Well, Senator, if there's one thing...": Ibid.

416 "My objections to Gates center on his...": Tom Polgar, "The See-No-Evil CIA Nominee," *The Washington Post*, June 23, 1991.

417 "The fact of the matter is that Casey...": Ibid.

418 "run like a covey of quail": "President: Senators Ought Not to Panic," *The Washington Post* (excerpts), July 14, 1991.

418 "I just don't think it's the American way...": Ibid.

418 including former Latin America Division chief Jerry Gruner: Ibid.

419 Boren remained confident: When Boren gave a press conference announcing the committee's decision to postpone the hearings, he mentioned that committee investigators would question Gruner. Later criticized for mentioning Gruner's name publicly, Boren defended himself by saying Gruner had already been named in books and articles. But he was clearly embarrassed by his slip. "It is absolutely no secret to anyone that he occupied a position at the CIA headquarters during the period of time of the contra resupply operation," Boren said. CIA officials told *The Washington Post*, however, that Gruner would be recalled from his overseas post because of Boren's identification.

420 in a new "Mustang and no money": "Excerpts from Questions and Answers at the Gates Hearings," *The New York Times*, October 4, 1991.

421 "Because of the great interest that this committee...": George Lardner, Jr., and Walter Pincus, "Gates Concedes Lack of Vigilance on Iran-Contra," *The Washington Post*, September 17, 1991.

421 "a solid performance": George Lardner, Jr., and Walter Pincus, "Hearings Point to Confirmation of CIA Nominee," *The Washington Post*, September 18, 1991, and Walter Pincus, "Gates's Solid Performance Follows a Cautious Script," *The Washington Post*, September 18, 1991.

422 "I thought you were just going to say...": Ibid.

422 "in all probability, he will be confirmed": Ibid.

422 he was "an exceptionally gifted analyst...": "Sworn Testimony of Alan Fiers Before the Select Committee on Intelligence," September 20, 1991.

422 purposely manipulated the Directorate of Intelligence: "Sworn Testimony of Hal Ford Before the Select Committee on Intelligence," September 26, 1991.

423 "But I guess what I find most important...": "Sworn Testimony of Mel Goodman Before the Select Committee on Intelligence," September 26, 1991.

423 "I take no satisfaction in sharing ... with you ...": "Sworn Testimony of Jennifer Glaudemans Before the Select Committee on Intelligence," September 26, 1991.

424 "Let me be clear," she stressed.: Ibid.

425 "I welcome the opportunity to modify...": "Sworn Testimony of Hal Ford Before the Select Committee on Intelligence," September 26, 1991.

425 Matthews inexplicably changed his testimony: Confidential interview.

426 "It has caused me some real pain...": "Sworn Testimony of Robert M. Gates Before the Select Committee on Intelligence," October 4, 1990.

426 "You're a bright fella," he said: "Statement of Senator Ernest F. Hollings," Select Committee on Intelligence, October 18, 1991. See also George Lardner, Jr., "Committee Approves Gates at CIA," *The Washington Post*, October 19, 1991.

427 "Charlie Allen and all the rest of them...": Confidential interview.

427 "I hope this sense of family...": George Lardner, Jr., "Gates Takes Over as Director of CIA," *The Washington Post*, November 13, 1991.

Epilogue

428 The bitterness and rancor sparked: Elaine Sciolino, "Gates Takes Over CIA Challenged to Lift Its Anxious Mood," *The New York Times*, November 12, 1991.

429 the politicization of intelligence reports: Elaine Sciolino, "CIA Panel Rejects View That Reports Were Slanted," *The New York Times*, February 7, 1992.

—— ★ ★ ★ ——
Bibliography

ARTICLES

Aikman, David, Sandra Burton, and Jaime A. Florcruz. "The Wrath of Deng." *Time*, June 19, 1989.

Anderson, Jack, and Dale Van Atta. "CIA Backed Qaddafi Assassination Try." *The Washington Post*, June 12, 1985.

Anderson, Jack, and Dale Van Atta. "FBI Learned of Arms Shipment to Iran." *The Washington Post*, August 29, 1989.

Anderson, Harry, and Carroll Bogert. "Deng's Great Leap Backward" (in "Upheaval in China"). *Newsweek*, June 19, 1989.

Anderson, Harry, with Melinda Liu. "An Army in the Middle." *Newsweek*, June 5, 1989.

Anderson, Harry, and Melinda Liu. "The Chinese Army's Uneasy Truce with Itself" (in "Upheaval in China"). *Newsweek*, June 19, 1989.

Associated Press. "CIA Beirut Chief Is Among the Dead." *The Washington Post*, December 25, 1988.

Associated Press. "Activists in Hong Kong Assist 4 Chinese Dissidents to Escape." *The Washington Post*, June 27, 1989.

Atkinson, Rick, and Dan Balz. "Bomb Strike Kills Scores of Civilians in Building Called Military Bunker by U.S., Shelter by Iraq." *The Washington Post*, February 14, 1991.

Atkinson, Rick, and Steve Coll. "Bush Orders Cease Fire." *The Washington Post*, February 28, 1991.

Bangkok Post, The. "Chavalit: Name Names or Go to Hell." November 10, 1988.

Bangkok Post, The. "U.S. Urged to Retract Charge Against Military." November 11, 1988.

Bangkok Post, The. (editorial). "Chatchai's Key Role in the Khmer Equation." March 15, 1989.

Becker, Elizabeth. "Cambodian Premier Sees Progress Toward Peace." *The Washington Post,* November 12, 1988.

Becker, Elizabeth. "The U.S. Finally Got It Right in Cambodia." *The Washington Post,* January 30, 1989.

Becker, Elizabeth. "Conference on Cambodia to Begin." *The Washington Post,* July 29, 1989.

Binder, David. "Yugoslavia Seen Breaking Up Soon." *The New York Times,* November 28, 1990.

Birnbaum, Jesse, and Howard G. Chua Eoan. "Despair and Death in a Beijing Square." *Time,* June 12, 1989.

Blumenthal, Sidney. "Whose Agents? The CIA and the War Debate." *The New Republic,* February 11, 1990.

Bowring, Philip. "Beware of Generals Bearing Peaceful Revolution." *The Far Eastern Economic Review,* June 25, 1987.

Branigin, William. "U.S. Protégé Reportedly Vows to Quit." *The Washington Post,* December 22, 1988.

Branigin, William. "Noriega Opens Bank, Perhaps for Laundering." *The Washington Post,* January 27, 1989.

Branigin, William. "U.S. Firms Seek Change in Panama Sanctions." *The Washington Post,* April 4, 1989.

Branigin, William. "Americans in Panama Complain of Harassment." *The Washington Post,* April 11, 1989.

Branigin, William. "Opponents of Noriega Warn of Electoral Fraud." *The Washington Post,* April 19, 1989.

Branigin, William. "Panama's Mean Season." *The Washington Post,* April 29, 1989.

Branigin, William. "Noriega's Force Attack, Club Opposition Candidates." *The Washington Post,* May 11, 1989.

Branigin, William. "Panamanian Captain Arrested in Coup Attempt Dies in Custody." *The Washington Post,* October 11, 1989.

Branigin, William. "Rebel Ignored Plea to Delay Coup." *The Washington Post,* October 14, 1989.

Branigin, William. "U.S. Assails Panama in Killing of GI." *The Washington Post,* December 18, 1989.

Bremner, Charles. "Asia Hand Holding Steady." *The Times* (London), June 14, 1989.

Cannon, Lou, and David B. Ottaway. "New Attack on Libya Discussed." *The Washington Post,* December 22, 1988.

Chanda, Nayan. "A Lethal Boost." *The Far Eastern Economic Review,* October 27, 1988.

Chongkhadikit, The. "Chawalit to Retire from Army, Enter Politics." *The Bangkok Post,* November 10, 1988.

Cody, Edward. "2 Chinese Form Exile Faction." *The Washington Post,* July 5, 1989.

Cody, Edward, and David B. Ottaway. "Pan Am Bomb Probe Focuses on Palestinian Held in Sweden." *The Washington Post,* December 22, 1989.

Coll, Steve. "Afghan Rebel Faction Decries Attack by Rivals." *The Washington Post,* July 20, 1989.

Coll, Steve. "U.S. Envoy Reassigned in Afghan Policy Clash." *The Washington Post,* August 10, 1989.

Coll, Steve. "U.S. Facing a Dilemma in Arming Afghan Rebels." *The Washington Post,* August 13, 1989.

Coll, Steve. "Afghanistan's Tribal Chiefs Struggle to Reassert Their Power." *The Washington Post,* August 17, 1989.

Coll, Steve. "The Rout of the Republican Guard." *The Washington Post,* March 2, 1991.

Cramer, Richard Ben. "How Bush Made It." *Esquire,* June 1991.

Delfs, Robert. "Tiananmen Massacre." *The Far Eastern Economic Review,* June 15, 1989.

Delfs, Robert. "Repression and Reprisal." *The Far Eastern Economic Review,* June 22, 1989.

Devroy, Ann. "U.S. Keeps Troops on Sidelines." *The Washington Post,* October 4, 1989.

Devroy, Ann, and David Hoffman. "White House Reveals Earlier China Mission." *The Washington Post,* December 19, 1989.

Devroy, Ann, and Molly Moore. "Noriega's Forces Attack, Club Opposition Candidates." *The Washington Post,* May 11, 1989.

Devroy, Ann, and David B. Ottaway. "CIA Director Under Fire." *The Washington Post,* October 16, 1989.

Devroy, Ann, and Joe Pichirallo. "U.S. Gives Refuge to Panama Dissidents." *The Washington Post,* October 10, 1989.

Devroy, Ann, and Walter Pincus. "Deputy CIA Head Chosen for National Security Post." *The Washington Post,* December 29, 1988.

Devroy, Ann, and Patrick E. Tyler. "U.S. Forces Crush Panamanian Military; Noriega in Hiding as Fighting Continues." *The Washington Post,* December 21, 1989.

Dobbs, Michael. "Afghan Pullout Marks Historic Reversal for Soviets." *The Washington Post,* February 13, 1989.

Dobbs, Michael. "Soviets Complete Pullout from War in Afghanistan." *The Washington Post,* February 16, 1989.

Dobson, Christopher, and Simon O'Dwyer-Russell. "Iraqi Leader Threatens to Gas Israel." *The London Daily Telegraph,* April 3, 1990.

Donnelly, Tom. "Terror in Panama." *Army Times,* March 20, 1989.

Drozdiak, William. "French Super-Magistrate Pursued Libyan Link." *The Washington Post,* November 15, 1991.

Drozdiak, William, and George Lardner, Jr. "French Seek 4 Libyans in Jet Bombing." *The Washington Post,* October 31, 1991.

El-Tahri, Jihan. "Terrorists Said to Seek Overthrow of Abu Nidal." *The Washington Post,* November 20, 1989.

Engelberg, Stephen. "Webster Names Ex-Agent to Top CIA Post." *The New York Times,* December 9, 1987.

Engelberg, Stephen. "Suspect in Murder of Drug Agent Is Seized in U.S. Trap in Honduras." *The New York Times,* April 6, 1988.

Engelberg, Stephen. "CIA Seeks Looser Rules on Killings During Coups." *The New York Times,* October 17, 1989.

Engelberg, Stephen. "Panamanian's Tale: '87 Plan for a Coup." *The New York Times,* October 29, 1989.

Fineman, Mark. "Jalalabad Devastated but Quiet." *The Washington Post,* May 11, 1989.

Frankel, Glenn. "No Charges in Sight in Pan Am Bombing." *The Washington Post,* December 16, 1989.

Fuller, Graham E. "Let's Not Blow It in Afghanistan." *The Washington Post,* November 27, 1988.

Fuller, Graham E. "Can Najibullah Be Nudged Out?" *The Washington Post,* June 18, 1989.

Fuller, Graham E. "When Gorbachev Fails . . ." *The Washington Post,* September 24, 1989.

Gazarik, Richard. "Flight 103 Victim on Sensitive Mission." *Greensburg (Pa.) Tribune Review,* June 1989.

Gazarik, Richard. "McKee Excelled in Career." *Greensburg (Pa.) Tribune Review,* June 1989.

Gertz, Bill. "U.S. Commandos Steal into Iraq to Spot Mobile Missiles." *The Washington Times,* January 25, 1991.

Gigot, Paul. "Iraq: An American Screw-Up." *The National Interest,* Winter 1990.

Gillette, Robert. "Third World Missiles Linked to German Firm, Italian Firms." *Los Angeles Times,* March 11, 1989.

Goodgame, Dan. "What If We Do Nothing?" *Time,* January 7, 1991.

Goshko, John M. "Poor Morale, Drift Seen at Baker's State Department." *The Washington Post,* March 6, 1989.

Goshko, John M. "U.S. Drafts 2-Stage Plan for Dealing with Panama." *The Washington Post,* April 30, 1989.

Goshko, John M. "State's Morale Improving 6 Months into Baker Era." *The Washington Post,* July 20, 1989.

Goshko, John M. "Left Alone by Plotters, Noriega Phoned Rescuers, Webster Says." *The Washington Post,* November 4, 1989.

Gugliotta, Guy, and Steve Coll. "Bush Says Iraq Has Agreed to Meet with Allies." *The Washington Post,* March 1, 1991.

Harden, Blaine. "Super Cop." *Washingtonian,* April 1984.

Harrison, Selig S. "Who Will Win the Bloody Battle for Kabul?" *The Washington Post,* January 29, 1989.

Hentoff, Nat. "Saint for Our Time." *The Village Voice,* April 7, 1987.

Hernon, Peter. "Strong Sense of History Drives Webster." *St. Louis Post-Dispatch,* March 16, 1987.

Hersh, Seymour M. "Panama Strongman Said to Trade in Drugs, Arms and Illicit Money." *The New York Times,* June 13, 1986.

Hersh, Seymour M. "Reagan Is Said to Have Let Israel Sell Arms to Teheran." *The New York Times,* December 8, 1991.

Hewitt, Gavin. "Did German Bungling Lead to Pan Am 103?" *The Washington Post,* September 24, 1989.

Hewitt, Gavin. "The Great Escape from China." *The Washington Post,* June 2, 1991.

Hockstader, Lee. "Baghdad Warns Insurrectionists 'They Will Pay.' " *The Washington Post,* March 8, 1991.

Hoffman, David. "Bush Gets Warm Reception in China." *The Washington Post,* February 26, 1989.

Hoffman, David. "Noriega Drug Questions Ignored, Report Says." *The Washington Post,* April 9, 1989.

Hoffman, David. "Bush Attacks Critics of Response to Coup." *The Washington Post,* October 11, 1989.

Hoffman, David. "Bush Sent Key Aide on Private Mission to China." *The Washington Post,* December 13, 1989.

Hoffman, David, and Ann Devroy. "U.S. Was Caught Off Guard by Coup Attempt." *The Washington Post,* October 6, 1989.

Hoffman, David, and Helen Dewar. "Baker Rules Out Early Bid to Aid Contras Militarily." *The Washington Post,* December 21, 1988.

Hoffman, David, and John M. Goshko. "Senate Panel Was Negative on Boosting Covert Aid." *The Washington Post,* October 11, 1989.

Hoffman, David, and Don Oberdorfer. "China Trip Defended by Bush." *The Washington Post,* December 12, 1989.

Hoffman, David, and David B. Ottaway. "Panel Drops Covert-Acts Notification." *The Washington Post,* October 27, 1989.

Hoffman, David, and Joe Pichirallo. "Rebels Held Noriega for Hours." *The Washington Post,* October 5, 1989.

Hoffman, David, and Maralee Schwartz. "CIA Director, Envoy Won't Be in Cabinet." *The Washington Post,* December 3, 1988.

Ibrahim, Youssef M. "Investigators Reach Wreckage of French Jet." *The New York Times,* September 22, 1989.

Ibrahim, Youssef M. "Arabs Say Deadly Power Struggle Has Split Abu Nidal Terror Group." *The New York Times,* November 12, 1989.

Ibrahim, Youssef M. "Libya Denies Link to Airline Blasts." *Los Angeles Times,* June 28, 1991.

Ignatius, David. "Why Bob Gates Is the Eeyore of Sovietology." *The Washington Post,* May 28, 1989.

Jenkins, Loren. "Honduran Riot Poses Setback for U.S." *The Washington Post,* April 16, 1988.

Kempe, Frederick. "The Noriega Files." *Newsweek,* January 15, 1990.

Kenworthy, Tom, and Joe Pichirallo. "Bush Clears Plan to Topple Noriega." *The Washington Post,* November 17, 1989.

Krauss, Clifford. "Failed Anti-Qaddafi Effort Leaves U.S. Picking Up the Pieces." *The New York Times,* March 12, 1991.

Kristof, Nicholas D. "Beijing Death Toll at Least 200; Army Tightens Control of City but Angry Resistance Goes On." *The New York Times,* June 5, 1989.

Kristof, Nicholas D. "Tiananmen Crackdown, Students' Account Questioned on Major Points." *The New York Times,* June 13, 1989.

Kurkjian, Stephen. "CIA Economists Are Key Players in Crisis Analysis." *The Boston Globe,* September 6, 1990.

Kurkjian, Stephen. "CIA Wages Quiet War on Iraq." *The Boston Globe,* February 11, 1991.

Lardner, George, Jr. "Webster: Not Lobbying to Keep Job." *The Washington Post,* November 18, 1989.

Lardner, George, Jr. "In a Changing World, CIA Reorganizing to Do More with Less." *The Washington Post,* July 5, 1991.

Lardner, George, Jr. "Committee Approves Gates at CIA." *The Washington Post,* October 19, 1991.

Lardner, George, Jr. "Gates Takes Over as Director of CIA." *The Washington Post,* November 13, 1991.

Lardner, George, Jr., and Walter Pincus. "Gates Concedes Lack of Vigilance on Iran-Contra." *The Washington Post,* September 17, 1991.

Lardner, George, Jr., and Walter Pincus. "Hearings Point to Confirmation of CIA Nominee." *The Washington Post,* September 18, 1991.

Lardner, George, Jr., and R. Jeffrey Smith. "Intelligence Ties Endure Despite U.S.-China Strain." *The Washington Post,* June 25, 1989.

Leppard, David, and Nick Rufford. "Lockerbie: The Final Reckoning." *The Sunday Times* (London), December 17, 1989.

Leppard, David, and Nick Rufford. "Police Close In on Lockerbie Killers." *The Sunday Times* (London), December 17, 1989.

Livingstone, Neil C. "Danger in the Air." *Washingtonian,* June 1990.

Malone, William Scott. "The Panama Debacle—Uncle Sam Wimps Out." *The Washington Post,* April 23, 1989.

Marcus, Ruth, and Ann Devroy. "Bush Faults Rules Governing Covert Action Against Noriega." *The Washington Post*, October 23,
1989.

Mathews, Jay. "Students Confront Tear Gas, Troops in Chinese Capital."
The Washington Post, June 4, 1989.

Mathews, Jay, and Marianne Yen. "Two Escaped Dissidents Plan Network for Chinese Exiles." *The Washington Post*, June 30, 1989.

McAllister, Bill. "Trap Set as Honduran Suspect Jogged." *The Washington
Post*, April 7, 1988.

McCollum, Bill. "Afghan Endgame: The CIA Has Bungled It." *The
Washington Post*, September 10, 1989.

McConnell, Jeff. "Coups, Wars, and the CIA." *The Boston Globe Magazine*,
May 13, 1990.

McDonald, Marci. "Power Tennis, Anyone?" *The Washington Post Magazine*, July 18, 1989.

McGee, Jim, and David Hoffman. "Rivals Hint Bush Understates Knowledge of Noriega Ties." *The Washington Post*, May 8, 1988.

McGee, Jim. "Senate Panel Raps FBI CISPES Probe." *The Washington
Post*, July 15, 1989.

Moore, Molly. "Cheney Predicts Gorbachev Will Fail, Be Replaced." *The
Washington Post*, April 29, 1989.

Moore, Molly, and Joe Pichirallo. "Cheney: U.S. Was Willing to Take
Custody." *The Washington Post*, October 6, 1989.

Moore, Molly, and George C. Wilson. "Bush's Maximum-Force Invasion
Still Entails Risks." *The Washington Post*, December 21, 1989.

Mulvaney, Jim. "Troops Vs. Troops." New York *Newsday*, June 7, 1989.

Mylroie, Laurie. "How We Helped Saddam Survive." *Commentary*, July
1991.

Naeo Na (Bangkok). "Ex-General Swings Timber Operations Trade Deal
with Vietnam." June 14, 1988.

Nation, The (Bangkok). "Politicians Dismiss 'Money Dumping' Charges."
May 25, 1988.

National Journal. "Tilting with Intelligence." May 9, 1987.

News Service Report. "Panama Arrests American." *The Washington Post*,
April 8, 1989.

Newsweek. "What Can Be Done About Kaddafi?" December 3, 1984.

Newsweek. "The CIA: A Straight Arrow for Director." March 16, 1987.

Newsweek. "Drugs, Money and Death." February 15, 1988.

Newsweek. "The Chinese Army's Uneasy Truce with Itself." June 19,
1989.

Newsweek. "Terror at 30,000 Feet." October 2, 1989.

Newsweek. "Conventional Wisdom Watch." August 20, 1990.

Newsweek. "The Moscow Connection." September 17, 1990.

Newsweek. "Have Rebels Will Travel." March 25, 1991.

New York Times, The. "Excerpts from Questions and Answers at the Gates Hearings." October 4, 1991.

Oberdorfer, Don. "Bush Urged to Select Strong Security Adviser." *The Washington Post,* November 12, 1988.

Oberdorfer, Don. "Scowcroft Provides Policy Anchor." *The Washington Post,* November 24, 1988.

Oberdorfer, Don. "U.S. Weighs Arms for Cambodian Resistance," *The Washington Post,* April 30, 1989.

Oberdorfer, Don. "U.S. Criticizes Deng but Seeks to Avoid Showdown on Dissent." *The Washington Post,* June 13, 1989.

Oberdorfer, Don. "Hill Chairmen Urging Review of Cambodia Aid." *The Washington Post,* September 9, 1989.

Oberdorfer, Don. "Peace Talks Sought on Cambodia." *The Washington Post,* September 30, 1989.

Oberdorfer, Don. "Baker Blocked Speech by NSC Deputy on Gorbachev Reforms." *The Washington Post,* October 28, 1989.

Oberdorfer, Don. "Was War Inevitable?" *The Washington Post Magazine,* March 17, 1991.

Oberdorfer, Don, and David Hoffman. "U.S. Orders Dependents to Leave China." *The Washington Post,* June 8, 1989.

Oberdorfer, Don, and Valerie Strauss. "Cambodian Resistance Seeks U.S. Military Aid." *The Washington Post,* April 19, 1989.

Oksenberg, Michael. "Confessions of a China Watcher" (in "Upheaval in China"). *Newsweek,* June 19, 1989.

Ottaway, David B. "Groups Fostered Atmosphere Conducive to Giving Rebels Modern Weapons." *The Washington Post,* February 12, 1989.

Ottaway, David B. "What Is 'Afghan Lesson' for Superpowers?" *The Washington Post,* February 12, 1989.

Ottaway, David B. "CIA Defends Reports on Soviet Moves." *The Washington Post,* March 1, 1989.

Ottaway, David B. "U.S., Pakistan Agree to Continue Afghan Rebel Aid." *The Washington Post,* June 11, 1989.

Ottaway, David B. "Vice President Urges Military Aid to Cambodian Resistance." *The Washington Post,* June 23, 1989.

Ottaway, David B. "Stingers Were Key Weapon in Afghan War, Army Finds." *The Washington Post,* July 5, 1989.

Ottaway, David B. "U.S. Increasing Arms Flow to Afghan Resistance." *The Washington Post,* July 16, 1989.

Ottaway, David B. "CIA Removes Afghan Rebel Aid Director." *The Washington Post,* October 2, 1989.

Ottaway, David B. "Zaire Is Said to Cut CIA Arms Flow to Angolan Rebels." *The Washington Post,* October 4, 1989.

Ottaway, David B. "Coming out of the Cold." *The Washington Post,* October 22, 1989.

Ottaway, David B., and Ann Devroy. "Bush Expresses Confidence in CIA Chief's Performance." *The Washington Post,* October 17, 1989.

Ottaway, David B., and Laura Parker. "Pioneering the Deadly Art of Airline Bombs." *The Washington Post,* April 2, 1989.

Ottaway, David B., and Laura Parker. "Pan Am Bomb Probers Differ on Courier Report." *The Washington Post,* April 14, 1989.

Ottaway, David B., and Laura Parker. "CIA Confident Iran Behind Jet Bombing." *The Washington Post,* May 11, 1989.

Parker, Laura. "Hijack Alert Issued Before Lockerbie." *The Washington Post,* March 20, 1989.

Parmelee, Jennifer. "Libya Holds Suspects in Fire Probe." *The Washington Post,* March 28, 1990.

Perry, Mark. "The Secret Life of an American Spy." *Regardies,* February 1989.

Perry, Mark. "William Webster Vs. the White House." *Regardies,* January 1990.

Perry, Mark, and Jeff Goldberg. "The CIA's Secret Plot to Oust Saddam Hussein." *Regardies,* November 1990.

Perry, Mark, and Jeff Goldberg. "Will Judge Webster Be Benched?" *Nation,* April 15, 1991.

Perry, Mark, and Scott Malone. "How Scandal Almost Sank Our Secret Cambodia War." *The Washington Post,* October 30, 1988.

Pichirallo, Joe. "U.S. Probes Panama Strongman on Drug Ties." *The Washington Post,* November 11, 1987.

Pichirallo, Joe. "Bush Broadens Noriega Explanation." *The Washington Post,* May 10, 1988.

Pichirallo, Joe. "Gregg Says Envoy Told Bush Noriega Was a Problem." *The Washington Post,* May 21, 1988.

Pincus, Walter. "Retired CIA Veteran Chosen to Head Clandestine Activities." *The Washington Post,* December 9, 1987.

Pincus, Walter. "CIA Aide Acts to Lift Reprimand." *The Washington Post,* January 1, 1989.

Pincus, Walter. "CIA Chief Criticized over Reports." *The Washington Post,* July 15, 1989.

Pincus, Walter. "Gates's Solid Performance Follows a Cautious Script." *The Washington Post,* September 18, 1991.

Podesta, Don. "Coup Attempt Against Noriega by Rebel Troops Fails in Panama." *The Washington Post,* October 4, 1989.

Polgar, Tom. "The See-No-Evil CIA Nominee." *The Washington Post,* June 23, 1991.

Reuters. "Libya Offers to Accept Controls on Suspect Plant." *The Washington Post,* December 25, 1988.

Reuters. "Panama Arrests American." *The Washington Post,* April 8, 1989.

Reuters. "U.S. Move in Panama Called Inept." *The Washington Post,* April 28, 1989.

Rezendas, Michael. "A 'Pussycat' with Claws, Sununu Leaving Mark in Home State." *The Washington Post,* December 24, 1988.

Rohter, Larry. "Military Infighting Seen Behind Honduran's Arrest." *The New York Times,* April 15, 1988.

Rohter, Larry. "Seized Honduran: Drug Baron or a Robin Hood?" *The New York Times,* April 16, 1988.

Rosenthal, Andrew. "Scowcroft and Gates: A Team Rivals Baker." *The New York Times,* February 21, 1991.

Rosenthal, Andrew. "Webster Leaving as CIA Director; Ex-Deputy in Line." *The New York Times,* May 9, 1991.

Rosenthal, Andrew. "Bush Picks Deputy for U.S. Security to Head the CIA." *The New York Times,* May 15, 1991.

Rupert, James. "Afghan Rebels Fail to Resolve Dispute." *The Washington Post,* February 11, 1989.

Rupert, James. "Arab Fundamentalists Active in Afghan War." *The Washington Post,* March 2, 1989.

Rupert, James. "Afghanistan Rebels Lose Key Battle." *The Washington Post,* July 8, 1989.

Schell, Orville. "China's Spring." *The New York Review of Books,* June 29, 1989.

Schemann, Serge. "German Is Charged in Libyan Case." *The New York Times,* March 22, 1990.

Schmitt, Eric. "Nuclear War Plan in 80's Skirted the Constitution." *The New York Times,* November 18, 1991.

Sciolino, Elaine. "U.S. Accuses Benin of Abetting Libyan Terrorism." *The New York Times,* May 20, 1988.

Shapiro, Fred. "Letter from Beijing." *The New Yorker,* June 5, June 19, July 3, 1989.

Sheridan, Michael, et al. "Libya Blamed for Lockerbie." *Independent,* November 15, 1991.

Siam Rat (Bangkok). "Chawalit Lectures on National Security." April 13, 1988.

Smith, Jeffrey R. "CIA Assesses Effect of Gorbachev Cuts." *The Washington Post,* December 13, 1988.

Smith, R. Jeffrey. "Webster Says Laws on Chemical Arms Exports May Be Too Weak." *The Washington Post,* February 10, 1989.

Smith, R. Jeffrey, and George Lardner, Jr. "Iraq Sanctions Seen Working Slowly." *The Washington Post,* November 24, 1990.

Smith, R. Jeffrey, and Patrick E. Tyler. "Fire Strikes Chemical Plant in Libya." *The Washington Post,* March 15, 1990.

Southerland, Daniel. "China Sending Friendly Signals to U.S." *The Washington Post,* April 2, 1989.

Southerland, Daniel. "Protestors Widen Aim in China." *The Washington Post,* April 24, 1989.

Southerland, Daniel. "Protesters Upstage Summit." *The Washington Post,* May 16, 1989.

Southerland, Daniel. "1 Million in Beijing Center Demand Democracy." *The Washington Post,* May 18, 1989.

Southerland, Daniel. "Signs of New Power Struggle Emerge in China." *The Washington Post,* May 22, 1989.

Southerland, Daniel. "Top Chinese Officials Meet to Resolve Leadership Crisis." *The Washington Post,* May 24, 1989.

Southerland, Daniel. "China's Premier Li Emerges; Hard-Liners Seen Ascendant." *The Washington Post,* May 25, 1989.

Southerland, Daniel. "Deng Intensifies Chinese Campaign Against Enemies." *The Washington Post,* May 26, 1989.

Southerland, Daniel. "Troops Roll Through Beijing to Crush Protesters; Hundreds Feared Killed as Chinese Fight Back." *The Washington Post,* June 4, 1989.

Southerland, Daniel. "Forces Loyal to Deng Tighten Hold on City." *The Washington Post,* June 8, 1989.

Southerland, Daniel. "China Presents Deng as Leader in Full Command." *The Washington Post,* June 29, 1989.

Southerland, Daniel. "China Denies U.S. Charges on Attack." *The Washington Post,* July 5, 1989.

Southerland, Daniel. "10,000 Chinese Detained in Crackdown on Dissent." *The Washington Post,* July 8, 1989.

Southerland, Daniel. "Chinese-U.S. Ties Seen Unlikely to Improve Soon." *The Washington Post,* August 26, 1989.

Southerland, Daniel. "Deng Resigns His Last Party Post." *The Washington Post,* November 10, 1989.

Southerland, Daniel. "U.S. Envoys Visit China to Improve Ties." *The Washington Post,* December 10, 1989.

Southerland, Daniel. "Chinese Cast New Dragnet." *The Washington Post,* December 23, 1989.

Sricharatchanya, Paisai. "Shy but Not Retiring." *The Far Eastern Economic Review,* January 21, 1988.

Sricharatchanya, Paisai. "The Army's New Role." *The Far Eastern Economic Review,* February 19, 1987.

Sricharatchanya, Paisai. "A 'Lean, Mean Machine.'" *The Far Eastern Economic Review,* February 19, 1987.

Tasker, Rodney. "Chaovalit's Chosen Men." *The Far Eastern Economic Review,* September 18, 1986.

Thatsaniyuawet, Banyai, and Rungruang Prichakun. "Chawalit's Plans." *The Bangkok Post,* January 16, 1988.

Thayer, Berta R. "U.S. Soldier Killed By Panama Troops." *The Washington Post,* December 17, 1989.

Thorton, Mary. "Casey Criticized at Funeral." *The Washington Post,* May 10, 1987.

Tyler, Patrick E. "High Link Seen in Cairo Spy Case." *The Washington Post,* August 20, 1988.

Tyler, Patrick E. "Mubarak Reassigns Key Deputy." *The Washington Post,* April 16, 1989.

Tyler, Patrick E. "Skeptic with Strong Views." *The New York Times,* May 15, 1991.

Tyler, Patrick E., and Molly Moore. "Soviet Defense Spending Cut as Promised, CIA Reports." *The Washington Post,* November 15, 1989.

United Press International. "Togo Thwarts Bomb Plot." *The Washington Post,* August 12, 1986.

U.S. News & World Report, "On the Trail of Terror." November 13, 1989.

U.S. News & World Report, "The New Spy Wars." June 3, 1991.

Walcott, John. "Jet-Bomb Probe Points at Radical Palestinian Unit." *The Wall Street Journal,* February 3, 1989.

Washington Post, The. "Panama: The Official Word." October 10, 1989.

Washington Post, The. "Upheaval in Eastern Europe, the Turning Points." January 14, 1990.

Washington Post, The. "Refugees Force a Fateful Choice." January 14, 1990.

Washington Post, The. "The Communists Lost Control of the Process." January 14, 1990.

Washington Post, The. "President: Senators Ought Not to Panic" (excerpts). July 14, 1991.

Waxman, Sharon. "PLO Says Arab Once Linked to Iraqi-Backed Group Killed 3." *The Washington Post,* January 14, 1991.

Weaver, Timothy. "Afghan Guerrilla Assault on Jalalabad Stalls." *The Washington Post,* March 26, 1989.

Weiner, Tim. "Targeting of Iraq is Complex and Inexact, Experts Say." *The Philadelphia Inquirer,* February 14, 1991.

Weiner, Tim, and Owen Ullmann. "CIA's Webster Criticized as Ineffective." *The Philadelphia Inquirer,* February 22, 1991.

Weisskopf, Michael. "Student Leaders Elude Police in New Chinese Underground." *The Washington Post,* June 24, 1989.

Weymouth, Lally. "Cambodia's Hun Sen Is No Savior." *The Washington Post,* April 16, 1989.

Weymouth, Lally. "The Cambodian Cockpit." *The Washington Post,* April 30, 1989.

Weymouth, Lally. "The Ex-King Offers Help." *The Washington Post,* September 10, 1989.

Weymouth, Lally. "An Afghan Rebel Chief Tells America 'No Deal.'" *The Washington Post,* September 17, 1989.

Weymouth, Lally. "The Business of Terrorism in Libya." *The Washington Post,* November 20, 1991.

Wilson, George. "U.S. Is Key to China's Military Modernization." *The Washington Post,* June 6, 1989.

Wilson, George C. "Lack of Information Hampered U.S. Response to Panama Coup Attempt." *The Washington Post,* October 15, 1989.

Wines, Michael. "An Inquiry in Hot Pursuit." *The New York Times,* January 1, 1989.

Wines, Michael. "Libya Now Linked to Pan Am Blast." *The New York Times,* October 10, 1990.

Wines, Michael. "After 30 Years in Shadows, a Spymaster Emerges." *The New York Times,* November 20, 1990.

Wines, Michael. "CIA Sidelines Its Gulf Cassandra." *The New York Times,* January 24, 1991.

Woodward, Bob, "CIA Paid Millions to Jordan's King Hussein." *The Washington Post,* February 18, 1977.

Woodward, Bob, and Walter Pincus. "CIA's Webster Disciplines 7 Employes over Iran Affair." *The Washington Post,* December 18, 1987.

Woodward, Bob, and Walter Pincus. "At CIA, a Rebuilder 'Goes with the Flow.'" *The Washington Post,* August 10, 1988. (One of five in a series.)

Xinhua News Agency. "Hong Kong, Macao Stowaway Helpers Arrested" (from Foreign Information Broadcast Service). December 26, 1989.

Yen, Marianne. "'Changan Avenue Was Full of Corpses.'" *The Washington Post,* July 1, 1989.

Yen, Marianne. "Chinese Abroad Urged to Seek Democracy." *The Washington Post,* July 29, 1989.

BOOKS

Agee, Philip. *Inside the Company: CIA Diary.* Harmondsworth, Eng.: Penguin Books, 1975.

Bamford, James. *The Puzzle Palace: A Report on America's Most Secret Agency.* Boston: Houghton Mifflin, 1982.

Barron, John. *KGB: The Secret Work of Soviet Secret Agents.* London: Corgi Books, 1975.

Barron, John. *KGB Today: The Hidden Hand.* New York: Reader's Digest Press, 1983.

Bradlee, Ben, Jr. *Guts and Glory: The Rise and Fall of Oliver North.* New York: Donald E. Fine, Inc., 1988.

Buckley, Kevin. *Panama: The Whole Story*. New York: Simon and Schuster, 1991.

Burrows, William E. *Deep Black*. New York: Random House, 1986.

Bush, George, with Victor Gold. *Looking Forward*. New York: Doubleday, 1987.

Byron, John, and Robert Pack. *The Claws of the Dragon*. New York: Simon and Schuster, 1991.

Cannon, Lou. *President Reagan: The Role of a Lifetime*. New York: Simon and Schuster, 1991.

Cline, Dr. Ray S. *The CIA Under Reagan, Bush and Casey*. Washington, D.C.: Acropolis Books, Ltd., 1981.

Cockburn, Andrew, and Leslie Cockburn. *Dangerous Liaison: The Inside Story of the U.S.-Israeli Covert Relationship*. New York: Harper Collins, 1991.

Cohen, William S., and George J. Mitchell. *Men of Zeal*. New York: Viking, 1988.

Colby, William. *Lost Victory*. Chicago: Contemporary Books, 1989.

Darwish, Adel, and Gregory Alexander. *Unholy Babylon: The Secret History of Saddam's War*. New York: St. Martin's Press, 1991.

Dinges, John. *Our Man in Panama*. New York: Random House, 1990.

Dobson, Christopher, and Ronald Payne. *The Dictionary of Espionage*. London: Harrap, 1984.

Draper, Theodore. *A Very Thin Line: The Iran-Contra Affair*. New York: Hill and Wang, 1991.

Emerson, Steven A., and Brian Duffy. *The Fall of Pan Am 103*. New York: G. P. Putnam's Sons, 1989.

Emerson, Steven A., and Cristina Del Sesto. *Terrorist*. New York: Villard Books, 1991.

Eveland, Wilbur Crane. *Ropes of Sand: America's Failure in the Middle East*. New York: W. W. Norton and Co., 1980.

Faligot, Roger, and Remi Kauffer. *The Chinese Secret Service*. New York: William Morrow and Co., 1987.

Ford, Gerald R. *A Time to Heal*. New York: Berkley Books, 1980.

Friedman, Thomas L. *From Beirut to Jerusalem*. New York: Farrar Straus Giroux, 1989.

Godson, Roy, ed. *Intelligence Requirements for the 1980s*, 5 vols. Washington, D.C.: National Strategy Information Center, 1979–1984.

Haig, Alexander. *Caveat: Realism, Reagan, and Foreign Policy*. London: Weidenfeld and Nicolson, 1984.

Hersh, Seymour M. *The Samson Option: Israel's Nuclear Arsenal and American Foreign Policy*. New York: Random House, 1991.

Hiro, Dilip. *The Longest War: The Iran-Iraq Military Conflict*. New York: Routledge, 1991.

Hourani, Albert. *A History of the Arab Peoples.* Cambridge, Mass.: Harvard University Press, 1991.

Jeffreys-Jones, Rhodri. *American Espionage: From Secret Service to CIA.* New York: The Free Press, 1977.

Jordan, Hamilton. *Crises: The Last Year of the Carter Presidency.* New York: Berkley Books, 1983.

Kempe, Frederick. *Divorcing the Dictator.* New York: G. P. Putnam's Son's, 1990.

Kessler, Ronald. *Moscow Station.* New York: Pocket Books, 1990.

Kessler, Ronald. *Escape from The CIA.* New York: Pocket Books, 1991.

Knight, Amy. *The KGB: Police and Politics in the Soviet Union.* London: Allen and Unwin, 1988.

Ledeen, Michael, and William Lewis. *Debacle: The American Failure in Iran.* New York: Vintage Books, 1982.

Mangold, Tom. *Cold Warrior: James Jesus Angleton, the CIA's Master Spy Hunter.* New York: Simon and Schuster, 1991.

Martin, David C., and John Walcott. *Best Laid Plans: The Inside Story of America's War Against Terrorism.* New York: Harper and Row, 1988.

Mayer, Jane, and Doyle McManus. *Landslide: The Unmaking of the President, 1984–1988.* Boston: Houghton Mifflin, 1988.

Melman, Yossi. *The Master Terrorist: The True Story Behind Abu Nidal.* New York: Adama Books, 1986.

Meyer, Herbert E. *Scouting the Future: The Public Speeches of William J. Casey.* Washington, D.C.: Regnery Gateway, 1989.

National Security Archive. *The Chronology.* New York: Warner Books, 1987.

North, Oliver. *Under Fire.* New York: HarperCollins, 1991.

Oberdorfer, Don. *The Turn: From the Cold War to a New Era.* New York: Poseidon Press, 1991.

Ostrovsky, Victor, and Clair Hoy. *By Way of Deception: The Making and Unmaking of a Mossad Officer.* New York: St. Martin's Press, 1990.

Persico, Joseph E. *Casey.* New York: Viking, 1990.

Powers, Thomas. *The Man Who Kept the Secrets: Richard Helms and the CIA.* New York: Knopf, 1979.

Prados, John. *The Soviet Estimate: U.S. Intelligence Analysis and Russian Military Strength.* New York: Dial Press, 1982.

Prados, John. *Keepers of the Keys.* New York: William Morrow and Co., 1991.

Ranelagh, John. *The Agency: The Rise and Decline of the CIA.* New York: Simon and Schuster, 1987.

Raviv, Dan, and Yossi Melman. *Every Spy a Prince: The Complete History of Israel's Intelligence Community.* Boston: Houghton Mifflin, 1990.

Richelson, Jeffrey. *The U.S. Intelligence Community.* Cambridge, Mass.: Ballinger, 1985.

Richelson, Jeffrey. *America's Secret Eyes in Space: The U.S. Keyhold Spy Satellite Program.* New York: Harper and Row, 1990.

Rushdie, Salman. *The Satanic Verses.* New York: Viking, 1989.

Sakharov, Vladimir, with Umberto Tosi. *High Treason: Revelations of a Double Agent.* New York: G. P. Putnam's Sons, 1980.

Salinger, Pierre, and Eric Laurent. *Secret Dossier: The Hidden Agenda Behind the Gulf War.* New York: Penguin Books, 1991.

Scott, Peter Dale, and Jonathan Marshall. *Cocaine Politics.* Berkeley: University of California Press, 1991.

Smith, Russell Jack. *The Unknown CIA.* Washington, D.C.: Pergamon-Brassey's, 1989.

Sterling, Claire. *The Terror Network: The Secret War of International Terrorism.* London: Weidenfeld and Nicolson, 1981.

Toobin, Jeffrey. *Opening Arguments.* New York: Viking, 1991.

Weiner, Tim. *Blank Check: The Pentagon's Black Budget.* New York: Warner Books, 1990.

Wise, David. *The Spy Who Got Away.* New York: Random House, 1988.

Woodward, Bob. *Veil: The Secret Wars of the CIA, 1981–1987.* New York: Simon and Schuster, 1987.

Woodward, Bob. *The Commanders.* New York: Simon and Schuster, 1991.

Wright, Robin. *In the Name of God.* New York: Simon and Schuster, 1989.

Yergin, Daniel. *The Prize: The Epic Quest for Oil, Money and Power.* New York: Simon and Schuster, 1991.

DOCUMENTS

"Report of the President's Special Review Board" (The Tower Report). Washington, D.C.: U.S. Government Printing Office, February 26, 1987.

"Report of the Congressional Committees Investigating the Iran-Contra Affair, 100th Congress, 1st Session." Washington, D.C.: U.S. Government Printing Office, November 1987.

"Report of the Congressional Committees Investigating the Iran-Contra Affair (U.S. Senate Select Committee on Secret Military Assistance to Iran and the Nicaraguan Opposition and U.S. House of Representatives Select Committee to Investigate Covert Arms Transactions with Iran), 100th Congress, 1st Session," Appendix B: Volumes 1–27. Washington, D.C.: U.S. Government Printing Office, 1988.

"Drugs, Law Enforcement and Foreign Policy: A Report of the Subcommittee on Narcotics, Terrorism and International Operations," Volume 1: Report. Washington, D.C.: U.S. Government Printing Office, April 13, 1989.

"Drugs, Law Enforcement and Foreign Policy: A Report of the

Subcommittee on Narcotics, Terrorism and International Operations," Volume 2: Exhibits. Washington, D.C.: U.S. Government Printing Office, April 13, 1989.

"Drugs, Law Enforcement and Foreign Policy: The Cartel, Haiti and Central America: Hearings Before the Subcommittee on Terrorism, Narcotics and International Operations, Committee on Foreign Relations, U.S. Senate, 100th Congress, 2nd Session," Parts 1–4. Washington, D.C.: U.S. Government Printing Office, 1989.

"Nomination of Robert M. Gates to Be Director of Central Intelligence: Report (with testimony and exhibits) of the Select Committee on Intelligence, U.S. Senate, 102nd Congress, 1st Session," October 24, 1991.

United States of America v. *Oliver L. North,* United States District Court for the District of Columbia (Criminal No. 88–0088): Stipulations of Fact and Exhibits.

United States of America v. *Abdel Basset Ali al-Megrahi, Lamen Khalifa Fhimah,* United States District Court for the District of Columbia, November 14, 1991.

Index